CANADIAN MARKETING

CANADIAN MARKETING
Cases and Concepts

Second Edition

KENNETH G. HARDY

> The University of Western Ontario

MICHAEL R. PEARCE

> The University of Western Ontario

ADRIAN B. RYANS

> The University of Western Ontario

Allyn and Bacon, Inc.

Toronto   Boston   London   Sydney

Library of Congress Cataloging in Publication Data
Main entry under title:

Canadian marketing.

    1. Marketing—Canada—Case studies. I. Hardy, Kenneth G., 1941–   . II. Pearce, Michael R., 1946–   . III. Ryans, Adrian B., 1945–   .
HF5415.12.C2C36   1984   658.8′00971   84-6501
ISBN 0-205-08154-1

Canadian Cataloguing in Publication Data

Hardy, Kenneth G., 1941–
    Canadian marketing : cases and concepts

ISBN 0-205-08154-1

1. Marketing—Canada—Case studies. I. Pearce, Michael R., 1946–   II. Ryans, Adrian B., 1945–
III. Title.

HF5415.12.C35H37 1984   658.8′00971   C84-098624-6

Printed in the United States of America.

10 9 8 7 6 5 4 3 2   89 88 87 86 85

We rededicate this book to our wives —
Rosemary, Janet, and Susan.

Contents

Preface

Canadian Marketing: Cases and Concepts is an integrated collection of cases, frameworks, and text for Canadian university courses in marketing. Our objective is to provide an opportunity for Canadian students to learn problem-solving skills and concepts in marketing. The distinctive benefit of this book is the demonstrated interest and learning value of the cases and text, which describe realistic Canadian situations.

The revised edition attempts to maintain the strategic positioning of our successful first edition. We paid careful attention to the marketing research conducted by ourselves and by our publisher. We were particularly attentive to the recommendations for cases that should be continued in the revised edition. Of the 52 cases in the original edition, 12 have been retained. However, it was difficult to achieve a perfect consensus of the specific cases to repeat. We hope that most of your favourites are contained herein, and we are sure that you will enjoy the 32 fresh new cases.

In selecting the cases, preference was given to those with demonstrated student interest. Generally speaking, shorter cases were chosen over longer cases, although each chapter contains at least one multi-issue case that is suitable for a report or presentation.

Perhaps the most notable change in the revised edition is the inclusion of six cases from outside Canada. We have done this deliberately on the premise that Canadian students should become comfortable with the context of marketing decisions in Europe and the United States. The authors share a belief that Canadian marketers must look outward for multinational and global marketing opportunities. Canadian marketing professionals must develop great skills in opportunity identification and follow-through—in short, to become great entrepreneurs.

The revised edition has been reorganized to bring buyer behaviour and marketing research together in one chapter. We have added a new section on how to use major reference works in conducting basic market research. The library has much to offer if marketing students know how to use it. Because the public policy dimensions of marketing tend to be treated in a separate course, the former chapter on marketing and public policy was deleted in favor of one major case on the topic.

We merged into one chapter the formerly separate chapters that provided an introduction to case learning and an introduction to marketing strategy. The financial analysis and financial exercise material was moved from its former position as an appendix to its current position as Chapter Two. We believe that basic financial skills are absolutely essential to the development of effective marketing strategies and plans.

You will find several new topics in this edition: several cases in retailing, cases on marketing services, agribusiness, export marketing, and sales promotion. We have tried very hard to provide regional and industrial sector representation across Canada without sacrificing any truly great cases.

Authors from coast to coast participated in this edition. We are grateful to the following professors for allowing us to print their cases: Stephen Arnold, Peter C. Bell, Alice Courtney, John Claxton, Bob Collins, Nick Fry, Christopher Gale, James Graham, Gordon H. G. McDougall, Robert E. M. Nourse, Richard Pollay, Philip Rosson, Ralph Sorensen, Ian Spencer, and George Touches. We are also delighted that each of our colleagues in Western's marketing area group contributed at least one case: Steve Ash, David Burgoyne, Terry Deutscher, John Kennedy, Blair Little, and Roger More. Also, several research assistants and casewriters assisted faculty members in preparing the cases. Each author's name is shown beneath each title in the table of contents.

We would also like to thank our reviewers, F. W. A. Bliemel, Queens University; George H. Haines, Jr., Carleton University; Stanley J. Shapiro, Simon Fraser University; and Ian S. Spencer, St. Francis Xavier University.

It was a great deal of work to bring this revision together; we collected and evaluated more than 100 cases through three attempted outlines—a process that spanned more than two years.

A great many people played significant roles in this revision. The Canadian editor of Allyn and Bacon, Jerry Smith, was just as responsible for the formulation of this edition as he was responsible for the successful selling of the first edition. Our production editor, Barbara Willette, was very patient with us even though we provided her with a sometimes faded and always multi-styled hodgepodge for a manuscript. Sue Danowski coordinated the typing of the teaching notes and the transmission of the manuscript and art. Ken Woytaz, Anna Currie, and Jean Fish programmed the teaching notes on their magical word processors.

We are indebted to our students on whom we tested this material, to the Plan For Excellence for funding, and to the administrators and faculty at Western, who make this a pleasant place to grow. Dean C. B. Johnston is an outstanding marketing professor and a tireless marketer for the School.

Unless otherwise indicated, the copyrights on the cases and text contained herein belong to The University of Western Ontario. These materials should not be reproduced without the express written permission of the School of Business Administration.

CANADIAN MARKETING

CHAPTER I
MARKETING STRATEGY FORMULATION: INTRODUCTION

A Guide for Students Using Cases

This book was designed to help you deal with marketing problems typically faced by practitioners. It is not a book designed to present theory in search of applications. Instead, our purpose has been to help you develop skills and concepts that will be useful to you when you face actual business problems. In fact, this book contains forty-four real problems which we call cases. A case is a factual description of a situation a manager faced at some point in time. Although we have sometimes disguised names, places, and numbers at the request of the organization involved, each case is a real decision that was faced by a real individual. The object of each case is to put you into the position of a decision-maker, facing the time pressure and having to cope with deficiencies in information.

In each actual situation, the manager had to analyze all the facts available, identify problems and opportunities, generate and evaluate alternative courses of action, make a decision, and then implement this decision. You will be expected to go through this same process with one exception: you will not have the opportunity to implement your decision nor to see the results.

You may wonder why you must struggle through numerous cases in order to learn the basic skills of marketing management. The answer lies in the way you developed skills in other endeavours. For example, how did you learn to throw a ball or play a piano? Someone showed you how to do it, you tried, your "teacher" commented, you tried again, and you got better each time you tried it. You can very effectively and efficiently acquire marketing management skills the same way. Each case is a practice session in a series—you will get better and better at them as you go along.

If anyone knew the precise method or formula that would fit all marketing decision situations, then we would give you this formula and you could approach marketing much like chemistry. Alas, so far no one has discovered such an approach. Instead, marketing professionals have discovered many generalizations and many approaches that have been proven useful in a wide variety of situations. Yet none of these methods are sure-fire in any specific situation. Thus, you might best think of marketing management as a disciplined way of making decisions, not as a science.

There is another reason for exposing you to cases. Real cases, carefully written, give you a genuine flavour of what happens in marketing, and thus you should have a far better idea of whether you wish to pursue marketing as a career choice. We caution you to remember, however, that each case is designed for one or two class sessions, whereas in actual fact the decision-maker had to grapple with it, often for several months. The case-writer has thus helped you considerably by distilling a lot of information into a few pages of reading. The case you read in about an hour or so typically took a month of time to research and write.

Uses of Cases

There is no one way in which cases are used. The general idea, however, is that we learn by doing, not by listening or watching. Doing can take several forms: (a) individual preparation, (b) small group discussion, (c) class discussion, (d) in-class presentation, (e) written report, (f) written examination. Each of these situations is somewhat different in terms of what you must do to perform well.

Individual Preparation for Class

Interesting and worthwhile cases are usually complicated and controversial. Each case in effect is a challenge to your ability to sort relevant information from irrelevant, to interpret facts and opinions, to create or at least to identify appropriate courses of action, and of course, to communicate your thinking clearly and persuasively to others.

Cases are written both to give you the essential facts available to the decision-maker and to give you some general background about the decision situation. You will learn a lot about contemporary business institutions and practices in this way. For this reason, we suggest you read through the case once quickly, getting a general impression of what the case is about and in general what sorts of problems or opportunities you face. During this reading, you will find frequently that the case describes in the first paragraph or two, and perhaps the last paragraph or two, the manager's view of the situation. Sometimes, the case even describes the manager's views of the alternatives available. Do not, however, rely on the manager's views—frequently you can and should improve upon these views.

After your first reading, it is time to pick up a pencil or magic marker and begin to go through the case again very carefully. You will find that a thorough preparation involves going through the case several times, each time perhaps with a different purpose in mind. During the second reading, underline key facts (for example: variable costs were . . .) and make marginal notes to help you find these facts in a hurry later (for example: var. costs). You may also jot down in the margins or on another piece of paper any thoughts that occur to you as you proceed through the case familiarizing yourself with case data.

The third step is to isolate key variables and make a few numerical calculations. For example, the case may not spell out too clearly how well the company's marketing strategy has been performing. In this instance, you may find it useful to calculate market share or rough out an income statement, etc.

Then, sit back a few moments and just think. Time spent at this stage is most important in using your total preparation time effectively and efficiently. Most cases are sufficiently complex to absorb all the preparation time that you have available—and then some. You cannot afford to waste time by doing unnecessary analysis or in simple "wheel-spinning." We have found the best way to organize preparation time is to identify as soon as possible the decision choices you face and then to choose analytical approaches you have found useful in the past. For example, suppose you realize that you must make a selection amongst alternative target markets. It is highly likely that your analysis must include careful examination of the segmentation in that market and of the behavioural characteristics of these segments. There's more, but you probably get the point. Over time, you will develop your ability to focus quickly on meaningful analysis to assist you in making decision choices. The text and occasional lectures will help you develop this facility.

Much of your preparation time should be spent in interpreting information. You must not only be acquainted with case facts but also have an opinion as to what they mean with reference to the choices that must be made. Essentially, always ask yourself of each case fact: "so what?"

A number of frustrations commonly plague decision-makers as they tackle marketing problems: a shortage of time in which to make decisions, a lack of good information on which to base decisions, and uncertainty as to how the results will work out. You will experience these same frustrations. There are a few things you can do about them however. First, seldom can you rearrange the time frame, so treat that as a given. Second, lack of information unfortunately is often not a sufficient reason to make no decision. In such instances, you have essentially two options: (a) proceed with your analysis by making an assumption or (b) plan to acquire the needed information (for example, via marketing research) and, if necessary, make an assumption now as to what that information will be. This may seem somewhat contrived, but let us assure you that this is exactly what practising managers must do all the time. It is critical that you be prepared to make assumptions in the absence of hard data and that you write them down so that you and others can follow your trail of logic. As your analysis proceeds, you should be able to assess how important to the outcome any particular assumption is. For example, suppose you assume that sales will go up 10 percent if price is dropped 5 percent. This could perhaps be examined via a test market. In any event, as you do your financial calculations, what if you are wrong by, say, 3 percent? Would it change your decision? Examining the importance of your assumptions by analyzing the sensitivity of decisions to changes in those assumptions is a very important management skill.

Fourth, although we have just encouraged you to make assumptions, we must also caution you about them. Be careful not to project your own values and life style to others. For example, business students often come from middle class backgrounds and have strong aspirations to join the upper classes. Accordingly, projecting their own values and habits onto other consumers is both inappropriate and dysfunctional.

Fifth, think before you put everything together. If you try to plug all the data, assumptions, and analyses into a framework mechanistically, you will end up with a filled-in chart which is of little real value. Such use of frameworks is worse than having no framework at all. Some marketing instructors believe for this reason that it is better to have students struggle with problems for a while without the benefit of any framework.

Sixth, we believe you should generate at least two or three alternative courses of action to examine in detail. One of the main differences between managers who have had professional training and those who have not is the ability of the trained manager to see several ways to achieve a particular objective. Scientific studies of decision-making behaviour show that all too often decision-makers lock in too early on particular pieces of data and therefore on particular courses of action to their disadvantage. Therefore, work hard at seeing several ways to meet your goals. Naturally, no one expects you to list and exhaustively analyze courses of action that are obviously inappropriate. Instead, list the major alternatives you think are worthy of examination. Then outline the decision criteria you are using. At this point, you are ready to write down the advantages and disadvantages of each of the best alternatives. A summary of the pros and cons is an excellent way to focus your attention and to communicate clearly and briefly your thinking to others.

Seventh, financial calculations are an essential part of marketing decision making. Whenever possible, you should calculate costs and revenues, project profit and investment implications, and do all this under optimistic, expected, and pessimistic conditions. Such analysis integrates and makes very concrete your marketing decisions and helps relate them to other functional areas within the firm.

Eighth, be brief and specific. One of the skills you must master is the ability to simplify the complexity of marketing decisions down to the key points and then deal with those key points. There is a great tendency to waffle when one puts down his/her own forecast of results following a recommended strategy. This often leads to vague suggestions of "increasing sales" or "investigating new channels." We look for recommendations such as:

> The target market should continue to be married females in the 24–40 age bracket. Mr. Humphrey should set his factory price at $2.52 per unit with margins of 40 percent to the retail trade and a cooperative advertising budget of $50,000. He should stay with the current channels of distribution, which are the chain discount stores in Canada. The thousand outlets will be served by ten salesmen who will call on them as shown in the first exhibit. The product line should not be expanded. The most likely contribution over the next five years will be $400,000 for this product line, as shown by the simplified profit and loss statements in the second exhibit.

Ninth, do not waste time repeating case facts. There is a great tendency for individuals preparing and presenting cases to restate the situation, often just under new headings. In your preparation, you might wish to write a few things down to help familiarize yourself with the facts, but this is solely for your own use. Your colleagues, your instructor, and later your boss should know the case facts. Just ask yourself after you have written something whether you have restated a fact or whether you have added something conclusive or interpretive to it. For example, instead of repeating the case fact "D.B. White's machinery is outmoded," you should draw a conclusion such as "D.B. White should avoid manufacturing-intensive types of businesses because their machinery is outmoded." Another conclusion might be "D.B. White should replace the outmoded machinery in order to open up manufacturing-intensive opportunities."

Finally, your instructor may or may not assign specific assignment questions with each case. When no questions are asked, the implicit assignment is to be ready as the decision-maker in the case to recommend what you would do and why. When questions are assigned, they should be considered as a means of assisting you in getting into the case and not as the limits of your preparation.

Watch out! The process of case preparation can be deceiving. Many students have done a *superficial* job in preparation yet fooled themselves into thinking they were on top of the situation. As a class discussion proceeds, they say to themselves, "I touched on that" or "I would have reached the same conclusion had I pushed the data a little further." When exam or report or presentation time comes along, these students have a rude awakening. This is not surprising because skills are acquired with practice—athletes and other performers spend hours in practice before they enter the important events. There is no substitute for *thorough* preparation.

Small Group Discussions

If possible, it is highly desirable to have a small group meeting of classmates prior to full class discussions. Many students find small group discussions the most rewarding part of case work. A good group discussion is a sharing experience for all involved. It is a time for trying out ideas, for getting new ideas, for getting help on analysis. Meetings are best if pre-arranged and if the group consists of four to six individuals who respect one another.

Many students have difficulty at the outset of a case discussion course in participating in the class discussion. The small group setting is an ideal way for such individuals to practise participation in the give and take of case discussion.

Class Discussion

In actual situations when managers address the issues represented in the cases, there are almost always different points of view on what action should be taken and what will happen. It is only natural then to have controversy in a case discussion. The essence of the case method is the process of stating points of view, defending positions, and actively listening so as to understand and constructively criticize the positions of others. A good class discussion is a lively discussion that is marked by well-reasoned and well-argued differing viewpoints.

The need to be a skillful communicator arises repeatedly in management, and the kind of class discussions we are referring to presents ideal opportunities to practise talking and listening skills. For some people, however, talking in large group settings is difficult and threatening. If you are one of these people, you must work at this problem because you will not gain full measure from a case course by being a silent nonparticipator. As suggested, you can practise in a small group setting. Alternatively, you may gather your courage up and one day just jump in. The best way to get in if you are concerned is to find a minor point or raise a question about something. Do not wait until you have a major presentation to do. Your classmates and your instructor will be supportive of your efforts. Remember, in the classroom we learn as much or more from one another's mistakes as we do from "correct" answers. We also must all remember the importance of listening carefully to what others say: too many of us simply wait our turn to talk and do not make an effort to relate our comments to those of the previous speakers.

In a typical class, what gets done is a function of several factors. Certainly, without the willing cooperation (both preparation and participation) of the students, a case class falls flat on its face. The instructor also has a role to play. It is his/her job to moderate the discussion—a kind of verbal traffic cop—and to help students with difficulties in analytical methods and communication skills. The instructor selects the order in which cases will be discussed and the focus in each discussion in accordance with his/her pedagogical objectives. It is not your instructor's role to show you his/her solution, but rather to help you develop your own approaches. Students, not surprisingly, are always interested in "what actually happened" as well as what the instructor would do. Your instructor may know the outcome and share it with you, but the learning is not in what others did, but in the process and habit of making good decisions that you are developing.

Reports, Presentations, and Examinations

During a sequence of cases in regular class sessions, your instructor will make decisions on what aspects of a case to emphasize one day to the next. The constraints of time often mean that your instructor will choose to focus on problem identification one day, a certain analytical technique another day, and so on. However, from time to time, it is useful to do a case from start to finish. Such occasions are written reports, formal presentations (often by small groups), and written examinations.

Reports, presentations, and exams all require the student to do a more thorough job in communicating his/her thinking about the case. In our view, reports are the most difficult because typically they are one-way communication but the student is given a good deal of time to prepare them and hence the expectations of the grader are high. Oral presentations are different by virtue of the opportunity usually given for two-way communication to clarify ambiguities and by a usual expectation that only the highlights will be presented. Examinations are of course the most time-constrained. Typically, we give four hours for reading, analysis, and final writing of a case exam. This is not much time as everyone involved realizes.

In all of these situations, you as the communicator must be very aware of the expectations of the "audience." Reports, presentations, and exams are not expected to be diaries of the thoughts you had as you worked through the case. Instead they are supposed to be concise, coherent, persuasive arguments for specific advocated courses of action. In fact, a good report, presentation, or exam usually starts where all too many students stop. It should be an organized, more fully developed version of your regular preparation.

All audiences vary in their expectations. In general, we recommend that you find out from your intended audience as much as you can about such expectations. Unless given other instructions, we suggest the following format: (a) executive summary of action to be taken and expected results (this is written last but appears first for the reader/listener), (b) statement of problem/opportunity and the performance objectives you are aiming at, (c) identification and analysis of alternatives (evaluation of alternatives is the bulk of the effort), and (d) your recommendations and their anticipated consequences in some detail.

Learning from Using Cases

We have discussed at length the basic philosophy underlying the use of cases. It remains for us to give you some final tips on how to learn from a sequence of cases. First, remember that cases are not given to you in the event you might find yourself exactly in the same situation that the case portrays. This is an extremely rare occurrence. Instead, each case was written to illustrate a broad class of problems. For example, you may spend several hours working on segmentation in the rice market. Instead of wondering "will I ever use my knowledge of the rice business," you should focus on the approach taken and the concept of market segmentation that can be applied to other situations. If the case was well done, you probably tackled such questions as the following:

1. "When is segmentation worth doing?"

2. "What dimensions are worth using in any particular situation and how do I choose from amongst a set of possibilities?"

3. "Where do we get the information necessary for a segmentation analysis?"

and so on. Your knowledge and your notes should reflect consideration of these kinds of issues. After you have done all the specific work, ask yourself, "What have I learned today that I can apply to other marketing problems?" Over time, you will see a distinct pattern of problems and appropriate kinds of analyses developing. You will then have your own way of dealing with marketing problems efficiently and effectively.

Developing a Marketing Strategy

A Marketing Framework

Developing an effective marketing strategy can often be very difficult. By its very nature, marketing is oriented towards the world outside the particular company or organization, an environment that is complex and continually changing. The very complexity of the environment makes it essential that we should have a specific conceptual framework to aid us in our decision making. If we don't, it is all too easy to miss a critical element in the environment and make a poor decision.

The marketing framework shown in exhibit 1 will provide a sequence of items for you to consider. As you can see, it is composed of two main parts: Analysis and Action. You analyze the internal and external factors, the buyers, the channels, and the competitors. Under the topic of Action, you create at least three marketing strategies, choose one, and indicate how the strategy will be implemented. The sub-items are self-explanatory. *One or several* of the sub-items may apply to your particular marketing problem. Although the framework is *conceptually* simple, as shown in the diagram below, the real test is how you use it in practice.

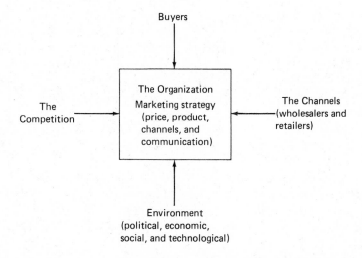

Exhibit 1 A Marketing Framework

ANALYSIS

Internal Factors

OBJECTIVES
Profit
Employee satisfaction
Share/sales
Product quality
Corporate reputation

STRENGTHS/WEAKNESSES
Expertise
People
Financial
Channels
Cost structure
Capacity
Reputation
Data/information

CURRENT RISKS
Morale of employees, channels,
  customers
Financial
Opportunity cost[a]
Image
Market position
Disclosure[b]

External Factors

BUYERS
Market size and growth
Segments, size, and
  accessibility
Influencers, buyers, users
Needs: kind, triggering,
  seasonality
Criteria: ranked sensitivity
Information sought, extent and
  type of search

COMPETITORS
Many or few
Leaders or followers: relative
  size, strength, share
Strong or weak: which products/
  territories, source of strength
Dimensions of competition

CHANNELS
Aggressive/passive
Receptive to change/traditional
Developed/underdeveloped
Effective/weak
Controllable/uncontrollable
Preference for margin or turnover
Centralized/decentralized
Financially sound

OPPORTUNITIES
Competitive weakness
Unmet needs of buyers or channels
Market growth
Cost advantage
Unused production or channel
  capacity
New laws
New technology

Exhibit 1 (continued)

ACTION

Common Suboptions for the
Four Elements of Marketing
Strategy

PRODUCT	PRICE
Quality level	Level
Superior	Premium
Competitive	Competitive
Less than competition	Low
Product line	Volume discounts
Broad	Yes
Deep	No
Both	
Package/warranty/service	
Superior	
Competitive	
Branding	
Yes	
No	

MARKETING COMMUNICATIONS	CHANNELS OF DISTRIBUTION
Amount	Number
High spending	Selective
Low spending	Extensive
Type	Mass
Mass advertising/promotion	Motivation
Personal selling	Margin
Publicity	Turnover
Control	Free goods
Manufacturer	Type
Channel members	Perform extensive tasks
Mutual	Perform few tasks

Note: You do *not* need to make a decision in *all* subitems for each case. This is only a list of variables to consider.

a. The rewards from an alternative venture.
b. Yielding damaging data or plans.

Internal Factors

Earlier in this chapter, we talked about major steps in making management decisions using a fairly general problem-solving framework. Now the marketing framework gives you more specific considerations to think about under the same topic headings. Don't worry about precise labels; use the framework as a check list to ensure that you have covered the major aspects of the case. You do *not* need to write something down from the case for each item in the check list. With practice, you will look for the major items automatically.

You will find that it is possible for one item to be both a strength and a weakness. The most usual situation is excess capacity, which is a weakness because the plant is not operating at the point of lowest total cost per unit, but is a strength because of the ability to produce added product(s) without further investment if someone can just sell the added product(s). Excess capacity also sets up an *opportunity*, so it can wear a third label.

Let's look at a particular example of how to use an analysis of internal factors in the case of D.B. White Limited, a small Canadian manufacturing company.

D.B. White Limited

D.B. White Limited was an old, family-owned company that formulated chemicals such as additives for concrete, tile and grouting chemicals, and floor hardeners for the construction industry. The market for these products was growing at a rate of 10 to 15 percent each year. D.B. White had 250 employees, annual sales of approximately $7 million a year, and offices in five countries around the world, although the overseas offices performed a negligible amount of business.

The plant was old and the machinery was becoming unreliable, but the company owned cheap manufacturing and storage facilities close to most major markets. The company had incurred a series of losses until 1973, when new management was found. After 1973 the company's before-tax profit averaged 10 percent of sales, and D.B. White became financially solid to the point of having cash for acquisitions.

There were well over 250 product categories among their various divisions, and no one category accounted for more than 10 percent of sales. D.B. White had a small share of the many markets in which the products were sold partly because the company sold their products on a pricing strategy of high service and high margins. D.B. White was the only all-Canadian company in markets dominated by foreign firms.

Most of the products were not new and were easily copied. Many of the products came from licences and agreements with other companies because the research and development laboratory was used primarily for testing chemicals as part of customer service. A new product committee was formed in 1975 with the objective of finding products that would possess some competitive advantage, have prospects of four or five years in the market, and be compatible with the D.B. White marketing and manufacturing resources.

Although the company had encountered two or three new product failures, the reputation among customers, distributors, and suppliers was excellent. The president and the executive vice-president were actively searching for new licences and acquisitions of other companies in related fields.

The twenty salesmen were reasonably knowledgeable concerning the products and their applications. The company had a strong distribution network of three hundred wholesalers and dealers across Canada and direct sales to one hundred large contractors. Even with four hundred accounts, the president judged that there were another one hundred accounts worth pursuing. The top executives held degrees in business administration. Through a program of early retirement and active personal assessment, the president judged that he had acquired a core of capable, hard-working people. However, he acknowledged that he was short of seasoned middle managers.

The board of directors set three objectives: to achieve a 12 percent return on equity before tax, to see the employees expand their abilities, and to maintain a good reputation with customers, distributors, and lending institutions. The shareholders had decided to take modest dividend payments and plow most of the money back into the company in order for it to grow.

Now as an exercise, let us take the partial information on the D.B. White organization and reorganize it into an analysis of internal factors. Exhibit 2 shows what it might look like.

Now that you have reorganized the information, ask yourself what type of marketing ventures this company should entertain. Here is a list of possible ventures the company could consider:

1. try to further expand their distribution overseas;

2. try to find new channels of distribution such as chain food stores in order to market their products to consumers;

3. invest in research and development to come up with their own new products rather than relying on licences;

4. lower the prices on their products in order to stimulate sales;

5. advertise their products to contractors, wholesalers, and retailers;

Exhibit 2 D.B. White Limited

Internal Factors

OBJECTIVES

1. 12 percent return on equity
2. To help employees expand abilities
3. To maintain a good reputation with customers, distributors, and lending institutions

CURRENT RISKS

1. Ability to find products offering a competitive advantage
2. Instability of construction business
3. Loss of key middle and top managers

STRENGTHS

1. Good reputation for products and service
2. Cheap manufacturing and storage facilities close to large markets
3. Good customer and distributor base
4. Good relations with suppliers
5. Good employees
6. An all-Canadian company in markets dominated by foreign-owned firms
7. Flexibility to move quickly because of small size

WEAKNESSES

1. Spread thin with small foreign operations
2. Insufficient seasoned middle managers
3. Do not dominate any market
4. Wide product line makes technical expertise more difficult
5. Products are losing competitive advantage, being copied
6. Deal in many small markets
7. Factory equipment is old and not totally reliable or efficient

6. advertise their products to the public;

7. acquire new product lines that have a distinctive competitive advantage and high margins;

8. mount an aggressive selling campaign to acquire additional accounts;

9. throw out any products more than ten years old or selling less than $5000 per year; and

10. stop buying many of the commodities in semiproduced form and manufacture a greater portion of each of the components themselves.

When we consider the information, there really are only two strong alternatives among the ten listed. You should be able to guess them from the company data which has been reorganized in exhibit 2.

They are options 7 and 8. Option 7 makes sense because it is clear that the majority of products are not offering the competitive advantage needed for the firm to survive. Option 8 is needed because the products rely on distribution and capture only a small share of any market.

Let us go through the other options and see why they do not seem feasible for this company.

1. Further expansion overseas—tends to spread the company personnel too thinly.

2. Food store channels—no expertise in consumer marketing or dealing with retail food chain store operations.

3. Invest in R & D—too long and too uncertain for a small company. D.B. White's strength is marketing to industry.

4. Lower prices—not consistent with high service strategy.

5. Advertise to channels—already well known to dealers and distributors.

6. Advertise to public—too expensive, no skills, no channels, no packaging.

9. Toss out old and small products—would cut their sales by half and most of the old products still contribute to overhead and profit.

10. More manufacturing—equipment is unreliable and *marketing* is the company's strength.

Let's stop for a moment and ask how this framework of internal factors helped in analyzing a partial case problem. You were able to discard some action options before you wasted time on them. As you saw from the evaluation of the ten options, you discarded several if the company did not have sufficient strength in a critical area to carry out the option. For example, there would be no point in a company with old, outmoded equipment attempting to manufacture a greater portion of the chemicals they processed. The manufacturing side was a weakness of the company rather than a strength.

We are not recommending that you immediately consider options after you have done an analysis of internal factors. As you will see from the next section, you should wait until you have analyzed the buyers, the competition, the channels of distribution, and the opportunities before you generate these strategic options. However, we have made the point that the analysis of internal factors can orient you and simplify the remaining analysis. This is why you should do a thorough analysis of internal factors as soon as you can see what some of the issues in the case might be.

It should be clear that a framework gives an enormous advantage in getting started on a marketing problem. You still have to make assumptions and build a logical analysis with a creative mind, but at least you have a road map.

To some degree, case analysis is a process of simplification. You must organize the facts and assumptions, and then you must weigh the most important facts and assumptions, paring away the less relevant so that you can focus on a few manageable items. You will understand frameworks better after you have done a few cases.

Buyers

The first thing to consider in a buyer analysis is the market size and growth potential. Most markets contain buyers who use substantially different processes and criteria for their purchase. A product or service cannot be all things to all people, so you should pick a homogeneous group with whom you can do well. When you have identified the process and criteria used by a particular segment of buyers, the implications for marketing strategy become fairly clear. Hence, you have an important piece of the data to develop strategy options.

One of the most common problems in using the buyer framework is the difficulty, in the absence of case data, of knowing how someone such as a hotel manager buys cleaning supplies. You probably have never worked in a hotel, nor do you know anyone who has hotel experience. You are forced to make assumptions, pretend that you are running a hotel, and think about the criteria and process you might use. Nine times out of ten you can guess fairly accurately about the behaviour of buyers. However, sometimes when you are making these assumptions about buyer process and criteria, you will find that you and a friend purchase the same item using two very different patterns. How does a buyer analysis accommodate this? You and your friend *may* typify different segments, but your analysis *may be too particular*. Most buyer analyses are done at a fairly high level of aggregation in which a lot of individual and small-group differences are ignored.

Channels

The dimensions listed for channels are not exhaustive. The same list could be used to compare the existing channels with the ideal channels for a particular product or service. With *new products*, the big question is: What do the desired channels want and can our product/service deliver enough to get on board? Another important question for new products is the maximum trial period before the reseller thinks about dropping the product.

At the risk of oversimplifying channel behaviour, we can list the criteria used by most wholesalers and retailers in evaluating a product line:

1. Does it meet a need? Will it sell?

2. Does it return good gross profit dollars (margin times turnover) for inventory and space used?

3. Is it largely service-free?

Resellers usually have some form of committee or group approach to evaluating products. Even the small independent talks to somebody before adding or dropping a line. Channel analysis tends to be fairly straightforward, and few students have difficulty projecting themselves into the role of a retailer or wholesaler.

Competitors

Almost everything you buy is set in some sort of competitive context. Even the telephone and utility companies compete with other modes of communication and energy. One of the first issues to identify is the directness of the competition. If the competitors attempt to satisfy the same customer needs with the same products in the same way, the competition cannot be more direct. However, often firms are only partial competitors with one another. For example, product lines and geographic markets may overlap. The competitive patterns in many Canadian industries turn out to be mosaics where partial competition between firms (as defined above) is more the rule than simple direct competition. The result is that competitive analysis has to be taken on a case-by-case basis and you must try to assess the extent of the competition.

It is important to know the strategic dimensions on which competition takes place: marketing communications? price? product innovation? service? channel control? You would like to know the apparent marketing strategy of each competitor and the potency or potential threat to your marketing efforts.

Why should you analyze competitors? How can they stop your project or organization? It is not a black-and-white matter of competitors preventing your project, but they may *limit* your degree of success. Moreover, in all your strategy, you are trying to find soft spots in the armor of the "enemy," soft spots such as poor service, incomplete lines, high prices in a price-sensitive market, weak communication, and ineffective channels of distribution. By improving upon one or several of these weak spots, your organization can gain a competitive advantage.

What do you do with cases that have relatively little data on competitors and the data seem rather judgmental? You will have to tolerate the sparse data and make whatever assumptions you feel are necessary. In practice you will have the opportunity to check these assumptions, but even then time pressures often limit you to researching only the most crucial ones. Competitors are moving targets, and today's data are not good for very long anyway.

Opportunities

Most cases will suggest several opportunities to meet the organization's objectives. We must recognize, define, and evaluate those opportunities in light of our analysis of internal and external factors.

Recognizing and defining an opportunity is one of the most important yet least structured activities in marketing analysis. Many entrepreneurs seem to have an intuitive sense of opportunity, but there are some techniques which may help the rest of us. Problems may be opportunities in disguise if we can solve the problem and thereby meet a buyer's needs or gain a competitive advantage. Our organization's strengths are the foundations for exploiting opportunities, and by reviewing these strengths, we may recognize some opportunities. Another source of opportunities is change in the political, economic, social, and technological environment, because change creates new game rules and competitors often are slow to adapt.

In the first stages of analysis we should define an opportunity broadly so that we do not miss significant possibilities. As we evaluate opportunities and develop strategies, the statement of opportunity will necessarily become more specific.

Earlier, we compared ten opportunities to the internal analysis of D.B. White Limited, and we immediately rejected eight of those opportunities. Rather than do this evaluation of opportunities at the conclusion of each piece of analysis, we should wait until the internal and external factors are analyzed. By then we should have thought of several opportunities which we may compare with our entire analysis.

An opportunity is nothing until it is exploited. The next step is to develop a set of marketing strategy options that will take the fullest advantage of the opportunity.

Marketing Strategy Options

Marketing strategy options are *combinations* of product, price, channels, and marketing communications, which includes advertising, personal selling, and sales promotion. You may have substrategies such as a promotion strategy, but each option in marketing strategy *should show all four strategic elements*. Using the strategy framework from exhibit 1, a marketing strategy option may contain a phrase from as many variables as needed, but you do not need to mention every item in the strategy check list. For example, one consistent strategy might be:

	Marketing strategy variables	Decision
Product	Quality	Superior
	Line	Deep
	Package/warranty/service	Superior
Price	Level	High
Channels of distribution	Number	Selective
	Motivation	Margin
Marketing communications	Amount	Low
	Type	Personal selling
	Control	Manufacturer

A second marketing strategy option might be identical to the above with the exception that communication might be raised to competitive levels. A third strategy would be the same as above but use *both* mass and personal communications. You can be very creative in generating marketing strategy options, but usually you hit upon a fundamental format and then vary *pieces* of the strategy.

Remember that this framework is just a crude shell, and although your recommendations follow the preferred option, the recommendations should be very specific and precise. For example, your choice of marketing strategy may be the price dimension listed as "high," but your recommendation says: "Price the shoe at $29.95, which is a premium of 20 percent over comparable styles."

Why must each strategy contain all four elements of marketing strategy? It is impossible to evaluate a marketing strategy if, for example, the price is unstated. Force yourself to be as explicit as you can. The frameworks are a double check to ensure that your analysis and strategies are comprehensive. After you have generated a marketing strategy, evaluate it in terms of its apparent feasibility, the extent and probability of meeting organizational objectives, exploiting a defined opportunity, taking fullest advantage of the total situation per exhibit 3, and its financial risk.

Exhibit 3 Marketing Strategy

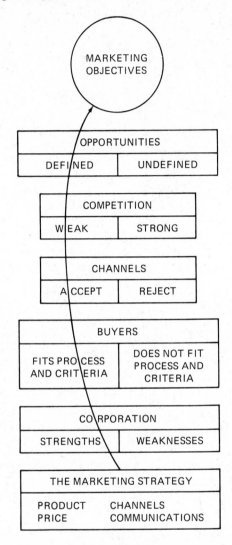

In your recommendations, you should describe the strategy in detail, show projected profit-and-loss statements that demonstrate the likely profit impact of your strategy, and show how you would *implement* the strategy. For example, who will initiate the strategy and when will he or she perform each part of the strategy? Try to be as specific as possible about the timing of the strategy parts such as the schedule of advertising and the frequency of sales calls. Thus, your strategy becomes an operational plan and potentially alive. You couldn't do any more in the actual situation!

Summary

The basic idea of marketing strategy is to meet marketing objectives in a way that takes best advantage of the organization's resources, the buyer's needs, the channels' abilities, the competitors' weaknesses, and the available opportunities. Exhibit 3 shows a highly simplified diagram of the skill you will learn as you practise solving the cases in this book.

1 Teledyne Canada Limited

In November 1975, the general manager of the Metal Products Division of Teledyne Canada Limited was faced with the problem of devising a marketing program for a household garbage-bag-handling system that might be added to the division's line of products.

Mr. Nutt, the division's general manager, had observed that plastic garbage bags were rapidly replacing the traditional garbage can, but storing these bags often posed a household problem. Plastic bags awaiting the weekly garbage pickup service gave off disagreeable odours, looked disorderly, were prey to animals, and provided a breeding place for flies.

To overcome this problem, Mr. Nutt had designed a special metal container. Despite the fact that the company's draftsmen had never developed a product similar to this, they were able to embody most of Mr. Nutt's ideas in a light, compact, and durable piece of household equipment (exhibit 1). The container was made of rust-resistant heavy-gauge steel, and the exterior faces had a green baked-enamel finish. It could be assembled in about five minutes with a slip-in corner system[1] that eliminated the need for tools and bolts to assemble the unit. The container had a bottom, a counterbalanced stay-open lid, and a bag support apparatus[2] that held the bag open for filling and sealed the bag when the lid was closed. There was enough storage area for at least four full bags.

The Company

The division's primary line was cabs for off-highway equipment such as front-end loaders, crane carriers, road graders, and large open-pit-mining trucks. The second product line was fuel tanks, hydraulic oil tanks, and other fabricated parts for the same type of vehicles. A third line was job shop pro-

1,2. Patent applied for.

duction of many different metal products for farm equipment. The plant was not at full capacity.

Production

Fabrication of the garbage-handling system was essentially a metalworking task. The component parts were stamped to shape, painted, and then packed unassembled into cardboard containers. The division's labour force was well acquainted with the necessary processes as a result of the division's experience in the production of its major lines.

Exhibit 1

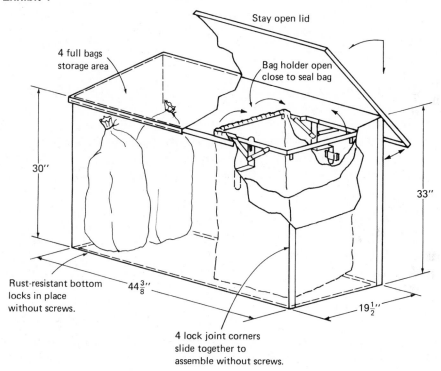

Stay open lid

4 full bags storage area

Bag holder open close to seal bag

30″

33″

Rust-resistant bottom locks in place without screws.

$44\frac{3}{8}''$

$19\frac{1}{2}''$

4 lock joint corners slide together to assemble without screws.

THE ALL NEW TELEDYNE HOUSEHOLD GARBAGE BAG HANDLING SYSTEM
The answer to every household's garbage bag handling and storage problem

1. A newly designed bag support which holds the bag open for filling and when closed, seals in odours and keeps flies out. (Patent applied for)

2. Extra storage area for a minimum of four full bags.

3. A self-stay-open lid.

4. Assembles in five minutes with the TELELOK corner system, eliminating the need for tools to bolt the assembly together. (Patent applied for)

5. Bottom locks in place to form support for bags.

6. Years of service through use of rust-resistant coated heavy-gauge steel.

7. Will stay colour bright in outdoor use because all exterior faces have baked enamel finish.

8. Keeps animals and vermin out.

9. Can be used for storage of garbage cans.

10. Attractive design to enhance a usually messy disposal area.

TELEDYNE   CANADA   METAL   PRODUCTS
460 Industrial Ave. (1 block north of Timberjack)
Woodstock, Ontario   Phone 519-537-2355

The unit variable costs were $15 in materials and $6 in labour. Reducing the thickness of the steel would save $1 per gauge. At $10 the gauge would be equivalent to the steel found in their competitor's product. However, Mr. Nutt felt that this lighter-gauge steel appeared flimsy.

Manufacturing and administration overheads directly associated with the garbage-handling system would vary with unit volume as shown below. The manufacturer's selling price would incorporate 12 percent federal sales tax.

Unit volume	Estimated total overhead ($)
0– 1,000	5,000
1,001– 5,000	10,000
5,001–25,000	20,000

Marketing

Although no quantitative estimates of the market had been made by Mr. Nutt or his staff, they believed that the product met the needs of a large number of Canadian homeowners.

Because the division had never marketed a household consumer product, it was decided to make a trial production run of two hundred units. The trial run was to try out the tooling and various means of advertising in the Woodstock area in order to map future national marketing programs. Mr. Nutt believed it was wise to use a test market and thus avoid the possibility of investing a large amount in a new product that could have hidden defects or could not be developed into a profitable item. For the trial run, he had purchased special tooling that cost $2700. The test market product was priced at $44.95 and sold directly to the consumer.

First Promotion

To decide on a name for the product, check consumer acceptance, and evaluate different advertising techniques, Mr. Nutt decided on a "Whatsit" contest. Anyone who had purchased a Teledyne Garbage Bag Handling System was eligible to enter the contest, and the prize was $100 for the best name.

One full-page ad (at a cost of $200) followed by a half-page ad (at a cost of $100) were placed in the *Oxford County Shopping Newspaper*, a free weekly tabloid (exhibit 2). Orders were to be placed at the plant for free home delivery in Woodstock. A sample of the product and contest signs (the cost of the signs was $225) was placed at branches of the Royal Bank of Canada and the Canadian Imperial Bank of Commerce in Woodstock as part of the bank's program of displaying local products of interest. In addition, company employees purchased the product and praised it to their friends.

Three days prior to the close of the contest, radio spot commercials at a total cost of $225 were used. These commercials ran for a minute each and were played twenty-eight times, evenly spaced throughout the three days. Sales of at least three units were directly attributable to the radio advertising.

Teledyne rented a booth at the Woodstock Fair for $40. The fair ran five days, and Mr. Nutt and his staff obtained a feel for consumer reaction to the new product. They learned that previous buyers were coming back to purchase a second container for uses Mr. Nutt had never thought of, such as a sail locker, tool storage bin, and oat bin for horses.

The winning name for the product was Garbage Geni. A picture of the winner receiving the cheque from Mr. Nutt was published in the local paper. In the announcement the winner said: "The product solved several garbage bag problems at my home. My wife can open the lid and operate the bag holder with one hand whereas before there was usually a mess because she did not have enough hands to hold the bag open and fill it at the same time."

The winner commented that he thought of the name because, like a geni, it made his garbage problems disappear. He suggested this as a slogan to Mr. Nutt.

The result of the promotion was 140 Garbage Genis sold in four months in the Woodstock area, which had a population in 1975 of approximately

Exhibit 2

CONTEST CLOSES SEPTEMBER 30TH.

LAST CHANCE TO **SAVE MONEY** BY

BUYING AT FACTORY PRICE & ENTER THE

TELEDYNE "WHATSIT" CONTEST

YOU COULD BE THE WINNER OF $100

BY SUBMITTING A NAME FOR TELEDYNE'S ALL NEW

HOUSEHOLD GARBAGE BAG HANDLING SYSTEM!

$100 PRIZE

FEATURES OF THE TELEDYNE SYSTEM INCLUDES:

1. A newly designed bag support which holds the bag open for filling and when closed, seals in odours and keeps flies out. (Patent applied for)

2. Extra storage area for a minimum of four full bags.

3. A self stay open lid.

4. Assembles in five minutes with the TELELOK corner system, eliminating the need for tools to bolt the assembly together. (Patent applied for)

5. Bottom locks in place to form support for bags.

6. Years of service through use of rust resistant coated heavy gauge steel.

7. Will stay colour bright in outdoor use because all exterior faces have baked enamel finish.

8. Keeps animals and vermin out.

9. Can be used for storage of garbage cans.

10. Attractive design to enhance a usually messy disposal area.

The answer to every household's garbage bag handling and storage problem.

Rules of the Contest Are:

1. You must have purchased a TELEDYNE GARBAGE BAG HANDLING SYSTEM from Teledyne Canada metal products at the reduced price of $44.95 provincial sales tax extra.

2. Submit your entry by mail on the contest card before the closing date.

3. In the event of the same name being submitted by more than one person, the one with the earliest postmark will be the winner.

4. In the event of the same postmark for the winning name from more than one contestant, the prize money will be divided accordingly.

5. Contestants must not be employees of Teledyne Canada or a member of their immediate family.

6. Decision of the contest judges will be final.

7. All names submitted become the property of Teledyne Canada Ltd.

CALL US AT 537-2355 FOR FREE DELIVERY IN WOODSTOCK

What can you do about that daily household headache? How do you keep the bags from spilling? How do you prevent the mess caused by rodents and animals? What can you do to eliminate the fly nuisance and the odours.

Answer! Use the Teledyne Household Garbage Bag Handling System with its neat and sanitary "open to fill, close to seal" bag manager.

YOU'LL LOVE THE NEW, HEALTHY, EASY TO OPERATE, COMPLETELY CHILD SAFE, GUARANTEED AND PROVEN DISCOVERY FOR HANDLING GARBAGE BAGS.

26,500 persons. Mr. Nutt commented that a large part of the sales were the result of owners of Garbage Geni selling its merits to friends.

To Mr. Nutt's knowledge, there was only one competitive product on the market. It was called Garbage Can House and had been distributed through Home Hardware stores for two years. Although it sold to the consumer for $29.95, it did not have Garbage Geni's features. This garbage container was made of a lighter-gauge steel than the test market Garbage Geni, had no bottom, used screws and bolts, had no bag manager, and required the additional purchase of two garbage cans. Mr. Nutt felt that the superior features offered by Garbage Geni gave it a sales appeal not matched by its competitor. Mr. Nutt had heard rumours of a second competitor beginning production, but the details of the product were not known.

Future Marketing

In November of 1975, Mr. Nutt was approached by three organizations seeking distribution rights to the Garbage Geni. During the initial test market period, a Garbage Geni had been displayed in the plant's reception area. Two manufacturers' agents saw the display and asked Mr. Nutt for the exclusive rights to market Garbage Geni in Canada. One agent was engaged in advertising for several products, and the other agent had a liaison with six agents across Canada. Although Mr. Nutt did not talk price with these two men, both agents indicated that they would sell the product to retailers for a commission of 10 percent of the selling price to retailers. The retailers would take a markup of 50 percent of the selling price to their customers.

Mr. Nutt also had been invited to make a presentation to a large well-known chain of automotive stores. Although the direct factory price to the consumer in the test market had been $44.95, Mr. Nutt suggested that the automotive chain sell the Garbage Geni for $56.95 based on a factory-to-retailer price of $39.90. However, the automotive chain store buyer said that the Garbage Geni was too expensive at $56.95 and a 30 percent markup was inadequate for his chain. The buyer wanted a minimum markup of 50 percent on suggested list price, even though the chain probably would lower the consumer price slightly for competitive reasons.[3] Despite this discouraging view of an acceptable price, Mr. Nutt and his

---

3. For example, if the manufacturer's selling price was $1, the retail organization would want to sell it for $2. This consumer price could be reduced to, say, $1.79 if the organization felt that it was necessary in order to give it a competitive edge.

staff were of the opinion that the product could fill a real need for a large number of families in the middle and upper income levels.

During this time, Mr. Nutt had requested the estimating department to develop a new cost based on fully tooling the unit at an additional cost of $6000. The extra tooling could reduce labour costs by $1 per unit.

Mr. Nutt believed that the spring and summer of 1976 would produce good consumer acceptance for the product, but if he was to capitalize on that potential, he would have to make a decision soon on feasibility and marketing. Despite that pressure, Mr. Nutt did not feel that he was ready for full-scale negotiations with the chain store buyers, who he felt "would squeeze every last cent."

Mr. Nutt wondered whether he should use lighter-gauge steel and/or invest another $6000 in tooling in order to achieve a lower price. He could sell directly to consumers, sell through agents, or reopen talks with the automotive chain store buyers.

Mr. Nutt thought that building supply stores, lumber yards, hardware stores, discount stores, and catalogue operations would demand a 50 percent retail margin on their selling price. Point-of-purchase materials for retail stores would cost $5000, and he was told that $30,000 in cooperative advertising would help the acceptance of a new product. If he assembled his own sales force to sell Garbage Geni through hardware stores, building supply, and lumber yards, each salesman would cost $25,000 per year including travelling expenses.

Mr. Nutt had not discarded the idea of a door-to-door sales force, perhaps employing students in the summer. The door-to-door salesmen might sell the Garbage Geni at $79.99 and take a 50 percent sales commission. Some recruiting and sales supervision would be necessary.

Mr. Nutt had considerable financial resources available from Teledyne Corporation provided he could foresee a reasonable financial contribution from the project. There were several combinations of options that he could visualize as alternative marketing strategies. He was enthusiastic about the prospects for the Garbage Geni, but he wondered what specific action he should take.

2 The Old Bridge Inn

One day in October 1981, Tim Agnew approached his friend and fellow classmate Tom Bauer with a problem. The Inn which Tim's mother owned and operated in Young's Point, Ontario, had encountered financial difficulties. Cash reserves had dwindled to zero. Creditors, including the federal government, had threatened to place a lien on the premises if payments were not met. At the same time, Mrs. Agnew had just taken ill and was unable to properly deal with the situation. As a result, Tim decided to leave school in order to run the business. He wondered if Tom might have any suggestions as to how the Inn's operations should be managed.

On the first weekend in November, Tom set out for Young's Point, which is located twenty kilometres northeast of the city of Peterborough (see exhibit 1). While the initial drive along Highway 401 was rather uninteresting, the scenery soon improved as Tom turned north onto Highway 115 outside Port Hope. After a 45-minute drive, Tom saw a weather-beaten sign indicating that his destination was near. Almost before he realized it, Tom drove through Young's Point and found himself in the country again. There was no sign of the Inn. Remembering Tim's description of the Inn as lying beside the Trent-Severn canal system, Tom retraced his route. Near the point where the highway crossed the Otonabee River, he saw, buried among a myriad of nameplates, a tiny sign for the Old Bridge Inn. Following the sign to the end of a short dead end road, Tom found himself in front of a large two-storey red-brick building. On the roof of the building stood a relatively small, simple sign stating: Old Bridge Inn.

Tom pulled his car into the empty parking lot adjacent to the building, got out, and approached the front door. The curtains were drawn, and inside there appeared to be no sign of life. Tom pulled on the door and found, much to his surprise, that it was open. He walked in, his eyes trying to accustom themselves to the darkness. "Good afternoon, can I help

Exhibit 1 The Old Bridge Inn Located Near "E"

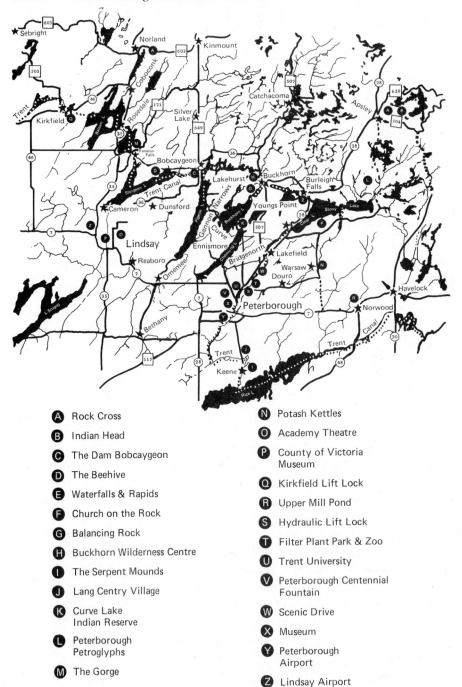

Ⓐ Rock Cross

Ⓑ Indian Head

Ⓒ The Dam Bobcaygeon

Ⓓ The Beehive

Ⓔ Waterfalls & Rapids

Ⓕ Church on the Rock

Ⓖ Balancing Rock

Ⓗ Buckhorn Wilderness Centre

Ⓘ The Serpent Mounds

Ⓙ Lang Centry Village

Ⓚ Curve Lake
Indian Reserve

Ⓛ Peterborough
Petroglyphs

Ⓜ The Gorge

Ⓝ Potash Kettles

Ⓞ Academy Theatre

Ⓟ County of Victoria
Museum

Ⓠ Kirkfield Lift Lock

Ⓡ Upper Mill Pond

Ⓢ Hydraulic Lift Lock

Ⓣ Filter Plant Park & Zoo

Ⓤ Trent University

Ⓥ Peterborough Centennial
Fountain

Ⓦ Scenic Drive

Ⓧ Museum

Ⓨ Peterborough
Airport

Ⓩ Lindsay Airport

you?'' a voice asked from the back. It was Mary, the 21-year-old cook. After explaining the purpose of his visit, Tom was shown upstairs, where he found Tim.

History of the Inn

Tim provided Tom with a brief background of the Inn. The main support beam dated back to 1887. The Inn had originally been built as a general store/roadhouse at the junction of the Otonabee River and the old Highway 28. Its clientele was composed mainly of loggers and raftsmen. Initially, business flourished; however, as Highway 28 was expanded and moved 50 metres to the west in 1940, business dropped off. The original bridge beside which the Inn stands was now closed to vehicular traffic and open only to pedestrians.

With the decline in business, the Inn fell into a state of disrepair. It changed ownership several times, being used exclusively as a private residence. In 1955, the Inn was bought by Mr. Russ Brooks. He obtained a liquor license, hired a honky-tonk piano player, and turned the Inn into a local drinking establishment. Tim summed up the Inn's previous reputation as being a ''booze-it-up joint.'' Although ownership of the Inn changed hands four times within the Brooks family, its operations remained essentially unchanged. Throughout this period, the Inn had a record of consistent, though minimal, earnings losses.

Agnew Family Involvement

In August of 1980, the Old Bridge Inn was purchased by Mrs. Annabelle Agnew. Mrs. Agnew, a widow, had been left a sizeable inheritance by her late husband. With her sons no longer living at home, Mrs. Agnew decided that she wished to try her hand at running a business. While visiting a real estate agent one day in her hometown of Toronto, she saw a picture of the Inn and immediately fell in love with it. Although she had no previous experience in the restaurant business, Mrs. Agnew had taken several Cordon Bleu cooking courses. She decided that the Inn presented a perfect opportunity to combine business with her love of cooking. As a result, a purchase agreement was drawn up in which ownership was transferred to Mrs. Agnew at a ''distress price'' of $75,000. A further $15,000 was invested to restore the Inn to its current condition.

Difficulties Facing the Inn

Although Mrs. Agnew had been able to increase gross sales from $10,000 to over $90,000, the Inn was still faced with financial difficulties (see exhibit 2). The Inn had narrowly succeeded in paying off its overdue accounts, and its cash reserves were now nonexistent (see exhibit 3). Mrs. Agnew was hoping to find a new buyer for the Inn, but sale of the Inn before the turn of the new year seemed highly unlikely. In order for the Inn to survive that long, a positive cash flow was badly needed. The cash flow problem was aggravated by the fact that most of the Inn's revenues were generated by tourists during the summer season (see exhibits 4 and 5).

While cash flow was the Inn's most pressing concern, profitability in the past had been hurt by a high level of operating expenses. Tim had taken several steps to reduce these expenses. Cost of food sold had been reduced drastically by arranging for weekly delivery from a large Ontario meat-processing firm rather than buying at retail from a local supermarket.

Exhibit 2 The Old Bridge Inn Income Statement
for the Year Ended October 15, 1981

REVENUES:

Food Sales	$62,995	
Cost of Food	19,821	$43,174
Beverage Sales	29,665	
Cost of Beverages	10,369	19,296
Other Revenue		2,108
Gross Margin		$64,578

EXPENSES:

Telephone	$ 695	
Utilities	5,512	
Services	3,396	
Advertising	4,272	
Office Supplies	592	
Kitchen & Bar Supplies	1,588	
Entertainment	5,497	
Wages	41,763	
Insurance	1,273	
Depreciation	4,220	
Taxes	789	
Interest	8,343	$77,940
Profit/(Loss)		($13,362)

Exhibit 3   The Old Bridge Inn Balance Sheet (October 15, 1981)

ASSETS:

Cash		$ 0
Inventory Food		1,900
Beverage		2,000
Bar/Dining Supplies		400
Office Supplies		500
Building	$44,459	
less Depreciation	2,046	42,413
Equipment	12,353	
less Depreciation	2,174	10,179
Land		35,000
TOTAL		$92,392

LIABILITIES:

A/P	$ 9,912
First Mortgage	42,000
Second Mortgage	8,000
	$59,912

EQUITY:

Agnew	$32,480
TOTAL	$92,392

Renegotiation of the Inn's first mortgage at 14 percent through a Small Business Development Bond from a chartered bank would save an additional $2450 annually. Tim also felt that the Inn's wage expenses were too high, although he was not sure how they might be reduced.

The Inn's Upstairs

Having explained the history of the Inn and the current difficulties facing it, Tim decided to give Tom a tour of the premises. They started off by viewing the second floor. This level consisted of two unattached sections, each accessible via its own staircase (see exhibit 6). The larger section consisted of seven single rooms and two bathrooms. Five of the seven rooms were currently inhabited by Mrs. Agnew, Tim, and their Great Dane, Abraham. The remaining three rooms were used to store various articles.

Exhibit 4   The Old Bridge Inn Income Statement
for the 6 Months Ended April 15, 1981

REVENUES:

Food Sales	$11,869	
Cost of Food	5,478	$ 6,391
Beverage Sales	6,723	
Cost of Beverages	2,494	4,229
Gross Margin		$10,630

EXPENSES:

Telephone	$ 484	
Utilities	3,227	
Services	1,616	
Advertising	1,602	
Office Supplies	342	
Kitchen & Bar Supplies	1,382	
Entertainment	1,630	
Wages	12,656	
Depreciation	4,220	
Interest	2,181	$29,340
Profit/(Loss)		($18,710)

The smaller upstairs section, consisting of four rooms and a bathroom, was available for rent on a nightly basis. Each room was simply furnished and contained a mirror and washbasin. Three of the four rooms held double beds, while the fourth held two single beds. The nightly charge per room was eighteen dollars. Income derived from the rental of rooms ac-counted for almost all that is listed under "Other Revenue" in the operating statements.

Kitchen Operations

The next stop on the tour was the kitchen (see exhibit 7). The kitchen area had been built onto the Inn in 1955. A long wood-topped counter ran down the middle of the kitchen, making maneuvering rather cumbersome. One side of the kitchen was lined with a counter containing a household dishwasher, three sinks, two ovens, one with six ranges and the other with a heating plate, a microwave oven, and a deep freezer. The other wall of the kitchen was occupied by three large old refrigerators and shelves containing numerous articles and memorabilia from the Agnew family past.

An outline of typical operations was obtained through discussion with Mary, the cook. The initial part of the day was spent on the preparation of food items prior to cooking. Such preparation was carried out on an ongoing basis from 10:00 A.M. until early evening. It was interrupted frequently as customer orders for meals were received.

Further discussion revealed the existence of several recurring problems which had been encountered in the past. A major concern was the limited cooking capacity. The two stove/ovens combined were able to heat only a maximum of twelve plates at any given time. The microwave oven presented an even greater bottleneck. It was able to accommodate only five individual servings of vegetables. Cycle time for the microwave was approximately three minutes, compared to five minutes for the oven. During banquets or the peak summer period, when up to 70 people might be

Exhibit 5 The Old Bridge Inn Income Statement
for the 6 Months Ended October 15, 1981

REVENUES:

Food Sales	$51,126	
Cost of Food	14,343	$36,783
Beverage Sales	22,942	
Cost of Beverages	7,885	15,057
Other Revenue		2,108
Gross Margin		$53,948

EXPENSES:

Telephone	$ 211	
Utilities	2,285	
Services	1,780	
Advertising	2,670	
Office Supplies	250	
Kitchen & Bar Supplies	206	
Entertainment	3,867	
Wages	29,107	
Insurance	1,273	
Taxes	789	
Interest	6,162	$48,600
Profit/(Loss)		$ 5,348

Exhibit 6 Second Floor Plan

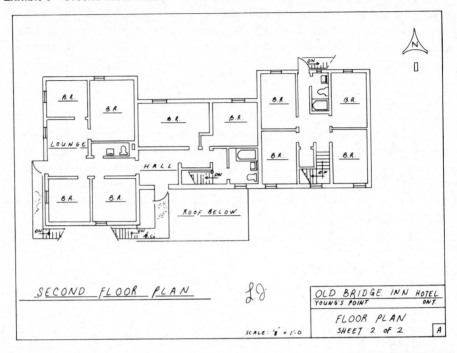

eating dinner at the same time, this lack of capacity became a definite problem. Maintaining enough clean dishes and glasses to serve customers also became a problem during busy periods, because the household dishwasher had a cycle time of 45 minutes. To help alleviate this problem, a student was sometimes hired to wash dishes by hand.

Another problem mentioned was the lack of space in the kitchen. In the summer, the kitchen was often staffed with five people: Mrs. Agnew acting as head cook, Mary as assistant cook, two kitchen helpers, and a dishwasher. In addition, waitresses would constantly walk in and out of the kitchen to place and pick up orders. As a result, it was "near impossible to make it from one end of the kitchen to the other without knocking someone or something over."

The Dining Area

The scene which he had just heard described contrasted sharply with the calm Tom found as he entered the dining area. Although it was 6:00 P.M.

Exhibit 7 First Floor Plan

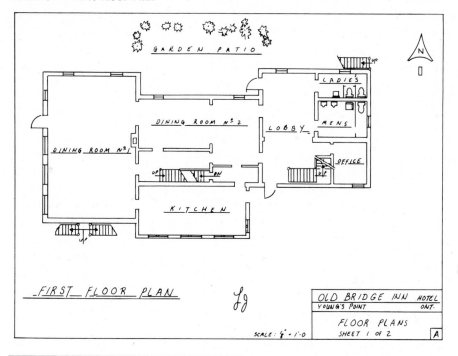

on a Saturday evening, there were only four couples in both dining rooms. Tom sat down at the polished wood bar and ordered a drink from the bartender, Karen. He chuckled to himself as he tried to picture what a group of fishermen in hip-waders would look like amidst the dark oak beams, Tiffany lamps, and spotless silverware. Apparently, hobby fishermen frequently walked over to the Inn from the nearby locks during the summer months, but few actually stayed for a drink or a meal after looking in the door.

A piano standing in one corner of the front dining room caught Tom's attention, and he inquired if it was ever used. Karen replied that during the summer, the Inn had a policy of providing live entertainment every Friday and Saturday evening. A singer/songwriter from the Peterborough musicians union was usually hired at a cost of $150 per weekend. Most of the performers played middle-of-the-road pop, although the Inn's most popular performers had been a country and western duet. Advertisements in the local newspapers and radio were used to notify the public of upcoming entertainers.

Through further discussion with Karen, Tom discovered that the low turn-out was a common occurrence in the off-season. In fact the Inn often closed its doors early owing to a lack of customers. The Inn's mainstay patrons during the winter season fell into three groups: young couples, families, and senior citizens. Of these, the last group seemed to represent the only steady repeat customers. Most customers lived outside a 10-kilometre radius from the Inn. When asked why this was so, Karen conceded that the Inn had earned a bad reputation amongst the local populace. Most disliked the high-class image which the Inn conveyed. Comments such as "The prices are too high," "I can't relax here," "Why don't you get rid of this silver and get some brighter tablecloths!" were typical of the local sentiment.

In addition, there were unflattering comments about the level of service, especially during the summer. One local banquet group was so upset by the slow service that its members had vowed never to return to the Inn. Word of such incidents spread quickly throughout the community, and as a result, Karen felt that the Inn would have to work hard in order to regain the confidence and business of the local population.

By this time, Tom was getting rather hungry, and Tim's offer of a complimentary meal was gratefully accepted. While glancing over the handwritten menu (see exhibit 8) and wine list, Tom mentioned the several points which Karen had raised previously. Tim agreed that the Inn did not have a strong local draw. He felt that its current operations were targeted at the middle and upper income groups living in the Peterborough area (see exhibit 9). The problem of poor service was probably the combined result of limited cooking capacity and inexperienced waitresses. Hiring waitresses with the desired level of experience from the local labour pool had proven to be difficult in the past.

With the arrival of the meal, the conversation broke off. Tom had ordered the soup of the day to start off his meal. The first spoonful of piping hot broth convinced him that the soup was definitely homemade. The main course turned out to be as pleasant a surprise as the appetizer. The seafood creole was warm, the vegetables crisp, and the potatoes plentiful. With the mention of dessert, Tom started to eye his waistline. However, within no time at all, he found himself ordering a second serving of a freshly baked pumpkin pie.

As Tim and Tom contemplated the day's progress over a second bottle of wine, their thoughts were interrupted by a vocal uprising from the side dining room. A table of four middle-aged customers was demanding that the waitress bring over Mrs. Agnew and the dog Abraham. Tim walked

Exhibit 8

THE
OLD
BRIDGE
INN

Good Evening!

Menu

Young's Point, Ontario
(705) 652-3661

Roast Beef	$10.50
Peter's Seafood Pot	$9.25
(Lobster, Shrimp, Crab in a Cream Sherry Sauce)	
Barbequed Ribs	$8.95
Striploin Steak	$9.50

Above Served With:

Homemade Vegetable Soup or Tossed Salad
Parsley Potatoe

Choice of: Creamed Carrots & Onions, Ratatouille
or Broccoli & Cauliflower in a Cheese Wine Sauce

Desserts

Pumpkin Pie ⎫
Raisin Pie ⎬ $1.50

Tipsy Trifle $1.75

Coffee, Tea, Milk   40¢
Enjoy Your Meal

---

over to the table and explained that Mrs. Agnew was sick and upstairs lying in bed. However, the group persisted with their demand until Tim grudgingly went upstairs to call his mother and the dog. Upon Tim's return, Tom eagerly inquired as to the nature of the problem. "No problem at all," replied Tim, "It's just a bunch of my mother's friends who get upset if they don't see her and the dog whenever they come here."

Exhibit 9 Census Agglomeration of Peterborough

Market: 34% above national average

Retail sales, 1979	$280,000,000
% Canadian total	0.37
Per capita	$4,265

Income: 7% above national average

Personal disposable income, 1979	$505,800,000
% Canadian total	0.30
Per capita	$7,706

Current Growth Rate: 2% per decade

Population, June 1, 1979	65,600
% Canadian total	0.28
% Change, '76–'79	+0.47

POPULATION

1976 Census:

Total		65,290
Male		31,450
Female		33,840

Age groups:	Male	Female
0–4	2,250	2,120
5–9	2,410	2,400
10–14	3,050	2,910
15–19	3,310	3,355
20–24	3,185	3,095
25–34	4,620	4,565
35–44	3,320	3,410
45–54	3,485	4,005
55–64	3,025	3,565
65–69	1,135	1,425
70 + ...	1,670	3,000

FAMILIES

	1976
No.	16,965
Aver. no. per family	3.3

LEVEL OF SCHOOLING

	1976 Census	% Total
Population, 15 yrs. + ...	50,210	100
Less than gr. 5	880	2
Grades 5–8	9,010	18
Grades 9–10	10,845	22
Grades 11–13	14,340	29
Postsecondary, nonuniversity . . .	7,740	15
University only . . .	4,390	9
University & postsecondary, nonuniversity . . .	3,015	6

Note: Level of schooling refers to the highest grade or year completed by the person. Those currently enrolled reported their present grade or year.

EMPLOYMENT

(1961 = 100)	Peter-borough	Canada
1974	140.8	142.8
1975	147.6	141.1
1976	140.6	144.1
1977	132.5	144.3
1978	136.0	146.5

Exhibit 9   (continued)

HOUSEHOLDS

	1976
No.	21,620
Aver. no. per household	2.9

HOUSING

	1976 Census	% Total
Occupied dwellings no.	21,620	100
Owned	14,320	66
Rented	7,300	34

MOTHER TONGUE

	1976 Census	% Total
English	61,755	94.6
French	530	0.8

RETAIL TRADE

1971 Census

Total sales, $000		133,569
Stores, no.		457

By kind of business group:	Stores No.	Sales $000
Food	74	33,934
Groceries, confectionery & sundries	14	1,105
Grocery	17	2,186
Combination*	22	28,955
Meat markets	5	702
General merchandise	18	21,352
Automotive	125	37,212
Apparel & accessories	59	9,112
Hardware & home furnishings	55	10,211
Furniture, TV, radio, appliance, etc.	13	6,374
Other stores	126	21,746

*Grocery stores with fresh meat.

TAXATION STATISTICS

Income class:	1977	% of Total
Under $2,500	6,893	16.0
$2,500–5,000	7,229	16.8
5,000–7,500	6,220	14.5
7,500–10,000	4,327	10.1
10,000–12,500	4,105	9.5
12,500–15,000	4,274	9.9
15,000–20,000	6,292	14.6
20,000–25,000	1,620	3.8
25,000–30,000	1,109	2.6
30,000 & over	952	2.2
Total returns, no.	43,021	100.0
Total Inc., $000	434,460	...
Average income, $	10,099	...
Total tax, $000	60,997	...
Average tax, $	2,276	...

EARNINGS

	Av. weekly earnings $	
	Peterborough	Canada
1974	183.61	178.09
1975	205.08	203.34
1976	225.25	228.03
1977	239.18	249.95
1978	250.22	265.37

NEWSPAPERS

Newspaper, daily:	1979
Examiner (Thomson)	
Circulation, total	23,712
city	15,388
outside	8,324
Newspaper, weekly: Review	29,700

RADIO STATIONS

CHEX, 10,000 watts.
CKPT, 10,000 watts.
CFMP-FM, 31,400 watts.
CKQM-FM, 50,000 watts.

TELEVISION STATION

CHEX-TV, Video, 163,000 watts ERP.

Exhibit 9 (continued)

PORT HOPE

POPULATION

1976 Census:

Total		9,785
Male		4,720
Female		5,065

Age groups:	Male	Female
0–4	425	380
5–9	400	360
10–14	425	435
15–19	415	420
20–24	420	415
25–34	745	720
35–44	475	460
45–54	500	555
55–64	450	540
65–69	180	235
70 + ...	285	555

FAMILIES

	1976
No.	2,590
Aver. no. per family	3.2

MOTHER TONGUE

	1976 Census	% Total
English	9,265	94.7
French	100	1.0
Netherlandic & Flemish	110	1.1

HOUSEHOLDS

	1976
No.	3,317
Aver. no. per household	2.9

HOUSING

	1976 Census	% Total
Occupied dwellings, no.	3,320	100
Owned	2,245	68
Rented	1,075	32

EARNINGS

	Av. weekly earnings $	
	Port Hope	Canada
1974	172.54	178.09
1975	199.22	203.34
1976	222.99	228.03
1977	245.28	249.95
1978	263.32	265.37

BUILDING PERMITS

	1978	1977	1976
		—$000—	
Value	10,963	2,174	1,706

EMPLOYMENT

(1961 = 100)	Port Hope	Canada
1974	189.3	142.8
1975	180.5	141.1
1976	183.5	144.4
1977	189.1	144.3
1978	188.7	146.5

LEVEL OF SCHOOLING

	1976 Census	% Total
Population, 15 yrs. + ...	7,370	100
Less than gr. 5	190	3
Grades 5–8	1,305	18
Grades 9–10	1,780	24
Grades 11–13	2,165	29
Postsecondary, nonuniversity ...	1,025	14
University only ...	545	7
University & postsecondary, nonuniversity ...	360	5

Note: Level of schooling refers to the highest grade or year completed by the person. Those currently enrolled reported their present grade or year.

The Patio

With the completion of the bottle of wine, Tim and Tom got up to finish their tour of the Inn. All that remained was the patio. Although it was dark outside, floodlights helped to illuminate the patio area. The patio was a recent addition to the Inn, having been set up by Tim the previous summer. Cedar tables and benches had been handbuilt by a local craftsman. The maximum number of customers allowed on the patio under the liquor licence was 66 people.

During the summer, the patio had been open every day from noon until 11:00 P.M. A portable bar had been set up outside. An additional bartender had been hired to take orders and serve both food and drinks. Four large vats filled with ice served to keep the drinks cold. A self-serve barbeque was set up for customers wishing to grill hamburgers, etc. Other items could be ordered via the bartender from the kitchen. These items were typically similar to those offered on the luncheon menu. No full course meals were offered outside. A small speaker system hooked into the main system indoors broadcast music or live performances from inside when they occurred.

Although the patio had been moderately successful, Tim felt that the Inn had not taken full advantage of its potential. Tim thought that most of the people using the patio were customers who were waiting for an empty table inside so that they could eat a full dinner. Tim also thought that the live entertainment offered on weekends in the front dining room served to draw customers from the patio to inside. As a result, the level of patio sales usually dropped abruptly after 9:00 P.M.

Competitors

Having completed the rather lengthy tour of the Inn, Tim suggested that Tom might want to take a look at the operations of the Chemong Lodge. The Lodge was an operation similar to the Inn located 14 kilometres away in Bridgenorth. En route to Bridgenorth, the two decided to stop off at the Commercial Hotel, the local watering hole. The Commercial was typical of most small town bars—loud, crowded, and unpretentious with entertainment provided by a guitar player dressed in cowboy attire. After a lively discussion with Fred, an elderly regular who also frequented the Inn, Tom and Tim continued on their way.

The Chemong Lodge was an interconnected network of log cabins built by its owner, with approximately twice the seating capacity of the Old Bridge Inn. Items offered on the menu were typically of the surf-n-turf variety, with entrees priced about $2 higher than the Inn's. At the time of the visit, the Lodge was slightly over one-quarter full. Most of the customers were well-dressed couples in their late twenties or early thirties. By eavesdropping on various conversations, Tim and Tom established that most of the customers were from Peterborough. After several more drinks, Tom decided that it might be wise to drive back to the Inn.

Advertising

The next day, Tom inquired about the Inn's advertising policy. Tim retrieved copies of newspaper advertisements which had been placed in the Peterborough Examiner and the local Kawartha Sun (see exhibit 10 for examples). Tom was unable to determine the exact frequency with which advertisements were placed as the Inn did not have a formal expenditure control system. He estimated that a daily listing in the Peterborough Examiner at a cost of $42 and a weekly listing in the Kawartha Sun at a cost of $35 was representative of the Inn's summer advertising expenditures. During the off-season, advertising dropped off substantially.

Exhibit 10 Sample Ads

Kawartha Sun, September 3, 1981

Exhibit 10   (continued)

Peterborough Examiner, October 1981

Kawartha Sun, Summer 1981

The Inn also placed occasional 30-second spots on the local AM and FM radio stations (see exhibit 11). Mrs. Agnew would phone the radio station to inform them of various events she wanted publicized. The announcer would then write a commercial and read it on the air without further consultation. Due to the ad hoc nature of the Inn's radio advertising, Tim felt it was largely unsuccessful in delivering an accurate picture of the Inn to potential customers. In addition to its local radio advertisements, the Inn had also received free publicity through a highly complimentary review broadcast throughout Ontario on CBC radio (see exhibit 12).

Exhibit 11   Sample Radio Commercial

Media Music 908/2/3.

Where Katchewanooka and Clear Lake Waters join, under the settler-trodden wooden bridge, stands the OLD BRIDGE INN. This Hallowe'en, enjoy the fun of an old-fashioned Box Lunch Social—just a dollar and a half per couple, with proceeds going to UNICEF. The ladies will prepare an attractive Box Lunch to be auctioned to the eager beaux at 6:30 P.M. Book now for your Christmas or New Year's party—and remember the Hallowe'en Box Lunch Social—at the OLD BRIDGE INN, just off Highway 28 at Young's Point.

Exhibit 12   CBC Commentary: *Young's Point—The Old Bridge Inn*

For Ontario Morning.—CBC

I think we have here at Young's Point what is probably the finest Inn in the province. I know there are others at Caledon East, Huntsville, Elora, Acton, Bayfield, Niagara-on-the-Lake, Jackson's Point, and possibly Deep River which, according to the Ontario Morning correspondent seems to have everything—but the *Old Bridge Inn* is surely the most beautifully situated. A two-storey turn-of-the-century house of warm and solid red brick. It stands guard over the Old Wooden Bridge which fords the Otonabee River and gives access to the locks of the Trent Canal and keeps a constant eye on the thundering waters of the Dam. The old bridge is closed to cars and so it is a walker's dream and an Oasis to those seeking peace, away from the world of the traffic that passes out of hearing on to the Kawarthas and Buckhorn Lakes. The Village of Young's Point cleverly hides under the new bridge comfortably enfolding its 300 or so regular residents. Not everybody here sounds like me but their ancestors all came from where this voice first sounded in Ireland in a house between the River Barrow and the Royal Canal in County Kildare. This Meeting of the Waters is Canada's version of that famous Vale of Avoca, not far from Dublin, that inspired Thomas Moore to write his immortal song *The Meeting of the Waters!*

There is not in this wide world a valley so sweet
As that vale in whose bosom the bright waters meet

the poem ends:

Sweet vale of Avoca, how calm could I rest
In thy bosom of shade, with the friends I love best
Where the storms that we feel in this cold world should cease
And our hearts, like thy waters, be mingled in peace.

So it is at Young's Point as I say to myself with Shakespeare's Falstaff: "Shall I not take mine ease in mine Inn?" If *location* is an essential of the good Inn so indeed is the Innkeeper, and let me tell you our Innkeeper Annabelle is as refreshing as the sight and sound of the waters alongside her Inn. She inherits a fine tradition following on the genial original Russ Brooks, now in retirement and on guard over the other end of that wooden bridge in the original family residence and the original post office, which in turn faces today's post office where despite the charm of Mrs. Jack Young, Winnie and Dorothy, the world intrudes in the mail as we all pick up there with the inevitable bill from Sears, Simpsons or Eaton's. After location and an Innkeeper I suppose the atmosphere of an Inn is the third element of the trinity of graces an Inn should possess. What I call Annabelle soup is always homemade although called by more accurate names from day to day or Jour to Jour. The food is always homely but imaginative and lends to your whiskey or wine a distinction it might not otherwise have. There are some rooms should you require to take your ease overnight.

An Inn is a serious matter and I wish there were more to act as an oasis and haven as we travel our long lonely roads.

As Dr. Johnson said in March of 1776, "There is nothing which has yet been contrived by man by which so much happiness is produced as by a good tavern or Inn." Anyway I wonder does your community boast an Inn that has that Trinity of Graces, each separate, none greater than the other, of LOCATION, INNKEEPER, BILL OF FARE? If you'll excuse me I'll get up from my chair and go down to the Inn and test out what G. K. Chesterton said in his *Song Against the Grocers*.

God made the wicked grocer
For a mystery and a sign
That men might shun the awful shop
And go to Inns to dine
The righteous minds of Innkeepers
Induce them now and then
To crack a bottle with a friend
Or treat unmoneyed men.

This is Tony Ross, your intrepid reporter from far Young's Point. Cheers, and Slainthe.

Tim was concerned that the Inn was not getting the maximum return from its advertising expenditures. He was unsure whether the frequency of advertising was optimal, especially the heavy weighting in the summer. On the whole, he suspected that the Inn advertised with about the same frequency as its competitors. Tim also wondered if the ads were conveying the right message to his customers and potential customers. He believed the Inn had a fairly widespread reputation for the quality of its food. However, he worried that many people who had heard of the Inn did not know where it was located. In order to help Tom formulate an advertising strategy, Tim had collected some information about the local media as shown in exhibit 13.

Exhibit 13 Local Media Information—1981

A. RADIO

1. CHEX-AM

60-SECOND SPOTS	1x	156x	312x
Class "AAA"	29.20	21.80	18.75
Class "AA"	19.95	18.15	14.50
Class "A"	17.20	14.50	12.10
Class "B"	14.60	12.10	9.70

30 seconds—75% of 60 second rate

CHEX-AM TIME CLASSIFICATIONS

CLASS "AAA"	(Rotation)
	6:00 a.m.–10:00 a.m.
	Monday to Saturday
CLASS "AA"	(Rotation)
	10:00 a.m.–3:00 p.m.
	Monday to Saturday
	Select hours Sunday
CLASS "A"	(Rotation)
	3:00 p.m.–6:30 p.m.
	Monday to Saturday
CLASS "B"	(Rotation)
	6:30 p.m.–Midnight
	5:00 a.m.–6:00 a.m.
	Monday to Saturday

REMOTE BROADCAST $95.00 per hour
plus lines and location costs

TAGS on National Announcements $5.75

ALL NIGHT RADIO   Midnight to 6:00 a.m.
Rates on Request

SATURATION CONTRACTS

150 × 60 seconds	15.95	30 seconds	13.45
300 × 60 seconds	13.95	30 seconds	11.45
500 × 60 seconds	13.30	30 seconds	10.90
750 × 60 seconds	12.70	30 seconds	10.35
1000 × 60 seconds	12.10	30 seconds	9.70

25% of spots in total to be aired each 3 months

NEWS & SPORTS-5 MIN.	1x	156x	312x
Class "AAA"	37.50	24.20	20.60
Class "AA"	35.10	20.60	18.15
Class "A"	32.60	18.15	16.00
Class "B"	30.25	15.70	13.30

10 minutes — 40% additional

TOTAL AUDIENCE PLAN

	10%—AAA	40%—AA	30%—A	20%—B
		10x	20x	30x
60 SECONDS		193.05	358.60	499.95
		19.30	17.93	16.66
30 SECONDS		166.65	292.82	399.30
		16.66	14.64	13.31

Exhibit 13   (continued)

Contracts are subject to cancellation by either party by a 30 day advance written notice.

Cancelled or interrupted contracts are subject to short rate.

Advertisers who reduce or interrupt their schedule must begin a new contract for discount purposes.

Accounts are due and payable in Canadian funds when rendered.

2.   CFMP-FM

CFMP - STEREO - FM - 101.5

ANNOUNCEMENTS		ONEx	104x	156x	312x
CLASS AAA					
	60 Seconds	18.00	13.00	12.00	11.00
6:00 a.m.–12:00 Noon					
	30 Seconds	15.00	10.00	9.00	8.00
Monday–Friday					
CLASS AA					
12:00 Noon–6:00 p.m.	60 Seconds	16.00	11.00	10.00	9.00
Monday–Friday					
	30 Seconds	13.00	8.00	7.00	6.00
Saturday & Sunday					
CLASS A					
	60 Seconds	14.00	9.00	8.00	7.00
6:00 p.m.–Sign-Off					
	30 Seconds	11.00	6.00	5.00	4.00
Monday–Friday					
NEWS & SPORTS			AAA	AA	A
(5 Minutes)					
	3x Weekly		16.00	14.00	12.00
(10 Minutes 40%					
Additional)	6x Weekly		12.00	10.00	8.00
SATURATION PACKAGES		10x	20x	30x	50x
Best available times	60 Seconds	13.50	13.00	12.50	12.00
to be used within					
2 weeks	30 Seconds	10.50	10.00	9.50	9.00
SATURATION CONTRACTS		300x	500x	750x	1000x
	60 Seconds	10.50	10.00	9.50	9.00
(to be used in					
12 Months)	30 Seconds	7.50	7.00	6.50	6.00
SPECIAL FEATURE & PROGRAM RATES ON REQUEST					

Card No. 5 Effective September 1, 1981

Exhibit 13 (continued)

B. NEWSPAPER
    1. *KAWARTHA SUN*

        Circulation: 20,000 in the Kawarthas and Lakeshore Districts.

Full Page: 31¢/line		($416.64)
1/2 Page & Up: 32¢/line	OR	$4.48/column inch
1/4 Page–1/2 Page: 33¢/line	OR	$4.62/column inch
1/8 Page–1/4 Page: 34¢/line	OR	$4.76/column inch
1/16 Page–1/8 Page: 35¢/line	OR	$4.90/column inch
Transient Rate: 37¢/line	OR	$5.18/column inch
Feature Rate: 37¢/line	OR	$5.18/column inch

    2. *PETERBOROUGH EXAMINER* (1979 information)

        Circulation: 23,391
        Full Page: 37¢/line ($1,025.64)
        All sizes at flat rate of 37¢/line
        Format: 9 columns × 308 lines each
        Position charge: 15% extra
        Colour (min. size 600 lines): 1 col. + $125;
                                    2 col. + $175

Summary

Before Tom left, Tim reiterated what he felt to be the Inn's most pressing problems. First amongst these was cash flow. Tim had initially thought that closing the Inn's doors during the winter would be a possible solution. However, in order to sell the Inn, he felt the onus would be on him to prove to a potential buyer that it was a viable ongoing business concern. Short-term funds of up to $5,000 could likely be obtained from a local bank to implement operational changes, provided that all expenditures were accounted for in advance. A plan to improve the long-term profitability of the Inn was also important, since Tim figured that there was only a 50 percent chance that the Inn would be sold before the following summer.

As Tom was getting into his car, Tim came running out with a letter his mother had just given him. It had arrived earlier in the day by registered mail (see exhibit 14). Tim felt that the tone of the second paragraph served to bring into focus the urgency of the situation currently facing the Inn and its operations.

Exhibit 14

Ontario
Ministry   Retail
of   Sales Tax
Revenue   Branch

208 Dundas St. East
Belleville, Ontario
K8N 1E3

(613) 962-9108
Zenith 71820

REGISTERED MAIL

Refer to: D. E. Graham
V.P. #47289651

November 4, 1981

The Old Bridge Inn
Youngs Point, Ontario
K0L 3G0

Attention: *Mr. Agnew*

Dear Sir:

We would like to thank you for the two cheques in the amount of $2,500.00 and $2,875.80 to clear your outstanding tax liability of $5,375.80. Your proposal to pay your outstanding tax liability is accepted on the conditions that your current return is filed on or before the due date and your cheques are honoured when presented for payment.

If the above conditions are not kept we will have no alternative but to take whatever legal action that we deem necessary to collect without further notification to you.

Interest will continue to accrue at 12 percent per annum on the unpaid balance.

Yours very truly,

T. O'Sullivan

Acting District
Compliance Supervisor

TOS:jb

3 Windsor Miniature Golf

In January 1974, John Smith and Jim Brown, two high-school teachers, had just finished their analysis of a proposal for a miniature golf course in Windsor, Ontario. They had initially thought of the idea after watching a miniature golf tournament (sometimes referred to as putt-putt, or "goofy," golf) on television. After collecting data on the viability of the proposal, they were discussing whether they should actually invest more time and money and make the proposal a reality. John felt the proposal would make money no matter where they located or how they promoted the venture.

"Look Jim, there's no real competition and there's lots of people who would love to play miniature golf in Windsor. I think we've got a potential gold mine on our hands. I've calculated that our maximum capacity for the course is 864 rounds per day, based on the assumption that there would be four people per hole and they would take one hour to play one round. Given that there are eighteen holes and the course will be open twelve hours a day, a total of $(4 \times 1 \times 18 \times 12)$ 864 rounds could be played every day."

Jim Brown was more cautious. "I think there are two important factors: the location, and how we market the idea to people. If we don't get the Devonshire Mall location, I wouldn't be too keen on the idea. Also, if we don't promote miniature golf properly, there's a chance that it won't succeed. I think we should have another look at our analysis and figure out if this idea could work and what's the best way to market it."

The Idea

John Smith and Jim Brown had often discussed ways of getting into business during their lunch hours at school. The two teachers felt they could invest $2000 each in a business venture if they could come up with a reasonable idea. After seeing the televised miniature golf tournament they decided to do some research on miniature golf in Windsor. The research included an analysis of: competition, potential locations, consumers' needs, the Windsor market, and the costs involved.

The Competition

A survey of the Windsor area revealed two existing miniature golf courses. The competitors were evaluated on a number of criteria (table 1), and the general conclusion reached by the partners was that both courses were of poor quality. It was felt that if a miniature golf course was constructed of high-quality materials and offered a fair degree of challenge, it would attract virtually all of the competition's customers. The partners decided that if they went ahead with the venture they should consider constructing the best possible course in terms of challenge, materials, and craftsmanship.

Potential Locations

After looking at a number of areas, the partners concluded that any location should be readily accessible to the public. The basic idea was to "bring the game to the people" by having a convenient location. They felt that a location in or near a shopping mall would be good because of the high traffic flows. The manager of Cambridge Investments, a company that

Table 1 Miniature Golf Courses in Windsor, 1974

		Competitor I (Gateway Plaza)	Competitor II (Suburban Go-Kart)
Location	Accessibility	excellent	poor
	Built-in clientele	very good	poor
Cost	Per eighteen-hole round	$0.75	$0.50
Course	Appearance	fair	poor
	Challenge offered	fair	poor
	Material quality	poor	very poor
Promotion	Advertising	little	none
	Tournaments	none	none
	Leagues	none	none
	Incentives	none	none
	Appeal to market segments	none	none
Return on investment		fair	in the red

controlled Devonshire Mall, was contacted, and the idea of a miniature golf course located at the mall was discussed. Devonshire Mall was considered an ideal site as it was the largest shopping centre in Windsor, with over forty stores in an enclosed mall located in the southern suburbs of the city. The number of people who shopped at Devonshire Mall each month was estimated at between 800,000 and 900,000. The mall had large areas of parking space and it was proposed that the golf course be located near one of the entrances to the mall (exhibit 1). The manager, while interested in the proposal, did not commit himself to the venture. He suggested that the two partners return after they had finalized their plans. If they were allowed to locate at Devonshire Mall their rental fee for the land would be 15 percent of gross sales.

Consumer Analysis

The next step in the project was to conduct a consumer analysis. The partners listed a number of consumer needs they felt miniature golf could satisfy and ranked them in terms of probable importance for three different consumer groups. The needs and rankings were:

	Preteen and teens	Male adults	Female adults
a. recreational enjoyment	1	1	1
b. family outing	4	4	2
c. relaxation	5	5	4
d. socializing	3	8	3
e. challenge/competition	2	2	5
f. time required to play	8	6	6
g. status	6	7	7
h. convenience	7	3	8

This analysis indicated the primary needs satisfied would be enjoyment, challenge, and socializing with friends or family. Further information was collected by conducting two consumer surveys. A questionnaire was drawn up and given to students at their school. The results, shown in table 2, indicated that most students would play miniature golf. Of the three hundred students interviewed, 196 said they would play miniature golf at Devonshire Mall if they were there. Approximately 50 percent would play miniature golf on a date, and 50 percent said they would come to the mall on Sunday and play. Approximately 76 percent said they felt that seventy-five cents was a reasonable price for golf. Only 17 percent felt seventy-five cents was too high a price.

Exhibit 1

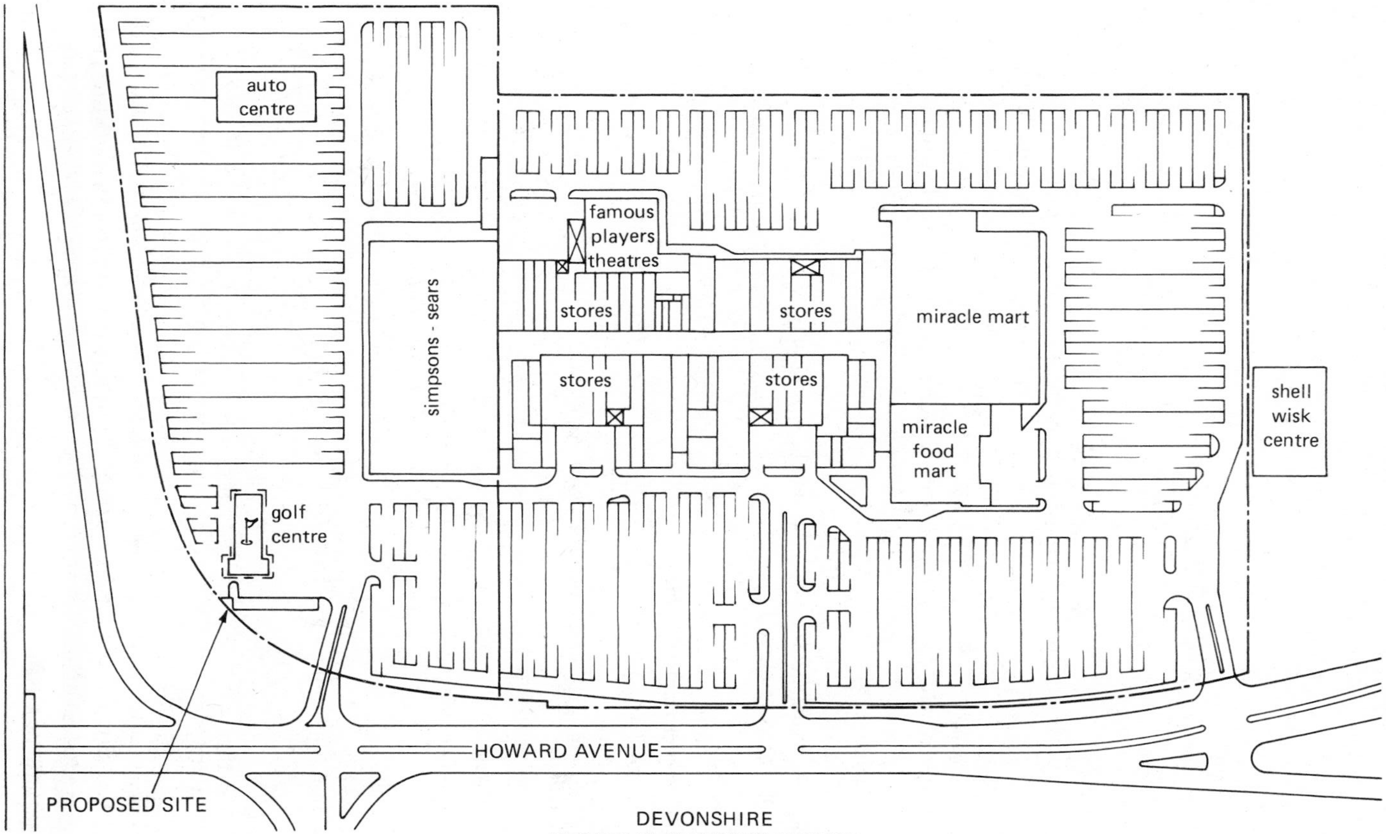

DEVONSHIRE
REGIONAL SHOPPING CENTRE
WINDSOR, ONTARIO

shell
wisk
centre

miracle mart

miracle
food
mart

stores

stores

famous
players
theatres

stores

stores

simpsons - sears

auto
centre

golf
centre

HOWARD AVENUE

PROPOSED SITE

57

Table 2 Student Survey Results—Age Six to Eighteen (Sample size = 300)

1. Sex?

Male	144
Female	156
Total	300

2. Do you go to Devonshire Mall in the summer?

Yes	253
No	47
Total	300

a. If yes: Would you play miniature golf there?

	Yes	No	Maybe
Male	99	12	7
Female	97	24	14

b. If no: Would you go to the mall for a recreational activity like miniature golf?

	Yes	No	Maybe
Male	4	11	11
Female	4	10	7

3. Do you think members of your family would play?

a. Older than yourself?

Yes	No	Maybe
85	61	154

b. Younger than yourself?

Yes	No	Maybe
126	33	141

4. Would you play miniature golf with your date?

	Yes	No	Maybe	No answer
Male	80	14	26	24
Female	82	10	32	32

5. Do you consider $0.75 a low price—reasonable price—high price—?

	Low	Reasonable	High
Male	14	96	34
Female	4	134	18

6. Would you come to the mall on Sunday to play?

	Yes	No	Maybe
Male	70	42	32
Female	80	31	45

The second survey, shown in table 3, asked one hundred adults if they could see any use for a miniature golf course at Devonshire Mall. The results indicated that consumers might participate in miniature golf while shopping at the mall.

Table 3   Adult Survey Results

1. (Sample size = 100; females = 50, males = 50)
2. Interviews were conducted at Devonshire Mall and with friends and colleagues.
3. The respondents were informed of the proposal (miniature golf) and asked if they could see any use for such a service.
4. Results—most frequent responses only. (Response was considered frequent if it occurred 10 percent of the time.)
   a. I could see it as an advantage in that my children wouldn't mind coming shopping with us.
   b. Could serve as a family activity.
   c. Would play while waiting for my wife.
   d. I really don't have the time.

The Windsor Market

Windsor, Canada's tenth largest city, was primarily a heavy-industry community with large automobile assembly and feeder plants. The average weekly earnings in the city of over 200,000 people were $183 compared to the Canadian average of $149 (table 4). The proposed site at Devonshire Mall would be within a fifteen-minute drive for most of the population of the city.

Table 4   Selected Statistics—Windsor Market

A. *Population*

Age Groups, 1971:	Metropolitan Windsor Male	Female	Windsor (City proper) Male	Female
0–4	11,355	10,860	8,440	8,125
5–9	13,585	12,840	10,190	9,590
10–14	13,785	13,075	10,395	9,850
15–19	12,465	12,370	9,680	9,600
20–24	11,550	11,500	9,310	9,330
25–34	16,905	16,105	13,190	12,405
35–44	15,020	14,435	11,870	11,540
45–54	13,590	14,570	10,920	11,835
55–64	9,860	10,470	7,975	8.665
65–69	3,995	4,705	3,340	3,985
70+	6,685	8,905	5,535	7,535
Total	128,795	129,835	100,845	102,450

Table 4 (continued)

Families, 1971:

Number	62,395	49,253
Average no. per family	3.6	3.6

Households, 1971:

Number	74,230	59,795
Average no. per household	3.4	3.3

B. *Income*[a]

Average weekly earnings

	Metro Windsor	Canada
1968	$128.92	$109.90
1969	137.28	117.64
1970	150.80	126.82
1971	163.30	137.64
1972	183.33	149.22

Taxation statistics

Income Class	1971
Under $2,000	19,777
2,000– 3,000	8,780
3,000– 4,000	9,256
4,000– 5,000	9,208
5,000– 7,000	13,226
7,000–10,000	21,977
10,000–15,000	16,816
15,000–20,000	4,078
Over 20,000	2,213
Total	105,331
Average Income	$ 6,870

C. *Weather*

	Rainfall	
Month	*Average number of days with rain*[b]	*Average number of days without rain*
May	12	19
June	10	20
July	9	22
August	9	22
September	9	21
Total	50	104

a. *Source: Financial Post,* Survey of Markets, 1973.
b. Based on an accumulation of at least .01″. Averaged over last thirty years. Most likely time of rainfall: 3:00 P.M. to 7:00 P.M. during these months.

An additional piece of information was collected: the average number of days with and without rain between May and September (table 4). On average, there were 104 days without rain during the period.

Cost Estimates

The partners calculated the costs of constructing the miniature golf course (table 5). The total estimated cost of $7260 included the cost of building the eighteen holes plus a pro shop, fencing, and miscellaneous expenses. No cost was included for labour because the holes could be built by the

Table 5   Cost Estimates for Miniature Golf Course

Material Cost
1. ¾″ plywood	$12.70 per sheet	
2. 2 by 4	0.20 per foot (linear)	
3. 2 by 8	0.42 per foot (linear)	
4. paint	10.00 per gallon	
5. carpeting	8.00 square yard	

Average cost per hole

Material cost:
2 by 4, 125′	$ 25.00
2 by 8, 60′	25.00
¾″ plywood (3 or 4 sheets)	45.00
Carpeting (Kentucky blue grass), 11.25 square yards	90.00
Miscellaneous (nails, sheet metal, batteries, motors, sand, shrubbery)	75.00
Paint (1 gallon per hole)	10.00
Total	$270.00

Labour cost per hole: nil.
All construction is to be done by the industrial arts class at the high school under the supervision of a qualified craftsman

Total cost for eighteen holes = 18 × $270.00		$4,860

Other Expenses
Pro shop	$ 1,000	
Fencing (150′ by 100′)	1,000	
Miscellaneous (putters, balls, cards, pencils)	400	
Total	$2,400	$2,400
Total Cost		$7,260

industrial arts class at the high school where they taught. The only operating expenses they would incur would be advertising expenses and hiring someone to run the course. The cost of hiring someone was estimated at $1872 based on paying them $1.50 per hour for twelve hours per day for the season of 104 days. They had planned to have the course open from 10:00 A.M. to 10:00 P.M. each day.

While they had collected some data on advertising rates, they had not decided on any advertising campaign. *The Windsor Star,* the local daily newspaper, had a citywide circulation of 58,000. Cost of advertising for a full page, a half page, a quarter page, and one-eighth page was $1292, $646, $320, and $160, respectively. Radio advertising costs ranged from $100 for a thirty-second spot in prime time on CKLW (the local rock station) to $28 for an equivalent spot on CKWW (a middle of the road station).

The Decisions

The partners faced a number of decisions. They had not decided on the price to charge, either fifty or seventy-five cents per round, what advertising should be done, if any, or what they should do if the manager of Devonshire Mall did not agree to their proposal. They estimated the total cost would probably be around $8000, which would mean they would have to borrow $4000 from the bank. Finally, the major decision had to be made. Should they invest in this venture?

CHAPTER II
FINANCIAL ANALYSIS OF
MARKETING DECISIONS

The ultimate goals of marketing management are usually (although certainly not always) financial in nature. Accordingly, financial considerations are important both when selecting among alternative marketing activities and when evaluating the outcome of a marketing course of action. This note pulls together several of the financial analysis techniques used in marketing decision making. Our intention is not to suggest that all marketing decisions may be reduced to quantitative financial analysis, but rather to suggest ways in which a little "number-pushing" can provide useful insights into the impact marketing decisions may or may not have on an organization's financial performance and position.

Marketing and the Income Statement

Most organizations record or anticipate their operating performance over a period of time by means of an income, or profit and loss, statement. An income statement typically consists of the following major categories:

Sales
Cost of goods sold
Gross margin
Marketing expenses
General and administrative expenses
Net profit before tax

If the goal of the marketing manager is to impact favourably on the "net profit before tax" figure, he or she must understand the relationship between marketing activities and the income statement.

Sales

Sales revenue is a function of unit selling price (net of returns, allowances, discounts, etc.) times unit volume. Sometimes total dollar revenue can be increased by raising the unit selling price or by increasing unit volume. The choice of price levels that will result in maximum dollar revenue is a difficult marketing decision. An important question in this regard is: How much must sales volume increase to maintain the gross margin level if there is a drop in unit price? Put differently, if unit selling price is dropped, how much more volume will be necessary to maintain the same dollar revenue position? Comparable questions may be asked when considering a price increase.

Central to most marketing calculations is the sales forecast. Accounts on the income statement are generally projected in relationship to a sales figure previously estimated. Contribution analysis judgments are made relative to anticipated sales.

A number of methods may be used to forecast sales levels. These can be divided into four categories:

1. what has happened in the past,

2. what people say will happen,

3. what has happened in test markets, and

4. estimates based on sound consumer analysis.

Each technique has both quantitative and qualitative dimensions. Forecasters typically run into trouble when they approach forecasting as strictly mechanical number-pushing.

1. *What has happened*. The two major techniques used in this category are extrapolation and statistical demand analysis. The former refers to continuation into the future of trends apparent in the past, whereas the latter refers to projections of sales based on projections of indicators of sales (factors thought to be related to sales levels). Extrapolation is relatively easy to do, but dangerous if no attempt is made to adjust for known or foreseen changes in the determinants of sales (such as changes in technology or competition). Statistical demand analysis can be a very complicated process depending on how elaborate a set of factors is examined in relationship to sales and how sophisticated the statistical methods used become. The dangers in this method are overreliance on someone else's projections of the indicators (such as population size) and overreliance on statistical skills versus managerial judgment. Each method that uses the past as a basis for anticipating the future must be tempered with judgment to assure any meaningful degree of accuracy in projection.

2. *What people say will happen*. Salesmen are often asked for estimates of sales, brand managers asked to predict share of market results, and customers asked whether and what they intend to buy in the future.

These are all methods of anticipating sales based on asking "experts" or the customers themselves. Obviously, these forecasting methods have much to recommend them, but they pose potential problems as well. The "experts" may be ill-informed or too generalized in their predictions. The salesmen and brand managers may have hidden motivations for estimating higher or lower than they really expect. Consumers may be difficult to locate, not really sure of their intentions, or just plain uncooperative. What customers say they will do is no guarantee of what they will actually do.

3. *What has happened in test markets*. Test markets are designed to answer specific questions such as: What price level is more appropriate? Does newspaper advertising affect sales? How often will people buy the product? A well-designed and executed test can be a very useful approach to sales forecasting, but there are several problems to consider. For example:

a. How should results from a test market using heavy saturation advertising be translated to a national market launch using overall light advertising?

b. How typical was the test area?

c. Was the test long enough?

d. Did competitors behave in ways to confuse the test market results?

e. Will distributors provide the same support to the product once it goes national?

4. *Estimates based on consumer analysis*. Often it is neither possible nor necessary to engage in formal market testing to predict consumer response. Managers who are constantly in touch with their customers develop a "feel" for the market and can thus anticipate with reasonable accuracy how these people will respond to changes in product or services. This sort of thinking can be made more disciplined by using a consumer analysis approach in which various characteristics of the target market are examined and forecasted relevant to market responsiveness.

There are no perfect methods for sales forecasting, and a combination of methods is bound to produce different projected figures. The important point is to try some method, adjusting the result on the basis of managerial knowledge and experience. Also, it is important to generate a sales forecast using one or more of the above methods before engaging in an arithmetic review of break-even volumes based on product costs and prices. Sales forecasts require a focus on customer acceptance which keeps the decision-maker market-oriented.

Cost of Goods Sold

Cost of goods sold refers to costs incurred in buying or in producing the goods (or services) sold to the firm's customers. These expenses are generally best considered as variable costs. Variable costs refer to expenses that change with production and/or sales unit volume. Generally speaking, such costs are constant per unit (within certain volume ranges) and vary directly with total unit volume. Two other types of costs, fixed and discretionary, will be discussed later.

Many marketing professionals fail to recognize fully the substantial impact marketing decisions may have on the cost of goods sold section of the income statement. For example, product policy decisions relating to the width of the product line, the product design characteristics, the importance attached to avoiding stock-outs, and so on, may affect the cost of goods sold. Distribution decisions, even as fundamental as the basic type of system to be used, may also impact significantly on the unit cost of goods sold.

Gross Margin

Gross margin (or gross profit) refers to the remainder after the cost of goods sold has been subtracted from sales revenue. Gross margin may be expressed either on a total volume basis or on an individual unit basis, in dollars or as a percentage of sales. Many marketing professionals pay particular attention to the gross margin figure as an indicator of pricing policies and operating performance.

There are a number of ways to express pricing policies, but the most common involve the use of margins, markups, discounts, and markdowns. These terms frequently are used in a confusing fashion, especially when a complicated method of distribution is involved or when they are not used carefully.

A margin is the difference between selling price and "cost." Gross margin as defined above is the difference between sales revenue and cost of goods sold where the latter is that portion of total cost which varies directly with volume. But net profit before tax is also a margin—in this case, the difference between sales revenue and total operating costs. Thus, when the term margin is used it is important to determine exactly what costs are being considered in order to arrive at that particular margin.

Markup is not necessarily the same as gross margin. Markup is used in direct reference to an item or product line and is the difference between cost and selling price before adjustments to either of these figures. Gross margin on the other hand involves additions and subtractions of costs such as discounts, alterations, etc. For example, suppose a seller has 100 items he bought at $10.00 each and plans to sell at $15. His planned markup per item is $5, 33⅓ percent on selling price, and we might expect his total markup and gross margin both to be $500. However, if he sells 480 items at $15, twenty items at $13, and incurs costs of $0.50 each for alterations, his total gross margin will be $500 − 50 − 40 = $410. Gross margin then is typically less than markup because it is arrived at after adjusting the selling price and the cost of goods sold. This distinction between margin and markup is confusing and often overlooked, especially in introductory marketing courses.

Another area where confusion often occurs is in the use of margin and markup percentages. For example, an item which costs a manufacturer $4 might be sold to a distributor for $5, yielding the manufacturer a markup of $1. This markup may be expressed as a percentage of the selling price ($5) or as a percentage of the cost ($4):

as a percentage of selling price

$$\frac{1.00}{5.00} \times 100 = 20 \text{ percent}$$

as a percentage of cost

$$\frac{1.00}{4.00} \times 100 = 25 \text{ percent}$$

These different results indicate the importance of knowing on what basis the markup percentage has been expressed. Retailers normally express markup on selling price, and unless otherwise stated, you should assume a markup percentage is based on selling price.

A frequent problem is the determination of what selling price to set if the cost and markup percentage are known. For example, suppose an item cost $10 and the desired markup is 40 percent on selling price; what should selling price be?

$$\$10 = 60 \text{ percent of S.P.}$$

$$\text{S.P.} = \frac{\$10}{.6} = \$16.67$$

To convert a markup expressed as a percentage of selling price into one expressed as a percentage of cost:

$$\text{markup percent of cost} = \frac{\text{markup percent of selling price}}{\text{cost percent of selling price}}$$

To convert a markup expressed as a percentage of cost into one expressed as a percentage of selling price:

$$\text{markup percent of selling price} = \frac{\text{markup percent of cost}}{100 \text{ percent plus markup percent of cost}}$$

For example, a 30 percent markup on selling price is equivalent to a 42.9 percent markup on cost.

The calculation of markups can become complicated if several middlemen are involved. For example, the following table shows a hypothetical situation:

	Unit cost of goods sold	Selling price	Markup percentage on selling price
Manufacturer	$1.00	$1.50	33.3 percent
Wholesaler	1.50	1.75	14.3 percent
Retailer	1.75	2.50	30.0 percent
Consumer	2.50		

It is important to realize that the net profit margin percentage is unlikely to be the same as gross margin percentage for a particular firm. Stated another way, the net profit margin is unlikely to be the same as the gross margin. The reason for this is that a seller's costs generally include more than just the cost of goods sold. In the example above, the manufacturer's variable costs were $1.00, leaving a gross margin of $0.50 per unit but of this $0.50 another $0.25 had to be allocated to cover other non-manufacturing costs of producing and selling the item. Thus, the net profit margin of the item was $0.25 per unit and the net profit margin percentage was 16.7 percent.

Prices are often expressed using suggested retail price and margins or using suggested retail price less discounts. Using the example above, price may be quoted as $2.50 less 30 percent for the retailer and less 30 percent and 14.3 percent for the wholesaler. This approach indicates clearly the expected selling price of the buyer (list) and the margin the buyer would get by selling at the suggested list price. For example, a buyer may be quoted "$100, less a discount of 30 percent." In this instance, the item is for sale to the buyer at $70, the buyer's suggested selling price is $100, and the buyer's markup on selling price would be 30 percent. This may seem like a complicated way to express costs and prices, but it enables the seller to vary terms to the "trade" without necessarily affecting trade resale prices. In other words, it allows a flexible pricing policy, with the flexibility in the amount of discount and the seller's selling price. Sometimes prices expressed in these terms get very complicated, as when one discount is piled on another: $100, less 25 percent, less 10 percent, less 5 percent, results in a buyer's cost of $64.12 (not $60.00).

$100 less 25 percent = $75
$75 less 10 percent   = $67.50
$67.50 less 5 percent = $64.12

Some discounts may relate to method or speed of payment, others to volume purchased, and yet others to services performed by the buyer in the distribution system.

A markdown refers to the reduction from original selling price to a new selling price. For example, suppose a retailer was offering an item purchased for $3.00 at $5.00 (a markup percentage on selling price of 40 percent) and then marks it down to $4.00 to improve prospect of sales. A $1.00 markdown has been made. To convert this to a percentage on selling price, the new selling price is used. Thus, the markdown percentage is 25 percent ($1.00/$4.00 × 100). Customers, however, would typically be told in this instance that the item was being offered at "20 percent off." Note that the new margin on selling price in this example is also 25 percent ($1.00/$4.00 × 100).

Gross margins, markups, discounts, and markdowns of individual items or product lines do not appear directly on the income statement. However, most marketers keep careful records of gross margins, etc. to assess marketing performance in general and of individual items in particular.

Marketing Expenses

Marketing expenses may be classified in two ways. First, they are either variable or fixed. Second, they are either discretionary or nondiscretionary.

Variable costs were defined previously. From a marketing standpoint they may include items such as salespeople's commissions or brokerage payments. Fixed costs refer to costs that are not volume sensitive over a range of volume. For example, rent is generally a fixed cost, as is depreciation, a sales manager's salary, and so on.

Discretionary costs refer to costs that vary according to management decisions, such as salesmen's commissions, advertising expenditures, and promotional aids. Nondiscretionary costs refer to costs which do not vary according to management decisions after an earlier major decision has been made. For example, if a company is in the business of importing merchandise for resale (major decision), then brokerage costs are nondiscretionary because the company cannot set the level of these fees. Similarly, if management builds a sales office, then the subsequent depreciation on that office is a nondiscretionary expense.

Thus, the above examples may be classified as follows:

Salesman's commissions	discretionary, variable
Advertising expense	discretionary, fixed
Brokerage costs	nondiscretionary, variable
Sales office depreciation	nondiscretionary, fixed

Most marketing costs are best considered discretionary in nature. Discretionary marketing expenditures are those designed to increase sales volume and sales revenue rather than those that result directly from changes in sales volume or revenue.

General and Administrative Expenses

These costs are similar to marketing expenses in that they too may be classified as variable or fixed and discretionary or nondiscretionary. General and administrative costs include items not directly attributable to the cost of the goods sold or to the marketing activities of the firm. Often these expenses are lumped together and called "overhead" by marketing professionals. Examples are management salaries, interest expenses, heat, light and power, and legal expenses.

General and administrative expenses and marketing expenses are often allocated to individual products or product categories to arrive at a "full cost" for each item or category. This process of allocation can become very misleading when (a) there are only very arbitrary methods of allocation available such as on the basis of proportion of total dollar revenue accounted for by each, and/or (b) the unit volumes involved are subject to significant change from one operating period to the next.

Net Profit Before Tax

This item is the margin which remains after all expenses (except income tax) have been deducted from sales revenue. Often it is expressed as a percentage of sales in order to gauge trends over several operating periods or to compare one firm's performance with another.

Summary

The net profit before tax is not determined solely by the marketing function, but marketing decisions and activities obviously can impact very significantly on this amount. Income statements can be prepared on individual products or product groups to compare their relative impact on overall firm profitability, but this approach can become overly cumbersome if many products or services are involved or misleading if full costing (including allocated costs in the calculations) is attempted. In order to simplify such analysis, a technique known as contribution analysis has been developed.

Contribution Analysis

Contribution refers to the difference between selling price and variable costs. It may be calculated on a per unit basis or for a given volume. For purposes of this technique, all operating costs must be divided into only two categories: variable and fixed. Discretionary costs, as defined previously, must be reclassified. Sometimes the separation of costs into variable versus fixed can be problematical because there are situations that are ambiguous.

Contribution is an important concept because it allows an easier examination of the relationships among costs, prices, and volumes for particular items or groups of items. First, it solves the "overhead" costs allocation problem by treating such costs as fixed. Second, it facilitates sensitivity analysis to see the profit impact of variations in costs, prices, and volumes.

One variation of contribution analysis is referred to as *break-even analysis.* The purpose of this technique is to determine how many units or dollars of volume must be sold to cover all the costs incurred in generating that sales volume, with no resultant profit or loss. The methodology is quite straightforward, as the following simplified example indicates.

Suppose a manufacturer is considering offering a product for sale at $5. Production costs are $1.50 per unit, general and administrative costs $10,000, and the proposed advertising budget for the year $2000. How many items must be sold to break even?

STEP 1: Calculate the contribution per unit.

Contribution = Selling price minus variable costs
Contribution = $5.00 − $1.50 = $3.50

STEP 2: Calculate the total fixed costs.

Fixed costs = general and administrative expenses plus advertising
Fixed costs = $10,000 + $2,000 = $12,000

STEP 3: Calculate break-even volume.

$$\text{Number of units to break even} = \frac{\$\text{Fixed costs}}{\$\text{Contribution per unit}}$$

$$\text{Break-even volume} = \frac{\$12,000}{\$3.50} = 3428.6 \text{ units}$$

Rounding it off: 3429 units (always round up the unit volume)

A related question might be what must the dollar sales volume be to break even?

APPROACH 1: If the break-even unit volume has been calculated, then dollar volume may be calculated by multiplying break-even volume by selling price per unit. Therefore 3429 × $5.00 = $17,145.

APPROACH 2: If the break-even unit volume has not been calculated, there is an alternative method.

STEP 1: Calculate the contribution percentage per unit on selling price.

$$\text{Contribution percentage} = \frac{\text{Selling price minus variable costs} \times 100}{\text{Selling price}}$$

$$\text{Contribution percentage} = \frac{\$5.00 - \$1.50}{\$5.00} \times 100 = 70 \text{ percent}$$

STEP 2: Calculate total fixed costs.

As discussed previously, these are $12,000

STEP 3: Calculate break-even dollar volume.

$$\text{Break-even dollar volume} = \frac{\$\text{Fixed costs}}{\text{Contribution percentage per unit}}$$

$$\text{Break-even dollar volume} = \frac{\$12,000}{0.70} = \$17,142.86$$

Rounding it off: $17,143.00

(The $2.00 difference from approach 1 is the result of rounding off the numbers during the calculations.)

This sort of analysis may be carried further on a number of dimensions. For example: What would break-even volume become if the selling price were dropped to $4.00?

STEP 1: Contribution = $2.50 per unit ($4.00 − $1.50)

STEP 2: Fixed costs = $12,000

STEP 3: Break-even = $\dfrac{\$12,000}{\$2.50}$ = 4800 units

What would break-even volume become if the advertising budget were increased to $4000 and the selling price remained at $5.00?

APPROACH 1

STEP 1:   Contribution = $3.50 per unit

STEP 2:   Fixed costs = $10,000 + $4,000 = $14,000

STEP 3:   Break-even = $\dfrac{\$14,000}{\$3.50}$ = 4,000 units

APPROACH 2

STEP 1:   Contribution = $3.50 per unit

STEP 2:   Additional fixed costs = $2,000

STEP 3:   Additional volume to break-even = $\dfrac{\$2,000}{\$3.50}$ = 571 units

STEP 4:   Total break-even volume = 3429 + 571 = 4000 units

What would profit be if units sold were 5000, selling price at $5.00, and fixed costs at $12,000?

STEP 1:   Break-even volume = 3429

STEP 2:   Amount sold over break-even = 5000 − 3429 = 1571

STEP 3:   Unit contribution = $3.50

STEP 4:   Profit = unit contribution × units sold above break-even
$$= \$3.50 \times 1571 = \$5,498.50$$

Notice that contribution can be thought of as "contribution to fixed costs and to profit." Thus, once all the fixed costs have been covered, the entire contribution per unit goes directly to profit.

In each of the above instances, the computations have been straight-forward and mechanical. The marketing manager must then examine these numbers in light of his or her experience and expectations. For example, if the issue is whether or not to spend $2,000 or $4,000 on advertising and the break-even analysis indicates that the additional $2,000 spent must generate an additional unit volume of 571, then the marketing professional can begin to assess whether or not it is reasonable to expect 571 (or more or less volume) from that additional advertising expenditure. Similarly, variations in other costs and in selling prices can be assessed.

It must be emphasized that the above calculations are not related to actual sales. For example, a calculation that 3429 units must be sold to break even is no guarantee that 3429 units will be sold.

Most marketing professionals are interested in profits, not break-even. Accordingly, the break-even approach can be extended to include profit.

One method is to add the required dollar profit level to the total fixed costs:

$$\frac{\$\text{Fixed costs} + \$\text{Profit}}{\$\text{Contribution per unit}} = \frac{\text{Number of units to be sold to achieve}}{\text{the profit target}}$$

Another method is to add the required profit into the variable costs on a per unit basis. For example, in an illustration we had variable costs of $1.50 per unit, and we might add an additional $0.20 per unit that we wish to achieve as clear profit. This will lower the contribution per unit left to cover fixed costs:

$$\frac{\$\text{Fixed costs}}{\$\text{Selling price per unit} - \$\text{variable costs} - \$\text{profit per unit}} = \frac{\text{Number of units to be sold}}{\text{to achieve the profit target}}$$

Using this approach, the actual dollar profit must be calculated by multiplying the required "break-even" volume by the profit target per unit. (In our example, the required volume becomes 3637 units and the target profit is $727.40.)

In this way, by trying different profit targets, we can examine what relationships must occur between volumes, costs, and prices to achieve desired objectives. This kind of examination of changes in results by changing some of the basic factors (such as price or profit target) is called sensitivity analysis.

Contribution analysis is also useful in assessing the *relative performance* of products. For example, suppose a firm offers two products, A and B, and the question is which is more profitable for the firm.

A		B
$5,000	$Sales	$4,000
1,000	Unit Sales	2,000
$1.50	Unit Variable Costs	$.75
$2,000	Overhead Costs	$1,000
$1,500	Profit	$1,500

From the above chart, it appears both products are equally profitable in total, although A is twice as profitable as B on a unit basis. Notice that our assessment of profitability is confounded by the allocation of overhead. This firm's fixed costs are $3000, and the real issue is which product contributes most to this overhead and then to total profits. On a per unit basis, A's contribution is $3.50, and B's contribution is $1.25 (selling price per unit less variable cost per unit). A's total contribution is $3500, and B's total contribution is $2500 (unit contribution times volume sold). Thus, on a per unit basis, A is almost three times as profitable as B, and on a total basis, A is $1000 more profitable than B. Notice, however, that if B is dropped, A must cover the total firm overhead (unless that overhead drops too) of $3000, and total firm profit (assuming no change in volume) would drop to $500 from $3000.

Another use of contribution analysis is in *cannibalization analysis.* Cannibalization refers to the relationship between two (or more) products (or services) when increased sales of one product mean decreased sales of the other. For example, Brand A's new diet soft drink sales may be at the expense of sales of Brand A's regular soft drink. Often the question in such cases is "How much cannibalization can we afford before we are better off with just our existing products?"

Suppose we had the following information:

Regular drink		*Diet drink*
$.25	Selling price	?
.10	Variable costs	$.13

The contribution per unit for the regular drink is $0.15. Leaving aside other considerations, we'd be willing to trade regular drink sales for diet drink sales so long as the contribution per unit received was equal to or greater than $0.15. Accordingly, a selling price of $0.28 or more per unit would be required. If we sold the diet drink at $0.25 (a contribution of $0.12), we would lose $0.03 on every unit of diet sold instead of regular drink. This sort of analysis can be extended by examining changes in fixed costs (such as incremental advertising to support the diet drink) and the extent of cannibalization versus new business expected. The latter point can get a little complicated. Continuing the example, suppose it is estimated that the diet brand will sell 75,000 bottles the first year at $0.25 each, and of that 75,000, 35,000 will be cannibalized from the regular drink. What is the impact on the Brand A's total contribution?

STEP 1: Diet drink contribution per unit = $0.12

STEP 2: Lost unit contribution from cannibalization = $0.15 − 0.12 = 0.03
Units involved = 35,000
Total contribution lost = 35,000 × 0.03 = $1050

STEP 3: Contribution gained from new units sold = $0.12
Units involved = 40,000
Total contribution gained = 40,000 × 0.12 = $4800

STEP 4:   Net impact on contribution = Contribution gained –
          Contribution lost = 4800 – 1050 = + $3750

In this example, Brand A would be ahead $3750 by introducing the diet drink. If, however, the incremental fixed costs, annualized, were more than $3750 or were at least so close to $3750 that the required profit would not be realized, then this introduction may have to be reconsidered.

Translating Strategy into Expected Operating Results

All marketing managers should attempt to translate their marketing strategy into a projected income statement. In this way, the marketing professional is forced to set down what results are expected and what costs must be incurred to achieve those results. This exercise, aside from the benefits for financial planning, requires the marketing professional to think through the costs and benefits of marketing activities, to think specifically about customer response to alternative strategies, and to focus clearly on the firm's financial objectives of profitability and growth.

Marketing and the Balance Sheet

Most organizations record or anticipate their financial position as at a particular point in time by means of a balance sheet. Marketing decisions both affect and are constrained by a firm's balance sheet. Here are a few of the ways in which marketing may affect a firm's balance sheet in terms of its financial goals of liquidity and stability.

Liquidity

Liquidity represents a firm's ability to meet short-term obligations. There are several measures of liquidity, such as the current ratio (current assets divided by current liabilities) and amount of working capital (current assets minus current liabilities). Key accounts in working capital management are typically cash, accounts receivable, inventory, and accounts payable. Marketing decisions may affect each of these. Decisions as to whether or not to offer credit and to what extent, influence the relative level of cash versus accounts receivable generated during a sales period. Frequently, marketing professionals are optimistic about credit and financial managers are pessimistic, and so it is common for the two to argue about credit. Decisions as to product policy (width of line, depth, features, new product introductions, product changes, etc.) may affect inventory substantially. Marketing professionals sometimes seem to forget that one of the categories of costs in a marketing program is inventory, both the original investment in plant and in the distribution system and the carrying costs associated with inventory. Finally, marketing decisions (e.g., advertising expenditures) may involve creation of obligations to pay suppliers (e.g., media) that cannot be met immediately out of cash and thus result in accounts payable. The financial manager will attempt to balance current assets and current liabilities, and the marketing professional should be aware of this and anticipate the financial impact of these decisions on the working capital position of the organization. All too often, marketing professionals propose a strategy that includes no provision for increases in working capital for the firm and hence includes no understanding of the total financial consequences of the proposed strategy.

Recently, a very important concern of managers has been inventory investment. Marketing professionals should be able to calculate inventory turnover rates, relate sales to inventory requirements, and think in terms of return on inventory investment. For example, suppose a firm has an average inventory level of $300,000 at cost, a gross margin of 20 percent and sales of $3 million. What is the inventory turn and the gross profit return on inventory investment?

STEP 1: Inventory turn $= \dfrac{\text{Net sales}}{\text{Average Inventory at retail}}$

or

Inventory turn $= \dfrac{\text{Cost of Goods Sold}}{\text{Avg. Inventory at cost}}$

or

Inventory turn $= \dfrac{\text{Number of units sold}}{\text{Average unit inventory}}$

Average inventory at retail $= \dfrac{\text{Inv. at cost}}{\text{Cost of Goods Sold \%}}$

Therefore, Inventory at retail $= \dfrac{\$300,000}{0.8}$

Therefore, Inventory turn $= \dfrac{\$3,000,000}{\$375,000} = 8$ times

STEP 2: Gross Profit Return on Inventory Investment

$= \dfrac{\text{Gross Profit}}{\text{Inventory Investment}} \times 100$

$= \dfrac{\$600,000}{\$300,000} = 200\%$

Stability

Stability is the firm's overall financial balance. For example, if too much short-term debt is incurred to make long-term asset purchases, the firm may run the risk of financial default if the borrowers request their money at an inconvenient time. Marketing managers must realize that marketing decisions involve both costs and investments and that these decisions may jeopardize unnecessarily a firm's position and/or not be possible because of a firm's current financial position. For example, suppose a marketing professional wished to introduce nationally a new product. From an investment standpoint, the firm will be required to invest in additional accounts receivable (e.g., one month's sales at "cost of goods sold" cost), in additional inventory (e.g., one month's production), and in additional equipment (e.g., to increase capacity). These investments may be partially offset by increases in accounts payable (e.g., one month's purchases of raw materials). Further, some of these investments may have associated carrying costs such as inventory handling, staff costs in the credit department, and maintenance on the equipment. To the extent possible, all of these financial factors should be included in the marketing professional's considerations. Often, a projected balance sheet showing the anticipated changes in a firm's position is a good way to summarize this sort of analysis, and of course today marketing professionals increasingly use projected cash flow analysis to manage their working capital.

Conclusion

There are many ways in which straightforward financial analyses can contribute to better marketing decisions. On the one hand, such analyses help the marketing professional better appreciate the overall consequences of his or her activities, and on the other hand, such analyses help the marketing professional better justify strategic choices and performance. It should be emphasized, however, that such analyses are a necessary complement to, not replacement for, marketing analyses, judgment, and experience.

Exercises in Financial Analysis of Marketing Decisions

1. An item sells with a markup of 42 percent on selling price. What is the markup as a percentage on cost?

2. Nora Chambers is preparing a new product analysis for a new product she has code-named L240. She has decided L240 should sell at $89.95 retail, based on her market research. Retailers customarily expect a 40 percent markup and wholesalers, a 20 percent markup (both expressed as a

percentage of their selling price). L240's variable costs are $28.50 per unit and estimated total incremental fixed costs are $75,000. At an anticipated sales volume of 5,000 units, will Nora's L240 make a profit?

3. A buyer was offered an item for his store with the following terms: "$150, less 35 percent, less 10 percent, less 5 percent." How much must he pay if he takes advantage of all the available discounts?

4. If a retailer reduces the selling price of items 25 percent and sells the items, what is the markdown percentage on net sales?

5. As Product Manager for electric razors you are developing an understanding of the financial situation of your product. Your assistant has given you the following information:

Retail selling price	$30
Retail margin	33⅓%
Wholesale margin	20%
Direct factory labour	$2/unit
Raw materials	$1/unit
All overheads	$100,000
Salespersons' commission	10% of manuf. selling price
Sales force travel costs	$200,000
Advertising	$500,000
Total market size	1 million units
Current yearly sales your brand	210,000 units

Calculate the following: (a) contribution per unit for your razor, (b) break-even volume in units, (c) current total contribution, (d) current before-tax profit, and (e) market share to contribute before-tax profit of $3 million.

6. Bob Allison imports roses from California for direct distribution to customers in Ottawa. Five sales girls sell the roses to shoppers in malls on Thursdays, Fridays, and Saturdays and receive 10 percent of the $2 selling price. Each rose costs $0.35 from the supplier. Air freight costs $0.15 a rose, while customs duty costs $0.15 a rose. Provincial tax laws require that 7 percent of the selling price be remitted to the government. Mr. Allison absorbs this cost rather than passing it on to his customers. Fifteen percent of the roses received are damaged and thus cannot be sold. Other expenses include $325 for the sales manager's weekly salary, $500 a week for promotion (newspaper ads and posters) and $100 a week for gas and maintenance on the company car. The automobile has just been purchased for $9360 and it is expected to last three years. For accounting purposes, Mr. Allison uses the straight-line depreciation method. Mr. Allison, who earns $30,000 a year, spends 20 percent of his time with the rose project

and he allocates this cost accordingly to the rose project. He hopes the company can earn $1000 a week before tax. He wonders how many roses he must sell to break even, how many to make the $1000 profit, and how many to order if he expects to sell at that profit target level. (Use a fifty-two week year.)

7. Bill Earner is unhappy about his latest sales results: his total dollar sales of products A and B have increased but his gross profit percentage has declined over the previous year. He wonders whether it is time to drop product B whose volume has declined to 2000 units versus the 10,000 units sold of product A. Bill's total sales for the year were $400,000, his total cost of goods sold was $325,000 and his total overhead $50,000. Product B was Bill's first product and sold last year at $75 per unit (at factory). Bill calculated that it cost him $100,000 in materials and labour to produce B last year and he allocated $22.50 per unit towards his general overhead. Product A has been on the market for the past two years and cost Bill $10 per unit in materials and $12.50 per unit in labour to produce. Product A is made in a similar fashion to Product B so Bill has been able to produce it with only an additional $25,000 investment in new equipment (estimated life—5 years). Since this investment was to be depreciated on a straight-line basis, Bill decided to have Product A bear this additional annual company overhead. No other overhead was charged to A. Should Bill drop B? Why?

8. Al Hoffman is wondering whether he should introduce a new dessert flavour, butterscotch, based on the test market information he has received. His new brand, that he produces for $0.14 per unit (variable cost), has sold for $0.25 per unit and has done well against his competitor's caramel brand. Al estimates his butterscotch would sell 250,000 units in its first year of which 125,000 would represent switches to his lower-priced butterscotch from the competing caramel. He is worried, however, since he also estimates 20 percent of the butterscotch volume will come from his own chocolate customers (chocolate had a variable cost of $0.13 per unit and sold for $0.23 per unit) and 20 percent of the butterscotch volume will come from his own strawberry customers (strawberry had a variable cost of $0.16 per unit and sold for $0.25 per unit). Last year, Al sold 1.5 million units of dessert, of which a third were strawberry. Al wants an improvement in his gross profitability of at least 10 percent, otherwise he will not introduce butterscotch. What should he do?

9. Nancy Brown is preparing her next year's marketing plan submission for her lighter fluid line. She is aware that the company comptroller is very concerned about inventory management and has decreed that he

would oppose any plan that resulted in a lower return on inventory investment than the previous year. Nancy has gathered some information: last year's inventory turn for lighter fluid was 5.2. Last year's sales at retail were $5 million. Her forecasted sales at retail are expected to be up 12 percent. Retail margins were 35 percent last year and she plans 38 percent this next year. She sells direct to retailers. Her gross margin is expected to be 22 percent as it was last year. The comptroller has suggested that she target at a stock turn of 6.75. If she reaches her turn target and if her other figures become actuals, what will be the incremental inventory of lighter fluid in dollars, and will the return on investment in inventory go up or down?

CHAPTER III
UNDERSTANDING
BUYER BEHAVIOUR

Introduction

Understanding buyer behaviour is a fundamental activity in developing marketing strategy. If the buyers have not heard of the product, cannot find it, or believe that it is too expensive, then the marketer will not sell many units. It is important to analyze buyers *before* significant resources are committed to a project. Furthermore, it is important to analyze buyers at several levels of aggregation. At the broadest level, buyers and potential buyers make up total markets or total demand. Usually, we can make estimates of total demand and then disaggregate those estimates into estimates for groups of products, groups of buyers, and even particular brands. In the first part of this section, we will look at analyzing market opportunities.

The second major aspect of understanding buyers is to learn what processes and criteria they use in their decision making. This is described in the second section. Here there are some general concepts that are useful, but eventually we must assess particular buyer behaviour in a certain case. For this judgment, we will use all the evidence provided by the case and our own calculations and assumptions. If there is time, we may supplement the case facts with our own research.

The third section deals with the process of obtaining information about market opportunities and buyer decision processes. The research might be conducted in a library using secondary sources such as books and magazines or it might take the form of a small survey or experiment conducted by the investigator.

Assessing Market Opportunities

The analysis of market opportunities should deal first with end users and secondarily with retail and/or wholesale customers. Knowing how the end users treat your product will help you make appropriate strategic decisions and detect trends as they develop. The purpose of assessing market opportunities usually is to estimate demand for a particular product or service offering. Sometimes the product is new, in which case the task is a little more difficult. Sometimes it is simply a matter of determining future demand for an established product. Notice that we are talking about a fairly certain product offering but trying to project user responses at some time in the future—a very uncertain set of events.

A market is a group of people who are able to buy a product or service for end use. These groups of people can be aggregated at the level of generic product/market such as automobiles, or at the level of specific product/market such as imported cars or at the level of brand product/ market analysis such as Porsche sports cars.

Generic Product/Markets

Generic product/markets are broad categories of products aimed at broad (or unsegmented) groups of customers. Examples are the auto market, the tent market, and the health care market. Many generic product/markets can be described by demographic factors such as age and income. There are well-developed statistics on trends in age and income which means that many generic product/markets can be forecasted reasonably well. For example, the coming bulge in the over-40-years-of-age group suggests that health care will be a growing market in Canada. Simple reflection will conjure up many of the basic factors which will apply to generic product/ markets. They are factors such as population growth, leisure time, attitudes toward the product, economic conditions and changes in demographic or life-style patterns.

Specific Product/Markets

Specific product/markets, as the name suggests, describe a more specialized product and/or a part of the total market. From a generic category such as tents we can look more specifically at party tents, travel tents, hiking tents, and accessories. The analysis of buyers and their criteria can become much more specific. For example, hiking tents must be compact, light, and easy to set up and take down. We can begin to speculate about who would buy hiking tents. Probably they tend to be younger, without children, and oriented toward outdoor physical sports. The next step is to analyze where those people shop, what they read, and how they would go about buying a new hiking tent.

At this stage in the analysis, it is useful to look for market segments, that is, groups of buyers who will respond in a similar way to a particular product. For example, it may be possible to segment hikers into casual and serious groups, the serious hiker being willing to buy a high-quality hiking tent because he or she will use it a great deal. Casual hikers might tend to be interested in lower-priced tents because hiking is neither a central sport nor a matter of prestige, and they will not use the tent more than two weeks each year.

Hiking can be considered as part of a life style, that is, a portfolio of activities, interests, and opinions that differentiate us from others. In many instances, a consideration of the likely life style of hikers will provide clues to their shopping and spending habits.

There are several ways to estimate demand for hiking tents. Industry associations may keep statistics which can be projected. A head count of hikers and their annual expenditures is a second approach. Sometimes an estimate of demand can be derived from a related index such as the usage of parks and recreation facilities.

Branded Product/Market

Now we are assessing the opportunity for a specific branded product such as a high-quality tent for serious hikers. We have a particular target segment and a particular package of benefits. It is important to recognize that the package of benefits contains psychic as well as physical benefits. For example, a tent capable of use on mountain climbing expeditions may be a great source of pride for the owner.

For specific branded products it is important to recognize that the market opportunity is limited by the reach of the channels of distribution. If sporting goods stores account for 50 percent of the sales of tents and a manufacturer is represented in outlets doing 50 percent of the sporting goods volume, then this manufacturer has access to only one-quarter of the total market.

Specific products are aimed at specific audiences in an attempt to find market niches. In fact, a great many product line extensions such as new models and new sizes are attempts to add market segments of a smaller and smaller size.

Forecasting sales for a branded product/market can be accomplished by a variety of techniques. A survey of the sales force is a typical bottom-up approach. A projection of last years sales in a time series analysis is another frequent approach. Sometimes correlation analysis is used to link sales with proxy events, events that are historically related to sales (and seem to be causally related to sales).

Six Steps in Buyer Analysis

1. *Define the "market," its size and growth.* One of the first tasks is to define the buyers and the relevant range of competitive products. For industrial products, this may involve a survey or sales force report on (1) all the products that perform much the same functions as our product, (2) the breadth of applications, (3) the increase in these applications, and (4) the companies that are buying these products.

In the case of Minute Rice instant rice, about 8 percent of the consumption is exclusive users of "instant" rice, and the main competition is Uncle Ben's "instant" rice. For another 30 percent of consumption, the buyers are dual users of instant rice and regular rice, and the competitors are all other instant and regular rices. In the dual user and exclusively instant user markets, Minute Rice tends to be used as a pudding or mixed with some other food to make a special dish. For the remaining 62 percent of consumption, the buyers use regular rice almost exclusively and they often use rice as a separate side dish or substitute for potatoes. So you can see that Minute Rice faces varying levels of competition—even from potatoes!

As soon as the market has been defined you can collect statistics or estimates of its total size and growth. For Minute Rice the relevant market may be defined as "instant and regular rice," which is a 50 million pound market in Canada and growing at about 8 percent each year.

It is also important to determine the source of growth in the market, such as new users or increased consumption per capita, and whether that growth is uniform or coming from particular geographic, demographic, or life-style segments. Sometimes the growth may be coming from a segment served by a particular channel of distribution because the channel is working so well.

The total market size will be needed for calculating the financial feasibility of your marketing strategy options. In addition, you should always look at the size of regional markets in Canada, because a regional market introduction (such as one province) is always a possibility. Because of the sparse population and high cost of securing distribution, a province-by-province roll-out may make more sense than a national introduction. Another way of attacking Canadian markets is to target the ten major cities in Canada, because they offer dense population, efficient distribution, and media accessibility—all important dimensions for many consumer and industrial products.

2. *Define buyer segments—their size, behaviour, and accessibility.* The rice market can be segmented into (1) exclusively instant rice users, (2) dual

users, and (3) exclusively regular rice users. We know that their relative share of consumption is 8, 30, and 62 percent, respectively, and we know that each segment uses rice somewhat differently from the other segments. For example, we might target the dual users with particular messages that would encourage them to use Minute Rice more often *in a planned way* rather than simply in emergencies, as they used to do in the past.

Industrial purchasers often can be segmented by industry or by the size of the company. The *application* of the product may be different by industry, and the *buying process* is almost always different between large and small companies.

3. *Identify buyers, users, and influencers.* It is useful to identify all the people who share in the decision making, because we may wish to communicate with influencers and users, as well as with the buyers. In the case of Minute Rice, we may wish to reassure the whole family that Minute Rice tastes good even though it takes less time to prepare than regular rice. For a new industrial product, we would like all the buyers, users, and influencers to have accurate information on the product.

4. *Identify the basic needs satisfied by the product, triggering sources, and any aspects of seasonality.* Another way to define the zone of competition for a product is to define the range of needs that it satisfies. Toothpaste can fight cavities or whiten teeth and milk can refresh or give health. As a *refreshing drink*, milk competes with all other beverages such as water, Kool Aid, soft drinks, and even alcoholic beverages. In a commercial context, a typewriter can process words and it can be a status symbol.

It's useful to look at what sparks the purchase, because the manufacturer or retailer would like to ignite the spark for their product or have their product available when the customer decides to buy. Furthermore, if there are seasonal sales, marketing professionals need to know so that they can supply enough of the right merchandise when it is required.

5. *Define the criteria of purchase in rank order of importance.* Because buyers usually have multiple criteria for purchasing a product, marketing professionals must know the criteria and their relative importance. For example, in dry cell batteries, surveys show that most consumers look for long life, a leakproof battery, and reasonable price, in that order. Accordingly, if you were advertising a brand of dry cell battery, you would be sure to stress the long life of your brand. Although you might not mention price in your advertisements, probably you would set the price of your battery at competitive levels.

6. *Describe the process of purchase, including the sources of product information, the reliance placed on those sources, and the extent of shopping.*

New buys in an industrial context usually involve several people developing criteria and analyzing data over a substantial period of time. It is important for an industrial marketer to know the staging of the purchase, the roles each person will play at each stage, and the information each person will want at each stage.

It is useful to know whether consumers insist on broad product availability or whether they are willing to shop for the product. If consumers will travel from store to store in order to get the "right dress," a dress manufacturer may be selective in the number and type of dress stores that he arranges to carry his line. Similarly, it is useful to know whether prospective buyers pay attention to newspaper, magazine, radio, and television advertisements. If they do, there is an opportunity to influence their choice through media advertising. Similarly, publicity stories, trial offers, coupons, point-of-purchase (POP), guarantees, product literature, labels, and even store clerks may be sources of information for customers. Almost all these information carriers represent opportunities for marketing professionals.

Obtaining Information About Buyers

We want accurate and detailed information in order to make marketing decisions, but we seldom have all the information we want. Most of our cases present some data derived from market research, but the cases typically leave several points of uncertainty. So far, we have been making marketing decisions by using the available data and filling in the gaps with explicit assumptions. In this chapter we look at the procedures for conducting marketing research activity.

Marketing research is "the systematic gathering, recording, and analyzing of data about problems relating to the marketing of goods and services."[1] By systematic we mean that the execution of research projects should be organized and planned. This involves laying out all aspects of the research design, such as the data analysis and report presentation, *prior to* undertaking the research. Because market research is meant to assist us in making decisions, the marketing issue must be carefully and correctly defined, and all aspects of the marketing research should be relevant to that issue. One company spent a great deal of money attempting to improve their advertising when a more careful investigation showed that awareness of the brand was high, but the repurchase rate was low because the product did not perform very well.

1.   Report of the Definitions Committee of the American Marketing Association (Chicago: American Marketing Association, 1961).

Classifications of Marketing Research

Marketing research may be classified as (1) exploratory, (2) conclusive, and (3) performance-monitoring research. Exploratory research is useful in helping us to identify situations calling for a decision and for identifying optional courses of action. It usually involves a research design intended to provide a preliminary reading on a situation within a short time and at a small cost. Typical exploratory research designs include the search of secondary data (available from libraries, Statistics Canada, and trade associations), interviews with experts, and case studies. Conclusive research provides information to assist us in evaluating options. The research designs for conclusive work tend to be more formal, more time consuming, and more expensive than exploratory research. Conclusive market research may include the use of detailed questionnaires and formal sampling procedures in surveys and experiments. Performance monitoring research is designed to provide control over marketing activity by measuring the outcome of a particular marketing activity.

Uses for Marketing Research

Marketing research can be used to gather factual information for analysis, to assess market performance, or to choose among options. In chart 1 we list several specific types of studies in each of these three categories.

Chart 1   Some Examples of Situations in Which Marketing Research May Be Useful

A. Gathering factual information for analyzing
 1. Market potential
 2. Consumer characteristics in a certain area
 3. Number and type of wholesalers
 4. Price levels of competitive products
B. Assessing performance on specific dimensions
 1. Buyer brand awareness
 2. Trial and repeat purchase rates
 3. Advertising impact
 4. Distribution penetration
C. Making choices among options
 1. Product characteristics
 2. Package size, package art
 3. Advertising budget level
 4. Advertising messages

Frequently, we can structure decisions into three options of GO, NO GO, and GET (MORE) MARKET RESEARCH (chart 2). The GET (MORE) MARKET RESEARCH option is not mutually exclusive from the GO and NO GO actions. For example, we may already be conducting market research in order to determine the likely consequences of various strategies. If we cannot develop any promising strategy options, then we should follow either the NO GO route or the GET (MORE) MARKET RESEARCH route.

If the decision is whether to use advertising *or* give samples to consumers, then one way to use marketing research to help make the choice is to assess the likely consequences of each option. For purposes of illustration, suppose the costs and the likely consequences in terms of profit of each option are as shown in chart 3. The best course of action, leaving aside other considerations, would appear to be "heavy sampling," followed closely by "medium advertising." Now, suppost it cost $20,000 to produce this piece of market research. Was it worth it? The answer depends somewhat on what management would have done without the research. For example, if management would otherwise have chosen "light sampling," the payoff from conducting the research that indicated "heavy sampling" is the incremental profit ($60,000) less the cost of the research ($20,000), for a net gain of $40,000. On the other hand, if management otherwise would have selected "medium advertising," the payoff of the

Chart 2   Schematic of Strategy Options and Likely Consequences

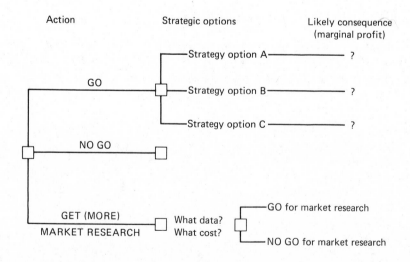

Chart 3 Using Market Research to Help Choose Between Options

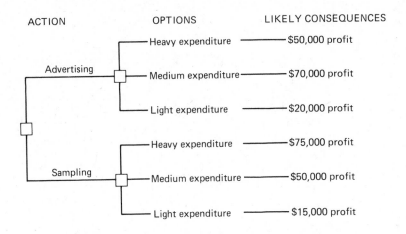

ACTION	OPTIONS	LIKELY CONSEQUENCES

Advertising
- Heavy expenditure ——— $50,000 profit
- Medium expenditure ——— $70,000 profit
- Light expenditure ——— $20,000 profit

Sampling
- Heavy expenditure ——— $75,000 profit
- Medium expenditure ——— $50,000 profit
- Light expenditure ——— $15,000 profit

research was the incremental profit ($5,000) less the cost of the research ($20,000), for a loss of $15,000. In short, doing market research is a trade-off between the cost of additional information and the value of that information in terms of decision making.

Steps in the Marketing Research Process

Very often an issue may be defined as "loss of market share," but we have no idea *why* we are losing share. We know from the marketing framework in chapter 2 that any number of things could be occurring in the external environment such as shifting buyer preference, a new competitor, improvements in competitive products, prices, channels, or marketing communications—or some failure in *our* marketing strategy. The point is that we need to generate some ideas about *why* we are losing share. Accordingly, we can conceive marketing research as a giant "detective funnel" in which we narrow down the possible causal factor(s) for our loss of share. After we have some idea of possible causes, we may want to conduct some quick, low-cost *qualitative* research such as depth interviews or focus groups[2] in order to check the basic validity of our ideas. We are not looking for representative samples or precise numbers; they should be obtained in the third stage when we really want some hard conclusions. Chart 4 shows the marketing research "detective funnel."

2. Focus groups are free-flowing group discussions conducted (or focussed) by an experienced discussion leader.

Chart 4   Marketing Research as a Detective Funnel

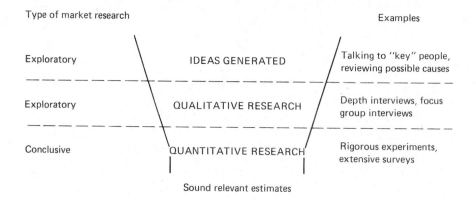

Type of market research   Examples

Exploratory   IDEAS GENERATED   Talking to "key" people,
                                                            reviewing possible causes

Exploratory   QUALITATIVE RESEARCH   Depth interviews, focus
                                                            group interviews

Conclusive   QUANTITATIVE RESEARCH   Rigorous experiments,
                                                            extensive surveys

Sound relevant estimates

The marketing research process can be divided into nine steps:

1. Define the issue and establish the need for information.
2. Specify the information needs and research objectives.
3. Determine the sources of data.
4. Develop data collection forms.
5. Design a sample.
6. Collect the data.
7. Process the data.
8. Analyze the data.
9. Present research findings.

The responsibility for the execution of these stages is shared by the marketing manager and the marketing researcher. First, they must be sure that the issue has been defined properly, that the research objectives make sense, and that the study is carried out in a proper fashion. The researcher holds primary responsibility for the technical details of carrying out the study, but he must be prepared to explain these aspects to the manager in nontechnical terms.

The Need for Information

The most critical and most difficult step in the research process is defining the issue and the need for more information. If the need for information is misdirected, then no matter how well the remaining steps in the research process are executed, we will have "the right answer to the wrong problem," and the research will be useless. Defining the need for information usually begins by the manager requesting the market researcher to conduct a certain study. Rarely does this request adequately specify the need for more information. It is up to the market researcher to question the marketing manager so that the researcher develops a good understanding of why the information is needed. This is seldom easy. Managers sometimes totally misdefine their real problems, and sometimes they hope that the research will support a decision they already have made. The market researcher must be careful to see that any research will be useful in aiding a real and meaningful decision; it is all too easy to rush into a piece of research without really specifying what difference the information would make. We should ask, "So what?" That is: "If demand was 100 units, so what? If it was 150 units, so what?" If it does not make any difference whether demand is 100 or 150 units, then perhaps we should not be wasting a lot of time and money in an attempt to forecast demand.

Market research costs money. There must be a high probability that the value of the information will justify the cost. For decisions with low risk and low cost there is probably little need for marketing research. High-risk/high-cost decisions are most likely to provide a positive payoff from marketing research. However, many decisions fall in between the two extremes and we have to assess the value of the information much the way we did in the earlier example of "advertising versus sampling." As marketing managers we must be prepared to state how much it is worth to reduce our uncertainty about a decision, but we should recognize that this judgment is subjective, and related to one specific manager (us) in one particular situation.

Determine Sources of Data

Much data can be obtained from work already completed. This secondary data may be held within the company (sales reports, special studies) or available through outside agencies such as Statistics Canada, commercial research firms, or academic studies. Alternatively, the study may call for primary data, which can be collected by mail, telephone or personal interviews, observation or experimentation. It is critical that the data fit the specified information needs of the issue.

All but the last of the steps in the marketing research process involve technical dimensions whose details are beyond our immediate scope. As marketing managers we should be aware of these technical steps, but basically we have to rely on the market researcher to see that the steps are executed properly. Thus, questionnaire design, sample selection, field work, data processing, and data analysis are not discussed in this overview except to urge that all these steps be undertaken with a clear view of the marketing issue and its associated information needs.

In doing these steps, we must recognize that the market researcher faces time deadlines and budget constraints. He often must compromise technical elegance for an "on time-on budget" report. In doing so, the market researcher should discuss the nature of the trade-off with the marketing manager before proceeding with the study.

Presentation of Results

The presentation of research results usually involves a written report and an oral presentation. The entire project can fail if the presentation is not executed properly. A report that is too technical or an oral presentation that misses the needs of the audience may cause management to ignore the study. The researcher must be prepared to give his findings in the language of a practising marketing manager, not the jargon of the technical researcher.

Summary

For the cases in this chapter we should focus on questions such as:

1. Is the issue defined properly?
2. Are the information needs related to the issue?
3. What type of research has been or should be conducted?
4. Are the data relevant to the issue?
5. Are the results presented in a useful fashion?
6. Is the study conducted in a technically correct fashion?

We have stressed the definition of the issue and specification of information needs because they are crucial activities; they are neither obvious nor easy and these steps frequently are done poorly or not done at all. However, with some careful thought and a logical sequence of steps, marketing research can be a valuable tool in the pursuit of the organization's marketing objectives.

Guide to Sources of Information on Canadian Markets

The following pages provide you with a step-by-step guide to working with the major references and periodicals concerning Canadian markets.

You may find these secondary sources of information to be extremely valuable when you are working on a project, analyzing a case or perhaps when you begin to think about starting a business of your own. You should be able to find most of these references and periodicals in your library.

CANADIAN BUSINESS INDEX
(formerly *Canadian Business Periodical Index*)
ISSN 0227-8669

Over 170 business periodicals and newspapers are indexed in this monthly publication which references articles in business, industry, economics, administrative studies and related fields.
The index is divided into four (4) main sections:

Introduction

Subject Index

Corporate Name Index

Personal Name Index

How to Use

1. Develop a list of words that describe the topic, industry, issues, etc. with which you are concerned.

2. Decide what time period is of interest to you.

3. Select the appropriate annual or monthly cumulation.

4. Look up the reference words in the SUBJECT INDEX and record the title, publication, and issue of relevant articles. Look up the name of any prominent person associated with the reference list in the PERSONAL NAME INDEX and record the appropriate information.

5. Arrange the articles by publication, issue, and page.

6. Select and review articles, recording relevant information and data, bibliographical requirements, and other reference sources.

CANADIAN NEWS INDEX

The CNI is a monthly publication with an annual cumulation that indexes the major Canadian newspapers.
The index is divided into three (3) main sections:

Introduction

Subject Index

Biographical Index (''people in the news'')

How to Use

1. Develop a list of words that describe the topic, industry, issues, etc. with which you are concerned.

2. Decide what time period is of interest to you.

3. Select the appropriate annual or monthly cumulation.

4. Look up the reference words in the SUBJECT INDEX and record the title, publication, and issue of relevant articles. Look up the name of any prominent person associated with the reference list in the BIOGRAPHICAL INDEX and record the appropriate information.

5. Arrange the articles by publication, issue, and page.

6. Select and review articles, recording relevant information and data, bibliographical requirements and other reference sources.

CANADIAN PERIODICAL INDEX
(formerly *Canadian Index to Periodicals & Documentary Films*)
ISSN: 0008-4719

Over 120 Canadian periodicals, books and works of art are indexed in this monthly publication which also publishes an annual cumulation.
The index is divided into three (3) main sections:

Introduction

Periodicals Indexed

Canadian Periodicals Index (author and subject index)
Note: Works of art are listed under artist's name
    Book reviews are sublisted under the subject title, "Book Reviews"

How to Use

1. Develop a list of words that describe the topic, industry, issues, etc. with which you are concerned.

2. Decide what time period is of interest to you.

3. Select the appropriate annual or monthly cumulation.

4. Look up the reference words in the CANADIAN PERIODICAL INDEX section and record the title, publication, and issue of relevant articles.

5. Arrange the articles by publication, issue, and page.

6. Select and review articles, recording relevant information and data, bibliographical requirements, and other reference sources.

DIRECTORY OF U.S. AND CANADIAN MARKETING SURVEYS & SERVICES
ISBN 0-917148-75-4

This directory lists 2150 commercially available reports and surveys from 149 consulting firms.

The publication is divided into four (4) sections:

Introduction

Alpha listing of Surveys & Services by Company name, subdivided into
Continuing services
Individual surveys less than $1000
Individual surveys more than $1000

Supplement for future additions and corrections

Index; an alpha subject listing providing title and number

How to Use

1. Develop a list of words that describe the topic, industry, issues, etc. with which you are concerned.

2. Look up the reference words in the INDEX and record the title and number of relevant surveys.

3. Select and review surveys, recording relevant price and contact data.

4. Acquire and review survey, recording relevant information and data, bibliographical requirements, and other reference sources.

FINDEX
ISBN 0-931634-02-4

U.S. directory of 2500 commercially available research reports from consumer and industrial studies.

The directory is divided into six (6) main sections:

INTRODUCTION
Reports arranged by topic

Company Reports (mostly investment reports)

Publishers, how to order a report

Supplement for future additions and corrections

Index; by subject

How to Use

1. Develop a list of words that describe the topic, industry, issues, etc. with which you are concerned.

2. Look up the reference words in the INDEX and record the title and number of the study.

3. Review the survey description in the REPORT section and record publisher of surveys you are interested in.

4. Identify publisher in PUBLISHER section and determine how to order survey.

5. Review survey and record relevant information, bibliographical requirements, and other reference sources.

PREDICASTS INC.

Predicasts Inc. publishes a number of information and data sources, the three main titles being:

Predicasts

Worldcasts

Predicasts Industry Studies

1. *Predicasts.* Predicasts is published quarterly and provides U.S. historical and forecast data on economic indicators, social statistics, supply, demand and contribution material. The data is compiled from publicly available sources.

2. *Worldcasts.* Worldcasts is a similar publication to Predicasts but covers most countries in the world to a lesser degree of detail.

3. *Predicasts Industry Studies.* Predicasts Industry Studies are detailed reports (100 pages) on trends within a wide range of industries. Projections are usually to 1985–1995 and are concerned with all aspects of the industry including markets, materials, prices, methods of manufacture and distribution. These are not annual publications and may become somewhat dated.

STANDARD INDUSTRIAL CLASSIFICATION MANUAL
Statistics Canada Catalogue 12-501, occasional

The SIC attempts to provide a "common framework" in which industry data can be compared. Periodic amendment is necessary from time to time to adjust for changes in the industrial structure. Amendments are kept to a minimum to help preserve the continuity of time series.

A SIC code is a number assigned to an industrial segment of a major industrial group. An industry is defined as: "A group of operating units . . . engaged in the same or a similar kind of economic activity . . . ". The term *industry* is used here in its broadest sense to include all economic activity from the primary industries such as agriculture and forestry to those concerned with the rendering of services such as barbers, beauty shops and the various levels of government.

The publication is divided into six (6) main sections:

Introduction

List of groups and classes

Description of Industries

Appendices   I: List of three and four digit Mining and Manufacturing Ind.
            II: Classification of Wholesalers by type.
           III: Industrial Classification on a company basis.

Classified Index

Alphabetical Index

Differences between the 1970 and 1960 editions of the SIC

How to Use

1. Develop a list of words that describe the topic, industry, issues, etc. with which you are concerned.

2. Look these words up in the ALPHABETICAL INDEX and record the corresponding SIC codes.

3. Look up the description of each recorded SIC number in the DESCRIPTION OF INDUSTRIES and eliminate those that appear irrelevant.

4. Look up the list of elements included in the remaining SIC codes recorded in the CLASSIFICATION INDEX. Note the number and nature of relevant and irrelevant elements contained in the classification.

5. Select those SIC codes that best describe your topic. Record the codes and description for future reference. Use the SIC codes when necessary to help identify appropriate data.

Note: Items included in the SIC codes may be more or less detailed than you want. This must be taken into account when researching data; for example, SIC 527—Other Storage & Warehousing includes furniture storage, grocery warehousing, and tobacco warehousing. Revenue information for SIC 527 will be for all businesses included in the category, not just grocery warehouses.

STANDARD COMMODITY CLASSIFICATION MANUAL VOLUME I
Statistics Canada Catalogue 12-502, occasional

The SCC attempts to provide a "common framework" in which commodity data can be compared. Periodic amendment is infrequent but may be made from time to time to adjust for changes in commodity structure.

The SCC code is a five digit number assigned to a specific commodity belonging to a commodity group and division. Although not defined in the manual, commodities are interpreted in the broad sense as any product, material resource, animal, vegetation or foodstuff involved in the Canadian economy.

The publication is divided into four (4) main sections:

Introduction & Summary of Classification Structure

List of Abbreviations, Divisions & Categories

Classification Sections I: Live Animals
                        II: Food, Feed, Beverages & Tobacco
                       III: Crude Materials, inedible
                        IV: Fabricated Materials, inedible
                         V: End Products, inedible

Appendices I: Alternative classification of Division 25
          II: List of the 1972 and 1959 edition codes and their differences.

Other Volumes:

Standard Commodity Classification Manual Volume II
Statistics Canada Catalogue 12-515, occasional

Standard Commodity Classification Manual Volume III
Statistics Canada Catalogue 12-516, occasional

How to Use

1. Develop a list of words that describe the commodity and the product(s) with which you are concerned.

2. Look these words up in VOLUME III and record the corresponding SCC codes.

3. Look up each recorded SCC code in VOLUME II and eliminate those that appear irrelevant.

4. Cross-check by referring to VOLUME I to ensure that it still fits. Note the number and nature of relevant and irrelevant items contained in these classifications.

5. Select those SCC codes that best describe your commodity. Record the codes and other items included in the code for future reference. Use the SCC codes when necessary to help identify appropriate data.

NOTE: Similar to SIC codes, SCC codes may be more or less detailed than you want, a fact that must be taken into consideration when researching data. SCC coding is not as popular as SIC coding, and there are not as many data coded by SCC as by SIC.

STATISTICS CANADA GUIDE
FINDING AND USING STATISTICS, A BASIC GUIDE FROM STATISTICS CANADA

The guide provides an introduction to the nature and purpose of Statistics Canada and statistical data, a summary of the services available from the agency, and some useful information on using the data.

Statistics Canada is the national statistical agency responsible for collecting and publishing data on almost every type of social and economic activity in Canada. The operations of the agency are governed by the "Statistics Act" which identifies specific areas for which data must be collected and published (e.g., the census), rules, regulations, and methods of collection and reporting, but it also allows for the pursuit of a wide range of data from other areas.

The guide is divided into five (5) main sections:

Introduction

Finding Data

Using the Data

Statistics Canada User Services

Appendices

How to Use

1. This is a valuable information booklet that should be read cover to cover at least once.

2. Refer to the guide for services and addresses available to the user.

STATISTICS CANADA CATALOGUE OF PUBLICATIONS
ISSN 0317-770X

The SCCP includes all current catalogue numbered titles available from the department as of a certain date (i.e., January 1, 1980). Previous and Historical Catalogues should be consulted for discontinued publications.

Statistics Canada Publications are catalogued using a five digit catalogue number. In addition to the traditional book or pamphlet form, some data is available on microfilm, microfiche, and from a computerized data base CANSIM (Canadian Socio-Economic Information Management System).

The SCCP is divided into three (3) major sections:

Introduction

Publications

Subject/Title Index

Statistics Canada Publications cover eight (8) topical areas:

General

Primary Industry

Manufacturing

Transportation, Communication and Utility

Employment, Unemployment, Labour Income

Education, Culture, Health & Welfare

Census of Canada: Population
                   Households & Family Dwellings
                   Labour Force

How to Use

1. Develop a list of words that describe the topic, industry, commodity, or product(s) with which you are concerned.

2. Look these words up in the SUBJECT/TITLE INDEX and record the corresponding catalogue numbers.

3. Review the description of each recorded publication in the PUBLICATIONS section and eliminate those catalogues that are not relevant.

4. Record the catalogue number, title, and description of each publication remaining for future reference.

5. Select and review publications and record relevant data.

Some Popular Statistics Canada Publications

11-003E   *CANADIAN STATISTICAL REVIEW*

Summarizes Canadian economic indicators and statistics showing monthly or quarterly figures for most recent two years. Includes seasonally adjusted major indicators, charts, and feature articles on general economic conditions and on special subjects.

11-203E   *CANADA HANDBOOK*

The annual handbook of present conditions and recent progress in Canada. Provides a description of the country's physical environment, the people, their heritage, the economy, the various levels of government, and their services.

11-511   *PERSPECTIVES III*

Presents information on a wide range of social concerns, including health, education, income, work, and the family. Text in each chapter describes the basic issues, reviews data presented, and suggests sources of further information on each subject.

12-501   *STANDARD INDUSTRIAL CLASSIFICATION MANUAL*

A manual for classifying establishments to industry classes on the basis of their principal activities.

12-502   *STANDARD COMMODITY CLASSIFICATION MANUAL VOLUME I*

A working manual for classifying commodity information on the basis of a systematical framework.

61-207   *CORPORATION FINANCIAL STATISTICS*

Contains aggregate balance sheet, income and expenses, profit and loss, and return on investment information for corporations classified in 182 industries.

61-517   *INTER-CORPORATE OWNERSHIP 1980*

A directory of who controls whom in Canadian business. This report traces ownership of corporations to the ultimate owner.

62-545   *URBAN FAMILY FOOD EXPENDITURE 1976*

Summary of family expenditure and detailed average expenditure in eight major cities classified by important family characteristics such as family type, income, age of head, etc.

63-224   *MARKET RESEARCH HANDBOOK*

Compilation of marketing information from various Statistics Canada sources with emphasis on provincial and subprovincial data. Includes general economic indicators, government revenues, expenses, and employment; population characteristics, personal income and expenditure; housing and household facilities, merchandising and services data, some breakdowns by metropolitan area and census agglomeration; extensive notes and a glossary of terms.

SCOTT'S INDUSTRIAL DIRECTORY OF MANUFACTURERS

Scott's is a directory of company addresses, size, and business information. Scott's is divided into four (4) volumes:

Western Canada

Ontario

Quebec

Atlantic Canada

Each volume is divided into four (4) sections:

Alphabetical listing of manufacturers by name with town locations.

Alphabetical listing of manufacturer's name, by town location providing information on
Manufacturer's name, address, telephone number
Executives
Products
Employees
Parent company, associated companies, head office, plants, and divisions.

Alphabetical listing of manufacturer's name with town location by SIC code.

Sundry information including
Business development services of provincial ministries
Municipal spokesmen interested in business development
Business development departments of Chartered Banks, Railways, and
Public Utilities
Maps

How to Use

1. Decide which geographical region you are interested in (Western Canada, Ontario, Quebec, or Atlantic Canada) and select the appropriate volume.

2. Identify and record companies of potential interest by SIC code in section III.

3. Review information provided in section II for each of the recorded companies. Eliminate those companies that are irrelevant and record pertinent information.

GUIDE TO CANADIAN MANUFACTURERS
Dun & Bradstreet Canada Ltd.

This publication is similar to Scott's but provides more detailed information on materials purchased and capital machinery employed. Information is provided on a smaller base number of companies.

The guide is broken down into four (4) volumes by manufacturing industry:

Food, Tobacco, Textile Apparel & Leather

Lumber, Wood, Furniture, Paper, Print, and Publishing

Chemicals, Petroleum, Rubber, Electrical and Miscellaneous

Primary & Fabricating Metal & Transportation Equipment

Each volume is divided into three (3) sections:

Alphabetical list of manufacturers by town providing detailed information on:
  Manufacturer's name, address, phone number, SIC code.
  Materials purchased
  Major products produced
  Major capital machinery
  Number of employees and size of office/plants
  Four key executives

Alphabetical listing of manufacturers by SIC code.

Alphabetical listing of manufacturers by name providing address.

How to Use

1. Determine the appropriate SIC codes for your topic and refer to the front of any of the volumes to determine which volume contains the appropriate information.
2. Identify the names and locations of potential companies by using the SIC code and section II.
3. Review the information provided in section I for each of the recorded companies. Eliminate those companies that are irrelevant and record pertinent information.

4 Blue Mountain Resorts Limited: The Night Skiing Decision

In mid-June 1979, Mr. Gordon Canning, President and Chief Executive Officer of Blue Mountain Resorts, was facing a major decision. He had to determine whether or not facilities for night skiing in the upcoming 1979–1980 winter skiing season should be installed on the Blue Mountain slopes. If he chose to do so, he would have to determine an appropriate pricing strategy for lift tickets and season passes. Since any promotions on night skiing would have to be included in the fall brochures, the decision had to be made by July 1.

Blue Mountain, located 136 kilometres (85 miles) north of Toronto near Georgian Bay, is Ontario's most prosperous ski resort. It is located a few miles from Collingwood, a city of 11,500 people with 40,000 people living in a 20-mile radius. It was started by Jozo Weider in 1941, and he continued to run the resort until his death in 1971. Since that time, his family has operated the business, making Blue Mountain the largest family-operated ski resort in Canada.

During the 1978–1979 season, Blue Mountain had 250 acres of ski trails in service. There were 27 different trails, serviced by 8 chairlifts and 10 other tows. Three quarters of the trails were covered with artificial snow.

Blue Mountain's skier market is primarily from South and Southwestern Ontario, with a small proportion coming from the U.S. Midwest. There are basically three types of skiers at the resort. The largest group is the day skier, who represents 38.4% of the skiers visiting Blue Mountain once or more during a year. Major markets for this skier are Toronto/Mississauga, the Collingwood area itself, and Hamilton/Burlington. The multi-day skier, who stays two to three days, accounts for 35.5% of Blue Mountain's skiers. Most of these people also come from South and Southwestern Ontario. The final category, vacationers (who stay four days

110

or longer), represents the remaining 26.1% of Blue Mountain's skiers. In a typical week, 65% of skiers at the resort ski on the weekend (Friday, Saturday, and Sunday). On the average, Blue Mountain's skiers visit the resort about ten times a season.

Mr. Gordon Canning, Jozo Weider's son-in-law, joined Blue Mountain Resorts in 1971 after completing his MBA studies at York University. Canning became Marketing Manager in 1972 and General Manager in 1975. In 1978, at the age of 35, Gordon Canning advanced to President and Chief Executive Officer of Blue Mountain Resorts Limited. He was also serving as Vice President of the Ontario Ski Resorts Association, Vice President of the Ontario Ski Council, and Chairman of the Tourism Development and Promotion Committee of Tourism Ontario. For an organizational chart of Blue Mountain Resorts, introducing the key people involved in the night skiing decision, see exhibit 1.

Exhibit 1 Abbreviated Organization Chart[a]—Blue Mountain Resorts Limited

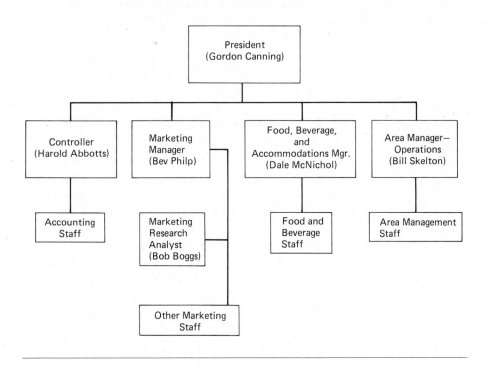

a. This chart contains only the people who would be involved to some extent in the night skiing decision.

Previous Investments (1970's)

Gordon Canning and the rest of the management were determined to maintain Blue Mountain's reputation for being innovative and successful. The organization's corporate strategy statement dictates that any proposed project must fit at least one of the following conditions before it can be undertaken:

1. A project that protects current earning power and minimizes any risks inherent to the business (e.g., weather conditions).

2. A project that expands primary earning power.

3. A project that helps to attain off-season use of facilities.

4. A project that offers new opportunities in (a) other ski areas or (b) other recreational areas.

In addition, it was very important to the business to maintain a "comfortable capacity" at the ski resort. Capacity at a ski resort roughly translates into the number of skiers per acre who can ski the hill in reasonable comfort; it depends on hill size, hill development, and lift facilities. As this skier-per-acre population rises, skiers become disgruntled over increasing lineups and waiting times. Blue Mountain had managed to keep this capacity at a comfortable level by increasing the number of lifts in 1974, 1977, and 1978 at a total cost of over $1 million. At the same time, they developed additional areas on the mountain to offer an increasing variety of ski runs.

In 1973, a $500,000 snow-making system was installed; since then, a further $1.75 million had been invested to upgrade snow-making and grooming facilities. This investment reduced the risk to Blue Mountain of insufficient natural snowfall's forcing closure of the facilities. As long as the temperature was low enough, the hill could be covered in artificial snow. Early in 1979, Blue Mountain installed the world's first computerized snow-making system to boost the efficiency and output of its snow-making plant. This computerized system was expected to increase the efficiency of the system for 1979–1980 by up to 30 percent over that of the previous season. With this snow-making facility, Blue Mountain's management felt that they could usually count on a skiing season from Christmas to mid-March.

In 1975, Blue Mountain installed "Get Moving Boards"—electronic boards to indicate which lifts were operating, the current waiting times, and which of the major restaurants were open. The next year, a ski shop complex was constructed at the central base lodge to house the ski repair and rental shops.

The first major diversification away from skiing occurred in 1977 when Blue Mountain introduced "The Great Slide Ride" at a cost of $500,000. A chairlift ride to the top of the mountain in combination with a 3000-foot descent on a plastic sled opened the way to the development of summer tourism for Ontario ski resorts.

The Night Skiing Opportunity

In the fall of 1978, Gordon Canning began to inquire into ways to increase utilization of the facilities in the off-hours of the winter skiing season. Night skiing, which involves lighting up the hill with artificial lighting, allows skiers to remain on the hill until late into the evening. However, the majority of night skiing facilities were located in private resorts near large urban centres. Since the nearest large city was 85 miles away, Canning and Bev Philp (who was in charge of the Marketing Division of Blue Mountain Resorts) were uncertain about whether skiers would be interested in night skiing at Blue Mountain.

Blue Mountain's management felt a responsibility and a commitment to offering skiers the highest quality and best value for their money. Canning felt, therefore, that if Blue Mountain were to introduce night skiing, their facilities would have to be better than any of their competitors. By lighting an entire slope, Blue Mountain could offer the longest run, the highest vertical,[1] and the best snow conditions for night skiing in Southern Ontario.

Gordon Canning's first move was to approach Harold Abbotts, Blue Mountain's Controller, to determine the incremental investment costs of this proposal. Abbotts and Bill Skelton, who was responsible for running the operations of the resort, agreed that $135,500 would be needed to install the necessary equipment (mostly lighting) on one area at Blue Mountain. If the decision were made to go ahead with the proposal, one of four separate areas would likely be chosen. Each of the areas was roughly similar in size; skier capacity would be easily adequate even if demand for night skiing was much higher than expected. Two of the possible choices were ski slopes at the intermediate level of difficulty, one (the North area) was advanced, and one (Big Baby/O-Hill) was beginner and intermediate. Canning was comfortable that $135,500 estimate was an accurate one because all construction would be done by the Blue Mountain staff themselves.

1. A "vertical" is defined as the difference in elevation between the top of the ski trails and the base of the mountain.

In addition, there would be operating costs involved in maintaining the facilities for the evening hours. The costs would involve payroll for cashiers and ski patrol, repair and maintenance costs for equipment and trails, printing costs for tickets, and an additional cost for utilities (lights and lifts). The total additional operating costs would be approximately $1000 per night plus a seasonal allocation of $20,000 for fixed costs, which would be shared with day skiing. These figures did not include the costs of additional liability insurance, which would depend on the number of skiers, or the cost of promoting night skiing. Current rates for liability insurance were $7.75 per thousand skiers. Incremental promotional costs for supporting night skiing were estimated at no more than $5000.

With this information, Gordon Canning approached Bev Philp and Bob Boggs (who designed and executed Blue Mountain's marketing research) and asked them to determine the market potential for night skiing. Blue Mountain already had an extensive marketing research programme, which enabled the management to keep up to date with the changing characteristics and needs of the approximately 30,000 different skiers who visited Blue Mountain annually.[2] Hill hosts and hostesses had been hired each winter since 1975 to aid in the distribution of surveys. After working approximately two hours per day, the employee was permitted to ski the rest of the day for free.

During each winter season, 4000 profile questionnaires are distributed. On designated sampling days (balanced according to skier frequency), the hill host or hostess approaches every third person in the ticket lineup and asks how many are in the skier's party and the age, sex, and residence of each member. There are four ticket wickets at Blue Mountain; the profiles are divided in proportion to the number of tickets bought at each wicket.

Also, during each winter season, a detailed seven-page "overall" skier survey is distributed to approximately 700 skiers. These questionnaires are distributed throughout the season in proportion to the number of skiers using the facilities during any one time period. In practice, this sampling plan means that more questionnaires are given out on week-ends than during the week, and more are distributed in January and February than in November and December. The questionnaires are given out by the Hill hostesses in the various cafeterias. The number distributed in each cafeteria is determined by the proportion of dollar sales across the food outlets. Hostesses are given specified quotas by age and sex to use in requesting skiers to participate in the survey. Their quotas are developed from the

2. Exhibit 8, which is discussed later in the case, shows a distribution of average number of days skied during the 1978–1979 season. It had been obtained from a survey of skiers during the following season.

results of the profiles. This plan ensures that the survey results are as demographically representative as possible.

The overall skier survey that had been conducted during the 1978–1979 skiing season already contained two questions on night skiing (see exhibit 2 for the results), but Blue Mountain management had felt that these data were not sufficient for an accurate determination of market potential for night skiing. Therefore, Bob Boggs subsequently developed a three-page questionnaire that focused exclusively on night skiing and distributed it to just under 200 people (see exhibit 3). This survey was conducted identically to the overall survey, except that the interviews were all done near the end of the season, in February and March. Consequently, it was expected that skier profiles would be somewhat different in the night skiing survey than the overall one. Exhibit 4 contains data on several demographics for the overall survey. Data from the entire night skiing survey was also available for analysis (see exhibits 3 and 3A). Refusal rates for the night skiing questionnaire were less than 5 percent, since, as in the past, most skiers were very cooperative and supportive of the questionnaires.

Exhibit 2 Night Skiing Questions on the Overall Survey

How likely would you be to use night skiing facilities on a regular basis?

Definitely would use	14.1%
Probably would use	15.9
Might/might not use	20.1
Probably would not use	30.9
Definitely would not use	19.0

How often over the season would you use night skiing facilities?
(Asked of those respondents who at least *might* use the night skiing facilities at Blue Mountain)

1 time	17.0%
2 times	18.5
3 times	11.8
4 times	5.8
5 times	8.8
6–10 times	15.5
11–15 times	3.5
16–20 times	2.8
Once every weekend	5.5
Occasionally	7.3
Weekends and holidays	3.0

Exhibit 3   Night Skiing Survey

Survey of Blue Mountain Skiers   DATE: _____

Dear Skier:

We would appreciate a few minutes of your time to give us your opinion of night skiing at Blue Mountain. This survey is designed to help us provide you with the facilities and services which will best meet your needs and help us plan for future development.

THANK YOU FOR YOUR ASSISTANCE.

HOW TO FILL IN THE QUESTIONNAIRE
In the box at the right, please write the number that is beside the answer you best wish to select.

EXAMPLE:

What is your age?
> (1) Under 15
> (2) 16/17
> (3) 18–24
> (4) 25–34   ⌐3⌐
> (5) 35–49
> (6) 50 or over

IN SOME QUESTIONS WE ASK YOU TO WRITE IN YOUR ANSWER IN THE SPACE PROVIDED.

1) Have you ever been night skiing before?
> (1) yes   70.7%
> (2) no   29.3%   ☐

2) Where, if yes?_____

3) Would you be interested in night skiing at Blue Mountain?
> (1) yes   44.4%
> (2) no   55.6%   ☐

4) How many times a year would you ski at night?
> (1) 1–5   33.7%*
> (2) 6–10   33.7%
> (3) 11–15   15.7%
> (4) 16–20   7.2%   ☐
> (5) 20–30   4.8%
> (6) 30 or more   4.8%

Exhibit 3 (continued)

5) What night of the week would you prefer to ski?

    (1) Monday   4.9%*
    (2) Tuesday   7.3%
    (3) Wednesday   9.8%
    (4) Thursday   11.0%
    (5) Friday   28.0%
    (6) Saturday   25.6%
    (7) Sunday   13.4%

6) How far would you drive to go night skiing?

    (1) less than five miles   7.3%*
    (2) 6–10 miles   11.0%
    (3) 10–25 miles   17.1%
    (4) 25–35 miles   13.4%
    (5) 35–75 miles   29.3%
    (6) more than 75 miles 22.0%

7) Would your trips be mainly:

    (1) Skiing at Blue Mountain for the night and returning home the same night. (16.0%)*
    (2) Skiing at Blue Mountain for one day and one night. (14.8%)
    (3) Skiing at Blue Mountain for two or more days combined with a night or more of skiing. (55.6%)
    (4) Other, please specify (13.6%) _____

_____

8) At what hour would you usually begin night skiing at Blue Mountain?

    (1) 3 P.M.   4.8%*   (4) 6 P.M.   25.3%   (7) 9 P.M.   4.8%
    (2) 4 P.M.   3.6%   (5) 7 P.M.   38.6%   (8) other _____
    (3) 5 P.M.   15.7%   (6) 8 P.M.   7.2

9) At what hour would you usually finish night skiing at Blue Mountain?

    (1) 5 P.M.   —   (5) 9 P.M.   4.9%*
    (2) 6 P.M.   —   (6) 10 P.M. 40.7%
    (3) 7 P.M.   —   (7) 11 P.M. 54.3%
    (4) 8 P.M.   —

*Tabulation based on the 83 respondents (44.4%) who replied "yes" to Question 3.

Exhibit 3 (continued)

10) a. Midweek skiing for the day costs $9.00. What do you think is a fair ticket price for midweek night skiing? [See exhibit 3A for a tabulation]

b. Weekend skiing for the day costs $12.00. What do you feel is a fair ticket price for weekend night skiing? [See exhibit 3A for a tabulation]

11) Would apres-ski entertainment be a factor in your decision to go night skiing?

    (1) yes   67.5%*
    (2) no   31.3%   ☐

12) At which area would you like to see night skiing at Blue Mountain?

    (1) North   11.4%*
    (2) Happy Valley/Apple Bowl   38.0%
    (3) Tranquility/Smart Alec   38.0%   ☐
    (4) Big Baby/O-Hill   12.7%

13) Would you be interested in ski lessons at night?

    (1) yes   24.1%*
    (2) no   75.9%   ☐

14) Would you require rentals at night?

    (1) yes   10.8%*
    (2) no   89.2%   ☐

15) How many times will you ski at Blue Mountain this year?

                  [See exhibit 3A for a tabulation]

16) Are you a season's pass holder?

    (1) yes   20.5%*   15.6%**
    (2) no   78.3%   84.4%   ☐

ABOUT YOURSELF

Finally, to help us classify the answers could you please answer these last few questions.

17) What is your age?

    (1) under 15   4.8%*   4.3%**
    (2) 16/17   7.2%   4.8%
    (3) 18–24   54.2%   52.7%
    (4) 25–34   25.3%   29.3%   ☐
    (5) 35–49   8.4%   8.5%
    (6) 50 and over   —   0.5%

---

*Percentages are based on the 83 respondents (44.4%) who replied "yes" to Question 3.
**Percentages are based on all respondents to the survey.

Exhibit 3 (continued)

18) Your sex?

    (1) Male   69.5%*   67.7%**

    (2) Female   29.3%   32.3%

19) Where do you live?   [see exhibit 3A for a summary]

(1) Toronto	(10) Sarnia
(2) Hamilton/Burlington	(11) Windsor
(3) Oakville	(12) Barrie
(4) Mississauga	(13) Collingwood and area
(5) London	(14) Owen Sound
(6) Guelph	(15) Detroit Area
(7) Cambridge	(16) Other Michigan
(8) Kitchener/Waterloo	(17) Ohio
(9) Oshawa	(18) New York
	(19) other

20) What is your occupation?

(1) Professional/ Managerial	35.8%*	(7) High School	25.9%
(2) Owner	1.2%	(8) Elementary Student	
(3) Sales	8.6%	(9) Housewife	1.2%
(4) Clerical	4.9%	(10) Unemployed	
(5) Skilled Labour	12.3%	(11) Retired	
(6) Univ./College Student	9.9%		

21) What is your marital status?

    (1) single   80.5%*

    (2) married 18.3%*

22) What is your total family income, before taxes?

    (1) under $12,000   8.8%*

    (2) $12,000–14,999   14.7%

    (3) $15,000–19,999   25.0%

    (4) $20,000–24,999   14.7%

    (5) $25,000–29,999   11.8%

    (6) $30,000–35,000   5.9%

    (7) over $35,000   19.1%

---

*Percentages are based on the 83 respondents (44.4%) who replied "yes" to Question 3.

**Percentages are based on all respondents to the survey.

Exhibit 3 (continued)

23) Do you have any general comments about night skiing at Blue Mountain?

_____

_____

_____

THANK YOU!

Exhibit 3A   Selected Frequency Counts from the Night Skiing Survey

Question 10

	Percent Judging the Price as "Fair" for Skiing*	
Price	*(A) Midweek Nights*	*(B) Weekend Nights*
Less than $4	13.2%	—
$4	19.7%	5.1%
$5	31.6%	16.7%
$6	17.1%	21.8%
$7	9.2%	15.4%
$8	5.3%	16.7%
$9	2.6%	6.4%
$10	—	11.5%
More than $10	—	5.1%

Question 15

Anticipated Skiing Days This Year at Blue Mountain	*Night Skier Respondents**	*All Respondents*
0	1.3%	1.7%
1–5	29.9%	34.5%
6–10	15.6%	17.2%
11–15	9.1%	9.8%
16–20	16.9%	10.9%
More than 20	27.3%	25.9%

*Tabulation based on the 83 respondents (44.4%) who replied "Yes" to Question 3.

Exhibit 3A   (continued)

Question 19

| | | *Percent of:* | |
Location of Home	Codes from Q. 19	Blue Mountain Night Skiers*	All Respondents
Toronto	1	48.8%	42.8%
Near Toronto	2,3,4,9	22.0%	20.3%
Southwestern Ontario	5,6,7,8 10,11	8.5%	11.2%
Collingwood Area	12,13,14	8.4%	13.4%
U.S.	15,16,17,18	12.2%	11.8%

Exhibit 4   Demographic Data from the Overall Survey

Age

Category	Percentage of Respondents
Under 15	6.1%
16 and 17	8.8%
18 to 24	41.6%
25 to 34	30.6%
35 to 49	11.6%
50 and over	1.3%

Sex

Category	Percentage of Respondents
Male	60.8%
Female	38.9%

Marital Status

Category	Percentage of Respondents
Single	67.2%
Married	25.1%
Separated/Divorced	7.6%

Season's Pass Holder

Category	Percentage of Respondents
Yes	17.8%
No	82.2%

*Tabulation based on the 83 respondents (44.4%) who replied "Yes" to Question 3.

Gordon Canning felt that from this questionnaire he could get a good idea of the price sensitivity of the different consumers. (Planned prices for daytime skiing are shown in exhibit 5.) If he went ahead with night skiing, he knew he would have to make pricing decisions on both single-night lift tickets and season passes. He wondered whether he should offer a special night skiing season pass or combine it with the season pass already offered. He expected 2100 skiers to buy the current season pass for the 1979–1980 winter season at the planned $250 cost. He knew he had the alternative of increasing the pass price and making it a day and night pass. On the other hand, he could offer three different passes—a night season pass, a combined night and day season pass, and the traditional day season pass. He would, of course, have to set appropriate prices for all passes.

Besides the pricing decision, Canning wanted to get a good idea of the profile of the potential frequent night skiers—age, marital status, place of residence, etc. If he decided to go ahead with the project, he felt that he needed this information for planning a successful introduction—both from a promotional standpoint (e.g., what sort of message should he try to communicate to what people living where?) and from a product line standpoint (e.g., how important was it to have apres-ski activities?).

In making his decision, Gordon Canning also thought that it might be worthwhile to review some information he had about day skiers, because this data could perhaps offer him some insights about patterns of behaviour that would emerge for night skiers. First, he was interested in skiers' spending patterns. Exhibit 6 presents a summary of the expenditures of the typical skier for a day on the slopes during the 1978–1979 season. It also contains rough estimates of the estimated gross margins for evening operations of services (food and beverage, ski rentals, etc.). Also, Canning wanted to review the data on frequency of skier visits during a

Exhibit 5   Planned Lift Rates for the 1979–1980 Season

	Weekends and Holidays	Midweek
All-Day Ticket	$13.00	$11.00
Red Lift*	$10.00	$ 8.00
Afternoon Ticket**	$10.00	$ 8.00
Rope Tow	$ 3.00	$ 3.00
Monday to Friday Ticket	N/A	$45.00
Season Ticket	$250.00	

*Surface lifts that go partway up the mountain
**Good for the period 1:00–4:30. All other tickets are usable between 9:00 and 4:30.

year. His marketing staff told him that the last accurate data that were available had been obtained from the recent overall survey, but the data were for the 1977–1978 season (exhibit 7).

Blue Mountain's management had observed a marked divergence between data obtained when skiers were asked to recall how much they skied last year and information given when they were asked to forecast how much they were going to ski in the future. On the average, people seemed to think that they would ski considerably more in the future than they had in the past. What Gordon Canning had to decide was to what extent any forecasts for the future reflected plans that would actually be realized rather than inaccurate optimism. With these reservations in mind, he sat down to begin his analysis of the night skiing decision.

Exhibit 6 Dollar Revenue Per Skier Visit[a] (1978–1979)

	Dollar Revenue	*Estimated Gross Margins for Night Skiing[b]*
Lifts	$10.15	—
Food and Beverage	3.82	20%
Blue Mountain Inn[c]	0.27	—
Ski School	0.39	10%
Rental and Repairs	1.15	40%
Ski Shop	1.06	30%
	$16.84	

a. Season passholders are excluded.
b. These figures are very rough estimates. They were obtained by taking the margins from daytime operations and adjusting them to reflect costs at projected service levels for night skiers.
c. During the ski season, the Inn operates at or near capacity.

Exhibit 7 Average Number Days Skied 1977–1978[a]

Number of Times Skied	*Percentage of Skier Population*
0	13.4%
1–5	20.3%
6–10	15.7%
11–15	12.2%
16–20	10.3%
21 + (avg. 26)	28.1%

a. These data were collected in the "overall" survey during the 1978–1979 skiing season, so these figures include a substantial fraction who had not skied at all during the previous year.

5 Federal Bermuda Line

The Federal Commerce and Navigation (1974) Ltd. is a Canadian company with its head office in Montreal, Quebec. As a subsidiary of Fednav Limited, a holding company, Federal Commerce and Navigation (1974) Ltd. offers various transportation services. The President of the company, Mr. Lawrence G. Pathy, is looking into the possibilities of expanding the company's operations. One of these possibilities is a shipping service from Halifax to Hamilton, Bermuda. In order to assess the potential of such a shipping service, Mr. Pathy commissioned a shipping consultant, Mr. John Grice, of Analytic Services Limited, Halifax, Nova Scotia, to perform a feasibility study. The study report was completed by March 1975 and presented to Mr. Pathy. A summary of the most important points for Mr. Pathy to consider is attached.

After reading the study, Mr. Pathy had to assess the potential of the proposed new shipping service for his company.

A Halifax–Bermuda Container Service—Feasibility Study

Bermuda is a British colony with responsible internal self-government. It has an area of 20.59 square miles and is located 756 miles south-southwest of Halifax and 697 miles southeast of New York. It lies astride the trade routes between Europe and the Gulf of Mexico, and those routes linking Europe to the Far East via the Panama Canal. Furthermore, it is located on the trade route between Eastern Canada and the Caribbean. Historically, it has been served by ships plying those trade routes.

Bermuda has a resident population of 60,000, including 3000 United States Air Force personnel and their dependents. Bermuda's trade flows are virtually all one-way, imports dominating almost nonexistent exports.

124

Industry and Trade

The principal local industry is tourism, which is the mainstay of the economy. Ranked second is the "exempted company" business, namely the use of Bermuda as an offshore financial centre and corporate base by international business organizations. These pay moderate annual licence fees, employ large numbers of local staff, and purchase or rent considerable office space and private accommodation, but their activities are *outside* Bermuda.

The relatively high cost of local labour—in a community where there are many more local jobs generated than there are Bermudians to fill them—has tended to reduce the effort to create local manufacturing industry in Bermuda (exhibits 1 and 2). Nevertheless, certain key industries do flourish—for example, the preparation of airline meals for all carriers serving Bermuda; the manufacture of paints, local arts and crafts including pottery, silkscreening and woodwork; the distillation of various perfumes, toiletries, and a liquor made from loquat juice; ships repair and servicing; printing and publishing. Service trades are also important and include banking and financial services; accountancy/audit preparation; wholesale and retail dealing in a wide range of goods and services. These all take advantage of Bermuda's stable political climate, absence of direct taxation, favourable geographical site close to the principal tourist and financial markets, and extremely well developed communications.

Exhibit 1 Total Bermuda Imports and Exports

| | Value in million U.S. dollars (F.O.B.) | |
Year	Imports	Exports
1938	9	1
1948	29	4
1958	48	22
1963	55	39
1967	68	60
1968	73	65
1969	83	77
1970	87	81
1971	108	92
1972	114	36
1973	123	30
1974	155	34

Source: Yearbook of International Trade Statistics, 1975, Vol. 1, United Nations.

Exhibit 2 Bermuda Imports and Exports for Selected Countries

Year	General Imports F.O.B. (Value in Thousand U.S. Dollars)				General Exports F.O.B. (Value in Thousand U.S. Dollars)			
	1971	1972	1973	1974	1971	1972	1973	1974
EEC (Nine)	34589	34147	37373	37450	47040	17135	6179	8816
EFTA	2127	1903	1826	2059	3623	307	2169	1003
U.K.	24192	22820	24665	23003	20546	4114	788	1072
U.S.A./ Puerto Rico	48747	54666	55372	68696	1535	2080	4172	4865
Canada	13063	13323	12082	13394	586	508	808	968
New Zealand	1911	2975	2924	3664	307	1190	2025	473
Australia	51	67	100	66	14673	2332	1014	1140
Japan	1522	2464	1947	2721	5413	2147	946	122
Hong Kong	963	1134	1291	1544	9	18	71	59

Source: Yearbook of International Trade Statistics, 1975, Vol. 1, United Nations.

Imports

The ten leading nations supplying products to Bermuda in 1973 were as follows: U.S. (45% share), U.K. (20%), Canada (10%), Aruba/Curacao and France (3% each), New Zealand, Venezuela, West Germany, Netherlands, and Denmark (2% each). The Aruba/Curacao and Venezuelan imports are largely of petroleum products. Thus 91% of Bermuda's imports are from 10 countries, and 75% are from 3 countries. The imports are almost totally of consumer goods that readily lend themselves to containerization. The U.S. trade is almost fully containerized, but this is not the case with U.K. and European cargoes, 80% of this trade moving on a break-bulk basis. However, Bermuda importers are now demanding a containerized service from European ports.

There are 34 product categories that are important for Canadian exporters to Bermuda. In each of these categories, Canada shipped $100,000 or more of goods and held the leading, second, or third highest share of imports. In two other categories—perfumes and cosmetics, and telecommunications equipment—the $100,000 or more imports criterion was met, but import share rank placed Canada fifth and fourth, respectively.

Hamilton is the port of entry through which all shipments are handled. The port has some 1500 square feet of wharf area and 70,000 square feet of shed space. The Bermuda Government has granted a monopoly to Stevedoring Services Ltd., which handles all ships at Hamilton. This company has two mobile cranes, each of which is capable of working a small container ship to a finish. In consort they can complete the discharge and loading of a 100-TEU[1] capacity ship in 12 hours. Yard equipment includes two Silent Hoist top lift trucks.

Some current port practices at Hamilton are of interest to the prospective operator. All reefer and chilled containers are immediately stripped at the dock and are loaded for the same ship. This avoids having a $25,000 container out of circulation until the next ship arrives. Also, 40-foot containers are not allowed on the road at all, are allowed on the dock only with special permission, and must be stripped to be returned to the same ship. In addition, a customs ruling requiring that all containers with more than one consignee must be stripped at the dock results in some 45% of the containers being stripped on the dock, with only 55% currently moving over the road on a house-to-house basis. All inland transportation is by road.

Existing Shipping Services to Bermuda

A. European cargoes to Bermuda. At present there are five shipping lines offering a service to Bermuda:

1. Ozean/Stinnes Linien: loading at Hamburg, Bremen, Antwerp, Rotterdam, and London—service to Bermuda and Mexico's east coast—every 3–4 weeks.

2. Deutsche Seereederei of Rostock: loading at Hamburg, Antwerp, and London—service to Bermuda, Nassau, and Mexico's east coast—every 2 weeks.

3. Intercontinental Transport: loading at Hamburg, Bremen, Rotterdam, Antwerp, and London—service to Bermuda and Mexico's east coast—fortnightly.

4. Pacific Steam Navigation: loading at Liverpool—service to Bermuda, Nassau, and South America's west coast—every 3 weeks.

The incremental break-bulk nature of the Bermuda trade for these lines creates certain problems. The first concerns service frequency; no line offers the weekly service that Bermuda importers desire, sailings ranging from every 2 to 4 weeks. This means that importers are unable to pipeline supplies in the way they would prefer. Instead, they have to make do with larger, less frequent consignments. The second problem

1. TEU = Twenty-foot container equivalent units.

centres on the lack of containerization. This leads to higher rates of pilferage and damage than the importers find acceptable.

Partly in response to these problems, United States Lines now offers weekly containerized shipments to Bermuda through a feeder service connection—the Bermuda Express Service. In this way, cargoes are transhipped from United States Lines ships in New York and loaded for the shuttle service to Hamilton, Bermuda.

5. United States Lines: loading at LeHavre, Antwerp, Hamburg, Rotterdam, Felixstowe, Liverpool—service to New York, Philadelphia, Baltimore, Jacksonville, Savannah, Los Angeles, San Francisco, Hawaii, Japan with a feeder ship connection (Bermuda Express Service) to Bermuda from New York—weekly.

The reaction of Bermuda importers to United States Line's containerized service out of New York is very positive, emphasizing the advantages of containers in reducing pilferage and damage and permitting goods to be pipelined and shipped in smaller consignments from the UK/Continent. Equally important is the weekly frequency of the service.

B. USA cargoes to Bermuda. There are two shipping lines offering shipping services from East Coast USA to Bermuda:

1. Bermuda Express Service: weekly shuttle service from New York to Bermuda—characterized by a high degree of reliability, fully containerized, with substantial reefer capacity (18–20 reefer or chilled containers per sailing).

2. Pan Atlantic Shipping Ltd.: fortnightly service from Miami and Jacksonville to Bermuda—also provides reefer containers.

C. Canadian cargoes to Bermuda. Only one shipping line—Saguenay Shipping Ltd. (a subsidiary of Alcan)—offers a service for Canadian cargoes Bermuda-bound. It serves the ports of Montreal and Halifax, Bermuda, the Caribbean islands, and Venezuela/Guyana. On the return trip to Canada, Saguenay carries bauxite that is loaded in Jamaica. Service frequency is monthly. In 1974–1975 the first winter sailing out of Montreal began. Before this, winter operations were run out of Halifax. The ship used is a large bulk carrier that carries containers in the holds south-bound and bauxite north-bound. This ship is not ideally suited for the nonbauxite cargoes it carries. Saguenay competes for Canadian business with the Bermuda Express Service over New York. Importers interviewed in Bermuda were unanimous in their severe criticism of Saguenay's service, characterizing it as irregular, unreliable, infrequent, and arrogant. They cited these as reasons for shipping Canadian cargo via the Port of New York and also for sourcing supplies (especially food products) in the United States that would otherwise be sourced in Canada (much of it in the Maritimes). Rates on the Saguenay service average well in excess of $1000 per 20-foot container.

D.   New Zealand cargoes to Bermuda. Sailings from New Zealand are coordinated by the New Zealand Shipowners Committee and their members are Blue Star Line, PRO, Shaw Savill, and New Zealand Shipping Line. These shipping lines offer three sailings per year from Timaru, Auckland, and Wellington to Bermuda. There is no fixed trading pattern for these vessels except that they come via the Panama Canal.

Potential for a Halifax-Bermuda Service

Potential exists for a shipping service between Halifax and Hamilton, Bermuda. The traffic would be (1) Canadian exports and (2) European and U.K. exports transhipped at Halifax from deep sea container lines. All the cargo would be containerized. The service would mirror that provided by Bermuda Express out of New York in combining local and distant cargoes.

Taking the deep sea container trade first, Atlantic Container Line and Dart Container Line serve all of Northern Europe and the United Kingdom. Between the two lines, three sailings per week to Halifax are offered, providing a veritable blanket coverage of all major European ports (see attached service patterns, exhibits 3a and 3b). Both lines are represented by substantial interests in these areas and have extensive sales forces and networks of consolidation depots already in place, allowing them to move quickly and effectively to generate cargo for a new system if they can be so motivated. In Southern Europe, the same can be said of Zim Container Service (see attached service pattern, exhibit 3c). This strength in Europe and the United Kingdom is absolutely critical to the success of the Halifax–Bermuda service inasmuch as Europe and the United Kingdom will be the most significant contributors to the service in terms of volume and revenue. Strategically, then the transshipment cargo (especially from Europe/UK) must be regarded as the base for the service and the Canadian cargo as an "add on."

The transhipment operation at Halifax has the advantage of serving all vessels from one dock, a situation which cannot be duplicated by Halifax's

Exhibit 3   Patterns of Ocean Container Ship Services

a. Atlantic Container Line

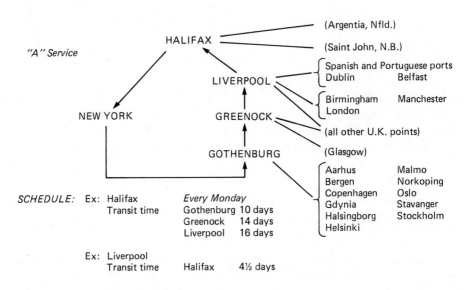

"A" Service

HALIFAX
— (Argentia, Nfld.)
— (Saint John, N.B.)

LIVERPOOL
— Spanish and Portuguese ports
  Dublin   Belfast
— Birmingham   Manchester
  London
— (all other U.K. points)

NEW YORK   GREENOCK
— (Glasgow)

GOTHENBURG
— Aarhus   Malmo
  Bergen   Norkoping
  Copenhagen   Oslo
  Gdynia   Stavanger
  Halsingborg   Stockholm
  Helsinki

SCHEDULE: Ex: Halifax   Every Monday
                Transit time   Gothenburg 10 days
                                Greenock   14 days
                                Liverpool   16 days

           Ex: Liverpool
                Transit time   Halifax   4½ days

b. Dart Container Line

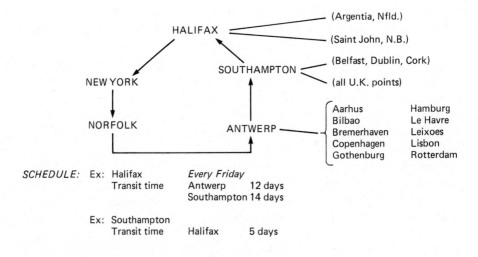

HALIFAX
— (Argentia, Nfld.)
— (Saint John, N.B.)

SOUTHAMPTON
— (Belfast, Dublin, Cork)
— (all U.K. points)

NEW YORK

NORFOLK   ANTWERP
— Aarhus   Hamburg
  Bilbao   Le Havre
  Bremerhaven   Leixoes
  Copenhagen   Lisbon
  Gothenburg   Rotterdam

SCHEDULE: Ex: Halifax   Every Friday
                Transit time   Antwerp   12 days
                                Southampton 14 days

           Ex: Southampton
                Transit time   Halifax   5 days

130   Understanding Buyer Behaviour

Exhibit 3 (continued)

c. Zim Container Service

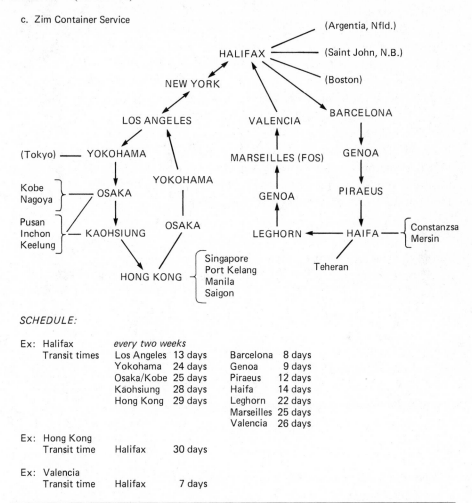

SCHEDULE:

Ex: Halifax   *every two weeks*
     Transit times

Los Angeles	13 days	Barcelona	8 days
Yokohama	24 days	Genoa	9 days
Osaka/Kobe	25 days	Piraeus	12 days
Kaohsiung	28 days	Haifa	14 days
Hong Kong	29 days	Leghorn	22 days
		Marseilles	25 days
		Valencia	26 days

Ex: Hong Kong
     Transit time   Halifax   30 days

Ex: Valencia
     Transit time   Halifax   7 days

Source: Atlantic Provinces Transportation Commission, *Directory of Ocean Containership Services.*

most formidable competitor—New York. At New York, containers must be loaded to or from mother ships at various points in New Jersey and then trucked to or from Pier #8 in Brooklyn (some 25 miles distant) to connect with the Bermuda-bound ship. This situation adds to the problem of control and contributes at least $150 in the form of gate charges and trucking charges per 20 feet container. As the first port-of-call for westbound services of ACL, Dart Container Line and Zim Container Service, Halifax also has an advantage over New York in terms of delivery time for containers originating in Europe.

On the matter of local Canadian cargo, substantial amounts now move via New York which can be recovered if a quality transportation service is available. Quality in this context implies container availability (including temperature controlled containers for reefer and chilled requirements), frequency (weekly appears to be the minimum acceptable frequency) and reliability. An outstanding example of a Canadian company shipping considerable volumes of food products via New York to Bermuda is McCain Foods of Florenceville, New Brunswick. If the level of service at Halifax were satisfactory, not only could the existing flow of traffic be captured, but it is likely that McCain would increase their penetration of the Bermudian market at the expense of U.S. suppliers.

Revenues and Costs

Bermuda General Cargo Imports by volume are shown in exhibit 4. The traffic base for a potential Halifax–Bermuda service has the following sources:

Source of imports	Tons
1. Europe/UK	24,830
2. Canada	11,838
3. New Zealand	2,446
4. West Coast U.S.A.	2,000 (est.)
5. Cargo originating in North New York State and Midwest U.S.A.	1,000 (est.)
6. Cargo that can be resourced from the U.S. East Coast	2,000 (est.)
Total annual tonnage for which Halifax system is competitive	44,114

We estimate that a Halifax-based service could capture 20,000 to 28,000 tons of this business. This is based on the following calculation:

Total annual tonnage potential: 44,114.

(Assume 100% trade containerized and average tonnage/TEU is 8 tons)

With 50 sailings per year, TEU available per sailing is 110, i.e.,

$$\frac{44,114}{8 \times 50}$$

Exhibit 4   Bermuda General Cargo Imports (in tons of 2240 lbs.)

Year	New Zealand	Canada	Europe/U.K.	U.S.A.	Total
1968	—	—	—	—	97,036
1969	1831	19,942	38,466	39,666 (1237)	105,932
1970	2085	20,774	39,142	48,529 (1539)	113,404
1971	1853	26,219	41,544	47,550 (775)	118,672
1972	2456	20,807	34,166	43,860 (1629)	104,148
1973	2059	16,057	30,204	46,618	96,025
1974	2446	11,838	24,830	49,603	89,707

1.   Figures in parentheses in the U.S.A. column are tonnage moved via West Coast U.S.A. (e.g. Los Angeles). Direct sailings from the West Coast to Bermuda terminated in 1972. Most of this cargo still moves over the ports of San Francisco and Los Angeles via the Panama on vessels of U.S. lines and is transshipped at New York.
2.   In recent years, total tonnage to Bermuda has declined owing to a moratorium declared on major hotel construction effective 1973 through 1978.
3.   The U.S. tonnages include a significant amount of Canadian, Far East, and Europe/U.K. cargo moving via New York, either by truck from Canada or transshipped from deep sea vessels in the case of Europe/U.K. and Far East.
4.   Cumulative totals of the annual tonnages for New Zealand, Canada, Europe, U.K., and U.S.A. do not equal "total" figures on the above chart. This is due to the existence of small tonnages (usually less than 1000 tons per annum) imported from countries other than those indicated.
5.   A significant amount of air freight also enters Bermuda. In 1974 it amounted to 6543 tons, 60% of which originated in the U.S.A. and 40% of which originated in the U.K.
Source: Analytic Services Limited, Halifax, Nova Scotia.

Based on a strong competitive position in Europe and Canada, as well as a good position with respect to California and New Zealand, one could expect a penetration of 50–70 containers per sailing, from a total of 110 available.

This forecast is based on a shipping rate of $800 round trip (Halifax to Hamilton and return) for a transhipped dry cargo twenty foot container. Reefer and chilled cargo would bear high rates (say $1000), as would dry containers originating in Canada. The $800 rate is predicated on cargoes being able to pay $1500 as a minimum rate from Europe/U.K. on a through rate to Bermuda, and deep sea lines requiring revenues of $700 per twenty foot container for the Europe/U.K. to Halifax portion.

Several comparisons suggest this to be a reasonable rate for a new service.

1. Bermuda Express quotes a round trip rate for non-volume movements of transhipped containers from New York to Bermuda of $1,017 per twenty foot container (exclusive of trucking charges and port costs).

2. On cargo from Europe/U.K., Bermuda importers have indicated that existing rates for a twenty foot container range from a low of $1400 to a high of $2600, according to origin and commodity. In fact, most of the freight is paying more than $1800 per container.

3. Saguenay rates for a twenty foot container are, on average, well in excess of $1000.

4. McCain Foods currently pays $1300 per twenty foot container to ship its frozen foods to Bermuda through New York on the Bermuda Express Service. In addition, it incurs trucking costs of $500 per container, that would be reduced if it shipped through Halifax.

A profit analysis based on 50–70 TEU per sailing is given in exhibit 5.

Exhibit 5   Profit Analysis based on 50–70 TEU per sailing

a. *Office costs*

Halifax office	Annual expenses
Manager	$20,000
Assistant Manager	12,000
Clerk	9,000
Boarding Officer	8,000
Secretary	7,000
Subtotal	$56,000
Office	7,000
Total	$63,000

Office costs per sailing based on 50 sailings per year: $1,260
This assumes that a separate office is established. If the service were integrated with an established agency, total cost would be less than half, i.e. less than $630 per voyage.

b. *Ship operating costs*

These are based on a two-year time charter for a 100 TEU full container ship (cellularized), with an operating speed of 13 knots, consuming eight tons of fuel daily.

Halifax–Hamilton sailing time = 756 nautical miles ÷ 13 knots per hour
= 58 hours

Exhibit 5 (continued)

> Halifax–Hamilton return = 116 hours, leaving 52 hours per week for
> port time at both ports, and an allowance for delays.

Per diem charter =		$2,500 – $2,800
Per diem fuel costs =	8 × $110	$ 880 – $ 880
	Range	$3,380 – $3,680

365 days × ($3,380 – $3,680)

Annual cost to operate vessel including fuel = $1,233,700 – $1,343,200
Cost per sailing including fuel   = $24,674 – $26,864

c. *Stevedoring costs*

Stevedoring at Hamilton ($60 average per TEU including overtime)
Based on 50 TEU per week = 3,000 × 2 = $6,000
Based on 70 TEU per week = 4,200 × 2 = $8,400

Stevedoring at Halifax ($65 average per TEU including overtime)
Based on 50 TEU per week = 3,250 × 2 = $6,500
Based on 70 TEU per week = 4,550 × 2 = $9,100

d. *Port charges*

Halifax Port Charges

Harbour Dues	$ 55
Pilotage	$150
Wharfage	$100
	$305

Hamilton Port Charges

Agency Fees	$200
Pilotage	$150
Other	$150
	$500

e. *Contingency*

Two hundred dollars per voyage is included to account for unforeseen
expenses such as the use of tugs during adverse weather conditions and
pilotage charges due to interharbour movages, as well as to pay for
charterers' liability insurance.

Maximum Total Cost per Voyage

a.	Office Costs	$ 1,260
b.	Shipcosts	26,864
c.	Stevedoring - Halifax	9,100
	Hamilton	8,400
d.	Port Charges	805
e.	Contingency	200
	Total	$46,629
Revenue $800 × 70 TEU		$56,000
	Profit	$ 9,371

Minimum Total Costs per Voyage

a.	Office Costs	$ 630
b.	Shipcosts	24,674
c.	Stevedoring - Halifax	6,500
	Hamilton	6,000
d.	Port Charges	805
e.	Contingency	200
	Total	$38,809
Revenue $800 × 50 TEU		$40,000
	Profit	$ 1,191

The profit per voyage ranges between $1,191 and $9,371.

Source: Analytic Services Limited, Halifax, Nova Scotia.

6 Domglas Inc.

In early 1978, Stan Pearce, Market Development Manager of the Foods Division at Domglas, Inc., had the idea of marketing ready-to-eat soup in glass jars for the convenience of microwave oven owners. The attraction of glass packaging for soup was that the soup could be heated in a microwave oven in its original container. However, ready-to-eat soup in glass was expected to cost one or two cents more per serving than conventional concentrated soup in cans. If Domglas were to go ahead with this idea, one of the major soup companies would have to be persuaded to install a glass-packaging production line and to test market the product.

Before deciding whether it was worth trying to sell this idea to the soup companies, Domglas had to estimate the potential market for ready-to-eat soup in glass.

Stan gave the task of investigating the feasibility of packaging soup in glass to Ken Bowlby, an MBA student at a major Canadian Business School, who had been hired by Domglas for the summer.

The Company

Domglas Inc., the largest supplier of glass containers in Canada, was a wholly-owned subsidiary of Consolidated-Bathurst Inc., one of Canada's largest newsprint and corrugated container manufacturers. Consolidated-Bathurst Inc. was, in turn, part of Power Corporation. The company operated six modern glass container manufacturing plants located in Montreal (Que.); Bramalea, Hamilton, Wallaceburg (Ont.); Redcliff (Alta.); and Burnaby (B.C.). Glass packaging was made at these plants for products ranging from soft drinks to peanut butter, from alcoholic beverages to salad dressing.

Domglas viewed its leadership in the industry as being based on quality products, excellent customer service, and modern facilities.

The Microwave Oven

Ken began his analysis by investigating ownership of microwave ovens in Canada. In 1972, only 12,000 Canadian households had owned a microwave oven, but the number had grown to 350,000 by 1978. The Electrical and Electronic Manufacturers' Association had developed domestic sales forecasts for major appliances and its forecasts for microwave oven sales and ownership were:

Year	Domestic sales	Total ownership	Percent of households
1979	110,000	458,000	6.1
1980	125,000	583,000	7.5
1981	150,000	733,000	9.2
1982	180,000	913,000	11.2
1983	220,000	1,133,000	13.5
1984	265,000	1,398,000	16.2

The expected surge in microwave oven ownership was attributed to the growth in the number of households in Canada (expected to exceed the population growth, at least through 1988) and to a changing life style, which was creating a need for new labour-saving devices.

Cooking with a microwave oven presented a problem in that metal utensils were impervious to microwaves and could not be placed in the oven. Even metal pigments in painted or glazed dinnerware could result in a damaged oven. Many microwave oven owners used special ovenware, but this resulted in extra dishes to clean.

Domglas had conducted extensive testing of soda-lime glass for microwave cooking and found that it was microwave compatible. Further tests by B.C. Hydro had found that "clear glass of sufficient strength to withstand the heated foods is best (for microwave cooking)."

The Questionnaire

Ken designed a questionnaire to evaluate customer attitudes to glass packaging for microwave oven cooking. In June 1978, this questionnaire was mailed to 600 names obtained from returned Litton-Moffat microwave oven warranty cards.

Of the 20 questions, numbers 15 and 20 most directly addressed the issue of ready-to-eat soup in glass:

15. Would you purchase ready-to-eat soup in a single-serving container (approximately 10 ounces) that could be put directly into your microwave oven and poured into a bowl after heating? Assume the same price per serving as canned soup.

    ☐ Yes   About how many individual servings per month? _____
    ☐ No   Why not? _____

20. Please review questions 15 to 19 and, for each one, indicate below whether or not you would be willing to pay 1c or 2c more per individual serving for the product described. *(Enter an X beside each question, under the appropriate column.)*

Question Number	Would pay 1c or 2c more per serving	Would not pay 1c or 2c more per serving
15		
16		
17		
18		
19		

Of the 600 questionnaires, 312 were returned. The responses to question 15 and that part of question 20 that related to soup in glass are summarized in table 1.

Ken's next task was to develop estimates for annual demand for this new product.

Table 1 Summary of Question Responses

Number of servings per month	Q. 15: No. of Responses	Q. 20: No. responding that they would pay 1¢ or 2¢ more per serving
0 ("No")	103	185
1	8	3
2	12	7
3	5	3
4	26	19
5	9	6
6	2	0
8	16	9
9	2	0
10	11	5
12	17	8
15	2	1
16	21	14
18	9	4
20	26	20
24	8	7
25	2	2
30	1	0
36	6	3
40	11	5
45	3	3
48	8	5
50	3	2
60	1	1

7 Paul Finney Takes Up Tennis

When Paul Finney started his new job teaching Economics at Fanshawe College of Applied Arts and Technology, he vowed to himself that he was going to make more time available for sports and other recreational activities. Paul, who was 25, viewed himself as a person who had always been interested in sports and for many years had participated actively in various kinds of athletics. As an undergraduate at Queen's University, he had been a member of the varsity basketball team as well as playing on intramural squads in volleyball, water polo, and touch football. After graduating from Queen's, Paul had spent two years studying for a Master's degree at the University of Chicago. There, the pressure of studies had been too intense to allow much free time. Consequently, he had done almost nothing in the way of sports activities. He often complained to his wife of feeling lethargic through lack of exercise. However, Paul now had a new job in a new city. To him, it was clearly time to resume active participation in sports.

During the fall and winter months, Paul Finney lived up to his self-made promise. He took up badminton—a game that he used to play before going to Chicago. Quite a few of the faculty at Fanshawe played badminton at noon in the gym, and there was never any trouble in finding a partner for a game. True, Paul did not play as often as he had intended but, after all, it was his first year of teaching in a new environment. Besides, it was a substantial improvement over doing nothing at all.

Around February, Paul began to think ahead to the coming summer months. Badminton was best played indoors. Paul suspected that most of his associates at the College gave up the game over the summer in favour of outdoor activities. He often had heard his friends express their interest in the arrival of warm weather. By the way they spoke, most of these people seemed to be looking forward to the opportunity to play one of two sports: golf or tennis.

Paul had played golf before, but he had never joined a golf club or played with any degree of regularity. Four years previously, while still a student at Queen's, he and several classmates had taken summer jobs with the Department of Industry in Ottawa. Using borrowed or rented clubs, they would occasionally drive to the Chaudière Club in nearby Hull and play nine holes in the early evening. Paul probably played golf a dozen times that summer but had played on only three or four other scattered occasions during his life. Both of his parents were avid golfers and had encouraged him to take up the game so frequently and forcefully that Paul sometimes wondered if he hadn't rebelled against the whole idea. Golf just didn't seem to be his "cup of tea." For one thing, he reasoned, it was far too time-consuming—at least three hours to play a decent round. He had never "broken 50" for nine holes and had been told by someone, he couldn't remember who, that the only way to improve was to play at least three times a week. At the same time, Paul had the impression that golf courses were always crowded and he invariably had the feeling of being rushed.

Tennis might well be different. Paul had never played a game of tennis, but he had watched Davis Cup matches on television. He reasoned that he could surely play a recreational game of tennis in an hour or less. This would allow lots of time in the day for other work. Furthermore, there were several tennis courts right on the campus at Fanshawe. Quite a few of his associates at the College seemed to be tennis players and, given his experiences with badminton, there would probably be no trouble in lining up a game at any time on a moment's notice. Paul began to think seriously about taking up tennis in the coming summer.

One night in March, he was sitting in his living room after supper checking through the day's mail. A sale catalogue had arrived from Eaton's mail order department. Paul picked it up to browse through. He enjoyed looking through mail order catalogues—particularly those advertising a sale—even if he had no specific purchase in mind. By habit, he always started at the back page and worked toward the front. The kind of things he might like to buy always seemed to be in the back half of the book while the front was always full of women's dresses and lingerie. Sure enough, just a couple of pages from the back, he spotted a tennis racket. It seemed to be a pretty good bargain—a Dunlop, regularly $17.95, on sale for $10.95. He decided to keep it in mind.

It was early April before the issue of a tennis racket arose again. Paul was visiting the home of Dave Babcock, a fellow teacher at Fanshawe, and recalled having heard that Dave was an active tennis player. He decided to ask Dave about the racket in the catalogue. "I've been meaning to ask you about something," he led off. "I've been thinking about taking up tennis this summer, but I've never played before and haven't the foggiest idea of what kind of racket to get. I saw one on sale the other day in Eaton's catalogue, but I just haven't any basis for evaluating whether the thing's any good or not. Have you any suggestion as to what I should be looking for in a racket?"

"It's really been some years since I bought a racket," Dave replied. "I'm not so sure that I'm the right person to ask. I don't really know what to tell you. The man you'd be best to ask is Bill Englander in the Math Department. He's played a lot of tennis and was the Junior Champion of British Columbia a few years ago."

The next day Paul attended a faculty meeting at Fanshawe. Arriving a little early, he noticed Bill Englander and thought to ask about the tennis racket. Paul had met Bill before and had spoken with him on numerous occasions during the year. It was not difficult, therefore, to broach the tennis racket question in much the same manner as he had with Dave Babcock the night before.

"I have to admit that I'm not too keen on Dunlop rackets," Bill offered. "I've seen a lot of people break them too easily. So I probably wouldn't be too enthusiastic about the racket you saw in the Eaton's catalogue. That is, not unless it happened to be a Dunlop Max-Ply. For some reason, the Max-Ply is way ahead of the other rackets Dunlop puts out and, in fact, is really a first-class racket. I rather doubt, however, that the one you saw was a Max-Ply. I think they run somewhat more expensive than $17.95 and aren't the kind of racket that's likely to go on sale."

Bill's remark came as somewhat of a disappointment to Paul because he had become quite interested in the Dunlop racket in the catalogue. Then, the thought crossed his mind that the racket was reduced to almost half price at a time when the tennis season was just coming up. "Why," he asked himself, "would there be such a large price reduction unless something was wrong with it?"

"A lot of people I know use Slazengers," Bill continued, "but I personally don't like them too well." He proceeded to explain what he didn't like about Slazenger rackets, but Paul was beginning to lose track of the conversation. He wondered to himself if Bill wasn't leading up to recommending a racket that would suit his own needs more than those of a beginner. At the same time, Paul sensed a definite tone of authority and expertise in Bill's remarks. There was little doubt that the fellow could be trusted to recommend a good racket—the only problem was that it might be *too* good.

Although nothing was said, Bill seemed suddenly to sense the hesitations that were running through Paul's mind. He paused for a moment, then began to speak again in a slower and more deliberate voice. "There are several good rackets on the market, but my choice for somebody starting to play for the first time would be a Spalding. The reason I say this is that Spalding started making their rackets in Belgium about two years ago. At that time, they really lowered their prices. I think that you'd get better value in a Spalding racket than in anything else. After you've been playing for a while, you'll find that you develop fairly distinct ideas about what you want in a racket—a certain type of grip, the weight, or any one of a number of things. But you have to play for some time before you find this out. If you're starting, I don't think you could go far wrong with a Spalding."

Paul had begun to listen intently again. "If I bought a Spalding," he asked, "what would be a reasonable price to pay for it?"

"Well, I would think that somewhere between $12 and $15 would buy you a decent racket. Of course, you'd also have to pay to have it strung. That would cost anywhere from $5 to $15, depending on what kind of stringing you get."

"Do you have any advice on that? I don't know the first thing about having a racket strung."

"For a starter, you should probably get braided nylon. Don't get the plain nylon—it's the cheapest and won't last very long before it breaks. The braided nylon is made up of a lot of strands of thin nylon fibre braided together. That gives it a lot of strength, but at the same time isn't too expensive. They'll probably also ask you what tension you want it strung at—the more tension you have, the more 'zip' there is to the racket when you hit the ball. I'd say about 50 pounds would be fine. If you get the tension much higher than that, it becomes quite difficult to control the ball when you hit it."

When he got home that night, Paul checked the Eaton's sale catalogue again. As Bill had suspected, the Dunlop racket that was on sale was not a Max-Ply.

For the next three or four weeks, Paul made no further move to buy a tennis racket, but he did think about it a lot. He mentioned to Bob Foulkes, a frequent badminton partner, that he was going to take up the game of tennis and was in the market for a racket. He also followed closely the newspaper accounts of upcoming Davis Cup matches between Canada and Mexico. Canada was supposed to have a good chance of winning but someone must have been too optimistic because they lost ignominiously in five straight matches.

In a casual conversation with a neighbour, Tom Norton, Paul discovered that Tom was also a tennis player. Tom mentioned that he had bought a new Dunlop Max-Ply the previous summer. He offered to sell Paul his old racket, which was not a Max-Ply, at a good price. Paul didn't encourage the idea and the matter of buying a used racket never developed further. Paul frequently met Bill Englander in the course of his work at Fanshawe, and Bill never failed to ask if Paul had bought a tennis racket yet. Each time, Paul replied that he had not, always adding that he certainly was going to in the near future.

On the morning of April 28, Paul slept in. He had no classes to teach until 11:30 that morning; so he decided to visit Tom Munro Sports on his way into work. Munro's was one of two sporting goods stores in the city. Of the two, it seemed to be the one that most of Paul's friends talked about patronizing. Paul himself had bought badminton shuttles at Munro's on several occasions. Knowing the approximate layout of the store, he quickly spotted the tennis racket section upon entering and started to walk toward it. He was the only customer in Munro's at the time and was intercepted by a youthful-looking sales clerk even before reaching the tennis rackets.

"May I help you, sir?" asked the clerk.

"Yes, I'm interested in buying a tennis racket," Paul began. "I particularly like the Spalding—you do string them right here in the store, I assume?"

"Uh . . . yes sir, we do, but . . . "

"Good. You have the braided nylon?"

"Yes indeed. But I'm sorry to say that we don't have any Spaldings. We dropped their line about a year ago."

"Oh . . . why did you do that?"

The clerk slowly began to walk the remaining short distance toward the tennis racket section. Paul followed as the young man continued to talk. "Well, about two years ago, they dropped the prices on all of their rackets by a really significant amount. They started making their rackets overseas somewhere—Formosa I think—they're not made in North America anymore, you know."

"No, they're made in Belgium."

"Is that it? . . . Well, anyhow, what happened to us, is that one day we were selling a Spalding racket for, say, $17.95. All of a sudden, we had the same racket being sold for about $7.95. Pretty soon, some of the people who had paid $17.95 began to notice this. Needless to say, they didn't like it one bit. We'd explain that it was Spalding who had reduced the price, but people were still pretty hostile. Eventually, we found that the only way to avoid this kind of situation was to drop the line altogether.''

"No kidding!"

"That's exactly what happened . . . Do you mind me asking if you're new to the city, sir?"

"Well, yes I am—I just moved here last summer."

"I thought so because I was really surprised when you asked specifically for a Spalding. I don't recall ever having anyone ask me for a Spalding before. They just aren't that popular with tennis players around here. . . . Did it have to be a Spalding, or could I show you something else?"

"Well, I'm not sure. I certainly had planned to buy a Spalding. What other lines do you carry?"

"Well, here in London, all the good tennis players use Dunlop Max-Ply. It's truly an excellent racket. The good players all swear by it."

"What does it run?"

"It's $26.95. Terrific value for a racket of that quality." The clerk removed a Max-Ply from the rack and held it loosely in his hand. Paul did not move to take it from him.

"I'd like to think about it for a while. I don't need the racket right away. What I really came in for was a pair of white shorts, size 36."

"By all means." Without looking further at tennis rackets, the two walked to a nearby counter containing the shorts. There was only one style of white shorts available. They were wrapped in a clear polyethylene bag.

Paul noted the price of $4.95 marked on the outside of the bag, but did not bother to remove the shorts. "I'll take a pair in size 36," he said. Immediately after paying for the shorts, he left the store.

During the next week, Paul was out of town on business. Soon after returning he happened to pass by College Sports, the only other sporting goods store of significant size in the city. He went in and walked over to the selection of tennis rackets. College Sports carried Slazenger, Wilson, and Dunlop rackets, but there were no Spaldings. Paul didn't bother to examine the rackets closely or to remove any from the rack. He left the store almost immediately, before a sales clerk had a chance to approach him.

Later in the week, Paul was shopping in Wellington Square Mall, an indoor shopping centre in the downtown area. Remembering that he had seen a small sporting goods department on the main floor of the Eaton's store there, he decided to see if they had any tennis rackets. There was only a limited selection. All except one of the rackets were prestrung, and there were no Spaldings. Again, he didn't bother to examine any closely and left the store quickly.

At about this time, Paul began to wonder if the whole business of buying a tennis racket wasn't taking up too much of his time. He tried to think of any other store in London that might have a large selection of rackets, but none came to his mind. He had visited three stores and had not found a Spalding racket in any of them. Paul began to think that he'd have to settle for some other kind of racket, but wasn't at all sure what it would be. He could feel himself getting quite confused.

On June 1, Paul took his young son to Simpson's department store to buy a new pair of running shoes. On entering the store, he realized that it would be relatively convenient to walk by the sporting goods department on the way toward getting his son's shoes. "They probably don't have any more of a selection than Eaton's," he thought to himself. "But there's nothing to lose by taking a look anyhow."

While still some distance away from the sporting goods department, Paul could see quite a large number of tennis rackets displayed on a vertical rack sitting upright on an island counter. This rather surprised him. He walked up to the rack and looked more closely. All of the rackets were of a single brand, Jelinek, which Paul had never heard mentioned before. Altogether, there were about 25 rackets displayed in various models of the Jelinek line; they ranged in price from $3.95 to $10.95. Looking more closely, Paul noticed from the label on one racket that the Jelinek brand was manufactured in Japan.

Paul walked slowly around to the other side of the island counter. There, he discovered a display of about two dozen additional rackets that he had not been able to see from his previous position. Most of them were Spaldings, although there were a few Dunlop Max-Ply rackets at one end. All were pre-strung except the Max-Ply. Stapled beneath each racket's position on the rack was a small white card indicating the name of the racket, its price, and the kind of material with which it was strung. Paul read each of the cards carefully, noticing at the same time that most of the rackets were not hung in the correct position corresponding to their card. One card identified the Max-Ply at $26.95, unstrung. Another indicated a Wilson racket at $16.95, but the store was apparently out of stock because Paul couldn't see any Wilson rackets at all. Of the remaining four cards, all identified various Spalding models. Three of the four were identified as being strung with twisted nylon; they were priced at $7.95, $9.95, and $12.95. The remaining Spalding racket was a Fred Stolle model at $15.95, strung with braided nylon.

Removing the Fred Stolle racket from the rack, Paul was surprised to note how heavy and clumsy it felt in comparison to a badminton racket. The grip was much thicker and the whole racket much heavier. He swung it through the air a couple of times.

Holding the Fred Stolle racket in his hand, Paul looked over the remaining ones still hanging on the rack. He reread the white cards beneath each one and, as he was doing so, a sales clerk approached him. The clerk said nothing. Finally, Paul pointed to the cards on the rack and asked the clerk to explain the difference between twisted nylon and braided nylon.

"I'm sorry sir, but I don't know very much about tennis rackets," the clerk replied.

" . . . Well, that's all right . . . I'm pretty sure this is what I'm looking for anyhow." Paul handed the clerk the Spalding Fred Stolle racket that he'd been holding.

While the clerk rang up the sale, Paul decided to look at tennis balls. The majority of the tennis balls stocked by Simpson's were various price lines of the Jelinek brand. Somehow Paul decided that he didn't want to start out by buying Japanese tennis balls. The only alternative was a large cellophane bag of twelve tennis balls for about $1.99. It was apparent to Paul that these were real "cheapies." Not only were they priced far below the other tennis balls, but they were also not packed in a vacuum cannister. Paul wasn't sure why tennis balls should be packed in a vacuum cannister, but the only ones he could ever recollect seeing had been in a container of that kind. He decided not to buy any tennis balls at this time.

However, after looking at the tennis balls, Paul remembered that he had intended to get a cover for his racket. No one had specifically suggested that he should have a cover. In fact, he had never kept his badminton racket in a cover. But Paul recalled having seen players walking to or from tennis courts at various times in the past. Most of them had a wooden press or cloth cover protecting the racket when it was not in use. Paul had ruled out the idea of a press, saying to himself that a press was heavy and that he'd never bother to take the thing on and off each time he played. Simpson's had several covers displayed on a counter near the tennis rackets. The first to catch Paul's eye was a white simulated leather cover with black trim and the word "Spalding" boldly emblazoned across each side. It was $3.95. A less expensive cover at $2.95 was available in several different colours, but it had "Wilson" written across each side. Finally, there was a plain blue nylon cover priced at $1.49 with nothing written on each side. He picked up the Spalding cover and plain blue one, examining them. A small label sewn inside the blue cover indicated that it was made in Japan. After a moment's hesitation, he decided to buy the plain blue cover.

A couple of days after buying the racket, Paul had commented on its purchase to Jack Bailey, a fellow member of the teaching staff at Fanshawe.

"Have you used it yet?" asked Jack.

"Hell no—I just bought it and haven't played a game of tennis in my life."

"Then it's about time you started. What are you doing right now?"

"Not a great deal. But are you willing to waste your time with a duffer like me?"

"Sure—I'll show you what little I know of the game. The only problem is that I don't have any tennis balls with me."

"I haven't bought any yet myself, but I'm willing to do so right now."

"Good enough. We can drive down to Munro's and pick some up. Then we'll drop back here and have a game."

The two drove to Munro's in Paul's car. There were no convenient parking places near the store, so Paul double-parked while Jack went into the store. He bought a cannister of three Slazenger balls for $2.59 on Paul's behalf.

Paul enjoyed his first game of tennis, although it was hardly a game in the true sense of the word. Paul quickly realized that he had a lot to learn yet and felt rather awkward at his seeming inability to hit the ball with any degree of accuracy. He noticed Jack also had a Spalding racket, although not a Fred Stolle model.

During the weeks that followed. Paul noticed that he came to think and talk about tennis quite a bit. For example, he told John Lowery, a teacher of Economics at Fanshawe, of his initial experience at Tom Munro Sports. Paul raised the question as to whether the store's logic in dropping the Spalding line was sound business practice and whether Spalding's own decision to reduce prices on its rackets so drastically was a good one.

Paul had dinner with a former Queen's classmate, Peter Doubless, and learned that Peter was thinking about taking up tennis. Peter said that he thought he'd invest about $5.00 in a racket. Paul then explained how carefully he'd considered the matter of a tennis racket purchase and why he decided to start out by spending around $15.00. Peter's response was that he hadn't really thought about it that way, but that he probably should reconsider and spend more than he had initially planned.

Paul also showed his new racket to his neighbour, Tom Norton, and explained the difficulty he had encountered in finding a local merchant who stocked the Spalding line. Tom replied that he wished he had known

Paul was looking for a Spalding because he knew that Sayvette, a local discount house, carried that brand. Paul didn't say anything, but the next time he was near Sayvette he went into the store and looked at their tennis rackets. He noted that there were two Spalding models, but that they were cheaper rackets priced at $3.95 and $5.95.

One one occasion, Paul showed his new racket to Bob Foulkes. Bob apparently played very little tennis but was very keen on badminton. During the winter months, it had been Bob with whom Paul had played badminton most frequently. Noting that Paul's tennis racket was a Spalding, Bob asked if his badminton racket was also a Spalding.

"I really don't know." Paul replied. "Let me think for a moment . . . about all I can remember is that it's called a 'Viceroy.' But I don't think that's a manufacturer's name. It's just the name given to my particular model of badminton racket. I don't remember ever looking to see who the manufacturer was. I've had the racket for about six years now. It was given to me second-hand by an old fellow named Gord who used to run the locker room in the gym at Queen's."

Paul's curiosity was sufficiently aroused by this question that, later the same day, he made a point of looking closely at his badminton racket. The model name was not "Viceroy," as he had previously reported to Bob Foulkes. Rather, it was a "Varsity" model. The racket had been manufactured by Spalding.

8 British Columbia Box Limited

On December 23, 1976, Mr. Paul Flynn, the Vancouver Plant Manager of British Columbia Box Limited, was about to make a half-million dollar decision. He and Mr. Wood, the plant Industrial Engineer, had narrowed the choice of suppliers for a new flexo folder gluing machine down to Andrews and Bale. In the final week of discussions the price cuts, negotiated by Mr. Flynn, had lowered the prices of the machines by $15–20,000 from earlier quotations. However, Mr. Flynn had to make a final decision in order to get a purchase order out before Christmas.

The British Columbia Box (BCB) plant was located in Vancouver with sister plants in Burnaby, Victoria, and Toronto. BCB was part of a large international company specializing in packages of all types. The main product of the Vancouver plant was folded cartons for consumer goods companies such as beer, foods, cosmetics and toys. The raw material for cartons was rolled paper, which was combined to form corrugated board that was cut, slotted, printed, folded and glued. One of the main machines in these operations was the folder gluer.

As early as 1972, Mr. Flynn and Mr. Wood had been conscious of the need for a flexo folder gluer machine that would combine flexographic printing with the folding and gluing operations. The existing machine was more than eighteen years old, did not print, and needed frequent repairs. Mr. Wood had analyzed the financial payout for a flexo folder gluer based on a volume of business going through the box plant in 1972. To his surprise, Mr. Wood discovered that the volume of business was not sufficient to justify the machine. All of Mr. Wood's estimates were based on the standard size machine which was 38″ × 80″.

In mid-1975, Mr. Flynn and the sales manager, Mr. Ray Dover, were developing a five-year plan that included a significant plant expansion for the Vancouver operation. Mr. Dover had assured Mr. Flynn that he could generate an additional $1,000,000 in sales, particularly if there was a larger flexo folder gluer such as a 50″ × 110″. Mr. Dover said that he was turning down business because of the absence of a larger machine.

In August of 1975, Mr. Flynn attended a conference put on by the Technical Association of the Pulp and Paper Industry (TAPPI) in which the major manufacturers of heavy equipment displayed their machines. The Bale brochure showed a new computer numerically controlled flexo folder gluer which was available in 38″ × 80″ and 50″ × 110″. The brochure stressed the low preparation time possible with computer numerical control. Computer numerical control (CNC) is a control system that provides automatic instructions, sensing, and feedback to a machine—all run by a computer.

Mr. Flynn returned to Vancouver and asked Mr. Wood to do a new analysis based on a 50″ × 110″ CNC flexo folder gluer. Mr. Wood discovered that the savings on setup time almost could justify the larger machine. With the CNC machine, the typical run time would remain constant at about 17 minutes, but the average setup time of 36 minutes could be cut to 18 minutes. A 50″ × 110″ machine would eliminate two existing machines in the Vancouver plant and would cost approximately $450,000 based on the phone calls which Mr. Wood had placed to several of the major manufacturers. At the conclusion of these phone calls, Mr. Flynn and Mr. Wood had concluded that they could justify a CNC 50″ × 110″ flexo folder gluer. Mr. Flynn issued a memo on September 25, 1975, which is shown in exhibit 1.

Exhibit 1

P.A. Flynn   Sept. 25/75

Canadian Division Office

Manufacturing Equipment—Vancouver

A very significant proportion of this plant's annual sales comes from the brewery market, a total value of approximately $1,200,000 gross sales out of a total sales budget of approximately $9,000,000. These sales generate a profit margin of $325,000 annually.

Nearly all these boxes are glued, and this operation is performed on our 38″ × 80″ Folder Gluer, which was installed in 1959 and has been in continuous use since. As is to be expected from a machine that has seen such service, major overhauls have to be performed from time to time. Such a major overhaul has been deferred on the 38″ × 80″ Folder Gluer for over 12 months pending the outcome of the Vancouver Plant Expansion Proposal.

Exhibit 1   (continued)

Since the Expansion Program may incur further delays, it now becomes critical that we take steps to safeguard our continued participation in the brewery business. We have recently had a manufacturer's erector review the 38″ × 80″ Folder Gluer and have received a quotation to completely update the machine. The cost of this work would be approximately $160,000.00.

There are three disadvantages to this proposal.

There are three disadvantages to this proposal.

1. A six- to eight-week shutdown of the Folder Gluer is required to complete the work, creating problems of supplying customers with their orders in that period.

2. $160,000.00 would be invested in a machine whose framework and structure is not as strong as modern equipment and would still be liable to breakdown.

3. Beyond maintaining present output levels, there is no return in terms of cost reduction or methods improvement through improved run speeds or reduced labour.

An alternative course of action, which would not have the disadvantages mentioned above and which I strongly recommend, is to move the proposed purchase of the 50″ × 110″ Two-Colour, Flexo Gluer from the Plant Expansion Program and to proceed with its installation separately and as soon as possible.

The installation of this 50″ × 110″ machine would provide backup for the present Folder Gluer until it can be finally phased completely out of production and scrapped, permit the removal of 04 and 06 V Type Printer Slotters, both over 25 years old, and generate substantial additional income from cost reductions through the elimination of Finishing Department equipment, such as the #22 Stitcher, #14 E Taper, and #13 VersaTaper. It would also lead to a reduction in labour within the Finishing Department of up to ten persons.

From analysis it is estimated that a cost reduction of $139,000.00, before taxes, could be achieved with the present volume. In addition, the 50″ × 110″ Folder Gluer would have the capacity to handle an additional volume over our present sales of 30,000,000 square feet.

The cost of a new 50″ × 110″ Two-Colour, Flexo Folder Gluer is estimated at $450,000.00, and savings described above would give a before-tax return of 25%. As the proposal is part of our long-term planning, it appears more sensible to invest this money on a new machine now than to spend $160,000.00 on our present outdated Folder Gluer.

It must be stressed that the action must be taken soon to ensure protection of our ability to service the brewery accounts. The purchase of a new Two-Colour 50″ × 110″ Flexo would do this as well as provide the additional advantages already described.

Exhibit 1 (continued)

I am sending a draft capital request to Mr. B. Davidson for consideration and would appreciate favourable consideration of this project so that we can target towards installation early in 1976.

P.A. Flynn
Plant Manager

cc: B. Davidson
    R. Smythe

N.C. Flexo Folder Gluer 50″ × 110″
Value of Surplus Equipment

	Size	Unrecovered Cost	Sales Value Estimate[a]
Kalder Printer Slotter 04 with Stacker	32″ × 70″	$ 5,369	$15,000
Kalder Printer Slotter 06 with Stacker	52″ × 122″	5,233	15,000
Rhone Folder Gluer	38″ × 80″	19,294	12,789
Folder–Taper	35″ × 90″	18,495	10,000
Semi-Auto Stitcher	—	4,259	4,000
Gang Saw	—	5,639	3,000
Semi-Auto Taper with Hoist	—	—	500
		$58,289	$60,289

a. Estimated sales value per machinery dealers sales listing.

Two months later, the task took on new urgency when Mr. Flynn received a memo signed by his Plant Superintendent and Quality Control Supervisor. The memo said that the existing folder gluer could break down any day, throwing the plant onto one shift and jeopardizing the beer business. Mr. Flynn responded to this warning in his memo of December 17, 1975, which is shown in exhibit 2.

Exhibit 2

P.A. Flynn   Dec. 17/75

Canadian Division Office

Folder Gluer—Vancouver

With reference to our proposal to purchase a Two-Colour Flexo Folder Gluer for this location to replace worn-out existing oil ink presses and our folder gluer, the following report has been compiled by the Plant Superintendent and Quality Control Supervisor regarding our existing folder gluer.

1. The complete kicker bar assembly is worn-out, and this is causing crooked cartons.

2. The main drive shaft assembly is badly worn at the point where it connects to the drive gear train; this is beyond repair and would have to be replaced.

3. The main gear train is so badly worn that there is a two-inch backlash in the slotting section, causing the slots to jump.

4. The slotting heads are sloppy on the shafts causing the heads to come out of line, and this causes chipping of the slotting knives and rings. This in turn causes ragged slots. After operating approximately 24 machine hours with a new set of slotting knives and slotting rings, they become worn to the point where they produce ragged slots.

5. The scoring heads are sloppy on the shafts, causing the scores to travel from side to side on the slots, producing crooked containers, toed-in containers, and cracked scores. The cracking of the scores is caused by the pulling action of the scoring heads moving back and forth on the shafts as the cartons are going through the machine.

6. The main folding panels of the machine are twisted and are out of mesh with each other and this is caused by a combination of worn screw guides, worn screws, and worn guide shafts.

All of these factors are causing loss of production, excessive spoilage, and serious quality problems. This results in considerable time waste and excessive labour being used in sorting and reworking orders before they can be sent out to customers.

Exhibit 2 (continued)

In view of the fact that this company's entire participation in the manufacture and sale of corrugated cartons to the brewery industry rests solely on our ability to keep this machine functioning, I request your support in preparing a Capital Request for replacement equipment without further delay.

P.A. Flynn
Plant Manager

cc: B. Davidson
     R. Smythe

In April of 1976, Mr. Flynn wrote a capital request of $586,800 for a CNC flexo folder gluer. In order to put appropriate prices in the capital request, Mr. Flynn asked the four major equipment manufacturers for serious quotations based on delivery of May 1977. Exhibit 3 shows the detailed capital request forms prepared by Mr. Flynn to justify the CNC flexo folder gluer.

In July of 1976, a new division general manager was appointed; he began to question the entire need for a CNC flexo folder gluer in the Vancouver plant. However, by late August 1976, Mr. Flynn had persuaded the division general manager that such a machine was warranted, and the capital expenditure request was forwarded to Canadian Division headquarters in Toronto and then to the parent company head offices in Los Angeles.

Even though the capital expenditure request had not been returned to him, Mr. Flynn had heard "on the grapevine" in early September that his capital request had been approved in Los Angeles. In mid-September, the division general manager suggested that Mr. Flynn consider using one of the underutilized 38″ × 80″ flexo folder gluers from the BCB plant in Victoria, B.C. It was early October before Mr. Flynn persuaded the general manager that the Victoria machine (which did not have numerical controls) would not be suitable for the volume and type of business that Mr. Flynn hoped to do in the Vancouver plant. Finally, in November 1976, the formal approval was received to purchase a CNC 50″ × 110″ flexo folder gluer. In the meantime, the four main suppliers had been active in attempting to persuade Mr. Flynn to specify their machine.

Exhibit 3 Capital Expenditure Request Prepared April 27, 1976

Proposed Expenditure Period | Estimated Cost

	Capital	Related Expense		Other Than Capital		Capital	Related Expense	Other Than Capital	Less Trade-In	Net Project Cost
1976	$125,000	19—	$—	19—	$—					
1977	$443,300	1977	$18,500	19—	$—	$568,300	$18,500	$—	$—	$586,800

Description

Purchase and Install 1 only 2 Colour 50″ × 110″ Numerical Control Flexo Folder Gluer.

Justification

		Average Added Income	Return on Investment
		After Tax	
Market Expansion	X	$ 54,800	7.8%
Cost Reduction	X	$ 97,700	13.8%
Non-Income-Producing		$152,500	21.6%

Explanation

Folding and gluing capacity at the Vancouver plant is now limited to one 16-year-old worn-out machine with no printing section, and several light, hand fold and feed finishers. All are awkward to set up, slow in operation, and costly to repair. Quality, consistent with the present day exacting standards, is difficult to maintain.

It is proposed to replace the existing 38″ × 80″ Folder Gluer together with 2 old oil-ink presses and 2 hand fed finishers, with a new 50″ × 110″ Folder Gluer having in-line 2 colour Flexo printing, and Numerical Control for automatic wash-up and size change.

The new high performance combination printing, slotting, folding, and gluing equipment will consistently produce a high quality container and will provide finishing capacity for an additional 20 million sq. ft. of board annually. A yearly income before taxes of $265,000 will be generated through reduced labour requirements and increased sales volume.

Suppliers

Each of the four main equipment manufacturers had been in the business for some time and maintained technically qualified sales representatives who travelled large territories. These representatives typically would telephone Mr. Flynn each month and visit his plant three or four times each year.

Each company produced several other pieces of equipment for the paper and box industry such as corrugators, folders, and die cutters. In any one year, approximately a dozen large flexo folder gluers would be sold in all of North America.

One of the newest companies, but a well-respected one, was the Bale Company based in Pittsburgh. In August 1975, Mr. Flynn had been attending a TAPPI conference when he talked with Dick Bateman, the Bale representative. Dick had handed him a brochure on the new Bale CNC flexo folder gluer and commented that Bale had three CNC machines out in the field. When Mr. Flynn had indicated some interest, Mr. Bateman had immediately made an appointment to visit the Vancouver plant. When he was in Vancouver, Mr. Bateman showed a film, offered approximate sizes, and gave rough prices. As he toured the plant, he made some suggestions on new layouts that could be used if the Bale machine was purchased. By this time, the new Bale machine had received considerable publicity in the industry's trade journal, *Boxboard Container*.

A few weeks later, Jim Castrelli, the Andrews salesman, visited the Vancouver plant. He mentioned that he had heard of BCB's interest in a CNC flexo folder gluer. Although Andrews had not developed a CNC flexo folder gluer, Mr. Castrelli's comment was "Just wait six months, and we will have a good CNC machine on the market." At that time, Andrews had an excellent flexo folder gluer, but it was not computer numerically controlled. Mr. Castrelli showed a film and left brochures. In addition, he indicated the ways in which the Andrews CNC machine would be better than the existing Bale machines. He invited Mr. Wood and the plant manager to see the Andrews manufacturing facility in Cleveland and installations of similar machines. Mr. Wood took up the offer and was on the road for more than a week with Mr. Castrelli.

The Rhone salesman, Mr. Dunnell, dropped in one day without any warning. He mentioned that he had learned of BCB's interest in a CNC flexo folder gluer. The Rhone company had a reputation for waiting until the specifications were well developed and then putting in a low bid. Mr. Flynn and Mr. Wood felt that Rhone had lost some of their reputation for high-quality machines. Mr. Flynn would be obliged to let Rhone bid simply because the company was a major manufacturer, but he would have to justify paying more for some other machine. It was not always easy to explain higher quality to nonproduction managers who were not familiar with the machines. The BCB Burnaby plant had several standard Rhone flexo folder gluers, and the Burnaby plant manager was pleased with them.

The Kalder Company had sent in a good salesman, who made several visits regarding BCB's need for a CNC flexo folder gluer, but he died from a sudden heart attack. He was replaced by an equally good man who made only one or two visits before he was promoted to sales manager. The replacement salesman was relatively new to corrugated board machinery, and he regaled Mr. Wood and Mr. Flynn with stories of his experiences in the Viet Nam war. Kalder was ruled out early because the company had not developed any expertise in numerically controlled machines.

A few weeks after Mr. Wood had visited plant sites with Mr. Castrelli of the Andrews Company, Dick Bateman appeared at the Vancouver plant and jokingly said to Mr. Wood, "I heard that you were out around the country with Jim Castrelli—I hope that you'll see our three installations!" After some discussion of who should go on this trip, Mr. Flynn agreed to go with Mr. Bateman. He spent the better part of a week inspecting Bale machines and the Bale headquarters in Pittsburgh. Later Mr. Flynn made a similar inspection of Andrews installations.

Purchase Process

When the official request for prices had been issued in April of 1976, the specifications had essentially been built around the Bale machine. However, each request for quotation had stipulated that the various options be priced separately so that Mr. Flynn and Mr. Wood could change options if necessary. Exhibit 4 shows the comparison of CNC features available from Rhone, Andrews, and Bale. Exhibit 5 shows their quotations as of April 1976. There were Japanese and European manufacturers of similar equipment, but Mr. Flynn had eliminated any non–North American suppliers because he wanted service and parts close at hand.

Andrews and Rhone could provide a variety of machines for the corrugated industry, while Bale had concentrated on converting machines. There were several Bale machines of a somewhat earlier vintage in the U.S. plants of BCB's parent company. All of them had performed satisfactorily.

In January 1976, Andrews had produced their first CNC flexo folder gluer. The main difference between the Andrews and Bale machines was that Andrews offered a Scotsman vacuum feeder, a safer and more reliable feeder. Bale had their own vacuum feed, but it was judged to have lesser

Exhibit 4 Numerically Controlled Functions by Manufacturer

Function Dial In:	Bale Co.	Andrews Co.	Rhone Co.
1. Box Depth—Lateral and Circumferential	*	*	*
2. Slot Register	*	*	*
3. L.H. Trim	*	*	*
4. L.H. Slot	*	*	*
5. R.H. Slot	*	*	*
6. R.H. Trim	*	*	
7. First Print Register	*	*	
8. Second Print Register	*	*	
9. Preset Powered Side Guides	*	*	*
10. Analogue Nip Control (Preset Control of All Roll Openings)	*	*	
11. Preset Dim's Setup of Next Run While Preceding Run is on	*	*	* Limited
12. First Blank Capability	*	*	
13. Soft Wire Open Loop		*	
14. Repeat Order Storage	*	*	
15. Feed Section Backstop (Scotsman)		*	
16. Storage Order Data for 100 Order	*	*	
17. Optional Additional Capacity	*	*	
18. Data From Other Computer or Storage	*	*	
19. Closed Loop—Hardwire	*		
20. Glue Lap Equipment and Creaser Control Panel Setup	*	*	
21. Manual Override	*	*	*
22. 8-Minute Wash-Up Cycle	*	*	
23. 2-Minute Setup (No Wash Up)		*	
24. Wrong Entry Control	*	*	*
25. Management Information System	*		
26. English/Metric System	*		

capability than the Scotsman. Andrews had an ink wash-up system that appeared to work well, whereas the Bale wash-up system was reputed to be less than 100 percent satisfactory. On the other hand, Bale had more experience in numerically controlled functions, which were developed, supplied, and serviced by the Cummings and Allen Company, headquartered in Minnesota. Any adjustments to the numerically controlled functions would be done by Cummings and Allen via a telephone hookup to their computer. By contrast, the supplier of CNC functions for Andrews had a Canadian office on the outskirts of Vancouver.

Exhibit 5 Summary of Quotations Received

Comparison of Prices Quoted for Delivery, January–March 1977
50″ × 110″ 2 Col. Flexo Folder Gluer ($000)

| | If Ordered Before December 31/76 | | |
	Bale Co.	Andrews Co.	Rhone Co.
Feed Unit Vacuum Motorized Opening	Inc.	79.7	Inc.
Flexo Point Units—2 Only	390.8	97.6	97.6
Slotter Section with Powered Heads	Inc.	63.3	Inc.
Scrap Conveyor–Slotter Section	5.2	Inc.	6.5
Folder Gluer with Counter Ejector	Inc.	128.1	250.9
Subtotal	396.0	368.7	355.0
Optional Items			
Power Side Guides (Feed Unit)	5.3	Inc.	Inc.
Wash & Run Feature	5.0	9.7	18.2
Chrome Plated Print Cylinders and Full Rolls	2.6	Inc.	Inc.
Haling Die Mount System	Inc.	Inc.	Inc.
Side Belt Scrap Conveyor	Inc.	Inc.	Inc.
Numerical Control with Memory	95.0	102.3	57.5 (without memory)
Skip Feed Provision to 60″	60″ 2.3	63″ Inc.	66″ 13.7
Drive System Inc. Transformer	40 HP. Inc.	60 HP. 15.7	60 HP. (not firm) 21.7
Inside or Out Glue Lap	Inc.	Inc.	6.9
Centre Support	Inc.	Inc.	1.2
Roll Back Slotter Section	Inc.	Inc.	6.2
Low Ink Warning	Inc.	Inc.	1.0
Independent Folding	55″	87″	70″ max.
Gap Detector—Skewed Sheet	Not Req'd	Inc.	1.9
Total Machine Including Optional Items	506.2	496.4	487.3
Total Brokerage Duty Freight	3.5	3.5	3.7
Net Delivered Price	509.7	499.9	491.0

The Rhone, Bale, and Andrews salesmen had telephoned Mr. Flynn periodically and asked if there was anything they could do. After the original quotations were received in April 1976, Mr. Flynn's response had been uniform, "Don't bug me, I'll call you if there is any major action in the wind." Mr. Flynn was still fighting to get a capital expenditure request approved for the machine.

In September 1976, Mr. Flynn had heard that the capital expenditure request had been "approved" in Los Angeles. It was then that Mr. Flynn and Mr. Wood saw that there might be a close race between Andrews and Bale. Andrews had recently sold a rotary die cutter to the BCB Burnaby plant, and Andrews had a reputation for building very solid machines. However, there was not one Andrews machine in the city of Vancouver.

Until September 1976, both Mr. Flynn and Mr. Wood had favoured the Bale machine because of Bale's experience in numerically controlled functions. Mr. Wood preferred the Bale machine because it offered a cathode-ray tube display control panel whereas Andrews offered a panel with digital readouts. The Bale machine could diagnose its own breakdown source. The only negative opinion came from Jack, the maintenance supervisor, who did not like the old Bale die cutter in the BCB Vancouver plant.

In the final days of the negotiations, the purchasing department attempted to tie down the suppliers to firm performance contracts such that if the machine did not perform by a certain date, such as July 1, 1977, there would be monetary penalties. However, Mr. Flynn was pessimistic about the value and viability of such performance contracts. He placed more reliance on the word of Archie, his factory superintendent, who had seen pictures of the machines and talked to the salesmen. Archie had said, "If you get that Andrews machine, I'll get it running for you." Mr. Flynn was of the opinion that if anyone could make a machine run, Archie could. Neither Archie nor the foremen had been drawn into the purchase process in a formal way. Mr. Wood had suggested that Archie might visit some plant installations, but Mr. Flynn had countered that his plant men would have to make any machine perform, regardless of the choice.

Mr. Flynn and Mr. Wood had made a commitment to the suppliers that they would settle the choice of machine by Christmas of 1976. The Rhone company was eliminated from the race because their machine's numerical functions were limited in scope. Mr. Flynn demonstrated that Rhone machines would not provide the output required in the BCB Vancouver plant. In early December, they invited Bateman and Castrelli to give them, the Manager of Engineering Services, and the Purchasing Agent for the Canadian Division a final presentation at the Canadian Division headquarters in Toronto.

In April 1976, the quotations had been Bale $509,700 and Andrews $499,000. On Thursday, December 16, the Andrews salesman, sales manager, and division manager made their presentation. The Andrews quotation for spring delivery of 1977 was $535,000—the price had risen from April because of inflationary factors. During dinner with the Andrews representatives that evening, Mr. Flynn pointed out that a number of Andrews' options were expensive by comparison to the same features on the Bale machine. As a result, the Andrews representatives agreed to take a look at their prices; by the end of the evening, they had lowered their price to $525,000.

On Friday, December 17, the Bale salesman, sales manager, and division manager visited the same BCB people and offered a price of $519,640. Mr. Flynn indicated that he would like to lower that price, and the Bale people threw in free installation. However, they were quite firm that they would not negotiate any further on price.

On Saturday morning, December 18, Mr. Flynn telephoned the Andrews sales manager and told him, "If you want to stay in the picture, you will have to look at your price in terms of including the installation of the machine and training of personnel as part of the $525,000 price." The Andrews sales manager immediately agreed to this arrangement.

On that same day, Saturday, December 18, the Manager of Engineering Services and the Canadian Division General Manager made a whirlwind trip to the United States in order to see each of the two machines in operation. The Bale CNC flexo folder gluer was installed in a BCB plant in Georgia. It was not functioning particularly well when the Canadian BCB executives arrived. After spending the morning in Georgia, the two men hurried on to Philadelphia to see an Andrews machine operating in a competitor's plant. The Andrews machine was functioning smoothly.

On Monday morning, December 20, Mr. Flynn wrote out a justification for spending an extra $5000 on the Andrews machine. This was sufficient for Andrews to fly a man to Toronto to write a revised quotation for the BCB Vice-President of Finance to review.

At 3:00 P.M. on Wednesday, December 22, the Bale sales manager telephoned the Canadian Division Purchasing Agent in Toronto and said, "We are putting two CNC flexo folder gluers into production; we can put a third machine into production and pass the economies on to you. We will let the third machine go at $490,000. Do you want it?" The Purchasing Agent contacted the Manager of Engineering Services, who telephoned Mr. Flynn. Mr. Flynn was surprised because the Bale people had made it very clear that the $519,640 was not negotiable. He talked it over with the Manager of Engineering Services, and they agreed that they could not justify a $35,000 difference in price, especially since the Andrews people had not shut the door on further price negotiations. Mr. Flynn told the

Manager of Engineering Services that he felt obliged to let the Andrews people have another look at their price.

Mr. Flynn telephoned the Andrews' sales manager, who called back 20 minutes later to say that Andrews' best price would be $510,000, and that would be their final position. At that point, the Bale machine was $20,000 less than the Andrews machine. Mr. Flynn knew that there were eight features on the Andrews machine that were not on the Bale machine. It would be difficult to place an exact value on those features. However, Mr. Flynn had to telephone the Manager of Engineering Services in Toronto with a decision by 4:30 P.M. that day.

CHAPTER IV
POSITIONING

A number of concepts are available to guide management direction of the marketing effort. This set of concepts includes product differentiation, market segmentation, and market positioning. *Product differentiation* refers to differences in the offerings of competitive firms. Sometimes these differences may be meaningful to customers and sometimes not. All aspects of the firm's marketing mix may be used to create or communicate differences among competing product or service offerings. *Market segmentation* refers to differences in the characteristics of customers. Sometimes these differences may be meaningful to a marketing professional (such as differences that bear on receptiveness to a particular advertising appeal) and sometimes not. The basic thrust of market segmentation is a focus on customer differences to determine specific market targets most appropriate and promising for an individual marketer. Once identified and understood, these segments enable the marketing professional to design specifically appropriate marketing strategies for those segments. Rarely can a marketer be "all things to all people."

We view *positioning* as a combination of product differentiation and market segmentation. In other words, positioning refers to the way in which specific customer segments *view* competitive product/service offerings. Notice that the emphasis in this definition is on the customer's perception or viewpoint. This emphasis is necessary because consumers make purchasing decisions based on their perception of competitive differences in product benefits.

Positioning is a relatively new word, but smart marketing professionals have been using the positioning concept for a long time. Positioning is becoming increasingly important because the marketplace has become more confusing, with more buyers and sellers involved, higher degrees of competition (increasingly for share points instead of for an overall increased market), increasingly technical products, and more marketing activities (such as the overall level of advertising). In this kind of environment, focussing on specific customer groups with a clearly identified and identifiable product offering (relative to competitive offerings) has become almost a precondition for marketing success.

There are a number of ways to approach the positioning task, which we regard as an essential step in formulating a marketing strategy. Exhibit 1 is a conceptual diagram of what is involved in positioning decisions. This exhibit shows that consumer analysis, competitive analysis, and corporate self-analysis are all critical elements of the positioning decision.

Market Analysis and Segmentation

As discussed in previous chapters, there are a number of ways to approach buyer (existing and potential) analysis. One basic distinction is between market statistics and buying/usage behaviour. *Market statistics* refer to

Exhibit 1   The Process of Positioning

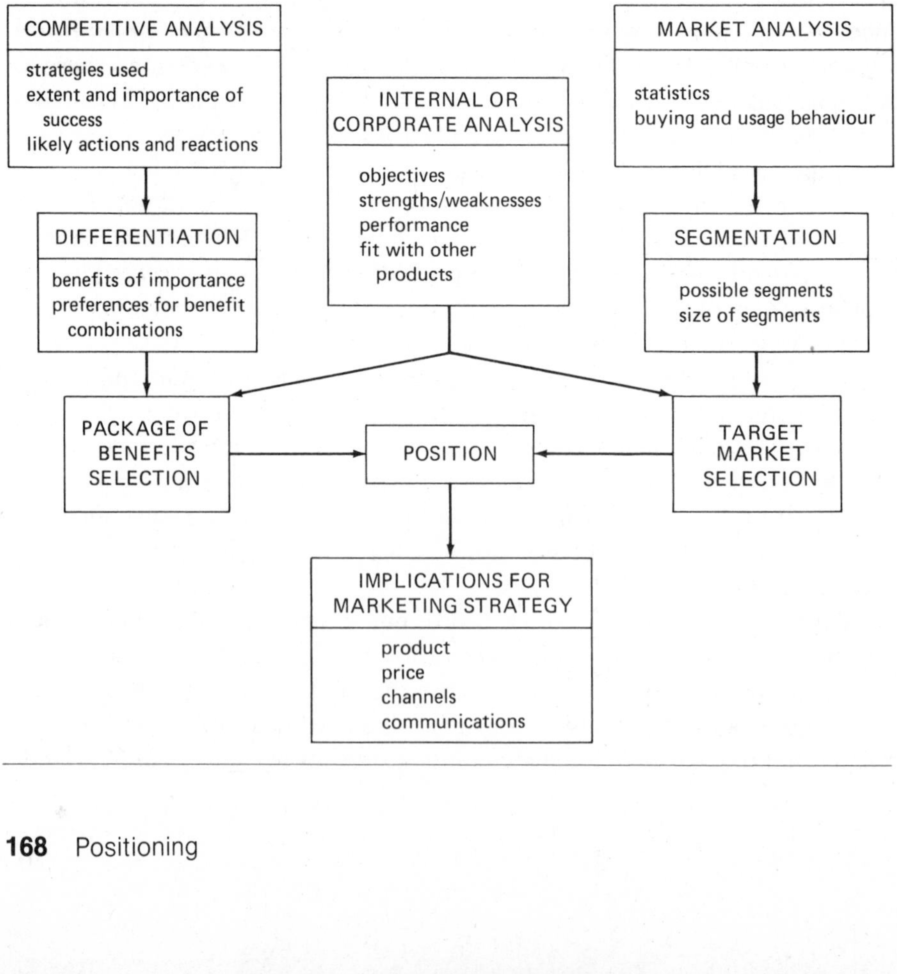

market size, growth rate, geography, discretionary income trends, and other characteristics of the customer that relate to who buys and how much is bought. *Buying/usage behaviour* refers to analysis of buying motivation (why buy), perceptions (what is being bought), attitudes and preferences (influences on the purchasing process), usage frequency and amount, and so on. Market analysis typically involves attempts to determine the size of a market, its potential, and the characteristics of buyers that enable the design of an appropriate marketing strategy.

Sometimes there are significant differences among buyers on dimensions such as location (geography), attitudes, income levels, life style, and usage behaviour, which in turn lead to significant differences in one or more of the following: interest in the product category; buying behaviour patterns; responsiveness to product variations; and responsiveness to other marketing variables such as advertising, price, availability of product, and so on. These differences may create difficulties in designing one strategy that satisfies all potential customers. At the same time, certain segments may offer attractive opportunities for a marketer prepared to tailor his or her strategy to the specific wants and characteristics of a specific market segment.

Ideally, we would like to identify segments that have maximum homogeneity within each customer group while having maximum differences among customer groups. This is seldom possible, particularly when there are no clear guidelines as to which segmentation dimensions or criteria to use in any particular case. For example, suppose you were asked to segment the breakfast cereal market, what segmentation criteria would you use? You might try income levels, age, sex, usage (amount eaten), and so on. Your assessment of whether your resulting representation of the market was appropriate or not should be on the basis of two questions:

1. Does the method used result in segments of meaningful size and potential to the extent that one or more of the segments could be selected as a *target market* (a group that will constitute the principal buyers or users of the product)?

2. Does the method used provide insight into a practical means of designing a marketing program to appeal to each segment with a reasonable likelihood of success?

In short, segmentation is only worth doing if it enables one to get some "marketing leverage" with a particular subset of the entire market.

Segmentation is not always appropriate. Sometimes, broad vague appeals to the entire market (a shotgun approach) make more sense than narrow appeals to a specific market segment (a rifle approach). For example, it seldom makes sense to segment the market for regular light bulbs. Sometimes there are no meaningful, useful ways in which to segment a market—but usually there are.

Competitive Analysis and Differentiation

Many questions may be asked about the competition when designing a marketing program. Some of these questions are general in nature, such as:

1. How many competitors are there in this business? (direct competition and indirect competition)
2. What are the financial and production strengths and weaknesses of these competitors?
3. How important is this particular business to these competitors? How are they likely to react to us?

Some questions are specific in nature, such as:

1. What are our competitors' marketing programs, in terms of product, pricing, distribution, sales effort, advertising, etc.?
2. Who are our competitors' customers? How satisfied are they with our competitors' offerings and methods?
3. Why are our competitors successful or not successful?

One useful way to address these questions is in terms of "product differentiation." A firm's entire marketing program can be thought of, from the customer's viewpoint, as a " package of benefits." This package of benefits includes more than the physical characteristics of the product or service provided: the extent of availability of the product (distribution decisions), the value attached to the product (pricing decisions), the image associated with the product and/or the user (advertising decisions), the warranty or after-sale service available (product decisions), and so on all add up to an overall package of benefits from the customer's viewpoint. This sort of analysis forces us to realize that the customer buys a product not because of its physical characteristics (such as the specific ingredients in a perfume) but because of the benefits those characteristics confer on the customer (such as an enhanced attraction to the opposite sex). We can use this notion of package of benefits to examine the differences in competitive approaches to a market. For example, we might think of a market from a benefit structure point of view and ask: "What possible combinations of benefits might appeal especially to a substantial number of customers?"

Suppose we were examining competitive approaches to the restaurant business in a particular city. One way to compare restaurants may be on their images as perceived by the city's inhabitants. Two such image dimensions may be "expensive" versus "inexpensive" and "modern/casual" versus "traditional/conservative." By looking at these two dimensions simultaneously and trying to locate the relative position of each restaurant on these dimensions, we can prepare a market structure diagram:

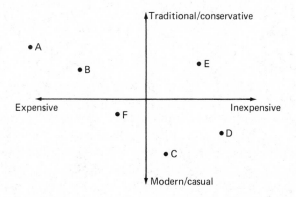

Again, in our hypothetical example, if we discovered the consumer perception of the six competing restaurants was as shown in our diagram, we could draw some conclusions regarding who competes most with whom. For example, it appears A and B are similar restaurants that as a pair are very different from C and D, and so on. A is said to have chosen a different market "position" from that chosen by, say, D.

It should be emphasized that sometimes firms choose their position and consciously strive to make the consumer identify the firm with the chosen position; other times, firms do not attempt to position themselves—but the consumer will nevertheless position them.

In the above example, only two positioning dimensions were used. Obviously a wide variety of dimensions may be used; it's just that it's difficult to show more than two or three on a piece of paper. While it is best to use "benefits" as dimensions along which to position relatively competitive offerings, sometimes it is easier to use product, price, and other characteristics. For example, here is a three-dimensional market structure diagram for a business jet market:

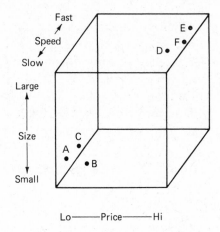

This diagram looks complicated but it's not really. First, notice that it shows the market as a cube with three dimensions—it may help to think of height, width, and depth. These dimensions, taken in combination, allow us to find a place in the cube space to put each of our competitors. For example, A is lowest in price, second smallest, and slowest, whereas E is much more expensive, fastest, and largest. Exactly where each competitor is placed is a matter of relationship among one another on the three dimensions selected. In our example diagram we can see two very distinct types of "packages of benefits"; these suggest that A, B, and C are one set of direct competitors, while D, E, and F are another set.

This form of analysis can be simple and rather straightforward (for example, based on content analysis of advertising) or quite sophisticated (for example, based on multidimensional scaling of consumer research results). The critical issue is identification of the appropriate dimensions to use when examining competitive differentiation. The dimensions selected must be of importance to the existing or potential consumer audience.

Positioning Equals Segmentation Plus Differentiation

The decision as to a target market position involves a blend of segmentation analysis and differentiation analysis. Essentially, the manager wishes to select an audience large enough to constitute a viable market and an audience to which he can appeal with a particularly attractive package of benefits. Diagrammatically, we may think of this process as follows.

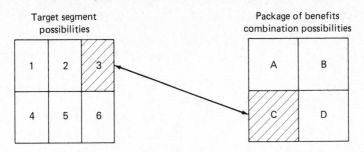

Segment 3 is target, and package of benefits most attractive to
segment 3 is combination C

Ideally, we would find a large market segment not being provided by the competition with a package of benefits in line with the benefits desired by that audience.

Implications for Marketing Strategy

The kind of analysis suggested in this chapter is a major component in the formulation of marketing plans and programs. Clearly, an analysis of corporate capabilities (marketing, finance, production, and people) as well as an analysis of the environment (for example, legal issues) must also be added into the considerations that precede the final decisions on a marketing program. With this in mind, however, we stress that *all* aspects of a firm's marketing strategy should be examined and managed so that they are consistent with one another and all are in harmony with the objective of reaching an identified target audience with a particularly appealing package of benefits. In this way, the firm will have a competitive advantage relative to the marketing programs offered by other firms.

9 Head & Shoulders

"When Head & Shoulders was introduced into Calgary in 1963 it almost immediately became the number one shampoo with over 15% of the market. Following the Calgary test, the brand was introduced nationally with virtually no change in the marketing plan and was a great success." The manager of the Head & Shoulders Brand Group, discussing the background of the brand's position in mid-1974, continued "By 1969, Head & Shoulders had captured more than 20% of the Canadian shampoo market. Since 1970, however, times have changed. We are still getting volume increases but our share of shampoo dollar sales has declined during the past four years. The decline is serious and we will have to do something to protect the long-term future of the brand."

The Procter and Gamble Co. Ltd. had spent nearly ten years and tested over 1000 preparations to come up with an anti-bacterial agent for an anti-dandruff shampoo that met consumer desires. Such a development effort was typical for Procter and Gamble and helped make it one of the world's most successful consumer goods companies. Procter and Gamble opened its first plant in Canada in Hamilton, Ontario, in 1915. The company's first successful consumer product was Ivory Soap, and early growth was based primarily on soap, laundry products, and household cleaners. Since World War II, the company had expanded into food, toilet goods, and paper products with such products as Duncan Hines Cake Mixes, Crest Dentifrice, and Pampers Disposable Diapers—all successful market leaders. Manufacturing facilities had been extended to: Point Claire, Quebec; Belleville, Ontario; and Grande Prairie, Alberta. Company sales in Canada in 1973–1974 fiscal year were $216 million, and sales worldwide were over $5 billion. In Canada, the company was by far the largest single advertiser, with 1974 media expenditures estimated at almost $12 million, virtually all on television.

Company products were developed to meet the following set of objectives: products must fulfill consumers' needs; they must have good volume potential and long-term growth prospects (the company was not interested in limited life cycle products); they must be technically the best products available and conform to rigorous quality control; they must be reasonably priced. The decision to develop a new product was based on a full understanding of a market, gained through extensive consumer research, exhaustive laboratory and consumer testing for safety and effectiveness. Before full scale introduction, the product had to undergo successful market testing.

Evolution of Head & Shoulders

Investigations into the hair care market in the early 1950's revealed that 70% of the population had a dandruff problem to some degree. The company's Market Research Department found that there was no truly effective dandruff control preparations then available to the consumer. In fact, no one really knew what caused dandruff although the predominant theory stated that it was caused by bacteria on the scalp.

Consumers at the time were using a number of preparations to control dandruff, although research indicated that they were not entirely happy with the results. There were a number of anti-dandruff shampoos on the market but they did have drawbacks. Most of them used coal-tar derivatives as the active ingredient, but this left the hair smelling unpleasant. Anti-dandruff shampoos were generally quite expensive, and many of them could be obtained only with a prescription. Additionally, many of these shampoos did not clean very well. Rinses and hair dressings such as Resdan were also used to control dandruff. The problem with these preparations was that they required an extra step after washing the hair.

The Procter and Gamble Research Department developed Zinc Pyrithion (or ZPT) and combined it with a shampoo base that had earlier been developed for a "beauty" shampoo. The resulting product was called Head & Shoulders. The company felt that an anti-dandruff shampoo should have a therapeutic image so a paste formula was prepared to be packaged in a white glass jar and in a white tube with blue and magenta label colours to convey that image. The perfume was also chosen to convey a therapeutic as well as a cleaning image in contrast to the coal-tar derivative shampoos which had a bad cleaning image with the consumer.

Introductory Marketing

With a product that research had shown to be an outstanding dandruff shampoo, the introductory strategy for Head & Shoulders was to convince consumers that the brand was an unsurpassed dandruff control shampoo. The name selected was thought to be descriptive and reinforcing of the anti-dandruff benefits. Advertising copy was aimed at both male and female adult users, and media were selected to ensure that the copy reached women (who controlled 85% of purchases) during the daytime on T.V. and reached all members of the household on nighttime T.V. Examples of Head & Shoulders advertising are shown in exhibit 1.

Originally, the product was sold in three sizes—Personal, Regular, and Family—in both jar and tube form. Shortly after the initial introduction, a lotion form was introduced, and it captured almost 30 percent of the brand's total business. Promotions were designed to support the Family and Regular sizes at the trade and retail level throughout the year, with emphasis during the fall and winter when dandruff awareness was thought to be at its peak.

The price was set to ensure that the company made a reasonable return on its investment. This was a higher price than for normal sham-

Exhibit 1 Head & Shoulders Anti-Dandruff TV Commercials

"DELIVERYMAN" 30-SECOND
ANNOUNCER: Some people who don't worry about dandruff should.
CO-WORKER: (thinking to self) Dandruff!
ANNOUNCER: Behind Tom's back, people were thinking . . .
CUSTOMER: (to self) Dandruff!
ANNOUNCER: Until Tom overheard Sally say to the boss . . .
SALLY: Tom would be good in Sales, but he has dandruff!
TOM: (overhearing and thinking to self) It shows?
ANNOUNCER: That did it. Tom started using Head & Shoulders regularly. Fixed his dandruff problem. Hair looks great, and Sally's more than pleased that Tom's been made a salesman.
ANNOUNCER: Head & Shoulders . . . really works.

"GET TOGETHER" 30-SECOND
ANNOUNCER: Some people who don't worry about dandruff ought to.
ESCORT: (thinking to self) Dandruff!
ANNOUNCER: Lynn never imagined that behind her back people were thinking . . .
WOMEN: (thinking to themselves) Dandruff!
WOMAN TO ANOTHER: Oh, I love Lynn's dress, but that dandruff!
LYNN:(overhearing) It shows?
ANNOUNCER: That is all she needed to make Head & Shoulders her regular shampoo. Fixed her dandruff problem. He (escort) sure noticed.
ESCORT: New hair style? Looks great.
ANNOUNCER: Head & Shoulders really works.

poos due to the high cost of providing the anti-dandruff benefits, but it was still less expensive than the specialized anti-dandruff shampoos on the market at that time.

The brand's record for the first six years until 1969 was as follows:

	1964	1965	1966	1967	1968	1969
Estimated total shampoo market index	100	105	111	120	135	162
Head & Shoulders market share %	12	15	18	19	20	21
Head & Shoulders advertising as a percentage of total shampoo advertising	15	22	18	20	21	24

The Hair Revolution

In the late 1960's, major changes began to occur in the shampoo market. This was the post-Beatle era, when people began to let their hair grow longer and to wash it more frequently. There was also a Baby Boom surge in the number of teenagers and young people in their early 20's, the age group most inclined to have long hair. The shampoo market grew rapidly and by 1969 had reached almost $25 million in retail sales.

With the increasing importance of hair to a person's overall image and with more frequent washing, people became more concerned with the cosmetic benefits of a shampoo. In the early 1970's, after a period of years when no important new brands had appeared, a number of new cosmetic-oriented brands were introduced with heavy advertising. Protein 21, for example, appeared with the claim that it could cure the "frizzies," and Bright Side was advertising as making your hair light up and shine.

The new brands made a strong initial impact, but after a short time they began to lose market share, possibly because consumers perceived that the products hadn't met their initial expectation. However, additional new brands sprung up as the early ones declined. Herbal Essence shampoo by Clairol was introduced with advertising emphasizing a wildflower fragrance. The "PH" shampoos such as VO5 and Earthborn were introduced with heavy advertising support and emphasizing mild scalp care. Johnson's Baby Shampoo expanded its target to all-family usage with a mildness claim, "If it's mild enough for baby, it's mild enough to be used every day."

During these changing years, shipments of Head & Shoulders continued to climb and advertising spending kept pace with sales volume. In the rapidly growing market, however, the brand's share of sales dollars and share of market advertising began to decline, reaching a low of 12 percent and 11 percent, respectively. By 1974 the Head & Shoulders Brand Group was concerned about the long-term future of the brand. They were very reluctant, however, to tamper with a product position that had been so successful and that still held the leading position among all shampoos, especially in light of continuing increases in shipments.

It was recognized by the Brand Group Managers that the strong therapeutic image that had been so important in building the Head & Shoulders share had also required some compromise in terms of consumer perceptions of the brand's mildness. Company technical research indicated, nevertheless, that the brand was actually as mild for the head and hair as the cosmetic shampoos.

As they began to reconsider the positioning of Head & Shoulders, Brand Management assembled the shampoo usage data shown in exhibit 2 and the 1974 brand image study summarized in exhibit 3.

Exhibit 2 Summary of Shampoo Usage: 1968, 1971, 1974

Households having the following shampoos on hand as a % of total households:

	1968	1971	1974
Head & Shoulders	20	27	30
Breck	13	15	14
VO5	11	13	12
Halo	14	12	11
Johnson's Baby Shampoo	5	10	20
Herbal Essence	—	—	23
All Others	57	63	75

Percentage who have used Head & Shoulders during past 4 weeks:

	1968	1971	1974
Adult Females	16	15	18
Adult Males	15	20	23
Teen Females	17	13	19
Teen Males	21	22	15
Someone in Household	22	27	28

Form of Head & Shoulders last used as a % of total Head & Shoulders users:

	1968	1971	1974
Tube	39	37	36
Lotion	29	41	44
Jar	32	22	20

Exhibit 2 (continued)

Number of times hair washed per week by age:

	1968	1971	1974
Adult Females	1.2	1.3	1.7
Adult Males	1.2	1.4	1.8
Teen Females	1.7	2.6	2.8
Teen Males	1.3	2.0	2.6

Percentage who have dandruff incidence or tendency:

	1968	1971	1974
Adult Females	66	65	57
Adult Males	61	65	64
Teen Females	58	56	53
Teen Males	54	52	48
Someone in Household	84	80	74

Percentage who have severe or moderate dandruff:

	1968	1971	1974
Adult Females	12	8	9
Adult Males	15	14	15
Teen Females	9	8	8
Teen Males	13	8	7
Someone in Household	25	21	21

Source: Procter and Gamble files.
Note: Some of these data are disguised.

Exhibit 3 1974 Brand Image Study Summary Ratings
of Shampoo Brands on Six Shampoo Benefits[a]

Shampoo Benefit	Head & Shoulders	Bright Side	Protein 21	Herbal Essence	Halo	Johnson & Johnson	Breck
Cleaning	65	64	64	63	65	71	70
Controls frizzies	31	35	50	30	36	32	29
Leaves hair shiny	69	72	60	65	65	57	69
Mild for hair	55	64	67	69	71	75	72
Controls dandruff	80	40	35	29	34	28	32
Leaves hair manageable	53	55	60	58	55	65	61

a. Ratings are on a scale from 0 to 100. Across brand differences (e.g., Head & Shoulders compared to Bright Side) are statistically more significant than across benefit differences (e.g., Frizzies rating as a ratio of Shiny rating).
Source: Procter and Gamble files.
Note: Some of these data are disguised.

10 Canada Packers—Tenderflake

In December 1973, Mr. Brian Burton, brand manager for Canada Packer's Tenderflake lard was writing the annual marketing plan for the fiscal year ending in March 1975. He had been assigned to Tenderflake one year earlier and his first action had been to initiate a basic attitude and usage study on Tenderflake and its competitors. With these data in hand, Mr. Burton was considering possible changes in brand strategy.

Background

Canada Packers Limited was incorporated in 1927 as a meat-packing company. The company had diversified into a wide variety of products, one of which was Tenderflake lard. Lard is a pork by-product produced by every major meat-packing company in Canada because it offers an opportunity to utilize raw materials fully.

Until 1970, Canada Packer's lard had been distributed in the same manner as the company's meat products. Canada Packers had divided the country into five regions, each of which had been serviced by a separate and autonomous plant. Each plant manager had set prices for his products and had operated a sales force that called on grocery stores in that region. The company had not advertised lard extensively because personal service and low price had been considered the important factors in selling to food wholesalers and supermarkets.

In 1969, top management at Canada Packers had felt that the company's packaged goods lines were not reaching their profit potential under this decentralized approach. In 1970, they established the Grocery Products Division; and by 1973, this division marketed the company's lines of shortening, margarine, lard, canned meats, cheese, soap, pet food, peanut butter, and salted nuts. Each product had been assigned to a brand manager whose responsibility was to develop strategy and monitor the performance of the brand.

Tenderflake Brand History

Tenderflake lard had never been advertised, but it benefitted from the high awareness and reputation of the Tenderflake name, the Maple Leaf family brand name, and the Canada Packers corporate name. Tenderflake lard had achieved sales of 25 million pounds in fiscal 1973, which represented 65 percent of the total lard market. This dominant share had been achieved by Canada Packers aggressive pricing, which few competitors could match. As a result, the brand had generated pretax profits of only 1¢ a pound in fiscal 1972, 1.6¢ a pound in fiscal 1973, and would be fortunate to break even in fiscal 1974.

Tenderflake was distributed across Canada by the 65-man Grocery Products sales force. Each salesman had a territory that included large and medium-size grocery outlets and a few wholesalers who serviced the very small grocery stores. Chain retail outlets took a markup of 16 percent on their selling price. In 1973, a standard co-op advertising program was offered to retail outlets whereby Canada Packers put 1 percent of the invoice value of a customer's purchase into a fund used for advertising. Standard volume discounts amounted to another 1 percent variable cost for the brand.

The Market

Mr. Burton knew that shortening and lard were used interchangeably. Company executives estimated that 84 million pounds of lard and shortening would be sold in fiscal 1975. The combined sales of lard and shortening had been declining at about 2 percent per year.

Of the 84 million pounds of lard/shortening to be sold to consumers in fiscal 1975, approximately 60 percent would be shortening. Crisco would sell 55 percent of the shortening poundage, and Tenderflake would sell 65 percent of the lard poundage.

Shortening was white and odourless because it was made with vegetable oil or from a mixture of animal and vegetable fat. Tenderflake was white and odourless (which was not true of all lards) because Canada Packers employed a superior refining process that completely removed all odour and colour from the lard. Regardless of colour or odour, lard tended to produce a flakier pie crust than shortening because lard created more layers of pastry, and most experts agreed that lard was easier to use. Major industrial consumers in the quality pastry area specified lard regardless of price.

The price of shortening appeared to influence the sales of lard. Mr. Burton had noted that whenever the price of lard was less than seven cents below the price per pound of shortening, consumers tended to switch from lard to shortening. Retail prices of lard and shortening had traditionally fluctuated with the price of raw materials. Only Crisco had maintained stable prices and growth in sales and profits despite the general market decline. The prices of competitive products as of December 1973 are shown below.

Lards	Retail price per pound
Tenderflake	$0.45
Burns	0.44
Schneider	0.44
Swifts	0.45
Shortenings	
Crisco	0.56
Average of cheaper shortenings	0.50
Average of all shortenings	0.53

Competition

Crisco shortening, marketed by Procter and Gamble, was the only major advertised brand of lard or shortening. Mr. Burton estimated that Procter and Gamble spent approximately $550,000 per year in advertising Crisco. Their campaigns had stressed that Crisco was all vegetable, that the product was dependable, and that it was desirable for deep frying and pastry making. Crisco was promoted by the Procter and Gamble sales force, which sold a wide line of paper, food, and soap products to grocery outlets and a few wholesalers. Procter and Gamble's only trade incentive on Crisco was a co-op advertising plan that paid eighteen cents on every 36-pound case. Crisco followed a premium price strategy that appeared to produce a profit of eight cents per pound on the product. The following table shows the estimated cost structures of Crisco and Tenderflake as of December 1973.

Crisco and Tenderflake both were packaged in one-pound and three-pound containers. Approximately 5 percent of Tenderflake's sales came from the three-pound container, the majority of these coming from western Canada, while 39 percent of Crisco's sale came from the three-pound size.

ESTIMATED COST STRUCTURE OF CRISCO AND TENDERFLAKE

	Crisco (per pound)	Tenderflake (per pound)
Retail price	$0.56	$0.45
Less retail margin	0.09	0.07
Factor price	0.47	0.38
Cost of goods sold	0.31	0.31
Gross margin	0.16	0.07
Expenses (including sales force, general administration, freight, distribution, trade allowances, co-op advertising, and volume discounts, but excluding media advertising)	0.06	0.06
Media advertising	0.02	
Profit	$0.08	$0.01

Mr. Burton believed that Crisco had higher sales on the three-pound size because it was priced at a lower cost per pound than the one-pound size. Because of the low margins and a higher per pound packaging cost on the larger size, Canada Packers sold the three-pound size at a slight premium to the one-pound package. Mr. Burton believed that the higher price was responsible for the low proportion of sales in the three-pound size.

Consumers

Mr. Burton's first action as brand manager of Tenderflake had been to commission a consumer study to determine the usage of lard and competing products, a profile of the consumer, and the consumer's attitude toward lard and its competition. A well-known market research company had conducted interviews with a representative sample of 1647 women across Canada and this research had been the basis of the "Fats and Oils Study"[1] that Mr. Burton had received in March 1973.

Women were asked about the time of year when they baked, and this led to the development of the baking seasonality index.

Spring	132
Summer	100
Fall	161
Winter	196

1. Lard, shortening, cooking oil, butter, and margarine are defined as fats and oils.

The report indicated that lard and shortening were used mainly for baking. Lard was used primarily for pastries, while shortening was used more for cakes and cookies. Exhibit 1 shows how consumers use various fats and oils, while exhibit 2 gives specific data on lard and shortening users.

Exhibit 1

CONSUMER USE OF FATS AND OILS (percent)[a]

	Salad/ Cooking Oil	Butter	Margarine	Shortening	Lard
Pan frying	43	6	21	13	13
Deep fat frying	24	1	2	14	11
Salad dressing	25	—	—	—	—
Baking cakes	8	8	20	24	4
Baking cookies	3	10	24	27	13
Baking pastries	1	2	3	49	62
Spreading	—	84	53	—	—
Total ever use	90	89	85	78	58

USERS OF LARD AND SHORTENING BY APPLICATION (percent)

Total (1565)[b]	Lard Only (287)	Shortening Only (609)	Dual Users— Use of Lard (669)	Dual Users— Use of Shortening (669)
Pastries	60.6	49.0	61.9	28.0
Cakes	4.9	14.6	4.0	23.1
Cookies	15.0	15.9	12.6	26.0
Pan frying	11.5	10.1	10.6	10.7
Deep fat frying	8.0	10.3	12.3	11.9

a. Tables may not sum to 100 percent because of multiple mentions.
b. Number of women responding.

Exhibit 2 Average Pounds of Lard and Shortening Used Per Week

	Total Users	Region				
		Maritimes	Quebec	Ontario	Prairies	British Columbia
Lard	.42	.45	.65	.35	.42	.25
Shortening	.49	.91	.60	.40	.32	.37

Exhibit 2 (continued)

	Language	
	French Quebec	*Remainder of Canada*
Lard	.70	.37
Shortening	.62	.45

	City Size			
	500,000 and Over	*100,000– 499,999*	*10,000– 99,999*	*Under 10,000*
Lard	.35	.35	.40	.52
Shortening	.35	.45	.47	.64

	Family Size		
	2	*3–4*	*5 and Over*
Lard	.35	.34	.57
Shortening	.33	.44	.70

	Income			
	Under $4000	*$4000– $6999*	*$7000– $9999*	*$10,000 and Over*
Lard	.57	.52	.35	.27
Shortening	.59	.59	.44	.36

	Age			
	Under 35	*35–44*	*45–54*	*55 and Over*
Lard	.42	.44	.39	.43
Shortening	.51	.58	.45	.41

	Heaviness of Use					
	Total Users	*Heavy*	*Heavy Medium*	*Medium Light*	*Light*	*Non- Respondents*
	(956)[a]	(174)	(206)	(209)	(354)	(13)
Lard	0.42	1.41	0.40	0.25	0.05	
Percent consumption	100	62	21	13	4	
Shortening	(1278)[a]	(300)	(271)	(295)	(364)	(48)
Usage per week		1–2 lbs.	1 ½ lbs.	1 lb.	1 lb.	

a. Number of women responding.

The attitude toward the product itself seemed to be largely rooted in the usage role of lard and the tradition of passing this role from one generation to the next. Exhibit 3 shows the data on consumer perceptions of lard as a product, perceptions of brands, and reasons for using or not using lard.

Exhibit 3

PERCEPTIONS OF BRANDS OF LARD

Perceptions		Total Users (956) (Percent)
All brands are equally good		55
One brand is better		42
Tenderflake/Maple Leaf	21	
Burns	3	
Schneiders	3	
Crisco[a]	8	
Miscellaneous	7	

a. Crisco frequently was mistaken as a brand of lard.

VOLUNTEERED REASONS FOR PREFERRING A PARTICULAR BRAND OF LARD

Volunteered Responses	Crisco (79), %	Tenderflake/ Maple Leaf (199), %	Burns (32), %
Baking End Benefits			
Flaky/light/better pastry dough	32	34	38
Excellent for pies/cookies/ doughnuts	13	13	6
Good/better tasting/baked product	11	13	3
Product Benefits			
Easier to handle/blend	14	11	3
Less greasy/not greasy	11	6	—
Better texture	5	11	9
Smells better	4	5	3

Exhibit 3   (continued)

Other Reasons

Good result	20	18	34
Always used it	5	18	9
Cheap	4	6	3
Miscellaneous	18	20	22

PERCEPTIONS OF LARD AND SHORTENING BY USERS

Perceived Product Performance	*Percent Lard Users Said*	*Percent Shortening Users Said*
"Best for pie shells"		
Lard	62	25
Shortening	30	68
No difference	8	7
	100	100
"Produces flakiest pastry"		
Lard	54	24
Shortening	38	69
No difference	8	7
	100	100
"Best for frying"		
Lard	38	20
Shortening	35	60
No difference	27	20
	100	100
"Cheapest"		
Lard	74	62
Shortening	6	14
No difference	20	24
	100	100
"Most tolerant"		
Lard	31	9
Shortening	46	71
No difference	23	20
	100	100

Exhibit 3 (continued)

VOLUNTEERED REASONS FOR NOT USING LARD (percent)

Volunteered Responses	Total Nonusers (691)
Prefer Other Product	
Prefer/use shortening/Crisco	26
Prefer/use oil/margarine/butter	12
Health Reasons	
Too much fat/animal fat	12
Not good for heart/liver	11
Difficult for digestion/too heavy	6
Too greasy	6
Do not eat fried things/grease	2
Dislike Product	
Do not like taste	7
Do not like it	6
Other Reasons	
Never tried it	9
Don't see need for it	4
Don't get good results	2
Miscellaneous Responses	12

Note: Tables may not add to 100 percent because of multiple mentions.

Crisco and Tenderflake showed uniform strength across the country, but smaller brands of lard and shortening demonstrated some regional strength (exhibit 4).

In addition to the fats and oils study, Mr. Burton had employed a commercial research firm to conduct several focused group interviews in order to obtain "soft," or qualitative, data on Tenderflake and its competitors. Typically, ten to fifteen women gathered and talked freely about baking and oils products under the leadership of a skilled psychologist. Little attempt was made to generalize from these interviews because the samples were small and were not selected randomly. However, the technique produced ideas for marketing strategy and could be verified by the fats and oils study.

The focused group interviews suggested that flakiness and fear of failure were the key areas of consumer concern. For pastries, lard was perceived as a better product than shortening among lard users, and Tenderflake seemed to have a premium-quality image. Among women who used only shortening, there was a strong perception that lard was an oily, cheaper product.

Attack by Crisco

Early in 1973, Crisco aired the television advertisement shown in exhibit 5. The commercial clearly attacked lard's major product advantage, and Mr. Burton felt that Tenderflake, as the major lard producer, might lose market share to Crisco. He saw this as the same type of approach directed at lard that Procter and Gamble had used previously to pull Crisco ahead of the cheaper shortenings. By December 1973, Mr. Burton had developed several options, and he was about to take action.

Options

Mr. Burton saw an opportunity to raise the price of Tenderflake and to begin advertising. The reasoning was that advertising could help to ensure

Exhibit 4[a]

BRAND OF SHORTENING BOUGHT LAST (percent)

			Region			
Brand	Total (1278)	Maritimes (122)	Quebec (345)	Ontario (487)	Prairies (193)	British Columbia (131)
Crisco	52	38	64	47	42	64
Fluffo	12	24	1	15	19	7
Domestic	8	10	9	7	6	6
Others	8	20	2	6	13	11
Don't remember	20	8	24	25	20	12

BRAND OF LARD BOUGHT LAST (percent)

			Region			
Brand	Total (859)	Maritimes (48)	Quebec (176)	Ontario (308)	Prairies (235)	British Columbia (92)
Tenderflake	53	69	49	60	51	36
Burns	13	2	2	7	23	30
Swift	7	—	5	5	6	22
Schneiders	5	—	1	12	1	—
Crisco	11	4	39	3	4	2
Miscellaneous	18	27	22	14	23	7

a. Tables may not add to 100 percent because of multiple mentions or rounding.

Exhibit 5 Crisco TV Advertisement

PRODUCT:	Crisco	
LENGTH:	30 seconds	
MONITORED:	Toronto	
	December 1973	

Frame No. 1	SCENE:	*Young man and woman in kitchen.*
	WOMAN 1:	John, you never have seconds of my pie.
	MAN:	Marie, this pie crust is so flaky.
Frame No. 2:	SCENE:	*Close-up of Crisco can on table.*
	WOMAN 1:	OK, Marie, how'd you make your pie crust?
	WOMAN 2:	With Crisco.
	WOMAN 1:	But isn't lard cheaper?
Frame No. 3:	SCENE:	*Close-up of ingredients being blended in a bowl. Crisco can in background.*
	WOMAN 2:	Maybe . . . but Crisco's worth the difference. It's softer than lard, so blending's easier.
Frame No. 4:	SCENE:	*Close-up of ingredients being blended in bowl. Crisco can in background.*
	WOMAN 2:	Even the bottom crust has such delicate flakes they blow away.
Frame No. 5:	SCENE:	*Two women talking in kitchen.*
	WOMAN 2:	And Crisco's one hundred percent pure vegetable.
	MAN:	Mmmm . . . really flaky.
Frame No. 6:	SCENE:	*Woman 1 and man in another kitchen.*
	WOMAN 1:	Seconds, John?
	MAN:	Mmmm.
	ANNOUNCER:	Use all-vegetable Crisco instead of lard. You'll think it's worth the difference.

the stability of Tenderflake volume while improving the gross margin in order to cover advertising and profit. Further decisions would be to define target audiences, brand positioning, and copy strategy for Tenderflake. Mr. Burton thought that the fats and oils study suggested a number of opportunities. In Mr. Burton's judgment, an advertising budget of $350,000 probably would receive management approval provided that it was well conceived and promised a financial payout.

The sales manager had pointed out that the chain-store buyers saw the main competition as other lards and that raising the price of Tenderflake would permit cheaper lards to erode Tenderflake's market share. He strongly advised that Tenderflake maintain its price position with other lards, rather than "chasing after Crisco."

The most difficult task would be to estimate the probable results of whatever marketing strategy Mr. Burton chose. However, senior marketing managers at Canada Packers would expect the annual marketing plan for Tenderflake to show sales and profit projections for the next five years.

11 Julius Meinl A.G.*

"When we opened our first PamPam discount food store four years ago in 1973," said Mr. Thomas Meinl, a Director of Julius Meinl A.G., a large Austrian food processor and retailer, "It meant that we were operating retail food stores under three completely different names. We are considering currently a change of one or two of these store names to bring a stronger and more coordinated image to our retail operations. At the same time, we are aware that such a move could result in lower consumer acceptance of one or more of the retail operations and certainly would have a negative effect on our business with other food outlets. However, any advantage that we would gain from a change of store names will decline with time. Therefore, it is important that we make an early decision."

Julius Meinl A.G.

The company was founded in Vienna in 1862 by Julius Meinl, who imported coffee beans and retailed them as roasted coffee under the Julius Meinl name. Over the years the company expanded on several dimensions. Many new stores under the Julius Meinl name were opened, primarily within the geographic area of what was then the Habsburg Empire. The company entered into other areas of food processing, with plants being built in suitable locations in the company's trading area. The products of these plants were sold under the Julius Meinl name, both in the company retail outlets and to other food retailers.

The breakup of the Habsburg Empire in 1918 led to the creation of several new states—Austria, Hungary, Czechoslovakia, and Yugoslavia. The USSR, Italy, Poland, and Romania also took possession of former Austro-Hungarian territories. These changes, together with the impact of the preceding war, created significant disruptions in the company's operations.

* Courtesy IMEDE Management Development Institute, Lausanne, Switzerland.

However, the company was rebuilt, and further expansion took place in the following two decades. This expansion included the acquisition of a chain of food stores, Brüder Kunz, which continued to be operated under the Kunz name. By 1937, the company had 572 stores located in eight countries in central Europe. In addition to this, over 1000 franchises sold Meinl brand products in these countries.

World War II and the subsequent political changes again brought severe disruption to the company. There was damage to the company's physical assets. The communist takeover in Eastern Europe resulted in a loss of virtually all assets in those countries. For the retail part of the company's operations, this meant a loss of about half of the prewar outlets. Once again, management was faced with the task of rebuilding the company. This they did, with primary emphasis on rebuilding and expansion of company-owned operations within Austria.

Austria

Austria is a country of 83,900 square kilometres. The population in 1976 was 7,500,000 and was growing very slowly. The principal city and capital, Vienna, is located in the east of the country and had an estimated 1976 population of 1,700,000. This was over six times the population of Graz and Linz, the next largest cities. The rate of migration to urban areas was less than in the more industrialized European countries.

The Austrian economy was dependent on agriculture, tourism, mining, and manufacturing. Industrial production, concentrated around Vienna, Graz, and Linz, had increased substantially since the mid-1960's, and most particularly in the period 1970–1974. Since that time, in common with most European countries, the rate of growth had slowed significantly.

While the standard of living in Austria was not as high as it was in Germany and France, it had risen rapidly prior to 1975, and in terms of comparisons such as private consumption per head, the gap had been narrowing. Passenger car ownership provides a good example. There were 45,000 cars in Austria in 1950. In 1960, there were 340,000; by 1970, the number had grown to 1,125,000. By comparison, the population per passenger car in 1970 was 4.4 in France and 7.6 in Austria. In 1973, the population per passenger car was 3.8 in France and 4.5 in Austria. This rapid increase in car ownership created very severe traffic and parking problems in urban areas, which, for the most part, had been designed and built in other eras of transportation.

Urban Living and Food Purchasing

Most Austrian cities had evolved slowly over a period of many centuries. In comparison with North American cities, a higher proportion of the population lived in multiple-unit dwellings. There were a great many more multiple-use dwellings with retail stores, cafés, garages, or business offices on the ground floor and residential units on the upper floors. Thus, the residential areas were spread more diffusely throughout the city, and it was possible to live a complete life in a very small geographic area. Further, while there were very few buildings over ten storeys in height, there were also very few single-storey buildings. The net result was that Austrian cities were more compact for a given population than a comparable North American city and that the people traditionally have had food and other stores within a short distance from their residence. For the retailer, the relatively concentrated population meant that a store could be viable economically with a small geographic trading area.

The Austrian housewife placed high importance on quality and freshness of food. When this factor is combined with limited residential refrigeration facilities and close proximity to shopping facilities, it is easy to understand why most women traditionally shopped for food on a daily basis.

The emergence of several factors in the mid-1960's led to some erosion of this tradition in the 1970's. Foremost of these was the rising standard of living. It made feasible the dramatic rise in automobile ownership. The development of manufacturing facilities occurred on the fringes of urban areas. Such development increased the distance between work and residence. The pressure for more and better housing led to the development of single- and multiple-dwelling housing on the fringe of the urban areas. This development was primarily single-purpose residential use of land. Demand increased for all types of consumer products. To meet these growing and changing needs, a large number of new stores carrying a wider range of goods, often at discount prices, sprang up both in downtown areas and on the fringes of Austrian cities. The shifting consumer expenditure patterns, wider choice of retail outlets, and increased mobility resulted in many people assessing the priority of their food expenditures in terms of quality, price, and place of purchase.

The Evolution of Julius Meinl Operations

Julius Meinl Branded Products

The Julius Meinl brand coffees on which the company was founded were of high and consistent quality. This policy was maintained over the years for all of the products that were added to the Julius Meinl line. In 1977, this line included coffee, tea, jams, wines, liquors, chocolates, cookies, cakes, fruit juices, candies, pasta, and cooking oil, most of which were processed in company plants. The total line contained some 900 items, and the average processing gross margin was 4 percent.

Some of these product lines were carried by other Austrian food retailers. Julius Meinl coffee, in particular, had wide consumer acceptance and was one of the leading Austrian coffee brands with an estimated 20 percent share of market. The jam, tea, and oil lines also had good acceptance in food outlets outside the company operations.

The pricing of Julius Meinl products was consistent with their high quality. This meant that the line historically had broad acceptance by upper income consumers and by those consumers in other income levels who saw the brand as providing good value. As income levels rose, the brands gained broader market appeal.

Wholesale Operations

The wholesale division sold Julius Meinl branded merchandise, packaged foods, and some nonfood merchandise to other Austrian food retailers and to institutions such as hotels and restaurants. Most sales to retailers were made to small and medium-sized independent food stores. Few of the food chain retailers purchased from the wholesale division, either because it was more advantageous for them to buy direct or, in the case of Julius Meinl branded products, they would not stock a brand name associated with a competitive retail outlet.

While the sales of the wholesale division had shown steady growth through the years, this rate of growth had declined in the mid-1970's. The division purchased Julius Meinl brand products from the processing operations at prices equivalent to those paid by the company's retail store operations. The gross margin for the division on these products was 14 percent, and they accounted for approximately 60 percent of the division's sales.

Julius Meinl Stores

Prior to the 1950's, the Julius Meinl stores were run as specialty service stores. They were relatively small in size and, for the most part, were located in areas easily accessible to upper-income customers. Early in the 1950's, delicatessen and fruit and vegetables were introduced. The new stores were larger than existing stores and carried a broader range of products, including nonfood items, all of which were of the high-quality standard associated with the Julius Meinl name. Increasingly, there was self-service.

By the late 1960's, emphasis had changed from growth in total number of stores to increasing the volume and size of existing outlets. While new stores continued to be opened, some small units made uneconomic by location and/or increased costs, were phased out. Parking space was acquired for some stores. Leased fresh meat departments were added to a number of the larger stores in the 1970's.

In 1977, there were some 300 stores under the name of Julius Meinl in Austria, southern Federal Germany, and northern Italy. Twenty of the stores had customer parking. Of the 270 stores in Austria, 122 were in Vienna, located both in the high pedestrian traffic central core area and in the many residential shopping areas. About 10 percent of the stores were renovated extensively each year.

The Julius Meinl stores ranged in size from 100 to 800 square metres, the average or typical store having an area of 200 square metres. The average store operated on a gross margin of 20 percent and carried 3000 food and beverage items and 500 nonfood items. Approximately 800 items were Julius Meinl branded products. For these product categories, they were usually the only brand carried. The line accounted for approximately one quarter of store sales. In addition to emphasis on Julius Meinl brand products, the stores were noted for the breadth and quality of their delicatessen products. In fact, the chain was one of Austria's largest delicatessen retailers.

The distinctive signs and logo on the stores were very closely coordinated with the packaging, labelling, and advertising of the principal Meinl line, coffee. There was also design coordination in the use of the Julius Meinl name across all the product lines. As a result, there was strong identification of the Meinl name with quality products, particularly coffee, and with stores that carried a high-quality range of products.

The rise in the Austrian standard of living during the 1960's and early 1970's led to a situation in which an increasing number of people were attracted as customers to the Julius Meinl stores. Further, given their interest in quality of merchandise and shopping environment, this clientele had relatively low interest in the appeal of the discount food operations that began to appear in the 1970's.

Kunz Stores

The Kunz stores were a chain of neighbourhood food stores in Vienna and eastern Austria located primarily in middle-income and lower-middle-income residential areas. Some of the changes that occurred in the Julius Meinl store operations in the 1950's, 1960's, and early 1970's also took place in the Kunz stores. New stores were larger than existing stores. The product range was broadened, and there was a change to self-service in many stores. Parking was added to some stores. However, the number of new stores opened was smaller than for the Julius Meinl chain, and because the average store size was smaller, more stores were closed because they were uneconomic to operate. There were differences also in the direction in which the product range was broadened. In the Kunz stores, there was greater emphasis on adding nonfood household items such as cleaning products and health and beauty care products, as well as certain textiles such as ready-to-wear clothing.

The changes in Austrian living and shopping behaviour that were occurring in the 1960's and 1970's affected the Kunz operations quite substantially. To a far greater extent than for the patrons of the Julius Meinl stores, the customers of Kunz stores took advantage of increased mobility and availability of alternative forms of store outlets and shifted their food purchase patterns. This shift made a number of stores unprofitable. Twenty-one stores were closed between 1972 and 1977.

Of the 90 stores in the chain in 1977, 64 were in Vienna, and 15 had parking facilities. The store size ranged from 50 to 800 square metres, the typical store being 100 square metres in size. About 5 percent of the stores were renovated each year. Some of the smaller stores continued to be full service operations. The average store carried 2500 items, of which 500 were nonfood. There was increased emphasis on branded food items and nonfood items such as ready-to-wear clothing. Stores operated on an 18 percent margin. The average Kunz store carried about 700 Julius Meinl branded items, which were featured somewhat less in display than in the Julius Meinl stores, and accounted for about 15 percent of sales. For product categories where Julius Meinl brands were available, other manufacturers' brands were seldom carried.

The PamPam Stores

Two factors led Meinl management in the early 1970's to look for new ways of increasing sales and profits. The first was the change in Austrian food-buying habits. The second was that coffee, historically the company's most profitable line, was being squeezed by extreme competition at both the retail and manufacturer level. The result was the development of the PamPam store concept, large area discount operations located within Vienna, approximately two thirds of the distance between the core of the city and the boundary. There would be parking for up to 200 cars (large by Austrian standards) and the store operations would be carried out in new single-storey, single-purpose buildings of inexpensive construction. For a number of reasons, one of which was land costs, the stores would be located in areas with a relatively high concentration of heavy commercial and industrial business. The self-service PamPam discount store would be located at the back of the building reached by a hallway lined with small service stores leased by other retailers.

By 1977, four PamPam stores were in operation in Vienna, each in a different quadrant of the city. The store sizes ranged from 2000 to 2500 square metres, and were in competition with several other discount food stores. Some 9000 food and beverage items and 6000 nonfood items were carried at any one time. Turnover in items carried, particularly for non-food merchandise, was quite considerable. The average gross margin on all items was 10.5 percent. The stores carried about 300 of the faster-moving Julius Meinl brands, which competed for sales against other manufacturers' brands. Sales of Julius Meinl brands accounted for about 2 percent of total sales. Exhibit 1 gives price data on selected Julius Meinl products sold in the three different retail chains.

The success of the PamPam stores was well beyond the planning esti-mates. Initially, there had been concern about possible heavy inroads by PamPam on Kunz and Julius Meinl stores. Experience after each store open-ing indicated that sales were affected by about 7 percent for Kunz stores within a 5 kilometre radius and by about 3 percent for Julius Meinl stores in the same radius. The impact on store sales for these two chains was related to geographic distance of stores from the PamPam location, although this relationship was not as strong for Julius Meinl stores.

Competition in the Retail Food Market

The Julius Meinl retail operations competed in the Austrian market with a number of chains and several thousand independent food stores. Informa-tion on size and branding policy of the principal chain competitors is given in exhibit 2.

Exhibit 1   Retail Prices for Selected Julius Meinl Branded Products
Sold in PamPam, Julius Meinl, and Kunz Stores

		Store		
Product	*Size*	*PamPam*	*Julius Meinl*	*Kunz*
Coffee	0.25 kg	35.00	40.00	40.00
Pasta	0.5 kg	8.00	10.00	10.00
Wine	0.7 litre	40.00	50.00	50.00
Jam	0.5 kg	12.00	15.00	15.00
Cooking oil	2.5 kg	37.50	39.90	39.90

Konsum and Spar were both consumer cooperatives. With the exception of Carrefour, all of these chains operated outlets comparable in size to Kunz and Julius Meinl stores. Aside from Carrefour, the dozen or so food discounters located in the Vienna area were independents operating out of stores ranging in size from 700 to 1400 square metres. Carrefour was associated with the French-based organization of the same name. It had opened a large hypermarché in 1976 in a new shopping plaza located about 5 kilometres south of the Vienna city boundary. The plaza was the first large one to be built in Austria.

Outside sources estimated that in 1977 the retail stores operated by Julius Meinl A.G. would obtain a 11.3 percent share of the Vienna food market and a 8.6 percent share of the Austrian market. Forecast data on 1977 operations are given in exhibit 3.

Exhibit 2 Information on Principal Chain
Competitors in the Austrian Food Market

Name	Estimated No. of Outlets in Austria	Carry Private Brands		Carry Julius Meinl Brands	
		Yes	No	Yes	No
Carrefour	1	X		X	
Konsum	900	X			X
Löwa	30	X		X	
Billa	167		X		X
Hofer	42	X			X
Spar	1000	X			X

Exhibit 3 1977 Forecast Data for Julius Meinl Retail and Wholesale Operations

	PamPam	Julius Meinl	Kunz	Wholesale
Index of Sales (Julius Meinl = 100)	30	100	25	20
Operating costs as a percentage of sales[1]				
Fixed	1.5	4.0	3.4	0.9
Variable	7.7	15.7	14.6	11.3

1. These data are disguised. However, the underlying relationships across the data are maintained. Fixed costs include depreciation, rent, and insurance. Variable costs include transport to the stores, repairs, direct store advertising, and store staff costs, many of which were not, in reality, variable.

The Future

"Yes, we've been very pleased with the growth of our PamPam stores," said Mr. Thomas Meinl. "Given current market conditions, we expect the annual sales growth of about 25 percent to be two and a half times that of our Julius Meinl stores and three and a half times that of the Kunz and wholesale operations. Of course, we were fortunate in our timing to arrive in the market when economic conditions were not very good and many consumers were becoming cost conscious."

"At the same time, I must say that we do have a sound concept for this stage of development of the Austrian market. We had an opportunity to put a Julius Meinl store in the new plaza south of Vienna, but stayed out because we could not see that there was going to be sufficient sales volume for several years to make it profitable. Now that the plaza is in operation, we have been able to confirm that our estimates of store traffic were accurate ones."

The success of the PamPam operations led Meinl executives to consider expansion of the operation, both in Vienna and in other Austrian cities. They were proceeding with some caution, however. Although there were relatively few large discount food operations in the country, there was still substantial strength in the traditional ways of food shopping, and they were concerned about the high economic cost of overbuilding. There was also some concern about the energy shortage situation forecast for the 1980's. They believed that the shortage, if it were severe and/or prolonged, would result in high sales losses for volume retail outlets dependent on private transportation.

The Change of Store Names

The idea of changing the PamPam name first came up in a discussion on the possible opening of a discount operation in another Austrian city. One of the executives suggested that acceptance of the discount concept in that city, in which the traditional shopping patterns were still widespread, would be speeded up if the store had a name that was associated with the familiar and well-accepted Julius Meinl name. He proposed the name "Meinl Market." The proposal started a more general discussion about the merits of associating the Meinl name with the volume discount stores, and even the Kunz stores.

There was reasonable agreement that the use of the Meinl name on the PamPam stores would increase patronage and sales by as much as 10 percent through the goodwill associated with the Meinl name. This would be reinforced through the more efficient use of advertising, which the name change would make possible. However, there was substantial disagreement as to where the increased patronage would come from. Some executives believed that the increase would come from a cross-section of the community that was similar in pattern to the existing PamPam stores. Others disagreed and expressed the view that the Meinl name would attract customers primarily from the Julius Meinl and Kunz stores. This was met with the response that if the Meinl name on PamPam stores would attract Kunz customers, then perhaps a Meinl name on Kunz stores would attract new customers to that operation and create stronger loyalty among existing clientele.

The idea of the Meinl name on the three retail chains led to a further round of discussion on the impact of the name on customer loyalty. It was in this part of the meeting that concern was raised that the use of the Meinl name on stores with very different merchandising approaches would result in buyer confusion and a blurring of the images of the three types of operation. Further there was concern expressed that the attachment of the Meinl name to the three operations would lead to coordination of merchandising and buying policies that would weaken the competitive strength that each chain had in the market.

Throughout the discussion, the manager of the wholesale division remained adamantly opposed to the use of the Meinl name in any form for the PamPam and Kunz operations. While he acknowledged that it was widely known in the trade that Julius Meinl A.G. controlled these operations, he was positive that his customers, most particularly the independents, would react strongly to any such change. He stated that if the Meinl name went on the PamPam operations, he could expect to lose 20 to 30 percent of his Julius Meinl brand name business within a year and 10 to 20 percent of his other business as well.

"While that meeting was very interesting and lively," said Thomas Meinl, "there was no consensus reached on the change of store names. However, we should make an early decision on the PamPam stores at least. Any advantage that the Meinl name can provide will be strongest now when the PamPam name is still not firmly established in the consumer's mind. To delay much longer will make the change less effective and more difficult to implement. Further, it is highly likely that we will be adding one or two units to the chain in the next year. A decision on store name is needed now as input into our planning for these decisions."

CHAPTER V
PRODUCT DECISIONS

Product and service decisions are some of the most critical for a marketing manager because the product or service must stand up to buyer and retailer scrutiny after the customer is persuaded to try it. Furthermore, long periods of development and large amounts of money frequently are invested in a product or service before it is introduced, and these decisions are not easily reversed. In addition, the product or service tends to be a focal point for every department of the organization: market research, engineering, production, marketing, and cost control. Also, almost every change in the product or service tends to demand a change in the rest of the marketing strategy—changes in pricing, communications, and sometimes distribution.

There are decisions concerning single products and entire product lines, and for each of these there are "add," "modify," and "drop" decisions. New product introductions are a very special case of "add"—a very critical activity because most organizations require a steady flow of new products in order to survive. First, let us look at how we might categorize the various products and services.

The first classification is between products and services (chart 1). Services are both goods and performance of tasks such as vacations, life insurance, health care, libraries, road maintenance, garbage pickup, tax advice, religion, and education. Services can be further subdivided into tangible (or touchable) and intangible services; public transportation is tangible and legal advice is intangible. Products are the physical goods we see around us—stereos, wines, clothing, cars, and houses.

Services differ from products in three major respects. First of all, because of the intangibility of many services, it is much more difficult to predict the availability and to control the quality of services than it is to forecast and control products. Even a tangible service (such as a reservation on an airline) exists for only a few hours and then is gone, whereas a

Chart 1 Schematic of Product and Service Classification

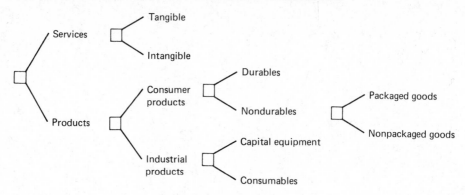

product tends to be physical and enduring. Time is an important element in tangible services because the service is produced and consumed at the same time. For example, paying a serviceman to repair a machine or change the tires on your car is a case of producing and consuming at the same time. From a consumer standpoint, it is very difficult to get a refund on a service *after* the service has been performed—most services are not reversible. A third important difference between services and products is the difficulty of measuring the value of services such as hospitals, public transportation, and legal advice. This creates a problem in pricing and communicating the service. How do you describe and quantify the peace of mind that a good doctor or lawyer can provide, especially in crisis situations? However, for the remainder of the book, we are going to use a shorthand and talk about "products" when we mean products *and* services.

The second classification is consumer and industrial (chart 1). Within consumer goods, further useful divisions can be made into durables, such as refrigerators, and nondurables, such as gasoline. The distinction is useful because the consumer's buying process, and hence the entire marketing approach to durables, is different from nondurables. For most durables, buyers are willing to shop around, and the manufacturer can get by with fewer retail outlets than a gasoline marketer who requires many outlets.

Within nondurables, packaged goods such as foods, cleaners, and cosmetics are different from nonpackaged goods such as clothing because of the food and/or drug channels and the opportunities for quality control and promotion by virtue of prepackaging.

Industrial products can be classified into capital equipment, such as presses, and consumables, such as raw materials, office supplies, and small tools. The decision process for capital equipment tends to be a "new buy" and involves more executives over more time than the purchases of consumables, which tend to be routinized straight rebuys.

Product Life Cycle

Product categories, such as calculators, and particular brands, such as Rapidman, appear to go through a life cycle beginning with market entry, a stage of growth, then maturation and decline. The familiar S-shaped curve of product category sales over time is graphed in chart 2, but there are numerous variations of this curve if you plot the sales of a product category or particular brand. Although this pattern of growth, maturation, and decline is fairly common for brands and product categories, it is not inevitable.

It is useful to understand some of the forces that contribute to the generalized product life cycle curve for a product category such as small pocket calculators. In the initial market entry, there is some time required for customers to build an awareness of the availability and usefulness of small calculators. Slowly, students and business people evaluate and try the product, and if they like the calculators, they tell their friends. This word-of-mouth advertising is the second step of the diffusion of a new product category in the market and may account for the steep climb in sales during the growth phase; many people are trying and rebuying the calculators over a relatively short span of time.

During maturation, the market growth for pocket calculators will slow and new entrants will compete for market share. The differential advantage or "unique selling proposition (USP)" of the original calculators becomes diluted by the presence of a variety of product types. In time, the amount of product differentiation in the product category tends to

Chart 2 Product Category Sales and Stages of the Product Life Cycle

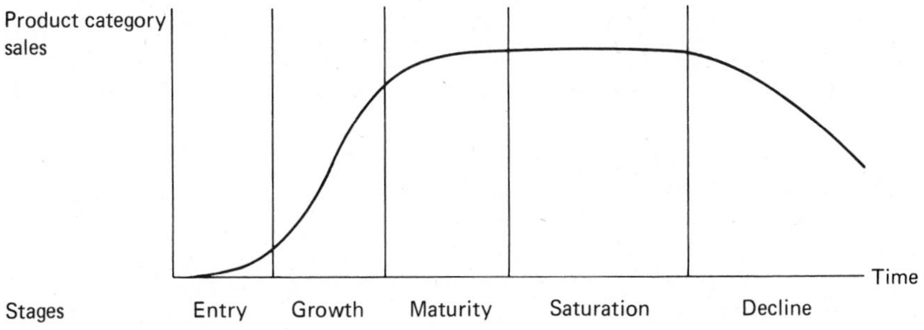

Product category sales / Time

Stages   Entry   Growth   Maturity   Saturation   Decline

diminish, with the exception of brands competing for special segments. At this stage, we think of the market as saturated. Price competition becomes increasingly intense and occasionally a "price war" erupts. As you might suspect, product profitability tends to decline in the late stages of a product life cycle. Chart 3 summarizes the market and marketing variables that generally tend to change during the life cycle of a product category.

Usefulness of the Product Life Cycle Concept

The above generalizations apply more often to a product category than to any particular product or brand in a category. However, the life cycle concept is of use to individual marketers. Most importantly, it shows us how competition tends to evolve over time in a product category. For example, the marketers of the first new brand in a market usually take some extra risks, but they have a brief period of time to reap some extra rewards before competitors enter. First new brands often have the option of pursuing a "premium" strategy consisting of unique brand, high price (skimming), selective channels, and high spending on marketing communications. The opportunities for such "premium" strategies are reduced as soon as the product category reaches maturity. Only the brands that specifically target

Chart 3   Characteristics of a Product Category Over Five Stages of the Product Life Cycle[a]

	Stages				
	Entry	*Growth*	*Maturation*	*Saturation*	*Decline*
Sales	Small	Growing	Peaking	Leveling	Declining
Buyers	Innovators	Early adopters	Early majority	Late majority	Laggards
Competitors	None	Few	Several	Many	Declining
Channels	Selective	Selective	Extensive	Mass	Mass
R & D	Much	Less	Little	None	None
Production costs	High	Less	Level	Level	Level
Price	High	Level	Declining	Declining	Low
Communications	High spending	High spending	Declining	Declining	Low
Product modifications and extensions	Few	Many	Many	Few	None
Profits per unit	Low	High	Declining	Declining	Low

a. For a more detailed chart, see Chester R. Wasson, *Dynamic Competitive Strategy and Product Life Cycles* (Challenge Books, 1974).

a quality-conscious, price-insensitive audience can pursue a "premium" strategy after maturity of the category has been reached.

In addition to the strategy options that may be closed off, the product life cycle concept helps us to know what factors to monitor and how those factors tend to behave. For example, competition tends to become more aggressive during the stages of maturity and saturation. Furthermore, competition may move from nonprice factors to price competition and thereby reduce profits further. As far-sighted marketing managers, we should be preparing some contingency plans for a new competitive environment.

The product life cycle concept for a brand is largely useful as a conceptual tool because we have no way of pinpointing where our product is on the curve, there is no universal time scale on the bottom of the graph, and there is no inevitable slip from one stage to the next. We must recognize that the product life cycle for a particular brand is not inevitable. Many products *do evolve* with their customers and competitors as a result of careful monitoring and intelligent support. Look at Listerine mouthwash, a product introduced more than 50 years ago and still a leader in its product category. Where products get into trouble, particularly packaged-goods products, is when the marketing professionals forget who is buying the brand and the customer's reason for buying it.

One of the important decisions for both industrial and consumer products is the timing of (1) abandoning support for the product and (2) dropping the product completely. There is a system of labelling products in accordance with their perceived position in the product life cycle and their responsiveness to marketing effort. "Stars" are dominant, profitable, and responsive to marketing effort. "Cash cows" are not economical to support with marketing effort and will be "milked" by withdrawing marketing support, thereby maintaining their profitability. "Dogs" are products with small shares, which are not sufficiently responsive to warrant relaunching but do contribute enough to warrant the management time spent on them. Classifications such as stars, cash cows, and dogs are useful because they provoke managerial judgment and/or experimentation regarding the responsiveness of a brand to further marketing effort.

Decision Criteria for Add, Modify, or Drop Decisions

There are financial, market, production, and organizational criteria for product decisions. The financial criteria usually begin with contribution and/or profits that are coupled with investment figures on new products and modified products to show a return on investment and/or a payout period. The market criteria are factors such as market dominance, customers' desire for a full line, voids in the market, or the need to position a product directly opposite a competitive product. The production criteria are considerations such as capacity, utilization of by-products or similar processes, and the sheer "opportunity" from owning a design or ability to make a product. "Opportunity" is in quotation marks because the product is not an opportunity unless someone wants to buy it. The organizational criteria are factors such as the management time that will be required to look after a product.

"Add" Decisions

The major considerations when adding a product or product lines are its "fit" with the company's manufacturing and marketing resources, retailer and consumer demand for the product, and its fit with the existing product lines in order to avoid cannibalizing existing products. Most of all, a product addition should promise a profit at least commensurate with the investment and risk involved in the product. Accordingly, most marketing managers spend a considerable amount of time working through projected profit-and-loss statements in order to assess the possible impact on profits from adding a new product. The usual approach is to forecast several possible sales ranges over a five-year period for the new product and any of the products that it may cannibalize. From these sales forecasts a series of hypothetical five-year profit and loss statements can be generated for the new product or the entire product line. Most product addition decisions can be cast in the framework shown in chart 4.

The burden is on us to develop all possible marketing strategy options, and at least one option should promise an acceptable financial return before we follow the GO route. In other words, we will work from right to left on the schematic of chart 4, first assessing the profit consequences of the various strategy options before we make a GO or NO GO decision. If none of the GO options seem sufficiently rewarding, then we should take the NO GO decision. In some circumstances there is justification for collecting more market data.

New Product Introduction Processes

Many companies have adopted a system for managing new product introductions. In these companies a definite system is established, assigned to a manager, and monitored by top management. Very often a sequence of stages are delineated as follows: idea generation, screening, business analysis, product development, product testing, test marketing, and market launch.

Chart 4 Schematic of New Product Decisions

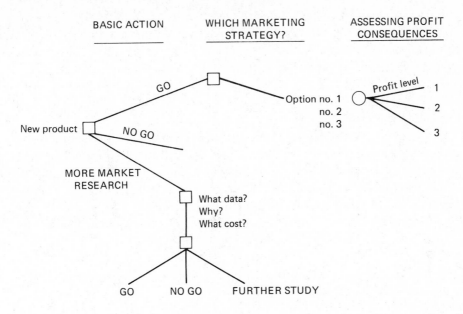

The concept of a modified product or a new product should stem from an analysis of the desired positioning of the product. All three stages of idea generation, screening, and business analysis should consider possible positionings. When we have tentatively settled on a product concept, we must design and test the product so that it does in fact deliver the benefits, *especially* whatever unique benefit(s) we wish to communicate. Then we should test prototypes or models of the product to make sure that the product works when used by a typical customer. The next step is to make whatever modifications are necessary and retest the prototypes. When the product performs well by itself in these "use" tests, we can find out how it fares against competition and how much customers will pay for it by arranging a test market in a few stores or a few cities. Now we are testing the entire marketing strategy, not just the product. If the strategy works well in a test market we can proceed to a regional or national launch.

In terms of numbers of new products, the process can be viewed as a giant funnel with many ideas for new products pouring in the top, being screened out at various stages until only a trickle of new products actually are launched on the market. Even then, the success rate for new products, however defined, is not very encouraging.

"Modify" Decisions

After a product is launched, it may be modified several times during its life span. Packaged goods are frequently strengthened on some dimension such as nutrition or taste, and industrial products are constantly being improved. Usually, these modifications involve some investment and a great deal of time. However, product modifications usually provide new opportunities to talk about the product, to target new customers, and sometimes to reposition the product against new competitors.

The motivation for product modifications usually is to (re)gain a competitive advantage in order to retain share and profits. Even though a product modification may be less significant than adding a new product, much the same considerations are involved: retail and consumer demand, cannibalizing existing products, continued fit with the organization's production and marketing resources, and the financial rewards in light of the investment.

"Drop" Decisions

There are a variety of reasons for dropping a product, but the main reason usually is lack of sufficient profit to compensate for the managerial time involved. Sometimes a product drifts into technical obsolescence and customer interest fades. Sometimes raw materials cease to be available, as in the case of a floor-hardening product; the main ingredient was a by-product from a chemical process operated by another company which stopped using that particular chemical process.

Sometimes products are launched and then found to fail under a full range of working conditions. This is not as unusual as one might think. A fabricating company in Toronto once launched a styrene folding bathtub enclosure which was supposed to fold back neatly against the bathroom wall when not extended for use. Unfortunately, styrene as it was developed at the time had a fairly high coefficient of expansion, so that when the tub enclosure was cold, it was so loose it would fall off the guiding tracks. However, when the hot shower water heated the styrene, the interlocking panels expanded so much that the panels would not fold back. The product died on the retailers' shelves.

Summary

Because the environment is constantly changing, our products and services must be managed very closely in order to remain competitive. We will have to develop a system of modifying existing products and replacing obsolete products with new ones in order for the organization to survive.

Within that system of managing products and services we will develop criteria and measures of how well those modifications or new products fit with our target market, organizational strengths and weaknesses, channels of distribution, and competitors. Recognizing the factors that probably will play on our product as it moves through the product life cycle for its category, we will be ready for the changing scene.

Chart 5   The Process of Positioning and Product Implications

COMPETITIVE ANALYSIS		MARKET ANALYSIS
strategies used extent and importance of success likely actions and reactions	INTERNAL OR CORPORATE ANALYSIS objectives strengths/weaknesses performance fit with other products	statistics buying and use behaviour

COMPETITIVE ANALYSIS
- strategies used
- extent and importance of success
- likely actions and reactions

↓

DIFFERENTIATION
- benefits of importance
- preferences for benefit combinations

INTERNAL OR CORPORATE ANALYSIS
- objectives
- strengths/weaknesses
- performance
- fit with other products

MARKET ANALYSIS
- statistics
- buying and use behaviour

↓

SEGMENTATION
- possible segments
- size of segments

PACKAGE OF BENEFITS SELECTION → POSITION ← TARGET MARKET SELECTION

PRODUCT IMPLICATIONS
- establish product concept
- test concept and prototypes
- modify, retest
- conduct test market
- launch

IMPLICATIONS FOR MARKETING STRATEGY
- marketing objectives
- product
- price
- channels
- communications

12 Windshark Wind Energy Conversion Systems Corporation

In the summer of 1980, principal designer Bruce Dean and his associates were in the final stages of completing the design and construction of a prototype wind energy conversion system (more commonly known as a windmill) for generating electrical power. Mr. Dean felt the system was worthy of being marketed in Canada and the United States, in view of the growing interest in renewable energy and the ever-rising costs of conventional energy. He was developing the mill with the technical assistance of an aerodynamicist from the University of Western Ontario. Although most of the engineering aspects of the system were virtually resolved, Mr. Dean and his associates were concerned with the marketing side of the proposed enterprise.

In late 1981, Windshark management seriously began to ponder the problems surrounding the type of sales and distribution strategy they should follow in light of the special procedures and equipment required to install the large mill, the timing of introducing the mill, the pricing of the mill, promotional techniques to use if any, types and amounts of advertising, and what initial marketing approach to take, to name a few.

Design and Purpose of the System

Although details of wind energy turbines and systems varied, the steps to provide a reliable source of electricity were essentially the same. The kinetic energy of the wind turned a propeller or rotor causing a generator or induction motor to rotate via a main shaft to generate an electric current. The Windshark system was designed to hook into a household service system and supply regular 120-VAC 60-Hz domestic service.[1] The

---

1.   120-VAC 60-Hz domestic service was the normal voltage and current supplied by the public utilities, such as Ontario Hydro.

generator was an 1800-r.p.m.[2] 20,000-watt induction motor capable of sufficiently supplying the total energy requirements of an average household, small business, or farm operation. The mill was a horizontal-axis downwind model positioned perpendicular to the direction of the wind. The hub and propeller system was allowed to rotate freely with the wind on a lollycom bearing on top of the tower.

The key innovation of the Windshark mill was its spring-loaded blade pitching mechanism. In the past, the difficulty in designing a constant speed mill had been the barrier to manufacturing a usable system for households that required 120-VAC 60-Hz electrical current. Traditional windmills had been used for purposes that did not require prescribed electrical specifications, such as water pumping and resistance heating. The pitching mechanisms operated as an upside risk to prevent the mill from spinning out of control during high winds and sustaining the generator at a rotational speed of 1800 r.p.m. As the wind speed increased, the blades of the propeller automatically pitched so that each blade effectively "cut" less wind and maintained its rotational speed to some maximum. Windshark's efforts at obtaining a patent on the design were unsuccessful since the mechanism was not considered a "new, significant technological innovation."

Industry and Competition

Currently, the alternative energy market was very small and undeveloped. Few manufacturers had experienced success—most manufacturers were primarily in the research and development stages of business development. Most attempts at household adaptation had been aimed at back up or supplemental use with low-power-yield systems. No one firm had surfaced in the Canadian or U.S. markets—probably because of lack of a good marketable product (exhibit 1). Nevertheless, one firm, Enertech Corporation based in Norwich, Vermont, was experiencing good success with a model visually comparable to the Windshark mill. However, the Enertech mill had a very low power yield and consequently provided only marginal savings on utility bills. The Enertech system utilized a speed brake to stop the propeller in high winds rather than limiting its speed as the Windshark mill did. Consequently, substantial potential energy was lost by not operating the mill at higher windspeeds where energy output reached its maximum. The Enertech mill produced a maximum of 1650 watts (enough for lights and

---

2. In order for the mill generator to produce this "grade" of electricity, it *must* spin at 1800 r.p.m.; this required a variable blade pitching mechanism.

Exhibit 1   Wind Energy Manufacturers and Distributors

Major U.S. distributor

Enertech Corporation
P.O. Box 420
Norwich, Vermont 05055

Canadian distributors:

Careful Eco Systems Ltd.
Box 1212
Whaletown, B.C. V0P 1Z0
(Dunlite 2 kw: $5,185 Canadian)

Amherst Renewable Energies Ltd.
Box 387
Perth, Ontario K7H 3G1
(Dunlite 2 kw and 5 kw: prices on
request)

DYNERGY CORPORATION
Box 428
1269 Union Ave.
Laconia, New Hampshire 03246
(603) 542-8313

MODEL 5M:
Maximum output: Not available
Vertical axis, Three blades
Rotor diameter: 15 feet
Cut-in wind speed: 10 mph
Rated output: 3300 watts at 24 mph
Price: $11,000 (U.S.) includes
alternator and base

ENERTECH CORPORATION
P.O. Box 420
Norwich, Vermont 05055
(802) 649-1145

MODEL 1500:
Maximum output: 1650 watts,
115 volts AC
Horizontal axis, Downwind, Three
blades
Rotor diameter: 13 feet
Cut-in wind speed: 9 mph
Rated output: 1500 watts at 22 mph
Price: $2900 (U.S.)

Other models: Sparco wind powered
water pump ($300 to $350 U.S.)
Wincharger 200 ($625 U.S.)
Sencenbaugh 500 ($2560 U.S.)

COULSON WIND ELECTRIC
RFD 1, Box 225
Polk City, Iowa 50226
(515) 984-6038

Rebuilt Jacobs, Winchargers and
Winpowers.
Accessories: towers, batteries,
appliances.

DAF INDAL
3570 Hawkestone Road
Mississauga, Ontario L5C 2V8
(416) 275-5300

Developing vertical axis Darrieus
wind generators in the 50 kw range.

DAKOTA WIND AND SUN
Box 1781
Aberdeen, South Dakota
(605) 229-0815

MODEL BC4:
Maximum output: 4000 watts (140
volts DC)
Horizontal axis, Upwind, Three blades
Rotor diameter: 14 feet
Cut-in wind speed: 8 mph
Rated output: 4000 watts at 27 mph
Price: $5,470 (U.S.)

Other models: 10,000 watt model
to be available this fall
Dealerships: 23 U.S. dealers; write
for list

Canadian distributor:
Massawippi Wind Electric
R.R. 3
Ayer's Cliff, Quebec J0B 1C0
(Dakota BC 4: $6,400 Canadian)

Exhibit 1   (continued)

DUNLITE ELECTRICAL
PRODUCTS
28 Orsmond Street
Hindmarsh, Australia 5007

MODEL 2kw:
Maximum output: 3000 watts at 24,
32, 48, and 110 volts
Horizontal axis, Upwind, Three
blades
Rotor diameter: 13½ feet
Cut-in wind speed: 8 mph
Rated output: 2000 watts at 25 mph
Price: $3,800 (Australian)

Other models: 5kw (110 volt)
$4,800 (Australian)
Sencenbaugh 1000 ($2,950 U.S.)
Dunlite 2000 ($4,020 U.S.)
Accessories: measuring equipment
and controls

Canadian distributor:
Energy Alternatives
2 Croft Street, Box 671
Amherst, Nova Scotia B4H 1B1
(902) 667-2790

FRIESEN INDUSTRIES
32032 South Fraser Way
Clearbrook, B.C.
(604) 859-7101
Control switches and inverters

FUTURE RESOURCES AND
ENERGY LTD.
Box 1358, Station B
Downsview, Ontario M3H 5W3
(416) 630-8343
Canadian distributor for Swiss-made
Elektro wind generators: 5 kw and
10 kw models, 110 volts DC. Prices
on request.

some small appliances) whereas the Windshark mill produced +20,000 watts, enough for an entire household. Inevitably, the mill would not operate in periods of no wind. It was estimated based on meterological data that the mill would on average eliminate 95 percent of the dollar amount of yearly energy consumption in Canada. Enertech reportedly sold more than 400 systems in 1980.

Windshark management also saw the public utilities as somewhat of a peripheral competitor, although they felt that little could be done other than compete on the basis of price.

Market Potential

Generally, Mr. Dean felt that the mill would have excellent market potential in both Canada and the United States. The mill system was originally designed with the rural and farming market as a focal point. Farmers and rural households paid higher prices for electrical energy and generally used more of it. Furthermore, this market usually had more available capital and would benefit greatly by the tax savings. Canadian Ministry of Agriculture studies indicated that "belt areas of strong winds coincide with where major farming and livestock production occurs on flat lands." Statistics from 1976 reports also indicated the total number of farm operations in Canada was 300,118 of which 25 percent were in Ontario. The total rural and farming population was in excess of 1,500,000 of the 22,992,000 people in Canada. The average equity of a Canadian farm operation was $341,000.

Public utility commission studies indicated the average Canadian household spent $1300–$1500 per year on total energy requirements in 1981, of which approximately 80 percent was devoted to heating, laundry, and cooking and 20 percent to lighting and small appliances. Eastern and Western Canadian households were considerably higher at more than $1800 per year. These figures had been increasing by roughly 10 percent or more per year. Similar trends were evident in the U.S. although energy costs on average were 10–15 percent higher. Mr. Dean felt uncertain about what would be involved in operating in the United States. Nevertheless, the U. S. market seemed very lucrative for reasons other than its higher energy costs. The prevailing exchange rate would enable American consumers to purchase a system for 15 percent less than the tentative Canadian retail price of $15,000. Also, the U.S. government enacted special provisions for accelerated capital cost allowances for those who purchased alternative energy equipment (50%/year for two years) in addition to an investment tax credit. The investment tax credit allowed a consumer to deduct 20 percent of the purchase price (after C.C.A. allowances) of alternative energy equipment from his calculated taxes payable in the year of purchase. Moreover, individual households in the U.S. were allowed to sell any surplus energy they generated as individuals to their local utilities at wholesale prices. This sort of legislation had not been, and was not expected to be, passed in Canada. Canadian alternative energy equipment purchasers were currently allowed a Class 8 20 percent reducing balance C.C.A. (new proposals considered accelerating that rate) and an investment tax credit. The investment tax credit was 10 percent in the Western Provinces, 7 percent in Ontario, and 20 percent in Quebec and the Eastern provinces. Overall, Ontario appeared to have the least market potential due to relatively cheaper energy costs and lower tax incentives. Mr. Dean was concerned about entering any other Canadian and American markets without a set sales, distribution or installation strategy and the lack of information regarding the potential receptiveness of those markets to such a revolutionary product.

Cost Data

Cost data are given in exhibits 2, 3, and 4. All costs were actual, based on prototype costs and should be similar in the future for production models. However, advertising was left out of the fixed cost section because Windshark management was uncertain about what type and how much advertising and promotion to do. The installation costs were thought to be fairly accurate—also based on prototype costs. However, the suggested selling price and selling commission were more arbitrary. Windshark

Exhibit 2 Total Variable Materials Cost

Hub grinding	$ 50
Three, 16-foot pine boards	
Kevlar fibrefill (15 yds.)	
Carbon fibre (15 yds.)	182
Main shaft—2″ cold rolled	46
Main bearings—2″ pillow block	27
Pitch mechanism—25 lbs. steel	19
Hub	27
Extra machine brackets, screws, etc.	45
Twelve lolly bearings	65
Framing	18
Shark cover—moulded fiberglass	136
Styrofoam cone	46
Paint	9
Rotating lollycom	182
10″ to 1/2″ wall steel column (95 ft.)	652
Gemini power monitor control box	1,200
20 kw morse induction AC generator	1,820
Helical 25-H.P. primary step-up gear box (8:1)	319
Packaging	5
Shipping (average)	40
Total Variable Materials Cost	$4,899
Total variable materials cost	$4,899
Replacement purchases	50
Dealer promotion	200
Mill insurance/water heater	175
Total Variable Cost	$5,324

Exhibit 3   Direct Labour

Direct Labour

  5 hrs. Blading, carbon and kevlar moulding
  5 hrs. Blade balancing and painting
  7 hrs. Welding
  5 hrs. Moulding shark cover
  8 hrs. Hub assembly
  _6_ hrs. Paint and package mill

  36 hrs. @ $10 per hour

Total Direct Labour = $360

Note: Direct labour is included in wages as a fixed cost, along with promotional
      work and research and development. It is, therefore, not included with total
      variable cost when calculating mill price.

  Suggested list price $15,000
  $2000 installation costs
  $1500 sales commission

---

management felt the $1500 commission was reasonable, although they
wondered if it should be raised or lowered. The issue of pricing was of
key importance to Windshark. Pricing suggestions varied from $10,000 to
$20,000 per mill. Mr. Dean knew that discount pricing would increase the
potential unit sales of windmills and the customer's return on investment.
However, he was concerned about "leaving money on the table" by pricing too low in light of the one-time purchase nature of the mill. The tentative $15,000 selling price seemed reasonable, considering the energy and
tax savings the mill provided as well as furnishing a handsome contribution for Windshark.

Key Marketing Issues

The major marketing problem the system posed was the issue of installation. This was a very involved task requiring a heavy crane, a backhoe
driller, and various qualified operators and electricians. This single aspect
of the product required significant consideration in developing a sales and
distribution strategy. Mr. Dean was in doubt as to how the bulky mill
could be distributed efficiently to its destination and be installed by locally
available personnel. He felt the tasks of selling, distributing, and installing
should be integrated somehow, although he was unsure of the criteria he
would use for deciding who should perform these functions.

Exhibit 4 Total Fixed Costs

Total Fixed Costs:

Administration (secretary)	$13,200
Wages (including direct labour)	40,000
Rent/insurance building	5,000
Rent/insurance office	1,000
Promotion	5,000
Supplies	1,000
Depreciation	313
UIC/CP/WC tax	2,400
Loan repayment	5,400
Other overhead	8,000
Advertising	?
Total Fixed Overhead	$81,313 + ?

Installation Costs:

Concrete (1.6 metres × $77/metre)	$ 123
50-amp service wire, $1.80/ft. (200-ft. average)	360
3 hrs. driller @ $182/hr.	546
8 hrs. crane @ $39/hr.	312
2 men, 8 hrs. lay wire @ $8/hr. wages	128
8 hrs. electrician, wiring @ $15/hr.	120
Building permit—$6/$1000 building costs	90
Wiring permit and inspection	17
6 hrs. welder @ $25/hr.	150
Assembly and assistance: 8 hrs. 2 men @ $8/hr.	128
	$ 1974

13 Schick Blades

In May 1970, Warner-Lambert Canada Limited acquired the Schick line of wet shaving products from the Eversharp Company. At the time of the acquisition, the Schick line consisted of two types of razor blades (double-edged and injector), razors, and shaving lathers and lotions. Marketing support was primarily directed at the double-edged razor blade line.

In August 1971 Warner-Lambert made a major change in the marketing strategy for Schick razors and blades. Marketing support was taken away from double-edged razor blades and placed instead on the Schick injector razor system. The thrust of advertising was directed toward the injector system, and the system was also supported with heavy consumer sampling.

Warner-Lambert was able to improve Schick market share substantially, from 23.0 percent in 1969 to 27.9 percent in 1972. However, heavy investments in advertising and promoting the Schick injector system had reduced profit margins significantly.

In the period since the Warner-Lambert acquisition, two major market developments had taken place:

1. In May 1971, Wilkinson launched a new form of razor blade, the Wilkinson bonded system. This was a single-edged blade bonded into a plastic cartridge. The resulting precise shaving angle was claimed to give a more comfortable "nick-free" shave.

2. In January 1972, Gillette launched Trac II, a shaving system consisting of *two* single-edged blades bonded into a cartridge. Gillette claimed the twin-blade Trac II system offered the closest available shave.

The Schick marketing group were concerned about the initial successes of these new shaving systems. In the November/December 1972 audit of retail sales, combined Wilkinson Bonded and Trac II share had reached 10.2 percent, the sixth consecutive period in which share had increased.

Schick had investigated introduction of a blade competitive with Trac

II. However, the new Schick blade, code named A3, would have a gross margin so low that any conversion of current Schick injector or double-edged system users to the new blade would result in reduced Schick profits.

In January 1973, the Schick product manager was asked to prepare a position paper on the brand which addressed the following issues:

1. Should Schick develop and launch a direct competitor to Trac II, and if so, how should it be positioned to consumers?

2. If such a recommendation was made, how should Schick injector and double-edge blades be marketed?

3. If a recommendation was made *not* to launch a Schick twin-bonded razor blade, how should the Wilkinson and Gillette market penetration be countered?

Background

Shaving Systems

The safety razor was invented in the 1890's by Geisman and subsequently commercialized and popularized by the Gillette Company in the early part of the twentieth century. The safety razor, using double-edged blades made of carbon steel, replaced the open "cutthroat" razor used for centuries, and represented a significant step forward in comfort and safety.

In 1926, Colonel Jacob Schick invented the forerunner of the injector razor; this consisted of a razor handle and single-edged carbon steel blades enclosed in a magazine under spring pressure. The handle was "loaded" with one of these blades, and the loading action automatically ejected the worn blade.

Four basic wet shaving systems were available to the consumer at the end of 1972:

Double-edged blades were the most popular, with 73 percent of the market. These blades, packed in dispensers of five, ten, or fifteen blades, had two sharp edges and fitted into permanent razor handles. Blades were standardized and would fit into any make of razor.

Injector blades accounted for 15 percent of the market. These were single-edged blades packed in dispensers of six, seven, ten, or eleven depending on metal type and manufacturer. Any make of blade would fit all available injector razor permanent handles.

Band blades consisted of long strips of blade which could be rotated within a cartridge. The cartridge fitted into a permanent handle, but the brand of blade had to match the make of the handle. These blades were premium priced and had reached a peak market share of 7.4 percent before declining in 1971 and 1972.

Bonded blades were the newest market entrants. They consisted of either one (Wilkinson) or two (Gillette Trac II) single-edged blades bonded into a cartridge. Five cartridges were packed into a dispenser, and a cartridge was attached to a permanent razor handle. The correct brand of blade had to be used to fit any brand of razor handle. The bonded blades were premium priced about 25 percent higher than double-edged or injector blades.

Metals Used for Razor Blades

The period of the 1960's was known in the industry as the period of the "metals war." During this period each manufacturer tried to outdo the other with "new, improved razor blades." Until 1963, all blades had been made of carbon steel. Between 1963 and 1970, however, a number of other metals were introduced.

1963	Wilkinson introduced the first stainless steel blade
1964	Gillette, followed by Schick, launched their own stainless steel blades
1965–1969	All manufacturers upgraded the quality of stainless steel used in blades
1969	Schick introduced the first plated blade, Krona Chrome, with a chromium-plated shaving edge. Gillette launched a chromium and platinum plated blade, Gillete Plus
1970	Both Schick (Super Krona Chrome) and Wilkinson (Wilkinson II) launched improved plated blades.

Each new product launched claimed shaving superiority in either closeness, smoothness, or comfort. Research indicated that it was very doubtful whether consumers were ever convinced of any tangible differences between the stainless steel and coated blades or were ever able to recall the claims made by the manufacturers.

While manufacturers considered that plated blades should last longer than stainless steel, research among consumers indicated that they expected to get an average of six shaves per blade, irrespective of type of shaving system or metal.

A large number of brands were marketed in 1972; confusion was generated by the four different types of shaving systems and the three types of metals used (carbon steel, stainless steel, and plated). Table 1 lists the principal brands of blades marketed at the end of 1972.

Table 1 Blades Actively Marketed—December 1972

Manufacturer	Brand Name	System Type				Metal Type		
		Double-edged	Injector	Bonded	Band	Stainless	Carbon	Plated
Gillette	Super Blue	X					X	
	Super Stainless	X	X			X		
	Plus	X						
	Trac II			X				X
	Techmatic				X			X
Schick	Super Stainless	X	X			X		
	Super Krona Chrome	X	X					
	Instamatic				X			X
Wilkinson	Super Sword	X				X		
	Wilkinson II	X						X
	Wilkinson Bonded			X				X

The Market

Unit sales of razor blades had averaged 2 percent annual growth in recent years. Trends toward more expensive plated blades had resulted in a 6 percent annual retail dollar sales volume growth through the 1960's. Table 2 shows retail sales of blades between 1970 and 1972.

Sales were neither seasonally or regionally skewed to any significant extent. Distribution was through a very wide range of outlets including food and drug stores (accounting for 70 percent of retail sales), department stores, "jug milk" outlets, variety stores, barber shops, etc.

Market Segments

Although double-edged blades accounted for 73 percent of blades sold in 1972, the injector and bonded segments had increased in importance in recent years. The growth of injector and bonded blades appeared to have come at the expense of the double-edged and band segments.

In both the double-edged and the injector segments, growth in recent years had been in the plated blades; however, stainless steel blades remained the major metal type in both segments. In part, this was believed to be a function of the lower distribution obtained for the plated blades and in part a reflection of the premium price (approximately 13 percent) that manufacturers charged for their plated blades compared with the stainless steel brands. Major segments of the razor blade market are shown in table 3, and competitive prices of razor blades are shown in table 4.

Competition

The Canadian razor blade market was dominated by three companies: Gillette (41 percent market share), Schick (28 percent), and Wilkinson (23 percent). Details of market share are shown in table 5.

Table 2   The Canadian Razor Blade Market (Retail Sales)

	1970	1971	1972
Blades (millions)	155.0	156.5	154.2
Dollars (millions)	21.3	23.0	24.1
Food store percent	40.7	40.0	40.1
Drug store percent	28.3	29.0	29.0
Other percent	31.0	31.0	29.9

Table 3 The Canadian Razor Blade Market

	1970		1971		1972	
	Blades (millions)	Percent	Blades (millions)	Percent	Blades (millions)	Percent
Double-edged						
Stainless	81.5	52.5	73.6	47.0	63.8	41.4
Plated	28.5	18.4	34.4	22.0	37.0	24.0
Carbon	20.5	13.3	18.8	12.0	12.3	8.0
Total double-edged	130.5	84.2	126.8	81.0	113.1	73.4
Injector						
Stainless	15.8	10.2	16.3	10.4	17.0	11.0
Plated	1.1	0.8	4.7	3.0	6.8	4.4
Total injector	16.9	11.0	21.0	13.4	23.8	15.4
Bonded	—	—	1.9	1.2	12.2	7.9
Band	7.4	4.8	6.9	4.4	5.1	3.3
Total market	154.8	100.0	156.6	100.0	154.2	100.0

Table 4   Comparative Prices of Razor Blades, January 1973

		Suggested Retail Price	Suggested Retail Price per Blade
Double-edged			
Stainless	5s	$0.79	$0.158
	10s	1.49	0.149
Plated	5s	0.89	0.178
	10s	1.69	0.169
Injector			
Stainless	7s	1.09	0.156
	11s	1.59	0.145
Plated	6s	1.09	0.182
	11s	1.79	0.163
Bonded			
Trac II	5s	1.10	0.220
Wilkinson	5s	1.10	0.220

Table 5   Competitive Division of the Razor Blade Market

	1970	1971	1972
Double-edged			
Gillette	40.0	37.8	33.7
Schick	13.9	13.7	12.7
Wilkinson	20.3	20.3	18.8
Others	10.0	9.2	8.2
	84.2	81.0	73.4
Injector			
Schick	9.8	12.1	14.5
Gillette	1.1	1.1	0.9
Others	0.1	0.2	
	11.0	13.4	15.4
Bonded			
Gillette			4.1
Wilkinson		1.2	3.8
		1.2	7.9
Band			
Schick	1.5	1.2	0.7
Gillette	3.3	3.2	2.6
Others			
	4.8	4.4	3.3

Gillette had lost overall market share in 1971 and 1972, despite the introduction of Trac II. Both Schick and Wilkinson had improved their positions in recent years. Table 6 shows share of market by company.

Wilkinson

Wilkinson Bonded was launched in May 1971 as a "unique" shaving system. This was a single-edged blade bonded into a plastic cartridge. It was positioned as offering "the most comfortable, the most cut-free shave that modern technology can offer." Advertising support for this positioning was based on the bonding of Wilkinson's best blade into a plastic cartridge at a precise angle for comfortable shaving.

In 1971, Wilkinson supported Wilkinson Bonded with $150,000 in advertising and $300,000 in trade promotion allowances to achieve distribution and display. Although no sampling was carried out, Wilkinson did offer "free shaves" at selected barber shops in major metropolitan areas. In 1972, Wilkinson spent $210,000 on media advertising and an estimated $440,000 in trade promotional allowances and consumer promotions.

During 1972, Wilkinson Bonded appeared to grow quite steadily in market share; however, the November/December 1972 sales period showed a decline in market share.

WILKINSON BONDED SHARE OF RETAIL SALES (BLADE UNITS)

1971 Year	1972 J/F	M/A	M/J	J/A	S/O	N/D	1972 Year
1.2	2.0	2.1	3.1	3.2	4.1	3.0	3.8

Wilkinson Bonded was also premium priced relative to double-edged and injector blades. Five cartridges sold for $1.10.

While Wilkinson's main marketing thrust had been behind the Wilkinson Bonded brand, the company had continued to support the Wilkinson

Table 6 Share of Razor Blade Market by Company (Retail Sales, Blade Unit Basis)

	1970	1971	1972
Gillette	44.4	42.1	41.3
Schick	25.2	27.0	27.9
Wilkinson	20.3	21.5	22.6
Other	10.1	9.4	8.2

II (plated) brand. Wilkinson II received $150,000 in media support in 1971 and $120,000 in 1972. In addition, the brand was supported with competitive trade promotional allowances. Wilkinson II was positioned as "a high-quality blade, giving a clean, close, and comfortable shave." Support for this positioning was based on "traditional, British craftsmanship." Wilkinson's stainless steel brand, Wilkinson Sword, had been supported only with trade promotion allowances through 1971 and 1972.

Gillette

In January 1972, Gillette launched Trac II, a shaving system consisting of two single-edged blades bonded into a cartridge. Gillette backed the launch of Trac II with strong consumer and trade advertising support, consumer promotions, and trade merchandising incentives:

1. In 1971, $300,000 was spent on magazine and television advertising.
2. A million free razor handles (demonstration quality) and single cartridges were distributed by mail. Along with these samples 1,000,000 refund offers were distributed. The refund offered 50¢ off the regular retail price of a Trac II kit (consisting of a regular razor handle and five cartridges).
3. In-store and magazine advertising offered a $1.00 refund to anyone purchasing a Trac II razor kit and sending such proof of purchase to Gillette.

The Schick marketing group estimated that Gillette spent $950,000 on Trac II in 1972. This compared with the $900,000 Schick spent that year on its injector system.

In addition to the activities mentioned above, Gillette offered discounts to retailers of between 8.3 percent and 20 percent in order to stimulate the initial distribution of Trac II, its display in prime locations in stores, and discounted pricing.

Trac II was positioned both to the consumer and to the trade as a major product innovation in wet shaving. Consumer advertising claimed that Trac II provided "the closest shave possible." Advertising copy stressed the advantages of twin blades.

Gillette built rapid distribution for Trac II; by the end of 1972, it was available in all major outlets. As distribution built, and the advertising and promotional programs were executed, Trac II began to increase its market share.

TRAC II SHARE OF RETAIL SALES (BLADES) 1972

J/F	M/A	M/J	J/A	S/O	N/D	Year
0.5	1.9	3.0	5.1	6.2	7.2	4.1

This share penetration was achieved despite a substantial premium price of $1.10 for five cartridges. This was 22¢ per cartridge compared with 16–18¢ for plated injector or double-edged blades and 15–16¢ for stainless steel blades.

While actively supporting the launch of Trac II, Gillette had not ignored the double-edged segment. Gillette Platinum Plus, its improved plated blade, was positioned as the brand that gave "the smoothest shave" and supported with $100,000 in television advertising plus trade promotional support. Gillette's Super Stainless blade, positioned as "the best selling blade that gives the most comfortable shave," was also actively supported with $110,000 in television advertising and trade promotional allowances.

Schick

Between 1969 and 1971, Schick invested heavy advertising and promotional support behind the Krona Chrome and Super Krona Chrome blades, hoping to capitalize on Schick's slender lead in the introduction of plated blades. However, the rapid response of Gillette and Wilkinson thwarted much of Schick's efforts. It became apparent to the Schick marketing group that concentration of marketing efforts on the double-edged Super Krona Chrome brand was not resulting in any increase in market share for the brand.

By the end of the second quarter of 1971, Schick had not increased its share of the double-edged segment at all compared with 1970, and factory sales had actually declined 5 percent compared with the first six months of 1970. In sharp contrast, the unadvertised Schick injector system was increasing its market share in response to promotional programs (limited sampling and trade promotion allowances to encourage display and feature pricing) and increased distribution. Factory sales were up 23 percent compared with the first half of 1971.

The major consumer usage and attitude study conducted for Schick in the first quarter of 1971 had yielded some important conclusions (exhibit 1):

1. The consumer was confused about the various types of metals used in razor blades and neither understood nor appreciated the claims made by manufacturers about their "new, improved products."

2. The image of injector razors held by double-edged blade users was generally good. However, double-edged users felt that they would get fewer shaves per blade with an injector razor. Despite this, research indicated that, on average, users of injector razors actually got the same number of shaves per blade as did users of double-edged blades.

3. Only 9 percent of blade users were actually using injector systems; it was estimated that less than 30 percent of all blade users had ever tried an injector razor.

4. Injector blade penetration was highest among young shavers, declining with increasing age.

The Schick marketing group also had available to it Australian research on the injector system. In Australia, a three-week in-home consumer test of the injector system had been conducted. Results showed that the number of people who indicated that they would probably or definitely buy the Schick injector system *doubled* following trial, from 37 percent pre-trial to 71 percent post-trial.

An additional factor helped determine Schick's marketing strategy. The cost-of-goods structure on Schick blades actually made it advantageous, in terms of gross profit per blade, for Schick to convert its double-edged users to the injector system.

Exhibit 1 Excerpts from the 1971 Study of Canadian Blade Consumers

The objective of this study was to determine which men used razors, how they used them and how they felt about different shaving systems. The study showed that, of men who shave, 57 percent shave daily, 20 percent between four and six times per week, and 23 percent between one and three times per week. Of these shavers, 52 percent used a blade exclusively, 32 percent use only an electric razor, and 16 percent used both depending on the circumstances. Two out of five current blade users had once used an electric razor but had switched to wet shaving "to get a closer shave." Over two thirds of present electric razor users had once used a blade, but had switched to electric "to get a faster shave."

On the average, consumers expected to get six shaves per blade. This average did not differ significantly among carbon, stainless, or plated blade users, nor did it vary between users of double-edged or injector systems. One in three wet shavers identified closeness as the most important characteristic of a shave. In addition, 21 percent identified comfort; 15 percent, safety; 11 percent, smoothness; 10 percent, speed; and 6 percent, long-lasting as the most important characteristic. Among the wet shavers, 86 percent used double-edged systems; 9 percent, injector; and 5 percent, band razors.

Respondents were asked to name the first brand of razor blade that came to mind (top-of-mind awareness) and all brands that they could remember (share-of-

Exhibit 1 (continued)

mind awareness). They were then asked to show the interviewer the blade they last shaved with (brand used last). See the first table below.

When asked why they preferred their particular brand, consumers generally expressed the view that they got "the best, closest shave" from their brand or that "it gave them the most comfortable shave," as shown in the second table below. Seventy-nine percent of all blade users stated that they always purchased the same brand. Respondents were asked what advantages they felt their current shaving systems had over other systems. The results are shown in the last two tables in this exhibit.

PERCENT OF RESPONDENTS NAMING EACH BRAND

	Top-of-Mind	Share-of-Mind[a]	Used Last
Gillette			
Blue/Super Blue	24	64	6
Stainless/Super Stainless	13	35	19
Plus	3	29	9
Unspecified	10	33	4
Schick			
Stainless/Super Stainless	13	36	17
Krona Chrome/Super Krona Chrome	4	24	6
Unspecified	5	21	2
Wilkinson			
Super Sword	17	48	20
Wilkinson II	3	12	6
Unspecified	3	23	1
Miscellaneous	5	21	10

a. Columns add to more than 100 percent because of multiple responses.

PERCENT OF RESPONDENTS STATING
REASONS FOR BRAND/SYSTEM PREFERENCE

	Double-Edged Users			Injector Users
	Schick	Gillette	Wilkinson[a]	All Brands
More shaves per blade	26	19	32	15
Better/closer shave	32	23	37	32
More comfortable shave	14	10	11	23
Generally prefer	28	38	30	30
No reason given	—	10	—	—

a. Columns add to more than 100 percent because of multiple responses.

Exhibit 1 (continued)

PERCENT OF RESPONDENTS STATING
ADVANTAGES OF INJECTOR RAZORS COMPARED
TO DOUBLE-EDGED SYSTEMS

| | Double-Edged Users | | | Injector Users |
	Schick	Gillette	Wilkinson[a]	All Brands
Convenient/easy to handle	8	9	12	42
Safer	4	12	6	34
Better/closer/cleaner shave	2	3	1	33
Faster	2	1	3	10
More shaves per blade	1	3	—	7
None	29	21	27	3
Never used one	29	21	27	—
No reason given	25	30	24	

a. Columns add to more than 100 percent because of multiple responses.

PERCENT OF RESPONDENTS STATING
ADVANTAGES OF DOUBLE-EDGED RAZORS COMPARED
TO INJECTOR SYSTEMS

| | Double-Edged Users | | | Injector Users |
	Schick	Gillette	Wilkinson	All Brands
Convenient/easy to handle	4	9	13	4
More shaves per blade	45	46	47	30
Better/closer/cleaner shave	17	13	16	8
Faster	9	7	9	2
Safer	9	4	5	3
No reason given	16	21	10	53

Based on these considerations, the Schick group recommended drastic alterations in the marketing strategy for Schick razor blades.

1. The thrust of advertising would be directed behind the Schick injector system. The system would be positioned as "the most convenient and easiest to handle shaving system." The major emphasis would be on the *system*, with only secondary emphasis on the blade metal type.

2. Advertising of the injector system would be accompanied by heavy sampling of an injector handle and two blades. Emphasis would be put on sampling younger shavers, whose shaving habits were not fully established.

3. Schick would sharply reduce advertising expenditures on its double-edged brands and support them only with trade promotion allowances to maintain distribution and competitive pricing.

Schick Marketing Activities, 1971–1972

Advertising

Schick spent $240,000 in measured media (all in television) in support of Schick Injector in the second half of 1971. In 1972, $450,000 was spent on television advertising. The advertising positioned the Schick injector system as giving "the closest, most comfortable shave because of its lightness, maneuverability, and convenience."

Advertising support for Schick double-edged brands was cut back in the second half of 1971. The first-half expenditure of $268,000 was reduced to $154,000 in the second half of 1971. Advertising on the double-edged brands was totally in the second half.

Sampling

In 1971, Schick sampled 475,000 injector razor kits to consumers, each consisting of a razor handle and two or three blades. This consumer sampling program cost $140,000, or 29.5¢ for each kit delivered. In 1972 the kits sampled were increased to 700,000 at a cost of $200,000 (28.6¢ per kit).

After direct cost of goods and all trade discounts were accounted for (but not contribution to corporate overhead, selling costs, advertising, or market research), the Schick group estimated that the profit per stainless steel injector blade was 4¢, and for a plated blade this increased to 5¢.

If a sample cost 30¢ and successfully created a *new* user who was not a user of any other Schick system, this new user would "pay back" the cost of the sample given to him in five-to-seven weeks. However, it was not possible to control within reasonable costs the distribution of samples. Therefore, it sometimes happened that samples were given to people who already used the Schick brand. In such cases, the real cost of sampling was the cost of the sample, plus the lost revenue the company would have realized from the blades that user would have bought at normal prices.

On balance, the Schick marketing group thought that the sampling program had been instrumental in increasing Schick's market share.

Trade Promotion

Trade promotional allowances were given on both the double-edged and injector brands. The purpose of these allowances was to allow Schick to remain competitive with both Wilkinson and Gillette in terms of retail pricing and the display space given to the brands by retailers.

Results

The changes in emphasis for the period can best be seen in the Schick operating results for 1971–1972 (table 7).

Table 7   Schick Double-Edged and Injector Operating Results

	1970 ($000)	Percent	1971 ($000)	Percent	1972 ($000)	Percent
Double-edged						
Net sales	1593	100.0	1604	100.0	1716	100.0
Cost of goods[a]	412	25.9	403	25.1	437	25.4
Promotion						
Trade	300	18.8	200	12.5	400	23.3
Consumer	69	4.3	78	4.9	34	2.0
Total	369	23.2	278	17.3	434	25.3
Advertising						
Measured media	572	35.9	422	26.3	109	6.4
Other	10	0.6	5	0.3	20	1.2
Total	584	36.6	427	26.6	129	7.5
Market research	40	2.5	11	0.7	20	1.2
Operating	18	1.1	18	1.1	19	1.1
Marginal profit	170	10.7	467	29.1	677	39.5
Injector						
Net sales	1322	100.0	1660	100.0	1994	100.0
Cost of goods[a]	308	23.3	404	24.3	471	23.6
Promotion						
Trade	100	7.6	106	6.4	150	7.5
Consumer	45	3.5	140	8.4	293	14.7
Total	145	11.0	246	14.8	443	22.2
Advertising						
Measured media			240	14.5	450	22.6
Other	12	0.8	40	2.4	80	4.0
Total	12	0.8	280	16.9	530	26.6
Market research			10	0.6	13	0.7
Operating	17	1.3	13	0.8	22	1.1
Marginal profit	840	63.5	707	42.6	515	25.8

a. Represents variable cost of goods only and does not include any overhead such as amortization of plant and equipment, indirect labour costs, contribution to corporate overhead (selling, administration, research and development, etc.), or indirect expenses.

Table 7 (continued)

	1970 ($000)	Percent	1971 ($000)	Percent	1972 ($000)	Percent
Total						
Net sales	2915	100.0	3264	100.0	3710	100.0
Cost of goods[a]	720	24.7	807	24.7	908	24.5
Promotion						
Trade	400	13.7	306	9.4	550	14.8
Consumer	114	3.9	218	6.7	327	8.8
Total	514	17.6	524	16.1	877	23.6
Advertising						
Measured media	572	19.6	662	20.3	559	15.1
Other	22	0.7	45	1.4	100	2.7
Total	594	20.4	707	21.7	659	17.8
Market research	40	1.4	21	0.6	33	0.9
Operating	35	1.2	31	0.9	41	1.1
Marginal profit	1010	34.6	1174	36.0	1192	32.1

a. Represents variable cost of goods only and does not include any overhead such as amortization of plant and equipment, indirect labour costs, contribution to corporate overhead (selling, administration, research and development, etc.), or indirect expenses.

Schick Cartridge Razor

Gillette Trac II was introduced into Canada in 1972. Prior to the launch, the Schick marketing group had commissioned some research involving a series of six group discussions. The shavers who participated in these groups were asked to compare the Trac II system with double-edged systems or injector systems.

The research indicated that Trac II gave a technically excellent shave. It was considered superior to double-edged shaves by double-edged users, but was only considered comparable to injector blades by regular users of injector systems. Most shavers expressed some cynicism about the Trac II concept, and some expressed strong resistance to cost.

On the basis of this research the Schick group concluded that Gillette could be successful if they could overcome resistance to the Trac II concept by inducing trial and overcome resistance to the high cost of sampling, offering incentives in the form of redeemable coupons or similar activities. Trac II's superiority over double-edged systems was more pronounced than over injector systems; therefore, it was felt that Trac II posed a greater danger to the double-edged brands than to the Schick injector system.

During 1972, Gillette Trac II market share increased from 0.5 to 7.2 percent. Concerned about this rapid market growth, Warner-Lambert Canada estimated the costs of producing a twin-bladed cartridge system similar to Trac II. Based on importing cartridges from the United States (where Schick marketed such a product under the brand name Super II), Warner-Lambert Canada would have a gross marginal profit of $5.00 per 100 blades compared with $7.10 per 100 for injector blades and $6.60 for double-edged blades.

Investigations were underway to determine costs involved in manufacturing a cartridge razor in Canada. Preliminary estimates indicated a capital expenditure of $500,000 for equipment, but a lead time of at least nine months before local manufacture could be established. However, with such local manufacture, it was believed that the cost of goods could be reduced to the level that, if priced at parity with Trac II and Wilkinson Bonded, the gross marginal profit could be $7.00 to $7.25 per 100 blades.

Schick in the United States had launched Super II, a direct competitor to Trac II, in March 1972. As shown in table 8, growth of this brand had been slow compared to the growth of Trac II.

In January 1973, the market group had to weigh the advantages and disadvantages of proceeding with a Schick Super II product in Canada. Whether or not they recommended such a move, there was a clear need to develop new strategies for the complete Schick line that would counter the Trac II market penetration.

**Table 8 Schick Super II and Gillette Trac II
Market Shares (U.S.) (1972, $U.S. basis)**

	J/F	M/A	M/J	J/A	S/O	N/D
Gillette Trac II	4.6	5.2	7.3	9.3	11.3	13.5
Schick Super II		0.2	0.5	1.3	2.1	2.5
Schick Injector	13.9	14.0	13.8	13.9	12.6	12.6
Schick double-edged	10.6	10.4	9.8	9.0	8.9	7.7
Total Schick	24.5	24.6	24.1	24.2	23.6	22.8

14 Jouets du Monde

In March 1976, M. Henri Jolivet, the buyer for Division 4 (metal, plastic, and wood model kits, construction toys, etc.) of Jouets du Monde, was considering what action to take on his Hi-brix line of construction toys, which were now facing new and significant Japanese competition. Decisions were required soon so that orders could be placed and plans firmed up for the fall selling season.

Jouets du Monde was a Canadian chain of toy and hobby stores with eight locations spread through the major urban centres in Eastern Canada—Toronto, Ottawa, Montreal, Quebec, St. John's and Halifax. The company had been immensely successful in the decades of the 1950's and 1960's and had developed a reputation for both breadth and depth in toy merchandising. It was, some observers noted, the *only* place in Eastern Canada where certain specialty toy and hobby lines could be obtained. While still profitable, the company in the early 1970's had come under increasing competitive pressure, particularly in the higher-volume standard toy lines, from department stores, other specialty retailers, warehouse type outlets, and so on. As a result, sales growth had slowed, and profitability as a percent of sales and return on operating assets had dropped. Attempts to find noncompetitive or unique lines had made some progress but at the cost of greater inventory investments due to slower turns and the emergence of what some called a cluttered look in the stores. Pressed by these circumstances, management was asking all personnel to give greater attention to returns on inventory investment and shelf space.

Hi-brix

The Hi-brix line of construction toys was based on a miniature rubber interlocking brick patented by a European manufacturer. By means of these bricks and several small accessories, such as windows, doors, etc., a child could construct model homes, castles, vehicles, even space ships. By purchasing progressively larger sets, more elaborate structures could be built.

The Hi-brix line had been marketed in toy stores and department stores in Canada for many years and was very well known as a high-quality high-priced toy that had certain educational benefits for the child. The European manufacturer had always provided advertising and promotional support and had controlled distribution to the end that recommended retail prices were by and large observed by all outlets. Sales were made throughout the year with a peak in the pre-Christmas period.

Hi-brix at Jouets du Monde

Jouets du Monde imported the Hi-brix line direct from Frankfurt, ordering the bulk of its estimated annual requirements in March for the subsequent year. Smaller orders could be placed throughout the year to fill in popular items, but this tended to be expensive in terms of shipping and order processing costs.

In preparation for placing his 1976 order, M. Jolivet compiled some historical data on the aggregate performance of the Hi-brix line (table 1).

As M. Jolivet well knew the Hi-brix line had come under competitive fire in the past two years from the entry of a Japanese toy set, which was apparently copied from the Hi-brix line. The Japanese product, branded O-hio, was of good quality and resembled Hi-brix in many ways, except that it was not compatible in use because square rather than round studs were used to interlock the pieces. It was imported by a distributor who operated in Western Canada and was priced to sell at retail at approximately two thirds of the price of an equivalent Hi-brix line.

In the first year after introduction, the O-hio line achieved distribution largely through nontraditional outlets for toys; but in the past year several

Table 1

Fiscal Year End Jan. 30	Units Sold	Average Per Unit Retail Price ($)	Gross Margin* ($)	Closing Inventory at Cost ($ × 1000)
1971	17,100	20.15	9.91	94.1
1972	19,700	17.50	8.58	98.9
1973	21,600	16.80	8.08	127.4
1974	23,200	19.10	8.88	130.8
1975	21,400	17.20	7.77	153.4
1976	16,100	18.40	9.02	139.7

*After transportation, brokerage, etc., but before promotional allowances.

department stores and other direct competitors had taken the line, and, in the process, some had dropped Hi-brix. M. Jolivet had discussed the Japanese line with the distributor and determined that the full line would be available to Jouets du Monde. Taking the average of several similar items, M. Jolivet came up with the following comparisons:

HI-BRIX		O-HIO	
Current retail price	*Current cost**	*Recommended retail price*	*Current cost*
$17.40	9.40	$12.60	5.40

*After transportation, brokerage, etc., but before consideration of promotional allowances.

M. Jolivet had appealed to the European manufacturer for lower purchase prices to meet the new competition, initially to no avail. Then, in the past year, the promotional allowance for Hi-brix had been increased from 5 to 15 percent of purchases. Jouets du Monde had traditionally spent the full promotional allowance provided for the line on media advertising and point-of-sale materials. There was no promotional allowance available on the O-hio brand.

Up to this point, M. Jolivet had rejected the notion of stocking both brands. He realized that if he did, unit inventories would have to be almost doubled (because most of the inventory was located on or under the shelves in the stores) and that shelf space as well would have to be expanded. M. Jolivet estimated that in fiscal 1976 Hi-brix inventory was stored in 175 square feet and that 100 linear feet of shelf space were given to the Hi-brix line. Table 2 shows comparable data for previous years. He felt it very unlikely that sales would increase correspondingly, although there was some hope for modest unit sales increases.

Table 2

Fiscal Year End Jan. 30	*Inventory Space (sq. ft.)*	*Shelf Space (linear feet)*
1971	100	80
1972	120	90
1973	170	100
1974	160	100
1975	180	100
1976	175	100

15 The Cold-flo_{TM} Ammonia Converter— Imperial Oil Limited

In Edmonton in May 1978, John Singer was considering an offer for the exclusive distributorship of an innovative fertilizer applicator called the Cold-flo Converter. As Field Services Co-ordinator of Agricultural Chemicals for Imperial Oil (the Exxon Canadian affiliate), he felt that the converter would be an improved method for applying the popular fertilizer, anhydrous ammonia. John wondered if prairie farmers would accept the new applicator and if Imperial Oil should be directly involved in selling the applicator.

Background Information

Imperial Oil entered the fertilizer market in 1963 with Engro fertilizer in granular form. This was done for two reasons. First, a major competitor, Federated Co-op Ltd. of Saskatchewan, sold both petroleum and fertilizer, while Imperial Oil distributed only petroleum. As a defensive move, Imperial Oil entered the fertilizer market with fertilizer purchased from Cominco. Second, Imperial Oil entered the fertilizer market to provide increased earning opportunities for its independent Esso agents. Prior to the introduction of fertilizer, Esso agents had depended on bulk petroleum and lubricants for their income.

In 1965, Imperial Oil realized that service demands for fertilizer had changed. A more efficient distribution system was needed. The company commenced a test building program for fertilizer warehouses and a manufacturing feasibility study.

In 1966 and 1967, Imperial Oil completed construction of the field warehouse network at a cost of seven million dollars.

In 1969, the company built a $57,000,000 fertilizer plant in Redwater, Alberta, with an annual capacity of 500,000 tons. Several bottlenecks in the plant had been worked out since 1969, and the plant's present capacity was about 700,000 tons.

In 1971, Imperial Oil added anhydrous ammonia (NH_3) to the Engro family of fertilizers. NH_3 was a big success. The total market for this product had grown from 20,000 tons in 1971 to about 155,000 tons in 1978. In 1978, the average ammonia customer purchased 13 tons. The total NH_3 market was expected to grow for many years at an annual rate of 10 to 11 percent. Imperial Oil's gross margin on NH_3 was more than twice the gross margin for granular fertilizers which was approximately 5 percent.

The total Prairie market for fertilizer was 1.5 million tons in the 1977–1978 crop year. Imperial Oil presently held about 21 percent of this market. In Alberta, Imperial Oil's severest competition came from Sherritt-Gordon, a large mining company, and Western Co-ops Ltd.[1] Sherritt-Gordon had a plant in Alberta and marketed aggressively through a network of independent dealers and wholesaled through the United Grain Growers (UGG) elevator chain. Another major competitor in Alberta was Cominco. Cominco, owned by one of Canada's largest firms, CP Investments, had a network of independent dealers who sold Elephant Brand fertilizer. In Saskatchewan, the Saskatchewan Wheat Pool had a major chunk of the market. The Prairie Wheat Pools, UGG, and Federated Co-op, all depended heavily on the "Co-op doctrinaire" segments of the prairie population (about 40 percent). John Singer estimated that half of the co-operative segment always patronized the Wheat Pools. The other half, primarily larger farmers, could be lured away by Imperial Oil if Esso agents offered equally attractive prices and better service. Compared to the Wheat Pools, Esso agents were more likely to have application equipment and products available when needed, and were more willing to work after hours to supply service to customers. The Wheat Pools, as farmer owned co-operatives, repatriated profits to customers at the end of the crop year. The dividends returned on fertilizer sales had been as high as 10 percent of the purchase price.

Anhydrous Ammonia and Other Fertilizers

There are three types of fertilizer: granular (crystals and pellets of fertilizer), solution (fertilizer mixed with water), and gas (NH_3). Imperial Oil did not sell solutions, although two of its competitors, Manitoba Wheat

---

1. Western Co-operatives Ltd. was owned by the Alberta, Manitoba, and Saskatchewan Wheat Pools and Federated Co-op. Western Co-ops and Cominco had both completed major expansions to their fertilizer production facilities in the last two years.

Pool and Simplot, did. John Singer knew that Imperial Oil had not found solutions profitable. Solutions were also the most expensive form of fertilizer to the farmer.

Consumption (in tons) of the best selling nitrogen fertilizers ranked as in table 1.

Granular fertilizer was used across the prairies. Anhydrous ammonia was used primarily in Alberta, although it was expanding rapidly into Saskatchewan and Manitoba. Solutions were prevalent in Saskatchewan and Manitoba.

These fertilizers could be distinguished from one another by the percentages they contained of the nutrients Nitrogen (N), Phosphate (P_2O_5) Potash (K_2O), and Sulphur (S). For instance, 21-0-0-24 indicated a fertilizer that contained 21 percent N, 0 percent P_2O_5, 0 percent K_2O and 24 percent S. While all crops were physiologically indifferent to their source of nutrients, different crops used varying amounts of nutrients. Also, soil types affected the form and amount of fertilizer required.

Granular fertilizers were applied by spreading them over the surface of the soil ("top dressing") or by drilling them into the soil with seed. Solution fertilizer was sprayed on the soil. Anhydrous ammonia was injected into the soil as a liquid using a specially equipped tillage tool that plowed the liquid in the ground.

Anhydrous ammonia application presently required an NH_3 tank and truck (for agent-to-farm delivery) and an NH_3 applicator. Conversion kits could be installed on conventional tillage equipment as well. These were

Table 1

Name	1974–1975 Season	1975–1976 Season	1976–1977 Season
Anhydrous ammonia	81,585	127,309	145,872
Ammonium nitrate	207,687	239,673	202,394
Ammonium sulphate	54,499	64,891	44,194
Urea	86,843	105,416	144,161
Urea ammonium nitrate solution	20,266	24,504	40,084
Total	450,880	561,793	576,705

less costly but less efficient than a standard NH_3 applicator. Presently, 90 percent of prairie ammonia customers used the conventional applicators, and 10 percent used the conversion kits.

Regardless of the application method used, it was important that the NH_3 be injected at least 6–8 inches (15–20 cm) in the soil. If the NH_3 was injected too shallowly or under adverse soil or moisture conditions, the liquid NH_3 quickly vaporized with the reduction of pressure and temperature increase and the gaseous NH_3 would escape from the soil.

Anhydrous ammonia could be applied in the fall or spring. In the fall, cooler soil temperatures reduced the loss of NH_3 due to evaporation. However, spring application was more popular. In the spring, farmers were more certain of their cropping plans and could judge accurately the amount of nitrogen that the soil required. Also, for sandy soils, spring NH_3 application reduced the risk of leaching loss. The seasonal demand for fertilizers has resulted in dealers' being unable to supply fertilizer and application equipment in sufficient quantities to meet demand during peak periods.

Anhydrous ammonia had to be carefully handled because it could burn exposed skin by freezing. Exposure to high concentrations of NH_3 vapour or liquid could be fatal. However, NH_3 was easily detected by its pungent odour and first aid was very simple: apply lots of water.

The Cold-flo Ammonia Converter

The Cold-flo Converter was developed by United States Steel (USS) in conjunction with researchers at Pennsylvania State University. USS had marketed the converter as part of its "conserve America's energy resources" advertising strategy. The offer by USS for exclusive distributorship of the Cold-flo system was made to Imperial Oil by accident: representatives of the two companies had met during rock phosphate negotiations in April 1977. A tentative verbal agreement giving Imperial Oil exclusive distribution rights for three years was made in June 1977. John Singer had to present his recommendations to the Field Services Manager, Doug Mackenzie, late in June 1978. A final decision had to be made at that time.

The Cold-flo Converter consisted of a small cylindrical chamber that changed NH_3 to a liquid at atmospheric pressure. The conventional application applies to NH_3 as a gas under slight pressure. The converter had two basic functions; it served as an expansion chamber for pressure release and separated liquid ammonia from ammonia vapour. Ammonia was metered into the converter from a nurse tank by means of a regulator. After conversion, the liquid ammonia flowed by gravity from the bottom of the converter through a manifold and hose system into the soil. Vapourized ammonia exited from the top of the converter to a second manifold and hose system into the soil. About 85 percent of the NH_3 was a liquid and 15 percent vapour.

The Cold-flo Converter had several advantages. It was a low-cost method of fertilizer application because the ammonia could be applied as the soil was tilled. This meant that one trip over the field was eliminated and time, equipment wear, labour, and fuel were saved.[2] Also, herbicides could be incorporated into the application procedure. The Cold-flo system could be used on soil too heavy for use of a conventional applicator for NH_3.

Because the Cold-flo Converter applied NH_3 to the soil as a liquid, sealing problems (holding the gaseous NH_3 in the soil) were minimized, and shallower application was possible. Ammonia could be applied to the soil as shallow as 4 inches (10 cm) deep near the feeder roots of most crops. Deeper placement was recommended for coarse-textured soils.

The Cold-flo Converter could be mounted on most standard field cultivators, chisel plows, or disc harrows. A farmer could purchase the mount or make one. In the United States, the Cold-flo Converter had been most widely used on field cultivators. The procedure for setting up the system varied only slightly for chisel plows and disc harrows.

The successful operation of the converter with any tillage equipment depended on four factors. First, there had to be proper calibration of the NH_3 regulator to the rate of application per acre to ensure proper rate of application. Second, liquid and vapour hoses had to be properly arranged so that the NH_3 flowed in a uniform and unrestricted fashion to ensure even application. Liquid hoses had to be downward sloping. Third, liquid and vapour attachments had to be properly placed to ensure complete coverage of the ammonia. Finally, the correct number of liquid and vapour outlets had to be used. United States Steel had developed tables for determining the proper number of outlets and the best application rates per hour per acre.

Some Considerations

The Cold-flo Converter had been tested by the Department of Land Resource Science at the University of Guelph. The results of the testing had been published by the Ontario Ministry of Agriculture and Food in

2. In the United States, the savings had been estimated at $1–2 per acre.

May 1978. The report found the converter to be simple and safe but also raised a number of questions.

The Ontario Ministry warned that heavy crop residues, wet soil conditions, or fine soil texture could increase the escape of vapourized NH_3 from the soil. Also, ammonia losses could result when the converter was used with a disc harrow because disc penetration was uneven and varied between 2 and 6 inches (5 and 15 cm). Further, the Ministry thought that the gravity flow system might be hampered when driving over sloped land. There was also a danger that the NH_3 would damage germinating seed if improperly applied. The Ministry acknowledged, however, that no published data existed that compared the Cold-flo system to other methods of nitrogen fertilizer application.

John Singer said any fertilizer was capable of damaging seed if improperly applied. He felt that the problem of seed damage had been satisfactorially solved by three methods used by American farmers familiar with Cold-flo. One method consisted of applying NH_3 at an angle or opposite to the direction of planting. Another method was simply to ensure that the NH_3 was applied at least 4 inches below the soil surface. Finally, a farmer could wait about a week after NH_3 application before planting.

It was possible that farmers, like the Ontario ministry, might overestimate the loss of vapourized NH_3 from the soil. This was because a white cloud could sometimes be observed rising from the soil where NH_3 had been applied. While some of this cloud could be gaseous ammonia, most of the vapour was water that condensed upon contact with the cold NH_3 liquid. Also, any loss of ammonia could be smelled around the tillage equipment.

Another aspect of Cold-flo merited consideration. If Imperial Oil marketed the system, the company would be able to associate itself with an innovative product. There was nothing to stop competitors from supplying NH_3 for the Cold-flo converter because the pressurized NH_3 tanks were standardized. Further, the demand for NH_3 exceeded supply in the prairie market. In the short term, Imperial Oil was unwilling to invest in storage and transportation equipment sufficient to supply all the present market in any one location because customers who "shopped around" for NH_3 would leave Esso agents once competitors had a local supply of NH_3 and were able to satisfy the customers in the area. John believed the NH_3 market to be dislocated due to these "growing pains," especially in Alberta.

An alternative existed to the Cold-flo system. A Nebraska firm had developed a "Can Converter" system that operated on the same principle as Cold-flo except that the cannister-like converters were small and mounted on each shank of the tillage equipment. USS had viewed the system as an infringement on its patent and had purchased the rights to the system, although the Can Converter system did not work nearly as efficiently as the Cold-flo system.

The Cold-flo Converter and Esso Agents

Imperial Oil had 450 Esso agents in the prairies, 70 of which sold anhydrous ammonia. These agents were independent businessmen who sold Imperial Oil products on a commission basis. They were serviced and supervised by 28 sales representatives in three areas.

Esso agents were encouraged by Imperial Oil to sell both petroleum and fertilizer products. Many agents, particularly in the small rural communities, had combined incomes. Along with Imperial Oil products, they sold everything from herbicides to insurance and equipment. Sometimes an agent was related to the farmers that he sold to.

Imperial Oil's best agent, located in Lacombe, sold 6000 tons of granular fertilizer a year. Two other Esso agents sold 5000 tons yearly. The vast majority of Esso agents sold between 1000 and 4000 tons of fertilizer yearly. Esso agents received a commission of $65 per ton of NH_3 sold and $10 per ton of bulk granular fertilizer sold. About 70 percent of the granular fertilizer sold by Esso agents was in bulk, rather than bagged.

Fertilizer sales were becoming an increasingly significant portion of agents' total income. This was due largely to the growth of NH_3 sales. An agent just starting to sell NH_3 could be virtually guaranteed of $25,000 in gross commissions in the first year with a $50,000 investment in equipment. Petroleum products did not have this growth factor. An agent earned 4–6¢ per gallon on fuels and lubricants and had to work all year to sell them. On both petroleum and fertilizer sales, agents would net about one third of their commissions.

In addition to selling Imperial Oil products, Esso agents rented fertilizer application equipment.[3] This service saved farmers from investing in little-used application equipment. Esso agents, along with farm radio and newspapers, were also a source of information. When fertilizer shortages

---

3.   Esso agents owned and financed all mobile equipment (e.g., fertilizer applicators, NH_3 nurse tank trailers, trucks). Imperial Oil owned all fixed equipment (e.g., warehouses, fertilizer tanks) and paid the depreciation and interest on mobile equipment. The pay-out period for mobile equipment was five years.

occurred in 1974 and 1978, the agents had advised farmers of the impending shortages and price increases.

This information service provided by agents could have a variety of effects. During fertilizer shortages, agents received a strict allocation of product. Naturally, the Esso agents wanted to ensure that their regular customers received fertilizer and so told them to order early. The agents hoped that this action would encourage their regular customers to remember them in the future if fertilizer prices dropped and the agents faced stiff competition. However, news of shortages caused farmers to "shop around" in an effort to obtain fertilizer. This behaviour heightened apparent demand.

As the price of fertilizer rose in a shortage situation, farmers often purchased more rather than less fertilizer. This was due in part to hoarding, but the major reason seemed to be the general economic outlook. In 1974 and 1978, the price of grain had risen; farmers believed that they could afford to purchase fertilizer and fertilizer purchases reduced their taxable income. The increase in yield resulting from the use of fertilizer more than offset the cost of buying and applying the product.

Esso agents also provided farmers with information concerning the safe handling of anhydrous ammonia. The agents could supply 20-minute audiovisual cassettes that explained NH_3 characteristics and handling procedures.

If Imperial Oil adopted the Cold-flo system, the agents would have to fulfill several requirements. These would be:

1. Supplying the NH_3 to existing nurse tanks and continuing to provide delivery of NH_3 to existing nurse tanks.

2. Using a Cold-flo installer from Esso Chemical to set up the initial unit at the agency and for troubleshooting thereafter. (Once the setup of the system was demonstrated, farmers would be able to install the equipment themselves.)

3. Encouraging farmers to request the installer early, since its availability would be limited prior to and during the fertilizer season.

4. Providing Cold-flo Converter kits to farmers composed of 1 Cold-flo Converter, liquid and vapour manifolds, and hoses.

5. Providing liquid and vapour dispensers designed for Cold-flo to be attached to the shanks of tillage tools.

6. Providing converter mounting stands.

7. Providing Cold-flo Splitters and extra manifolds for extra-wide tillage equipment.

Esso agents would obtain Cold-flo equipment from Esso Chemical. They would be invoiced on their 30-day merchandise accounts. Parts for Cold-flo equipment would be ordered by telephone. Delivery of parts from inventories held in Calgary and Winnipeg would normally take two to five days.

The selling price for the Cold-flo equipment could be kept under $1000.00. If the price was more than $1000.00 the agents would have to be licensed under the Provincial Farm Implements Act to sell farm equipment. Licensed dealers were controlled in that they were required to service equipment sold and meet other requirements such as keeping up repair parts for as long as one year after the sale of the equipment.

Customers should be aware that Imperial Oil was willing to refund the price of any Cold-flo unit found to be unsatisfactory with normal use. This guarantee would be good for 12 months after the date of purchase.

The Cold-flo Converter and Farmers

The rural areas of the prairies had undergone some major changes. Farms had decreased dramatically in number and increased in size (exhibits 1 and 2). There was an accelerating movement away from ownership of farm land and toward full tenancy and part tenancy and ownership.

The prairie farmer's investment in equipment was significant. A heavy-duty chisel plow (33-foot cultivator) could cost about $8600.00, and a 30-foot disc harrow could cost about $13,000.00. Four-wheel-drive tractors cost between $40,000.00 and $125,000.00, and harvesters could cost

Exhibit 1 Number of Farms in Canada

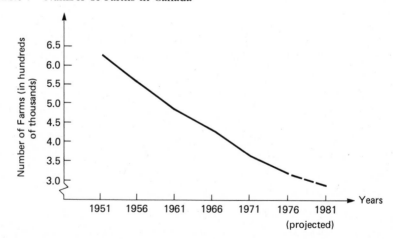

Exhibit 2   Size of Farms in Canada

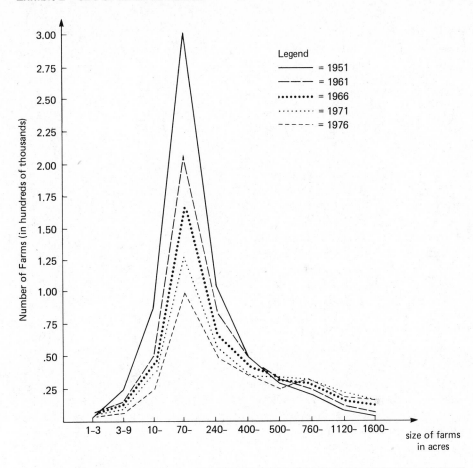

Legend

————	= 1951
– – – –	= 1961
••••••••	= 1966
··········	= 1971
– - – - –	= 1976

Number of Farms (in hundreds of thousands)

size of farms in acres

1-3   3-9   10-   70-   240-   400-   500-   760-   1120-   1600-

as much as $65,000.00. Farmers easily have $250,000.00 to $500,000.00 worth of equipment. A complete Cold-flo unit would cost a farmer about as much as the tires for his combine (see exhibit 3).

Fertilizer demand over certain periods was also strongly correlated to farm incomes. Increases in fertilizer demand typically lagged one year behind increases in farm income. Small farmers especially were often reticent about purchasing new equipment. They tended to purchase equipment when they could pay cash because a poor year could leave them with bills that could not be paid. For many Alberta farmers, owning modern equipment was a point of pride rather than a pure economic decision.

In order to convert a tillage tool to Cold-flo, a farmer would have to obtain Cold-flo equipment from an Esso agent. Some of this equipment

Exhibit 3 Pricing of the Cold-flo System

		Price Delivered To Agent	Suggested Retail Price
System 16	Converter package with 16 liquid outlets	$500.00	$560.00
System 24	Converter package with 24 liquid outlets	$530.00	$595.00
System 32	Converter package with 32 liquid outlets—This is a system 16 plus a flow splitter and an extra 16 outlet liquid manifold	$660.00	$745.00
System 48	Converter package with 48 liquid outlets—This is a system 24 plus a flow splitter and an extra 24 outlet liquid manifold	$750.00	$845.00
Type 1	Liquid dispenser for field cultivator	$ 3.25	$ 3.65
Type 2	Combination dispenser for chisel plow	$ 9.25	$ 10.40
Type 3	Combination dispenser for cultivator with trailing hose (for use in difficult soil conditions)	$ 5.65	$ 6.35
Type 4	Vapour dispenser for field cultivator	$ 3.25	$ 3.65
Converter mounting stand		$ 84.00	$ 94.50

could be made by the farmer (i.e., the converter mounting stand) or purchased from other suppliers (i.e., liquid and vapour dispensers). The Cold-flo system also required other ammonia equipment that was not normally supplied by Esso agents. This equipment included:

1 ammonia flow regulator

1 breakaway quick couple for the pressurized ammonia line from the nurse tank

vapour hose

vapour system hose clamps (2 per vapour line)

liquid system hose clamps (2 per liquid line)

4 U-bolts for mounting vapour manifolds to the implement frame

2 ammonia pressure hoses

1 hitch

Other prairie companies such as Agwest, Westeel, Rosco, and Norwesco supplied hoses, regulators and quick couples. Hose clamps and bolts were available from any hardware store.

The cost per ton of NH_3 would be reduced by $10 to Cold-flo users because the agent would not have to supply a conventional applicator. If a farmer already happened to own a nurse tank trailer as well, the cost per ton of NH_3 would be reduced by $20. In addition to the reduced cost of fertilizer, farmers with their own applicators should be less affected by shortages in equipment during peak application periods.

The Current Situation

USS had sold about 3000 units since the Cold-flo Converter had been introduced two years ago. USS had encountered some production constraints and claimed that an additional 4000 units could have been sold. Imperial had four alternatives with regard to Cold-flo:

1. Exclusive distribution through Esso agencies.
2. Marketing by Esso Chemical on a wholesale basis through the Esso agency system.
3. Nonexclusive distribution through Esso agencies.
4. Nonparticipation.

A preliminary testing of the Cold-flo system was done in the fall of 1977. Two units had been installed on a farm near Beiseker, Alberta. The units were reported to be running well after some modifications to the dispensers.

Three units had been tested in Manitoba near Portage, Winkler (a heavy soil area that restricted the use of conventional application equipment), and Brandon. The farmers were pleased with the performance of Cold-flo. Several inquiries about the Cold-flo system were generated, including inquiries by a Co-op and an Agwest dealer. A Hutterite colony near Beiseker requested two units for the spring of 1978. In total, 3000 acres were tested. Twenty-five to fifty units had been sold for the spring of 1978.

The distribution of the Cold-flo system in the Prairie could have the following benefits:

1. Increased ammonia volume for Esso agents: diversified approach (conventional applicators and Cold-flo) to serve a wider range of customer needs; sales of Cold-flo to customers whose needs do not justify tying up the agent's applicator; Cold-flo sales may draw in potential ammonia customers.

2. Enhancement of profitable ammonia sales versus less profitable granular fertilizer sales.

3. Reduction of the required agent investment per ton of fertilizer sales. Agent could build sales volume quickly.

4. Promotion of Imperial Oil's image of progress and leadership: innovative product, energy and labour saving.

Mr. Singer wasn't certain that all of the factors involving the Cold-flo decision had been considered. Basically, he wanted to know, "Should Imperial Oil market the Cold-flo converter and if so, how?"

Exhibit 4   Engro Posted Price History—Alberta Bulk ($/ton)

Date	82-0-0	34-0-0	46-0-0	21-0-0-24
Mar. 1971	$150.00	$ 71.00	$ 91.50	$41.00
June 1971	150.00	71.00	99.50	41.00
Sept. 1971	150.00	75.00	94.00	39.00
Dec. 1971	150.00	75.00	94.00	39.00
Mar. 1972	155.00	75.00	94.00	39.00
June 1972	155.00	75.00	94.00	39.00
Sept. 1972	155.00	76.00	92.00	42.00
Dec. 1972	155.00	76.00	92.00	45.00
Mar. 1973	155.00	76.00	92.00	45.00
June 1973	155.00	76.00	92.00	45.00
Sept. 1973	170.00	82.00	103.00	54.50
Dec. 1973	185.00	89.00	113.00	59.50
Mar. 1974	185.00	89.00	113.00	59.50
June 1974	185.00	89.00	113.00	59.50
Sept. 1974	215.00	100.00	135.00	75.00
Dec. 1974	285.00	100.00	182.00	95.00
Mar. 1975	255.00	135.00	169.00	95.00
June 1975	255.00	120.00	169.00	95.00
Sept. 1975	265.00	132.00	175.00	93.00
Dec. 1975	265.00	119.50	159.00	87.00

Exhibit 4   (continued)

Date	82-0-0	34-0-0	46-0-0	21-0-0-24
Mar. 1976	280.00	122.00	159.00	75.00
June 1976	280.00	132.00	164.00	83.00
Sept. 1976	260.00	122.00	159.00	74.00
Dec. 1976	250.00	122.00	159.00	74.00
Mar. 1977	270.00	125.00	159.00	79.00
June 1977	255.00	128.00	157.00	78.00
Sept. 1977	240.00	122.00	152.00	78.00
Dec. 1977	240.00	125.00	155.00	82.00
Mar. 1978	260.00	136.00	169.00	85.00

16 Bartaco Industries Limited

In September of 1978, Mr. Mel Element, Vice-President and General Manager of Bartaco Industries Limited, was reviewing the position of the company's Otaco seating division. Despite the development of an advanced product and an intensive selling effort, the Otaco seating division was not meeting Mr. Element's expectations for sales and profits.

Sales of buses had come to a grinding halt as the entire U.S. mass transit market paused to see whether President Carter would support the elderly and the handicapped, who had demanded and won, at least temporarily, more accommodating designs in mass transit vehicles. The pressure for new designs to permit total access of wheelchairs on all transit vehicles followed a move by the U.S. Department of Transportation (DOT) to develop a set of standard specifications for advanced Design Buses via the Transbus project. The RTS-2 bus designed by General Motors was meeting more acceptance from the city transit properties than the government-designed Transbus. However, the uncertainty in specifications was causing a number of bus purchases to be postponed.

The Otaco seating division held 95 percent of the Canadian market, which amounted to about two buses per day, most of them made by General Motors Canada. However, most of the Canadian sales had been for Otaco's traditional transit seat in which the margins were modest. After three years of development, Otaco people had designed a new public transit seat, the Innovator I, which appeared to have significant competitive advantages. The new seat already had been sold to a few Canadian and American transit companies, but the sales objectives for 1976 and 1977 had not been reached. The 1978 sales probably would be $3 million in traditional seats and $3 million in the Innovator—still below projected sales.

Because of other management pressures, Mr. Element wanted to cut back the amount of time that he and the sales manager, Mr. George Daniels, were spending on the United States marketing effort, but he was concerned about the possible impact on sales. On the positive side, Mr. Element believed that earlier market forecasts of 6000 buses per year over the next five years had been extremely pessimistic, and recent developments led him to believe that a market expansion would eventually take place that would result in total market sales of 40,000 buses per year. However, he was not sure when that expansion would take place, nor if he should wait for it.

Company Background

Bartaco Industries was a wholly owned subsidiary of Galt Malleable Iron (GMI), a Canadian company headquartered in Galt, Ontario. Of $10 million sales in 1969, $6 million of GMI sales had gone to the United States auto industry, almost exclusively to the Ford Motor Company. In 1971, under a new president, GMI had begun to seek opportunities for diversification. The acquisitions were intended to lessen the company's dependence on one customer and one industry. In February of 1974, GMI purchased Bartaco Industries Limited for $600,000. At that time, Bartaco was a near-bankrupt conglomerate with sales of $25 to $26 million in fields ranging from foundries to health spas. With Mr. Element as vice-president, the new management pruned Bartaco's unprofitable lines and divisions. In only one year, Bartaco turned from major losses to modest profits. By 1977, Bartaco was earning pre-tax profits of $754,000 on total sales for the company of almost $9 million (exhibit 1).

One area of Bartaco that Mr. Element had originally believed to have very high potential was the Otaco seating division, which produced the traditional transportation seat used in most Canadian and American buses, trains, and subways. The seat was made of tubular steel construction with a padded seat and back and was covered with either vinyl or cloth. Because of rights, lefts, wheel humps, and back seats, there could be as many as 200 different parts in a traditional bus seat. This type of seat, which was manufactured in Otaco's Orillia plant, was labour-intensive and did not readily lend itself to assembly line production. A similar low-cost functional seat was produced by American Seating in the United States. Although American Seating had 80 percent of the traditional seat market, the lack of product differentiation had led to competition based on price, resulting in low margins and low profits in 1974. However, Mr. Element thought that he could design a totally new seat that would satisfy market needs and utilize assembly line production methods, leading to better margins and profits.

Exhibit 1   Bartaco Industries Limited

Abbreviated Income Statement, 1977
(000)

Sales		$8,785
Cost of goods sold	$6,405	
Selling, administrative and general	1,394[a]	
Interest	232	
Income before taxes		8,031
		$ 754

Abbreviated Balance Sheet, September 30, 1977
(000)

Current Assets		Current Liabilities	
Cash	$ 7,416	Bank loan	$ 2,900
Accounts receivable	6,672	Accounts payable	5,608
Inventories	7,275	Income tax payable	859
Marketable securities	212	6% debentures	453
Prepaid expenses	319	Maturing principal on	
	$21,966	long term debt	95
			$ 9,915
Fixed Assets		*Long-Term Debt*	$ 5,457
Land	$ 321	Deferred income taxes	415
Buildings	3,515	Minority interest in subsidiaries	7,560
Machinery	8,425		$13,432
	$12,261	*Capital Stock*	$ 4,579
Less depreciation	6,427		
	$ 5,833	Retained earnings	1,195
Deferred charges	1,322		$ 5,774
	$29,121		$29,121

a. About $500,000 of selling general and administrative cost could be assigned to the Otaco seating division.

The Innovator I Concept

Mr. Element had envisioned potential for a new seating concept that was quite different from traditional or plastic seats. His automotive background led him to seek a modular seat with a simple manufacturing and assembly process that could be mass produced. Starting in mid-1974, Mr. Element and Thomas Faul, a consulting engineer designer, began to develop the new concept with $250,000 in funding from the federal Department of Industry, Trade and Commerce's Industrial Design Assistance Program (IDAP). In a later presentation to Mr. Element, Mr. Faul indicated the objectives that should be set for the Innovator I.

> Now, in our initial considerations, we looked at the present method of constructing seats and it quickly became apparent that the seat is quite inflexibly built out of tubing, plywood, foam cushions, vinyl, etc.—and it pretty well has to leave the factory exactly in the manner in which you install it, which is rather bulky, difficult to coordinate, difficult to schedule, and difficult to get on time.
>
> In order to simplify matters, we have to devise a unitized technique of making seats which is not frozen all the way down the production line; that is Objective No. 1.
>
> Objective No. 2 is to be able to deliver varying colours easily and quickly because your customer changes his mind maybe two weeks before delivery of the vehicle and there isn't a hope of the factory ever getting the right colour in the last two weeks and your installing it on the vehicle. So something has to be done to prevent this bottleneck from being a menace and a money-consuming problem for both you and Otaco.
>
> The 3rd objective in the program is to design a seat that would basically maintain its fundamental construction right from the beginning from let's say a streetcar seat which is the most austere, heavily travelled seat to the most deluxe kind of seat that you would find in the railway coach.

Stainless steel was chosen for the seat base because of its strength-for-weight characteristics. Unlike the traditional and plastic seats, the new design was much stronger, more durable, and more fire resistant. Foam inserts provided the required padding and molded plastic added a styling touch.

Mr. Element considered the qualities of durability and strength very important to the market potential of the new seat. Transit seats, because of high usage, had to endure a considerable amount of daily wear and tear. This factor, combined with vehicle vandalism, especially in larger cities, made them a constant cleaning and repair problem for the property maintenance department. In large cities, a bus would last for ten years, but seats might last for only five years. The transit properties had repair shops with as many as 50 to 60 people, who were paid ten to twelve dollars an hour to replace torn cushions, to reweld frames, and to replace smashed fiberglass and wood. Good repair people were scarce.

The Innovator I seat was developed over a three-year period of interaction between transit managers and Bartaco's design and production people. The prototype seat was displayed at transit association conventions as a means of inviting constructive comment. Throughout development, computer models were utilized to pinpoint areas in which to add or remove strength. It was the only seat thus designed. Production factors were also in constant review, to enable the design of a marketable seat that could take advantage of an assembly line manufacturing process.

Many obstacles had to be overcome during early development. In late 1976, General Motors had announced the completion of a new bus, the RTS-2. Because of General Motors' interest in developing second sources of supply, Otaco was invited to supply the display bus with new seats. At that time, the plant had not passed the prototype stage for the Innovator I, and the seats did not meet the expectations of General Motors executives because the colour was poorly matched to the rest of the bus interior and the plastic styling inserts were not fitted properly.

During the development period, the plant was still producing traditional seats, but not without difficulties. The city of Canton, Ohio, ordered traditional seats from Otaco. After accepting the order, Mr. Element was forced to cancel it midway through production because of problems at the plant. Later, when a major U.S. order was received for the traditional seats, the plant welders proved to be too unskilled to complete the job. Housewives had to be brought in from the local area and trained as welders. However, even when the manufacturing problem was solved, Otaco was limited by the availability of trainable people to expand its traditional seat line into the U.S. market.

By the spring of 1977, more than $1 million had been spent on development and tooling for the new seat (exhibit 2). The Innovator I was in its final stages of development, and a new assembly line had been set up in Galt with a capacity of 500 seats per eight-hour shift. Otaco designers had developed two shell sizes, a mini or low-back shell for rapid transit vehicles and a high-back shell for buses. From his experience in the transit market, Mr. Element had developed a simple pricing strategy. The prices in table 1 are cost-plus estimates for a high back fully optioned seat and for a low back seat with no options.

Exhibit 2

Innovator 1

SEATING SYSTEMS FOR BUS, RAIL AND TROLLEY

United States Transit Market

Mr. Element had estimated that the United States transit market was some five times larger than the Canadian market. As well, 80 percent of the price of all transit vehicles was subsidized by the United States federal

Table 1   Costing for the Innovator I

	High-Back Fully Optioned Seat[a]	Low-Back Seat With No Options[a]
Materials	$ 40	$27
Labour	10	7
Variable overhead	25	16
Depreciation	5	4
Total variable cost	$ 80	$54
Selling and administration[b]	12	8
Total	92	62
Selling price estimate	120	80
Target pre-tax profit	$ 28	$18

a. Source: Mr. Element's estimates.
b. An average bus has 50 seats.

government through the Urban Mass Transit Administration (UMTA). Applications from individual transit properties for UMTA funding were made public through trade magazines before vehicle specifications or bids were accepted (exhibit 3).

Mr. Element divided the total market for seats into bus and light rail vehicles. These markets could be divided again into original equipment (80 percent) and retrofitting. For Otaco's purposes, the bus market could be divided again into city bus (80 percent) and tour bus markets because Otaco seats were aimed primarily at the city bus market.

The two major builders of city buses were General Motors and Grumman Flxible, each holding almost 50 percent of the market. A third bus builder was American Motors General, but their executives had recently become embroiled in a bitter lawsuit with UMTA, and the company (not having a product that would meet the specifications) withdrew from the advanced design bus market.

The light rail market could be divided into subway and train, although the seats used in these vehicles were almost identical. There also were airports, malls, and marine craft that offered opportunities to sell seats. Exhibits 4 and 5 show the stock of transit vehicles and the annual deliveries of new vehicles. Based on APTA's projections for purchases of transit vehicles (exhibits 6 and 7), Mr. Element made his own projections for the sale of transit seats (table 2).

Exhibit 3 Bus Bidding Schedule, September 1978

Property	Bid Date	Quantity	Size	Delivery
Los Angeles, CA	Protest Indefinite Delay	230[2]	40′ × 102″	59 weeks
Cleveland, OH	Protest Indefinite Delay	157	40′ × 102″	52 weeks
New York, NY	Protest Indefinite Delay	838[3] Opt. 89–100	40′ × 102″	52 weeks first 100
Santa Clara, CA	Protest Indefinite Delay	50[1]	35′ × 102″	60 weeks
Memphis, TN	12/15/78 10:00 A.M. CST	30	40′ × 102″	40 weeks
Roanoke, VA	12/18/78 2:00 P.M.	10	35′ × 96″	60 weeks
New Orleans, LA	1/10/79 2:00 P.M.	175 10[1]	40′ × 102″ 40′ × 102″	40 weeks
Dallas, TX	1/15/79 10:00 A.M.	75	40′ × 102″	40 weeks
Stockton, CA	1/15/79 5:00 P.M.	5	35′ × 96″	60 weeks
Detroit, MI	1/18/79 2:00 P.M.	167[1]	105- 40′ × 102″ 36- 40′ × 102″ 17- 35′ × 102″ 9- 35′ × 102″	52 weeks
Billings, MT	1/23/79 11:00 A.M.	15	35′ × 102″	52 weeks

1. Wheelchair lift specified.
2. Wheelchair lift deleted/lift provision/securements required.
3. Three separate bids in one package.

Buying Process

In the United States, the purchase of transit vehicles and their components was primarily the responsibility of the individual property manager. He was influenced by the property maintenance department and the property directors. The maintenance manager's input was often a strong influence in the decision. His day-to-day tasks and his long experience with the durability and maintenance of different vehicle packages made his advice very valuable to the younger, less closely involved general manager. The

Exhibit 4   Transit Passenger Vehicles Owned and Leased 1966 to 1975

Calendar Year	Railway Cars			Trolley Coaches	Motor Buses	Total Revenue Vehicles
	Light Rail	Heavy Rail	Total Rail			
1966	1,407	9,273	10,680	1,326	50,130	62,136
1967	1,308	9,257	10,545	1,244	50,180	62,069
1968	1,355	9,390	10,745	1,185	50,000	61,930
1969	1,322	9,343	10,665	1,082	49,600	61,347
1970	1,262	9,338	10,600	1,050	49,700	61,350
1971	1,225	9,325	10,550	1,037	49,150	60,737
1972	1,176	9,423	10,599	1,030	49,075	60,704
1973	1,123	9,387	10,510	794	48,286	59,590
1974	1,068	9,403	10,471	718	48,700	59,889
P 1975	1,061	9,608	10,757[a]	703	50,811	62,271

P = Preliminary.
a. Includes 45 PRT transit vehicles, 39 cable cars, and 4 inclined plane cars.

Exhibit 5   New Passenger Vehicles Delivered 1966 to 1975

Calendar Year	Railway Cars			Trolley Coaches	Motor Buses	Total Revenue Vehicles
	Light Rail	Heavy Rail	Total Rail			
1966	0	179	179	0	3100	3279
1967	0	85	85	0	2500	2585
1968	0	384	384	0	2228	2612
1969	0	650	650	0	2230	2880
1970	0	308	308	0	1442	1750
1971	0	250	150	1	2514	2764
1972	0	360	360	1	2904	3265
1973	0	238	238	1	3200	3439
1974	0	92	92	0	4818	4910
P 1975	0	127	127	1	5261	5389

P = Preliminary.

property directors were more removed from the purchase decision. Directors were either elected or appointed, and they were responsible to the city or region for the performance of the property. Although the directors controlled the property finances, they usually did not become directly involved in supplier selection.

Exhibit 6 U.S. Transit Industry Demand Estimated by The American Public Transportation Association (APTA) 1976–1980 Projected Orders

Calendar Year	Total Transit Buses		Heavy Rail Cars		Light Rail Cars		Trolley Coaches		Self-Propelled		Commuter Rail Cars Locomotive-Hauled	
	Minimum	Maximum	Minimum	Maximum	Minimum	Maximum	Minimum	Maximum	Minimum	Maximum	Minimum	Maximum
1976	6239	8315	386	386	50	60	62	70	36	76	70	70
1977	5179	6580	175	175	143	143	110	173	32	40	0	20
1978	4973	6280	302	401	0	0	0	0	32	40	0	39
1979	3765	4985	100	119	0	0	0	0	32	40	5	5
1980	3782	4635	268	431	210	250	0	0	32	60	5	5
Five-year average	4788	6159	246	302	81	91	34	49	33	51	16	28

Note: The APTA United States Transit Industry market survey was distributed to all APTA transit system members on June 15, 1976. Data from all responses received through August 4, 1976, were tabulated and projected to represent the entire U.S. transit industry. Summarized data from the respondents was multiplied by an expansion factor in order to obtain demand for the entire U.S. transit industry. The expansion factor is a ratio of the entire U.S. transit industry fleet, for example, of 50,811 motor buses divided by the portion of that fleet, 33,335 motor buses, owned or leased by the reporting transit systems for an expansion factor of 1.52.

Exhibit 7 U.S. Transit Industry Demand Estimated
by APTA 1981–1985 Projected Orders

Type of Vehicle	Minimum Total Order for Five-Year Period	Minimum Yearly Average	Maximum Total Order for Five-Year Period	Maximum Yearly Average
Transit bus	16,108	3,222	22,502	4,500
Heavy rail car	218	44	1,693	339
Light rail car	62	12	122	24
Trolley coach	0	0	0	0
Commuter rail car	(a)	(a)	(a)	(a)

(a) = Sample size insufficient to make projection.

**Table 2 Mr. Element's Forecast of the
North American Transit Seat Market**

	($000,000)			
Markets:	1978	1979	1980	1981
Bus	$ 30	$ 36	$ 36	$ 36
Subway	$ 2–5	$ 2–5	$ 2–5	$ 2–5
Train	$ 5–10	$ 5–10	$ 5–10	$ 5–10
Airports and malls	$ 5	$ 5	$ 5	$ 5
Marine (small craft)	$10–20	$10–20	$10–20	$10–20

The actual buying process was a multiple-stage purchase. An individual property would take the initial step by placing a request for funds to UMTA. Once the first stage approval was secured, the property manager was required to set detailed product specifications, not only for the vehicle chassis and body but for all options, including seats.

Vehicle specifications usually were set with the help of all competing suppliers, each trying to influence the specifications in favour of its own product. As soon as the vehicle specifications were decided, a detailed proposal was sent to UMTA for final approval. The main function of UMTA was to ensure that the product performance specifications would be adequate. After UMTA agreement was received, suppliers were selected on a product-bid basis, and the contract was finalized. Each competitor was involved from the initial fund request to the final supplier selection, a period usually of six months or more.

However, in 1971, the United States Department of Transport (DOT), through UMTA, had moved to set standard specifications for buses on what was known as the Advanced Design Bus (ADB) or Transbus as described and appraised in the following excerpts from the May 1976 issue of *Commercial Car Journal*.

Transbus

The American taxpayer has paid out $25 million for a federally-funded transit project, that has been a colossal failure. According to the Department of Transportation publicity attendant to the project, TRANSBUS was to represent the first "basic changes in urban transit buses in more than 15 years." TRANSBUS was not designed as a "remake" of existing buses, DOT said, "but was to be all new, from its sleek exterior and low profile to countless passenger comforts and high-speed operation."

Today the TRANSBUS project is in a shambles. And after more than a year of demonstration service in Miami, Kansas City, Seattle and New York, the Urban Mass Transportation Administration finds itself struggling to decide what to do with the embarrassing results of the four demonstrations . . . while at the same time trying to keep the results from the American public.

And while UMTA was pouring millions of taxpayer dollars into the project that has, in a word, flopped, General Motors was developing what the major coach-builder calls the "RTS-2." GMC in the U.S. plans to have the bus in production by this summer. The RTS, according to GM officials, is the first completely new production transit bus designed since 1959. In addition to an optional kneeling feature, the RTS has a new independent front suspension and automatic transmission, automatically controlled air conditioning and heating, new electrical system designed for greater durability and easier maintenance and new seat designs.

The RTS uses a lot of corrosive-resistant stainless steel alloy initially developed for catalytic converters and acrylic windows that resist impact up to 10 times better than safety glass.

Greater parts interchangeability and faster removal and replacement of the fiberglass body panels offer potential for repair economies. Already transit authorities from coast to coast in the U.S. are beginning to clamor for permission to purchase this exciting new city coach designed originally around a Detroit Diesel Allision GT-404 gas turbine.

Because GMC Truck and Coach has been the predominant supplier of transit coaches to U.S. cities, the majority of local transit authority officials want to go with a proven winner. And they have found out through the transit grapevine that TRANSBUS has proved itself to be anything but that.

Veteran transit officials expressed deep reservations over the TRANSBUS project in these areas: costs due to design change; initial purchase price; specific design features such as reduced seating capacity; the "kneeling" feature and maintenance accessibility, coupled with UMTA's emphasis on accommodating non-ambulatory handicapped riders. The comments of these officials reflect a recognition that TRANSBUS did not accomplish its stated objectives.

The most startling revelations of all, however, were in the area of fuel consumption. One of the prime objectives of UMTA's TRANSBUS project was to produce a city coach with greater fuel economy benefits than existing transit coaches, but this was never realized.

The issue among the three bus manufacturers is this. The U.S. Federal Government, through UMTA, picks up 80 percent of the tab when a city or a metropolitan agency buys buses. But there's a catch. To get the money, the city or agency must draw up bid specifications that allow all three companies to bid for the contract. Then the low bidder must be chosen. The problem arises when some cities want to buy the RTS-2 yet under federal procurement regulations, the UMTA is obligated to see that any purchase is bid competitively. UMTA administrator Patricelli has stated he doesn't want any applications for RTS-2; he would prefer a performance specification, which the RTS-2 meets, but to which other manufacturers can also bid. The two smaller bus makers fear that GMC with its almost ready RTS will make off with all the business before they can even be sure of reliability for production prototypes.

Clearly, whatever UMTA does will make some of the companies furious.

The essential question in all of this is whether the government should continue to provide federal funding for bus purchases on a strict low-bid basis, or on the basis of long-term cost effectiveness.

Eventually here in Canada a similar question will need to be answered.

More on Transbus

Since the earlier article was written, UMTA has made a decision to fund the interim bus. UMTA, the transit properties and the Bus Technology Committee of the American Public Transit Association (APTA) have been cooperating to develop a performance oriented specification which will allow these new "interim" buses to enter the market and still keep the same opportunities for competition which have characterized the bus market for several years.

In January, 1975, the UMTA administrator declared that in the interim before the decision on TRANSBUS, UMTA would fund high floor, two-axle buses incorporating styling and design changes consistent with the TRANSBUS, should manufacturers desire to provide such changes. Two manufacturers in the U.S. decided to do exactly that and UMTA has agreed to allow these buses on the market.

UMTA has worked toward the development of a modified bid procedure centered around the use of performance oriented specifications to facilitate competition among different manufacturers with somewhat different buses.

It is believed that these new performance specifications will provide the means for introducing life-cycle costing evaluation; a better, more effective approach which makes sense to most people who are seriously concerned with effective procurement.

As part of the total bid procedure, provision will be made for any bidder to offer his own systems or components and make the case that they best satisfy the performance requirement of the specification.

On May 19, 1977, Secretary Adams ordered that the Advanced Design Bus specifications become mandatory on all buses offered for bid after September 30, 1979. He added that if one manufacturer should beat the September 30, 1979, date substantially, DOT would "consider sole source procurements to get Transbus on the streets as soon as it is available." The same announcement indicated that there would be a 15-month delivery, which meant that it would be three-and-a-half years from the May 1977 date before *delivered* buses would have to meet the new specifications. There were rumours that DOT might give manufacturers some financial aid in moving ahead with Transbus, either progress payments on early tooling costs or funds for research and development.

Seat Manufacturers

The three bus builders, General Motors, Grumman Flxible, and American Motors General were producing 12, 12, and 10 buses per day, respectively. Only Grumman Flxible had ever had any connection with a seat manufacturer, but Flxible buses were not restricted to their own supplier because customers could choose any supplier's seat as part of the bus package. A third seat manufacturer, Lear Ziegler, produced only automotive seats, but their executives had announced that the company would soon produce a stainless steel seat directed at the subway or rapid transit market. Mr. Element felt that Lear Ziegler could not pose a serious threat for at least one year. Table 3 provides some comparisons of the various basic types of seats.

Table 3 Transit Seat Comparison

	Otaco Seat	Standard Upholstered Seat	Standard Plastic Seat
Original price	$120–130 (fully loaded)	$120–130 $120–130	$80–90
Life cycle estimate	10 years	10 years	5 years
Life costs	low	medium	high
Refitting	fast	medium	medium
Safety	crash pads fire resistant		

Otaco's Marketing Effort in the United States

When Mr. Element decided to actively pursue the United States market, he was faced with a number of options. He initially wanted to develop his own sales force because he felt they could be more easily controlled than sales agents. In addition, the specialization of handling only one line would enable a more concentrated effort to exploit the market before the competition could develop a similar seat. Mr. Element could foresee some difficulties with this approach, primarily in attracting proven sales people who had a strong background in the transit vehicle market place. He felt that the task of learning the marketplace and developing the detailed knowledge of the product and process might prove too lengthy even for experienced salesmen.

The second option Mr. Element considered was to offer nonexclusive sales agreements to a number of U.S. agents. The major benefit to this option was the immediate and very intensive coverage of the entire American market. The greater number of sales agents would increase the difficulties of controlling a major thrust, but Otaco would not be faced with the financial investment required to develop a company sales force.

As a third option, Mr. Element had considered a single sales agent with exclusive sales rights to the U.S. market. This arrangement would immediately provide Otaco with an experienced sales force that understood the public transit vehicle market. The sales agents would still have to learn the Otaco product line and production process, but this option would provide the broad geographical coverage that Mr. Element believed necessary for a major market thrust.

During this time, Mr. Peter Redding was suggested to Mr. Element as a possible sales agent. Mr. Redding was described by Mr. Element as "a suave, aggressive, and competent salesman." At 41, Mr. Redding had been involved in the transit market for five years as a sales agent, selling bus bumpers and bus washers. Although Mr. Element had encouraged Mr. Redding to become an Otaco employee, he had turned down the offer, preferring both the freedom of a sales agent and his own company, Fairfield Corporation.

After careful deliberation, Mr. Element decided to hire Fairfield Corporation as exclusive sales agent for the U.S. market. Mr. Redding, from his headquarters in Chicago, was to expand Fairfield as necessary to cover the U.S. market as it opened up. The agreement was based on a commission structure of sliding percentages to sales volume. In the first year, Mr. Redding was given an $80,000 retainer fee or 4 percent of sales, whichever was the greater of the two. After the first year, Mr. Redding received 4 percent of sales to $2.5 million, 2 percent of sales from $2.5 to $20 million, and 1 percent of sales over $20 million. Mr. Element and Mr. Redding set what they believed to be realistic and achievable sales targets of $2.5 million, $5 million, $10 million, $15 million, and $20 million for the first five successive years. Fairfield's first year of association with the Otaco division was 1976, and seat sales of $1.5 million were achieved.

In terms of roles, Mr. Redding said that he did a lot of "bird-dogging," particularly on the top twenty properties that account for 74 percent of the market. He said that he visited each major property manager three to four times per year, of which one or two times might be at meetings. In addition, he said that he made occasional telephone calls and mailings when he had something of real value to communicate.

Mr. Redding said that he spent his time chasing federal grants issued through UMTA. He knew most of the people involved in property purchases. When he saw a property about to buy some seats, he made telephone contact. He followed up with a presentation usually accompanied by Otaco executives such as Mr. Element, Mr. Daniels (Otaco Sales Manager) and a technical expert from Otaco.

"When it comes to the closing phase," Redding said, "there must be a meeting of minds, that is, that the property managers must be almost convinced that this is the product for them." He suggested that any hard-sell would not be tolerated and that the person would never get an opportunity for repeat calls. With this problem-solving approach, Mr. Redding said that he took a problem in Denver and actually wrote out the specifications for the order.

Mr. Redding described his role as to

orchestrate as I see fit for the particular sale, but each sale is different in terms of the people who actually make the decisions. As an example, the Chicago transit property has one person who is really a decision maker for all equipment, but his name doesn't show in the telephone directory that lists about 40 names. Similarly, in Portland, Oregon, there is one person, and in Denver it is a case of consultant plus one or two other people.

Boards are not likely to change the decision of an operating management team. And boards only get involved if they are switching from one seat supplier to another. In that case, the board likes to see a sample of the seat but they seldom change very much. In the case of Cleveland, we made a presentation before management and the board, but it was obvious that the minds of the decision makers had been made up in favour of American Seating long before the presentation by Otaco. We were wasting our time, and it became obvious. The man who had invited us to make the presentation was embarrassed.

St. Louis Order

Of the attempted sales during the three year development of the Innovator I, the St. Louis order typified the buying procedure. The first lead came as a result of a notice in *Public Transit Magazine* in June 1976. The city of St. Louis was seeking approximately $9,500,000 of UMTA funds for the purchase of 170 buses.

Mr. Redding travelled to St. Louis for two introductory meetings. There he met Mr. Jerry Eddy, the St. Louis property's general manager, a man in his late thirties who provided Mr. Redding with the basic information and agreed to meet Mr. Element and Mr. Daniels. The evening before the third meeting, the three Otaco representatives had dinner with Mr. Eddy. During the evening, Mr. Eddy was very friendly, and Mr. Element was able to discover that the main competition for the order was from American Seating's traditional fully optioned seat, which was fully padded and vinyl-covered with a metal back plate. Mr. Eddy was using the American seat in his buses, but Mr. Element was hopeful that the seat's shortfalls in the areas of wear and difficulty of padding replacement would open the way for the Innovator I.

The following day, when Mr. Eddy was presented with the prototype seat, he seemed rather unresponsive; after a brief examination, he asked a number of clerical employees from surrounding offices for their comments. His next step was to ask his maintenance manager to join the group in his office. The maintenance manager, Mr. Bill Newman, carefully examined and tested the seat while questioning the Otaco representatives. Mr. Newman seemed very impressed with the Innovator's durable design and ease of replacing the cushions and moldings. After more discussion between the two managers and the Otaco representatives, Mr. Eddy indicated that he was interested in the Innovator I, and the meeting ended.

A short time later, Mr. Element and Mr. Redding returned to St. Louis to help Mr. Eddy establish the seat specifications. Although Mr. Eddy wanted the Innovator I, he was concerned about UMTA reaction if the seat specifications were too restrictive. Mr. Element suggested that Mr. Eddy should contact UMTA executives to test their reaction. Mr. Redding, however, first called some of the UMTA authorities whom he knew and prepared them for Mr. Eddy's call.

In early August, Mr. Eddy again called Mr. Redding, indicating a renewed concern about the seat durability. Mr. Eddy asked for the names of previous customers and was given three satisfied customers, including the Toronto Transit Commission in Canada. In addition, Mr. Eddy was shown a thirty-minute film of the durability testing of the Innovator I. From what Mr. Redding and Mr. Element could discover, the American Seating salesman, who was also in contact with Mr. Eddy, had suggested that the welding in the Innovator seat would break too easily.

About the same time, a Regional Transit Convention was held in St. Louis. The Bartaco representatives hoped to display the seat to the St. Louis directors and gain their support. Unfortunately, few of the St. Louis directors were in attendance, and little was accomplished to further Otaco's position.

In late August of 1976, the bid specifications were completed and sent to UMTA and $9.5 million in funding was approved. Although the bid had been approved, the specifications still allowed American Seating to bid using their traditional seat.

In October 1976, a national UMTA convention was held in San Francisco. Just prior to the convention, Mr. Element had purchased the rights to a "molectrics" process, which gave stainless steel a chrome-like finish. Using the process, Mr. Element was able to finish a prototype seat for the San Francisco display. When Mr. Newman and Mr. Eddy arrived at the convention and saw the new molectrics finish on the Innovator I, both men were very impressed.

Another factor that strengthened Otaco's position was the large number of St. Louis directors who attended the San Francisco convention. For three days, Mr. Eddy brought individual directors to Mr. Element's hotel suite to examine the seat and to ask their opinion. Near the end of the convention, Mr. Eddy seemed to have decided in favour of the Innovator I, with the molectrics finish and an added handle on each seat for standing passengers. Although Mr. Element had no "on-line" production experience to estimate the cost of the molectrics feature, Mr. Eddy was pressuring him for an immediate total price. Mr. Element and Mr. Daniels decided to add $5.00 per seat and presented the new offer to Mr. Eddy. He accepted the bid on the spot.

After the convention, Mr. Element learned that one of the St. Louis directors was against the Otaco seat because he thought that it was "too plush" (although he drove a luxury car himself). Other directors may have considered the seat too untested for a major commitment. For whatever reasons, Otaco was awarded only 50 bus sets (of 50 seats each), while American Seating received the order for the other 120 bus sets. Mr. Element made one last attempt to sway Mr. Eddy but was unable to do so. In retrospect, Mr. Element rationalized that the smaller order had given Otaco more time to gear up their production line.

Marketing Strategy

The Otaco sales manager, George Daniels, always had indicated some misgivings about Redding's strategy. Because there was some tendency for the smaller property owners to follow the larger ones, Mr. Redding had concentrated on the largest American properties. Mr. Daniels had pointed out the problems of financing and scheduling the larger orders, and he believed that more concentration on the smaller properties would alleviate many of Otaco's problems, an opinion not shared by Mr. Redding. Mr. Daniels acknowledged that the Innovator I had made significant inroads in larger properties in the United States as well as in Canada. Many of the U.S. transit properties relied on decisions made by the Toronto Transit Commission because of the TTC's careful testing of all equipment. The Toronto Transit Commission had standardized on the Innovator I. Occasionally, American transit properties were reluctant to deal with a Canadian supplier, but everyone involved in the selling effort asserted that such a bias could be detected almost immediately before any large amount of selling effort was expended.

Upon DOT's issuance of the baseline specifications for the Advanced Design Bus in March of 1977, Mr. Daniels had initiated a testing program with the Ontario Research Foundation in order to develop test reports on the Innovator I in three mounting configurations. The test data would demonstrate to UMTA, bus builders, and property managers that the Innovator I met all the required specifications. On August 29, 1977, he wrote:

> One of our major challenges in the United States is and will be the base line specification. In addition to that will also be the "Who has the procurement power, the bus builder or the property."
>
> In the latter regard, the price offset strategy employed by UMTA and the appropriate credits applied to seating will play a very significant part.
>
> Otaco's challenge will be to sell and very accurately define to bus builders, UMTA and properties that our Innovator will have price offset advantages in the following areas that we are given credit for. These will be: weight reduction, a long life cycle cost saving due to stainless steel construction (necessity to not continually repaint), low profile transit cushions of an economical nature that do not have to be manually repaired—and can be of a throwaway nature.

In fact, the Innovator was on the UMTA approved list, and Mr. Redding had secured price offsets of $30,000 on a $130,000 bid, which resulted in Otaco winning the contract over a bid of $110,000.

September 1978

Mr. Element could not help but feel uneasy. The Flxible bus building company had just been sold to Grumman Corporation. The new Grumman Flxible, as well as introducing a new advanced design bus called the 870, had just come out with a new plastic seat that could sell for $3500 per bus set. Although the Innovator I represented a major product advantage over the competition, Peter Redding believed that Otaco executives might be forced to go with a "minimum specification" product in order to approach the $3500 price range. In order to reduce the Innovator's weight for the Transbus specification, Mr. Element already had designed a low-backed shell.

Lear Ziegler had just produced prototypes for a padded steel seat very similar to the Otaco Innovator. Most orders for transit seats still required a high degree of custom manufacturing, and Mr. Element predicted, "The guys at Lear Ziegler will blow their minds when they really discover the cost of custom manufacture." However, the bus builders were pressing to offer two or three standard seat options in order to streamline their own assembly lines.

Mr. Element was still spending 25 percent of his time and Mr. Daniels was spending 40 percent of his time in the sales effort to the United States market. The vice-president no longer wanted himself or his sales manager so deeply involved in actual selling to the United States market. Many transit properties would be in the market for vehicles in 1979, but the specifications were still in flux, and Mr. Element still was anxious about the arrangements for marketing the Innovator I.

It was no particular comfort to Mr. Element that no North American manufacturer of seats for mass transit vehicles seemed to be making profits. He knew that Otaco was a solid number two, a "backup" supplier to American Seating, but he wondered whether he should redirect the selling effort from buses to some other transit vehicles. The imminent "Buy America Act" did not particularly concern Mr. Element because he could arrange for assembly of the seats in the United States and thus meet the requirements of this possible legislation. The President of Galt Malleable Iron was looking for cash to put into the foundry division of Bartaco and anyone offering $5 million probably could buy the Otaco seating division.

17 London Regional Children's Museum

Mrs. Carol Johnston paused in her work to sip her coffee. As she did so, she looked out on the scene just below her crowded loft/office. Two eight-year-old boys were alternately pumping water vigorously to make the big water wheel spin. A young mother rested on a stool while her little girl made snow goggles using the scissors, glue, string, and cardboard provided in the Inuit display. The whole place was alive with children doing things, discovering their world. Mrs. Johnston, Chairman and founder of the London Regional Children's Museum (LRCM), returned to her work.

The fifteen-person Board of Trustees had recently decided to purchase a permanent site for the LRCM, a decision that meant a tremendous leap forward for Canada's first children's museum. It also meant a monumental fund-raising challenge for Mrs. Johnston and her supporters. Total revenues from all sources for the LRCM in 1978–1979 were approximately $90,000. The new site would require an estimated $1,100,000 to become operational. Mrs. Johnston and her board had been hard at work with major government sources and foundations. By March 1981, they had received commitments from government sources and private sources for more than half the goal. Of the $750,000 LRCM needed from private sources, approximately $300,000 had already been pledged, leaving Mrs. Johnston to formulate a fund-raising strategy to get the remainder. Only four months remained until the closing date on the LRCM's planned purchase of an old public school building. Working out the specifics of a fund-raising campaign thus became Mrs. Johnston's top priority activity.

Concept and Activities of the LRCM

The LRCM began in 1975 in London, Ontario. A small group of individuals sharing an interest in children and a belief in education through hands-on experience steadily developed the foundations of the LRCM. From a modest beginning in city park recreational programs, the LRCM had moved to donated space in a downtown shopping mall in 1976. The 2000-square-foot "storefront museum" soon proved inadequate for the growing popularity and programme activities of the LRCM. In late 1978, the LRCM moved into 5000 square feet of donated temporary space in another downtown office and shopping centre. By late 1979, the Board established a committee to search for even larger, permanent quarters. After careful search, the committee recommended Riverview School, a recently closed public school with 27,000 square feet of space owned by the London Board of Education. This site met all the LRCM's criteria but required substantial renovation. The London Board of Education agreed to sell the property to LRCM for $300,000 with a closing date of July 8, 1981. The renovations and setup would take another six months and an estimated $800,000, enabling an opening at the new location in mid-January 1982.

The LRCM was a participatory museum aimed at children from three to fifteen years of age. Exhibits were designed to invite children to learn about the past, present, and future by touching, doing and making. For example, children were encouraged to try the typewriters, to pump the bellows to work a windmill, to crawl through the skeleton of a house, to dig for fossil bones, and so on. Staff and volunteers developed major themes such as "People and Machines" and minor, seasonal themes such as "An Old-Fashioned Christmas" to create a constantly changing museum environment. Artifacts were virtually never put behind glass because the basic philosophy was "look and touch."

The displays and activities were designed both for the walk-in visitors and for programmed, guided tours of school classes. In addition, the LRCM had developed a large extension service. Forty kits were developed at a cost of over $100,000 for use by school teachers, youth groups, and parents for a rental fee of $5.00 per week. Each kit was a portable museum display in a box, focusing on a specific theme such as a foreign culture or a career. These kits conformed with the basic concept of the LRCM, containing items to touch, taste, try, make, wear, etc.

The LRCM also offered its facilities for community groups such as weavers or astronomers to meet and exhibit their skills. STAY (Science Technology and You) became associated with the LRCM and committed itself to raise money for science exhibits.

The staff of LRCM were in constant demand as workshop leaders and demonstrators for other groups throughout Ontario. Requests for comments and assistance on children's programming were received from across Canada.

The LRCM operated six and one-half days per week with four full-time employees and a number of part-time employees who, in total, constituted the equivalent of one additional full-time employee. In addition, there were 60 volunteers who helped in all the LRCM's activities.

In 1977, the LRCM was incorporated as an Ontario nonprofit charitable organization managed by a board of trustees elected by the voting membership. Later that year the LRCM was registered as a charitable institution with the Department of National Revenue.

LRCM Audience

Mrs. Johnston believed the LRCM was for all people residing or visiting in Southwestern Ontario. Its appeals were to school and children's groups to augment curricula and general experience. Adults found the museum helpful in interpreting the environment for their children and themselves. Mrs. Johnston also thought industry, local ethnic groups, government groups, and others could also share their talents and resources with visitors to the LRCM.

In Mrs. Johnston's view, the audience for the LRCM could be described in many ways. From a geographical viewpoint, the primary audience was located in London and Middlesex County, totaling over 300,000 people in early 1981. The secondary audience was located in the contiguous counties of Perth, Oxford, Elgin, Lambton, and Kent, which had a combined population of over 500,000, most of whom were within one hour's drive of London. About 20 percent of the population were children between the ages of five and fourteen. Out-of-town visitors were harder to calculate. The best figures available showed about five million visitors spending about $142 million in the London area in 1976. Mrs. Johnston knew that in the 1980 summer season, just over one third of LRCM's visitors were tourists.

Visitor response to the LRCM steadily increased as shown in the following chart:

Year	Total visitors	Groups (average size about 25 people)
1975	250	15
1976	9,550	75
1977	19,000	350
1978	20,150	400
1979	29,077	760
1980	39,751	1,084

This meant that in 1980, the LRCM drew almost two fifths of the audience attracted to London's new Regional Art Gallery, as shown in the following chart of visitors to some other London cultural activities:

	Total visitors
Centennial Museum	15,003
Eldon House Museum	15,872
Lawson Museum	2,325
London Regional Art Gallery	100,000 (estimate)
London Regional Children's Museum	39,751
Museum of Indian Archaeology	4,250
Strathroy Middlesex Museum	4,000

Past Funding and Support

The operation of the LRCM was funded from a variety of sources. In fiscal 1979 and 1980, with budgets of approximately $40,000 and $90,000, respectively, about half of these amounts were raised from admissions, programmes, kit rentals, memberships, and government grants. The balance in both years was provided through fund-raising activities of the Board and volunteer groups. Exhibit 1 details the sources and uses of funds for these two years and the budget for fiscal 1981.

As demands for museum services grew, fund raising continued to be a major priority of the Board. In 1980, the funding base was broadened to include appeals to service clubs, a modest corporate fund-raising campaign and special projects such as children's theatre productions, an evening with Peter Ustinov, Wheel-Around-the-World (a bicycle-based fund-raising ride), a Pepsi-Cola booth at the Western Fair, and the sale of Christmas cards.

Since 1976, the LRCM received a wide range of grants from government and private groups as the following chart shows:

Government of Canada	Local Initiatives Project and Canada Works	$67,935
	Canada Council Explorations Grant	11,600
	Young Canada Works—1977, 1979	20,982
	International Year of the Child 1979	3,000
	Summer Youth Employment Program 1980	9,476
	Canada Community Development Project 1981	32,160
Province of Ontario	Ministry of Culture and Recreation Experience Grants—1977, 1978, 1979	11,730
	Wintario	23,454
	Ministry of Culture and Recreation Design Grant	19,000
	Museum Maintenance Grant—1979	11,910

	Museum Maintenance Grant—1980	11,910
	Experience '80 Grants	4,884
Private	May Court of London	2,000
	Kiwanis Club of North London	3,000
Foundations	Laidlaw Foundation	30,000
	The Birks Family Foundation	400
	Sir Joseph Flavelle Foundation	1,000

Mrs. Johnston was very proud that throughout its development years, although operating with very tight funding, the LRCM had never been in debt except for current payables. Bills were paid on time, and no expenditures were undertaken without a reasonable certainty that funds were available or forthcoming.

The LRCM benefited greatly from extensive support from many institutions and groups both in the London area and in the Canadian museum community. Exhibit 2 outlines this assistance given to the LRCM.

The LRCM also sought members. Two types of annual membership were offered: voting at $15 and nonvoting at $5 for a child, $10 for an adult, and $20 for a family. Memberships entitled individuals to newsletters, a 10 percent discount at the Museum Shop, and free admission to the museum for the year. All volunteers were expected to be members. Mrs. Johnston hoped to increase dramatically the number of members in the years ahead.

The LRCM requested an admission fee, but no attempt was made to ensure that each visitor paid it. Mrs. Johnston had preferred to use available people doing other work, relying instead on visitors putting money in a box at the entrance to the exhibit area. The requested fees were 50¢ per child and 75¢ per adult. During fiscal 1979–1980, general admission fees collected were $8505. Additionally, LRCM generally charged a flat fee of $10 per group for school groups coming through the museum. In 1979–1980, such fees amounted to $6060.

Plans for the Future

Mrs. Johnston described her plans for LRCM programming as follows:

> The participatory approach to museum exhibits is basic to each of the galleries planned for the permanent site. The concepts for these galleries were the result of a Canada Council grant which the Museum has been working from to develop prototypes during the past two years.
>
> Major galleries will include: Things in Caves, The Street Where You Live, If I Were a Child Long Ago, Inuit, Planetarium, People and Machines.

Exhibit 1 London Regional Children's Museum Operating Statements

		September to August		
Revenues:		1978–1979[a]	1979–1980[b]	1980–1981[c]
Admissions		$ 6,620	$14,565	$17,200
Kit rentals		348	494	2,000
Membership dues		405	1,130	1,800
Donations		9,162	7,758	7,500
Special projects		—	—	
Spring Festival	527			
Wheel Around the World	2,735		2,906	
Discovery Train	2,999		—	
Western Fair	—		4,428	
Christmas Cards	380		257	
Museum Shop	—		274	
Children's Theatre	—		21,474	
		6,641	29,339	17,000[d]
Ministry support grant		—	11,910	12,000
Project grants		9,229	17,065	16,000
Interest		4,823	6,376	3,000
Miscellaneous		634	404	4,700[e]
Total revenues		$37,862	$89,041	$81,200
Expenses:				
Salaries and benefits		25,441	47,699	57,350
Materials and supplies		2,192	3,522	6,000
Programming and promotion		1,228	4,481	5,100
Telephone		685	625	800
Travel		939	2,100	2,000
Equipment, cleaning, maintenance		19	998	1,600
Moving and storage		557	472	500
Insurance		370	704	700
Special projects		2,089	17,876	—
Bank charges		234	329	150[f]
Miscellaneous		142	2,732	1,700
Leasehold improvements		—	1,040	100
Taxes		—	129	
Exhibit development		—	815	4,400
Total expenses		$33,896	$83,522	$80,800
Surplus		3,966	5,519	400
		$37,862	$89,041	$81,200

a. Audited.
b. Unaudited.
c. Budget.
d. Net figure.
e. Includes property tax rebate of $4,300.
f. Includes moving and storage and utilities and maintenance 2 months of new building.

Exhibit 2   Groups Supporting the LRCM

A. INSTITUTIONAL

Use of space:
The University of Western Ontario
Richardson's Real Estate
London and Middlesex Historical
  Society
City Centre Mall
London Towers

Loaning of artifacts:
Computer Circuit Limited
3M Canada Limited
Antique stores in London
Theatre London
Private citizens
Public Utilities Commission
The University of Western Ontario

B. SERVICE CLUBS

Kiwanis Club of North London
Kiwanis Club of Forest City (London)
Lion's Club of East London
Lion's Club of West London
The May Court Club of London
The Junior Service League of London

C. SPONSORING CORPORATIONS

Allpak Ltd.
Almatex Chemical Coatings
EMCO Ltd.
Ex-Cell-O Corp. of Canada Ltd.
John Labatt Ltd.
Lawson & Jones Ltd.
London Free Press Printing Co. Ltd.
Sifton Properties Ltd.
3M Canada Ltd.

D. INDUSTRY SUPPORT: GOODS AND
     MATERIALS CONTRIBUTED

Thames Valley Beverages Ltd.
Canadian International Paper Company

Somerville Belkin Industries Ltd.
Eddy Match Co. Ltd.
Copp's Buildall
D. F. Johnston Ltd., Canadian Tire
  Corporation Associate Store
Kingsmill's Ltd.
Borden Co. Ltd.
D. H. Howden Co. Ltd.
Wright Lithographing Co. Ltd.
Fine Papers London Ltd.
M & T Insta-Print Ltd.
General Steel Wares
3M Canada Ltd.

E. MUSEUM SUPPORT

Centennial Museum has sponsored
  theme exhibits
Children's museums in the U.S.,
  (e.g., Boston Children's Museum)
The Ontario Science Centre supported
  the LRCM from the beginning:
  It funded a three-day workshop for
    Trustees
  It brought the Science Circus to
    London under LRCM sponsorship
  It loaned many artifacts and exhibit
    materials
  It provided consulting advice on
    mounting programs and exhibits
Royal Ontario Museum loaned artifacts
National Museum of Natural Sciences
  loaned artifacts

F. MEDIA SUPPORT

Both print and broadcast media in the
  London area provided widespread coverage and support of LRCM activities

Each permanent gallery, although designed around a basic theme, will provide opportunities for a wide range of programming.

Smaller galleries will include: Discovery Room, Festival Room.

This Discovery Room will be developed as a starting place for younger children with shelves and boxes and intriguing spaces packed with interesting natural science materials. The Festival Room will house seasonal exhibits such as the Haunted House or Christmas or exhibits developed in cooperation with a local group such as Theatre London or the London Symphony.

In addition to the galleries, space will be available for a multi-use auditorium to allow presentation of children's theatre, movies, and concerts and to house temporary and traveling exhibits.

Two "extension" exhibits, "Orchestra Pit" and "Habitat," are planned for temporary showing in the Auditorium and for traveling to other museums.

Visitor space will also be designated for museum kits, a Recycle Shop, and a Museum Shop. The Junior Service League of London will run the Museum Shop as a volunteer activity.

"Behind the scenes" space, essential for building and storing exhibits and artifacts, will include a workshop and large storage area.

LRCM staff had prepared some projections of audience response (exhibit 3), membership response (exhibit 4), and kit rentals (exhibit 5). These projections in addition to a great deal of financial analysis led to the

Exhibit 3 London Regional Children's Museum, Projected Admissions Numbers, Charges and Revenues for the Period 1981–1986

	1981–1982	1982–1983	1983–1984	1984–1985	1985–1986
Number of groups	1,000	1,200	1,500	1,750	1,900
Casual Visitors:					
Adults	7,000	10,000	15,000	17,500	20,000
Children	14,000	20,000	30,000	35,000	40,000
	21,000	30,000	45,000	52,500	60,000
Admission charges:					
Groups	$15.00	$15.00	$17.50	$20.00	$20.00
Adults	1.25	2.00	2.50	3.00	3.00
Children	.75	1.00	1.00	1.25	1.25
Revenues:					
Groups	$15,000	$18,000	$26,250	$ 35,000	$ 38,000
Casual Visitors	19,250	40,000	67,500	96,250	110,000
	$34,250	$58,000	$93,750	$131,250	$148,000

Exhibit 4 London Regional Children's Museum, Projected Memberships and Fee Revenue for the Period 1981–1986

	1981–1982	1982–1983	1983–1984	1984–1985	1985–1986
Number					
Child	25	50	100	200	300
Adult	15	30	40	50	60
Family	50	100	200	300	400
Voting	20	25	25	25	25
Fee					
Child	$ 5	$10	$10	$15	$15
Adult	10	15	15	20	20
Family	20	25	25	30	30
Voting	20	20	20	25	25
Revenues					
Child	$ 125	$ 500	$1,000	$ 3,000	$ 4,500
Adult	150	450	600	1,000	1,200
Family	1,000	2,500	5,000	9,000	12,000
Voting	400	500	500	625	625
	$1,675	$3,950	$7,100	$13,625	$18,325

Exhibit 5 London Regional Children's Museum, Projected Kit Rentals for the Period 1981–1986

	1981–1982	1982–1983	1983–1984	1984–1985	1985–1986
Number of rentals	250	300	335	375	400
Fee per rental	$10	$15	$15	$15	$20
Total revenues	$2500	$4500	$5025	$5625	$8000

development of a detailed statement of projected operating revenues and expenditures for the 1982–1986 period (exhibit 6).

As soon as the LRCM board recognized that they faced a projected operating deficit of $54,750 for the first three years in the new location, they decided that it was critical to cover this amount with a specific donation. A commitment was received from a private donor to cover these deficits to a maximum of $55,000.

The Fund-Raising Challenge

In early 1977, the LRCM received a capital commitment in principle from Wintario (a resource operated by the Ontario Government's Ministry of Culture and Recreation) to provide one third of the cost of acquiring and

Exhibit 6 London Regional Children's Museum, Estimated Operating
Revenues and Expenditures[1] for the Period 1982–1986

	Fiscal Years September to August				
	1981–1982	*1982–1983*	*1983–1984*	*1984–1985*	*1985–1986*
Revenues:					
Admissions	$ 34,250	$ 58,000	$ 93,750	$131,250	$148,000
Memberships	1,675	3,950	7,100	13,625	18,325
Kit rentals	2,500	4,500	5,025	5,625	8,000
Donations	6,000	6,500	7,000	7,500	8,000
City of London grant	9,500	10,200	10,900	11,650	12,450
Ministry support grant	12,000	17,000	19,250	21,900	23,875
Fund raising projects (net)	25,000	27,500	30,000	33,000	37,500
Miscellaneous	1,000	1,100	1,200	1,350	1,500
Total revenues	$ 91,925	$128,750	$174,225	$225,900	$257,650
Expenditures:					
Salaries and benefits	$ 68,000	$ 88,000	$110,000	$121,000	$133,000
Materials and supplies	9,500	11,500	13,000	17,500	22,500
Exhibit development	3,700	5,200	5,700	6,300	7,000
Resource materials	1,500	2,000	2,200	2,500	2,750
Freight/moving	2,000	750	600	500	550
Equipment maintenance	500	550	600	650	700
Telephone	1,500	1,650	1,800	2,000	2,200
Travel/staff development	2,500	3,000	3,000	3,500	3,500
Insurance	3,350	3,700	4,050	4,450	4,900
Heat, light, and water	12,000	13,800	15,800	18,300	20,000
Building maintenance	1,000	1,500	2,000	2,500	3,000
Grounds maintenance	1,200	1,300	1,400	1,550	1,750
Taxes	9,500	10,200	10,900	11,650	12,450
Legal and audit	100	100	125	125	125
Bank charges	150	175	200	225	250
Miscellaneous	500	550	600	650	700
Contingency (10% of nonsalary)	4,900	5,600	6,200	7,250	8,250
Total expenses	$121,900	$149,575	$178,175	$200,650	$223,625
Surplus (deficit)	($ 29,975)	($ 20,825)	($ 3,950)	$ 25,250	$ 34,025

1. An inflation factor of approximately 10 percent per year has been used.

renovating an existing building and a commitment to provide half of the cost of furnishings and equipment and some aspects of the galleries. This commitment was still current and formed part of the funding plans of LRCM. National Museums Canada expressed an interest in receiving an application for funding of renovations needed for receiving, storage, and shipping of special traveling exhibits. Together, Wintario and National Museums Canada were expected to contribute $374,700 to the LRCM relocation and expansion. This left $725,300 to be raised from other sources. As of March 1981, LRCM had accomplished the following: (a) $33,000 was in hand from earlier capital fund raising, (b) over $15,000 was pledged by members of the LRCM Board of Trustees, (c) the Richard Ivey Foundation and the Richard and Jean Ivey Fund had pledged $150,000 and $50,000, respectively.

"We've still got a long way to go," thought Mrs. Johnston. She believed that LRCM faced a particularly tough environment in which to raise such substantial funds. She listed on the pad in front of her the following notes:

We're still quite new and not well-known—awareness of need for LRCM?

Does being a museum for children limit our appeal?

Do people think, "Aren't there enough attractions in town?"

During the last year the new Art Gallery, the new theatre, the symphony, the university, St. John's Ambulance, the "Y" and others all have had major fund-raising drives—is there any money left!?

We've learned how to approach governments and foundations, but how do we approach the general public?

Should we go after many small donations or focus our efforts on a few big ones?

She paused and thought, "I know we have to show we are professional, competent, responsible managers who provide an important service to our community. The question is, how do we do that? In the past, we did our best; but if we didn't get enough money, we were flexible and adjusted our activities to fit our financial resources. Now we're taking a big step. We need a lot of money, and we need it all in a certain time frame." Her thoughts were interrupted by the loud protests of a young boy being pulled out of the seat of the test cockpit of the F33 jet fighter—his mother had decided it was time to go home, but he wanted to stay even if it meant missing dinner.

18 Northern Telecom (A)

In early 1975, a three-person task force, with representatives from Northern Telecom Limited, Bell-Northern Research Limited, and Bell Canada, was asked to develop a strategy for Northern Telecom in the central office switching market. Central office switching equipment is the telephone exchange equipment owned by telephone companies that connects a user with the telephone at the number he or she has dialed. This equipment includes both local telephone exchanges and toll or long distances exchanges that connect all the local exchanges together. The decisions about Northern Telecom's central office switching strategy were viewed as crucial ones, since research and development expenditures in excess of $50 million and revenues of hundreds of millions of dollars were at stake.

Northern Telecom's major entry in the central office switching market, the SP-1, was experiencing rapid growth, but competitors were aggressively introducing new products that threatened to cut into future sales of the SP-1.

The task force was faced with two major alternatives:

1. Introduce all or part of a new digital central office switching line as soon as possible, with the first major elements of the product line being available in 1979, the exact timing depending on how quickly R&D and human resources were built up in the programme. The technical and business risks associated with such a strategy were viewed as being very large. If the decision to proceed with an early introduction of one or more digital central office switches was made, decisions also had to be made about the relative priority to be given to the various digital switches under development and their associated software packages. Furthermore, the timing of any announcement of one or more of the digital switches competitive with Northern Telecom's

existing product line might have an adverse effect on new sales of the existing line, leaving only extension sales for existing SP-1 offices.

2. Delay the introduction of the digital switching line until 1981 or later. This would alleviate Northern Telecom's short-run cash flow problems, and would probably extend the product life cycle of the SP-1 switch. Since the SP-1 switch was under increasing competitive pressure, one possibility was to introduce an updated enhanced version of the SP-1 switch (perhaps called the SP-2). Depending on the number and type of enhancements selected, this upgraded switch could be announced within a few months and could be available to customers by 1977.

The Company

Prior to 1956, Northern Electric Company Limited (as Northern Telecom was formerly called) was 40 percent owned by Western Electric, the manufacturing arm of American Telephone and Telegraph (AT&T), and in the words of a Northern Telecom executive, "operated very much like a branch plant." Its prime mandate was to manufacture Western Electric products for Bell Canada, and its product line generally lagged Western Electric's by two to three years. During this period, Northern Electric had only a very small R&D staff.

In 1956, Western Electric signed a consent decree with the U.S. Department of Justice, in which it agreed, among other things, that it would relinquish any ownership of Northern Electric. Northern Electric then became a wholly owned subsidiary of Bell Canada. Having no product line of its own, Northern Electric agreed to license many Western Electric products on the same basis as several other independent companies. The close working relationship between Northern Electric executives and engineers and their Western Electric counterparts soon began to weaken. Northern Electric, at this point, was essentially a company with no product line of its own and no R&D expertise in key technology areas, but with a firmly established business base in Canada and excellent engineering and manufacturing skills.

The Development of a Central Office Switching Product Line

In 1958, Northern Electric Laboratories was established in Belleville, Ontario, with a staff of 30–40 people. This operation was moved to new facilities in Ottawa, Ontario, in 1960, and a priority task became the acquisition of expertise in switching and transmission and the development of a product line that would meet Canadian needs. One of the first switching products developed by the Laboratories was the SA-1, a 1000-line crossbar system using Western Electric-type components.[1] Introduced in the early 1960's, over 1000 SA-1 switches were sold, mostly in Canada. Two other switches, the N5-1 and N5-2, were the result of modifications to a Western Electric product to reduce its line capacity to meet the Canadian market's needs.

In the early 1960's, it became apparent to Northern Electric management that the next generation of products would make extensive use of electronics to replace electromechanical components. Bell Canada had continued to have a working relationship with AT&T through a service contract. Before this relationship ended, Bell Canada was anxious to get access to the latest technology AT&T had to offer. AT&T had announced an electronic central office switch (the #1 ESS) in the early 1960's, with the first installation to occur in 1965 in New Jersey. Bell Canada was able to negotiate an arrangement whereby Northern Electric would manufacture under licence a #1 ESS switch for the World's Fair in Montreal (Expo '67). This provided a world showcase for AT&T's technology. This contract resulted in Northern Electric's becoming involved with both Bell Laboratories (the R&D arm of AT&T) and Western Electric as part of the development team. A switch was manufactured and installed for the World's Fair site by Northern Electric. Ultimately, a total of eleven of these #1 ESS switches were built under licence from Western Electric for Bell Canada. The switch was a large local switch able to handle from 10,000 to 60,000 lines. It was designed for major metropolitan areas such as Toronto and Montreal, and was expensive to manufacture on Northern Electric's scale. The product was phased out of the Northern Electric product line in the early 1970's.

Northern Electric's experience with the #1 ESS switch reinforced management's desire to develop a product line attuned to the needs of the Canadian market—particularly products that would be economical at low line sizes and would continue to be economical over a wide range of line sizes. By 1964, the basic architecture of such a product had been outlined. The SP-1 (Stored Program 1st System) had stored-program-control and an electromechanical network using a miniature crossbar (MINIBAR[2]) switch designed by Northern Electric. This promised to be a robust system; for example, if there were problems with the computer system, connections would be maintained during the problem (i.e., telephone conversations

1. An overview of central office switching technology is contained in a later section.
2. Registered trademark of Northern Telecom.

would not be cut off because of the computer problem). In 1965, a commitment was made to proceed with the SP-1, and the product development team grew from half a dozen people in 1965 to well over a hundred by the end of the decade. The first trial office (a switch installed in a telephone company exchange) was installed near Ottawa in November 1969; and on the basis of this trial, the product details were finalized. Detailed manufacturing engineering was then begun, manufacturing capacity was installed, and the first commercial office was placed in service in November 1971. During this period, the introductory marketing campaign for the SP-1 began. Seminars were held across Canada for telephone company executives. The first sale outside Bell Canada was to Alberta Government Telephones.

By 1975, versions of the SP-1 switch were available that could handle local exchanges from about 3000 to 25,000 telephone lines, medium-sized toll exchanges, and a combination of both. In the toll exchanges, operator positions were tied directly into the exchanges, allowing small telephone companies to play a bigger role in handling their own profitable toll business. This was an important selling point to independent telephone companies in the United States, who were always in conflict with AT&T Long Lines over toll revenues. By 1975, every major telephone company in Canada had bought the switch, and the SP-1 achieved about a 90 percent market share of the addressed segments of the switching market in Canada. Sales through 1975 were much higher than expected, with 25 percent of 1974 sales being made in the United States, and the SP-1 was viewed by non-AT&T companies in North America as the premium stored-program switch. Some sales were also made in the Caribbean. The sales history and some sales forecasts for the product are shown in exhibit 1. The expected flattening of sales in 1975 in the United States was due largely to the 1974–1975 recession, which was having a significant impact on capital expenditure programs in the telephone industry.

Bell-Northern Research

By 1970, Northern Electric Laboratories had become a major research and development organization, employing about 2000 people. At that time the decision was made to incorporate it as a separate entity. On January 1, 1971, Bell-Northern Research Limited (BNR) came into being, and the employees of Northern Electric Laboratories became employees of the ''new'' company. BNR did research and development work for both Northern Telecom and Bell Canada, with about 70 percent of its funding coming from the former and the remaining 30 percent from the latter. A very close working relationship continued among the three organizations.

Exhibit 1   Sales History and Sales Forecasts for SP-1
Central Office Switches (in Millions of Dollars)

Year	Canada	United States	Other Exports	Total
1971	6	0	0	6
1972	15	0	0	15
1973	33	2	0	35
1974	76	26	0	102
1975 (estimated)	148	27	0	175
1976 forecast	137	12[a]	0	149
1977 forecast	171	8[a]	8	186
1978 forecast	183	9[a]	7	198
1979 forecast	192	10[a]	12	214
1980 forecast	202	12[a]	15	229

a. Northern Telecom was to begin manufacturing some SP-1 switches in the United States beginning in 1976. These forecasts only include exports from Canada to the United States. Forecasts of shipments from the U.S. plant were not available.
Source: Company records.

The Telephone Industry

At the end of 1974, 357 million telephones were in service around the world, and that number had been growing by about 8 percent per year. About 44 percent of the world's telephones were located in the United States and Canada, with a further 27 percent and 12 percent in Western Europe and Japan, respectively. The total investment in telecommunications plant and equipment to support the North American telecommunications network alone exceeded $110 billion in 1975. Construction expenditures by telephone companies in North America, which included expenditures on switching equipment, had grown (in nominal dollars) at over 15 percent per year in Canada and 9.5 percent per year in the United States during the period 1965–1975. Expenditure growth rates were even higher outside North America.

Canada

Bell Canada, its subsidiaries, and its affiliated companies (New Brunswick Telephone Co., Maritime Telegraph and Telephone Co., Newfoundland Telephone Co., and Island Telephone Co.) provided most of the telephone services in Ontario, Quebec, the Atlantic Provinces, and the Northwest Territories. Together, these companies operated about 8.4 million telephones and were expected to spend approximately $225 million on central office switching equipment in 1975.

There were four major non-Bell telephone companies operating in Canada. British Columbia Telephone Company, a subsidiary of the U.S.-based General Telephone and Electronics (GTE), had about 1.5 million telephones in service. Alberta Government Telephones, Saskatchewan Telecommunications, and Manitoba Telephone System together had about 2.0 million telephones in service. Several hundred smaller telephone companies served about 300,000 telephones. Between them, the non-Bell companies were expected to spend about $150 million on central office switching products in 1975.

All the major Canadian telephone companies were members of the Trans-Canada Telephone System (TCTS), which coordinated transcontinental telephone service, data communications, and television network facilities. In 1973, TCTS members had put into operation the world's first commercial national digital data transmission facility called Dataroute, demonstrating the Canadian telephone companies' leadership in, and belief in, digital technology.

United States

About 144 million telephones were in service in the United States in early 1975. AT&T (Bell System), which included 24 Bell System and associated operating companies, provided service to about 82 percent of the telephones in the United States. Western Electric was wholly owned by AT&T and, as a matter of policy after the 1956 consent decree with the U.S. Justice Department, with very few exceptions sold its products exclusively to Bell System operating companies and to the U.S. government. The operating companies were accustomed to purchasing their equipment from Western Electric. Western Electric's total sales in 1974 were $7.4 billion, and it had a net income of $310 million. AT&T was expected to spend $1650 million on switching equipment in 1975.

The remaining 18 percent of the telephones in the United States were served by about 1600 independent telephone companies. While many of these companies were tiny, some were very large companies. General Telephone and Electronics (GTE) serviced about 45 percent of all telephones served by the independent telephone companies and had telephone-related revenues of almost $2 billion. The major independent telephone companies, the number of telephones they served, and their estimated 1975 expenditures on switching equipment are shown in exhibit 2. The large independent telephone companies provided a full range of telephone services. Smaller independent telephone companies typically relied on others,

Exhibit 2 Major U.S. Independent Telephone Companies in 1975

Company	Number of Telephones Served (000's)	Estimated Expenditure on Central Office Switches in 1975 (millions)
General Telephone Company	11,800	$218
United Telecommunications	3,236	70
Continental Telephone	2,246	} 240
Central Telephone	1,222	
Other independent telephone companies	7,500	

particularly AT&T Long Lines, for the provision of toll services. The two largest of the independent telephone companies, GTE and United Telecommunications, had their own major manufacturing companies, GTE Automatic Electric and North Electric, respectively, which supplied much of the central office switching equipment to their owners.

The independent telephone companies generally served the more rural areas of the United States, not the major concentrations of population (although a GTE operating company did serve much of Los Angeles). This resulted in a higher proportion of their central offices being in smaller line sizes relative to the Bell System. The Bell System, through AT&T Long Lines, serviced the long distance and international markets, which required a large number of large toll central offices. In fact, while only 23 percent of AT&T's central offices had less than 1000 lines, 64 percent of the independent's central offices were this size. Conversely, 43 percent of AT&T's central offices had over 5,000 lines, whereas only 8 percent of the independent's central offices were this large.

Europe

The European market for central office switching equipment was growing rapidly, with total expenditures on central office switching equipment in 1974 amounting to $3 billion. The European market was more fragmented than the North American market, since each country had its own government postal telegraph and telephone company (PTT's). Most of the PTT's had restrictive technical standards and took other steps to protect their domestic telecommunications equipment manufacturers. Furthermore, Europe had quite different technical standards for telephone switching equipment than North America and Japan, which meant that a manufacturer had to extensively modify its switching equipment if it wanted to sell in both markets. The development cost of these general modifications for the overseas market was estimated by Northern Telecom to be up to $20 million for a particular type of central office switch, with at least an additional $1 million to meet the idiosyncrasies of each individual PTT. Nevertheless, despite these barriers, the European market was an attractive market with a lot of future potential. Telephone service penetration was typically only one third to one half of the U.S. penetration of 60 telephones per 100 people. Much of the European telephone plant and equipment was obsolete and was ripe for replacement. In much of the rest of the world, the situation was similar, except that telephone penetration levels were even lower in most countries.

Northern Telecom's View of the 1975 Market

Northern Telecom executives generally viewed their North American customers as falling into three major segments: (1) Bell Canada, its subsidiaries and affiliated companies; (2) system telephone companies (the other telephone companies in TCTS, the Bell System operating companies in the U.S., and the major independent telephone companies in the U.S.); and (3) the smaller independent telephone companies in the United States and Canada. The first two of these segments operated full telephone systems, including local and major toll (long distance) switching systems.

Northern Telecom's close relationship with Bell Canada gave it access to operating company information which was very useful in setting product specifications and planning production. These two companies also shared the same knowledge base with Bell-Northern Research. Many executives viewed this close working relationship as providing a major advantage to both corporations. Bell typically identified its approximate requirements for switching equipment from Northern Telecom about two to three years in advance and provided detailed specifications of its needs about one year in advance. Northern Telecom provided firm price quotations at this point, and such prices were required to be as low as or lower than those provided to any other customer.

Alberta Government Telephones (AGT), Manitoba Telephone, and Saskatchewan Telecommunications used a more competitive buying procedure, AGT being the most extreme on this dimension. AGT typically developed tender documents with a detailed set of specifications, and Northern Telecom and other interested manufacturers would be asked to submit bids. B.C. Telephone and Quebec Telephone were special cases in the Canadian market, reflecting their status as subsidiaries of GTE. Since GTE had its own manufacturing subsidiary, GTE Automatic Electric, B.C.

Telephone and, to a lesser extent, Quebec Telephone bought most of their switching equipment from GTE Automatic Electric. B.C. Telephone bought switching equipment from Northern Telecom only when Automatic Electric didn't manufacture the required type of switch or when Automatic Electric couldn't meet its delivery requirements. Overall, Northern Telecom's share of the Canadian central office switching market, excluding British Columbia and the market for add-on extensions to non-Northern products, was about 90 percent. Most of the remaining 10 percent went to GTE Automatic Electric.

In the United States, the major independent telephone companies, except the GTE and United Telecommunications operating companies, generally used competitive tenders to buy equipment. This left about 8 percent of the U.S. market being awarded on a competitive tender basis. Their needs and buying criteria were generally similar to the major Canadian telephone companies; hence, they were usually seeking similar benefits from the switching products. These customers typically bought switching equipment from more than one supplier.

Many of the smaller independent telephone companies used low-interest loans from the Rural Electrification Authority (REA) to buy switching equipment. The REA set specifications for switching equipment, and telephone companies using REA money to purchase switches had to use a competitive tender against specifications, the business being awarded to the lowest bidder who met the specifications. However, a 6 percent penalty was applied to the bids of suppliers with insufficient U.S.-manufactured equipment in their proposals. In total in the United States, about 80 percent of Northern Telecom's switching equipment sales were the result of competitive tenders, the remainder being directed orders. Many of the smaller independent telephone companies did not have a sophisticated engineering capability within their organizations. Thus, in making major decisions about what equipment to buy, they often relied on what the respected larger telephone companies were doing, particularly those that seemed to be in a position to make an "unbiased" choice.

The Bell System operating companies and the GTE operating companies generally bought almost all their central office switching equipment from Western Electric and GTE Automatic Electric, respectively. Only in rare circumstances, when these manufacturing subsidiaries were unable to supply required equipment in a timely manner, did they go to outside vendors.

In dealing with all segments of the market, Northern Telecom executives believed customers preferred to deal with a supplier who could offer a full line of switching equipment to meet their needs. For large telephone companies, this would include everything from small local exchanges to large local and toll exchanges.

The sales of central office switching systems was comprised of two parts: the sale of the initial switch and the extension sales that allowed the basic switch to be expanded to meet the growth in the market served by the exchange. In the case of the SP-1 switch, the average initial installation was approximately 8000 lines, and the average ultimate capacity of each exchange sold was expected to be 20,000 lines. In other words, for every $1.00 spent on an SP-1 initial office, another $1.50 or more in extension sales would occur in subsequent years. Once a customer purchased an initial office from Northern Telecom or another vendor, they were committed to purchasing the extension equipment from the same vendor. Thus, the product life cycle for a central office switch such as the SP-1 was made up of two subcycles, the first being initial sales and the second being extension sales. With respect to the SP-1 sales in Canada, shown in exhibit 1, 100 percent of the sales in the period 1970–1973 had been initial sales, this percentage declining to 90 and 82 in 1974 and 1975, respectively.

The importance of extension sales to the customer also made it difficult for new suppliers, particularly foreign suppliers without local manufacturing and support facilities, to break into the central office switching market. Telephone companies had to be convinced that a supplier was in the market for the long term so that the telephone companies would be able to expand their switches and obtain spare parts many years into the future.

Central Office Switching Systems Technology

A central office switching system is the equipment that connects a telephone user's telephone with the telephone number dialed. Sometimes, as in the case of a long distance call, connections might have to be made through several central offices (local or toll exchanges) before the two telephones are connected (see exhibit 3a). Essentially, a central office switching system has two major components: the switching network and the central control system. The switching network is the electromechanical or electronic equipment that connects two telephone lines together and provides the dial tone, ringing, and busy signals. The control system activates the switching functions.

Digital Transmission of Speech and Data

Human speech shows up on an oscilloscope as an analog wave (see exhibit 3b). The height of the wave is directly proportional to the level of the signal transmitted. The number of waves in a given time period is a representation of the pitch or frequency of the signal. Thus, the analogue wave is a direct electrical representation of the sound waves used to generate it and is readily converted back to sound waves at the earpiece of the receiving handset.

In a digital system, the analog wave from the transmitting source is sampled at constant intervals, represented by the dots on the wave in exhibit 3c. A digital signal is then generated to describe the position of the dot on the wave. The digital signal takes the form of a binary word of eight bits (which can describe 256 different positions of the dot). A sample signal is shown in exhibit 3d. In order to get an accurate representation of the original analog wave, it must be sampled several thousand times every second by a codec (*co*der and *dec*oder)—a specialized electronic circuit. Technically, this process is called pulse code modulation (PCM).

After a conversation had been digitized, it looks like exhibit 3e, with one path for transmission in each direction. This compares to only one path required to transmit analog signals. At first glance, this might seem uneconomical, but digital communication can utilize multiplexing to dramatically cut transmission costs. Multiplexing simply involves the interleaving of several conversations on a single communication path (two wires). A sample is taken from the first conversation, then one from the second conversation, and so on, forming a frame of a predetermined number of samples. Each succeeding frame contains samples of the same conversations in the same sequence. At the receiving end, the samples are removed from the frames by a demultiplexer, and the multiple analog signals are reconstructed by a codec. Thus, all the conversations share the same two wire transmission path, but are separated by time (see exhibit 3f). Technically, this approach to signal transmission was called time division multiplexing (TDM).

Switching Systems

Space division switching (SDM), with different conversations being transmitted over separate wires, was the method the telephone industry had used prior to the mid-1970's to switch its analog signals. The earliest SDM switches were electromechanical step-by-step systems (S × S systems). While these systems were cheap, were relatively simple in design, and had large line capacity, they required large amounts of space, had few features, had high labour and maintenance costs, and were "noisy," making them satisfactory for voice communications but not "clean" enough for data communication.

Exhibit 3 Digital Technology

Exhibit 3a

To connect two telephones, connections might have to be made through local and toll exchanges (collectively called central office switching equipment) and perhaps through a private automatic branch exchange (PABX).

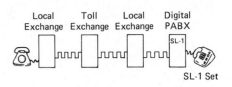

Exhibit 3b

Human speech as it shows up on an oscilloscope.

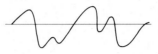

Exhibit 3c

In a digital system, the analog wave from the transmitting source is sampled at constant intervals. If the location of just the dots is transmitted, the analog wave can be accurately reconstructed at the receiving end.

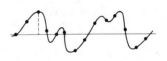

Exhibit 3d

Each sampled point on the wave is converted into an eight-bit binary word.

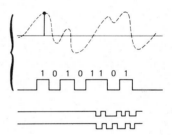

Exhibit 3e

A digitized conversation is transmitted in this form.

Exhibit 3f

Multiplexing can be used to transmit several conversations over one pair of wires. Each conversation is assigned to its own time slots. Here, one conversation occupies one time slot, and a second conversation (marked "x") occupies a second time slot. Thus, both conversations can share the same transmission path without any interference.

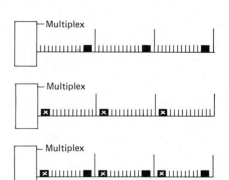

Source: Company records.

The next generation of SDM switches, first introduced by L.M. Ericsson of Sweden and later by AT&T in the 1930's, were electromechanical crossbar switches. These crossbar switches had several advantages over S × S switches, including more features, a more compact size, and lower labour and maintenance costs. However, these systems were difficult and expensive to extend. An evolutionary improvement over the basic crossbar system was one using reed relays rather than regular relay connections for connection points in the crossbar system. The reed relays operated more rapidly, consumed less power, and were easier to control than the earlier electromechanical switches.

A major advance in switching was the development of electronic switches, the first commercial model of which was the #1 ESS switch developed by AT&T and introduced commercially in 1965. The #1 ESS switch again used SDM signal path technology.

Modern exchanges, such as the SP-1 switch, used stored-program-control systems. Here, the software program controlling the system is stored in the alterable memory. This allows changes in the control system to be readily made. The availability of stored-program-control systems meant that a switch could be given a variety of features by making changes in the software. The computer could be readily programmed to handle maintenance, traffic analysis, and a host of other tasks that have to be done by a telephone company.

Northern Telecom and other industry executives believed that a successful all-digital system would provide significant benefits to users and telephone companies beyond those of state of the art stored-program-control analog systems. Being able to move many times as many signals over one transmission line would lead to better utilization of communication lines. Being digital, the information being sent was always uniform; that is, it was a bit of information, either a pulse or no pulse (again, see exhibit 3e). When a signal of this type became degraded through line loss, etc., it could readily be regenerated through the use of a digital repeater. These repeaters were tuned to look for bits and didn't blindly reproduce all signals in their inputs. Thus bits having lost their square shape could be regenerated to their original format resulting in a clean, interference-free signal. This was particularly important when transmitting data.

Northern Telecom first made use of the TDM-PCM technology in the T1 carrier, which was commercially demonstrated in 1963. The T1 carrier was used for interexchange transmission of signals, but it was expensive to manufacture and was economically practical only on heavily used portions of a telephone company's network.

By 1972, the first laboratory samples of large-scale integrated (LSI) circuits were becoming available. This allowed very complex circuits of hundreds or thousands of individual components to be put on a tiny electronic chip. By 1975, Northern Telecom had been able, with the assistance of LSI technology, to incorporate time division multiplexing, pulse code modulation, and stored-program-control into a private automatic branch exchange (PABX), the SL-1. A PABX is essentially a small switching system that controls the private telephone system within a company or other organization's office or factory facility.

Northern Telecom executives and engineers could envision fully digital switching and transmission systems in the future with digital switches, transmission systems, and digital PABX's all linked together. In this environment, a subscriber set generates an analog signal, which travels to a line interface at the local exchange containing the codecs and multiplexers. The conversation, now in a digital format, travels through one or more toll offices to a local digital exchange. Here it could be converted to analog for a local line, or it could be forwarded in digital form to a digital PABX, where it is finally converted to analog form for the subscriber.

Competition

The market for central office switching products was intensely competitive, with North American, European, and Japanese companies competing for shares of it. The major manufacturers and their estimated sales of telecommunications equipment (including central office switching equipment) are shown in exhibit 4.

Western Electric was the largest manufacturer of central office switching equipment in the world. As a result of the 1956 consent decree, it was not generally a factor in non-AT&T markets. A high proportion of its 1975 switching equipment sales were stored-program-control ESS switches of different sizes (#1 ESS, #2 ESS, and #3 ESS). In the mid-1970's, AT&T had announced a very large digital toll switch, the #4 ESS, which was for sale to non-AT&T companies in the United States and Canada. This was a specialized toll switch for use in the largest metropolitan areas (e.g., Toronto, Montreal, and Vancouver in Canada) and had a fairly limited market. The product was expected to be available in 1976 or 1977.

Both GTE Automatic Electric and North Electric (the United Telecommunications manufacturing subsidiary) also had large captive markets in their own companies. GTE Automatic Electric's sales of its #1 EAX stored-program-control analog switch were growing, even though Northern

Exhibit 4 Major Manufacturers of Telecommunications
Equipment and Worldwide 1974 Sales and Net Incomes

Company	Sales	Net Income
Western Electric (U.S.A.)	$7400 million	$311 million
ITT (U.S.A.)—telecommunications equipment only	3000 million	176 million
Siemens A.G. (West Germany) —telecommunications equipment only	1600 million	—[a]
L.M. Ericsson (Sweden)	1500 million	79 million
Nippon Electric Company (Japan)	1500 million	18 million
Northern Electric (Canada)	958 million	54 million
GTE Automatic Electric (U.S.A.)	700 million	42 million
—Canadian subsidiary	117 million	6 million
North Electric (U.S.A.) —subsidiary of United Telecommunications	290 million	7 million
Stromberg-Carlson (U.S.A.) —subsidiary of General Dynamics	234 million	10 million

a. Income on total sales of $6600 million was $92 million.
*Source: Telecommunications Market: Operating Telephone Company and Manufacturers
        Statistics,* Northern Electric Company Limited, 1975.

Telecom executives believed that the SP-1 switch had better architecture and features that allowed it to be used in a wider range of applications. The announced #2 EAX switch, which was expected to be commercially available in 1978, was expected to be a very formidable competitor to the SP-1. Automatic Electric had also announced a digital medium-size toll switch, the #3 EAX. This switch was scheduled for introduction in late 1978. This switch was expected to have some impact on sales of the SP-1 in toll applications. In many ways, the first serious competition for the SP-1 in 1973 and 1974 had been provided by North Electric's NX-1E stored-program-control analog switch. Several versions of the switch were available, including local and toll switches.

International Telephone & Telegraph (ITT) was the largest European-based supplier of telephone equipment. It had market shares of about 15 percent, 32 percent, 25 percent, and 42 percent of the switching markets in Italy, West Germany, the United Kingdom, and France, respectively. In 1974, ITT had introduced its Metaconta-L line of stored-program-control analog switches into the North American market, and this line was beginning to provide new competition for Northern Telecom.

In 1974, Ericsson was developing and promoting its AXE stored-program-control analog switch in Europe, and some industry observers believed that this product's architecture had benefited from knowledge of the strengths and weaknesses of the SP-1 architecture, and was superior to it. Ericsson was believed to be developing digital switches that would be integrated into the AXE line.

NEC America, a subsidiary of Nippon Electric Company, manufactured a stored-program-control analog switch, the D-10. In 1974 and early 1975, NEC had been very aggressive in its pricing on some bids in North America.

A brief description of the major competitive stored-program-control analog switches that were available or had been announced for the North American market are included in exhibit 5. While these switches had a nominal size range, they were usually most competitive within a more limited range of line sizes. These switches generally cost between $150 and $300 per line, depending on the size of the switches, its features, etc. Exhibit 6 contains the particular switches Northern Telecom executives viewed as being most competitive in each of the major market segments. They did not view the SP-1 as being competitive in really large local and toll applications because of its maximum line size capacity. Furthermore, Stromberg-Carlson had a stranglehold on the small switch segment of the independent market with their old technology X-Y step-by-step equipment. SP-1 and other stored-program-control switches could not compete at the smaller line sizes with the X-Y system.

Digital Switch Development Efforts at Northern Telecom

Prior to 1969, digital switching had been regarded by the telecommunications industry as possible but too expensive to be practical. The rapid advances in electronics in the late 1960's led Bell-Northern Research (BNR) Systems Engineering to reexamine the status of digital switching in 1968. In early 1969, they reported:

> The feasibility of integrated (TDM-PCM) switching has been demonstrated in many countries and the successful results show, without a shadow of a doubt, that such a system is technically viable. Digital switching in the present situation can hardly compete with conventional switching systems. . . . However, the near availability of large scale integrated circuits will probably change the competitive position in favour of digital switching within 5 years, and definitely within 10 years. In addition, the development of the pulse code modulation transmission system, which is now well underway in most industrialized countries, will eliminate the need for interface equipment, and, therefore, will give integrated switching a decisive advantage over conventional systems, both from economic and technical viewpoints.

Exhibit 5 Competitive Stored-Program-Control
Analog Switches —Available and Announced

Company	Product	Nominal Size Range (in lines)	Comments
Northern Telecom	SP-1	3,000–25,000	
GTE Automatic Electric	#1 EAX	4,000–40,000	Competitive with SP-1 in large line sizes. Northern Telecom felt architecture inferior to SP-1. Doesn't have all the features of SP-1.
	#2 EAX	4,000–40,000	Introduction expected in 1978. Viewed as a very serious threat to SP-1.
ITT (Europe)	Metaconta-L	5,000–60,000	Introduced in 1974. Active bidding for orders in the U.S. and Canadian markets.
North Electric	NX-1E	1,000–20,000	Significant sales to U.S. independents.
Stromberg-Carlson	ESC-1	2,000–20,000	Significant sales to U.S. independents.
Siemens (West Germany)	ESK	500–3,000	Field trial underway in North America.
Philips (Netherlands)	PRX	5,000–25,000	No sales to date in North America.
Nippon Electric	D-10	2,000–40,000	Introduced in Japan in 1971. First North American installation expected in early 1977.

Source: Company records.

They recommended that Northern Electric consider very seriously the development of an integrated digital switching system to be available for domestic sales within 7–10 years.

The report and its recommendations were not accepted by all managers in Bell Canada and Northern Electric. A great deal of money and manpower was then being used to bring the SP-1 stored-program-control analog switch to market. Since it incorporated the latest technology, many

Exhibit 6   Competition—by Size and Type of Exchange and Market Segment—Available and Announced

	Small	Medium	Local	Toll
			Large	
Bell Canada and subsidiaries and affiliates	None[a]	None	None	Auto. Electric #3 EAX[b] Western Electric #4 ESS[c]
Other Canada	Auto. Electric #1 EAX	Auto. Electric #1 EAX Auto. Electric #2 EAX	Auto. Electric #1 EAX ITT Metaconta-L	Auto. Electric # 3 EAX[b]
United States	Auto. Electric #2 EAX North Electric NX-1E Stromberg-Carlson ESC1	Auto. Electric #2 EAX Auto. Electric #1 EAX North Electric NX-1E ITT Metaconta-L		

a. Bell Canada would likely buy only Northern Telecom products in these sizes and types of switches.

b. The Automatic Electric #3 EAX was an announced digital toll switch and was expected to be able to handle 10,000 to 20,000 trunks.

c. The Western Electric #4 ESS was a huge digital toll switch that could handle 25,000–100,000 trunks (i.e., it was suitable only for very large metropolitan areas such as Toronto, Montreal, Vancouver, and major U.S. cities). Western Electric had begun to market this product to non-AT&T companies, including companies in Canada.

Source: Company records.

managers were convinced that this switch would meet the telephone companies' switching needs for the next 15 years, and they were not convinced that there was a need to spend money on the exploratory development of a digital switch.

In early 1971, Bell Northern's Systems Engineering Group notified selected individuals in Bell Canada, BNR, and Northern Electric that technological advances in memories, logic, crosspoints, etc., now convinced them that the SP-1 system would be obsolete for new local and toll installations by 1980. Exploratory development work on digital switching had been under way in other countries for as long as 12 years. In late 1971, work began at BNR to build a laboratory "test bed" to demonstrate the technical feasibility of digital switching, and to demonstrate solid state digital switching and circuit design techniques. The "test bed" would also assist in providing estimates as to the costs of developing a digital switch. In 1972, an initial budget for digital research was proposed by the switching division to the Board of Northern Electric calling for expenditures of $22 million over 7 years with $1.5 million firm for 1974.

In 1972, BNR demonstrated a Large-Scale Integration (LSI) codec that would be a key element in any digital switching product. This codec was a key element in the SL-1 PABX, which was to be available by late 1975. By 1973, BNR concluded that its exploratory development programme had successfully demonstrated the technical feasibility of digital switching and that the SP-1 programme was providing a solid base of experience in stored-program-control techniques, much of which would be applicable to a digital switch. In late 1973, market research on the non-Bell North American market began. At the same time, a detailed economic analysis of the impact of using digital switching in Bell Canada's Montreal switching network suggested by projection that Bell Canada might be able to reduce its capital expenditures in the metropolitan areas in its service area by $100 million in the period 1982–1992, if it moved to digital switching. BNR Systems Engineering was now convinced that a digital switch had good potential.

In November 1974, the Digital Switching Division was formed in Northern Telecom Canada to begin developing a product plan for the digital line. A similar organizational change occurred within BNR Development. In December 1974, the realization began to spread that development of a line of digital switches was going to require huge expenditures on research and development (much more than the $22 million envisioned in 1972), and that these expenditures might have a major negative impact on Northern Telecom's earnings. Some executives pointed out that delaying development of the digital switches for two or three years would relieve Northern Telecom's tightening cash flow situation. Selected financial data for Northern Telecom is shown in exhibit 7.

These financial concerns precipitated a major review of Northern Telecom's whole digital switching strategy. Three people were appointed to develop a marketing strategy for central office switches. A presentation was to be made to the Tricorporate Policy Coordinating Committee (which includes top executives from BNR, Northern Telecom, and Bell Canada). The task force was composed of Dr. Donald Chisholm from BNR, Mr. Lloyd Webster from product line management at Northern Telecom, and Mr. Bill Anderson from Engineering at Bell Canada.

Exhibit 7   Northern Telecom Limited Selected Financial Data 1971–1974

	1974	1973	1972	1971
Earnings and Related Data (millions of dollars)				
Revenues	957.7	608.1	531.3	573.8
Revenues of company manufactured products	799.8	512.9	448.5	473.4
Reseach and development expenses	44.0	32.7	28.0	29.7
Provision for income taxes	49.6	30.5	21.0	14.5
Net earnings	53.8	32.0	20.1	12.6
Financial Position at December 31				
Assets				
Cash and equivalent	14.1	69.4	52.3	27.4
Accounts receivable	144.9	100.1	85.5	104.5
Inventories	255.0	177.3	112.5	112.2
Current assets	433.7	360.1	260.1	253.6
Gross plant	278.2	261.5	237.5	230.0
Accumulated depreciation	158.2	142.5	128.4	124.4
Net plant	120.0	119.0	109.1	105.7
Investments in affiliates	9.0	6.5	5.5	5.0
Other assets	5.1	6.7	1.7	1.3
Total assets	567.8	492.3	376.4	365.6
Liabilities				
Current liabilities	150.6	149.7	84.9	83.3
Long-term debt	104.5	69.6	73.5	77.1
Owner liabilities	27.5	28.0	25.9	21.4
Shareholder's equity	285.2	245.0	192.1	183.8
Total liabilities	567.8	492.3	376.4	365.6

Source: Company records.

The Situation in March 1975

While the telephone industry was still strongly feeling the effects of the 1974–1975 recession, economists were beginning to forecast robust growth in the Canadian and U.S. economies in 1976 and 1977. Most Northern Telecom executives, in early 1975, believed that the degree of competition in the central office switching market would increase markedly during this same period of time. GTE's #2 EAX, and other similar second generation stored-program-control analog switches as well as late market entrants such as ITT's Metaconta-L, were expected to have a negative impact on new initial orders for the SP-1. Executives also believed that one or more of several competitors might introduce digital switches in North America in the 1978–1982 time frame. Stromberg-Carlson, IBM, North Electric, Philips, ITT, Ericsson, and Nippon Electric Company were all believed to be doing some development work on digital switches and might be able to introduce such a product in the North American market by 1980. Something had to be done to maintain and improve Northern Telecom's position in the central office switching market. Two major alternatives were open to Northern Telecom.

Alternative 1: Delay Introduction of the Digital Switching Line

To make no firm commitment to a major research and development effort on a digital switching line yet and to merely continue with exploratory research on digital switching. Given the increasing competitive pressure on SP-1, the SP-1 could be upgraded or enhanced to make it more competitive with the second generation stored-program-control analog switches that were becoming increasingly available. Several enhancements were possible, including increasing the line capacity of the switch with a new processor, improved memories, and replacing the MINIBAR electromechanical network used on the SP-1 with a sealed reed network. Northern Telecom's own tests suggested that their MINIBAR switch was cheap to manufacture and outlasted and outperformed reed networks, but many customers viewed sealed reed systems as the newer and better technology. Development costs for an enhanced version of the SP-1 (perhaps called the SP-2) might vary from $5 million to $20 million or even more depending on the particular enhancements incorporated. The risks associated with this alternative would depend on the particular enhancements selected, but were in all cases significantly less than those associated with a digital product line, since no major new advances in technology or manufacturing capability were required to bring it to market.

Alternative 2: Move Rapidly to Introduce the Digital Switching Line

To commit immediately to a heavy research and development programme to introduce some or all of the digital switching products as rapidly as possible. As of March 1975, exploratory or development work was either being considered or was underway on five separate digital products:

1. D256: This was a digital switcher-concentrator that would be used in a small community to switch calls in that community and to concentrate the outgoing/incoming calls for digital transmission to/from the central office serving the community. The product was designed to serve from 24 to 256 lines. The earliest this product could be available was 1976.

2. SL-1: Development work was well advanced on Northern Telecom's SL-1 PABX, which was to be available to customers in late 1975. It was considered possible to develop a small central office switch from this product by 1979.

3. DMS (no number assigned): This was another digital switch designed to serve small local offices with 1500 + lines. It could be available in 1979.

4. DMS (no number assigned): This was a large digital toll switch handling up to 50,000 trunks. It could be available in 1980.

5. DMS (no number assigned): This was a large digital local switch with the capacity to handle up to 100,000 lines. It could be available in 1981.

The work to date on the last three of these products had been only very exploratory, and no firm commitment to develop them in any time frame had been made.

This line of digital products, when fully available, would greatly improve Northern Telecom's coverage of the central office switching market. Executives expected the line to provide major benefits to telephone companies in terms of low space requirements, substantial reductions in outside plant, particularly cable (given that many digital signals could be handled on one transmission line), and lower maintenance and operating costs. The proposed digital line could accommodate growth from a very small number of lines to very large line sizes, would allow telephone companies to service small communities cost effectively through the satellite switchers-concentrators, and, in general, would provide the customer with a very flexible system.

While most observers of the telephone industry expected that the industry would eventually move to all digital systems, the conventional wisdom was that such a change would not really begin to occur until the early to mid-1980's. Bell Laboratories and AT&T executives, who met frequently with the executives of independent telephone companies to set equipment standards, regularly voiced this view. AT&T was heavily committed to stored-program-control analog switches (and was, in the mid-1970's, installing almost one #1 ESS office every working day, somewhere in the United States). Since digital transmission of signals between exchanges was increasingly prevalent in North America, Bell Labs and Western Electric people claimed that the logical point of entry for digital switches was in large toll switches, since the digital machines could be directly tied into the digital transmission network without the need for any analog-to-digital interfacing. This was where Western Electric's #4 ESS and Automatic Electric's #3 EAX switches would fit. Thus, it was generally believed that, at that time, digital switching provided few advantages at the local exchange level.

Within Northern Telecom's digital alternative, there were options. Work on parts of the line could be accelerated by increasing expenditures on R&D, or cash could be conserved in the period 1975–1978 by initially focusing development on the small local offices (products 1–3). Two of the possible plans under consideration were:

Plan A. Focus major development efforts on the small local office switch only. With this option, R&D expenditures on the digital line would be $32 million. The small office would be available in 1979.

Plan B. Develop the architectural concepts for the total line initially with a phased introduction of the digital line (small local office in 1979, large toll office in 1980, and a large local office in 1981). Under this plan, R&D expenditures were expected to total $66 million.

Some managers were also concerned that a major acceleration of the digital line could have a negative impact on its future competitiveness. In one internal memorandum to members of the task force, it was pointed out that "the timing of the digital switch affects the technology/manufacturing plateau on which the design will be based—too soon may result in noncompetitive costs after initial introduction. Too advanced a technology base may result in a high-risk design, delays, and subsequent field problems." In the same memorandum, the Vice President of Marketing pointed out that the realization of the full potential of a digital switch would be realized only in a digital transmission environment. The greater the amount of digital transmission equipment in place, the less interfacing needed between analog and digital switches and the more economical the digital switch would be. However, the Vice President of Marketing stated that he felt that even in early 1975 the mix of digital/analog transmission circuits was such as to make the cost savings significant for most telephone companies.

If the decision was made to proceed rapidly with the digital switching line, top management realized that an integral part of their decision was when and how to time announcements of the various products. Sales of the SP-1 were growing rapidly, and management wanted to sell as many initial offices as possible in order to generate the largest volume of subsequent extension business. This extension business was captive business and was typically more profitable than the initial orders, since competitive pressures were less and costs were lower. Furthermore, announcement of a digital switch competitive with the SP-1 would probably have a negative impact on the sales of this product and its product life cycle.

Preparing for the Presentation

As the members of this task force began putting together their presentation for the Tricorporate Policy Coordinating Committee meeting on March 6, 1975, they realized that this was perhaps the most critical decision Northern Telecom would make in the 1970's. The R&D costs involved in developing the digital switching line were very large compared to other projects Northern Telecom had been involved in in the past. The technological problems associated with the digital switches were huge—one executive, who was familiar with the technical problems involved, suggested that the development of the digital toll switch alone was about eight times as complex as the problems of developing the SP-1. But the market potential for central office switches was huge. One study done by Northern Telecom market researchers suggested that the market available to Northern Telecom in North America alone would be about $1.5 billion between 1980 and 1984 (see exhibit 8). This excluded any extension sales and possible sales to the telephone operating companies of AT&T, GTE (including B.C. Telephone in Canada), and United Telecommunications. In one confidential internal memorandum that the task force had just received from a member of their staff, the manager stated:

> Can Northern afford the program? Central office switching is the real strength of the industry. It is the most difficult to get into because of the high investment needed and the depth of experience to reduce (customer risk). It also represents essentially a captive long-term business once the initial offices are sold. *Northern Telecom cannot really afford not to be in digital switching*—it is a matter of minimizing

Exhibit 8 Estimated Size of Available North American Market (millions of dollars)

| Year | Canada[a] | | U.S.A.[b] | | Total | Number of Equivalent Lines (000's)[c] |
	Local	Toll	Local	Toll		
1980	73	17	86	4	180	630
1981	82	18	196	5	300	1100
1982	93	19	205	5	322	1240
1983	105	20	210	5	340	1290
1984	112	21	220	5	358	1365
Total	465	95	917	23	1500	5640

a. Canadian available market excludes B.C. Telephone requirement, SP-1 extension sales, and all crossbar and step-by-step extension sales.
b. U.S.A. available market excludes AT&T, GTE, and United Telecommunications markets and the SP-1 extension market. The toll market includes only the one U.S. independent telephone company, which had previously bought a medium-sized toll switch from Northern Telecom. This was believed to be a conservative estimate of the available toll market in the United States.
c. Equivalent lines were calculated by adding the number of local lines to five times the number of toll trunks.
Source: Company records.

investment and selecting the right time. If it comes to a choice of priorities, there are many other product investments that should be cancelled before Northern's position in the central office switching business is jeopardized.

The week before the March 6 meeting, Mr. Lloyd Webster, the Northern Telecom representative on the task force was to meet with the top management group of Northern Telecom to hammer out their position with respect to digital switching for the Policy Coordinating Committee meeting. As he reviewed all the inputs provided by a large number of Northern Telecom managers, he wondered what position he should take in the meeting with Northern Telecom top management. As he thought about the decision, he kept coming back to the risks involved for Northern Telecom. "Are we sure we can build a digital line? Are we right that this is the time to go digital, when Bell Laboratories and others think it is premature? Are we willing to bet $70 million of Northern Telecom's money that this is the right time to go digital? What is the probability, if we do choose a digital option, that all we do is kill a successful profitable product line?"

CHAPTER VI
PRICING DECISIONS

Price differs from the other elements of the marketing mix in two important respects: we can change prices relatively quickly; and our competitors can and will react quickly with their own price changes.

New communication programs usually take *weeks or months* to develop, product changes take *months or years* to make, and changes in the sales force or the channels of distribution take *years* to implement. Price changes often can be implemented in a matter of *days*. Although price is the most flexible element of the marketing mix, we should change prices only after careful consideration of likely competitive reactions.

In setting prices, the major focus usually falls on the company, the buyers, and the competition. We will look at each of these areas in turn. Chart 1 provides a conceptual framework for price decision making showing the main issues to be covered in each of the three areas.

Buyer

The value of the product or service to the buyer is a key factor in making a pricing decision. The value to the buyer becomes especially important in situations where direct competition is weak or nonexistent. Usually, the value of the product or service is different for each market segment, resulting in some segments of the market being willing to pay considerably more for the same basic product than other segments.

There are a number of ways we can take advantage of this variation in willingness to pay. Often we can charge different prices for different classes of buyers (student ticket prices for different seating locations at a hockey or football game) and for use of the product or service at different times (electrical utilities charging industrial users different rates for peak and off-peak power consumption). Other companies find that if they bring

Chart 1   A Conceptual Framework to Aid in Price Decision Making

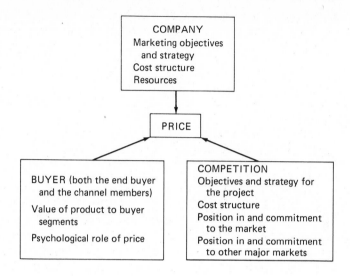

out the same basic product in several models, some buyers will be willing to pay disproportionately more for minor improvements in the basic product. This is a very common practice in many durable-good product classes, such as automobiles and electrical appliances. The product extensions will be introduced as the product proceeds through the life cycle for the product category (chapter 5).

In some product classes where product or service quality is difficult to evaluate, price can play an important psychological role in helping the buyer judge the quality of the product. In such a case, we should be sure to set a price that communicates the desired quality image to the target segments. Price is an important device to position the product in the market. We can extend the basic process of positioning that was developed in chapter 4, and we can make the price support the product positioning (chart 2).

In addition to looking at the end buyer for the company's product, we must also look at a proposed price from the viewpoint of any channel members (retailers or wholesalers) who are involved. Will the proposed price margins fit in with their pricing policies? And will there be sufficient incentive for the channel members to carry and promote the product effectively?

Competition

The high probability of competitive reaction to pricing policy makes it crucial to look at any possible price changes from the point of view of all the major competitors before actually initiating any pricing action. To assess the likely reaction of each competitor, it is essential for us to place ourselves in the position of each of the major competitors. To do this in a realistic manner, we need a thorough understanding of such issues as the competitor's commitment to, and dependence on, the market; the competitor's resources; and the competitor's commitment to, and position in, other major markets in which the competitor is involved. For example, we might believe that one of our major competitors in a particular market has a large market share, has a cost structure similar to ours for this product, and is already making substantial money in the market. The competitor has

Chart 2   The Process of Positioning and the Implications for Pricing

COMPETITIVE ANALYSIS		MARKET ANALYSIS

strategies used
extent and importance of
  success
likely actions and reactions
	INTERNAL OR
	CORPORATE ANALYSIS
	
	objectives
	strengths/weaknesses
	performance
	fit with other
	  products
		statistics
		buying and usage behavior

DIFFERENTIATION benefits of importance preferences for benefit combination		SEGMENTATION possible segments size of segments
PACKAGE OF BENEFITS SELECTION	POSITION	TARGET MARKET SELECTION
PRICE CONSISTENT WITH comparative product quality benefits claimed competitors' benefit claimed product *line* quality anticipated shifts in strategy	IMPLICATIONS FOR MARKETING STRATEGY marketing objectives product price channels communications	

no other strong positions in, nor heavy commitments to, other major markets that would require its financial and managerial resources. In this situation, we might very well conclude that if we initiate a significant price cut, the competitor would match us immediately in order to protect its share of the market, because it is dependent on this market.

Company

Pricing decision making should begin with our marketing objectives and strategy for the product (chart 2). It is essential that the price set for the product or service be consistent with the other elements of the marketing mix. This is especially true when the quality of the product or service is difficult for the typical buyer to evaluate and when the company's reputation is not well known to the buyers. In this situation, it will be difficult for a company marketing a high-quality product or service to charge a low price and still maintain the product's high image.

Strategy of Penetration Pricing

In some new growth markets, we see some competitors pursuing a marketing objective of building a large market share relatively quickly. In recent years, several companies in the electronic calculator and digital watch markets apparently have pursued this objective. The successful accomplishment of this objective in many markets requires an aggressive penetration pricing strategy, with some companies occasionally selling below their full costs in the first few years. By aggressive pricing, the market often grows very rapidly (if it is price sensitive), competitors are discouraged from entering the market, and a company can gain a large market share. In later years, as the market matures, the company with the largest market share is often able to reap better profits, since its large market share usually allows it to produce and market its products or services at a significantly lower cost than its competitors.

Skimming Strategy

Skimming and penetration pricing are polar opposites in a continuum of pricing strategies. For example, in the calculator market, some competitors had different objectives, followed different marketing strategies, and hence had quite different pricing policies. Hewlett-Packard, an American manufacturer that markets its calculators in Canada, followed a strategy of producing technologically advanced calculators for specific segments of the market. Since it had a stronger research and development capability than most of its competitors, it often could place an advanced calculator on the market for a year or two before anyone else could imitate it. It therefore tended to price its products high and made much of its profits in the period before competitors could effectively enter the market. Once an aggressive price competitor introduced a competing product, Hewlett-Packard often quietly withdrew from that segment of the market or offered a new more advanced product. Because firms pursue different marketing objectives and different marketing strategies, they will follow quite different pricing strategies, even in the same markets.

In some situations, often where a firm has a monopoly or temporary monopoly in a market, it can sequentially appeal to increasingly price-sensitive market segments by first introducing a deluxe version of the product at a very high price, then a year or two later a more basic model at a significantly lower price. Polaroid, with its SX-70 camera, has provided a recent example of this type of skimming pricing strategy. Starting with the original SX-70 model at over $200, it has since introduced three additional, increasingly less sophisticated models, the cheapest model often selling for less than $70.

Cost Structure

Clearly, our company's cost structure for a particular product or service does have an impact on our marketing strategy in a particular market. While in the short run we can sell a product or service below its full cost, in the long run a market is only worth entering or staying in if we believe that we can price our product far enough above cost to provide a reasonable return on investment. It is important to note that the real cost of producing a given product (costs after adjustment for inflation) decline as we gain experience in producing a product. For some products there is evidence that real costs decline by 20–30 percent every time cumulative production doubles; that is, if the one-millionth digital watch cost the company $100 to produce, the two-millionth digital watch will only cost $70 to $80 to produce. In markets where there is price competition, the price of the product eventually tends to parallel the underlying decline in costs. This is an example of a life cycle for a product category, which we discussed in chapter 5, but this life cycle is very compressed in time compared to most product life cycles. In new growth markets, where cumulative production may double every few months, it is essential that we anticipate how costs and prices are likely to evolve over time both for ourselves and for our key competitors in the market.

In developing pricing policy, as in developing the firm's overall marketing strategy, we must pay careful attention to the firm's resources, especially financial resources. An aggressive pricing strategy of the type adopted by Texas Instruments for electronic calculators requires significant financial resources in the early years when the company must invest heavily in expanding capacity, and when it is obtaining little or no cash flow from its product. This is one of the reasons a leading Canadian manufacturer of electronic calculators got into serious difficulties—it simply did not have the financial resources to follow the pricing policies of companies like Texas Instruments for a long period of time. We should give careful consideration to this issue before deciding on the marketing and pricing strategy.

We have focused on the most general type of pricing decisions. There are, however, a number of specialized areas that could be discussed, including competitive bidding, product line pricing (pricing a line of related products such as the Simpson-Sears line of washing machines), and setting prices in periods of rapid inflation. But even in these areas, most of the major considerations fall in the same three basic areas. In summary, in making pricing decisions, we should pay particular attention to the company itself, particularly its objectives, marketing strategy, resources, and cost structure; to competitors; and to the various buyer segments. Each of these three basic areas undergoes constant change, and we must constantly stay abreast of changes in each of the areas if our pricing strategies and policies are to be optimal.

Price Leadership

In many markets in Canada, we have only three or four manufacturers making products for those markets. In these oligopoly situations, each manufacturer may be very sensitive to the pricing actions of its "partners" in the market, and they watch each other very closely. In these situations, price stability is maintained by one firm's taking over as a price leader or price setter in the market.

Overt agreements among competitors in Canadian markets are not allowed under Canadian legislation if it can be shown that these agreements lessen competition. However, a practice may be established in which one firm will almost always be the first to change prices, followed quickly by its competitors. The test of leadership is that there are some followers. The characteristics of the price leader are *power* through market dominance; *credibility* through organizational, financial, and marketing strengths; and *predictability* through consistent behaviour.

Methods of Setting Prices

One of the most common methods of setting prices is the "cost-plus" method, whereby some satisfactory margin is added to a predetermined cost for the product. Retailers, the construction industry, and many industrial marketers use this method extensively. Two issues arise with regard to cost-plus pricing. The first is that demand may be so strong that a price higher than the cost-plus price could be achieved with little or no loss in unit sales; that is, demand is inelastic in economic terms. In this situation, cost-plus pricing may throw away potential profits. The second issue is the dilemma of agreeing upon the definition and components of product cost. Economic theory says that you should use marginal (variable) cost for pricing decisions, but many managers adopt a long-term outlook and insist on pricing to cover *total* costs. Regardless of whether we agree to use variable or total costs, there is more than a trivial accounting issue about what will be regarded as fixed and variable costs.

A second method is to set prices based on profit targets. We may forecast that we can sell a certain number of units at a particular price. If that price and unit volume do not meet our profit objectives, we may explore the unit volumes we could achieve at various other prices until we find a price and a volume that promise to produce our target profit.

A third approach to pricing is to match competitors. If the product is largely undifferentiated and customers are believed to be sensitive to price, then matching our competitors is usually a safe approach. If we undercut a competitor's price and we are not the established price leader, we may trigger a price war. However, to the extent the product is differentiated by market or by nonprice factors such as product quality, packaging, or advertising, we should be cautious about simply following competitors' prices.

The fourth method is demand pricing. We try to determine how much our particular customers and the channel members are willing to pay for our product. If this price does not meet product costs and some target level of profit, we probably will not market the product. Thus, to some degree, the demand method of pricing includes the cost-plus and target profit methods. The main difference is that we begin with the price we believe the market will bear.

Determining Sensitivity to Price

For products already on the market, we can get a feel for the products' sensitivity to price changes as we observe actions and volume reactions.

We can reasonably predict the price sensitivity of a target segment of buyers just by looking at why they buy the product and how they use it. For example, if there are strong safety or esteem needs associated with the product, the buyers probably will *not* be very sensitive to price.

But what about new products, especially new product categories where there are no established price levels? How can we set prices with no bench marks? Again, we can look at how and why buyers purchase the product. We can conduct test markets in which we experiment with three or four price levels and attempt to hold constant all other marketing variables. A third technique is to set up simulated shopping situations for consumer goods. With industrial goods, we can calculate the objective economic benefits from using the product and then calculate a range of possible prices. We can also interview prospective buyers and ask them how much they would pay for a product that would perform a specified set of activities.

We have used this survey technique with prospective purchasers of luxury condominiums, a totally new concept in a particular city. First, we found which apartment model and features the potential customer wanted and then we asked if he would pay, for example, $75,000 for the apartment. If he rejected the first price, we asked $70,000 and so forth until we trickled down to the price the prospective customer would be willing to pay. A more direct approach would be to simply ask the respondent what he would be willing to pay for the apartment. The reason for using the more elaborate approach was to offset the respondent's tendency to state hypothetical prices for significant purchases.

Summary

The three parties that have to be considered in all pricing decisions are buyers, competitors, and the company. Within the company, the cost structure is a major determinant of pricing strategies that the company can pursue. A structure yielding low costs creates the possibility of taking advantage of a lower price to gain a larger share of market—a penetration strategy. Nonprice advantages, such as a visibly superior product or uniqueness in the market, set up opportunities for premium pricing or skimming. Uniqueness in a market poses a problem of determining the amount buyers are willing to pay. Judgment and experiments such as test markets can aid in solving that problem. However, in many oligopolistic markets, price leadership exists, and price may be set aside in favour of other forms of competition.

19 Assembled Products Limited

"How much nerve can one guy have? That little ——— has destroyed the whole market for all of us!" exploded Bill Boyd as he paced around behind his desk. His predecessor as president of Assembled Products, Phil Caplan, now his archrival, had just cut the factory price of steel utility sheds by another 10 percent. This was the third cut of 10 percent that Caplan had announced in the last year, and it was only a little more than two years since Caplan had left Assembled Products to start his own company.

Background

Assembled Products was one of the oldest fabricators of aluminum and steel products for residential use. It was a division of an independent extruding company that had annual sales of $30 million and net assets of about $6 million. In addition to steel utility sheds, Assembled Products manufactured and marketed aluminum ladders, pole clothes lines, metal tables, filing cabinets, and steel shelving. Utility sheds accounted for about 75 percent of Assembled Product's dollar volume in 1976.

Assembled Products had been the first manufacturer and marketer of steel utility sheds in Canada. These were the small, prepainted, user-assembled sheds that had become very popular in the early 1970's for storing garden tools, lawn mowers, pool equipment, and bicycles. By 1974, Assembled Products was selling 60,000 sheds each year at an average factory price of $100, which Mr. Boyd believed to be about three-quarters of the dollar and unit market for small utility sheds in Canada. The total market was believed to have leveled off at 75,000 sheds per year; and as of January 1977, the relative shares of the market for utility sheds were believed to be Assembled Products 40 percent, Caplan's 33 percent, Hobo Products 15 percent, with miscellaneous regional manufacturers accounting for the remaining 12 percent. At the same time, most manufacturing variable costs such as raw materials and labour were rising by about 10 percent each year.

Most utility sheds were sold directly to chain, discount, catalogue, and department stores, building supply dealers, and buying groups in a knock-down condition; most retailers priced the sheds at double their cost. During the 1960's, many independent dealers had closed, had been purchased, or had joined some form of buying group. The remaining 400 independent dealers accounted for 20 percent of the market at most. Assembled Products had a sales force of five men making contact with head offices and with building supply dealers.

There had been relatively few significant changes in the features of utility sheds over the years, except that the number of different sizes increased each year. The vast majority of utility sheds were prepainted steel with a peaked roof and one or two sliding doors. None of the three major manufacturers conducted any consumer advertising, but Assembled Products spent $20,000 in sales aids and trade journal advertising on the utility sheds.

When Phil Caplan left Assembled Products in January 1975, he took the Major Department Store account with him. In fact, Major provided the financing for Caplan's new plant, which was set up to produce only steel utility sheds. In 1974, Major had purchased 15,000 utility sheds from Assembled Products, but Caplan supplied that volume in 1975.

January 1976

At the peak of the buying-in season for steel sheds in January 1976, Caplan, the only salesman in the company, mailed a price list to all major buyers of utility sheds. On all sizes of sheds, the price was 10 percent lower than Assembled Products' price list. The only difference was that Caplan's price list specified a minimum order of 1000 sheds, whereas Assembled Products' price list showed prices for orders of 10, 25, 50, and 100 sheds; any orders for 1000 or more were negotiated with the sales manager, Mr. Park. Four weeks after Caplan mailed his price list, the Assembled Products' salesmen were issued new price lists, which matched Caplan's price and showed a 10 percent price reduction on smaller quantities as well. Hobo Products followed suit at the same time as Assembled Products.

June 1976

Six months later Caplan issued a second price list, featuring prices 10 percent lower than the previous list on all order quantities. As soon as the first Assembled Products salesman walked in with Caplan's new price list, Charlie Park groaned and then raced for Bill Boyd's office. A few minutes later they were joined by Doug Reimer, the manufacturing manager.

After the initial round of expletives, Boyd hauled out his cost book, which showed that Assembled's total cost was $75 for the same standard steel shed that Caplan was offering for $81. Park said that the $75 was loaded with $20 overheads, of which $10 was general overheads and $10 was directly attributable to steel sheds. Reimer, his face reddening with anger, speculated that Caplan's specialized assembly line gave him at most a 10 percent advantage on variable costs.

"Let's really chop our price and run that turkey right out of business," blurted Park. Reimer pleaded, "What's the best we can do, Bill?" After a few calculations, Boyd said, "The best we can do is match him, Charlie. Why not hold for a few weeks and maybe he will come to his senses. Surely this is the end."

Park disagreed. "Bill, his first inroads were the chain stores, but now he's starting to get some of our buying groups for the building supply dealers. We've got to do something right away, and I think Doug is right. We should cut our price five dollars below his eighty-one dollars and show him that he can't fool around with us."

Boyd was aghast. "And take a profit of one dollar per unit? We might as well quit right now! Charlie, outside of the buying groups, most of our remaining accounts are independent dealers buying in smaller quantities who are willing to pay a little bit more. Caplan has gone as far as he can go." Park retorted, "How can a dealer compete with a chain store across the street who is selling the same shed for twenty dollars less? Jeez, can you imagine the flak?"

Two weeks later the salesmen were issued new price lists that matched the Caplan prices on all quantities.

January 1977

In January of 1977, Caplan mailed a new price list showing a further 10 percent reduction on standard steel utility sheds in any quantity.

20 Romano Pizza Limited

In May of 1977, Mr. W.R. Bruce, the marketing manager of Romano Pizza Limited, was reviewing the facts and figures before he made his recommendation on pricing levels to Mr. A.L. Scott, the president of the company. In the western provinces, where there were strong local producers, the competition was so severe that the frozen pizza operations had lost money in 1975 and 1976 and promised to lose money in 1977 (exhibit 1).

The low level of profits from Romano's frozen pizza was totally unacceptable, and it was almost certain that some type of price increase would be required. Mr. Bruce would have to decide the timing and extent of the price increase and whether to introduce it regionally or nationally. To add further complications to his decision, Dominion Stores Limited had launched a new private brand of frozen pizza. On the other hand, Mr. Bruce was concerned that any pricing move would jeopardize Romano's share of the market.

The Frozen Pizza Market

Frozen pizza was sold in sealed packages in the frozen section of most supermarkets and convenience stores. On the basis of the 1975 Consumer Usage and Attitude Study the company had commissioned, Mr. Bruce believed that almost all housewives understood the concept of frozen pizza. The study suggested that frozen pizza was purchased as a substitute for pizzeria or homemade pizza and often was an impulse purchase. Two thirds of Canadian housewives had purchased frozen pizza at one time or another, and 58 percent purchased some frozen pizza each year.

The predominant package in frozen pizza was the 21-ounce size, followed by the 15-ounce size. The 21-ounce package usually contained one large pizza, and the 15-ounce size contained four small pizzas.

ANNUAL PENETRATION OF FROZEN PIZZA

	Percent
Total Canada	58
The West	62
Ontario	64
Quebec	49
Maritimes	40

One of the important factors in the frozen pizza market was that 35 percent of the users purchased 78 percent of the volume (exhibit 2). The heavy users had larger families; the mothers had part-time work and purchased lower-priced brands in larger quantities. The light-user group

Exhibit 1   Profit and Loss Statements for the Frozen Pizza Business for East and West, 1975, 1976

WEST

	1975 (000)	1976 (000)
Net sales[a]	$2,102	$1,833
Variable costs	1,551	1,315
Fixed costs	344	298
Gross margin	207	220
Advertising and sales promotion[b]	201	314
Other expenses	106	50
Profit before tax	(100)	(144)

EAST

	1975	1976
Net sales[a]	$3,915	$3,871
Variable costs	2,556	2,422
Fixed costs	376	441
Gross margin	983	1,008
Advertising and sales promotion[b]	386	647
Other expenses	198	314
Profit before tax	399	47

a.   Volume discounts already have been deducted.
b.   Includes cooperative advertising, trade and consumer promotions.

Exhibit 2 Consumption and Usage by Heavy, Medium, and Light Users

	Percent of Total Users	*Percent of Total Ounces Consumed*
Light users	40	9
Medium users	25	13
Heavy users		
A	18	11
B	11	19
C	6	48
Total heavy users	35	78

Usage by Occasion[a] *(percent)*	*Heavy*	*Medium*	*Light*	*Total*
Serve occasionally	26	48	42	42
Serve as a "treat"	11	29	37	35
Buy it as a stand-by for quick meals	7	17	23	22
Buy it for regular family usage, inexpensive meal	70	35	10	16

a. Columns sum to more than 100 percent because of multiple mentions.
Source: Usage and Attitude Study, 1975.

bought higher priced brands, had higher annual income, bought in small quantities, and tended to have smaller families.

The major reasons for using frozen pizza in order of mention were family enjoyment, flavour, convenience, simplicity, and good value (exhibit 3). The nonusers of frozen pizza gave the following reasons for nonuse.

	Percent[1]
Apathy	46
Dislike frozen foods	21
Price too high	18
Inferior taste	22
Not enough room in the freezer	15

In another question, which asked why they would not buy frozen pizza in the future, the major reason came back as "inferior taste," especially when compared to homemade or pizzeria products. "Inconvenience" was a distant second reason, and only 4 percent said that frozen pizza was too expensive. The sale of all frozen foods had risen rapidly during the 1960's but had tapered off during the early 1970's.

1. Adds to more than 100 percent because of multiple mentions.

Brands

Romano pizza was the first frozen pizza introduced in Canada when the production techniques first became feasible in the mid-sixties. Romano manufactured from a plant in Calgary and a plant in Hamilton. Manufacturing costs as a percent of sales were 4 percent higher in the West because of freight rates and other costs. Romano had gained distribution in 80–90 percent of all food outlets in Canada.

To the original plain cheese pizza, Romano had added a pepperoni and a deluxe variety. Romano executives believed that their pizza was superior in smell and appearance. Except for the Royal private brand, which was very strong in the western provinces, most of the private brands used cheaper ingredients and consequently did not offer the same rich aroma coming out of the oven.

Romano, McCales, Royal, and Aida were the only brands with national distribution. The company did not purchase standard store audit data on sales, share, and inventories, but the consumer panel data available suggested that Romano pizza held 64–75 percent of the frozen pizza market and that the closest competitor held only about 13 percent of the market (exhibits 4 and 6). These relative shares were confirmed by store reports and evidence of shipments. The mentions of "current trial" were believed to understate the Romano brand share but gave some indication of relative strength in various regions.

Exhibit 3   Reasons for Using Frozen Pizza by Type of User (percent)

Reason	Total[a]	Light	Medium	Heavy
Family enjoys it	72	69	89	94
Good flavour	58	54	71	90
When no time to order in	56	54	62	65
Simple, easier than homemade	45	42	62	60
Good value for money	35	30	58	70
Low price	19	17	29	40
Good aroma	32	28	49	58
Like to serve to guests	27	25	41	41
Nutritious	22	19	37	44
Stays hot	20	16	35	54
Right size	20	18	28	34
No additives	8	6	14	26

a. Columns sum to more than 100 percent because of multiple mentions.
Source: Usage and Attitude Study, 1975.

Exhibit 4 Brand Shares Based on Consumer Panel Data, Sept. 1975–Aug. 1976

Brand	1975 Sept–Nov	Dec–Feb	1976 Mar–May	June–Aug
Romano	67.9	66.6	64.0	67.3
McCales	11.4	13.0	12.1	6.8
Pizzo	1.2	4.3	2.6	1.3
Alonzo	1.4	1.2	1.0	1.6
Canadia	1.4	1.7	.6	.3
Mamma Mia	.8	1.0	.5	2.7
Capiche	1.2	.4	.7	—
All other brands	2.5	2.8	3.8	7.4
	87.8	91.0	85.3	87.4
Royal[a]	7.1	5.2	8.9	5.1
Aida[a]	3.6	.9	3.5	2.0
Tasty Treat[a]	.5	1.6	.7	3.2
Dominion[a]	.1	—	.6	1.0
All others	.9	1.3	1.0	1.3
Total private brands	12.2	9.0	14.7	12.6
Total market	100.0	100.0	100.0	100.0

BRAND SHARES BASED ON MENTIONS OF "CURRENT TRIAL"[b]

Brand	Total	Maritimes	Quebec	Ontario	Manitoba	Sask.	Alta.	B.C.
Mamma Mia	1.6	—	—	—	—	2.0	10.0	—
Royal	2.4	—	—	—	2.5	5.0	5.5	3.4
Capiche	4.4	2.0	—	7.0	—	—	—	—
Antonio	2.2	—	—	4.9	—	—	—	—
Tasty Treat	0.8	—	—	—	—	—	—	—
Alonzo	6.2	—	20.7	—	—	—	—	—
Romano	39.8	47.7	29.3	43.7	41.7	35.0	30.0	27.6
McCales	5.5	17.6	8.7	3.1	4.2	6.0	8.2	3.4

a. Private brands.
b. Responding to the question "What brands of frozen pizza have you tried in the last four weeks?"
Source: Usage and Attitude Study, 1975.

None of the food companies, including Romano, used media advertising to support their brands, although cooperative advertising occasionally was provided. In order to obtain and hold distribution, every nonprivate brand offered trade deals. In 1976, Romano offered 2 percent of sales for co-operative advertising allowances, and offered volume rebates, periodic case allowances, and free goods. Romano also selectively issued a high-value consumer refund offer in which consumers were given $3 if they sent five Romano labels to the company.

The data in exhibit 5 show how the major brands were perceived by consumers. Exhibit 6 shows the degree to which Romano buyers switched from one brand to another. Buyers of Romano frozen pizza showed extensive loyalty in Quebec and the Maritimes, but that loyalty eroded rapidly moving westward to Ontario and the prairies. Of the people who bought private brands of frozen pizza, approximately 50 percent of them bought only their private brand product, and this was uniform across the country. Among the private brand buyers who did buy other brands, Romano accounted for 40 percent of the volume and McCales for about 7 percent.

Trade margins varied from province to province, with a low of 20 percent in British Columbia to a high of 30 percent in the Maritimes. However, the Maritimes were a special situation in which a few distributors supplied most of the large retailers and added 12 percent to their distributor's cost. Romano's price for a case containing a dozen 21-ounce cheese pizzas was $21 for any orders less than 250 cases. The quantity discounts were 2 percent for 250 to 499 cases, an *additional* 1 percent on orders up to 1499, and a further 1 percent on orders of 1500 cases or more. McCales followed the same volume discount structure.

Although competitive products retailed below Romano prices, the competitors were believed to offer the same percentage trade margins. Exhibit 7 shows a survey of pizzeria and frozen pizza prices in one city, while exhibit 8 shows Romano and competitive pricing across the country.

The difficulty in pricing frozen pizza resulted in part from the absence of a stable price base for frozen and pizzeria pizza. Numerous specials and coupons caused wide fluctuations in prices on a weekly or even daily

Exhibit 5 Brand Profiles (percent)

Brand	"Easiest to Make"	"Best Tasting"	"Least Expensive"	"Best Quality"	"Best Value"
Romano	39.6	39.8	30.8	37.3	37.7
McCales	11.0	11.1	4.8	11.0	7.5
Capiche	6.6	5.5	4.3	4.4	4.6
Mamma Mia	.9	1.2	2.6	0.9	1.2
Royal	2.1	1.9	5.8	2.1	3.7
Alonzo	5.3	9.8	3.6	3.0	2.7
No brand	34.7	36.0	43.2	40.3	39.0

Source: Usage and Attitude Study, 1975.

Exhibit 6 Frozen Pizza Brand Duplication/Exclusivity Among Romano Buyers, 1976

	Canada	Maritimes	Quebec	Ontario	Manitoba/ Saskatchewan	Alberta	British Columbia
	Lbs. Vol. (000)	Lbs. Vol. (000)	Lbs. Vol. (000)	Lbs. Vol. (000)	Lbs. Vol. (000)	Lbs. Vol. (000)	Lbs Vol. (000)
Total Romano Sales (000s)	4365	250	492	1768	424	307	1124
Their purchasing of:							
Romano	74.9	91.3	89.4	82.9	66.9	58.1	59.9
McCales	8.1	8.1	5.6	13.6	4.5	—	3.9
Capiche	0.8	0.5	2.1	1.2	—	—	—
Alonzo	0.2	—	2.1	—	—	—	—
Pizzo	3.5	—	0.2	—	—	—	13.6
Pensa	0.5	—	—	—	—	—	1.0
Mamma Mia	0.7	—	—	—	2.4	2.0	1.5
Canadia	1.0	—	—	—	—	—	3.8
Maria Elena	0.6	—	—	—	—	—	2.4
All other mfrs.	0.7	0.1	—	1.6	—	—	0.1
Private labels							
Royal	4.8	—	—	0.4	7.3	20.0	9.8
Aida	2.2	—	—	—	18.7	3.7	0.7
Dominion	0.1	—	—	0.3	—	—	—
Rosa	0.7	—	—	—	—	9.4	—
Handee bake	0.3	—	—	—	—	3.6	—
Tasty Treat	0.8	—	—	—	—	—	3.1
All other private labels	0.1	—	0.6	—	0.2	—	0.2

Exhibit 7   Survey of Pizza Prices by Size in London, Ontario—May, 1977

Frozen Pizza

Brand	Total Ounces in the Package	Number of Pizzas in the Package	Type	Price	Price/ Ounce
Royal	22½	1	Deluxe[a]	$2.19	$0.097
	21	1	Pepperoni	1.99	0.094
Capiche	15	4	Cheese	1.79	0.119
	18½	1	Cheese	2.49	0.135
	21	1	Pepperoni	2.59	0.123
	23	1	Deluxe[a]	2.89	0.126
Alonzo	20	2	Pepperoni	2.18	0.109
	21	6	Cheese	2.08	0.099
McCales	14	4	Cheese	1.79	0.128
	14	4	Bacon	1.89	0.135
	15	4	Deluxe[a]	1.89	0.126
	20	1	Cheese	2.09	0.105
	30	1	Supreme	2.93	0.098

Pizzeria Pizza

Type	Small (about 15 ounces)		Medium (about 21 ounces)		Large (about 30 ounces)	
	Store 1	Store 2	Store 1	Store 2	Store 1	Store 2
Cheese	$2.95	$2.75	$3.50	N/A	$3.75	$3.95
Cheese, pepperoni	3.80	3.65	4.45	N/A	4.90	4.95
Deluxe	4.35	3.95	4.85	N/A	5.35	5.60

a. Deluxe tended to include cheese, pepperoni, and mushrooms.

Exhibit 8   Competitive Retail Pricing: Average Prices for 21-Ounce Cheese Pizza in Major Chains as of May 1977

City	Romano	McCales	Royal	Tasty Treat	Alonzo	Mamma Mia	Aida	Dominion
Vancouver	$2.22	$2.12	$2.12	$2.12	—	$2.12	$2.12	—
Edmonton	2.29	—	2.12	—	$2.29	2.12	2.12	—
Calgary	2.45	—	2.12	—	2.12	2.12	2.12	—
Regina	2.29	2.12	2.12	—	2.29	2.12	2.12	—
Winnipeg	2.29	2.19	—	—	—	2.12	—	—
Toronto	2.19	2.19	—	—	—	2.17	—	$1.96
Ottawa	2.45	2.12	—	—	—	—	—	—
Montreal	2.42	2.12	—	—	—	—	—	—
Halifax	2.52	2.29	—	—	—	—	—	—

basis. In addition, prices of both frozen pizza and pizzeria pizza had risen dramatically because of cost increases. Romano's most recent price change had been December 1974, when the case of a dozen 21-ounce cheese pizzas was moved from $18 to $21. In June 1973, the factory price for the same case of pizzas had been only $11. As of 1977, cost of goods was composed as follows:

	Percent
Tomatoes	10
Meats	10
Cheeses	20
Spices, other ingredients	8
Labour	13
Packaging	9
Distribution, fuel, delivery, taxes, hydro, selling	30
	100

Pricing Options

A number of factors would influence any price change decision for the Romano brand. Mr. Bruce believed that a price increase of 3–5 percent would be followed by their competition. Reports from brokers and other trade people had indicated that the frozen pizza competitors were facing reduced profit margins; some, such as Alonzo and Capiche, already had been forced to increase their prices. However, in September 1975, Dominion Stores had launched a private brand priced at $1.99 for a 21-ounce cheese pizza.

   Another major option would be to delay any price increase until the competitors were forced to move. Mr. Bruce was extremely reluctant to incur any major erosion in the price relationship of Romano compared to other frozen pizzas.

   A third option would be to put heavy advertising support behind the brand and raise the price. The promised benefit would be better taste, and the media budget would be $770,000. If company executives chose to conduct a test market of this strategy prior to national roll-out, Mr. Bruce thought that Calgary or Edmonton would be likely test cities.

   An important factor would be the federal government's anti-inflation guidelines. Under the guidelines, Romano Canada Limited would be limited to an increase of $2.10 to $3.45 per case. One option would be to take the full price increase available under the anti-inflation guidelines and try to avoid any further increases in costs and expenses.

According to Canada's applicable pricing legislation, any differential in prices between regions in the country would have to be cost-justified if that price differential could be deemed to lessen competition unduly. Mr. Bruce had to reach a decision that would spell out the extent and timing of any price increases. He knew that Mr. Scott would be very interested in the profit impact of any proposed changes in prices.

21 S.C. Johnson and Son, Limited

Four months ago, in November 1980, George Styan had been appointed Division Manager of INNOCHEM, at S.C. Johnson and Son, Limited[1] (SCJ), a Canadian subsidiary of S.C. Johnson & Son, Inc. INNOCHEM's sole product line consisted of industrial cleaning chemicals for use by business, institutions, and government. George was concerned by the division's poor market share, particularly in Montreal and Toronto. Together, these two cities represented approximately 35 percent of Canadian demand for industrial cleaning chemicals but less than 10 percent of INNOCHEM sales. It appeared that SCJ distributors could not match the aggressive discounting practised by direct selling manufacturers in metropolitan markets.

Recently, George had received a rebate proposal from his staff designed to increase the distributor's ability to cut end-user prices by "sharing" part of the total margin with SCJ when competitive conditions demanded discounts of 30 percent or more off the list price to end-users. George had to decide if the Rebate Plan was the best way to penetrate price-sensitive markets. Moreover, he wondered about the plan's ultimate impact on divisional profit performance. George had to either develop an implementation plan for the Rebate Plan, or draft an alternative proposal to unveil at the 1981 Distributors' Annual Spring Convention, three weeks away.

The Canadian Market for Industrial Cleaning Chemicals

In 1980, the Canadian market for industrial cleaning chemicals was approximately $100 million at end-user prices. Growth was stable at an overall rate of approximately 3 percent per year.

"Industrial cleaning chemicals" included all chemical products designed to clean, disinfect, sanitize, or protect industrial, commercial, and institu-

1. Popularly known as "Canadian Johnson Wax."

tional buildings and equipment. The label was broadly applied to general purpose cleaners, floor maintenance products (strippers, sealers, finishes, and detergents), carpet cleaners and deodorizers, disinfectants, air fresheners, and a host of specialty chemicals such as insecticides, pesticides, drain cleaners, oven cleaners, and sweeping compounds.

Industrial cleaning chemicals were distinct from equivalent consumer products typically sold through grocery stores. Heavy-duty industrial products were packaged in larger containers and bulk and were marketed directly by the cleaning chemical manufacturers or sold through distributors to a variety of end-users. Exhibit 1 includes market segmentation by primary end-user categories, including janitorial service contractors and the in-house maintenance departments of government, institutions, and companies.

Building Maintenance Contractors

In Canada, maintenance contractors purchased 17 percent of the industrial cleaning chemicals sold during 1980 (end-user price). The segment was growing at approximately 10–15 percent a year, chiefly at the expense of other end-user categories. *Canadian Business* reported, "Contract cleaners have made sweeping inroads into the traditional preserve of in-house janitorial staffs, selling themselves on the strength of cost efficiency. . . ."[2] Maintenance contract billings reached an estimated $1 billion in 1980.

Frequently, demand for building maintenance services was highly price sensitive, and since barriers to entry were low (small capitalization, simple technology), competition squeezed contractor gross margins below 6 percent (before tax). Variable cost control was a matter of survival, and only products bringing compensatory labour savings could command a premium price in this segment of the cleaning chemical market.

A handful of contract cleaners did specialize in higher-margin services to prestige office complexes, luxury apartments, art museums, and other "quality-conscious" customers. However, even contractors serving this select clientele did not necessarily buy premium cleaning supplies.

In-House Maintenance Departments

Government

In 1980, cleaning chemical sales to various government offices (federal, provincial, and local) approached $2 million. Typically, a government

2. "Contract Cleaners Want to Whisk Away Ring-Around-the-Office," *Canadian Business,* 1981, p. 22.

Exhibit 1 S.C. Johnson & Son Limited, Segmentation of
the Canadian Market for Industrial Cleaning Chemicals

By End-User Category

End-User Category	% Total Canadian Market for Industrial Cleaning Chemicals (End-User Value)
Retail outlets	25
Contractors	17
Hospitals	15
Industrial and office	13
Schools, colleges	8
Hotels, motels	6
Nursing homes	5
Recreation	3
Government	3
Fast food	2
Full-service restaurants	2
All others	1
Total	100% = $95 million

By Product Category

Product Category	% Total Canadian Market for Industrial Cleaning Chemicals
Floor care products	40
General purpose cleaners	16
Disinfectants	12
Carpet care products	8
Odor control products	5
Glass cleaners	4
All others	15
Total	100% = $95 million

body solicited bids from appropriate sources by formally advertising for
quotations for given quantities of particular cleaning chemicals. Although
bid requests often named specific brands, suppliers were permitted to offer
"equivalent substitutes." Separate competitions were held for each item
and normally covered 12 months' supply with provision for delivery "as
required." Contracts were frequently awarded solely on the basis of price.

Institutions

Like government bodies, most institutions were price sensitive owing to
restrictive budgets and limited ability to "pass on" expenses to users.

Educational institutions and hospitals were the largest consumers of cleaning chemicals in this segment. School boards used an open bid system patterned on the government model. Heavy sales time requirements and demands for frequent delivery of small shipments to as many as 100 locations were characteristic.

Colleges and universities tended to be operated somewhat differently. Dan Stalport, one of the purchasing agents responsible for maintenance supplies at The University of Western Ontario, offered the following comments:

> Sales reps come to UWO year 'round. If one of us (in the buying group) talks to a salesman who seems to have something—say, a labour-saving feature—we get a sample and test it. . . . Testing can take up to a year. Floor covering, for example, has to be exposed to seasonal changes in weather and traffic.
>
> If we're having problems with a particular item, we'll compare the performance and price of three or four competitors. There are usually plenty of products that do the job. Basically, we want value—acceptable performance at the lowest available price.

Hospitals accounted for 15 percent of cleaning chemical sales. Procurement policies at University Hospital (UH), a medium-sized (450-bed) facility in London, Ontario, were typical. UH distinguished between "critical" and "noncritical" products. Critical cleaning chemicals (i.e., those significantly affecting patient health, such as phenolic germicide) could be bought only on approval of the staff microbiologist who tested the "kill factor." This measure of effectiveness was regularly retested, and any downgrading of product performance could void a supplier's contract. In contrast, noncritical supplies, such as general purpose cleaners, floor finishes, and the like, were the exclusive province of Bob Chandler, purchasing agent attached to the Housekeeping Department. Bob explained that performance of noncritical cleaning chemicals was informally judged and monitored by the housekeeping staff:

> Just last year, for example, the cleaners found that the floor polish was streaking badly. We (the Housekeeping Department) tested and compared five or six brands—all in the ballpark price-wise—and chose the best.

Business

The corporate segment was highly diverse, embracing both service and manufacturing industries. Large-volume users tended to be price sensitive—particularly when profits were low. Often, however, cleaning products represented such a small percentage of the total operating budget that the cost of searching for the lowest-cost supplier would be expected to exceed any realizable saving. Under such conditions, the typical industrial customer sought efficiencies in the purchasing process itself—for example, by dealing with the supplier offering the broadest mix of janitorial products (chemicals, paper supplies, equipment, etc.). Guy Breton, purchasing agent for Securitech, a Montreal-based security systems manufacturer commented on the time-economies of "one-stop shopping."

> With cleaning chemicals, it simply isn't worth the trouble to shop around and stage elaborate product performance tests. . . . I buy all our chemicals, brushes, dusters, towelling—the works—from one or two suppliers. . . . Buying reputable brands from familiar suppliers saves hassles—back orders are rare, and Maintenance seldom complains.

Distribution Channels for Industrial Cleaning Chemicals

The Canadian market for industrial cleaning chemicals was supplied through three main channels, each characterized by a distinctive set of strengths and weaknesses:

1. distributor sales of national brands.
2. distributor sales of private label products.
3. direct sale by manufacturers.

Direct sellers held a 61 percent share of the Canadian market for industrial cleaning chemicals, while the distributors of national brands and private label products held shares of 25 percent and 14 percent, respectively. Relative market shares varied geographically, however. In Montreal and Toronto, for example, the direct marketers' share rose to 70 percent and private labelers' to 18 percent, reducing the national brand share to 12 percent. The pattern, shown in exhibit 2, reflected an interplay of two areas of channel differentiation—namely discount capability at the end-user level and the cost of serving distant, geographically dispersed customers.

Distributor Sales of National Brand Cleaning Chemicals

National brand manufacturers, such as S.C. Johnson and Son, Airkem, and National Labs, produced a relatively limited range of "high-quality" janitorial products, including many special purpose formulations of narrow market interest. Incomplete product range, combined with shortage of manpower and limited warehousing, made direct distribution infeasible in most cases. Normally, a national brand company would negotiate with middlemen who handled a broad array of complementary products (equipment, tools, and supplies) by different manufacturers. "Bundling" of goods

Exhibit 2 S.C. Johnson & Son Limited, Effect of Geography
on Market Share of Different Distribution Channels

Supplier Type	Share Nationwide (percent)	Share in Montreal and Toronto (percent)
Direct Marketers	61[1]	70
Private label distributors	14	18
National brands distributors	25[2]	12

1.	Dustbane	17%
	G.H. Wood	13
	All Others	31
	Total	61%
2.	SCJ	8%
	N/L	4
	Airkem	3
	All Others	10
	Total	25%

brought the distributors' cost efficiencies in selling, warehousing, and
delivery by spreading fixed costs over a large sales volume. Distributors
were therefore better able to absorb the costs of after-hour emergency service, frequent routine sales and service calls to many potential buyers, and
shipments of small quantities of cleaning chemicals to multiple destinations. As a rule, the greater the geographic dispersion of customers and the
smaller the average order, the greater the relative economies of distributor
marketing.

Comparatively high gross margins (approximately 50 percent of
wholesale price) enabled national brand manufacturers to offer distributors
strong marketing support and sales training along with liberal terms of payment and freight plus low minimum order requirements. Distributors
readily agreed to handle national brand chemicals, and in metropolitan
markets, each brand was sold through several distributors. By the same
token, most distributors carried several directly competitive product lines.
George suspected that some distributor salesmen only used national brands
to ''lead'' with and tended to offer a private label whenever a customer
proved price sensitive or a competitor handled the same national brand(s).
Using an industry rule of thumb, George estimated that most distributors
needed at least 20 percent margin on retail sales to cover sales commission
of 10 percent, plus delivery and inventory expenses.

Distributor Sales of Private Label Cleaning Chemicals

Direct selling manufacturers were dominating urban markets by aggressively discounting end-user prices—sometimes below the wholesale price national brand manufacturers charged their distributors. To compete against the direct seller, increasing numbers of distributors were adding low-cost private label cleaning chemicals to their product lines. Private labeling also helped differentiate a particular distributor from others carrying the same national brand(s).

Sizable minimum order requirements restricted the private label strategy to only the largest distributors. Private label manufacturers produced to order, formulating to meet low prices specified by distributors. The relatively narrow margins (30–35 percent wholesale price) associated with private label manufacture precluded the extensive marketing and sales support national brand manufacturers characteristically provided to distributors. Private label producers pared their expenses further still by requiring distributors to bear the cost of inventory and accept rigid terms of payment as well as delivery (net 30, FOB plant).

In addition to absorbing these selling expenses normally assumed by the manufacturer, distributors paid salesmen higher commission on private label sales (15 percent of resale) than national brands (10 percent of resale). However, the incremental administration and selling expenses associated with private label business were more than offset by the differential savings on private label wholesale goods. By pricing private label chemicals at competitive parity with national brands, the distributor could enjoy approximately a 50 percent gross margin at resale list while preserving considerable resale discount capability.

Private label products were seldom sold outside the metropolitan areas where most were manufactured. First, the high costs of moving bulky, low-value freight diminished the relative cost advantage of private label chemicals. Second, generally speaking, it was only in metro areas that distributors dealt in volumes great enough to satisfy the private labeler's minimum order requirement. Finally, outside the city, distributors were less likely to be in direct local competition with others handling the same national brand, reducing the value of the private label as a source of supplier differentiation.

For some very large distributors, backward integration into chemical production was a logical extension of the private labeling strategy. Recently, several distributors had become direct marketers through acquisition of captive manufacturers.

Direct Sale by Manufacturers of Industrial Cleaning Chemicals

Manufacturers dealing directly with the end-user increased their gross margins to 60–70 percent of retail list price. Greater margins increased ability to discount end-user price—a distinct advantage in the price-competitive urban marketplace. Overall, direct marketers averaged a gross margin of 50 percent.

Many manufacturers of industrial cleaning chemicals attempted some direct selling, but relatively few relied on this channel exclusively. Satisfactory adoption of a full-time direct selling strategy required the manufacturer to match distributor's sales and delivery capabilities without sacrificing overall profitability. These conflicting demands had been resolved successfully by two types of company, large-scale powder chemical manufacturers and full-line janitorial products manufacturers.

Large-Scale Powder Chemical Manufacturers

Economies of large-scale production plus experience in the capital-intensive manufacture of powder chemicals enabled a few established firms, such as Diversey-Wyandotte, to dominate the market for powder warewash and vehicle cleansers. Selling through distributors offered these producers few advantages. Direct selling expense was almost entirely commission (i.e., variable). Moreover, powder concentrates were characterized by comparatively high value-to-bulk ratios and so could absorb delivery costs even where demand was geographically dispersed. Thus, any marginal benefits from using middlemen were more than offset by the higher margins (and associated discount capability) possible through direct distribution. Among these chemicals firms, competition was not limited to price. The provision of dispensing and metering equipment was important, as was 24-hour servicing.

Full-Line Janitorial Products Manufacturers

These manufacturers offered a complete range of maintenance products including paper supplies, janitorial chemicals, tools, and mechanical equipment. Although high margins greatly enhanced retail price flexibility, overall profitability depended on securing a balance of high- and low-margin business, as well as controlling selling and distribution expenses. This was accomplished in several ways, including:

1. centering on market areas of concentrated demand to minimize costs of warehousing, sales travel, and the like;

2. increasing average order size, either by adding product lines that could be sold to existing customers or by seeking new large-volume customers; and

3. tying sales commission to profitability to motivate sales personnel to sell volume, without unnecessary discounting of end-user price.

Direct marketers of maintenance products varied in scale from established nationwide companies to hundreds of regional operators. The two largest direct marketers, G.H. Wood and Dustbane, together supplied almost a third of Canadian demand for industrial cleaning chemicals.

S.C. Johnson and Son, Limited

S.C. Johnson and Son, Limited (SCJ) was one of 42 foreign subsidiaries owned by the U.S.-based multinational, S.C. Johnson and Son, Inc. It was ranked globally as one of the largest privately held companies. SCJ contributed substantially to worldwide sales and profits and was based in Brantford, Ontario, close to the Canadian urban markets of Hamilton, Kitchener, Toronto, London, and Niagara Falls. About 300 people worked at the head office and plant, while another 100 were employed in field sales.

INNOCHEM Division

INNOCHEM (Innovative Chemicals for Professional Use) was a special division established to serve corporate, institutional, and government customers of SCJ. The division manufactured an extensive line of industrial cleaning chemicals, including general purpose cleansers, waxes, polishes, and disinfectants, plus a number of specialty products of limited application, as shown in exhibit 3. In 1980, INNOCHEM sold $4.5 million of industrial cleaning chemicals through distributors and $0.2 million direct to end-users. Financial statements for INNOCHEM are shown in exhibit 4.

INNOCHEM Marketing Strategy

Divisional strategy hinged on reliable product performance, product innovation, active promotion, and mixed channel distribution. Steve Remen, Market Development Manager, maintained that "customers know our products are of excellent quality. They know that the products will always perform as expected."

At SCJ, performance requirements were detailed, and tolerances precisely defined. The Department of Quality Control routinely inspected and tested raw materials, work in process, packaging, and finished goods.

At any phase during the manufacturing cycle, Quality Control was empowered to halt the process and quarantine suspect product or materials. SCJ maintained that nothing left the plant "without approval from Quality Control."

"Keeping the new product shelf well stocked" was central to divisional strategy, as the name INNOCHEM implies. Products launched over the past three years represented 33 percent of divisional gross sales, 40 percent of gross profits, and 100 percent of growth.

Mixed Distribution Strategy

INNOCHEM used a mixed distribution system in an attempt to broaden market coverage. Eighty-seven percent of divisional sales were handled by a force of 200 distributor salesmen and serviced from 50 distributor warehouses representing 35 distributors. The indirect channel was particularly effective outside Ontario and Quebec. In part, the tendency for SCJ market penetration to increase with distances from Montreal and Toronto reflected Canadian demographics and the general economics of distribution. Outside the two production centres, demand was dispersed, and delivery distances were long.

Distributor salesmen were virtually all paid a straight commission on sales and were responsible for selling a wide variety of products in addition to S.C. Johnson's. Several of the distributors had sales levels much higher than INNOCHEM.

For INNOCHEM, the impact of geography was compounded by a significant freight cost advantage: piggybacking industrial cleaning chemicals with SCJ consumer goods. In Ontario, for example, the cost of SCJ to a distributor was 30 percent above private label, while the differential in B.C. was only 8 percent. On lower-value products, the "freight effect" was even more pronounced.

SCJ had neither the salesmen nor the delivery capabilities to reach large-volume end-users who demanded heavy selling effort or frequent shipments of small quantities. Furthermore, it was unlikely that SCJ could develop the necessary selling and distribution strength economically, given the narrowness of the division's range of janitorial products (i.e., industrial cleaning chemicals only).

The Rebate Plan

The key strategic problem facing INNOCHEM was how best to challenge the direct marketer (and private label distributor) for large-volume, price-sensitive customers with heavy service requirements, particularly in

Exhibit 3 S.C. Johnson & Son Limited, INNOCHEM Product Line

Johnson Wax is a systems innovator. Frequently, a new product leads to a whole new system of doing things—a Johnson system of "matched" products formulated to work together. This makes the most of your time, your effort, and your expense. Call today and see how these Johnson systems can give you maximum results at a minimum cost.

—for all floors except unsealed wood and unsealed cork

Stripper:	**Step-Off** — powerful, fast action
Finish:	**Pronto** — fast drying, good gloss, minimum maintenance
Spray-Buff Solution:	**The Shiner Liquid Spray Cleaner** or **The Shiner Aerosol Spray Finish**
Maintainer:	**Forward** — cleans, disinfects, deodorizes, sanitizes

—for all floors except unsealed wood and unsealed cork

Stripper:	**Step-Off** — powerful, fast stripper
Finish:	**Carefree** — tough, beauty, durable minimum maintenance
Maintainer:	**Forward** — cleans, disinfects, deodorizes, sanitizes

—for all floors except unsealed wood and unsealed cork

Stripper:	**Step-Off** — for selective stripping
Sealer:	**Over & Under-Plus** — undercoater-sealer
Finish:	**Scrubbable Step-Ahead** — Brilliant, scrubbable
Maintainer:	**Forward** — cleans, disinfects, sanitizes, deodorizes

General Cleaning:	**Break-Up** — cleans soap and body scum fast
	Forward — cleans, disinfects, sanitizes, deodorizes
	Bon Ami — instant cleaner, pressurized, or pump, disinfects
Toilet-Urinals:	
Glass:	**Go-Getter** — "Working Foam" cleaner
Disinfectant Spray:	**Bon Ami** — spray-on foam or liquid cleaner
	End-Bac II — controls bacteria, odors
Air Freshener:	**Glade** — dewy-fresh fragrances
	Johnson's Pledge — cleans, waxes, polishes
	Johnson's Lemon Pledge — refreshing scent
Spot Cleaning:	**Bon Ami Stainless Steel Cleaner** — cleans, polishes and protects
All Purpose Cleaners:	**Forward** — cleans, disinfects, sanitizes, deodorizes
	Break-Up — degreaser for animal and vegetable fats
	Big Bare — heavy duty industrial cleaner
Carpets:	**Rugbee Powder & Liquid Extraction Cleaner** — cleans
	Rugbee Soil Release Concentrate — for pre-spraying and bonnet buffing
	Rugbee Shampoo — for power shampoo machines

Furniture: Rugbee Spotter — spot remover
Johnson's Pledge — cleans, waxes, polishes
Johnson's Lemon Pledge — refreshing scent
Shine-Up Liquid — general purpose cleaning

Disinfectant Spray: End-Bac II — controls bacteria, odors

Air Freshener: Glade — dewy-fresh fragrances

Glass: Bon Ami — spray-on foam or liquid cleaner

Cleaning: Break-Up — special degreaser designed to remove animal and vegetable fats

Equipment: Break-Up Foamer — special generator designed to dispense Break-Up Cleaner

General Cleaning: Forward — fast-working germicidal cleaner for floors, walls — all washable surfaces
Expose — phenolic disinfectant cleaner

Sanitizing: J80 Sanitizer — liquid for total environmental control of bacteria. No rinse necessary if used as directed

Disinfectant Spray: End-Bac II Spray — controls bacteria, odors

Flying Insects: Bolt Liquid Airborne, or Pressurized Airborne, P3610 through E10 dispenser

Crawling Insects: Bolt Liquid Residual or Pressurized Residual, P3610 through E10 dispenser
Bolt Roach Bait

Rodents: Bolt Rodenticide — for effective control of rats and mice, use with Bolt Bait Box

—for all floors except unsealed wood and cork

Stripper: Step-Off — powerful, fast stripper

Finish: Easy Street — high solids, high gloss, spray buffs to a "wet look" appearance

Maintainer: Forward — cleans, disinfects, deodorizes
Expose — phenolic cleaner disinfectant

—for all floors except unsealed wood and unsealed cork

Stripper: Step-Off — for selective stripping

Sealer: Over & Under-Plus — undercoater-sealer

Finishes: Traffic Grade — heavy-duty, floor wax
Waxtral — extra tough, high solids

Maintainer: Forward — cleans, disinfects, sanitizes, deodorizes

—for all floors except asphalt, mastic, and rubber tile. Use sealer and wax finishes on wood, cork and cured concrete; sealer-finish on terrazzo, marble, clay and ceramic tile; wax finish only on vinyl, linoleum and magnesite.

Sealer: Johnson Gym Finish — sealer and top-coater cleans as it waxes

Wax Finishes: Traffic Wax Paste — heavy-duty buffing wax
Beautiflor Traffic Wax — liquid buffing wax

Maintainers: Forward — cleans, disinfects, sanitizes, deodorizes
Conq-r-Dust — mop treatment

Stripper: Step-Off — stripper for sealer and finish

Sealer: Secure — fast-bonding, smooth, long-lasting

Finish: Traffic Grade — heavy-duty floor wax

Maintainer: Forward, or Big Bare

Sealer-Finish: Johnson Gym Finish — seal and top-coater

Maintainer: Conq-r-Dust — mop treatment

Exhibit 4 S.C. Johnson & Son Limited,
Profit Statement of the Division

Profit Statement

	$000
GROSS SALES	4682
Returns	46
Allowances	1
Cash discounts	18
NET SALES	4617
COST OF SALES	2314
GROSS PROFIT	2303
Advertising	75
Promotions	144
Deals	—
External marketing services	2
Sales freight	292
Other distribution expenses	176
Service fees	184
Total direct expenses	873
Sales force	592
Marketing administration	147
Provision for bad debts	—
Research and development	30
Financial	68
Information resource mgt.	47
Administration management	56
Total functional expenses	940
TOTAL OPERATING EXPENSES	1813
OPERATING PROFIT	490

markets where SCJ had no freight advantage. In this connection George had observed:

> Our gravest weakness is our inability to manage the total margin between the manufactured cost and consumer price in a way that is equitable

and sufficiently profitable to support the investment and expenses of both the distributors and ourselves.

Our prime competition across Canada is from direct selling national and regional manufacturers. These companies control both the manufacturing and distribution gross margins. Under our pricing system, the distributors margin at end-user list on sales is 43 percent. Our margin (the manufacturing margin) is 50 percent on sales. When these margins are combined, as in the case of direct selling manufacturers, the margin becomes 70 percent at list. This long margin provides significant price flexibility in a price-competitive marketplace. We must find a way to profitably attack the direct marketer's 61 percent market share.

The rebate plan George was now evaluating had been devised to meet the competition head-on.

"Profitable partnership" between INNOCHEM and the distributors was the underlying philosophy of the plan. Rebates offered a means to "share fairly the margins available between factory cost and consumer price." Whenever competitive conditions required a distributor to discount the resale list price by 30 percent or more, SCJ would give a certain percentage of the wholesale price back to the distributor. In other words, SCJ would sacrifice part of its margin to help offset a heavy end-user discount. Rebate percentages would vary with the rate of discount, following a set schedule. Different schedules were to be established for each product type and size. Exhibits 5 and 6 outline the effect of rebates on both the unit gross margins of SCJ and individual distributors for a specific product example.

The rebate plan was designed to be applicable to new, "incremental" business only, not for existing accounts of the distributor. Distributors would be required to seek SCJ approval for end-user discounts of 30 percent or more off resale list. The maximum allowable end-user discount would rarely exceed 50 percent. To request rebate payments, distributors would send SCJ a copy of the resale invoice along with a written claim. The rebate would then be paid within 60 days. Currently, Innochem sales were sold by distributors at an average discount of 10 percent off list.

Proponents of the plan maintained that the resulting resale price flexibility not only would enhance INNOCHEM competitiveness among end-users, but would also diminish distributor attraction to private label.

As he studied the plan, George questioned whether all the implications were fully understood and wondered what other strategies, if any, might increase urban market penetration. Any plan he devised would have to be sold to distributors as well as to corporate management. George had only three weeks to develop an appropriate action plan.

Exhibit 5 S.C. Johnson & Son Limited, Distributors' Rebate Pricing Schedule

Code	Product Description	Size	Pack
04055	Pronto Fast Dry Fin	209 Ltr	1

Eff. Date: 03-31-81
Resale List Price 71   613.750
Distributor Price List 74   349.837

Disc %	Quote (FST) (Incl)	Rebate %	Rebate Dlrs								

Percent Markup on Cost with Car Load & Rebate

Disc %	Quote (FST) (Incl)	Rebate %	Rebate Dlrs	2% Net	2% MU-%	3% Net	3% MU-%	4% Net	4% MU-%	5% Net	5% MU-%
(1)	(2)	(3)	(4)	(5)	(6)						
30.0	429.63	8.0	27.99	314.85	36	311.35	38	307.86	40	304.36	41
35.0	398.94	12.0	41.98	300.86	33	297.36	34	293.86	36	290.36	37
40.0	368.25	17.0	59.47	283.37	30	279.87	32	276.37	33	272.87	35
41.0	362.11	17.5	61.22	281.62	29	278.12	30	274.62	32	271.12	34
42.0	355.98	18.0	62.97	279.87	27	276.37	29	272.87	30	269.37	32
43.0	349.84	18.5	64.72	278.12	26	274.62	27	271.12	29	267.63	31
44.0	343.70	19.0	66.47	276.37	24	272.87	26	269.37	28	265.88	29
45.0	337.56	20.0	69.97	272.87	24	269.37	25	265.88	27	262.38	29
46.0	331.43	20.5	71.72	271.12	22	267.63	24	264.13	25	260.63	27
47.0	325.29	21.0	73.47	269.37	21	265.88	22	262.38	24	258.88	26
48.0	319.15	21.5	75.21	267.63	19	264.13	21	260.63	22	257.13	24
49.0	313.01	22.0	76.96	265.88	18	262.38	19	258.88	21	255.38	23
50.0	306.88	23.0	80.46	262.38	17	258.88	19	255.38	20	251.88	22
51.0	300.74	24.0	83.96	258.88	16	255.38	18	251.88	19	248.38	21
52.0	294.60	25.0	87.46	255.38	15	251.88	17	248.38	19	244.89	20
53.0	288.46	26.0	90.96	251.88	15	248.38	16	244.89	18	241.39	19
54.0	282.33	28.0	97.95	244.89	15	241.39	17	237.89	19	234.39	20
55.0	276.19	30.0	104.95	237.89	16	234.39	18	230.89	20	227.39	21

1. Discount extended to end-user on resale list price.
2. Resale price at given discount level (includes federal sales tax).
3. Percentage of distributor's price ($613.75) rebated by SCJ.
4. Actual dollar amount of rebate by SCJ.
5. Actual net cost to distributor after deduction of rebate and "carload" (quantity) discount.
6. Effective rate of distributor markup.

Exhibit 6 S.C. Johnson & Son Limited, Effect of End-User Discount Level on Manufacturer and Distributor Margins Under Proposed Rebate Plan

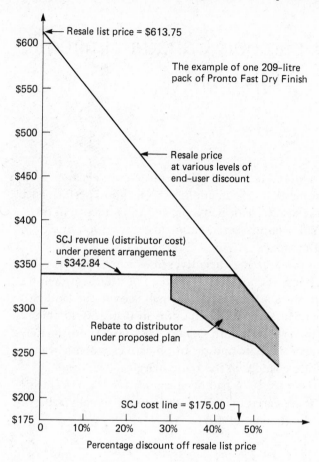

22 Warner-Lambert Canada Limited: Efferdent

Warner-Lambert Canada Limited launched Efferdent denture cleanser tablets nationally on October 9, 1973. In addition to its good performance in the Canadian test markets, Efferdent had a proven track record in the United States, where it had been marketed nationally since 1966 by Warner-Lambert's parent company.

In March 1976, the top marketing executives at Warner-Lambert Canada Limited met to review the marketing strategy of Efferdent denture cleanser. In the Canadian test markets, the brand had shown outstanding promise by reaching 8 percent share in five months in British Columbia and 27 percent share in the twelve-month Quebec City test. Unfortunately, the brand had failed to meet its share and profit objectives when it was launched nationally, despite changes in the trade margins. The original share objective of 26 percent by 1976 had been reduced to 21 percent in November of 1974, and it appeared that the brand would actually achieve about 18.5 percent share by the end of 1976.

The Company

Warner-Lambert Canada Limited was a subsidiary of Warner-Lambert Limited of Morris Plains, New Jersey. In 1975, the parent company ranked ninety-fifth in terms of sales ($2.17 billion) on the basis of *Fortune* magazine's review of the top 500 industrial companies in the United States. Net income was $165 million. The Canadian company manufactured and marketed pharmaceuticals, toiletries, and confectionaries. Some of Warner-Lambert's well-known products are Listerine mouthwash, Dentyne chewing gum, Rolaids, and Certs.

Warner-Lambert executives believed that the North American culture had become "a culture of abundance, of leisure, of consciousness of personal care and personal appearance, and of the outdoors." The nature of the company's line of consumer products reflected management's intention to respond to that culture. Accordingly, they believed that Efferdent denture cleanser fit the profile of the typical Warner-Lambert consumer product.

The Product

Efferdent tablets were about the size of a nickle in diameter, and when placed in very warm water, they produced bubbles and turned the water a blue colour. The denture wearer placed the dentures in the blue effervescing solution; after 12–15 minutes the solution cleared, indicating that the dentures had been cleansed. Competitive denture cleansers were marketed in tablets, powders, and creams.

In May 1973, the Block Drug Company had dominated the Canadian denture cleanser market with a national market share of 66 percent, consisting of Polident Tablets (36 percent), Polident Powder (9 percent), and Dentucreme (21 percent). Block Drug had followed a strategy of calling on the dentists and leaving them samples and information that might lead them to suggest Block products to their patients. Block Drug had a line of dental products, such as toothbrushes and gum desensitizers, which were sold direct to drugstores and food outlets across Canada by a sales force of eight to ten people.

A second competitor marketed Ansodent Powder, which had a 19 percent national market share with regional strength in the West. Steradent held a 9 percent market share, and a number of minor brands held the remaining 6 percent.

U.S. Experience

The parent company had test-marketed Efferdent in the United States in 1965 and had expanded nationally in 1966. The brand had gained an 8 percent market share in the first year in a market dominated by Block Drug with a 67 percent market share. Efferdent had eroded Block's franchise, gaining a 28 percent share by 1970 and a 40 percent share by 1973.

Efferdent's U.S. success was attributed to utilization of a "stain removal" advertising claim (versus Block's "natural look"), superior packaging, strong growth in food outlets because of the merchandising orientation of Warner-Lambert's sales force, and the company's trial-oriented consumer promotions.

Warner-Lambert (U.S.) had developed an "extra strength" formula with increased bleaching action and had introduced this formulation in the United States in June 1973. Coincident with this introduction, the brand had adopted new carton graphics utilizing a photo of an effervescing tablet on the face of the package. Although Warner-Lambert executives believed that Efferdent's chemical action was superior to competitive products, they acknowledged that the difference might not be visible to an ordinary consumer.

Canadian Test Markets

Efferdent had been test-marketed in Quebec City beginning in February 1972 and in British Columbia (B.C.) beginning in September 1972. The two test markets had been staggered in order to dilute the financial impact of any test-market losses.

Quebec City had been chosen as an area where a relatively small percentage of denture wearers (18 percent) used a commercial denture cleanser, while British Columbia represented an area where the use of commercial denture cleansers was quite high (63 percent). Warner-Lambert executives believed that Efferdent's potential users were quite price conscious, since they were generally older, in the lower to middle socioeconomic range, and frequently on fixed incomes. Warner-Lambert had no consumer research on denture wearers in Canada, and senior managers judged that Efferdent's profit expectations were too small to justify a $50,000 consumer usage and attitude study.

In the test markets, Efferdent was priced at parity with Polident tablets on a per box basis. Exhibit 1 gives the market penetration as a percentage of denture wearers of each form of denture cleanser prior to, and six months after, the introduction of Efferdent in each of the two test markets.

Exhibit 1   Market Penetration of Denture Cleansers as a Percent of Denture Wearers

	Before Efferdent		Six months after Efferdent launch	
	Quebec City (percent)	British Columbia (percent)	Quebec City (percent)	British Columbia (percent)
Tablets	5	16	15	25
Powders	12	25	9	26
Paste	1	22	1	13
	18	63	25	64

Before the introduction of the 42-tablet size, the product had been marketed in two sizes, 14 tablets per box and 28 tablets per box. Boosted by the introduction of a 42-tablets-per-box size in August 1972, Efferdent's market share in Quebec City had reached 26 percent by February 1973, and 42's were becoming the brand's largest-selling size six months after introduction. Exhibit 2 shows the mix of package sizes sold in each test market.

The brand's first-year share objective had been set at 10 percent. In British Columbia, Efferdent's market share had reached 7.6 percent after five months in test market. Warner-Lambert executives found the fact that this share level had been reached without the assistance of the 42's most encouraging. In addition, Efferdent had hurt Polident's B.C. market share in January–February 1973 (down 2.1 percent from November–December 1972) despite a special bonus tablets offer made by Polident in B.C. Exhibit 3 gives the competitive share trends during the test market period February 1972 to February 1973.

In September 1972, Miles Laboratories had introduced Vivact, a denture-cleansing tablet, into a Calgary test market. Polident had increased its price by 8 percent, and added a fourth size (66's). In addition, media spending for denture cleansers had almost doubled in some areas of Canada. Based on Polident's defensive action in Efferdent's test markets—"buy one, get one free" in Quebec City and bonus tablets in B.C.—it was expected that Block Drugs would defend its Polident sales nationally with the funds generated from their recent price increase.

Canadian National Launch

In May 1973, Canadian marketing management approved a recommendation to launch Efferdent nationally beginning October 9, 1973. They reasoned that it would be advantageous to launch Efferdent in October 1973 in order to spread the heavy initial investment of the national launch

Exhibit 2 Efferdent Share by Size and
Test Area, February 1973

Package Size	Quebec City— after 12 months (percent)	British Columbia— after 5 months (percent)
14's	13.7	2.4
28's	8.7	5.2
42's	4.4	—
	26.8	7.6

Exhibit 3 Test Market Competitive Share Trend

	J/F	M/A	M/J	J/A	S/O	N/D	J/F	Average (12 Months)	Gain/Loss (J/F73–J/F72)
QUEBEC CITY									
Tablets									
Efferdent	0	34.1	27.9	18.8[a]	25.9	27.9	25.9	26.8	+ 25.9
Polident	44.6	36.6	48.2	49.9	45.4	45.3	45.8	45.2	+ 1.2
Steradent	3.3	1.3	1.2	1.2	1.2	1.0	1.6	1.3	– 1.7
Total	47.9	72.0	77.3	69.9	72.5	74.2	73.3	73.2	+ 25.3
Powders									
Polident	16.4	9.2	7.0	11.1	10.8	7.1	7.8	8.8	– 8.6
Ansodent	11.3	4.8	4.6	5.2	3.6	3.1	4.0	4.2	– 7.3
All others	18.8	9.8	5.9	9.2	8.7	10.5	9.1	8.7	– 9.7
Total	46.5	23.8	17.5	25.5	23.1	20.6	20.9	21.9	– 25.6
Dentucreme	5.6	4.2	5.2	4.5	4.4	5.0	5.8	4.9	+ 0.2

BRITISH COLUMBIA

				Average (5 Months)	Gain/Loss (J/F73–S/O72)
Tablets					
Efferdent	3.6	7.6	9.6	7.6	+ 6.0
Polident	25.4	27.3	25.2	26.1	– 0.2
Steradent	1.8	1.3	1.4	1.4	– 0.4
Total	30.8	36.2	36.2	35.1	+ 5.4
Powders					
Ansodent	28.0	27.2	29.3	28.2	+ 0.2
Polident	6.3	6.6	4.9	5.9	– 0.4
All others	9.1	6.6	7.1	7.3	– 1.7
Total	43.4	40.4	41.3	41.4	– 3.0
Dentucreme	25.8	23.7	22.4	23.6	– 2.2

a. Temporary share decline results from major competitive promotion.

357

over two fiscal years and to preempt any further increase in competitive brand activity.

Despite the threat of aggressive action by Block Drug, the marketing executives at Warner-Lambert Canada felt that the denture cleanser market provided an excellent opportunity for Warner-Lambert to enter a new market category and to develop a potential series of lines relating to denture care. They judged that this was a prime opportunity because of Efferdent's proven ability in the Canadian test market and continuing strength in the United States, a very underdeveloped Canadian market with only 29 percent of denture wearers using a commercial cleanser, a low level of competitive spending and lack of strong competitive copy, and the Warner-Lambert sales force superiority and strength in the as yet underutilized food outlet segment. Competitive sales force orientation was said to be heavily skewed toward drug outlets with a very low level of merchandising and promotion activity. The marketing executives at Warner-Lambert believed that competitive packaging reflected a drug orientation and was antiquated in appearance. Exhibit 4 gives the major competitive brand profiles.

Efferdent entered the national market with the achievement of leadership in the denture cleansing market as its major long-term objective. Specifically, the 1974 objective was to achieve a 17 percent market share, growing to 29 percent by 1978 (exhibit 5).

The target market was defined as current users of competitive products and nonusers of commercial denture cleansers. The marketing strategy aimed to build high brand awareness with national television advertising; convince consumers that Efferdent tablets were superior to competitive products; obtain wide distribution of all sizes; achieve high consumer trial and interest through mass sampling, couponing, and advertising; maximize the shelf impact with superior package graphics; and obtain trade support by offering attractive incentives. The advertising campaign called for a combination of network and spot television in sixteen prime markets across the country with a timing schedule as shown below. The summer months would be avoided because of the reduced television audience at that time of year.

	(Oct. Nov. Dec.)	(Jan. Feb. Mar.)	(Apr. May June)
Weeks on air	— — 4	5 4 4	5 4 —
Media cost ($000)	40	115	75

	(July Aug. Sept.)	Total
Weeks on air	— — 5	31
Media cost ($000)	40	270

Exhibit 4 Major Competitive Brand Profile

Sales/Spending/ Market Share (1972)	Polident Tablets	Dentucreme	Ansodent
Retail sales ($000)	$1670	$900	$900
Retail share (percent)	36	21	19
Spending			
Media	250	125	90
Promotion	70	45	30
Total	320 (35 percent)	170 (35 percent)	120 (30 percent)
Regional strength	Ontario	B.C.	B.C./Prairies
Regional weakness	Prairies	Quebec	East
Copy positioning	Stain removal	1. Positioned against normal toothpaste 2. Dentist endorsement	1. Cleans, freshens 2. Natural looking, fast

	Polident		Dentucreme		Ansodent	
Usage and Attitude Results	Quebec (percent)	B.C. (percent)	Quebec (percent)	B.C. (percent)	Quebec (percent)	B.C. (percent)
Awareness	23	23	1	25	2	14
Trial	19	29	1	39	4	23
Trial within three months	17	18	1	26	3	17
In-home	15	16	1	24	3	16
Used last	14	12	—	24	3	13
Advertising awareness	45	63	N/A	22	N/A	N/A

Warner-Lambert executives planned six trade promotions and two consumer promotions (exhibit 6). In November, a direct-mail consumer programme would offer a high-value coupon to induce consumer trial and strong retail movement. This coupon had been very effective in British Columbia. In July of 1974, the 63's size would be launched with a trade incentive and a 25-cent cash refund offer to consumers. In addition, $50,000 was budgeted for a consumer sampling programme.

For the first six months after the national introduction of Efferdent, Efferdent tablets were imported into Canada and packaged in Canadian bilingual cartons. The tablets were based on the extra-strength formula that

Exhibit 5 National Projected Profit and Loss, October 1973 (000)

	1974	1975	1976	1977	1978
Market size	$5900	$6100	$6600	$7100	$7600
Percent change	+ 10	+ 4	+ 8	+ 8	+ 7
Efferdent share (percent)	17	22	26	28	29
Retail dollars	1000	1350	1730	2000	2200
Net sales	$ 670	$ 900	$1150	$1328	$1470
Direct costs (including direct cost of goods sold, freight, and research)	320	312	365	416	461
Trade and consumer promotions	254	185	140	160	175
Advertising	320	385	360	390	410
Total costs	$ 894	$ 882	$ 865	$ 966	$1046
Marginal profit	(224)	18	285	362	424
Test-market loss	(134)				
Cumulative	(358)	(340)	(55)	307	731
Payback	12	12	12	2 = 38 mos.	

had been introduced in the United States in June 1973. Canadian production began in April 1974, following the installation of the necessary equipment. Although the Canadian product also used the extra-strength formula, Warner-Lambert was not allowed to use the "extra-strength" claim because consumers across the country had not had an opportunity to purchase the original strength product. In the area of plaque removal and stain-removing ingredients, Extra Strength Efferdent was an improvement over the formula that had been test-marketed in Canada. The Canadian packaging closely resembled the U.S. cartons except for the addition of French and the deletion of the extra-strength claim.

Efferdent's pricing strategy was to maintain parity pricing with Polident *on a per box basis,* but to have fewer tablets per box in order to achieve premium pricing on a per tablets basis. This same strategy had been used in the test market. Once the brand had an established franchise in the category, the pricing strategy probably would move toward price leadership (lower than competition) on the belief that "pricing in the denture cleanser category was underdeveloped and elastic." Exhibit 7 shows the prices of the various competing products as of October 1973.

In addition, the Efferdent brand manager planned to match the Polident trade margin, which Warner-Lambert executives believed to be a 33.3 percent margin on the pharmacist's price to the consumer. Warner-

Exhibit 6 Trade and Consumer Sales Promotion Plan for the Efferdent National Launch, 1973

Month	Region	Promotion	Volume (000) Cases 000	Dollars 000	Weeks	Cost 000
October 1973	National	10/12's billing on 14's, 28's, and 42's	20.7	$155	8	$ 26
November	National	Coupon (direct mail)		154[a]		
January 1974	National	11/12's + $1.00 on 14's and 28's[b]	5.4	45	8	9
		11/12's + $1.50 on 42's	2.9	30	8	6
April	National	11/12's + $1.00 on 14's and 28's	10.8	90	8	18
		11/12's + $1.50 on 42's	5.8	60	8	12
July	National	11/12's + $1.50 on 63's + consumer offer of cash refund	5.7	80	8	29
						$100

a. Consumer couponing programme   96
   Sampling   50
   Merchandising material   8
b. Per case $254

Exhibit 7 Competitive Pricing, October 1973

	Size	Unit Price	Tablet Price	Index	Index Versus Polident Size
Polident tablets	16	0.65	4.06¢	100	100
	32	1.05	3.28	81	100
	48	1.49	3.10	76	100
	66	1.95	2.96	73	100
Efferdent	14	0.65	4.64	100	114
	28	1.05	3.75	81	114
	42	1.49	3.55	77	114
	63	1.95	3.10	67	1.05
Polident powder	3.0 oz.	0.65	2.71	100	67
	6.65 oz.	1.05	2.28	84	70
Ansodent	3 oz.	0.59	2.45	100	73
	6 oz.	0.98	2.45	83	75
	11 oz.	1.59	2.24	76	72
	16 oz.	1.95	1.82	62	61
Dentucreme	2.6 oz.	0.75	2.88	100	70
	4.2 oz.	0.98	2.33	81	71

Lambert distributed their proprietary products such as Efferdent directly to the drug and food trade. Wholesalers played only a minor role and bought at the same price as retailers.

Early Results

Efferdent did not penetrate the national market as quickly as Warner-Lambert executives had hoped. The product's market share during 1974 appeared to be falling 3 percentage points short of its target of 17 percent. Furthermore, based on the estimates available in mid-November 1974, it seemed that Efferdent's 1975 market share would be 15 percent rather than the 22 percent predicted in the plan for the product.

Upon further investigation, Warner-Lambert executives discovered that they had erred in their calculation of the Polident trade margin. In fact, Polident offered a 44.5 percent trade margin rather than the 33.3 percent assumed earlier by Warner-Lambert executives. Warner-Lambert salesmen had looked at a Block drug-price list that apparently did not show the 11.2 percent quantity discount that was, in fact, applicable to relatively small orders.

As a result of the discrepancy in the margin and subsequent greater profit per box available from Polident, the trade's merchandising support for Efferdent had been minimal. Although Efferdent was listed in almost as many food and drug outlets as Polident, Efferdent had been much less successful than Polident in obtaining multiple-size listings. Exhibit 8 gives the distribution of the two products as a percentage of the total number of stores in each category listing a particular product size.

Warner-Lambert district managers and sales supervisors also had observed that Efferdent generally was being sold at a per-box premium price of as much as 40 percent over Polident. The trade was believed to be doing this in order to compensate for the difference in trade margins between Efferdent and Polident. Exhibit 9 compares retail shelf prices for the two products.

Increased Trade Margin, November 1974

In November 1974, Warner-Lambert executives adjusted the trade margin on Efferdent to 44.5 percent so as to be on a par with Polident. The premium pricing (on a per-tablet basis) to the consumer had been maintained. Management had hoped that Efferdent's superior cleaning action and superior promotional activity would offset the 14 percent premium price.

Before November 1974, many retailers had sold Efferdent tablets at a price per box as much as 40 percent higher than the suggested retail price on Efferdent in order to compensate for the 11.2 percent discrepancy in trade margin between Polident and Efferdent. Following the adjustment in trade margins, Efferdent retailers had reduced the price per box to provide *box price parity* with Polident, and Efferdent had gained increased trade support. Although the reduction in price to both the retailer and the consumer had helped to improve Efferdent's sales by 33 percent in 1975, the increase had not been sufficient for the brand to meet its growth objectives of 21 percent share by 1976.

In December 1974, Block Drug had raised the price of Polident by 8 percent, but the price change had not been reflected on the shelf until August 1975. Although this competitive price increase had helped to reduce the per-tablet price discrepancy between Efferdent and Polident, Efferdent had continued to be at a premium price per tablet because of heavy deal activity on Polident. The per-box prices of the two products immediately after the Polident price increase are shown in exhibit 10.

Exhibit 8   Distribution Analysis—July–August 1974
Percent of Stores Listing One or More Sizes

		DRUG			
Efferdent	14's	28's	42's	63's	Total[a]
	65	74	73	21	94
Polident	16's	32's	48's	66's	Total
	88	87	81	55	100
		FOOD			
Efferdent	14's	28's	42's	Total	
	15	48	22	62	
Polident	16's	32's	48's	Total	
	37	54	32	69	

a. One or more sizes.

Exhibit 9   Retail Shelf-Pricing Analysis November 1974

Efferdent	14's	28's	42's	63's
Box basis	$0.56–0.65	$0.93–0.97	$1.19–1.39	$1.79–1.95
Tablet basis	0.04–0.046	0.033–0.035	0.028–0.033	0.028–0.031
Polident	16's	32's	48's	66's
Box basis	$0.45–0.65	$0.77–0.87	$0.97–1.33	$1.37–1.79
Tablet basis	0.028–0.041	0.024–0.027	0.02–0.033	0.021–0.027

Exhibit 10 Per Box Prices of Efferdent and Polident in August 1975

Polident	16's	32's	48's
Regular shelf price	$0.65	$0.95	$1.35
Feature price	0.59	0.85	1.23
Efferdent	14's	28's	42's
Regular shelf price	$0.60	$0.89	$1.25
Feature price	0.55	0.83	1.12

Immediately following the Efferdent launch in October 1973, Polident's share (tablets and powders) dropped to 33 percent and remained there.

As soon as it had become apparent to Warner-Lambert executives that Efferdent would not meet its share objectives in 1976, advertising expenditures had been reduced from $360,000 to $100,000 pending a decision on the brand's future strategy. However, trade and consumer promotions had been sustained, as shown in exhibit 11.

Strategy Options, March 1976

Warner-Lambert marketing executives reviewed the situation in March 1976, and four strategy options appeared. First, they could resize the Efferdent packages to conform with Polident sizes and thereby obtain both box and tablet price parity. Second, they could drop the price of the existing packages below the price of the corresponding Polident package, which would yield tablet price parity and a price advantage on a per-box basis. Third, they could increase promotional spending in order to support the existing premium pricing. Fourth, they could drop the brand.

Exhibit 12 shows the sales and costs anticipated for Efferdent in 1976 if the brand was held to the existing strategy.

1. *Resizing the Efferdent package.* Plant management had estimated that resizing the Efferdent package would require a $2400 expenditure for changes in machinery parts. In addition, management thought that resizing would provide an excellent opportunity for the introduction of a new glued-end carton. This would require the expenditure of $5200 for the purchase and installation of a hot-melt glue unit to seal the new style carton. The glued-end cartons were expected to provide an annual cost saving to the brand of $33,000. This saving would result from increased packaging efficiencies. Resizing also would require $2000 expenditure on artwork and a $13,000 write-off on unused cartons.

Any resizing would be accompanied by additional short-term advertising and promotional spending of about $90,000 in order to obtain trade acceptance and consumer awareness of the new sizes. It would be par-

Exhibit 11 Trade and Consumer Promotion Plan, 1976

Month	Size	Deal	Discount (percent)	Cases (000)	Expected Sales ($000)	Allowance ($000)	Total ($000)
February	42's	$1.25 per case merchandising allowance on 1–9 cases	12.5	1.5	13.3	1.9	1.9
		$2.00 per case merchandising allowance on 10 cases	20.0	8.5	75.6	17.0	17.0
					88.9	18.9	18.9
April	28's	$1.00 per case merchandising allowance	14.3	20.0	125.4	20.0	20.0
November	42's	$1.40 per case merchandising allowance	12.5	12.0	119.6	16.8	16.8
		Consumer sampling				84.3	
						Total	140.0

Note: 14's or 16's would be packed twenty-four to the case, 28's/32's and 42's/48's would be packed twelve to the case, and 63's/66's would be packed six to the case.

Exhibit 12 Projected Sales and Costs for Efferdent in 1976

		($000)
Net factory sales		665
Direct costs (including freight, direct cost of goods sold and research)	330	
Trade and consumer promotions	140	
Advertising	100	
Total direct costs		570
Marginal profit		95

ticularly important to get food trade distribution on the 42's size up from 25 percent to the 65 percent distribution enjoyed by the 28's. According to projections, the resizing might boost annual sales by $205,000 at factory prices.

2. *Reducing the price per box.* In October 1975, the Canadian government had introduced legislation aimed at curbing the country's two-digit inflation rate. Under the legislation an Anti-inflation Board (A.I.B.) had been established to control wages and profits. Any company wishing to increase the price per unit of any product would be required to justify this increase before the A.I.B. Thus, the anti-inflation legislation had placed constraints on Efferdent's future pricing strategy. In particular, it seemed risky to adopt any strategy that called for a reduction in the price of existing products. There was the possibility that once prices were reduced, the A.I.B. might not grant permission to raise those prices again.

The main argument for reducing the price per box below Polident prices would be to enhance the value of Efferdent in the eyes of the consumer. Although the per-tablet price would be identical, the shelf price comparison would tend to favour Efferdent.

3. *Additional advertising or promotional spending. Without* price parity per tablet, several executives thought that Efferdent would require additional advertising and promotional support of at least $200,000 per year. The key decision would be to choose between additional advertising that would be expected to have a long-term impact and further deal activity that would provide immediate sales increases. If increased deal activity was initiated, there would be a further critical decision between trade-oriented deals such as twelve cases for the price of ten versus consumer-oriented deals such as "10 cents off" which would be flashed on the package. Exhibit 13 shows one possible set of extra trade and consumer promotions that could be conducted in 1976.

Exhibit 13   Possible Additional Trade and Consumer Promotions for 1976

Month	Size	Deal	Discount (percent)	Cases (000)	Expected Sales ($000)	Allowance ($000)	Total ($000)
May	42's	$1.25 per case merchandising allowance	20.0	16.0	139.5	20.0	39.2
		$1.20 per case special					
July	14's	$1.00 per case merchandising allowance	12.0	1.5	10.7	1.5	1.5
September	28's	$1.00 per case merchandising allowance 1–9 cases	14.1	2.0	14.2	2.0	2.0
		$1.50 per case merchandising allowance 10+ cases	21.1	12.0	85.2	18.0	18.0
							60.7
		Consumer sampling					28.0
						Total	88.7

4. *Drop Efferdent.* A final option would be to eliminate Efferdent from the Warner-Lambert product line. After two and a half years on the Canadian market, the brand just passed the share objective established for its first year of national launch. However, Warner-Lambert executives believed that only 50 percent of all denture wearers were now using a commercial denture cleanser, a figure suggesting that there was a large potential market for Efferdent. A decision would have to be reached at the March 10 meeting because the president's midyear review of plans was scheduled for the following week. The president would expect a detailed marketing plan that would forecast sales and profits for Efferdent over the next five-year period.

23 Computron, Inc.[1] (R)

In January, Mr. Thomas Zimmermann, manager of the European Sales Division of Computron, Inc., was trying to decide what price to submit on his bid to sell a Computron 1000X computer to König & Cie., AG, one of Germany's largest chemical companies. Were Mr. Zimmermann to follow Computron's standard pricing policy of adding a 40 percent markup to factory cost (including transportation), 2 percent for installation, and 14 percent for import duty, the bid he would submit would be DM 203,000. Mr. Zimmermann was afraid that a bid of this magnitude would not be low enough to win the contract for Computron.

Four other computer manufacturers had been invited by König to submit bids for the contract. Mr. Zimmermann had received information from what he considered to be a "reliable trade source" indicating that at least one of these four competitors was planning to name a price that would undercut Computron's normal price by about 30 percent. In conversations he had had with König's vice-president in charge of purchasing, Mr. Zimmermann had been led to believe that Computron would have a chance of winning the contract only if its bid were no more than 10 percent higher than the bid of the lowest competitor.

Because König was one of Computron's most important customers, Mr. Zimmermann was particularly concerned about this contract and was wondering what strategy to employ in pricing his bid. He had exactly two weeks before the deadline for bid submission.

Background on Computron and Its Products

Computron, Inc. was an American firm that had several years ago opened a European sales office in Paris with Mr. Zimmermann as its manager. The

---

1. Names of all individuals and companies have been disguised. Data have been disguised but essential relationships maintained. Courtesy IMEDE Management Development Institute, Lausanne, Switzerland.

company's main product, both in North America and Europe was the 1000X, a medium-sized computer.[2]

Though it could be considered a general purpose computer, the Computron 1000X, which sold in the medium price range, was designed primarily for solving scientific and engineering problems. Ordinarily, it was not used for the solution of general business problems such as those of payroll accounting, inventory control, and production scheduling. Rather it found its basic applications in chemical and aircraft companies, public utilities, and nuclear engineering. In these fields, it was typically used to solve problems of chemical process control, aircraft and missile design, and design and control of electrical power plants and nuclear reactor stations.

In addition to its 1000X computer, Computron manufactured a small line of accessory equipment. These accessories, however, constituted a relatively insignificant share of the company's overall sales volume.

Computron's European sales constituted only about one-tenth of total company worldwide sales. Germany accounted for about one quarter of Computron's European sales. Last year, Computron sales in Germany had placed it fourth amongst competitors in its segment of the market.

Computron computers sold to European customers were manufactured and assembled in the United States and shipped to Europe for installation. Because of their external manufacture, these computers were subject to an import duty that varied in amount from country to country. The German tariff on computers of the type sold by Computron was 16 percent on the U.S. sales price.

Prompted primarily by a desire to reduce this importation duty and encouraged by recent European sales growth, Computron was constructing a plant in Frankfurt, Germany. This plant, which would serve all of the EEC, was scheduled to open in mid-March of this year. Initially, it would be used only for the assembly of 1000X computers. Assembly in Germany would lower the German importation duty from 16 percent to 14 percent. Ultimately, the company planned to use the plant for completely manufacturing computers in Europe to avoid all import duties.

The initial phase of the plant would occupy just under 1000 m[2] and would have an estimated annual overhead of approximately DM 1 million. As of January, the European sales office only had contracts for about one quarter of plant capacity, although it was anticipated that training and pilot assembly would keep the plant busy for one to three months from

2. Small computers sold in Germany in the price range up to DM 100,000, medium from DM 100,000 to DM 600,000, and large from DM 600,000 to DM 2,500,000.

the date of opening. Mr. Zimmermann felt under some pressure to generate additional business soon for this new facility.

Company Pricing Policy

Computron had always concentrated on being a high-quality, high-prestige company in its segment of the computer industry. The company prided itself on manufacturing what it considered to be the best all-around computer of its kind in terms of precision, dependability, flexibility, and ease of operation.

Computron did not try to sell the 1000X on the basis of price. The price charged by Computron was very often higher than that being charged for competing equipment. In spite of this fact, the superior quality of Computron's computers had, to date, enabled it to compete successfully in its segment in both North America and Europe.

The European price for the 1000X computer was normally figured as follows:

U.S. "cost"	(includes factory cost and overhead)
+ 40 percent markup	(for profit, research and development, selling expenses, and delivery)
+ 2 percent	(for installation)
+ duty	(varied by country and by specific components used in each individual 1000X machine)
European price	

Mr. Zimmermann's calculations following this approach are shown in exhibit 1. He arrived at a price of DM 203,000 for the 1000X, based on it being assembled in Germany.

The normal markup on cost used by the company was company policy. Top management had stated it was clearly against cutting this markup in order to obtain sales volume. Management felt that the practice of cutting prices "not only reduced profits, but also reflected unfavourably on the company's quality image." Mr. Zimmermann also knew that Computron's president was especially eager not to cut prices at this particular moment because Computron's overall profit before tax had dropped by half this past year compared to the previous year. In fact, the president had indicated he hoped to raise the standard markup on cost.

In spite of Computron's policy of maintaining prices, Mr. Zimmermann was aware of a few isolated instances when the markup on cost had been dropped to as low as 20 percent in order to obtain important orders

Exhibit 1   Calculated Normal Price for a 1000X Computer for König[a]

Factory cost	DM 125,000
40 percent markup	50,000
U.S. list price	DM 175,000
Installation (2% of list price)	3,500
Import duty (14% of list price)	24,500
Total normal price	DM 203,000

a. One CPU (60K), two 10 million character discs, 1 printer (300 lines per minute), and 3 visual display-interaction screens.

in the United States. In the European market, however, Computron had never yet deviated from the standard company policy markup level.

The Customer

König & Cie., AG, was one of the largest manufacturers and processors of basic chemicals and chemical products in West Germany. It operated a number of chemical plants throughout the country. To date, it had purchased three computer systems from Computron and one competitive system. Last year, König was Computron's biggest customer.

Mr. Zimmermann felt that the primary reason König had purchased Computron computer systems in the past was because of their proven reputation for flexibility, accuracy, and overall high quality. So far, König officials seemed well pleased with the performance of their Computron computers.

Looking ahead, Mr. Zimmermann felt that König would continue to represent more potential future business than any other single German customer of Computron's. He estimated that during the next year or two, König would have a need for another two complete computing systems.

The computer on which König was presently inviting bids was to be used in the training of operators for a new chemical plant. The training programme was to last for approximately four to five years. At the end of the programme, the computer would be either scrapped or converted into other uses. The calculations that the computer would be called upon to perform were highly specialized and would require little machine flexibility. In the specifications that had been published along with the invitations to bid, König management had stated that in buying this computer, König was primarily interested in dependability and a reasonable price. The latest technology in allowing machine-operator interaction was important to König for training purposes. Machine flexibility and pinpoint accuracy were listed as being of very minor importance, inasmuch as the machine was to be used primarily for training purposes and not for design work.

Competition

In Germany, approximately nine companies were competing with Computron in the sale of medium-priced computers designed to perform scientific and engineering calculations. Four companies, now including Computron, typically accounted for 80 percent of the business in any one year.

In preparing his bid for König, Mr. Zimmermann was primarily concerned about the following three competitors.

Ruhr Maschinenfabrik, AG: A very aggressive German company that was trying hard to expand its share of the market. It was number two last year. Ruhr sold a medium-quality general purpose computer at a price generally 95 percent of that Computron asked for its 1000X computer—but the import duty on the 1000X lowered this to 79 percent because the Ruhr machine was manufactured entirely in Germany. Though to date, Ruhr had sold only general purpose computers, reliable trade sources indicated that the company was currently developing a special computer in an effort to win the König bid. The price which Ruhr was planning to place on this computer was reported to be in the neighbourhood of DM 142,000.

Elektronische Datenverarbeitungsanlagen, AG: A relatively new company that had recently developed a general purpose computer of comparable quality to that of the Computron 1000X. Mr. Zimmermann felt that Elektronische Datenverarbeitungsanlagen presented a real long-range threat to Computron's aspirations as the "high-quality" company in the industry. In order to get a foothold in the industry, it had sold its first computer "almost at cost." Since that time, however, it had undersold Computron only by the amount of the import duty to which Computron's computers were subject.

Digitex GmbH: A subsidiary of an American firm, this company had complete manufacturing facilities in Germany and produced a wide line of computer equipment. The Digitex computer that competed with the Computron 1000X was only of fair quality. Digitex often engaged in price-cutting tactics, and the price it charged for its computer had sometimes, in the past, been as much as 50% lower than that charged by Computron for its 1000X. In spite of this difference, Computron had usually been able to compete successfully against Digitex because of the technical superiority of the 1000X.

Mr. Zimmermann was not overly concerned about the remaining competitors, inasmuch as he did not consider them to be significant factors in Computron's segment of the computer industry.

Mr. Zimmermann's Position

The total German market for medium-priced computers in the Computron segment could be expected to increase at an annual rate of 8–10 percent for the next several years. As Mr. Zimmermann considered this and Computron's aspirations in Europe, he wondered what price to bid on the König contract. With the deadline for bids only two weeks away, he knew he would have to reach a decision in the next few days.

24 Bavaria Manufacturing*
International (BMI)

In April 1976, the president of Bavaria Manufacturing International (BMI) met with members of the company's new products task force at the firm's Munich head office. The purpose of the meeting was to discuss the European market introduction of the company's newest product line (see exhibit 1). Present were BMI's marketing, production, sales and engineering managers. At the meeting the president made the following statement:

> BMI has traditionally been one of the most profitable companies in the Winchester group. Winchester are looking for big things from us this year, and we are staring down at red figures on our income statement. They are pressing us to introduce the Titan faucet line now. As there is no immediate end in sight to the recession in the construction industry across Europe, we must find new ways of increasing sales. Accordingly, I am moving the Titan introduction date up from January 1977 to September 1976. I think we all believe in this product and we must make every effort to get it to market as soon as possible. Our objective is to sell DM 25 million[1] worth of Titan in the first twelve months. . . . Karl, I must have your final marketing plan by the end of next week.

This last statement was addressed to Karl Schonfeld, BMI's marketing manager. Schonfeld, a recent MBA graduate from an internationally known Swiss business school, felt all eyes on him. He sensed that the successful introduction of this economy faucet line at this time of need for the company was an opportunity for him to make his mark at BMI.

After the meeting, Schonfeld retired to his office to begin work on the plan. He began by reviewing materials on the company, the industry, and the market. He then set about examining aspects of the new business BMI was about to enter.

* Courtesy IMEDE Management Development Institute, Lausanne, Switzerland.
1. The average exchange rate during 1976 was US$ 1 = DM 2.48.

Exhibit 1 Bavaria Manufacturing International (BMI) Titan Faucet

The Company

BMI was one of the major water faucet manufacturers in Europe. Begun as Bavaria Manufacturing in 1924 by two brothers, Hans and Otto Weidemann, the company started producing faucets for consumer and commercial use and never significantly diversified. It grew as a family business, survived World War II, and by the 1970's was considered to be one of the "big five" faucet manufacturers in Europe. In 1976, BMI marketed a full line of classical[2] faucets, as well as lines of "one-hand

---

2. There were two general classifications in the faucet industry: "classical" faucets and one-hand mixers. Classical faucets had two separate mounts for hot and cold water controls and either two separate spouts or a common spout into which both hot and cold water were fed. One-hand mixers were single-spout faucets in which hot and cold water were mixed in preset amounts selected by turning a single faucet handle. These were a recent innovation and represented a rapid growth segment of the market.

mixers"; thermostatically controlled faucets for use in homes, institutions, and hospitals; bathtubs; and other accessories for the bathroom (see exhibit 2). Faucets comprised 96 percent of its sales.

BMI's head office was in Munich; all its factories were located in West Germany. The company distributed its products through marketing subsidiaries in Europe and through agents around the world. In 1958, the Weidemann family sold 60 percent of the company to Winchester Holdings of London, England, and it was renamed Bavaria Manufacturing International. The Weidemanns retired from active management in 1961.

BMI had built its business on the basis of a high-quality product backed up by good service. Over the years, its faucets had gained a reputation for their ease of installation and durability. Many plumbers tended to use BMI faucets because they had apprenticed on them. Among plumbers it was commonly said, "If it's BMI, it's *quality.*"

The company had traditionally been an innovator. For example, it had pioneered faucets that used fewer connections than older products, to facilitate installation. However, in recent years, the industry had matured, and BMI's competitors had matched the company's innovations. By the 1970's, it manufactured products for the upper and middle segments of the faucet market, stringently maintained its reputation for quality, and sold its products at premium prices. It held 14 percent of the European market for faucets.

The Faucet Industry: The Big Five et al.

The faucet industry in Europe was not highly concentrated, with the five largest producers controlling only 50% of the market. (See exhibit 3 for data on sales and industry structure. Exhibit 4 presents data on market share held in selected markets by major competitors.) Aside from BMI, the major producers were as follows:

Grohe

Grohe was unquestionably the industry leader. A full-line German producer specializing in high-quality faucets for the upper end of the market, it was a family concern that had been in the faucet business for 50 years. Grohe, like BMI, was an innovator; its one-hand mixer had been one of the first marketed in Europe. The company's 1975 sales were estimated at DM 150 million. Grohe was strong in classical faucets, one-hand mixers, and hospital fittings. It maintained an in-house sales force and subsidiary sales and service organizations in Great Britain, Spain, France, Italy, Holland, Japan, and the United States.

Exhibit 2 BMI Products and Parts Diagramme

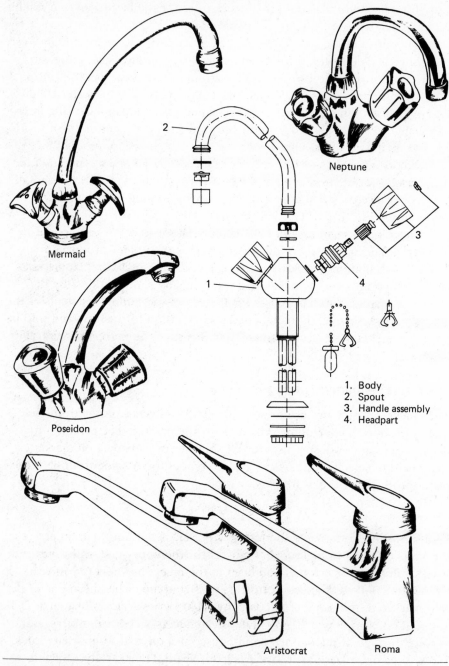

1. Body
2. Spout
3. Handle assembly
4. Headpart

Mermaid

Neptune

Poseidon

Aristocrat

Roma

Source: Company publications.

Hansa

Hansa was a full-line, family-owned German producer of high-quality faucets with a particular strength in one-hand mixers and medium-priced classical faucets. It maintained its own sales force. Hansa exported faucets all over Europe, but the firm had no really dominant position in any country other than Germany. Sales were estimated to be DM 62 million.

Pangaud

Pangaud was a privately held full-line French producer. This firm had its own sales force but was a strong factor primarily in France, particularly in

Exhibit 3 Bavaria Manufacturing International (BMI), 1975 Sales of Major Faucet Manufacturers

Company	Base	Total Sales (million DM)	Sales of Standard Faucets (million DM)	Relative Price Index [a]	Unit Sales (standard faucets)
Grohe	Germany	150	42	100	1,300,000
BMI	Germany	125	30	100	1,000,000
Hansa	Germany	62	19	100	550,000
Pangaud	France	60	28	70	1,000,000
CEC	France	52	20	75	750,000
Ideal Standard	Germany	32	10	100	300,000
Mamoli	Italy	24	12	70	700,000
Kludi	Germany	23	18	70	800,000
Damixa	France	22	0	0	0
Porcher	France	19	12	70	600,000
Venlo	Holland	15	5	85	200,000
Buades	Spain	13	8	65	400,000
SGF	France	12	5	70	200,000
Zuchetti	Italy	12	5	70	200,000
Rocca	Italy	10	5	70	200,000
Rapetti	Italy	10	5	70	200,000
Seidl	Austria	8	3	90	100,000
Schmidl	Germany	7	12	90	100,000
Others		214	86	70	4,000,000
		DM 870	DM 325	80	12,600,000

Source: Company records.

a. *Case note:* This column represented management's judgment of the relative price levels for similar faucets where the most expensive product in the market was assigned a value of 100.

Exhibit 4 Bavaria Manufacturing International (BMI),
Market Shares of Manufacturers in Major European Markets (percent)

Manufacturer	Price Segment	West Germany	France	Italy	Spain	Total Europe
Grohe	Standard	22	4	2	7	13
BMI	Standard	19	4	1	2	9
Hansa	Standard	6	0.5	—	4	6
Pangaud	Standard	1	5	1	18	9
	Substandard	—	2	—	4	3
CEC	Standard	—	5	—	14	6
	Substandard	—	1	—	3	2
Ideal Standard	Standard	2.5	0.5	0.5	5	3
Mamoli	Standard	—	0.5	12	1	3
	Substandard	—	—	3	6	3
Kludi	Standard	4	—	—	—	5
Porcher	Standard	—	7	—	—	4
	Substandard	—	2	—	—	2
Venlo	Standard	0.5	—	—	—	—
Buades	Standard	—	—	—	12	2
	Substandard	—	—	—	36	11
Percent Total	Standard	55	26.5	16.5	63	61
	Substandard	0	5	3	49	21

Source: Company estimates.

the low medium-quality segment of the classical faucet market. Sales in 1975 were DM 60 million.

CEC

CEC was a union of several French producers that offered a full range of faucets from low-priced classical faucets up to thermostats. This group was a major factor in the French market but had no significant position outside that country. It maintained a small sales force. Sales were DM 52 million in 1975.

One German manufacturer, Ideal Standard, a subsidiary of the U.S. giant American Standard, was a fast-growing firm that had recently introduced a popular one-hand mixer. All of these firms concentrated almost exclusively on the production of water faucets for the European and export markets.

The remainder of the market was supplied by some 200 smaller manufacturers, many of whom operated on a regional basis. In Italy alone, there were more than 100 faucet manufacturers, many of them low-overhead operations catering to local markets. These manufacturers specialized in cheaper-quality products and supplied much of the "substandard" segment of the market.

The Market for Faucets

Faucets were a DM 870 million business in Europe in 1976.[3] The market could be divided up according to the following price segments:

Medium- and high-price segment	DM 130,000,000
Thermostats and hospital fittings	225,000,000
Standard products	325,000,000
Substandard products	90,000,000
Accessories and spare parts	100,000,000
Total	DM 870,000,000

The "standard" segment was defined by BMI management as that part of the market in which function and price were the main factors affecting the brand decision and in which quality (durability) and service were important considerations. Style and general appearance were less important than in the medium- and high-price sector. Management defined the "substandard" segment as that part of the market in which products were below normal German government standards with respect to noise and flow control, price was a major consideration, and quality and service were less important. However, these segments were not clearly distinct from each other. Certain products could be considered to be in the standard sector in one European country and in the substandard sector in another because different countries had different accepted norms with regard to sanitary fitting installations.

Markets could also be classified according to whether they were residential or institutional. Approximately 90 percent of faucets were sold

3.   1976 estimate at factory wholesale prices, excluding the United Kingdom.

for residential buildings, while the remaining 10 percent went to the institutional market (hospitals, offices, hotels, etc.). On the average, a residential dwelling unit had five faucets, while the number of faucets in an institutional building varied according to its function. In the residential sector approximately 45 percent of the fittings were purchased for new construction, and 55 percent for the repair and replacement (R&R) market. Of those fittings purchased for new construction, 50 percent were for individual units, and 50 percent for collective residences (apartments and condominiums). These estimates represented averages, as the rate and type of construction in individual countries varied according to economic structures and domestic government policies (e.g., with regard to social housing projects).

There was an increasing trend in the wealthier countries of Europe, such as Germany, for families to undertake construction of their own homes. In approximately 60 percent of new private home construction, a family or individual financed the project. The remainder was developer-financed. The social housing (state-financed) segment of the residential new construction market was virtually all collective housing and represented 70 percent of all collective housing construction. The remainder was financed by private sources.

In the residential repair and replacement (R&R) market, half of sales were for use in collective housing units and half for individual dwellings. There was a broad tendency toward upgrading the quality of the fittings used when replacement was needed, especially when the owner was also the occupant.

In the institutional market, approximately 70 percent of faucets were purchased for new construction and the remainder for the R&R market. Approximately 10 percent of new construction was state-financed (hospitals, administrative buildings) and 90 percent privately financed (hotels, offices, factories, clinics). In old institutional construction, the sales of faucets were spread proportionally between state-constructed and privately constructed buildings.

During 1975, there was a near-collapse of the construction market across all of Europe. In 1974, 714,000 new dwelling units were constructed in Germany; in 1975, this number dropped to 500,000, and predictions for 1976 hovered around the 400,000 mark. The recession occurred in most European countries to a comparable degree. It affected faucet manufacturers to the extent that they were tied to the construction sector—and at a time when many were planning capacity expansions. The decline was attributed primarily to overspeculation in real estate during the early 1970's. This applied especially to units being built by private sources for investment purposes. Social housing was virtually unaffected.

Distribution

Ninety-five percent of all faucets in Europe were sold through sanitary wholesalers. Normally, a wholesaler would carry the complete range of products of one or two of the major faucet manufacturers, along with products of three or four local suppliers. The wholesaler did not normally enjoy an exclusive franchise from a manufacturer to sell its products in a particular area. A wholesaler stocked some 30,000 separate plumbing items, of which faucets represented between 2 and 8 percent of DM sales. His inventory thus represented a substantial capital investment. There were 4000 wholesalers in the EEC. Though there was a diversity of size among companies in this trade, an average wholesaler would do a sales volume of DM 4,500,000 per year.

Wholesalers sold primarily to plumbers, installers, and building contractors. An independent plumber would generally buy a faucet for a specific application and install it directly. In making the selection, the plumber would take into consideration the type of building requiring the faucet, the characteristics of the plumbing attachments, and the owner's wishes. In residential housing, the owner might prefer an expensive and attractive unit or a cheap functional one. The plumber preferred to work with faucets that were easy to install and would not need service or repair for a long time.

Installers were business people who employed a number of plumbers and took on larger plumbing contracts. They would characteristically buy a number of faucets for a contract and would be concerned about the profit margins on these, the volume discounts, and the quality of the products themselves. The majority of installers' business was in new residential and institutional construction. An installer would generally take into consideration the opinions of the plumbers when making purchase decisions, if the installer were allowed a free choice when purchasing faucets. However, the faucets to be used on a given contract would often be specified by the contractor.

Building contractors undertook construction projects independently, for private developers, or under government contract. On a small project a contractor/developer would commonly make purchase decisions on faucets himself, or delegate it to the installer with certain guidelines. The contractor would take price, quality and appearance into consideration, according to the type of building being constructed. On a larger project the developer would usually approve the faucets the contractor or installer selected. Occasionally, an architect would specify a certain brand of faucet for his building, though these did not generally occupy a significant part of his attention because they did not represent significant construction costs.

On government contracts, a government specifier would commonly select the faucets to be used by the contractor, with occasional input from an architect. Government specifiers were primarily concerned with the price and quality of a faucet. In the social housing sector, it was important that a faucet meet price restrictions and the government norms in terms of noise and flow control. BMI management felt that of these two considerations price was probably more important.

While "quality" was an important consideration among many purchasers, BMI management felt that it was difficult to define precisely. BMI marketing executives believed that quality was closely related to the amount of hand polishing and brass (by volume) in a faucet but that these characteristics were not easily apparent to all users. However, plumbers and installers generally stated that they "could tell quality when they saw it and felt it."

Costs, Prices, and Margins

Production costs of faucets varied according to how much brass was used in a given unit, the quality of the headpart (see exhibit 2), the amount of hand shaping and polishing that was required, the types of handles used, and the quality of the chrome plating. With so many variables, production costs would fluctuate considerably according to the unit produced and the corporate structure of the company producing it. Full-line manufacturers would manufacture several faucet lines of varying qualities and market them at varying prices.

A manufacturer would generally sell to wholesalers at a price that would allow an average contribution over variable factory costs of 33 1/3 percent. In turn, a wholesaler generally priced in order to enjoy a 16 2/3 percent markup on selling price to plumbers, installers and contractors.

The individual plumber or installer dealing with the public would sell the faucet at a price that would allow a 26 percent markup.

Since no two manufacturers produced faucets of exactly the same quality or appearance, prices for competing products could vary considerably. In this regard, BMI tended to price its products high in relation to those of its competitors.

BMI Product Lines

BMI produced and sold three classical faucet lines in 1974—the Poseidon, Neptune, and Mermaid. In addition, it produced the Aristocrat and Roma lines of one-hand mixers, a line of thermostatically controlled fixtures for home use, and another for institutional use. The classical faucet lines were differentiated as follows:

Poseidon Line

This was BMI's top line. It was characterized by its elegant shape, distinctive styling, and brilliant (transparent plastic) handles. The Poseidon line had been introduced three years earlier and was aimed at the luxury market for sanitary fittings. It was available in both chromium- and gold-plated editions. A representative chrome faucet in this line sold for approximately DM 60 to wholesalers. The Poseidon line comprised approximately 3 percent of BMI's sales.

Neptune Line

The Neptune Line was BMI's middle line. It had equally distinctive styling but used slightly less brass than the Poseidon and had attractive metal handles. A representative faucet from this line sold for DM 40 to wholesalers. The Neptune line had been introduced eight years earlier and accounted for 8 percent of BMI's sales.

Mermaid Line

The Mermaid line was BMI's only entry in the standard faucet market. It was of comparably high quality but was of a more economical design than the Poseidon and Neptune. A representative faucet from the line sold for DM 30 to wholesalers. Although the Mermaid line was over 20 years old, it was still BMI's top seller, comprising 24 percent of total company sales.

Each of the product lines included, in addition to the basic faucets, spouts, and shower heads, attachments to adapt them to various plumbing installations. Differing specifications in each of the countries of Europe (e.g., the distance between hot and cold water pipe centers) and abroad required that those producers who exported made available a large number of attachments with each line. Thus, although there was some commonality, BMI's product lines generally consisted of some 150 separate manufactured parts, made from 500–600 component parts.

The Titan Project

The Titan line was BMI's newest line of classical faucets. It was an economic faucet line (EFL) aimed at the low-cost and public housing markets, where BMI had no market offering.

The product had been conceived as early as 1973. At that time, management was becoming increasingly concerned about the number of small firms that imitated BMI designs and undersold it in the marketplace. These "copycat" producers would modify BMI's basic design, manufacture a cheaper-quality product that looked similar, and sell it for 30–40 percent less. These producers had for some time been making inroads into BMI's markets, especially into sales of the Mermaid line. The EFL was BMI's response to this threat.

The impetus to turn the EFL concept into a reality was provided by the recession in the construction industry. BMI, along with most of its competitors, had not anticipated the drop in demand and was caught with excess manufacturing capacity on its hands. The search for new market opportunities caused the company to again turn its eyes to the "low end" of the market. An internal study was done that indicated that the copycat products eating into BMI's sales generally used less brass by volume than did BMI's products. It also indicated that over 30 percent of the labour costs of BMI's faucets were in the hand polishing operations, and 20–30 percent in the handles. The study recommended that BMI design a line that could be produced entirely by automated processes and that would use a comparable amount of brass as the imitation products. Costs could thereby be reduced by approximately 25 percent. BMI would then be able to drop its prices so as to be competitive with copycat products and would break into the social housing and substandard markets it had thus far been excluded from.

As originally conceived, the EFL was to have replaced the existing Mermaid line. It was to have been marketed under the BMI name as a high-quality, low-cost faucet line. Sold at prices 20 percent below the Mermaid, it would rely on BMI's reputation for quality, and BMI's service and distribution organization would assure its acceptance in the marketplace. BMI expected the EFL—now dubbed Titan—to pick up Mermaid's sales and take market share away from competitors in the low-price standard and substandard faucet markets.

Product Development

Product development began in August 1975 with the formation of a task force comprised of BMI's marketing, sales, production, and engineering managers. This was BMI's first experience with such group management. The production manager, Mr. Rolf, was chosen to head the force, as it was his responsibility to bring the Titan into production and achieve necessary cost reductions. The engineering manager was instructed to design an EFL that looked distinctly different from existing BMI lines but that maintained BMI's standards of quality. He was to sacrifice design for function and economy where this became necessary. The marketing manager, Schonfeld, was to develop a detailed marketing plan for the EFL, to be approved by Winchester. The sales manager was to work with Schonfeld on marketing aspects of the line.

In September 1975, the first drawings were received from the engineering department. These were shown to the managers of various BMI subsidiaries across Europe to indicate the exact specifications and physical characteristics of the new line. Some of the managers indicated different specifications that would be required in their home markets. BMI engineering staff made it clear that lower costs had been achieved not by diminishing the quality of the product but by developing a line from standard parts. The development of a completely new line that used the smallest possible number of standard parts would enable the company to achieve economies of scale on the long production runs.

By October, models were produced for costing; and by November, the first prototypes were ready. These deadlines were all met in record time for BMI product development. Among the members of the task force, there was a shared commitment to the project, which was manifested in a strong feeling of confidence about the future of the line.

Consumer Testing

Once the prototypes were received from engineering in November, two consumer surveys were conducted. Schonfeld wished to use these to pinpoint any problems with public acceptance of the Titan. Any alterations in the product would have to be incorporated in the near future if the EFL was to meet its target introductory date.

In the first test, 150 people selected at random were invited into BMI's factory showroom in Munich to examine the prototypes. The Titan line was displayed alongside similar lines of French, Austrian, and Spanish manufacture. All lines were unmarked. After allowing each respondent time to view and test the faucets, BMI staff interviewed the respondent in order to record perceptions of the products. Each interview took up to half an hour, and results were recorded on survey sheets.

Results of the first consumer test did not reveal any particular bias for or against the Titan line. It was noted that the consumer apparently judged the quality of a faucet by the handles and that his or her overall response to the appearance was also closely related to perception of the appearance and feel of the handles. The only notable finding in the report was that respondents commonly indicated a preference for one line over another based on color. Since the handles on most, but not all, faucet sets were chrome and not colored, and since the hose and head of the shower sets were either black or white, it was not altogether clear what this meant. The problem was further compounded by the fact that Titan had plastic handles that were of a dark green color but that could easily be mistaken for black.

The BMI board of directors discussed the research results but could not come to any firm conclusion. Since it was known from experience in past consumer tests that the characteristics of the faucet handles strongly influenced consumer perception, it was decided to remove the variable from the test data. Accordingly, a second consumer survey was run; this time, all the faucets tested were supplied with identical chrome handles. Thus the only color differences were in the hose and head of the shower sets.

Results from the second survey were again inconclusive. Although there seemed to be some preference for shower sets with a white hose over those with a black hose, there was still no clearly stated consumer preference for the Titan line (with black hose) over its competitors or for any of the competitors over Titan. From this, Schonfeld and the task force felt that the only reasonable conclusion they could draw was that there was no particular feature of the Titan that would incline the consumer to select another faucet in preference to it when the consumer was presented with an alternative choice. Armed with this information and mindful of the approaching introductory date, Schonfeld set about making up his marketing plan.

Sizeup

Schonfeld began by accumulating relevant data on the countries of Western Europe (see exhibit 5). He quickly eliminated Britain from the list of available markets because he knew that its plumbing installations were so different from those of Continental Europe as to make that market totally inaccessible to Continental manufacturers. In order to account for differing European faucet standards, he divided prospective countries where the Titan could be sold into Class 1, 2, and 3 markets. These classifications he outlined in a memo:

Exhibit 5 Statistics on European Market (1975)

Legend:

1. BMI's market classification
2. Population
3. Growth in population over 5 years
4. Per capita income
5. Housing completions in 1975
6. Housing as a % of GNP
7. EEC member or not

Note: There were no tariffs on faucets in the EEC.
Tariffs in other countries averaged 5%.

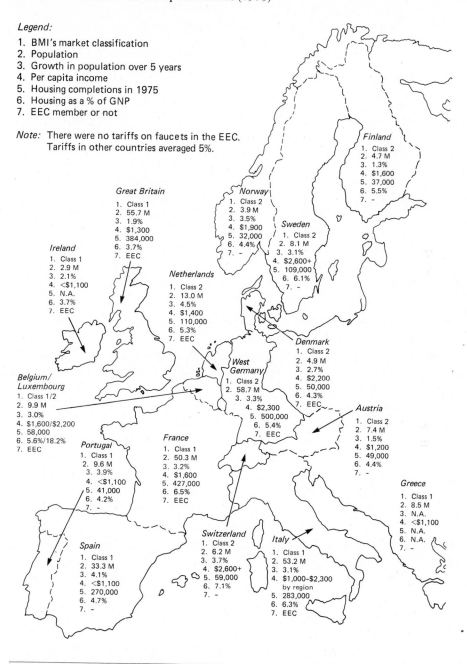

Finland
1. Class 2
2. 4.7 M
3. 1.3%
4. $1,600
5. 37,000
6. 5.5%
7. -

Great Britain
1. Class 1
2. 55.7 M
3. 1.9%
4. $1,300
5. 384,000
6. 3.7%
7. EEC

Norway
1. Class 2
2. 3.9 M
3. 3.5%
4. $1,900
5. 32,000
6. 4.4%
7. -

Sweden
1. Class 2
2. 8.1 M
3. 3.1%
4. $2,600+
5. 109,000
6. 6.1%
7. -

Ireland
1. Class 1
2. 2.9 M
3. 2.1%
4. <$1,100
5. N.A.
6. 3.7%
7. EEC

Netherlands
1. Class 2
2. 13.0 M
3. 4.5%
4. $1,400
5. 110,000
6. 5.3%
7. EEC

Denmark
1. Class 2
2. 4.9 M
3. 2.7%
4. $2,200
5. 50,000
6. 4.3%
7. EEC

West Germany
1. Class 2
2. 58.7 M
3. 3.3%
4. $2,300
5. 500,000
6. 5.4%
7. EEC

Austria
1. Class 2
2. 7.4 M
3. 1.5%
4. $1,200
5. 49,000
6. 4.4%
7. -

Belgium/ Luxembourg
1. Class 1/2
2. 9.9 M
3. 3.0%
4. $1,600/$2,200
5. 58,000
6. 5.6%/18.2%
7. EEC

Portugal
1. Class 1
2. 9.6 M
3. 3.9%
4. <$1,100
5. 41,000
6. 4.2%
7. -

France
1. Class 1
2. 50.3 M
3. 3.2%
4. $1,600
5. 427,000
6. 6.5%
7. EEC

Greece
1. Class 1
2. 8.5 M
3. N.A.
4. <$1,100
5. N.A.
6. N.A.
7. -

Spain
1. Class 1
2. 33.3 M
3. 4.1%
4. <$1,100
5. 270,000
6. 4.7%
7. -

Switzerland
1. Class 2
2. 6.2 M
3. 3.7%
4. $2,600+
5. 59,000
6. 7.1%
7. -

Italy
1. Class 1
2. 53.2 M
3. 3.1%
4. $1,000-$2,300 by region
5. 283,000
6. 6.3%
7. EEC

Source: Business Atlas of Western Europe, 1975.

Class 1. Class 1 countries include France, Italy, Spain, Portugal, and Greece. These are countries where there is a substantial market for substandard faucets. In total volume the substandard market represents DM 84 million, and the standard market DM 52 million at factory prices. BMI's sales in the standard sector of Class 1 countries amounted to some DM 12.4 million in 1975.

Class 2. Class 2 markets are those in which few, if any, substandard products are sold, and include Germany, Austria, Belgium, Holland, Luxembourg, and the Scandinavian countries. The total standard market size in these countries is estimated to be DM 265 million in 1976, of which DM 111 million will come from Germany. BMI's sales into this sector were DM 22.5 million in 1975.

Class 3. Class 3 countries, of which the Middle East and Eastern Europe are prime examples, are those in which all products, be they standard or substandard, are sold at roughly the same price. Total market size is estimated to be DM 100 million. BMI sales (Mermaid only) amounted to DM 5 million in 1975. Large portions of this market are protected by government policies or trade treaties and are therefore inaccessible to BMI.

Since the Titan line was intended to allow BMI to penetrate the substandard markets, Class 1 countries were to be a major focus of the marketing effort. The Titan would be positioned as close as possible to the low-priced competition in these countries. Schonfeld was aware that the product line had to be positioned in all markets in such a way as to maximize *incremental* sales to BMI and to minimize cannibalization of other lines. The president's remarks at the task force meeting had underlined this, since overall corporate sales were slumping substantially.

However, this was a complex issue, since a management decision had recently been made not to withdraw the Mermaid line from the market. Senior management at BMI believed that since the Titan was intended to enable BMI to penetrate markets it had previously been excluded from, it could be positioned in such a way as to pick up incremental sales without cannibalizing Mermaid's sales in the market segment in which it was still selling strongly. The Titan line was clearly differentiated from the Mermaid and other BMI lines on the basis of appearance alone, and it was felt it could be priced sufficiently below Mermaid so as to be considered an addition to the BMI family of products.

The pricing issue was highly influenced by the economics of the investment, however. Schonfeld had recently received a report from the production department stating that the target reduction of 25 percent on variable Mermaid costs was no longer attainable. He had had reports to suggest this in the past, but this latest one indicated that costs of the Titan line were unlikely to be more than 10 percent below those of the Mermaid. Schonfeld was disturbed by this. Earlier predictions of rises in costs had been based on the fact that the production department had been unable to cast two faucets in a single mould as planned (something BMI had been unsuccessful at on previous occasions) because hand polishing operations could not be fully eliminated and because fully automatic production (i. e., the purchase of some major machinery) would not be feasible until substantial sales volume materialized. These factors had resulted in predictions of costs 17 percent below Mermaid. However the new cost increases were based on the increased tooling, setup, operating, and working capital costs associated with increased parts requirements to meet specifications in Class 1 countries such as Italy and Spain. In fact, the number of product variations for the line had expanded from the 20 originally envisaged to 80 to cover French, Italian, and Spanish plumbing specifications.

Schonfeld was aware that to date, DM 2,975,000 had been invested in the Titan project. Of this, DM 1,740,000 had been spent on product development, DM 750,000 on production machinery, and DM 485,000 on tooling. One thousand prototype Titan faucet sets had been produced for test market purposes. The expected costs per unit submitted in the latest report were based on assumed unit sales of 1,000,000–2,500,000 faucets per year. If sales were 10 percent below the one million mark, costs per unit could be expected to rise 5 percent. This trend would continue down to a sales level of 500,000 units, after which per-unit costs would escalate rapidly. Therefore, if sales were only 800,000 units, costs would be equal to those of the Mermaid line.

The basic faucet from the Titan line would have to be sold to wholesalers at DM 24 in order to be 20 percent below Mermaid in price. However, in light of the new cost figures, variable manufacturing cost at this price increased from the originally projected 69 percent to 75 percent. This was before expected variable packaging and shipping costs of some DM 2.5 per unit. Schonfeld was thus caught in a cost/price squeeze and had to decide whether or not to risk raising the price of the Titan. If he did raise the price, he wondered by how much this should be done and in what markets. He estimated that at DM 24, Titan sales would be 1,000,000 units and that Mermaid sales would drop from 1,000,000 to 800,000 units. He estimated that Mermaid sales would drop by 4 percent below 800,000 for every 5 percent decrease in Titan prices below DM 24 and that Titan sales would increase by 7.5 percent for every 5 percent drop in price. If he raised the price of Titan, he estimated that sales would decrease by 10 percent for each 5 percent increase over DM 24 but that Mermaid sales would remain virtually unaffected. This was due to his belief that Titan and Mermaid would be perceived as different brands. Finally, Schonfeld did not believe the market would accept a price increase on Mermaid.

He also had to wonder if cost reduction strategies might be employed. The most obvious one would be to recommend full automation immediately. However, this would take time and would require a further capital outlay of DM 1 million. The degree to which costs would be further reduced was uncertain. From the data available to him, he estimated that full automation might reduce Titan's costs by 3–4 percent. Another alternative would be reducing the number of countries the Titan would be introduced in, in order to curb the proliferation of variations (estimated at an incremental 20 for each of Spain, France, and Italy).[4] A further option involved implementing a cost reduction programme on the handles of the Titan line. He believed that by moving to a plain handle, costs on this item could be reduced by 5–8 percent. However, be believed that the plain handles would be less attractive to end-consumers than the existing plastic Titan handles.

Because of the cost/price issue and the positioning issue, the countries in which Titan was to be distributed assumed paramount importance. From the beginning, it had been intended that the line would be targeted at the social housing sectors of the French and Italian markets. However, Schonfeld had to consider how many additional markets would be required to enable BMI to reach its sales target. Germany itself was BMI's stronghold where it held the greatest market share and had the best distribution, highest reputation, and best relations with the trade. Spain was the other market for which parts were already available. However, Spain and Austria were not EEC members, and wholesalers would have to pay a tariff of 5 percent of the landed cost of the faucet in these countries. There were no tariffs on faucets in EEC. Tariffs in Class 3 countries averaged 10 percent of the landed cost of the units. Schonfeld knew that BMI's distributors provided good market coverage in all European countries with the exception of Great Britain and Ireland. He also had to consider the possibility of selling Titan through innovative marketing channels such as "do-it-yourself" retail outlets. These were expanding rapidly in some countries such as Germany and Switzerland.

4. There would be few incremental product variations required if Titan were sold in more Class 2 countries.

Branding was also an important issue. Schonfeld had considered selling the Titan under a brand name other than BMI in order to avoid cannibalization of Mermaid sales. It would thus clearly be differentiated in the eyes of BMI's traditional customers and could be marketed to the substandard, standard, and social housing sectors of European countries, perhaps at a price higher than that at which it could be sold under the BMI name. If, on the other hand, the BMI name were used, customers would be assured of the quality of the product. Schonfeld considered some compromise positioning, where Titan would be sold as a "subsidiary brand" to the BMI family of products.

Schonfeld's Marketing Plan

Schonfeld decided to recommend to the production department that cost reduction measures be investigated, but he knew he would have to work with the figures presently available to him. He took one last look at the results of an attitude survey that had been conducted by BMI in Germany the previous year (exhibit 6) and proceeded with his task. With time pressures mounting, he did not have available to him the results of the Titan test market, which had been under way for several weeks in Vienna.

After a week, Schonfeld felt he had a workable proposal. Titan would be sold as a BMI line, using the BMI sales force, and would be backed up by the BMI service organization. It would be positioned at the low end of the BMI product range and distributed through wholesale channels exclusively. The EFL would be sold in Germany, France, Italy, and Spain in the introductory 12 months. Schonfeld decided to add Austria to the list of introductory markets, since there was already a full test market being conducted there.

After much deliberation he had elected to raise the factory price of the Titan by an average of 15 percent in order to assure the profitability of the line. However, he concluded from talks with salesmen in the field that buyers were more price-sensitive in Class 1 markets than in Class 2, where the name BMI on Titan would probably be perceived as a genuine opportunity to buy BMI quality at a lower price than Mermaid. Accordingly, he decided on a three-tier pricing scheme, whereby Titan prices were raised by 10 percent in Class 1 markets to DM 26.50 and 17 percent in Class 2 markets to DM 28; on the average, the Class 3 price (excluding tariffs) was to be DM 30. This would optimize the overall margin for the product. (See exhibit 7 for his sales projections and expected cannibalization of Mermaid sales over the next two years.)

Exhibit 6 Bavaria Manufacturing International (BMI), Company Assessment of Target Groups and Factors They Consider In Selecting Standard Faucets

					Potential Customer			
					Developer/		Government	
Concerns	Wholesaler	Plumber	Installer		Contractor	End-User	Specifier	Architect
Quality	X	X			X			X
Price			X		X	X	X	
Function		X	X		X	X	X	X
Appearance					X	X		X
Profit	X	X	X					
Ease of								
installation		X	X					
Brand	X	X						

Source: Derived from company records.

Exhibit 7 Bavaria Manufacturing International (BMI),
Titan's Projected Sales and Cannibalization of Mermaid
If Titan Is Sold For an Average Price of DM 27.6/Unit (DM 000,000)

| | 1976 | 1977 | | 1978 | |
| | | 1st Year of Titan | | 2nd Year of Titan | |
	Mermaid	Mermaid	Titan	Mermaid	Titan
France	2.1	2.0	6.1	1.6	9.7
Italy	1.5	1.1	3.0	.8	5.5
Spain	0.9	0.5	2.3	0	2.8
Austria	0	0	0.7	0	0.9
Germany	16.4	14.6	8.4	7.0	18.1
Other	4.6	3.8	0	2.6	0
Class 3	5	0	4.5	0	5
Product total	30	23	25	12	42
Total sales (DM 000,000)	30	48		54	

Source: Company records.

In order to minimize cannibalization of other lines, Schonfeld decided on a direct mail campaign for promotional material, aimed at specifiers and buyers for "standard" and "low-quality" building projects. Brochures advertising the Titan line would be directed to clients who were not likely to consider purchasing another line of BMI faucets (specifically Mermaid) and would bypass those buyers who would normally purchase Mermaid. The promotional message in these brochures would be: "Titan: BMI quality at an attractive price."

The selling emphasis, in comparison with Mermaid, would be as follows:

	Titan	Mermaid
Plumbers	20%	50%
Wholesalers	20	30
Planners, architects, specifiers	60	20
	100%	100%

The total promotional budget was DM 1,250,000.

Schonfeld finished with a summary of his plan for achieving his first year sales objectives (see exhibit 8). After completing it, he sat back and reflected that if his reasoning were correct, this would be one of the most successful new products in BMI's history. He noted that the first test results had come in from Vienna. The report stated that there had been no complaints whatever with any of the Titan faucets that had been installed

Exhibit 8   Bavaria Manufacturing International (BMI),
Summary of Schonfeld's Marketing Plan

1. First Year Sales Objective: DM 25,000,000

2. Brand Name: TITAN—One of the BMI Family of Products

3. Distribution Channel: Sanitary wholesalers

4. Markets:

Market	Sales	
France	DM	6,100,000
Italy		3,000,000
Spain		2,300,000
Austria		700,000
Germany		8,400,000
Class 3		4,500,000
Total	DM	25,000,000

5. Pricing:

Class of market	price
1.	DM 26.50
2.	28
3.	30

6. Positioning: Social Housing, Substandard and low end of Standard Markets.

7. Promotion: Printed material (leaflets)—aimed primarily at Architects, Specifiers, Wholesalers; Specially-trained sales support— Total Budget DM 1.25 mio.

8. Message: "TITAN: BMI quality at an attractive price."

---

in the two months since the test began. It also reported that Titan was selling well in the test market area. Schonfeld was pleased by this but did not wish to be overly optimistic.

Before turning in his plan, Schonfeld decided to go over it one more time. He knew that it would be scrutinized carefully by executives at Winchester House in addition to BMI top management in Munich. He would have to explain why he had elected to proceed as he had and what alternatives he had considered. If he were called to London, he knew he would have to defend his proposal in front of the Winchester senior management committee.

CHAPTER VII
DISTRIBUTION DECISIONS

Few marketing decisions are more significant and permanent than decisions on distribution. In particular, channels of distribution are costly and time-consuming to establish and are not easily or quickly changed. Seller-reseller relationships take time to develop to efficient and effective levels. Stores, particularly large ones, deliberate carefully about their choice of location and do not readily move from site to site.

The usual approach to distribution decisions in marketing texts is from the viewpoint of a manufacturer selling through wholesalers and retailers to the ultimate customers, as sketched in chart 1.

This sketch oversimplifies most channels of distribution, but there is some value in having a simple prototype as a base point. As examples of more complex channels, there may be several levels of wholesalers as in the automotive aftermarket, or retailers may combine to create buying groups that function somewhere between the wholesaler and retailer in our simplified chart. To make matters even more complex, manufacturers

Chart 1   Simplified Manufacturer's View of Channel of Distribution

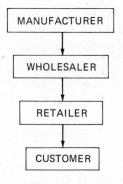

sometimes bypass various members of the distribution channel and sell direct to retailers or even to customers (e.g., factory outlets).

There are three fundamental ways to discuss distribution decisions. First, we may examine the *system* in terms of selection of alternative channels from manufacturer to final customer, relationships among channel members, tasks performed by each channel member, and so on. Second, we may focus solely on the *physical distribution* of product, which involves inventory, transportation, packaging, customer service, and so on. Or, third, we may take the perspective of a *channel member* trying to formulate a marketing strategy to improve the member's own performance.

The bulk of this chapter is about channel selection and management. We believe this to be appropriate for three reasons. First, it is a necessary starting point for any discussion of physical distribution or of any channel member's individual position. Second, we believe that there is a great deal of similarity between the marketing decisions faced by manufacturers and those faced by distributors. This point will be elaborated further later on. Third, the constant evolution of distribution systems and institutions can best be understood from this channel system viewpoint. Such understanding is critical for anyone involved in marketing.

Channel Behaviour

It is important to view a channel of distribution as a living, dynamic, evolving organism. Channel members are organizations run by people who are looking out for their own profit-motivated interests. More often than not, channel members need a strong reason why they should carry our new product or continue to carry our existing products. They have limited funds, limited storage space, and limited selling time. If a manufacturer's product cannot yield as many gross profit dollars as the products of competing manufacturers, most wholesalers and retailers will drop the product unless there is some other offsetting reason to keep it, such as a constant flow of customers asking for the product by name.

Channels of distribution perform functions such as storage, insurance, credit, sorting, transportation, inventorying, and repackaging. Although one person may be able to "cut out the middleman," the entire market cannot do this. Channel functions must be performed by some organization.

In fact, in many channels of distribution, there is aggressive competition within and between channel members as to which one will perform particular channel functions. Chart 2 illustrates this competition within and between channels of distribution. This competition *within* the channel

Chart 2   Competition Within and Between Channels of Distribution

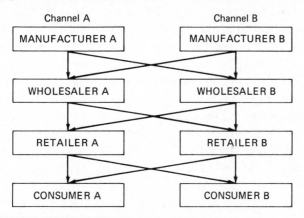

could be a situation in which Manufacturer A attempts to take over Wholesaler A's functions and sell directly to Retailers A and B. Retailers sometimes band together in groups in order to take over some of the wholesaler's functions, such as buying in large quantities.

Competition *between* channels occurs when manufacturers struggle against each other to gain a larger share of the market. Manufacturers A and B may sell through many of the same wholesalers, but they will encourage each wholesaler to push their goods rather than those of the other manufacturer. Similarly, Wholesalers A and B compete for retail accounts and sales just as Retailers A and B compete for customers and sales.

The ability to *control* or significantly influence a channel of distribution is a major advantage to anyone in the channel. That is why retailers buy wholesalers and vice versa, manufacturers buy wholesalers and retailers, and large retailers such as Simpsons-Sears buy manufacturing companies. Control of a channel gives the controlling manufacturer, for example, guaranteed access to the market. This power from channel control provides much greater flexibility in all the elements of the controlling firm's marketing strategy: for example, more merchandising, fuller representation of its product line, coordinated advertising, possibly better margins, and better locations.

Power is an important dimension of channels. In conflicts between manufacturers and wholesalers or retailers, the power issue often can be resolved by asking, "who needs whom?"—that is, does the retailer need this product or does the manufacturer need this retailer? Who would be hurt most if a change was put into effect? More often than not, a retailer or wholesaler does not need a particular product or even an entire line.

If there is a tendency for vertical integration within the channel, why do any wholesalers continue to exist? In a number of markets, wholesalers have been squeezed out of the market and their functions divided between retailers and manufacturers. Where wholesalers exist, it is because they specialize in their function and do it better, meaning more efficiently and more fully, than either the manufacturer or retailer could do it.

If the wholesaler carries several thousand items, the manufacturer cannot ask the wholesaler (or retailer) to spend all its time promoting a few of the manufacturer's products. The major reason for adopting *wholesale* distribution is to obtain broad coverage, local inventories, and some on-site representation. Few wholesalers are able to supply depth selling of complex technical products—they have too many lines and not enough time. If missionary selling is required, the manufacturer may have to provide that sales activity or at least underwrite it.

In all the discussion of conflict within channels, it should be noted that few wholesalers or retailers take kindly to being assigned a reduced role or a reduced margin or being totally bypassed by another channel member. Most channel members try to prevent these threats to their activities, and they react quickly with whatever weapons available whenever they are threatened. For example, if a manufacturer reduces wholesale margins, wholesalers may drop the manufacturer's product line.

Channel members such as wholesalers and retailers are usually motivated to maximize gross profit dollars per square feet of selling space, which they calculate by multiplying margin times turnover for the amount of space occupied.[1] To improve the equation for the retailer or wholesalers, the manufacturer can take steps to:

1. improve the margin through a greater discount, periodic case allowances or free goods, such as "two free with twelve";

2. increase the turnover through regular advertising or cooperative advertising with the retailer;

3. decrease the space required by reducing the number of sizes or the number of shelf facings;

4. reduce the cost of inventory by placing the goods "on consignment," which means the manufacturer owns the goods until they are sold by the middleman; or

1. There are many other performance measures in wholesale and retail trade. For example, with any increase in interest rates, there has been increased attention to "return on investment in inventory," usually measured at the gross profit level.

5. reduce the amount of inventory that the retailers or wholesaler is required to carry. Reducing the required inventory can be accomplished by lowering the minimum order or providing more frequent shipments.

Retailers in the food and drug business are deluged with requests to carry additional products. In order to cope with these requests, many chains have screening committees. Even when a new product line is accepted, it has to offer healthy case allowances to obtain trade acceptance, and then it must move off the shelves fairly well during the first six months in order to keep its listing with wholesalers, chains, and retailers.

Channel Decisions

Channel decisions can be divided into issues of managing existing channels, changing channels, and setting up entirely new channels. In managing existing channels, you may find it useful to view the channel members as extensions of the manufacturing organization. Thus, the manufacturer is selling *through* the channels, not just selling *to* the channels. Selling *through* the channels implies an aggressive stance of getting the most out of the channels by organizing, planning, and controlling their performance, as opposed to selling *to* the channels, which implies dropping the product at their doorstep and forgetting about it. Although retailers and wholesalers often are independent organizations, the owners/managers appreciate manufacturers who do market research, provide incentive, support their products, service their products, and provide literature and merchandising help. Exhibit 1 shows the list of items a wholesaler or retailer negotiates in the "contract" with a manufacturer or other channel member.

From the manufacturer's side, selling *through* the trade implies defining selling tasks, hiring good salespeople and supervising them, providing good products, providing good support for the products, and understanding the viewpoint of the retailer or wholesaler. Exhibit 1 shows that there is a natural conflict between the manufacturer and the retailer or wholesaler. For example, if the manufacturer could have everything its way, the "ideal" wholesalers and retailers would carry all the inventory, do all the merchandising, handle all the service—and never ask for price concessions, free goods, and more advertising allowances from the manufacturer. Conversely, if the middlemen could set all the terms of the contract, they might have the manufacturer carrying all the inventory, doing more advertising, providing more credit—and giving even larger margins and other incentives. The actual contract is negotiated within the guidelines of

Exhibit 1   Framework for Negotiating Items and
Their Implications in the Channel "Contract"

Negotiating Items	Implications for Manufacturer	Implications for Wholesaler/Retailer
1. Product line, branding	Determines ability to sell through more than one set of accounts	Determines exclusiveness of offering—ultimate is private brand
2. Number of outlets	Dependence on few versus cost of establishing, supervising many accounts	Determines amount of competition for product line
3. Type of outlets	Fit with product line and buyer habits should be good	Determines directness and nature of competition for product line
4. Task to be performed	Determines tasks needed to sell product line and what middlemen can/will do. Supplements middlemen with own sales force	Determines amount of work—type and number of staff, cost structure, financing
5. Assistance in tasks	Should fit product line requirements, overall marketing strategy, and resources. Bears on number, type of salesmen, and aiding material	Needed? Where and how, to fit with organization and strategy
6. Rewards	Cost—attempt to minimize in relation to net tasks	Margin times turnover, incentives, allowances, rebates
7. Risks of unsold goods, inventory, credit, reputation, extra service	Share risks in relation to ability, necessity, and rewards	Compares to industry standard. Expects extra rewards for extra risks
8. Supervision/ control by manufacturer	As requested and required to obtain proper effort, good selling	Ongoing or sporadic? Help versus infringement and rigid policies that miss opportunities
9. Evaluation and measures of performance	Usual annual evaluation in terms of sales, returns, cooperation, tasks performed	Nature of contract determines. Annual review sales, share, new products

historical industry practice and the balance of power between the negotiating parties.

In managing existing channels, we must periodically determine how well the channel members are performing in terms of total sales, selling the full line, service, new accounts, or whatever criteria we have mutually agreed upon. If we have good supervision, good relations, and good records, we can compare each channel member's performance to the predetermined target, to the average, or to some industry statistics on the same criteria. If the channel member is performing satisfactorily, the next step may be to negotiate next year's targets. However, if the targets are not being met, then we as manufacturers may haul out our "carrots and sticks." One "stick" is that the wholesaler, for example, may not receive its volume rebates because it failed to reach the target, or we may remove part or all of our product line. If dissatisfied with a manufacturer, the wholesaler may decide to drop the manufacturer's product line or may demand more margins, incentives, or additional assistance. The list below shows some of the "carrots" and tools that manufacturers can use to assist wholesalers and retailers.

Money	Margins
	Allowances
	Paid display/shelf space
	Co-op allowances
	Volume discounts
Skills and services	Merchandising training
	Clerk training
	Technical advice
Physical items	Display racks
	Display cartons
Physical help	Take inventory
	Prepare order
	Set up displays

There are numerous reasons for wanting to change channels of distribution, such as wanting more intensive effort, better credit risks, better coverage, better fit with products, more control, or lower cost. In changing channels of distribution, we should compare the performance of existing channel members (1) with the tasks and performance that we want and (2) with the tasks and performance available from other channel members. When a decision has been reached to change channels, the explanation of the change to existing channel members and the timing of the change are critical decisions. As a manufacturer, we want to minimize the existing channel members' desire and opportunity to retaliate against us.

In setting up a new operation, we have both the problem and opportunity of setting up a channel of distribution—"opportunity" because we are not bound by historical relations with selected channel members and "problem" because it is a great deal of work to identify, check credit, check reputation, persuade, set up, and support new accounts. However, in a new situation, we can picture ideal outlets and compare the available outlets against our ideal profile. Some of the criteria on which we might judge retail or wholesale outlets are:

type of clientele	credit
share of market covered by each	reputation
service	traffic flow
display	advertising
salesmanship	location
product knowledge of staff	margins expected
fitting	other incentives expected
delivery	

Before we go very far in establishing new channels of distribution, we must decide the breadth of coverage required to execute our marketing strategy. We define three categories in chapter 2: selective, extensive, and mass coverage. Selective channels would be relatively few stores appropriate for specialty goods such as stereos, automobiles, jewelry, and high-line furniture. Extensive channels would provide somewhat broader coverage for shopping goods such as appliances, shoes, sporting goods, televisions, and middle-quality furniture. Mass distribution channels are appropriate for common everyday items (convenience goods) such as standard clothing, small appliances, low-quality furniture, toys—the type of products sold in a discount store.

The breadth of the channel and the type of retailers must fit with the rest of the marketing strategy. It makes sense to establish mass channels for low-price products that have wide appeal but require little sales help and little after-sales service. Very often, these same products are supported by advertising to make them more acceptable to customers and thereby "pull" the product through the channel.

The next issue is to determine the process and criteria used by the desired wholesalers or retailers in deciding whether or not they will add our product line. This brings us back to the entire list of items we will negotiate with the middlemen (exhibit 1). It is also important to know the *process* of adoption. Does a committee decide? Do we prejudice our chances if we miss in the first attempt at gaining a listing? It is also important to learn the length of time our products will be "on probation" before the retailer or wholesaler makes a decision on adoption or rejection.

Finally, we must realize the profound importance that channel selection will have upon the number and skills of salespeople whom we hire. Mass channels usually require more salespeople than either extensive or selective channels. But because the convenience goods sold through mass channels usually are prepackaged, presold, high-volume, low-price, lower-margin items, a manufacturer's salesperson selling to mass retailers emphasizes gaining orders and troubleshooting, whereas a salesperson who is selling to selective channels may spend more time with each account on matters such as clerk training, merchandising aids, and after-sales servicing.

Physical Distribution

Physical distribution management has been variously defined, but we prefer to think of it as the management of goods from the point at which they leave the factory to their final acceptance (perhaps after delivery and installation) by the ultimate customer. This area of marketing thus includes transportation, inventory, storage facilities, packaging, and other tasks that relate directly to the movement of goods. Further, there are associated flows of information such as stock position, freight rates, and delivery times. In essence, physical distribution management (sometimes called logistics management) involves trade-offs among marketing, production, and financial objectives and resources. Should high inventories be maintained with their attendant high carrying costs in order to minimize stockouts? Salespeople typically want high inventories, whereas financial controllers do not. Should we produce a very wide product line and ship in small quantities or standardize and ship only in full truck loads? Physical distribution management involves making these kinds of trade-offs in order to minimize costs yet maximize customer satisfaction. Though it is a complicated area of management with a considerable set of analytical techniques, it is an aspect of management that holds much promise for improved productivity.

Reseller Marketing

Middlemen are very much concerned with marketing. Wholesalers, for example, rely extensively on salespeople. Thus, the material in our section on sales force decisions is as pertinent to them as to any manufacturer.

Similarly, because retailers also engage in advertising and promotion efforts, our chapter on marketing communications is geared to them as well as to manufacturer-marketers. In other words, we believe that marketing principles and methods as outlined in this book are just as appropriate to resellers as to manufacturers. Increasingly, we are observing practitioners embrace this position.

Yet this is not to say the manufacturer and the retailer see the marketplace in the same way. There are some important differences. First, and perhaps most important, is the distinction between *product motivation* and *patronage motivation*. When marketing management is approached from the manufacturer's viewpoint, we usually confine ourselves to product motivation, meaning why customers buy certain products and services and how to influence that behaviour. However, from the retailer's perspective, we must also consider patronage motivation, meaning where customers go to buy and how to influence that aspect of behaviour. In other words, retailers must deal with both types of marketing issues.

Second, there is a difference in terminology. Here are a few generalized examples related to the marketing mix concept:

Manufacturer term	*Retailer term*
Product policy	Assortment policy
Price increase/decrease	Markup/markdown
Market	Trading area
Distribution channel selection	Site selection/location
Advertising and promotion	Advertising, promotion, display signage, layout, atmosphere, etc.
Selling	Merchandising
Consumers	Customers/clients

There are more examples, but it is important to note that we will increasingly see a greater commonality as retailers recognize the conceptual distinction between "merchandising" and "marketing."

Third, while both manufacturers and retailers are concerned about market share and profit, they measure these performance dimensions differently. Large general merchandise retailers, in particular, typically have more complicated income statement structures that reflect:

broader lines (that is more items which they call stock-keeping units—SKU's);

more transactions, each of relatively small dollar value;

greater use of part-time employees in a more labour-intensive business;

greater decentralization and hence more management control problems.

In retailing, we find performance measures relating to the use of space, people, and inventory investment. While a manufacturer may be interested in getting maximum shelf space, display, sales attention, and advertising for one brand of peanut butter, the retailer must worry about how many different brands to carry; how shelf space, display, and so on will be divided among those brands; and, of course, how much attention and investment will be given to peanut butter versus salad dressings and all the other product categories. We will not go further here with this discussion, but we believe that any marketer who wishes to sell through middlemen must learn how those middlemen view the world, what performance goals they have, and the like.

Summary

Distribution is one of the most fundamental aspects of marketing. Indeed, one can observe a lot about the development of an economy by observing the stage of development of its distribution systems. Marketers realize that channels of distribution are characterized by continuous tension and change. Channel members constantly seek better ways to perform their functions and to take over or unload functions in the pursuit of profits.

25 ROLM Corporation

In October 1973, Kenneth Oshman, President of the ROLM Corporation, and other members of ROLM's top management team were finalizing a business plan to market a private branch exchange system (PBX), thereby entering the telecommunications industry. The plan was to be presented to ROLM's Board of Directors at their November meeting in order to obtain approval for market entry. The initial product was to be a computer-controlled electronic PBX with capacity to handle from 100 to 800 telephone extensions. This market entry would bring ROLM into direct competition with AT&T, ITT, Northern Electric, Philips, Nippon Electric, and many others.

The Company

ROLM Corporation had been founded in 1969 by four electrical engineers: Mr. Richeson, Mr. Oshman, Mr. Loewenstern, and Mr. Maxfield. In fact, the name of the corporation was an acronym based on the first letters of their surnames. All were in their late twenties to early thirties at the time of the founding, and all were, or had been, employed by electronic or computer firms in the San Francisco Bay Area. As Bob Maxfield recalled, "The company was the result of four guys deciding they wanted to go into business for themselves and having a couple of ideas about the kinds of products they might offer." Their original ideas were basically commercial applications of systems developed originally for the military and included a system for police departments to keep track automatically of the location of every police vehicle. Another idea was a system that would allow toll bridges to monitor regular users of the bridge automatically by means of a transponder attached to each vehicle, thus permitting bills to be issued to each regular user at the end of the month. A business plan was developed around these ideas and presented to venture capitalists, but it did not arouse much enthusiasm among potential suppliers of capital.

In the fall of 1968, Bob Maxfield and Gene Richeson attended the Fall Joint Computer Conference. This particular show in many respects heralded the coming minicomputer boom. Data General, subsequently to become a major factor in the minicomputer industry, and a dozen other new manufacturers announced their first products at this show. A few months later, while the four of them were sitting around "blue-skying" about potential businesses, Gene Richeson suggested that what the world really needed was a low-cost off-the-shelf military minicomputer.

No standard computer could withstand the severe environmental conditions encountered in military missions. At that time, the major manufacturers of militarized computers ("mil-spec") were IBM and Sperry Univac, who manufactured the computers on a custom basis resulting in long lead times and high cost—often $150,000[1] for a system. The Data General commercial NOVA minicomputer, on the other hand, cost about $10,000; Gene Richeson, on the basis of his knowledge of the requirements of the various military applications, felt that such a computer would have sufficient power for most of these applications. Bob Maxfield, who had the most experience with computers, felt that a militarized version of the Data General computer could be manufactured to sell for less than $30,000. As they discussed the possibilities further, they decided that it would be ideal from the customer's viewpoint if a militarized computer could be made software compatible and input-output compatible with an existing commercial minicomputer. This would allow the user to do the development work and system testing on the lower-cost commercial machine in a laboratory environment, using the "mil-spec" computer only when the system was actually deployed in the military equipment.

The next question they addressed was which commercial minicomputer they should choose. They selected the Data General NOVA computer for two reasons. First, Data General was a start-up company and thus might be interested in licensing the design and software to ROLM; also, given its small size, the decision would probably be made quickly. The second reason was that the Data General machine used the latest technology, which required a smaller number of components than competitive minicomputers. This was an important factor in designing a reliable machine for military applications. They phoned Edson de Castro, President of Data General, told him they were thinking of starting up a

---

1. All dollar amounts in this case are in United States dollars.

company to manufacture "mil-spec" computers, and asked him if he would be interested in licensing hardware and software designs to them. Mr. de Castro was interested, so they flew to Data General's home office in Boston and negotiated an agreement with him.

On the basis of their idea, they developed a business plan and were successful in getting sufficient money to start the business. ROLM began operation on June 1, 1969, and a working model was displayed at the Fall Joint Computer Conference in 1969. The first production unit was shipped in March 1970. In the first quarter of fiscal year 1971, which began in July 1970, ROLM showed a profit and remained profitable thereafter. Subsequent computers were based on ROLM's own designs.

The ROLM "mil-spec" computers typically were purchased by contractors of the U.S. Department of Defense, the Defense Department itself, and certain industrial customers who required computers that could operate in severe environments. The computers were generally used in research, development, and testing applications. Individual purchase orders were usually for small quantities. The company generally provided a central processing unit (CPU), a main memory, a chassis, a power supply, and a variety of input-output equipment, peripheral equipment (terminals, printers, magnetic discs, and tapes), and software. The customer could thus configure a system to meet its own needs. The company employed a direct sales organization which totalled about eight people in 1973. Kenneth Oshman, besides being President of ROLM, also acted as head of the marketing organization.

The Decision to Diversify

By fiscal 1973, sales had reached $3.6 million. An income statement and balance sheet for ROLM are included in exhibit 1. Early in 1973, top management of ROLM became concerned about the potential size of the segment of the military computer market in which ROLM competed. There was a strong feeling among ROLM's top management that their market segment would be saturated by the time their annual sales reached $10 to $20 million. Given that they had an objective to build a major company, they began to look for areas of diversification that would allow ROLM to continue its growth. They felt that any diversification should build on their main technological expertise in computers, so they investigated other computer-related businesses that they might enter. The PBX market was an obvious candidate. As Oshman pointed out, "The computer-based PBX is very much a computer system, and we already had 80% of the technology; we figured we could get the other 20% easier than the telephone companies could get the computer technology." The idea was initially abandoned when they realized that the cost of setting up a national sales and service organization would be beyond ROLM's resources. Nevertheless, the proposal kept resurfacing during the following months. As Bob Maxfield recalled, "We all felt it would be fun to develop a computer-controlled

Exhibit 1 ROLM Corporation Financial Data

Income Statement for Fiscal Year Ending June 29, 1973

Net sales	3,637,000
Costs and expenses	
Cost of goods sold	1,572,000
Product development	455,000
Marketing, administrative & general	964,000
Interest	14,000
Total costs and expenses	3,005,000
Income before taxes	632,000
Provision for income taxes	311,000
Net income	$ 321,000

Balance Sheet for Quarter Ending September 28, 1973

Current Assets		*Current Liabilities*	
Cash	$ 202,000	Accounts payable &	
Receivables	442,000	accrued payroll	$ 306,700
Inventories	994,600	Income tax payable	139,400
Other current assets	43,100	Other current liabilities	31,900
		Notes payable	24,400
Total current assets	$1,681,700	Total current liabilities	$502,400
		Lease Contracts Payable—	
Other Assets		*Long Term*	$ 97,500
Capital equipment	$ 440,700		
Accumulated depreciation	228,300	*Stockholders' Equity*	
		Capital stock	$ 170,800
Net capital equipment	212,400	Paid in surplus, net	610,800
Other assets	24,100	Retained earnings	436,700
Total other assets	$ 236,500	Total equity	$1,318,300
Total Assets	$1,918,200	Total Liabilities and Equity	$1,918,200

Source: Company records.

telephone system, so we decided to look at it more carefully in March 1973." Once the decision had been made to look at the PBX business more closely, it was decided to set up a separate organization to do the product development and market analysis. They felt either the "mil-spec" computer business or the proposed PBX business would receive second-class treatment if personnel attempted to work in both areas simultaneously.

To head the product development side of the project, Maxfield was successful in recruiting Jim Kasson from Hewlett-Packard. Kasson, whom Maxfield had known socially for a number of years, had a background in data acquisition and control systems and was very knowledgeable about computers. He also brought with him from Hewlett-Packard another very good engineer. Together with ROLM's top computer software specialist, they became, in June 1973, the three-person ROLM PBX technical feasibility team. In August 1973, Dick Moley, a marketing manager in Hewlett-Packard's computer division, joined ROLM to do the market analysis for the PBX.

Telecommunications Industry in the United States

The telecommunications system in the United States was operated by American Telephone and Telegraph (AT&T) and some 1760 independent telephone companies. AT&T was split into five major operations:

1. The General Department, which provided staff assistance in advertising, finance, engineering, legal, and marketing areas to the rest of the corporation.

2. Western Electric, which manufactured telephone equipment for the Bell System operating companies. Under the terms of a 1956 consent decree with the Justice Department, Western Electric sold its products exclusively to the Bell System operating companies and to the U.S. Government. In 1972, Western Electric's total sales were greater than $7 billion.

3. The Bell Telephone Laboratories, which conducted basic research and designs equipment for manufacture by Western Electric.

4. The Long Lines Department, which installed and operated the interstate long distance network and handled all international calls. It received revenues from both the Bell System operating companies and the independent telephone companies for providing these services.

5. The twenty-four Bell System operating companies, which provided and operated the telephone system at a local level. They covered about 85 percent of the telephones in the United States. Sixteen of the operating

companies were wholly owned by AT&T, and it owned a majority interest in six of the others.

In 1972, AT&T had telephone operating revenues of $21.4 billion and had 109 million phones in service, of which some 14 million were business phones connected to PBX, or functionally similar, systems.

The 1760 independent telephone companies provided local telephone service in areas not served by AT&T. These companies, as well as the Bell System operating companies, were regulated by state public utility commissions. They varied greatly in size from very small rural telephone companies to major corporations such as General Telephone, which had operating revenues in the United States of almost $2 billion. The ten largest independent telephone companies are shown in exhibit 2.

The Emergence of the Telephone Interconnect Industry

Prior to 1968, all telephone company tariffs in the United States had contained a blanket prohibition against the attachment of customer-provided terminal equipment (such as telephones, answering machines, and PBX's) to the telecommunications network. The historic 1968 Carterfone decision of the Federal Communications Commission (FCC) held that these blanket prohibitions were unreasonable, discriminatory, and unlawful, and the FCC required that the telephone companies file new tariffs that did not contain such blanket prohibitions. This decision opened up the vast market for terminal equipment to a variety of new competitors.

The Carterfone decision did allow the telephone companies to take reasonable steps to protect the telephone system from any harmful effects of interconnected equipment. New tariffs filed in early 1969 by the telephone companies required that protective connecting arrangements be installed on each line to protect and insulate the public network. In the next few years, these connecting arrangements became a major bone of contention between the suppliers of customer interconnect equipment and the telephone companies. Interconnect equipment suppliers charged that the connection arrangements sometimes caused technical problems, that the telephone companies used delaying tactics in installing them, and that they unnecessarily raised costs (an average charge by the telephone companies of $7–10 per line per month) for the users of the interconnect equipment. The telephone companies responded to these charges by pointing out that they had rapidly developed a large number of protective connecting arrangements for different types of terminal equipment and had installed several hundred thousand of them by 1974.

Exhibit 2   Ten Largest Independent Telephone Companies

Names and Addresses	Telephones	% of Total Independent Telephone Industry	Total Operating Revenues
1. General Telephone & Electrics Corp. (U.S. only), New York, N.Y.	10,622,000	45.81	$1,881,000,000
2. United Telecommunications, Inc., Kansas City, Missouri	2,642,300	11.40	448,684,000
3. Continental Telephone Corporation (U.S. only), Chantilly, Virginia	1,774,200	7.65	299,536,000
4. Central Telephone & Utilities Corporation, Lincoln, Nebraska	1,059,600	4.57	194,055,000
5. Mid-Continent Telephone Corporation, Hudson, Ohio	593,500	2.56	82,842,000
6. Rochester Telephone Corporation, Rochester, New York	535,100	2.31	89,502,000
7. Puerto Rico Telephone Company, San Juan, Puerto Rico	357,400	1.54	64,277,000
8. Lincoln Telephone & Telegraph Company, Lincoln, Nebraska	239,800	1.03	37,176,000
9. Commonwealth Telephone Company, Dallas, Pennsylvania	154,900	67	18,857,000
10. Florida Telephone Corporation, Ocala, Florida	143,600	.62	29,068,000

PBX's and Key Systems

Interconnect equipment was any equipment attached to where incoming telephone company lines terminated on a customer's premises. Although such equipment took a wide variety of forms, including answering and recording devices, most of the sales volume in the business market was in two product classes: private branch exchanges (PBX) and key telephone systems.

A PBX is a local telephone switching system within a company that handles incoming, outgoing, and intraoffice calls.[2] As shown schematically in exhibit 3, a PBX consists of four major parts:

1. Switching equipment and control system. The switching system is the electromechanical or electronic equipment that connects the various internal (telephone extensions) and external lines in the system and provides ringing, busy signals, dial tone, and intercom services. The control system is the system that actuates the switching functions.

2. Trunk circuits. These are lines connecting the PBX to the public switched network.

3. Attendant console. This is the equipment used by an inside operator to complete or transfer calls, to determine which lines are busy, and to handle a variety of other tasks such as taking messages and paging.

4. Telephone station equipment. These are the individual telephones and key systems (a telephone that allows a person access to several lines with a single illuminated push-button set) located throughout the building or organization.

While key systems were commonly part of the PBX telephone system in large companies, stand-alone key systems were commonly used in smaller organizations (typically those with 40 or fewer telephones) as the sole system. Here they connected the outside lines directly to the user's extension telephone. Usually one pushbutton on each telephone was connected to a common line providing an intercom capability.

The technology involved in automatic PBX's had evolved in recent years—from electromechanical step-by-step systems, to electromechanical crossbar systems, to electronic systems.[3]

Step-by-step Systems were first offered at the beginning of the century and were the primary PBX product of the telephone companies for many years. These electromechanical systems could be expanded indefinitely as long as the customer had space for the very bulky equipment. If maintained well, they provided economical and reliable service but offered only very

2. Some companies distinguished between PBX, a manually switched private branch exchange, and PABX, an automatic PBX, in which all switching was done without operator intervention. Here PBX will be used to cover both types of equipment.
3. A brief description of the switching and control systems technology can be found in Appendix A.

Exhibit 3   PBX System Including Key System

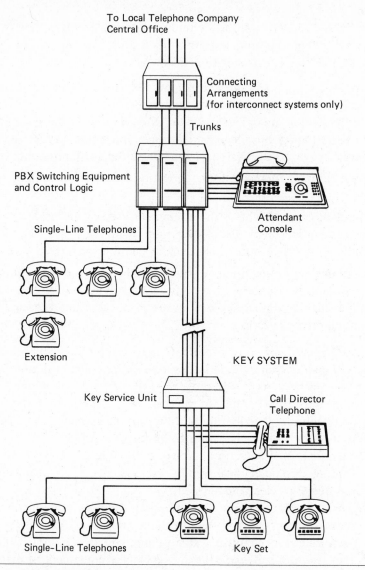

To Local Telephone Company
Central Office

Connecting
Arrangements
(for interconnect systems only)

Trunks

PBX Switching Equipment
and Control Logic

Attendant
Console

Single-Line Telephones

Extension

KEY SYSTEM

Key Service Unit

Call Director
Telephone

Single-Line Telephones

Key Set

Source: SRI Long Range Planning Service.

limited features. They were also expensive in terms of installation labour
and maintenance and generated a large amount of "noise," making them
unsuitable for data communications.

   Crossbar Systems were the next step in PBX evolution. These were
again electromechanical switches, and variations of them had been

available for years. These systems were much more compact than the step-by-step systems, being housed in cabinets, and had lower labour and maintenance costs. Once they were set up and adjusted, they provided very reliable service but were costly to expand beyond the capacity of the original installation. Modern crossbar systems offered the user a number of features such as:

Selective toll restriction. The system could be set up so that only certain individuals could dial long distance calls.

Station transfer. The user could transfer an incoming call from outside the company to another extension within the system without going to the switchboard operator.

Consultation hold. An incoming call could be held while the person dialed another number to secure information for the caller. This procedure did not require the telephone to be a key telephone equipped with a hold button.

Add-on conference. A third person could be dialed so that a three-way conference could be held. Again, a key telephone was not required.

Electronic Telephone Switching Systems were the most recent technological development. The original work on electronic switching systems had been done at Bell Laboratories in the mid-1950's, and the first commercial electronic central office (i.e., a switching system within the Bell system) was opened in 1965. Electronic switching technology only began to be used in the PBX market in the early 1970's, and by 1974 there were about 20 electronic PBX models on the market. Most of these electronic systems used space division multiplexing (SDM).[4] Electronic systems with time division multiplexing (TDM), which allowed several signals and calls to go over one pair of wires, promised to significantly simplify and reduce the costs of cabling a building for the PBX system. Electronic systems contained both memory and logic capabilities. The control logic—that is, how the appropriate circuits were interconnected during use—was implemented in two basic ways. The method greatly affected the flexibility of the equipment. The two ways were:

1. *Wired logic.* Here the logic was stored on printed circuit cards, and control actions were predetermined by the wiring connections on the cards. This limited the flexibility of the system and the ease with which it could be modified.

4. Again see Appendix A for explanation of technology.

2. *Stored-program logic (computer controlled).* Here all logic was stored either in exchangeable memory or by programming. Changes in the control logic could be readily made by changing the program.

Stored program logic gave a PBX great flexibility and the potential to meet future demands that wired logic systems could not match. Besides providing the normal control (connection) functions and a range of features to aid the telephone user, a computer-controlled electronic PBX could be used to record details of all toll calls (call detail recording), could monitor usage of the system, and could even perform self-diagnostic functions if there were problems with the equipment. In addition, if a company placed Tie Lines and WATS (Wide Area Telephone Service) lines on direct access (i.e., no operator was needed), the electronic switch could be programmed to seek the least cost route for a long distance call. With additional memory, a wide range of features could be made available on an electronic PBX, including all of those available on a crossbar system. Thus, in an electronic PBX, the systems features were in the central switching unit rather than the particular telephone or key unit. The user could make use of a particular feature by either dialing a code or pressing a couple of buttons on the telephone. Some of the features that could be offered on electronic systems included:

Classes of service. Each telephone station could be given access to only those services necessary for the person to perform his or her job. For example, some telephones could be allowed to call only certain long-distance area codes.

Automatic dialing and speed calling. Each user could store frequently called numbers in the system. The switch dialed the number when the user dialed a code. The stored numbers could easily be changed by the user.

Call forwarding. A code instructed the switch to forward any incoming call to a specified number.

Station number changes. When the user was relocated and wished to retain his or her current number, this change could easily be entered into the system. No telephone moving charges would be incurred as long as a telephone existed at the user's new location.

Automatic call distribution. A number could be set up for a particular department and any incoming calls to that number were distributed by the switch to any free department telephone.

Electronic systems could therefore provide a range of useful features to the user. While basic electronic systems were more costly than similar electromechanical systems, the marginal cost of adding features after installation was much lower. They promised to be more reliable than electromechanical systems, although experience with electronic systems was not yet large enough to provide a convincing maintenance and reliability record. Electronic systems, particularly those based on the TDM technology, were also more suitable for tying into data communication terminals. This was expected to become an increasingly important consideration by the late 1970's, when many more users were expected to be using their telecommunications system for both voice and data transmission.

Competition in the PBX and Key Systems Market

After 1968, a customer could purchase a PBX or key system from one of two basic types of suppliers: (1) the telephone company providing service in that area or (2) an interconnect company. As exhibit 4 suggests, the structure of the interconnect market was quite complex. In some cases, companies manufactured the equipment and distributed it through one or more suppliers who installed and serviced the equipment. In other cases, the manufacturer might be a manufacturer-supplier selling directly to the end-user or through a separate supplier subsidiary. These subsidiaries would often distribute the products of other manufacturers also.

Manufacturers of PBX and Key Systems

The manufacturers of PBX equipment were a pretty diverse group. Western Electric, the supplier of the Bell System; Northern Telecom, the U.S. subsidiary of Northern Electric, the Bell Canada manufacturing arm; and the major suppliers to the independent telephone companies, such as GTE-Automatic Electric, North Electric, and Stromberg-Carlson, were all well-established in the North American market—having supplied equipment to the various telephone companies since before the 1968 Carterfone decision. The PBX equipment manufactured by these suppliers for the independent telephone companies was, in 1968, generally similar to Western Electric's and offered only traditional features.

The Carterfone decision provided an opportunity for another group of manufacturers to enter the U.S. market. These were largely European and Japanese manufacturers who had extensive experience with PBX's and key systems in other markets. With the encouragement of the interconnect suppliers (i.e., the companies selling to the end-users), they modified their equipment and were able to offer end-users features previously unavailable in the United States. By the early 1970's, the Japanese and European companies had captured about 75 percent of the U.S. PBX and key system

Exhibit 4 Structure of the Market for PBX's and Key Systems

Telephone Companies

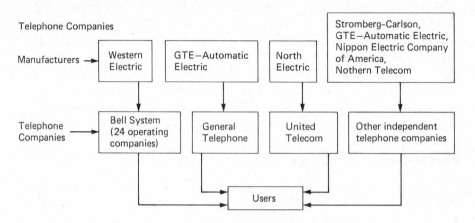

Interconnect Industry

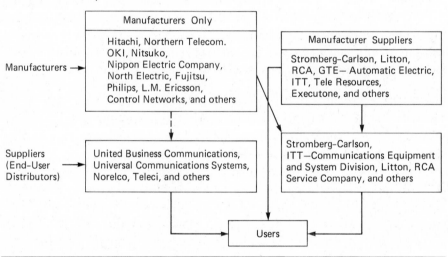

Source: SRI Long Range Planning Service.

interconnect market.[5] The major companies in this group were OKI, Nippon Electric, Hitachi, Nitsuko (all Japanese), and L.M. Ericsson (Swedish). International Telephone and Telegraph (ITT) also entered the U.S. market after the Carterfone decision; by 1973, some industry observers felt it had the best line of PBX equipment available in the United States. A list of the

5. That is, 75 percent of PBX and key system market that was not serviced by the AT&T operating companies or the independent telephone companies.

422 Distribution Decisions

major manufacturers ranked in terms of their estimated 1973 sales to U.S. interconnect suppliers is shown in exhibit 5. As exhibit 4 also suggests, some of these companies had also been quite successful in selling their products to some of the telephone operating companies. This resulted, in some cases, in end-users being able to obtain identical equipment from either the telephone operating company or an interconnect supplier.

The opening of the interconnect market had also brought a number of new U.S. manufacturers into the market. Wescom, Tele/Resources, and Philco Ford had all developed electronic PBX's and were supplying them to the independent telephone companies or to interconnect suppliers. Litton and RCA, which had entered the market as national interconnect companies, were buying PBX's from others and were both rumoured to be developing electronic PBX's. Other large manufacturers, active in foreign

Exhibit 5 Major Manufacturers of Interconnect Equipment Ranked in Order of Estimated 1973 Sales to U.S. Interconnect Companies

Company	*Manufacturing Locations*
OKI Electronics of America/OKI Electric of Japan	Japan and U.S.
Nippon Electric Company	Japan and U.S.
Hitachi	Japan and U.S.
Nitsuko*	Japan
International Telephone and Telegraph (ITT)	U.S. and Spain
L. M. Ericsson	Sweden
Northern Telecom (subsidiary of Northern Electric of Canada)	Canada and U.S.
Stromberg-Carlson	U.S.
North Electric (subsidary of United Telecommunications)	U.S.
Fujitsu	Japan
General Telephone and Electronics (GTE)-Automatic Electric	U.S.
North American Philips-Norelco	Netherlands and U.S.
CIT/TELIC	France and U.S.
Iwatsu*	Japan
Meisei	Japan
Siemens	Germany
Lynch	U.S.
Toshiba*	Japan

*Key systems only.
Source: SRI Long Range Planning Service.

markets, were also believed to be ready to enter the market. IBM was also viewed as a possible entrant, since it had developed a very strong position in the European PBX market with two expensive electronic PBX's. The major manufacturers of electronic PBX's and a brief description of their equipment and market position are listed in exhibit 6.

Notable in their absence from the list of manufacturers in exhibit 6 were the Japanese and European manufacturers. The major Japanese manufacturers (Nippon, Hitachi, Fujitsu, and Oki) and the leading European manufacturer, L.M. Ericsson, produced high-quality electromechanical PBX equipment. Until the devaluation of the dollar in 1973, the Japanese PBX equipment had been very competitively priced. Ericsson had always sold its equipment at premium prices in the United States. Both the major Japanese manufacturers and Ericsson were rumoured to be developing electronic PBX's.

Interconnect Companies

The number of interconnect companies had grown rapidly since 1968; by 1973, there were thought to be about 300 of them in the United States. These interconnect companies analyzed customer needs for PBX's and key systems, designed and recommended a system, installed it and serviced it. Interconnect companies could be subdivided into two basic groups—national suppliers and small regional or local suppliers. Estimated sales for the major interconnect suppliers in 1973 are shown in exhibit 7.

The four largest national companies—Litton, Stromberg-Carlson, ITT, and United Business Communications—had offices throughout the United States and were divisions of much larger corporations. In 1973, ITT was the only one of the four that had a wholly owned manufacturing subsidiary. Stromberg-Carlson Communications was the result of the acquisition by General Dynamics, in June 1973, of Arcata Communications, Inc. and Arcata Leasing from Arcata National. The two Arcata National units had offices in twenty major metropolitan areas across the United States and had generated losses of close to $4 million after taxes on sales of $25 million in the final year before General Dynamics acquired them. Eventually, as the acquired interconnect supplier was integrated with the Stromberg-Carlson manufacturing unit, Stromberg-Carlson would, like ITT, have an integrated manufacturing and distribution organization.

There were also three other companies that were national in scope. Universal Communications Systems, a subsidiary of American Motor Inns, and Teleci, a subsidiary of Holiday Inn, both specialized in the hotel/motel segment of the market, and RCA Service Company specialized in hospitals and universities. Industry observers believed that these companies were profitable. The hotel/motel segment of the market had some unique characteristics that made it a good candidate for specialization. It required only a voice communications system, phones were not moved, key sets were rarely used, most calls were ingoing or outgoing, and a record of all outgoing calls had to be made for billing purposes. Universal Communications Systems and Teleci chose to meet the needs of this segment by importing Japanese electromechanical PBX's that could meet these requirements at low cost.

The regional interconnect suppliers were generally small companies that typically served a geographical area within a 50- or 100-mile radius of their home office. Many had originally been in the sound and/or communications equipment business and had simply diversified into the interconnect market. Some of the major regional interconnect suppliers were Tele/Resources (New York), The Other Telephone Company (Minnesota), Fisk Electric (Texas), and Scott-Buttner Communications (California). Most of the interconnect companies were very small, telecommunications sales generally being less than $2 million. Tele/Resources, believed to be the largest of these companies, had sales of about $4 million. Industry observers believed that these companies, unlike many of the national suppliers, were profitable. This was probably the result of lower overheads, knowledge of local requirements, and the flexibility of small companies. Many of these companies were seriously undercapitalized.

Some industry observers felt that the interconnect suppliers had been unable to exploit fully what they believed to be the major weaknesses of the telephone companies—namely, their fairly obsolete product line and their inability to respond quickly to the changing market and technology. Much of the Japanese and other PBX equipment the interconnect suppliers were handling was only marginally superior in terms of features to the equipment manufactured by Western Electric. Thus they were forced to compete largely on the basis of lower price, more flexible pricing arrangements, and greater installation flexibility. Even the Tele/Resources PBX, while fully electronic and easy to install, was not a great deal more flexible than conventional PBX equipment and, in addition, required expensive special phones. Also, it was said to be difficult to maintain. Nevertheless, the first two years of production of this PBX was sold out within a few months of its being introduced.

Interconnect companies, both regional and national, stocked spare parts for their customers' PBX's so that they could rapidly get a customer's malfunctioning telephone system operating again. The faulty parts were

Exhibit 6 Electronic PBX Manufacturers and Their Product Offerings in 1973

Manufacturer	Model	Technologies Used[a]		Number of Lines PBX Can Handle	Comments
		Control	Switching		
Western Electric	801A	Electronic-wired logic	Space division (SDM)-reed relay[b]	46–270	Western Electric produced a very broad line of PBX's, most of which were still electromechanical. The 801A and 812A were both semielectronic. In the 101 systems, all switching was actually done in a Bell System central office, not on the customer's premises. An electronic central office was needed for the ESS. Only a small proportion of Bell central offices were electronic.
	812A	Electronic-wired logic	SDM-crossbar	400–2000	
	101 ESS (3A)	Electronic-computer	Time division (TDM)-electronic (PCM)[c]	400–800	
	101 ESS (4A)	Electronic-computer	TDM-electronic (PCM)	2000–4000	
ITT	TD-100	Electronic-wired logic	TDM-electronic (PAM)[d]	40–100	ITT's fully electronic PBX's covered all line sizes. Many observers felt it had the best line of PBX's on the market in 1973. Shipment of the TD-100 PBX was expected to begin in early 1974.
	TE-400A	Electronic-wired logic	SDM-electronic	100–400	
	TE-400G	Electronic-wired logic	SDM-electronic	400–800	
	TCS-2	Electronic-computer	SDM-electronic	600–6000	
Stromberg-Carlson	400A	Electronic-wired logic	SMD-reed relay	100–400	Both were semielectronic PBX's.
	800A	Electronic-wired logic	SDM-reed relay	400–800	

Company	Model	Technology	Switching	Lines	Comments
Wescom	501	Electronic-wired logic	SDM-electronic	40–120	This PBX was being sold to independent telephone companies. Shipments were expected to begin in early 1974.
Tele/Resources	TR-32	Electronic-wired logic	TDM-electronic (PAM)	40–164	This PBX required unique and expensive phones and was sold only to interconnect suppliers. There were large order backlogs in late 1973.
Philco Ford	PC-192	Electronic-computer	SDM-electronic	64–192	The PC-512 was introduced in 1972 and was marketed to independent telephone companies. It was very expensive in relation to competitive offerings and was not believed to be selling well.
	PC-512	Electronic-computer	SDM-electronic	128–512	
IBM	2750	Electronic-computer	SDM-electronic	256–756	IBM had been successfully selling these very expensive PBX's in Europe. They were really feasible only for installations requiring more than 500 telephones.
	3750	Electronic-computer	SDM-electronic	256–2264	
Northern Telecom	SG-1	Electronic-wired logic	TDM-electronic (PAM)	40–80	The SG-1 was introduced in 1972 and had been selling very well in the U.S. and Canada. The SG-2 was not yet in production.
	SG-2	Electronic-wired logic	TDM-electronic (PAM)	80–120	
ROLM	Proposed	Electronic-computer	TDM-electronic (PCM)	100–800	

a. See Appendix A for a brief discussion of the technological issues.
b. Reed relay was an evolutionary switching approach that bridged the gap between electromechanical crossbar and fully electronic switching.
c. PCM—pulse code modulation. Here all signals that are transmitted are digital signals.
d. PAM—pulse amplitude modulation. Here all signals that are transmitted are analog signals.

Exhibit 7 Estimated Sales by Interconnect Companies in 1973

Company	Sales (millions of dollars)
Litton Business Telephone Systems	25
Stromberg-Carlson Communications[a] (subsidiary of General Dynamics)	25
ITT-Communications Equipment and Systems Division	18
United Business Communications (subsidiary of United Telecommunications)	14
Universal Communications Systems (subsidiary of American Motor Inns)	9
RCA Service Company	8
Norelco Communications[a] (subsidiary of North American Philips)	5
GTE-Automatic Electric[a]	7
Teleci (subsidiary of Holiday Inns)	3
Tele/Resources	4
ITT-Terryphone[b]	4
Others (about 300, mostly local)	60
Total	$182

a. Excluding sales to local suppliers, figures for which are included under "Others."
b. Key system sales only.
Source: SRI Long Range Planning Service.

then returned to the manufacturer for repair. Since this could take weeks—even months—the interconnect companies generally carried substantial inventories of spare parts.

The Response of the Telephone Companies

The AT&T operating companies and the independent telephone companies were vigorously resisting the encroachment of the interconnect suppliers into the PBX and key systems market. In 1970, AT&T had established a huge task force with people from Bell Labs, Western Electric, and AT&T marketing and engineering at a new facility in Denver, Colorado, to develop a new, more competitive PBX product line. This resulted in the introduction of four new competitively priced electronic or semielectronic PBX's (shown in exhibit 7) between 1971 and 1973. But even this progress was not rapid enough for some of the AT&T operating companies, and they began to buy PBX's from outside suppliers. General Telephone had also taken similar steps to remain competitive.

The telephone operating companies also modified their pricing structures to improve their competitive position. Traditionally, telephone companies only leased equipment to users; thus the user paid an installation charge and a monthly rental/service fee (which could, of course, be increased from time to time) that continued as long as the customer had the equipment. By 1973, some of the telephone companies were giving their customers the option of paying for the use of the equipment with a "two-tier" pricing arrangement. With a "two-tier" pricing scheme, the customer signed a lease for the equipment for a specified number of years (usually between 5 and 10 years). Then the cost of the equipment was split into two portions—the "capital" cost of the equipment, which could be paid off immediately, and the maintenance/administrative charge, which was paid over the life of the lease and which could be increased during this period.

Current Status of the Interconnect Market and Future Prospects

In a proprietary report published by the Long Range Planning Service (now the Business Intelligence Program) of SRI International, it was estimated that sales by interconnect suppliers had grown from virtually zero in 1968 to $182 million (at end-user prices) in 1973. Manufacturers' selling prices were approximately 50 percent of end-user prices, and given that there was a substantial amount of inventory at the supplier level, manufacturers' shipments were expected to total $120 million in 1973.

The $182 million sales estimate was broken into three categories:

1. $130 million in PBX sales. This included 3300 PBX's with 248,000 telephones. This was estimated to be 12.4 percent of the dollar value of all new and replacement PBX installations in 1973.

2. $47 million in key systems sales. This included 6000 key systems with 72,000 telephones. This was estimated to be 6.7 percent of the dollar value of all new and replacement key system installations in 1973.

3. $5 million in service and maintenance revenues, which included charges for telephones added to the original system, moving telephones within an office, etc.

SRI also attempted to project the market growth through 1985. Given the uncertainties surrounding the interconnect market, both conservative and optimistic projections were made. These projections took into account probable shakeouts in the industry, stronger competition from the telephone companies, regulatory factors, and a shortening life cycle (hence more frequent replacement) for this type of equipment.

On the basis of SRI's assumptions, total interconnect supplier sales were expected to be in the range of $1.1 to $1.7 billion by 1985; this was expected to give interconnect suppliers an installed base penetration of 21–30 percent for PBX's and 15–21 percent for key systems. During this period, SRI expected rapid technological development to continue with computer-controlled or stored-logic electronic switching systems being standard in PBX and key systems by 1980.

PBX and Key Systems Customers

One of the first things Dick Moley had done after joining ROLM in August 1973 was to talk to several large companies about their communication problems. Commenting on these interviews, Moley said, "What they came up with was very interesting—because what they said their problems were were problems that were not being addressed by the interconnect equipment or the Bell System equipment at the time, and that is where we saw our opportunity. What they said was that the largest portion of their bill, frequently 70–80%, is toll expenses. If you are a large electronics company, for example, you have Foreign Exchange lines, Tie lines, and WATS lines. Trying to get people to use these—to get them to go to the proper tables and look up how to call a number in a particular city, say, Los Angeles—to dial 76 for Los Angeles, then dial 9 for an outside line, then dial the telephone number—is very difficult. Even if a person does all this, the line frequently will be busy. Similarly, to gain access to a WATS line, the caller may have to call a special operator and wait for a line to become available.

"So what happens in many companies, of course, is that many people make many long distance calls without bothering to use these expensive facilities. Furthermore, many companies wish to keep track of who was calling which numbers, both to control abuse and to bill departments for their real use of facilities, rather than simply making an arbitrary allocation. Many people also felt restrictions on toll calling on a telephone-by-telephone basis and automated queuing for WATS lines seemed to be needed features. The equipment available in 1973 simply did not address these needs, and the Bell System obviously didn't have a great incentive to optimize the use of toll calling facilities, since it would negatively impact its revenues."

A second major area of concern that surfaced in these interviews was the cost of making, and the time required to make, changes in the telephone system when people were relocated. This was particularly true in firms that used a project type of organization or in organizations that were experiencing rapid growth, where the average times between moves of a phone could be as short as six months. Every time personnel changes were made and people were relocated, the telephone company had to be called in to change wires and relocate the phones, and sometimes the companies had to wait quite a long time for the changes to be made. Furthermore, the Bell System and independent telephone company tariffs to make these changes varied across the country. In some areas, it cost about $15 to move a phone, whereas in other areas, such as New York, it might cost $75 for the same service. ROLM estimated that on the average, the real cost of performing this service was about $50. Many large companies operating in several parts of the country were aware of these differences and realized that under pressure from the Public Utility Commissions for the telephone companies to stop "subsidizing business," these charges would probably rise in areas where they were low. One very large firm of consultants operating in San Francisco, where the cost of moving a phone was only about $20, was already spending over $400,000 per year on these moves and changes.

"Another area that was an absolute nightmare was key phone systems," commented Dick Moley. "We saw that in our own offices last year when Ken Oshman's office had to be relocated. Two men spent a whole day recabling 125-pair cables to the new location for the key phone system. The cost was nominal, but it clearly cost the telephone company a lot of money to make these changes. We then asked ourselves, Why are key systems so difficult to move? The reason is that each light on the call director's push-button set takes six wires to activate, so you may need a very thick (1 inch in diameter) 125-pair cable from the switching equipment to the call director telephone with 20 or so lines, and you clearly can't afford to run such a cable all over the building. So essentially, the wiring is customized for the key system. That seemed to us to be totally insane with the available electronics. So we said we can do it differently. What we can do is use a key phone with a three-pair cable—one pair for voice, one pair to power the electronics, and the third pair to digitally signal which button is depressed and to indicate which button to light. Thus, if we standardize the building wiring completely on three-pair cables which connect to wall sockets much like electrical wiring, the user will not have to rewire the building if some phone is moved. They might have to plug in a special box and make an arrangement back in the switching equipment to make sure it was connected to a switch to drive a key phone rather than a single line phone, but no rewiring will be necessary."

Large customers would be critical to ROLM's success in the marketplace, since the computer-controlled PBX system that they were developing was designed to handle 100–800 lines. This line range had been chosen because cost-effective computer-controlled models that would provide the kind of benefits customers desired could not yet be cost competitive for installations of less than 100-line capacity. In 1973, only a very small number of Fortune 500 companies were buying from interconnect suppliers. Most of the sales by the interconnect companies had been made to smaller organizations. In fact, about 75 percent of the interconnect equipment, was sold to hotels and motels, wholesalers and retailers, stockbrokers, insurance agencies, hospitals and clinics, attorneys, banks, manufacturers, and service industries. Few of the installations made by the interconnect companies had more than 100 lines.

For these reasons, a final issue Dick Moley raised in his interviews with the large companies was why they had not bought equipment from interconnect suppliers. A major reason the companies cited was that they saw few economic benefits from buying from interconnect suppliers. The main benefit was that they could purchase the equipment and hence freeze their equipment cost (since they would be unaffected by telephone company rental rate increases). But since equipment was usually only 20–30 percent of their costs, and when a discounted cash flow analysis of the purchase versus rental choice was made, the savings often turned out to be minor. Meanwhile, if the equipment was purchased, the company was locked into equipment that might soon become obsolete. It seemed that smaller companies were much less likely to do a discounted cash flow analysis and seemed to be largely attracted to the interconnect PBX's by their marginally better features and the belief that they would get better service from these companies than they would from the telephone operating companies. An additional factor that might help explain the failure of the interconnect companies to penetrate larger companies was that few of the interconnect suppliers appeared to have sales organizations that were capable of conducting a multilevel sales campaign at several levels of decision making in prospective large companies.

From his discussions with the large companies, Mr. Moley also gained a better appreciation of the decision-making process for PBX's and key systems. Voice communication decision makers were generally low-level office managers or communication managers. These decisions had historically been made at a low level because the decisions to be made with respect to telecommunications equipment were generally of a minor nature. Until 1968, the Bell System operating company or the independent telephone company was a monopoly supplier, and hence there was no choice of vendor. The office or communications manager often relied greatly on the recommendations of the telephone company salesperson, and, in fact, the manager was frequently a former Bell System employee. The main responsibilities of the manager were largely those of placing orders with the telephone company and coordinating installation and service activities. When alternative suppliers to the telephone companies became available, these managers were very cautious about recommending them, since the risks of poor service and the possibility of the interconnect supplier going out of business were not inconsequential. Furthermore, since switching to an interconnect supplier typically required that the equipment be purchased rather than leased, the managers usually lacked the authority to make the decision themselves, and the capital expenditure had often to be approved at very high levels in the organization—sometimes even at the Board of Directors level. The communication managers were not usually accustomed to preparing these types of proposals and doing the necessary internal selling to get the proposals approved.

The results of the customer interviews made ROLM management very enthusiastic about their potential entry into the telecommunications market. As Mr. Moley remarked, "Out of our discussions, I and the others in ROLM management became really enthusiastic, because clearly here is a vast market where we potentially have the capability to solve meaningful customer problems and save companies large amounts of money. Computer technology was the key to solving these problems—we could optimize call routings, handle toll restrictions, etc. If there are telephones in place, handling moves and changes becomes simply a matter of remotely reprogramming the switching equipment—nobody needs to visit physically the customer's office or plant."

The ROLM PBX

By October 1973, Jim Kasson and his two associates had made considerable progress on the technical aspects of the ROLM product. The conventional wisdom in the telephone industry trade magazines at the time was that time division multiplexing (TDM) with pulse code modulation (PCM) switching technology and stored-logic (computer control) control technology would not be viable, cost-effective technologies until the late 1970's or early 1980's. Jim Kasson was now convinced that it was a viable technology in 1973. As a result of some clever circuit work and ROLM's knowledge of minicomputers, software, and PCM technology, they were convinced that their approach would work and would be cost-effective.

They had already "breadboarded" (i.e., laid out the electronic circuitry in a crude way) key technology elements that were new to ROLM, and they even had a couple of telephones in the laboratory working with their switching circuitry. In effect, the technological advances they were taking advantage of promised to change the nature of PBX manufacture from a labour- and capital-intensive operation to a technology-intensive electronic assembly operation that would require the manufacturer to have minicomputer, software, and solid-state switching expertise. These were all technologies in which ROLM management felt their company had significant strengths.

The management of ROLM was convinced that the flexibility of a computer-controlled PBX built on a TDM technology would change the economics of a business communication system's installation, maintenance, and operation, besides providing excellent user convenience. For example, with their PBX it would be possible to prewire a building with standard three-pair cable connected to wall outlets. Then all that would be necessary to install a complete system would be to connect the cables to the PBX, plug the standard telephone sets into the sockets, and enter into the computer the locations and extension numbers of the telephones. In the case of a multiline key set, the information entered into the PBX would include information on all the extensions that are to be routed to the set. Moves and changes of extensions would be a straightforward matter of entering the new configuration information into the computer. No longer would it be necessary to have the wiring tailored to the specific configuration and have ancillary keyset switching equipment located remote from the PBX. The features, both standard and optional, that they proposed to offer on the ROLM PBX are listed in exhibit 8.

Thus their proposed product was a minicomputer-controlled TDM system that could handle both voice and data communications. In essence it had all the capabilities of the successful IBM computer-controlled PBX's, plus the additional capability of handling key telephones without requiring large cables and key service units. Furthermore, unlike the IBM PBX's, which cost two to three times as much as conventional systems, the ROLM PBX was expected to be price competitive in the range of 100–500 extensions, a range that, they estimated, accounted for 60 percent of the dollar value of all PBX systems.

Decisions Facing ROLM in October 1973

Although many of the technical uncertainties with respect to the product had been resolved, there were several dark clouds on the horizon. The Bell

Exhibit 8   Features and Services to Be Offered on the Proposed ROLM PBX

A. *Station Features—Standard*

Direct Outward Dialing
Station-to-Station Dialing
Nonconsecutive Station Hunting
Programmable Class of Service
Consultation Hold—All Calls
Call Forwarding, Unlimited
Flexible Station Controlled Conference
Group Call
Indication of Camp-On to Station
Individual Transfer—All Calls
Lockout with Secrecy
One-Way Splitting
Outgoing Trunk Camp-On
Processor-Controlled Changes—
   Type A
Trunk Answer from Any Station
Tie Trunks
Toll Restriction
Trunk-to-Trunk Connections-Station—
   Type B
Trunk-to-Trunk Consultation

Station Features—Optional

Alternate Routing (toll call
   optimization)
Automatic Redial
CCSA Access
Dictation Access and Control
Direct Inward Dialing
Direct Inward System Access
Discriminating Ringing
Plug-in Station (with Keyset Adapter)
Secretarial Intercept
Station DTMF to Rotary Dial
   Conversion
Tenant Service
Automatic Identification of Outward
   Dialing
Redundancy
Off Premises Extension
Private Lines
Music on Hold—Attendant
Music on Hold—System
Music on Camp-On
Reserve Power—Inverter
Speed Calling
Area Code Restriction
Traffic Measurement
Paging Interface

B. *Attendant Features—Standard*

Attendant Camp-On
Attendant Conference
Attendant Console
Attendant Transfer of Incoming
   Call
Attendant Transfer—Outgoing
Attendant Trunk Busy Lamp
   Field
Switched Loop Trunk Selection
Switched Loop Station Selection

Flexible Intercept
System Alarm Indications
Multiple Trunk Groups—
   Unlimited
Attendant Key Sending—Touch
   Tone

Attendant Features—Optional

Busy Lamp Field
Busy Verification of Stations

System was aggressively attempting to stop the competitive erosion both by moves on the regulatory front and by improving their equipment, developing new pricing schemes, etc. In June 1973, at the urging of the telephone companies, the North Carolina Utility Commission had proposed banning all interconnect equipment from the state. Although the Federal Communications Commission ruled in January that its own ruling pre-empted state regulation of interconnect equipment, the issue was still in the courts. ROLM management was also concerned about other regulatory actions the Bell System might take. On the pricing front, the Bell System and the independent telephone companies had made their pricing structures more competitive and had the potential to make further moves in that direction. Furthermore, the Bell System's intensified product development efforts were likely to result in products that were technically much more competitive with the proposed ROLM offering than was the current product line, although ROLM would probably have a year or so lead time. Other interconnect manufacturers would probably be into the market with more competitive offerings even earlier than the Bell System.

ROLM's Board of Directors, in preliminary discussions of the proposed entry, were not totally convinced of the wisdom of ROLM, a $4 million company, moving against such formidable competitors and openly questioned whether this was the best area in which to invest the company's limited resources. Investment bankers also raised similar concerns. Even within the top ranks of ROLM management, there were executives who were quite unsure about whether a move into the telecommunications market was in ROLM's best interest. The Treasurer and the Director of Manufacturing had both formerly worked for Arcata Communications and had seen at first hand the problems in the interconnect business. They were among those expressing concern.

From a manufacturing cost viewpoint, ROLM management was not concerned about the disparity in size between ROLM and its competitors, whose manufacturing experience base for the most part was built on electromechanical equipment (which was labour and capital intensive), whereas ROLM's equipment was largely electronic. In their view, this made it feasible for ROLM to compete with the likes of Western Electric.

Pricing the PBX

Kasson and his team had concluded that with a further investment of $500,000 in engineering and manufacturing, they could get the product into production. If given the go-ahead, they expected to have a prototype working in the laboratory by mid-1974 and to begin shipping systems in early 1975.

Detailed estimates of manufacturing costs had been developed by Kasson and others on the PBX team. With a sales price based on two and one-half times manufacturing cost (direct materials, direct labour, and overhead based on direct labour cost), the ROLM PBX promised to be cost competitive with the most closely competitive models available in the United States. They anticipated that volume discounts would be given to customers ordering multiple PBX's if they decided to market the product through telephone companies or interconnect companies. Since the ROLM PBX made heavy use of electronic components (e.g., the minicomputer, the computer memory, and integrated circuits), the cost of the PBX was expected to decline over time as the cost of electronic components continued their decline. Electromechanical PBX's, and even electronic PBX's based on analog technologies, were expected to experience a much more static cost future.

Channels of Distribution for the PBX

In many respects, ROLM's management felt that the most crucial decision facing them in 1973 was the choice of channels of distribution for their PBX system. Dick Moley felt they had several alternatives open to them:

1. *Sell to the Bell System.* The operating companies of the Bell System had traditionally relied exclusively on Western Electric for all their equipment. However, as a result of competitive pressures from the interconnect companies, several of the operating companies, including the largest one, Pacific Telephone, now bought equipment from other suppliers. Pacific Telephone had bought electromechanical PBX systems from Japanese suppliers, and more recently it had bought Northern Telecom's fully electronic PBX, which handled up to 120 lines. The former move was not a very radical one, since the Japanese designs were similar to Western Electric designs and could be installed and maintained by their field service force without any extensive retraining. The Northern Telecom purchase was more significant, since this did require retraining the field service force. Since the Bell operating companies were still believed to control some 80 percent of the installed PBX base, even a small share of this market would represent a huge sales volume to ROLM.

2. *Sell to the independent telephone companies, such as General Telephone.* While the independent telephone companies covered about

15 percent of the phones in the United States, they were more concentrated in rural areas and were growing about 50 percent more rapidly than AT&T. This reflected the movement of industry and population away from major metropolitan areas. Since larger companies still tended to concentrate in major metropolitan areas, the independent telephone companies' share of the large PBX (greater than 100 lines) market was much less than 15 percent. Their captive manufacturing subsidiaries were not as strong as Western Electric, and the independent telephone companies had never relied on them as much. But even taking into account that the independent telephone companies were a much smaller factor in the market than the Bell System, they still represented a large, burgeoning market—with companies like Stromberg-Carlson and several Japanese and European manufacturers very active in it.

3. *Sell to the interconnect companies.* These were concentrated in the larger metropolitan areas. Here ROLM had two alternatives: (a) The national companies such as Litton Business Systems, ITT, RCA Service Company, United Business Communications, and Stromberg-Carlson Communications or (b) the regional companies such as Tele/Resources, Fisk Telephone Systems, and Scott-Buttner Communications. Many of the national suppliers were in trouble owing to the lack of experienced managers, higher than anticipated investments, heavier than anticipated installation and maintenance expenses, too rapid geographic expansion resulting in loss of control, and the difficulty of providing quick and adequate service capability on a nationwide basis. These problems were exacerbated by the fiercely competitive nature of the markets, the heavy legal expenses, and the drain on management time necessary to challenge some of the telephone companies' new pricing schemes before the regulatory commissions. These chaotic market conditions had resulted in some companies getting into difficulties and being forced to merge with others. Some of the regional interconnect companies were doing quite well in their local markets. They bought their equipment from a variety of manufacturers including Nippon, Stromberg-Carlson, and Tele/Resources. Generally, the manufacturers required them to handle the equipment on a nonexclusive basis, so two or more interconnect companies in the same market area might carry the same PBX line. The regional companies typically were undercapitalized and sold small systems. It was very seldom that one handled a PBX with a capacity larger than 100 lines. Most of the equipment they were handling was still electromechanical. While marketing through regional interconnect companies had some advantages, par-

ticularly from a servicing perspective, there was a real question of whether large companies with multiple locations would want to deal with multiple interconnect companies. Some of the other manufacturers, including Northern Telecom, handled large sales directly and simply subcontracted with the regional interconnect companies for installation and maintenance services.

4. *Sell direct*. ROLM had given little thought to this alternative, since they felt they were simply too small. But from a sales viewpoint it had some obvious advantages, especially when it came to dealing with large accounts with multiple locations around the country.

Dick Moley's Task

Dick Moley had to make decisions about channels of distribution and pricing and also about such closely related issues as the amount and nature of advertising and sales promotion to be directed at end-users. By the November 1973 Board meeting, he hoped to have selected and laid out in some detail the marketing plan for the ROLM PBX. He hoped he would be able to present a convincing case for ROLM's entry into the PBX market.

Appendix A: PBX and Key Systems Technology

Much of the technological change in PBX systems was occurring in the switching and control systems. The technological alternatives in both the switching and control systems are shown in exhibit A1. With respect to the switching system, two major alternatives were possible: space division multiplexing (SDM) and time division multiplexing (TDM). An SDM system was one in which separate individual transmission paths were set up for the duration of the call. A TDM system was one in which the speech on each active line was sampled at a very high rate, so that no information was lost, and the samples were assigned to unique time slots on a common transmission line. The original signal could be reconstructed from these samples when needed. The ability to handle many calls on one line promised to lower costs. In a TDM system, the samples could be transmitted as either an analog (pulse amplitude modulation (PAM)) signal or a digital (pulse code modulation (PCM)) signal. If pulse code modulation was used, then all signals were digital—making such a system ideal for transmitting data as well as voice. This was expected to be an increasingly valuable feature by the late 1970's, as more and more companies wished to transmit

Exhibit A1 PBX Technological Alternatives

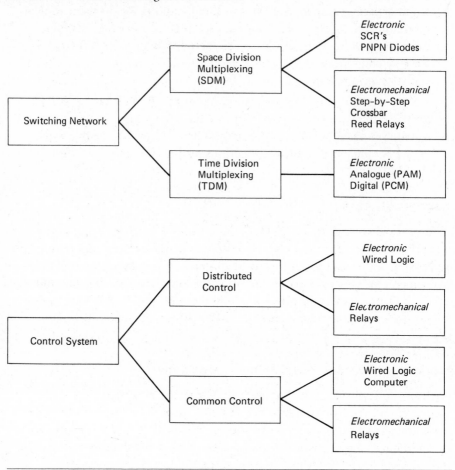

both data and voice over the same telecommunications system. Furthermore, if a digital signal was sent over a reliable transmission line, there was no cross-talk or distortion, which one could get if an analog system was used. ROLM engineers believed that a PBX with a TDM analog system could not (with the technology then available) be designed to handle more than 120 lines without excessive cross-talk. Partly for this reason, TDM with pulse code modulation was carrying an increasing share of the Bell System's long distance traffic. Nevertheless, many observers in the early 1970's did not expect that the pulse code modulation technology would be cost effective in PBX's until the late 1970's.

The control system could be either distributed control or common control. A distributed control system was one in which the control logic was distributed throughout the PBX system (e.g., if key phones were used, some of the control logic was in the key phone unit), whereas a common control system was one in which all the control functions were centralized in one set of logic. With a common control system, the control equipment was tied up only during the time the connection was made and not during the conversation. A wired logic common control system basically did with electronic components what was otherwise done by electromechanical relays. On the the other hand, a computer-controlled common control system added a new dimension to the PBX. New circuits had to be added to a wired logic system in order to alter its properties and capabilities, but a computer-controlled system's functions could be altered by changing its program. This gave a computer-controlled system great flexibility and the potential to meet future demands that wired logic systems could not match.

26 Hayes-Dana—Perfect Circle/Victor Division

Mr. Frank Peterson sat across the desk from Mr. Tom Moore, aftermarket sales manager for the Perfect Circle/Victor Division of Hayes-Dana Limited. Mr. Peterson was an independent automotive parts jobber who had been carrying the Perfect Circle/Victor line of piston rings, gaskets, and oil seals for more than twelve years. Mr. Peterson had just organized ten independent automotive parts jobbers in the southern Ontario and Niagara area into a buying group. He was in Mr. Moore's office to request direct shipment to members of the group and additional discounts.

In October 1972, Perfect Circle/Victor distributed its products through thirty-two warehouse distributor locations to over 2000 jobbers. Several executives in Perfect Circle/Victor were opposed to granting discounts or direct shipments to jobber buying groups on the grounds that to do so would entail a complete change in the distribution policy of the company. However, they recognized that all of Perfect Circle/Victor's competitors were selling direct to buying groups and that there were significant advantages from this method of distribution. As a result, Mr. Moore was giving careful thought to Mr. Peterson's request.

Company Background

Hayes-Dana Limited was one of the largest Canadian parts suppliers to the automotive industry. The company was organized under five autonomous divisions with each division operating under central corporate guidelines in order to ensure flexibility. One division, Perfect Circle/Victor, manufactured and distributed parts primarily to the automotive aftermarket.[1] The major products were piston rings sold under the Perfect Circle brand name

---

1. The aftermarket was the replacement service market as distinguished from the original equipment market (OEM).

442

and gaskets and oil seals sold under the Victor brand name. The company offered some 15,000 items in the three major lines, although about 20 percent of the items accounted for almost 80 percent of the volume. Products are illustrated in exhibit 1.

Channels of Distribution

The channels of distribution for automotive parts from the manufacturer to the consumer varied considerably. Perfect Circle/Victor operated its own warehouse beside their manufacturing plant in St. Thomas, Ontario. Parts were shipped from there to a few small direct OEM accounts or to warehouse distributors across the country. Sales to warehouse distributors accounted for over 90 percent of the division's business.

Exhibit 1   Hayes-Dana—Perfect Circle/Victor Division Product Examples

PRODUCT EXAMPLES

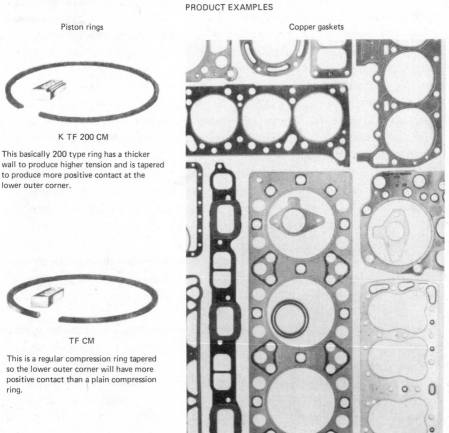

Piston rings

Copper gaskets

K TF 200 CM

This basically 200 type ring has a thicker wall to produce higher tension and is tapered to produce more positive contact at the lower outer corner.

TF CM

This is a regular compression ring tapered so the lower outer corner will have more positive contact than a plain compression ring.

A warehouse distributor (WD) provided facilities for storage, physical distribution, and sales representation for a number of noncompeting manufactures (as many as thirty or more manufacturers). Some WD's operated regionally, some nationally. The largest had sales of $50 million to $100 million in automotive parts. Several also distributed nonautomotive lines such as hardware, machinery parts, and electrical goods. Some WD's sold only to independent jobbers; others sold to both independent and franchised jobber outlets, and some sold also through owned jobber outlets.

A jobber was a local wholesaler who was prepared to make small-lot deliveries on a daily (or even more frequent) basis to trade accounts such as gas stations, repair shops and other automotive service outlets, fleet repair shops, and industrial firms. The jobber maintained limited inventories of automotive repair parts—enough to ensure that virtually all *routine* orders from trade accounts could be met—and replenished stocks with frequent (perhaps daily) orders from one or more WD's. Sales for jobber outlets ranged from $200,000 to $1 million annually. Employees included warehouse people, delivery drivers, field sales people, telephone order takers, and counter help (to serve those accounts that picked up their own orders). Trade accounts might buy from several different jobbers, and the business was thought to be very competitive. A number of jobbers also operated machine shops to which trade accounts could send motors, driveshafts, etc., for major repair and overhaul. There were an estimated 3000 jobbers in Canada.

An *independent jobber* typically was sole owner and manager with no formal ties to warehouse distributors. Orders would usually be concentrated with one WD, but two or more WD's might be utilized to obtain a wider selection of brands and to maintain flexibility in supplier relationships.

A *franchised jobber* owned the outlet but utilized certain facilities supplied by the WD such as inventory control systems, accounting services, order procedures, trade name, etc. In turn, the jobber placed virtually all purchases with the WD.

An *owned jobber* was an outlet owned by a warehouse distributor and managed by an employee of the WD according to centrally established policies and procedures.

Dealers for the major automotive manufacturers acted as distributors for the auto manufacturer's repair parts, acting, in a sense, as a jobber for a limited parts line. The automotive distribution system is outlined briefly in exhibit 2.

The structure of automotive parts distribution had changed over the years. Jobbers had joined together as "buying groups" since the 1940's. They grouped their purchases to present a more powerful position to their suppliers. They sought extra volume discounts, and later, when WD's appeared to provide the manufacturer with warehouse facilities, the buying groups sought to bypass the WD and obtain "drop shipments" from the manufacturer. Buying groups sometimes lasted only briefly, however, for the problems of managing a group were difficult for small business entrepreneurs to handle. Some groups, nevertheless, survived. Some built a group warehouse and began to operate it, in effect, as a jobber-owned WD.

Other factors also affected the distribution system. The huge growth in the number of automobiles, the proliferation of models (and hence of parts), and changing auto technology all served to magnify problems of inventory carrying costs, stock obsolescence, sales training, out-of-stock frequency, and so on. To tackle such problems with new management techniques was usually beyond the capabilities of small jobbers, but progress could be made with larger units and a more integrated systems approach to distribution. Hence, the number of independent jobbers had declined substantially by 1972, and many independents had formed buying

Exhibit 2   Outline of Automotive Aftermarket Distribution Channels

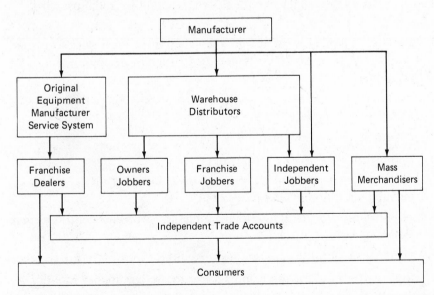

1. Hayes-Dana Perfect Circle/Victor Division sold only to warehouse distributors.
2. The main business of franchise dealers was in selling automobiles.

groups to gain better margins, terms, and other services from manufacturers. Many other independents sold out to WD's or switched to franchise operations.

Of the thirty-two WD locations utilized by Perfect Circle/Victor, eight were branches of Canadian Automotive Warehousing Limited, and three were branches of Automotive Warehousing Limited. This latter company also owned V.M. Redistribution Incorporated in the province of Quebec, which operated four warehouse distributor locations in that province and one in Nova Scotia. In addition, there were Auto Electric and Acklands Limited, each of which operated four warehouses. The remaining locations were separate firms.

Mr. Moore believed that from a warehouse distributor's point of view, the most important considerations in the decision to handle and distribute a manufacturer's product were price and margin, and then the manufacturer's record in terms of ability to supply demand, a willingness to maintain policies, and "a willingness to face mutual problems." The warehouse distributor, in turn, was expected by manufacturers to provide[2]

1. maintenance of an adequate stock of inventory of the manufacturer's merchandise both fast-moving and slow-moving items, at the exclusive cost of the warehouse distributor for warehousing and labour;

2. absorption of inventory taxes, floor taxes, and personal property taxes;

3. making available for the manufacturer a trained local sales force not only to call on established trade, but to attempt to open new accounts;

4. distributing, updating, and replacing the manufacturer's catalogues and price lists (located in jobber outlets);

5. dissemination of new product literature;

6. training of wholesaler's salesmen;

7. assistance in special promotions and distribution of the manufacturer's point-of-sale material;

8. responsibility for handling the manufacturer's product obsolescence program;

9. handling of all billings to wholesalers and responsibility for all credit;

10. freeing of capital for the manufacturer to use at a higher rate of

2. Taken from a 1972 survey by Automotive Warehousing Distributors Association, a U.S. organization.

return in his own business rather than in the above performed by the warehouse distributor; and

11. promoting a prosperous industry by efficient service to the thousands of small wholesalers who could not otherwise survive.

Pricing Practices

Price structures for the company's product lines varied slightly, but a typical schedule in the industry was:

Price paid by		Example
Consumer	Suggested list price	$1.00
Trade accounts	Suggested list price less 30 percent	0.70
Jobbers	Trade price less 35 percent	0.455
WD	Jobber price less 22 percent	0.355

In some trade circles, price schedules were treated as volume discount schedules, but Mr. Moore preferred to think of them as functional allowances—a return for distribution and selling services rendered. Some buying groups, by pooling their purchasing strength, commanded a price of about 15 percent off the jobber price, but Mr. Moore's view was that if they didn't perform all or most of the WD functions, they should not have more than a jobber price.

Mr. Moore recognized four categories of distribution with regard to functional allowances. The first category was the "legitimate warehouse distributor" who attempted to provide the eleven expected services in return for the full warehouse distributor discount. The second category was the "illegitimate warehouse distributor" who provided warehouse storage for the jobbers serviced but did not perform all the functions of the legitimate warehouse distributor. Some firms in this second category received the full warehouse distributor discount from some manufacturers.

The third and fourth categories were "formal" and "loosely knit" buying groups. The discount given to a group depended upon how the manufacturer viewed the group's worth and what functions were performed. A group's purchases could constitute a sizable portion of a manufacturer's output, and the group might agree to maintain a certain minimum volume, provide prompt payment, assure that, say, 85 percent of purchases would be made exclusively with the manufacturer, and so on. In negotiating prices, the group might attract bids on a competitive basis.

Since few groups had warehouses, arrangements with manufacturers usually called for direct shipments from manufacturer to jobber (bypassing the WD). Because of the jobber's need to provide prompt delivery to trade accounts, group members (or any jobber receiving direct shipments from the manufacturer's plant) generally had to carry larger inventories than jobbers using WD's. The possible profit effects of higher inventory levels is presented in exhibit 3 by an opponent of direct buying.

Competition

Perfect Circle/Victor had total sales of about $2.8 million at factory prices, or $3.6 million at jobber prices. In the Canadian *piston ring aftermarket*, Perfect Circle and General Piston Company Limited each had about 35 percent of the estimated $2.8 million (at factory prices) market. General Piston also manufactured oil filters and service tools. The company had eleven district managers servicing five legitimate WD and fifteen illegitimate WD outlets, and two major loose buying groups.

Exhibit 3   Excerpts from Brochure by Opponent of Direct Buying

The Profit Magic of Turnover versus the Empty Promise of "Extra Discount"

Manufacturers are practising false economics in saying that profit and discount are synonymous. They would have you forget service and availability, turnover and classification, carrying costs and costs of inventory protection, and return on investment. They would have you forget everything essential to sound jobbing.

   Let's do a comparison with three jobbers doing the same volume, assuming that the greater the discount, the greater amount of shelf stock that must be carried to earn this discount.

	Jobber Buys Direct at Extra 20 Percent Off	Buying Group Member Buys Direct at Extra 10 Percent Off	Jobber Buying Through Warehouse Distributor
Sales	$240,000	$240,000	$240,000
Percent gross profit	42	35	30
Gross profit	$100,800	$ 84,000	$ 72,000
Cost of sales	$139,200	$156,000	$168,000
Turnover	2	2.8	4
Inventory	$ 69,600	$ 55,715	$ 42,000
Capital released	$ 0	$ 13,885	$ 27,600
Return on investment	144 percent	150 percent	171 percent

Victor was the largest among four major competitors in the Canadian *gasket aftermarket,* with 58 percent of the estimated $3 million (at factory prices). One major competitor, Bel-Pro Inc., through their Canadian agents had 25 percent of the market. Their agents, Clark Bros., had several product lines and employed twelve salesmen with twenty illegitimate WD outlets and one loose buying group.

The Canadian *oil seal market* was estimated at $1.2 million at factory prices, and Victor had about 10 percent. Of two major competitors, Chicago Leather obtained about 50 percent of the market through fifteen legitimate WD outlets and five illegitimate WD outlets.

Perfect Circle/Victor Policy

Perfect Circle/Victor had offered functional allowances only to organizations that attempted to perform all the WD services. During a September 1972 industry conference, Mr. Moore had the opportunity of discussing distribution structures and allowances with other manufacturer executives. He noted the following comments were made during the discussion:

"Jobbers in loosely knit buying groups were strong, independent businesses with good machine shops."

"Buying groups represented a good share of the market in several areas."

"If a manufacturer hadn't done business with them, they'd have gone elsewhere."

"The trend is fifty-fifty whether or not a loosely knit buying group becomes a formal buying group by building its own warehouse and thus receiving the full discount that warehouse distributors receive."

"Most manufacturers seem to have contribution margins of forty percent."

"The seven or eight percent discount that one group received represented what a manufacturer considered fair value for warehousing."

Several Perfect Circle/Victor executives opposed the servicing of loose buying groups because they would be giving seven or eight percentage points or more for nothing. WD's, on the other hand, put up a large investment for space, personnel, computers, and salesmen. Too much WD business would be lost, it was felt, if a loose buying group was accepted. Some executives estimated a cut of *at least* 20 percent of the division's total sales as a result of an adverse reaction from perhaps half the WD's.

In addition, in order to ship directly to jobbers, additional warehouse facilities would have to be built at St. Thomas at a cost of $100,000 to

$200,000, additional stock of $300,000 to $500,000 would have to be carried, and warehouse operating expenses would have to be increased by an estimated $30,000 to $70,000, the extent of the added operation depending on how many jobbers would be served.

The executives who opposed a change in policy were anxious to maintain their reputation for being, as they termed it, "the manufacturer with the most integrity." Adherence to a hard line on loose groups would, they thought, enhance their position with their WD's. They also felt that if a loosely knit group became a formal group, built a warehouse, etc., Perfect Circle/Victor would be the first manufacturer to be invited for business. While their current policy might mean a few lean years, they felt the company would get the business back, and more, in the long run.

The Niagara Buying Group

Most of Mr. Peterson's group were located in the Niagara Peninsula, but three were located further north. In 1972, Perfect Circle/Victor had no WD's situated in the Niagara region and relied on distribution from Toronto and Hamilton WD outlets. The company's market penetration of the Niagara area was about one half of the national level, and this poor performance was attributed to the lack of a local warehouse carrying Perfect Circle/Victor lines.

When Mr. Peterson approached Mr. Moore, he alleged that his members were the strongest jobbers in the region and held a very large proportion of the aftermarket business in this area. They represented something over $190,000 of business to Perfect Circle/Victor (at factory prices). He explained to Mr. Moore that with the extra discount the group expected from all its supplying manufacturers, more salesmen would be hired and those manufacturers the group represented would get excellent sales representation. This also would mean, Mr. Peterson continued, that manufacturers not represented by the group would have a difficult time maintaining any sales in the region. Finally, he outlined the group's plan to build a central warehouse within two years to handle the anticipated extra volume and to perform full services.

Mr. Moore thought it would cost the group about $1.5 million to build a warehouse for a full line of aftermarket parts. He realized that a warehouse would permit prompt service for group members, but he wondered if there were enough business in the region to warrant a distribution warehouse being built by the group.

Perfect Circle/Victor had lost the business of a number of jobbers in steadfastly holding to the policy of refusing extra discounts. There were at least seven major and six minor buying groups in Canada whose business Perfect Circle/Victor had, in effect, turned away from because of the rigid policy. The request from Mr. Peterson was only the latest of a series of requests that had been made over the years, and it seemed likely there could be more buying group organizations attempted as independent jobbers sought means of competing with WD franchised and owned outlets. Existing buying groups represented sales at factory prices of about $2 million, and Mr. Moore thought it would be possible to obtain a substantial share of that amount if it was decided to change the company's distribution policy. The $2 million in additional sales included the Niagara/Southern Ontario sales to the Peterson jobbers.

While analyzing Mr. Peterson's proposal, Mr. Moore reviewed the performance of his thirty-two WD outlets. Seven, he judged, were doing an inadequate job, but it was not a simple matter to appoint a replacement. In some cases, the poor performers were branches of large WD organizations, and single branches could not be dropped. In some cases, even if the outlet could be dropped, there were no suitable replacements available or competitors had tight ties with possible replacements. In a number of areas where his outlets were performing poorly, Mr. Moore noted that there were buying groups he did not service. In Quebec, the major buying groups were often more aggressive and more successful than the WD's, in part because they were constituted by very strong jobber members.

Mr. Moore summarized:

> It would be nice to have the best of both worlds, and some outsiders have suggested we could accomplish that by giving extra discounts to buying groups and keeping it quiet. We would never do that in this company. It's not a way of doing business that we believe in. And anyway, in this business, everyone would know about it within a week. If we do decide to change, the tough part would be figuring out how to make the transition. Maybe there is some middle ground that would be fair to all parties, that would enable us to pick up buying group business without jeopardizing our WD relations. You know, our current policy, if nothing else, is clear and easy to administer.

27 Imperial Oil Limited: Packaged Specialty Products Distribution

Mr. Stuart Finlayson sat back in his chair to reflect on the consultants' draft report. He was in charge of a major study intended to result in the most cost-efficient distribution network possible for packaged specialty products for Imperial Oil Limited. Mr. Finlayson, Specialty Products Analyst, was assisted by a team of consultants and by representatives from several areas within Imperial Oil. The overall study had been divided into four stages; the first stage, Western Canada, was nearing completion as of early 1979. Mr. Finlayson was anxious to devote more attention to the work being done in the Atlantic, Quebec, and Ontario regions. He knew, however, that before be could do so, analysis and recommendations for the packaged specialty products distribution system in the West would have to be presented to senior management in both the West and Imperial's Head Office in Toronto, Ontario. With this task in mind, he was reviewing the information that had been collected.

Imperial Oil Limited

Imperial Oil Limited was one of Canada's largest companies as of 1979, with over $5 billion in revenues and approximately $4 billion in assets. Over 14,000 employees worked in Imperial's three main businesses: natural resources (crude oil, natural gas, natural gas liquids, minerals), petroleum products (gasoline, motor oils, lubricants, solvents), and chemicals (petrochemicals, plastic resins, agricultural chemicals, etc.).

As of 1978, approximately 10 percent of the company's petroleum products sales volume was specialty products. These products, contributing about 28 percent to the petroleum products margin, included motor oils, industrial and process oils, solvents (e.g. naphthas, varsol), greases, and waxes. In Western Canada, lubricating and process oils accounted for about 80 percent of the packaged specialty product sales. Imperial produced and distributed these products both in bulk and in packages. Over 1200 distinct product/package combinations existed, ranging from 500-ml plastic bottles to 205-litre (45-gallon) drums. In Western Canada, almost 60 percent of the packaged sales were 205-litre drums, and 547 of the product/package combinations accounted for 85 percent of the sales by volume. In addition to packaged sales, Imperial sold roughly the same amount of specialty products in bulk (via tank car or tank truck) direct to customer storage facilities. Although Imperial had been attempting to encourage a switch to bulk purchases by its major customers, the ratio of bulk to packaged had remained relatively stable for some time.

Mr. Finlayson's study of specialty products distribution was confined to packaged products and also incorporated packaged fuel products. The study focused on the distribution stage from filling completion to final customer or to commissioned agent warehouse.

As shown in the organization chart (exhibit 1), Mr. Finlayson was part of the Distribution Group, under the Marketing area in the Petroleum Products Group. At Imperial, a distinction was made between the activities of Logistics and those of the Marketing/Distribution group with regard to packaged specialty products. Logistics encompassed production and packaging of all specialty products and fuels and encompassed the distribution operations of the refinery warehouses up to the point the products left these warehouses. Physical distribution referred to all the activities in operating Imperial's other warehouses, all transportation of products, some local drum filling, and in general the distribution activities up to the point the products reached the end-user or the commissioned agents' doors.

Genesis of the Distribution Study

In 1978, top management at Imperial Oil developed and promoted the "pacesetter concept" for all aspects of company operations. Essentially, this concept meant that each activity in the company was to be performed as well as anyone else in comparable businesses was able to do it. For example, Imperial's truck fleet should be as efficiently managed and operated as the fleet of any other petroleum company. As this concept spread through the company, it triggered self-examinations by Imperial managers, stretched performance objectives, and meant consideration of different operating methods.

The pacesetter concept as it was applied to packaged specialty products distribution methods immediately raised several questions:

Exhibit 1   Imperial Oil Limited Organization Chart: Abbreviated[a]

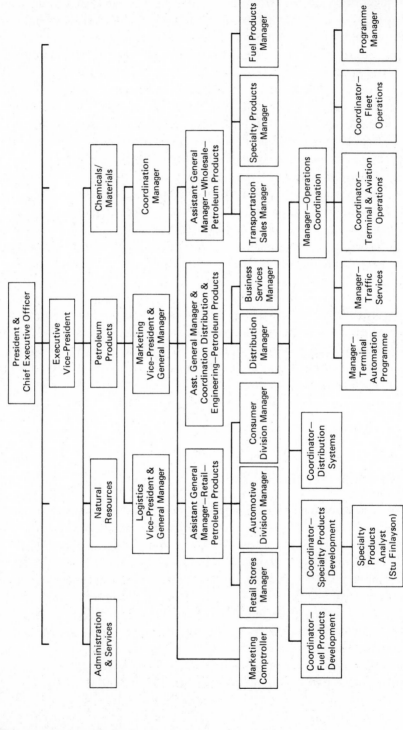

a. Many positions have been excluded from this chart, which was based on corporate documents. The intent is to show where the distribution group, and specifically the Specialty Products Development people, fit in the overall organization.

What is the most effective level of service—by customer type, by region, by product?

Where should warehouses/terminals be located and what facilities and operating methods should be incorporated?

What routing should products follow from source to customer and what modes of transport should be used over each "leg" of the network?

What is the most efficient set of operating rules throughout the system, covering such issues as order processing and production sequencing and scheduling?

Mr. Finlayson discovered that such questions were not easily or quickly answerable. Any studies of the physical distribution system for packaged specialty products to date had been based on individual elements of the system, not on a comprehensive examination of trade-offs amongst the elements. Performance data were limited at best, so Mr. Finlayson decided that the first step would be an assessment of how well the current physical distribution system was operating.

Any comprehensive study of the physical distribution system for Imperial Oil was bound to be difficult in Mr. Finlayson's opinion, if for no other reason than that it cut across so many departmental boundaries. To facilitate data gathering and analysis and ultimately to ease the change process any recommendations would require, Imperial Oil management established a working committee consisting of Mr. Finlayson and appropriate individuals from several areas in the company. The committee consisted of a representative from each of the four Imperial sales divisions (automotive, industrial, consumer, and retail stores) plus representatives from logistics, physical distribution, information systems, and comptrollers. They also hired, as of September 1978, a team of management consultants to guide and train the committee in doing such a study. Another committee, called the "steering committee" was also established that consisted of more senior-level management in the various departments and divisions involved. Mr. Finlayson knew from the outset that any recommendations he might make would need both the endorsement of head office and acceptance by regional senior management before they would be implemented.

The study was divided into four pieces on the basis of geography: Western Canada, Atlantic Canada, Quebec, and Ontario. Western Canada was selected as the first phase for a number of reasons, including Mr. Finlayson's assessment that several problems in the western physical distribution system deserved immediate attention. The steering committee decided that the consultants would work with him on this part of the national study and that the study approach taken in the West would be adopted by company personnel in the other three regions.

Mr. Finlayson noted the distribution study objectives which had been set in mid-1978:

1. To identify the most cost-efficient distribution network (at the specified level of service) for packaged petroleum products in Canada.
2. To detail the chronological changes and improvements required to the existing network to attain this status. (What key events might trigger action?)
3. To provide an action plan aimed at maintaining this status over the next decade (to 1990).
4. To identify short-term efficiency improvements.

The remainder of this case describes the Western Canada physical distribution study.

Study Organization and Approach

The working committee divided the study into six major parts: analysis of current distribution operations, demand forecasting, evaluation of customer service, identification of feasible future options, evaluation of options, and implementation plan.

An early task faced by the study team was specification of the information they felt necessary. Exhibit 2 provides an outline of the list developed by them. A variety of approaches were taken to gather information ranging from analysis of existing marketing data to in-field interviews with commissioned agents. The various methods used will be described more fully in subsequent sections.

Current Distribution in Western Canada

Packaged specialty products were provided to the Western Canada market from several Imperial sources, but almost nine tenths of the volume originated from their two major refineries in Canada. Packaged specialty products reached the ultimate customer through any one of four possible channels:

Refinery direct to customer

Refinery to salaried warehouse to customer

Exhibit 2 Study Data Requirements List: Condensed

A. Most Recent Product Flows and Costs: Overall

Sources of product
Location of warehouses/terminals
Location of agents
Volumes from each source to each destination
Volumes by each mode of transport
Cost by mode
Service (order frequency, delivery lead time)
Sales by product type, by package type, by type of customer, and by sales territory

B. Commissioned Agents

Sales for assigned and unassigned accounts
Average inventory levels
Inventory management—turns, damaged product, dead and surplus stock
Sources of product
Method of placing order (e.g., mail)
Frequency of ordering
Scheduled versus emergency ordering
Order lead time
Delivery mode—in and out
Special arrangements (e.g., drum collection)
Warehouse space and facilities
Service level—target and actual

C. Direct Sales Customers

Locations
Volumes
Sources
Method of placing order
Frequency of ordering
Order lead time
Delivery mode and cost
Service level—target and actual

D. Salaried Package Terminals

All costs (e.g., freight, warehousing, taxes, salaries, and benefits)
Warehouse size—space including usable height
Inventory levels and composition
Inventory management—turns, etc.
Order processing—number handled, average order size, etc.
Misc. activities
Service level—target and actual

Exhibit 2 (continued)

E.   Inflation Factors—Cost Increases
   Manpower and labour
   Transportation by mode
   Inventory carrying costs
   Commissions to agents
   Construction
   Land
   Equipment

Refinery to agent to customer

Refinery to warehouse to agent to customer

Imperial had six warehouses called salaried package terminals in the following locations: Winnipeg, Regina, Calgary, Lougheed (Vancouver), Prince George, and Price Rupert. With the exception of the Calgary warehouse, these terminals shared the same grounds as the regional bulk fuel terminals. The personnel were Imperial employees, and in all respects these terminals were company owned and operated. Approximately one third of the sales volume of packaged specialty products passed through these six terminals either directly to the final customers or to the commission agents.

There were 559 commission agents in Western Canada in 1977, and of these the majority were in Saskatchewan and Alberta. These agents served as the final distribution points for bulk fuel products, fertilizer, and packaged specialty products. In general, packaged specialty products constituted 10 percent or less of an agent's volume. An agent was an independent businessman operating in many cases out of facilities and land owned by Imperial Oil. Imperial Oil paid commissions ranging from 15¢ to 30¢ a gallon on packaged goods sales and distribution.

Agents engaged in basically two types of activities. The majority of their work (about 70 percent on the average) was providing distribution coverage for Imperial's industrial and automotive divisions. A customer would recognize a particular agent as a point of supply and place an order with the agent. Agents had no responsibility for sales coverage, cash, collections, etc. and were therefore paid a lower commission on this "assigned account" business. The remainder of their business was for the consumer division. This business was "unassigned accounts," involving both sales and distribution activities. Agents were responsible for all aspects of this business and were therefore paid a much higher commission rate.

An attempt to show product flow in millions of pounds in 1977 through all the channels is contained in exhibit 3. Not shown are a number of transfers interrefinery, interterminal, and interagency. The latter was estimated to be only 2–3 percent of total volume in 1977. The volume in pounds was thought to be representative of value in dollars. There were no differences in channel of distribution taken by specific product in the packaged specialty products mix.

The study team estimated that in 1977, distribution costs in Western Canada were $10.2 million, about 38¢ per gallon (1 gallon = 10 lbs.):

	$ million
Transportation	
to agents	2.1
remainder	2.1
Warehousing (excluding cost at agencies)	1.3
Order processing (people only)	0.3
Inventory carrying cost (includes agents' inventory; all inventory at 15% cost)	1.2
Agent commissions	
assigned	1.8
unassigned	1.4
	$10.2

Warehousing

The study team examined warehousing at both agencies and Imperial terminals. The team discovered wide variations in warehouse space, number of people involved in warehousing, and use of space and labour. Exhibit 4 provides summary statistics collected on the six terminals for 1977. Terminals accounted for about one eighth of the total square footage devoted to storage of packaged specialty products. Agents were located in all of the cities in which Imperial had terminals and refineries with the exception of Vancouver, the Lougheed terminal. The study team reported: "All warehouses are reasonably well laid out and are adequately equipped. . . . No major changes are warranted in handling methods at the warehouses."

Exhibit 3 Physical Product Flow 1977 in the West (millions of pounds)

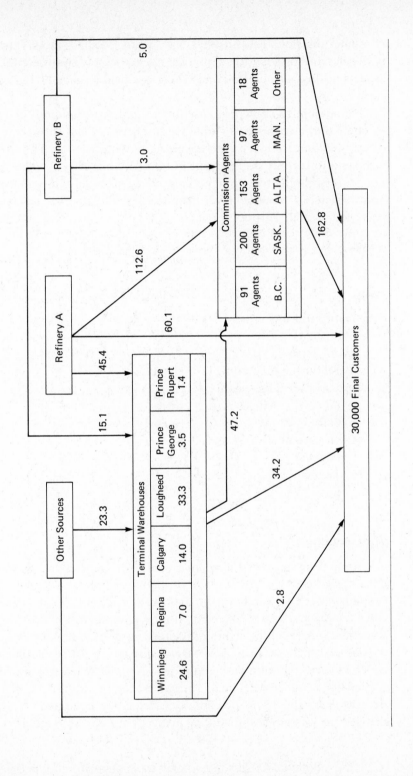

Exhibit 4 Terminal Warehouse Statistics, 1977

	Winnipeg	Regina	Calgary	Lougheed	Prince George	Prince Rupert
Warehousing area (ft²)	29,800	9,700	16,500	38,000	8,000	4,300
Throughput, 000 gals/ft²	83.9	72.7	84.6	86.8	44.1	33.0
Inventory						
Gals/ft²	6.4	7.4	8.4	7.5	3.6	3.7
$/ft²	9.09	10.72	12.06	11.24	4.25	3.72
Turns	10.9	11.4	7.6	9.9	10.1	8.1
Warehouse costs, ¢ per gal	7.9	12.2	11.1	7.1	8.5	28.9

Inventories

Inventory was held in the West at the refineries, terminals, and agencies. All of this inventory was owned and financed by Imperial Oil. As of October 31, 1978, 4.8 million gallons of packaged specialty products inventory were in the West, which valued at $1.70/gallon meant inventories of $8.2 million. The study team assumed an inventory carrying cost of 15 percent. Exhibit 5 shows the inventory in gallons in 1978 and the 1977 turnover statistics for the various locations of inventory.

The study team gathered data from a sample of 23 prairie agents to explore agent inventory management in more depth. Exhibit 6 shows highlights of the findings. Despite wide variations in inventory levels, the team's statistical analysis did not reveal any clear relationships between inventory and sales volume or warehouse size. Therefore, the team conducted field interviews with eleven representative agencies. The findings of these visits were reported to Mr. Finlayson as follows:

1. *Agents Carry Too Much Nonproductive Stock.*
   Agents routinely carry in inventory a large number of packaged products in various package sizes. In general, much of the inventory is nonproductive. A large portion of the typical agent's inventory turns over

Exhibit 5 Inventory Statistics, 1977–1978

	Oct. 31, 1978 Inventory in Thousands of Gallons	1977 Turns
Refinery A	637	20.4
Other Western sources[a]	123	8.7
Winnipeg		10.9
Regina	334	11.4
Calgary		7.6
Lougheed		9.9
Prince George	312	10.1
Prince Rupert		8.1
Prairie agents	2700	3.8
Pacific agents	712	4.5
Total	4818	5.5[b]
Value at $1.70/gal $8.19 million		

a. Refinery B excluded.

b. System sales were 26.5 million gallons, average inventory 4.8 million gallons.

Exhibit 6 23 Agent Inventory Survey in 1978 Highlights

Throughput range	13,000–147,000 gallons
Turnover range	1.4–10.4 times
Average inventory range	2,600–25,400 gallons
Storage space	790–4,800 ft^2

Note: For the 23 agencies studied, inventory level did not correlate with either volume or warehouse size.

very slowly, supporting an extremely small portion of agency packaged sales.

The ——— agency is a good case in point. During the 13 months ending August 1978, this agency sold 90 distinct packaged products (product packages or SKU's) for a total of 18,200 gallons. Twenty of the items accounted for 82 percent of the sales but for only 39 percent of the inventory. Thirty of the packaged items, which accounted for only 3½ percent of the sales, made up 42 percent of the inventory.

A number of factors contributed to this phenomenon, including:

There are no guidelines in place to determine what products to stock;
procedures that are established for the return of unwanted product are not followed;

agents will stock items without firm orders;

good inventory management has not been a priority at the agency level.

2. *Agency Stock Replenishment is Unsystematic.*

Most agents place replenishment orders on scheduled order days. Higher-volume agents reorder every week, or once every two weeks. Lower-volume agents reorder at three-, four-, or five-week intervals.

The exceptions to this rule are:

some city agents pick up stock from salaried terminals daily;

scheduled ordering has not been followed consistently in southern Manitoba;

all agents can place "rapid service" orders on the refinery for small-volume requirements between scheduled ordering days—some agents place similar nonscheduled orders on regional terminals.

Agents are not systematic in deciding what items to reorder and in what quantities. In general, an agent will walk through the warehouse, pick a number of items that seem to be low in stock, and order enough to fill the space usually assigned to these items. There is little attempt made to match order quantities to likely sales requirements.

The agents appear to operate an informal "order-up-to" system. At present their "order-up-to" levels are too high.

Beyond the agents' "feel for their business" the only device that might be used to determine reorder quantities is the sales data that are part of the Station Stock Report. None of the agents we interviewed use this report for this purpose.

Mr. Finlayson noted that these observations varied from inventory practices at the salaried terminals where managers had specific performance targets such as average inventory, amount of dead and surplus stock, service requirements, etc.

Customer Service

Imperial's major measure of the performance of its physical distribution network from the customers' viewpoint was a service level measure. This measure compared product orders with actual product shipments, by product category, by location where the order was received. The reported service levels for the terminals were in the range of 95–99 percent. Another standard, called the service standard, existed. This referred to the time between receipt of an order and shipment of the order. No formal measurement of this standard was done.

Mr. Finlayson was not comfortable relying on these indicators of service level performance. He knew that some Imperial sales representatives and some agents were unhappy with the typical eight-day or longer delay between order placement and order receipt between the refinery and terminals and agents. He knew too that there was no back-order system. Almost 100 percent of the orders were telephoned. If an order clerk receiving the call knew that an item was unavailable, the clerk would tell the customer or agent to order later. If the clerk did not know, the customer or agent was called and told when the order was filled. Mr. Finlayson knew that agents were most concerned with sales coverage, market penetration, and retaining customers at the expense of good inventory management.

Agents in the West were scheduled for both order and delivery from both refineries and terminals. This usually meant that on a specific order day, an individual agent would order from a terminal or refinery and would receive the order approximately two days later from a terminal and eight to ten days from the refinery. In addition, Imperial offered a "rapid service" system whereby the agent could order anytime and receive the order in 48 hours, usually from the nearest terminal but possibly from the refinery. Mr. Finlayson was quite concerned that the use of rapid service had increased dramatically as it was approaching $100,000/year and was intended to be an emergency service only.

Transportation

Imperial moved packaged specialty products using virtually every possible carrier. Each individual shipment was sent by the best method at the time; but according to the study team, no attention had been given to looking at the whole system. Including shipments by the agencies, approximately $6 million was spent on transportation of packaged specialty products in the West in 1977. The study team discovered that transportation "blocking" was being attempted. Blocking referred to consolidating several agency orders into a single large shipment to effect freight economies. It was used principally for shipments from the Western refinery to agents in Alberta, Saskatchewan, and central British Columbia. According to the study team, blocking resulted in substantial freight cost reductions; for example, the freight cost of blocking was sometimes less than half the less-than-truckload (LTL) cost. While the study team was generally pleased with the management of transportation, especially from the refineries to the terminals, they were concerned that "rapid service" deliveries to agencies were usually LTL.

Information and Control Systems

The study team learned that neither Imperial nor its agents had data on physical distribution in a format or single location that would be useful for decision-making purposes. Mr. Finlayson knew, however, that Imperial had most of the data available somewhere that a decision maker would need. Problems appeared especially acute at the agency level. For example, Imperial provided weekly reports, called Station Stock Reports, to its agents. These reports indicated for the previous week what had been shipped, what had been sold, and what should be in inventory to help the agents plan orders. Imperial did an inventory audit in each location approximately once a year. Beyond that, inventory records and management in the agencies appeared to Mr. Finlayson to be largely "back of the envelope." Mr. Finlayson believed that improvements must be made in the entire physical distribution information system.

After looking at these aspects of the current physical distribution system in the West, the study team then turned to forecasting future demands on the system.

Demand Forecasting

As the study team looked toward the future, several major questions occurred, including:

How much warehouse space will be required through to 1990 to handle future volume of sales?

Where should this space be located?

Therefore, the team prepared a series of sales forecasts to determine product flow through the system. The essential steps followed in preparing the forecasts were as follows: segment products and markets, assemble 1977 year sales data as base year data, estimate annual growth rates, project sales volumes by applying the growth rates to the base year data, and calculate the extent of movement through facilities under various location, size, and operating assumptions.

This whole process had not been attempted previously at Imperial. The study team defined eighteen geographical districts for Western Canada using the following criteria:

an area currently treated as a distinct area by operating personnel;

an area that could conceivably become distinct over the next 10–12 years; an area possibly subject to a differential growth rate compared to other areas over the planning period.

Similarly, the team selected eight sales categories (for example, distinguishing marine sales from automotive sales), six product categories (for example, greases), and two package categories (205-litre drum and all other packages).

The study team next used the head office sales records to calculate base year sales volumes in pounds (assuming 1 gallon equaled 10 pounds) for all packages, product categories, sales categories, and geographical areas. These charts were then reviewed with three divisional analysts (automotive, industrial, and consumer sales) to arrive at estimates for growth rates. These analysts, who had not seen sales data presented in this way before, assisted the study team in preparing forecasted volumes by year through to 1990. The divisional analysts were able to help the study team take into account anticipated trends such as an expected substantial growth in volumes of automotive oils sold through mass merchandising channels at the expense of the traditional service station outlets. A large number of tables were prepared showing forecasts by region, district, sales category, product category, and package type. Exhibits 7 and 8 show a total sales forecast by region and an example of a sales forecast for a geographic district.

Mr. Finlayson had not finished analyzing all of these forecasts. For example, he had noted that district sales annual growth rates varied from a high of 4.5 percent in Northern Alberta to a low of 0.3 percent in Edmonton. The team had, however, projected throughput volume by source and warehouse terminal as shown in exhibit 9.

Exhibit 7 Sales Forecast by Geographic District (000 gallons)

	1977		1978		1980		1982		1984		1986		1988		1990	
	D	O	D	O	D	O	D	O	D	O	D	O	D	O	D	O
Industrial	712	279	683	260	697	264	730	277	776	292	820	312	870	332	926	354
Automotive	14	109	16	124	18	138	18	142	18	142	18	140	18	136	16	127
Consumer	23	32	25	35	28	38	31	39	33	41	35	44	38	46	42	51
Retail stores	0	0	0	0	0	70	0	72	0	80	0	80	0	80	0	80
Aviation	4	6	4	6	4	6	4	7	5	7	5	7	5	7	5	8
Supply sales	56	619	56	619	56	619	56	619	56	619	56	619	56	619	56	619
Rail and marine	172	44	176	45	185	47	194	50	204	52	215	55	226	58	237	61
Total	981	1089	960	1089	988	1182	1033	1206	1092	1233	1149	1257	1213	1278	1282	1300
Total	2070		2049		2170		2239		2325		2406		2491		2582	

District: A major urban centre in the prairie region.
Average annual % growth through 1990: Drum = D = 2.1%; other package size = O = 1.4%. Total = 1.7%.

Exhibit 8 Sales Forecast by Region for the West (000 gallons)[a]

	1977		1978		1980		1982		1894		1986		1988		1990	
	Drum	Other	Drum	Other	Drum	Other	Drum	Other	Drum	Other	Drum	Other	Drum	Other	Drum	Other
Region 1																
All sales categories	4678	3006	4841	3129	5112	3598	5307	3887	5508	4083	5684	4170	5936	4266	6167	4362
Total	7684		7970		8710		9194		9591		9854		10202		10529	
Region 2																
All sales categories	12603	9150	13015	9688	13080	9794	13981	10321	14923	10890	15922	11297	17001	11709	18183	12142
Total	21753		22703		22874		24302		25813		27219		28710		30325	

a. These numbers include radiator antifreeze and imported products not shown in other exhibits.

Exhibit 9 Projected Throughput Volumes by Facility (000,000 gallons)

Facility	1977	1982	1986	1990
Refinery A	22.41	23.74	26.38	30.87
Refinery B	3.51	4.02	4.42	4.95
Other	2.61	2.90	3.12	3.34
Winnipeg	2.46	2.75	3.00	3.27
Regina	0.70	0.80	0.88	0.99
Calgary	1.40	1.70	1.91	2.28
Lougheed	3.33	3.86	4.20	4.53
Prince George	0.35	0.40	0.45	0.50
Prince Rupert	0.14	0.16	0.18	0.20

28 Ellis and Howard Limited

In November, 1976, Mr. Robert Wilson, General Manager of the major appliance division of Ellis and Howard Limited (a Kitchener, Ontario, wholesaler), was in a real dilemma concerning the recent sale of his only supplier, the appliance division of Westinghouse Canada Limited. The new owner of the division had just offered Ellis and Howard a contract that, Mr. Wilson felt, would not be advantageous in the long run, if accepted. If he could not soon secure a more suitable commitment from the new owner or from another well-known supplier, the major appliance division of Ellis and Howard could lose more than $8 million in sales.

For fifty-five years, with a handshake as a contract, Ellis and Howard had represented the appliance division of Westinghouse Canada Limited in the major part of Western Ontario and had built a dealer and service network that gave Westinghouse a share of the market almost double its national average. It was a tribute to this performance that Ellis and Howard had been the only wholesaler retained by the Westinghouse appliance division; all 1500 Westinghouse dealers across Canada, except Ellis and Howard's 160 dealers, were called on directly by Westinghouse salesmen. The new owner had offered Mr. Wilson a one-year contract for representation in the same Western Ontario territory. Mr. Wilson knew that a meeting scheduled for the end of the week with Mr. Ellis, the president of the company, was going to focus on his own recommended strategy, its rationale, and the implications for immediate action.

The Sale of the Appliance Division of Westinghouse Canada

In January 1976, White Consolidated Industries of Cleveland, Ohio, had purchased the appliance division of Westinghouse Incorporated, U.S.A. White executives had assumed that with this purchase came ownership of the appliance division of Westinghouse Canada Limited as well. However, the Canadian government, through the Foreign Investment Review Agency (FIRA), had insisted on Canadian ownership of the appliance division of Westinghouse Canada and had vetoed this part of the sale.

In September 1976, The Canadian Appliance Manufacturing Company Limited (CAMCO) had been created through the merger of the appliance divisions of American-owned Canadian General Electric Limited (GE brand) and Canadian-owned General Steelwares Limited (GSW and Moffat brands). This ownership arrangement had satisfied FIRA, and CAMCO had been allowed to purchase the plant, equipment, and land of the Westinghouse Canada appliance division and to have access to Westinghouse personnel and its distribution system. This acquisition had made CAMCO by far the largest and most powerful manufacturer of major appliances in Canada, with approximately $350 million in sales at retail and 37 percent of the Canadian market.

White Consolidated Industries of Canada Limited (WCI), however, had retained access to the Westinghouse brand name, trademark, and certain patents and technology to complement its existing Kelvinator, Gibson, Roy, and Hupp brands and divisions. In effect, CAMCO had acquired a division without a brand, whereas WCI had acquired a brand without a division. CAMCO had made the contract offer to Ellis and Howard.

The Ellis and Howard Major Appliance Division

The Ellis and Howard Company consisted of three wholesaling divisions: the wiring supply division, which was the largest; the major appliance division; and the housewares division. The major appliance and housewares divisions operated out of a relatively new, company-owned, 50,000-square-foot warehouse-office building and together employed 70 of the firm's 200 employees.

Major appliances (refrigerators, stoves, washers, dryers, freezers, dishwashers, and air conditioners) generated 90 percent of the division's $8 million in sales. Parts and servicing accounted for the remainder. Mr. Wilson estimated that the average appliance unit sale to the dealer in 1976 would be $300 and that the average Ellis and Howard margin would be 14 percent. Gross margins on parts and servicing varied widely, but Mr. Wilson estimated that they averaged 20 percent.

Thirty factory-trained service people and five experienced sales people covered the major part of Western Ontario, a territory that contained 1.7 million people or 20 percent of the population of Ontario. For historical reasons, the company did not represent Westinghouse in the cities of Toronto, Hamilton, and London or in the Niagara Peninsula. The Ellis and Howard service department was considered to be one of the best in the industry. The department operated twenty-five trucks and always offered delivery and service to dealers and to dealers' customers within 24 hours. All five sales people had been employed by Ellis and Howard for at least fifteen years and were well regarded by its dealers. Sales people were paid a base salary and performance bonus, while service people were on straight salary. The average sales person made $15,000 per year in salary and bonus and accumulated $5,000 per year in expenses. The average service person made $12,000 per year. Each company-owned truck cost an average of $4000 per year. Of the remaining thirty division employees, twenty-five worked in the parts or appliance warehouse or in the office, and five were managers. Nonmanagement personnel averaged $10,000 per year, while management averaged $20,000.

In Western Ontario, the Ellis and Howard Company was by far the largest major appliance wholesaler and the only one offering a full range of dealer services. Most manufacturers, particularly the larger ones, chose to sell directly to the dealer through their own sales forces. Nationally, 80 percent of appliances were sold directly to the dealer and 20 percent through wholesalers. Generally, wholesalers were more prevalent in the less populated regions of Canada.

The Appliance Dealer

To help assure the success of its selected dealers, Ellis and Howard provided sales training assistance, display and cooperative advertising ideas and materials, liberal credit arrangements, one-day delivery, and full customer servicing. In return, the dealers were expected to stock inventory and to support Westinghouse products aggressively in order to meet mutually determined sales targets. As was typical of the industry, the franchise agreement contained no clause restricting the dealer from selling competing brands. Thus, most Ellis and Howard dealers carried at least one other medium-priced line and usually a higher- or lower-priced line as well. Average dealer gross margin on major appliances was 28 percent.

The number of Westinghouse dealers in a particular market was constrained by the necessity of providing each dealer with some market protection and by Ellis and Howard's desire to sign up only those dealers who had good overall reputations and who appeared able to promote the product properly. Ellis and Howard was also conscious of a duty to shoppers to have at least one dealer in each market where consumers normally shopped, and in most markets to offer two or more dealers from which to choose.

It was Mr. Wilson's belief that the large number of appliance retailers made it possible for Ellis and Howard to meet these constraints and yet distribute one of the more widely available brands. For instance, in Windsor, Ontario, there were approximately twenty Admiral dealers and ten dealers each for Westinghouse, Canadian General Electric, GSW, and Moffat. Another five manufacturers each had about six dealers and the remaining 10 manufacturers each had from one to four dealers. Several of these manufacturers offered only one, or perhaps two, of the major appliances.

Like Mr. Wilson, the 160 Ellis and Howard dealers also faced a real dilemma following the sale of the Westinghouse appliance division. For many, Westinghouse was their largest-selling brand. For all, Westinghouse was a significant contributor to sales. Because both brand loyalty and store loyalty were thought to be important in major appliance sales, these dealers anxiously awaited news from CAMCO and WCI, particularly regarding the branding strategies, pricing strategies, and warranty and servicing plans. The dealers regretted losing Westinghouse, but they wanted to know as quickly as possible how the phase-out would proceed and, more importantly, what would be phased in.

The CAMCO Position

Mr. Wilson understood that the purchase agreement between Westinghouse and CAMCO specified that CAMCO would be allowed to produce all Westinghouse lines under the Westinghouse name until June 30, 1977, and would be responsible for parts and the servicing of existing Westinghouse products thereafter. He had also heard, to no surprise, that on July 1, 1977, CAMCO would be launching a new brand to replace Westinghouse. By November 1976, CAMCO had not announced the name of the new brand nor a new name for the Westinghouse division. However, it was strongly rumoured in the trade that "Hotpoint," a U.S. General Electric brand name that had not been sold in Canada for many years, would be used for both the brand and the division.

Although Mr. Wilson's old contacts at Westinghouse had advised him to carry on as normal, he could see that the new CAMCO-appointed management would probably want to liquidate all Westinghouse inventory as quickly as possible to prepare for the July 1 launch of Hotpoint. Mr.

Wilson could also see that CAMCO ultimately might want to eliminate Ellis and Howard, in spite of its excellent performance, because Ellis and Howard was the only Westinghouse appliance wholesaler. The one-year contract offer might easily be perceived by his employees and dealers as a first step in the direction of a phase-out.

The WCI Position

Rumours also persisted with regard to WCI's plans. The most frequent ones, and the most likely to be true, from Mr. Wilson's perspective, suggested that WCI would create a totally new White-Westinghouse division in Canada to produce and market White-Westinghouse brand name appliances, and that WCI would attempt to secure as many of the 1500 existing Westinghouse dealers as possible. It appeared to most observers that a serious battle for these dealers between the Hotpoint and White-Westinghouse brands would soon begin.

Mr. Wilson realized that if WCI were to create a separate White-Westinghouse division, it would have to import the appliances from the United States until a new Canadian plant or expansion was ready because the WCI subsidiaries in Guelph and Cambridge, Ontario, and L'Assomption, Quebec, could not produce the additional volume required. He further realized that WCI would soon have to contact the current Westinghouse dealers through the sales force of one of its existing divisions, through a totally new sales force, or through regional wholesalers. Otherwise, CAMCO (Hotpoint) might obtain too large a lead in signing the dealers.

The Frigidaire Division of General Motors: A Potential New Supplier

During the spring of 1976, the Frigidaire division of General Motors had decided to return to Canada and had approached several regional wholesalers, including Ellis and Howard. The offer had included 17 percent margins and an exclusive territory that covered all of Ontario except the Ottawa Valley and the Lakehead—an area that contained four times the population of the existing Ellis and Howard territory. Mr. Wilson believed that Frigidaire had a high-quality line that would produce an average unit sale price to the dealer of $500, but he also knew that to maintain consistency with its prestige line image, Frigidaire had a policy to have only one dealer in an area where Westinghouse had five. All Frigidaire products would be imported from the United States.

Comments from some of Ellis and Howard's dealers in Western
Ontario indicated that perhaps two out of three would not take on the
Frigidaire line if they were offered it because they viewed it as inappropriate for their clientele. These comments caused Mr. Wilson to
wonder whether the dealers in large urban markets such as Toronto would
feel the same. He was also concerned about the significant changes that
might be required to cover all of Ontario: new warehousing space, new
sales people and sales territories, and additional merchandising support.
On a more positive note, Mr. Wilson recognized that Ellis and Howard had
been offered an exclusive territory far larger than the major part of
Western Ontario and the freedom to merchandise in its own way.
Although no specific contract length had been discussed, he doubted that
Frigidaire would replace acceptable distributors with company salesmen
for many years to come.

The Ellis and Howard Position

Mr. Wilson calculated that if he was able to arrange for Ellis and Howard
to represent either Hotpoint or White-Westinghouse in the existing Ellis
and Howard part of Western Ontario, the appliance division would have to
retain 90 percent of its 160 dealers in order to support the existing level of
personnel, inventory, and overhead and to turn a modest profit. Both WCI
and the CAMCO partners had been Ellis and Howard's (Westinghouse's)
competitors for many years, but Mr. Wilson was certainly ready, if given
the opportunity, to negotiate with either and to point out the many advantages of working with his company.

He believed that CAMCO (Hotpoint) initially would offer greater continuity because Ellis and Howard would be dealing with the former
Westinghouse personnel but that WCI (White-Westinghouse) would be
more likely to employ wholesalers because few of its brands were dominant in Canada. In either case, he knew that he would have to successfully
negotiate for a larger territory or face cutbacks in the major appliance division. He seriously doubted whether CAMCO (Hotpoint) or WCI (White-
Westinghouse), even with Ellis and Howard's assistance, would be able to
secure 90 percent of the Westinghouse dealers in the existing Western
Ontario territory. He also knew that he would have to successfully
negotiate a reasonably long-term commitment or risk being dropped just as
soon as the new brand became established. Because the future relationship
between Ellis and Howard and either CAMCO or WCI was not totally
under Mr. Wilson's control, he knew that both speed and flexibility were
most important in determining the division's plans.

In fact, the Frigidaire offer also required speed and flexibility. Mr. Wilson knew that the launch was scheduled for early in 1977 and that Frigidaire could hardly be expected to wait much longer for a decision. He also knew that a decision to take on the Frigidaire line would mean major changes to the division almost immediately.

With reference to Ellis and Howard's dependence upon Westinghouse, somebody had once joked to Mr. Wilson that sleeping with an elephant might be exciting but that if it ever rolled over, he'd be dead. As he prepared for the meeting with Mr. Ellis, Mr. Wilson knew only too well how true the "joke" could be.

29 Warner-Chilcott Canada Limited

In June 1974, the senior executives at Warner-Chilcott Canada Limited gathered in the panelled boardroom at 2200 Eglinton Avenue East in Toronto to make the final decision on direct distribution. Warner-Chilcott was one of the largest pharmaceutical companies in Canada, and for some years the company had employed a dual distribution system whereby retail pharmacies could order from a drug wholesaler or direct from Warner-Chilcott. The wholesalers had been supported by Warner-Chilcott sales people and protected by a preferential wholesale discount of 10–12½ percent. If Warner-Chilcott executives shifted to a system encouraging direct orders from retail pharmacies, the preferential discount to wholesalers would be removed, and Warner-Chilcott sales people would stop placing retail orders through the wholesalers. If the sales projections were accurate, Warner-Chilcott executives saw a substantial saving over the period from 1975–1977 just by eliminating the wholesale discounts.

If Warner-Chilcott executives made this change in distribution policy, not only would they have to invest in facilities to perform wholesale functions, but they risked alienating the wholesalers, many of which were owned cooperatively by retail pharmacies. Among the senior managers of the worldwide Warner-Chilcott company, the Canadian decision to investigate direct distribution was generally regarded as the issue of the year because of the major ramifications for the company and the industry.

The Pharmaceutical Industry

The broad classification of pharmaceuticals was divided into prescription drugs and over-the-counter (OTC) drugs such as antacids, laxatives, and cold medicines. OTC products typically were branded packaged goods supported by extensive advertising, sales promotion, and personal selling effort.

New government regulations were changing the nature of prescription sales. Until 1971, the doctor had been the major influencer of prescription drug sales. Accordingly, most pharmaceutical companies employed special detail people to call on doctors and provide them with information that would lead the doctors to prescribe their company's product. In 1972, new provincial government legislation required pharmacists to give government-aided customers (e.g., old-age pensioners) the lowest-cost product available.[1] Pharmacists were required to substitute cheaper products unless the physician had already prescribed the lowest-cost product. As the number of government-aided customers grew, the pharmacist was becoming a larger influencer in prescription drug sales. For example, of the roughly eight million people living in Ontario in 1974, almost 1.2 million people were receiving some form of government aid.

Retail Pharmacies

The majority of the 4715 retail pharmacies across Canada were independently owned, although buying group operations and chain stores were increasing in importance each year. On OTC products, most pharmaceutical manufacturers provided a suggested list price that allowed a 40 percent margin for the retailer. However, with substantial price competition at the retail level, the margin was frequently less than 40 percent. On prescription products, the pharmacist's margin was obtained largely from the dispensing fee, which was established by the College of Pharmacists in each province.

Most retail pharmacies were judged to be good credit risks, but pharmacists often were relatively unsophisticated in their inventory management. Pharmacy outlets enjoyed same-day or next-day service when they ordered from a wholesaler and expected the same service when ordering directly from a pharmaceutical company. Chain store pharmacies tended to order much of their business directly from pharmaceutical companies and use the wholesalers for "fill-ins." A high percentage of orders from pharmacies to wholesalers were placed by telephone.

Wholesalers

There were twenty-three wholesale drug companies in Canada, each carrying five to ten thousand drug items. Many of these drug wholesalers were cooperatively owned by the pharmacies they served. For example, in

---

1. Provincial legislation in this regard varied from province to province.

Alberta, Ontario, and Quebec, the largest drug wholesale house in each of those provinces was a retailer-owned co-op organization. There was one large privately owned national wholesaler. The remaining wholesalers were relatively small regional organizations with their own warehouses, deliveries, credit facilities, and one or two salesmen. Exhibit 1 shows the Warner-Chilcott wholesalers and the pharmacies available by province. Most pharmacies bought from more than one wholesaler.

Wholesalers tended to be good credit risks, and they almost invariably took the 1 percent discount for prompt payment. Most wholesalers had sophisticated inventory management systems, and they tended to order on a two-week cycle. Wholesalers expected delivery of merchandise within one week of placing their order with the manufacturer. Because of the extensive price competition at the retail level, most wholesalers did not attempt to quote their margin in terms of the suggested retail selling price. Instead, the drug wholesalers simply added a markup that provided a 10–12½ percent margin on their price to the retailer.

Warner-Chilcott

Warner-Chilcott Canada Limited was a division of Warner-Lambert Canada, a wholly owned subsidiary of Warner-Lambert U.S.A. Warner-Chilcott

Exhibit 1 Wholesalers and Retailers Recognized by Warner-Chilcott as of June 1974

Province	Recognized Whole-Salers	Add Branches	Total Whole-sale Distri-bution Points	Retailers (Pharmacies)
British Columbia	3	—	3	499
Alberta	2	2	4	512
Saskatchewan	2	1	3	312
Manitoba	2	—	2	265
Ontario	2	7	9	1560
Quebec	7	—	7	1144
New Brunswick	2	—	2	115
Nova Scotia and Prince Edward Island	1	—	1	210
Newfoundland	2	—	2	98
Total	23	10	33	4715

manufactured about thirty OTC and prescription branded products, which tended to dominate their product category. Each of the thirty brands was available in an average of five sizes for a total brand/size list of 150 items. Warner-Chilcott put extensive promotional support behind their OTC products as part of a strategy to boost their OTC business. Many customers would ask for Warner-Chilcott OTC products by brand name, and they would be annoyed if a pharmacy did not have the brands in stock.

In 1973, Warner-Chilcott had factory sales of $6 million in OTC products and $4.8 million in prescription products. Wholesale drug houses billed 60 percent of the OTC sales and 75 percent of the prescription sales.

On OTC products, Warner-Chilcott gave the wholesalers a 10 percent discount on the price to the pharmacist plus occasional trade promotions, such as twelve cases for the price of ten (known as 10/12's), which might apply to as much as 30 percent of OTC sales. On prescription products, the base discount was 12½ percent to wholesalers. In addition, Warner-Chilcott offered a 1 percent discount if bills were paid within fifteen days. The minimum order quantity was set at $100, and Warner-Chilcott paid freight on all wholesale orders. Freight costs had tended to be about 2.4 percent of the order value.

Warner-Chilcott pricing to retail pharmacies provided a 40 percent discount for suggested retail selling price as shown in the table below. For orders direct from pharmacies, there was an additional 5 percent discount on orders of twelve dozen units, the 5 percent discount taken after the 40 percent discount. Pharmacies were eligible for display allowances to the extent of one to two dollars per case and for co-op advertising allowances, all of which amounted to less than 1 percent of sales. The minimum order for pharmacies was $100.

All Warner-Chilcott billing was centralized in Toronto, and the invoice was sent to the customer after the merchandise had been shipped. Shipments for Ontario, Quebec, the Maritimes, and the West were handled from Toronto. Fewer than 50 percent of the orders destined for the prairies and British Columbia were shipped from Winnipeg or Vancouver. In 1973, 16,000 orders were placed by retail pharmacies, and 2000 orders were placed by wholesalers.

In 1973, Warner-Chilcott had fourteen and a half OTC salespeople and thirty-three prescription drug detail people.[2] The OTC salespeople called on 53 percent (2550) of the pharmacies, which accounted for 73 percent

---

2. For OTC products there were thirteen full-time salespeople and three managers who spent 50 percent of their time selling.

Index of Price Structure for Direct and Wholesale Orders, June 1974

	Pharmacy Orders through Wholesaler	Direct Orders from Pharmacies
Suggested retail price to customer	100	100
Less retail discount of 40 percent	40	40
	60	60
Less retail discount of 5 percent on direct orders of twelve dozen or more	—	3
Less wholesale discount of 10–12½ percent, average 11 percent	7	—
Price to Warner-Chilcott	53	57

of total drug sales in Canada. The detail people called on doctors and occasionally on pharmacists and wholesalers. The total annual cost per salesperson was approximately $20,000.

Competitors

There were 150 pharmaceutical manufacturing companies, of which seventeen could be classified as large multiproduct operations. Like Warner-Chilcott many were subsidiaries of large multinational pharmaceutical companies. Exhibit 2 shows a summary of the selling terms of the seventeen major competitors. Nondirect companies gave a wholesale discount and shipped the majority of their merchandise through wholesalers. Direct companies gave no preferential discount to wholesalers, and the pharmacy could purchase from either the wholesaler or the pharmaceutical company. "Partially direct" companies combined the two systems so that the manufacturer gave the wholesalers a discount but the manufacturer would sell and ship merchandise direct to pharmacies as well as to wholesalers.

Direct Distribution

The management at Warner-Chilcott Canada were less than satisfied with the sales effort they had been receiving from their wholesalers. They felt that most of the wholesale salespeople could be more aggressive and progressive in their approach to customers. In fact, several senior executives at Warner-Chilcott believed that almost all the OTC products were actually sold by Warner-Chilcott salespeople, including 60 percent of volume billed through the wholesalers. They estimated that 70 percent of their prescription business was generated by their own salespeople.

The lack of push by wholesalers became particularly serious in the introduction of new products, which was an important way of increasing sales in the pharmaceutical business. A new product could be purchased by a wholesaler and then sit for months before any pharmacy bought it. Hence, Warner-Chilcott was required to spend more heavily on advertising and promoting new products to the pharmacies in order to create a retail demand.

Another difficulty was in monitoring sales. Once merchandise went to a wholesaler, Warner-Chilcott had no way of knowing where it was ultimately sold. Warner-Chilcott executives felt that wholesaler discounts were very expensive when looked at in light of the services provided by the wholesalers.

In 1970, Warner-Lambert U.S.A. had purchased the Parke-Davis Pharmaceutical company, which included the Canadian Parke-Davis subsidiary.

Exhibit 2 Competitive Selling Policies, June 1974

Company	Sales ($000,000)	Terms	Minimum Order[a]	Service Charge Under Minimum	Wholesale Discount (percent)
Direct Companies					
1	24.1	Net 30	$20.00	All freight	None
2	19.0	Net 30	25.00	$1.00	None
3	15.0	Net 30	25.00	All freight	5
4	14.4	Net 30	25.00	All freight	5
5	12.7	Net 30	20.00	$0.75	8
6	12.6	Net 30	15.00	Not accepted	None
7	11.0	Net 30	30.00	$0.75	None
8	10.0	Net 30	15.00	Postage	None
9	10.0	Net 30	25.00		None
10	9.4	Net 30	15.00	$0.50	8.33
11	8.8	Net 30	25.00	$1.00	Quantity discount
Nondirect Companies					
12	12.2	2/30/60	100.00	—	16.66
13	11.8	1/15/30	N/A	—	16.66
14	10.5	2/10/30	200.00	—	15
15	6.7	Net 30	200.00	—	40
16	7.0	2/10/30	50.00	—	15
17	5.2	2/20/30	100.00	—	15

a. Warner-Chilcott executives had learned that companies 6, 8, and 10 planned to raise their minimum order to $20 by September 1974.

In Canada, Parke-Davis gave wholesalers an 8 percent discount and sold directly to retail pharmacies from facilities located in Winnipeg, Edmonton, Vancouver, Toronto, and Montreal. This acquisition in the United States set up the opportunity for Warner-Chilcott Canada to share the distribution facilities of the Canadian Parke-Davis operation.

The first tentative discussions of such a move were made in 1971. Between 1971 and 1973, Parke-Davis closed their Toronto branch and opened a distribution branch in Brockville, Ontario. A full-scale proposal for direct distribution was prepared and evaluated in 1973. It was scrapped on the grounds of cost and risk.

In 1972 and 1973, two major pharmaceutical companies eliminated the preferential discount to drug wholesalers. The second changeover had occurred in early 1973 and had resulted in a massive wholesaler backlash against the pharmaceutical manufacturer involved. Wholesalers had purchased a six-month supply of the company's products and had aggressively sold it at prices lower than the new retail price the manufacturer was offering the pharmacies. Accordingly, in the first six months, the pharmaceutical manufacturer sold very little directly to pharmacies. However, the wholesalers' inventory eventually ran out, and the manufacturer then offered the best prices to the pharmacies because the wholesalers reverted to a standard markup on their cost.

The proposed terms for direct distribution would be to offer retail pharmacies a 40 percent discount (instead of 40 and 5) and a $20 minimum order (instead of $100). The invoice would accompany the shipment on terms of net 30 days (instead of 1/15, net 30 days), and any orders less than $20 would be charged a $0.75 service fee. The terms would be identical for wholesale drug houses except that they would be eligible for co-op advertising money and display allowances when they could show proof of performance. Normally, this proof of performance, such as a tear-sheet from a newspaper, could be administered only by the integrated wholesale/retail operations such as the co-ops.

Any major reorganization of the distribution channel would require considerable effort and planning. Exhibit 3 shows the proposed schedule to "D day," tentatively set for January 2, 1975. In anticipation of the project's approval, the systems design for the computer order handling already had been set in motion.

There were several considerations involved in the evaluation of selling direct. If the experience of the last pharmaceutical company that abandoned wholesale discounts was any guide, executives at Warner-Chilcott estimated that wholesalers would buy approximately $1.2 million worth of inventory as soon as the change was announced. This would be added to the $.96 million inventory already held by wholesalers and would inhibit direct sales to pharmacies for the first year. They further estimated that wholesalers would end the year with $360,000 in stock. It would take retail inventories two years to make up the net wholesale inventory reduction. In the first year, the net change in wholesale and retail inventories would be a negative $180,000.

The second consideration would be the difficulty of the sales force servicing all the pharmacies, even if five salespeople were added and the detail people were "borrowed" to make calls on pharmacies during the first months of direct distribution. Exhibit 4 shows a comparison of calls per year between the current and the proposed system.

Shipping could no longer be accomplished from the three locations. Regional warehouses would be required in order to give pharmacies the service they demanded. The number of orders was expected to jump from 18,000 to 100,000 per year. The Parke-Davis facilities offered an opportunity to add three distribution points in Edmonton, Montreal, and Brockville to the existing distribution branches in Toronto, Vancouver, and Winnipeg (although Toronto might be dropped if Brockville was

Exhibit 3   Timing for Change to Direct Selling
(D = change to direct selling January 2, 1975)

Sales

D minus 6 months	Reorganize sales territories
D minus 4 months	Hire new salespeople
D minus 2 weeks	Inform wholesalers of proposed change

Manufacturing

D minus 7 months	Start to increase inventory to provide three months extra stock to cover expected wholesale loading

Branch distribution

D minus 6 months	Begin to expand Parke-Davis facilities
	Hire 43 people to handle distribution

Systems

D minus 10 months	Begin systems design
D minus 7 months	Begin programming
D minus 3 months	Begin testing
D minus 1 month	System running parallel to old system

Exhibit 4 Number of Calls Per Year

	Current System	*Proposed Direct Selling System*
Calls	22,000	30,000
Salespeople[a]	14.5	19.5
Pharmacies visited	2,550	3,391
Percent coverage	53	70
All commodity percent coverage	73	90

a. The three sales managers would continue to spend 50 percent of their time selling.

added). In addition, Parke-Davis already employed a computerized ordering and sales reporting system.

It was anticipated that pharmacists might not be pleased by a move to
direct selling. It would mean more work for them because they would be
required to order Warner-Chilcott products separately from their regular
order with the wholesaler, thereby having to spend time filling out order
forms and seeing Warner-Chilcott salespeople. Also, pharmacies might fear
less service than that offered by wholesalers.

With these considerations in mind, projected sales volumes were set
out as shown in exhibit 5. Most Warner-Chilcott products carried a suggested retail price that would remain the same as before direct distribution. However, for the first three years of direct distribution, unit sales
were projected to be 4 percent less than unit sales under the existing
distribution system. However, because Warner-Chilcott would retain the
wholesale and 5 percent extra retail margin, factory dollar sales were
forecast to be greater under direct distribution. Exhibit 6 compares the
cost structure of the current distribution system with the estimated cost
structure of direct distribution.

In June 1974, the management at Warner-Chilcott met to make a final
decision. A wide variety of objections to direct selling were raised. The
executives wondered if they would realize any long-term increase in sales
through selling direct. The OTC sales force did not have the technical
knowledge required to sell prescription drugs to pharmacists. In areas
remote from any of the five proposed distribution points, the delivery time
from the date on which the order was mailed could be anywhere from two
to six days (exhibit 7).

Some executives believed that retailers would demand equal if not faster service from Warner-Chilcott than from their local drug wholesaler. In metro areas, orders in by 3:00 P.M. could be delivered the next day, which was slightly better than most competing pharmaceutical manufacturers could offer. The two days shown beside metro areas in exhibit 7 allowed one day for the mailed order to arrive.

Management believed that all the above factors intensified the threat of severe negative reaction at the pharmacy level and could result in widespread loss of accounts. In addition, costs were only estimates, and it was felt that costs could go as much as 10 percent higher. If costs rose and sales fell, the company would quickly find itself in a very serious profitability situation. However, time was running out because the proposal called for direct distribution to begin on January 2, 1975.

Exhibit 5

SALES VOLUME AND CHANNEL UNDER CURRENT AND DIRECT DISTRIBUTION

	Current (percent)				Expected Under Direct Distribution (percent)		
	Whole-sale	Direct	Total		Whole-sale	Direct	Total
Prescription	75	25	100	Prescription	20	80	100
OTC	60	40	100	OTC	10	90	100

PLANNED FACTORY SALES WITH CURRENT DISTRIBUTION
(000)

	1973	1974	1975	1976	1977
Prescription	$ 4,800	$ 5,700	$ 6,700	$ 7,300	$ 7,800
OTC	6,000	7,500	8,900	9,800	10,700
Total	$10,800	$13,200	$15,600	$17,100	$18,500

PLANNED FACTORY SALES WITH DIRECT DISTRIBUTION
(000)

	1975	1976	1977
Prescription	$ 7,200	$ 7,900	$ 8,400
OTC	9,600	10,600	11,600
Total	$16,800	$18,500	$20,000

Exhibit 6 Index of Cost Structure Under Current and Direct Distribution

	Current Distribution	Estimated for Direct Distribution[a]
Factory sales	100	100
Variable cost of goods sold and freight out	25	24
Less expenses		
Advertising	10	9
Sales promotion (including case allowances and co-op allowances)	14	14
Less divisional allocations		
Salespeople, sales administration, and marketing	23	23
Other overheads	21	24
Profit before tax	7	6

a. Includes all annual incremental costs

Exhibit 7 Delivery Points and Times to Customers in Selected Areas (in days from date of customer mailing the order)

Before direct distribution, June 1974

Area Shipped to	Shipping Point		
	Toronto	Winnipeg	Vancouver
Maritimes	6–9		
Montreal	4–5		
Alberta		4–6	
Metro areas	3–4	3	3
Same province but outside metro area	4–7	4–7	4–7

Expected times after direct distribution, January 2, 1975

Area Shipped to	Shipping Points				
	Brockville	Montreal	Winnipeg	Edmonton	Vancouver
Maritimes	5–8				
Metro areas	2	2	2	2	2
Same province but outside metro area	3–5	3–5	3–5	2–5	3–6

30 The Bin Stock Proposal

In November 1980, representatives of The Arrow Company and the Bay were preparing to meet about a proposed change in their relationship. Mr. David Whitehead, Principal Buyer for Men's Furnishings at the Bay, had proposed a men's dress shirt buying programme called bin stock, which would mean changes for both his company and for the vendor, The Arrow Company. Mr. Whitehead was examining the merits of this programme for the Bay, while Mr. Lionel Griffith, Vice-President—Sales at The Arrow Company was doing the same for his organization. Both gentlemen had discussed the idea recently, sounding one another out; both knew a decision had to be made this month for the 1981 fall selling season.

The Principals

The Arrow Company was a division of Cluett, Peabody and Company of Canada, a large clothing manufacturer. The Arrow Company manufactured and sold under its own name a wide range of shirts as well as pajamas, boxer shorts, and handkerchiefs. Its shirts were classified into several categories: dress (including formal wear), sports, and knits. Within dress shirts, Arrow offered a wide variety by colour and style, by fabric, and by cut. As of fall 1980, Arrow offered 332 different cutting ways (style, colour, fabric, cut combinations) in its dress shirt line. A large department store such as the Bay typically carried roughly one fifth of this dress shirt line at any one time. Mr. Griffith described his company as the best-known shirt producer in Canada among consumers and as a well-regarded resource among Canadian retailers. "We're a very service-oriented company," he said, "and this is the key to our success. We're not simply bookers and shippers." Arrow's manufacturing was in Kitchener, Ontario, while its marketing offices were in Toronto, Ontario.

One of Arrow's major customers was the Bay, a full-line department store with 50 stores across Canada. With headquarters in Winnipeg, Manitoba, the Bay was a division of The Hudson's Bay Company, a very large, diversified company with major holdings in the Canadian natural resources sector. "I've heard different views on our position in the marketplace," said Mr. Whitehead, "but internally we view our major competitors to be Eaton's, Simpsons and Woodwards, followed by Sears and others." The Bay, similar to many large department store operations, was organized with a central office, the General Merchandising Office (GMO) in Montreal, Quebec, and a field operations group, consisting of seven regions with focal points in Vancouver, Calgary, Edmonton, Winnipeg, Toronto, Ottawa, and Montreal. The key people in the Bay organization concerned with men's dress shirts were (1) at GMO, Gloria Ben-David, Group Merchandising Manager—Men's Wear; David Whitehead, Principal Buyer—Men's Furnishings; and Ron Gross, Buyer—Men's Shirts and Neckwear; and (2) in the field, the seven Regional Department Managers, who had responsibility for shirts and other merchandise.

Dress Shirts at the Bay

"We have three merchandise categories for dress shirts," said Mr. Whitehead, "330: regular cut, long sleeve; 331: regular cut, short sleeve; and 332: tapered shirts. These categories accounted for about 70 percent of our total men's shirt and neckwear volume in 1980. We've changed over the past few years in our buying from being almost completely de-centralized to a mixed system where GMO and the regionals each have major inputs into commitments."

As of 1980, GMO was responsible for all assortment planning; but all budgeting, and hence ability to commit funds, rested with the regional department managers. GMO staff prepared assortment strategies, based on their understanding of style and fashion directions, for each region and then each store. A commodity marketing plan was developed for each category detailing a recommended blend of products and resources, sales and margin histories and projections, turnover and average inventory statistics, and a buying plan detailing the required commitment of funds, nature of agreements with resources, advertising and promotion plans, and product knowledge training for the sales staff. In addition, GMO staff suggested for each store an opening model stock, replenishment schedules, methods of replenishment, and a variety of suggestions on how to present the category for merchandising impact. The GMO staff had established an assortment classification scheme called National Stock Assortment List (NASL), which enabled them to set priorities for each store in its assortment. Priorities ranged from "core" (all stores must carry the item), to "core large store" (the big downtown stores must carry), to "complementary" (an optional category of distinctly fashion-oriented items, usually offered only in the very high-volume stores). "We've all got the message," said Mr. Whitehead, "that senior management wants us to put top priority on reduced inventory investment and improved return on that investment. This means we need an improved flow of business, which will require that we work even harder on our relationships with our resources. We've had traditionally somewhere over 1000 SKU's in dress shirts alone; we're trying to bring that down dramatically."

The assortment parameters and plans formulated by GMO staff were discussed at length with the regional department managers. "This approach has had its problems," said Mr. Whitehead. "As one might expect, it has been difficult to get consistency in our assortment and merchandising, to get economies in our buying, and so on. Even our inventories are completely decentralized. Each region keeps its own item records. But I think we're getting much better now. The commodity marketing planning system really helps."

Dress shirts were purchased from five major sources: Arrow, Forsyth (best known lately for the Pierre Cardin line), Yves St. Laurent, Hathaway, and the Far East on a direct import programme. The Bay carried both manufacturer brands (such as Arrow) and its own Baycrest line. As of 1980, Arrow and Forsyth were very close together as the leading suppliers in terms of dollar volume sales at the Bay. Dress shirts was the third largest volume department in Men's Wear, and Mr. Whitehead had hopes of making it the leader in the near future. The dress shirt category had been growing recently at an annual average of 18–20 percent.

Actual procurement was typically done in one of two ways for dress shirts. The traditional method was a seasonal commitment. GMO would send out an assortment strategy and suggested quantities. The regions would commit for a season, tying up dollars for the season. A typical flow of events would be as follows for a fall season: preliminary discussions with the vendor in November, a preview in December, commitments in March for delivery in the summer. "This worked reasonably well, I suppose," added Mr. Whitehead, "but in addition to the problems of getting everybody on side, the OK growth rate and profit rate is really getting crunched as interest rates climb. We've had limited repeats; our money has been in inventory for the whole season."

The second method of procurement was vendor-assisted automatic reorder programmes. This was added to the seasonal commitment approach. The regional representative of the vendor met with the Bay regional department manager to ratify a vendor assistance agreement, which in part meant that the vendor sales representative became responsible for physical counting of store inventories and for repeats based on rate of sale in the store. The intent of this arrangement was to provide a more constant flow of merchandise from the resource into the individual stores. This system required more tasks of the vendor's sales force and shifted some of the inventory risks to him. As of 1980, approximately 40 percent of all dress shirts were on this "automatic" reorder system basis at the Bay.

Bay Relationships with Dress Shirt Vendors in General

"Like any other retailer, I guess, we've had our share of problems over the years with our resources," said Mr. Whitehead. "Whenever our relationships weren't open, trusting, and backed up with a flow of information, we've had misunderstandings about the terms of our agreements." The Vendor Assistance Agreement (VAA) was regarded by Mr. Whitehead to be absolutely critical to the relationship the Bay had with its resources. The VAA spelled out what the Bay required of all its major suppliers and was an integral part of all purchases with them. Excerpts from the basic VAA are shown as exhibit 1. "We have additional attachments as part of the agreement spelling out any specifics," commented Mr. Whitehead. "We also add a copy of pertinent sections of our commodity marketing strategy. We share this strategy with the vendor because we now believe that it is critical the vendor knows where he stands with us, what he can expect of us, and how we intend to grow this business."

Mr. Whitehead went on to say that one of the key issues in the Bay's relationship with any large resource is that vendor's ability to provide timely, accurate in-store item counts. "If a vendor stopped doing this, we'd be very unhappy, but we could do it ourselves. In fact, I suppose as our electronic systems capability increases, that item counting service will no longer be necessary," said Mr. Whitehead. "Overall, we know each vendor has strengths and weaknesses on dimensions such as service, fashion, etc. In fact, our quarterly assessment of each vendor, based on our GMO files and regional reports, shows this clearly. We also have different needs in each merchandise category. So we try to match vendor strengths with our particular needs in each category in our vendor selection."

Exhibit 1   Excerpts from the Bay's Vendor Assistance Agreement

Vendor Responsibilities:

1. Representatives will call on stores as per the schedule determined by the Regional Merchandise Information Manager, Department Manager and representative. The representative will report to each store's Item Records Office upon arrival and sign the vendor register (a record of representatives' visits showing date of visit, vendor, and representative's signature).

2. All regular merchandise in vendor's line will be regularly and accurately counted. Counting will be done once a month or more often if indicated in the agreement.

3. Merchandise return privileges will be exercised 2 times a year or as noted in the agreement.

4. Unless otherwise arranged by the General Merchandise Office (GMO), counts will be made in Hudson's Bay Company Item Records Books.

5. All new products, colour changes, price changes, etc., must be presented to GMO for authorization. GMO, through a National Stock Assortment List revision, will advise the Regions of changes.

6. The Item Records Office is charged with determining reorder quantities by using the Company's standard reorder formula. Representative suggested order quantities are subject to Item Records Office review. Normally, representatives should work with IRO clericals in preparing suggested orders.

Hudson's Bay Company Responsibilities:

1. Department Manager or designate must acknowledge and cooperate with Vendor's representatives when they call.

2. Arrangements other than those specified in the National Agreement will not be made in the Regions unless GMO, the Office of the Vice-President, Department Stores, and the representative's head office are notified.

3. Problem stocks, overstocks, etc., must be reviewed when representatives call.

4. Under normal circumstances, representative will receive his order (if merchandise is required) the day the count is made.

5. No returns will be made to supplier without authorization.

6. HBC staff will count:

    (a) between supplier visits if rate of sale warrants action.
    (b) if representative does not appear for a scheduled count.

7. Stock levels must be reviewed by the Department Manager or Sales Manager in conjunction with Vendor's representative every third month.

8. Any complaints or problems arising from VAA will be made in writing by the Regional Merchandise Information Manager to GMO to be taken up with supplier.

Arrow Relationships with Retailers in General

"There are many dimensions to our relationships with retailers," said Mr. Griffith, "but the key one that's really important is that all our programmes are available to everyone. We know independents are different than major department stores—they have different problems but different capabilities too. We have lots of programmes, but we're always careful to remember that two thirds of Arrow's business is with independents."

Arrow management regarded itself as a "one-price house," meaning that their terms were one wholesale price for everybody, net 30, no cash discounts and no advance order discounts. Arrow's competitors varied in the terms they offered, for example, some offered 9–10 percent discount for early orders. As was industry practice, Arrow offered quantity discounts. Orders were F.O.B. Kitchener with some exceptions when delivery problems occurred. Unlike its one-location competitors, Arrow maintained regional warehousing in Vancouver and Winnipeg to expedite repeat orders on basic items. Arrow did not offer push money or display space money, and according to Mr. Griffith, it was against company policy to provide markdown money or to buy display fixtures for retailers.

Arrow's practice of putting a suggested retail price on its shirts was contentious. All its shirts were so marked except some higher-priced sportshirts and other specialty items. Some retailers liked this practice, especially the independents, while some retailers apparently did not. According to Mr. Whitehead, this practice was of no concern one way or another to the Bay. Arrow was undecided about the future of suggested price marking. "We've also had conversations about doing price ticketing for some retailers using their tickets, but we haven't done this yet," added Mr. Griffith.

"Our greatest competitive strength," Mr. Griffith commented, "is our experienced field sales force." Arrow salesmen were spread across the country (nine of them dealt with the Bay), constituting a very experienced group in Mr. Griffith's opinion. "Unlike the big retailers such as the Bay who are constantly moving their people around, we leave our's in place," he added. "The average experience base of our sales representatives is 20 years. They know the business. Their job involves continuous data gathering. We want field reports constantly on business conditions in all their stores, in all their territories." The sales job included item counting whenever a retailer would allow it. "Even if the Bay's VAA didn't require this, we'd want to do it," said Mr. Griffith. "It tells us what's happening with each item in our line on a store-by-store basis for all our customers in the nation."

Arrow offered many services to its customers, which will be detailed further with specific reference to the Bay-Arrow relationship. A source of great pride to Mr. Griffith was Arrow's strong consumer marketing programme. Arrow engaged in extensive consumer mass media advertising, promoting both the Arrow name and specific Arrow products such as the Mark II collar line. Mr. Griffith felt this was a definite advantage in obtaining retailer support. "There's no question in my mind he's right," commented Mr. Whitehead. "Our last Bay market survey showed that brand recall in shirts was 67 percent. We've interpreted that as meaning the customer cares about shirt brand names, especially national brands. While we care about growing our Baycrest line, we also believe we should be strong in the names the customers want. That's why Arrow has roughly 80 percent of our volume in 330, 70 percent in 331, and 40 percent in 332."

The Bay-Arrow Relationship

"I'd say we have a good relationship with the Bay, from the top on down," ventured Mr. Griffith, "and I'm pleased they have a principal buyer in place now who cares about what's happening to them and to us." Mr. Whitehead added, "Arrow has grown with us at about or above the departmental average rate, because they've demonstrated flexibility in meeting our changing requirements." Asked to elaborate on the specifics of their relationship, Mr. Whitehead and Mr. Griffith identified ten important dimensions of it.

1. *New product development.* Arrow and the Bay typically worked closely together in the very early stages of new product development. The Bay formulated their dress shirt strategy in part on price-point segmentation. Ron Gross, the buyer, commented: "I spend a lot of time with Arrow discussing specifications on cloths, qualities, etc. We want appropriate products in our assortment, so we tell them exactly what we want based on our sales and even on our in-house testing programmes." For its part, Arrow sought early comments from its major customers like the Bay on innovations such as the Mark II collar in order to design better products and marketing programmes.

2. *Preview meetings.* For the past six to seven years, Arrow had made a practice of having preview meetings with all its major customers approximately three months before a line was released to Canadian retailers in general. Such meetings allowed discussion of a new line, thus encouraging early commitments by retailers in return for good selection and higher certainty of on-time delivery. Arrow normally did

not offer previews to smaller customers unless requested to do so by them.

3. *Backup stock.* Arrow ordinarily provided some limited backup stock for its major customers. This meant that Arrow allowed a margin of error for such customers by keeping aside extra inventory on an order, earmarked for a specific customer. This stock was owned by Arrow, and the retailer was not obliged to take it.

4. *Stock adjustments.* All retailers have peaks and valleys in sales. Arrow allowed its customers to build inventories for a peak selling period such as Christmas, then to bring inventories back down to agreed-upon predetermined levels by returning goods to Arrow. Arrow limited this privilege to those categories of merchandise that usually had some seasonal carryover. This service, which Arrow also provided to all its customers, sometimes involved a cost to the retailer. If Arrow had to refurbish shirts to bring them back to salable quality, the company charged $12 a dozen to stock adjust.

5. *Product knowledge sessions.* Both the Bay and Arrow staff felt that the periodic (at least annual) sessions offered by Arrow salesmen and management to Bay employees, especially in-store selling staff, were most valuable. These sessions typically were done in the regions to keep the Bay staff up to date on fashion directions in general, qualitative dimensions of shirts, Arrow product features, and Arrow advertising and promotional developments. "If we get their selling staff nodding their heads about our merchandise before it even gets to the store, we're way ahead of the usual lack of commitment and understanding a supplier's merchandise receives by in-store personnel," explained Mr. Griffith.

6. *Advertising, promotion, and visual presentation.* According to Mr. Whitehead, all the major dress shirt resources offered essentially the same cooperative advertising and promotional programmes. Such programmes, from Mr. Whitehead's viewpoint, were expected of the vendor by the retailer, but their offer was not critical in the selection of vendors. "Besides," he added "we're continuously negotiating on this. Arrow appears to have overall parameters, and we move inside these depending on the opportunities we mutually see." In conjunction with Arrow's national consumer advertising programme, Arrow offered its retailers advertising mats to enable them to tie into that campaign. Further, Arrow had two separate co-operative programmes, catalogue and media advertising. Each was a percentage contribution to the retailer's

advertising expenditures based on the dollar volume of regular ("first") quality shirts sold. In other words, these programmes did not apply to off-price sales. As exhibit 2 indicates, the Arrow cooperative advertising programme applied only to advertising in newsprint and on radio and television. Arrow also generally offered point-of-sale promotions such as signs and racks (which remained Arrow's property), although its activities in dress shirts had not been as extensive as in sportshirts and knits. Recent promotional programmes had included giveaways of Polaroid cameras and free monogramming. In the latter instance, Arrow loaned monogramming machines to participating stores. The Bay had offered this service to customers at its downtown stores.

7. *Special promotions.* Special promotions referred to jointly preplanned, controlled offers of off-price merchandise. Arrow and the Bay arranged such deals on a "buy to sell-out basis" for promotional events such as Father's Day. "Probably the best way to think of this is we're jointly supporting some off-price business, which gives each of us a quicker turn but a lower margin," explained Mr. Whitehead.

Exhibit 2   Excerpts from Arrow's Cooperative Advertising Programme

The Arrow Company

45 St. Clair Avenue West, Toronto, Ontario M4V 1K9

CO-OPERATIVE ADVERTISING PROGRAMME
EFFECTIVE—January 1, through June 30, 1980

The Arrow Company offers to you and all retailers of Arrow shirts in your trading area, a cooperative advertising plan for Spring 1980.

BASIS OF COMPENSATION: The programme provides an allowance for advertising, based on a percentage of your total purchases of first quality shirts purchased from The Arrow Company. This allowance is based on the preceding corresponding season (i.e., January 1, 1979 to June 30, 1979).

NEWSPAPER ADVERTISING: Arrow will pay, up to the limits of your allowance, 50% of the actual and reasonable net rate paid to the newspaper (after any discounts or rebates). Supporting newspaper invoice(s) and tearsheets must be submitted.

Newspaper inserts, supplements, rotogravure inserts, or reprints distributed in the paper are paid on the same basis as any other newspaper advertising.

Exhibit 2 (continued)

PRODUCTION COSTS ARE NOT COVERED

ONE EXTRA COLOUR will be additionally compensated (within the limits of your allowance) at 100% of the newspaper's actual colour surcharge; providing that at least 60% of the colour advertisement is devoted to products carrying the ARROW label.

TO QUALIFY, ADS MUST

1. DISPLAY THE ARROW LOGO in a headline or sub-headline.
2. MUST NOT include products competitive to those offered by The Arrow Company.
3. FEATURE ARROW merchandise exclusively. Should other merchandise appear in the same ad, there must be clear separation of Arrow advertising in both copy and illustration. Arrow's participation will be determined on a pro rata basis.
4. APPEAR IN ANY NEWSPAPER that publishes in an approved marketing area, between January 1, 1980 and June 30, 1980.

   Every consideration will be given to requests to use other suitable newspapers, e.g., weeklies. Submit a copy of a recent issue of the paper, a notarized statement of circulation, and local rate card, to The Arrow Company.

CANADIAN RADIO AND TELEVISION: Up to the limits of your allowance, The Arrow Company will pay 50% of the actual reasonable cost of air time, for spot commercials featuring ARROW merchandising, which are aired in an approved marketing area. Sponsorship of programmes is not covered. Net local rates (after any discounts and rebates).

PRODUCTION COSTS ARE NOT COVERED

The Arrow name must be prominently mentioned in the audio. T.V. commercials must also include the Arrow logo.

TO QUALIFY, COMMERCIAL MUST

1. The radio or television commercial must be supplied by The Arrow Company.
2. Any other commercials must have approval of The Arrow Company's Advertising Department prior to airing.

OTHER CO-OP ADVERTISING

1. Any customer may participate, up to the limits of their allowance, in any or all of the advertising media or material described in this programme.
2. Favorable consideration will be given any other advertising media or point of sale promotions in which the values are comparable to Arrow's promotional values and to those specifically available under this programme.

   NOTE: In these instances, PRIOR APPROVAL MUST BE OBTAINED from Arrow's Advertising Department.

Exhibit 2 (continued)

LIMITATION: Arrow's share of the cost of all advertising and advertising materials on any season's merchandise lines shall not exceed the dollar value equal to the established percentage for co-operative advertising in your region. Only Net Shipments on first quality shirts are used in calculating co-operative allowances. "Net Shipments" means merchandise invoiced, less returns. Excludes: Close-outs, Clearances and Special Production.

HOW TO COLLECT FOR ADVERTISING: All claims are to be sent to:

The Arrow Company
45 St. Clair Avenue West,
Toronto, Ontario M4V 1K9

Attn: Cooperative Advertising Department

FOR NEWSPAPER ADS — SEND:

1. Full tearsheet with the invoice claim.
2. An invoice based on the rate sheets or an invoice for 50% of the actual amount paid to the newspaper, net of discounts or rebates, with supporting newspaper invoice(s).

FOR RADIO AND T.V. — SEND:

1. Copy of Radio or T.V. script aired.
2. Copy of station's invoice for time with log of spots aired.
3. Station's affidavit of performance.

CLAIMS SHOULD BE SUBMITTED WITHIN 60 DAYS FROM THE DATE ADVERTISING IS RUN.
Credit will be issued within 60 days of receipt of an approved claim. DO NOT DEDUCT FROM MERCHANDISE REMITTANCES.

No "deductions" or "credits" for the cost of advertising are permitted to be taken against any outstanding indebtedness to The Arrow Company. Any such deductions from merchandise invoices will be considered a violation of this programme and may result in withdrawal of this offer.

If your purchases from the preceding corresponding season are not approximately in line with your current purchases in relationship to other merchants in your marketing area, Arrow will adjust your allowance accordingly.

Your Arrow representative will be able to advise you of the allowance available to you.

Retail promotional programmes are also available.

8. *Contact with Arrow sales organization.* "We try to have points of contact at several levels with the Bay," said Mr. Griffith. "For example, our regional representatives call on the stores monthly or even weekly in the major centres while I'm in contact much less often with their PB and buyer in Montreal. That much would be usual in our business, but in addition we have a fulltime man called our Regional Sales Manager located in Montreal. His job is to be in virtual constant contact with our key accounts at the buyer and PB level. He's almost a Bay employee, he works so closely with them." "Their man in Montreal is important to us too," added Mr. Whitehead, "because he's at a sufficient level in Arrow's organization to make important decisions quickly. Other suppliers either don't have such an individual or, if they do, have him in a less convenient location for us; for example, Forsyth's man is in Toronto."

9. *Arrow local warehousing.* Arrow shipped shirts directly to the Bay's seven regional receiving centres, either from Kitchener or its warehouses in Vancouver or Winnipeg. "This is a definite plus that Arrow offers," commented Mr. Whitehead, "because none of the other sources have such warehouses." "We try to stock the automatic reorder merchandise in the warehouses," added Mr. Griffith. "Anything special, we source directly from Kitchener."

10. *Merchandise flow improvements.* "An extremely important aspect of our relationship," said Mr. Whitehead, "is our efforts to improve the information flow between us and in that way improve the flow of merchandise." Typically, the Arrow salesperson in conjunction with the Bay department managers set up a model stock programme for each store and established a replenishment procedure. When the salesperson visited the store, he would count the Arrow inventory, then record it for the Bay in its store item record books and also send it to Arrow management in Toronto. Sometimes the salesperson received a fill-in order based on rate of sale figures on the spot and sometimes the Bay staff followed up later. "Our salespeople telephone in their orders each night to our computer," explained Mr. Griffith, "in order to get our process moving as quickly as possible."

The data gathered by the regional salespeople was an integral part of the quarterly or bimonthly review discussions between the Bay and Arrow management. Arrow prepared by hand movement statistics for each commodity item on a national, regional, and store-by-store basis for the Bay management. Further, these reports were used to identify the blend of regular and off-price goods, any problems in receiving or delivery of orders, etc. "This system provides both of us with invaluable information," added Mr. Griffith, "and we probably know at a national level what's happening in the Bay's shirt departments faster than they do." "We also share general market information based on our market research here, our activities in the U.S., and our trips abroad to Europe and other sources," said Mr. Whitehead.

The Bin Stock Proposal

"We're looking at a variety of options to improve our ROI and to increase flexibility in our relationships with vendors," said Mr. Whitehead. "We're looking now at three options, but there are probably more. First, we might negotiate a slight variation in our seasonal commitment approach. We would predetermine with Arrow some promotional programmes on selected cuts, styles, and patterns. We would commit systemwide for an inventory from which the regionals would draw repeats. We've done something like this with other vendors in other merchandise categories. There would be a lot of details to work out. Second, we might focus on vendor deals. Arrow occasionally has off-price offers intended for deal-selling. Ideally, we'd get these in early, sell at regular prices during the peak season, then go with promotional dumps when sales slackened off. We do this, too, with some of our other vendors. Third, we could try again the bin stock programme. Essentially, we would sit down with Arrow earlier than usual in the sequence of events to select specific items. We would get an exclusive on a few items in terms of cloth, style, cut, etc. We'd commit the entire Bay system to these items and put them on an automatic reorder basis, based on rate-of-sale in our stores. The usual VAA terms would apply. We'd be assured of repeats being available, even though we'd have unique merchandise. There are lots of details to work out, but the big question is whether Arrow wants to do this again after our at best semisuccessful attempt at bin stock in 1976 with them. I suspect they're less than enthusiastic."

Mr. Whitehead was referring to earlier experiments with forms of a bin stock programme with Arrow and other shirt vendors. The first such trial was in 1976 when the Bay and Arrow agreed to try three items (eight cutting ways) in category 330. The idea came up just before the usual buying commitment point for the fall 1976 season. The major question posed to Arrow as Mr. Griffith recalled was not what items would be best, but rather what items could be obtained in sufficient quantity to support such a programme. "In retrospect," said Mr. Griffith, "we should never have agreed. We tried to do too many numbers in too short a time. The fabric and style choices were wrong." "I wasn't in this job at the time," explained Mr. Whitehead, "but the files show that we sold only 52 percent of what we expected to sell. A lot of inventory was left over."

Both men advanced a variety of additional opinions why that bin stock programme failed and was discontinued. Mr. Whitehead: "Our organization was in limbo, which meant there was no continuity, no systemwide support for the programme. We weren't really into planning. Our regionals just didn't repeat as we'd expected." Mr. Griffith: "Somehow their regionals never really understood the programme or supported it. The items didn't get the exposure they needed. I mean, the Bay didn't make a strong statement to its customers about these numbers. Not only wasn't there enough volume to make this attractive to us, but the repeat rate was below what we would normally get. The programme would have been even less successful had we not told our salespeople to really birddog it. We were often in the middle, between what GMO said would happen and what the regional people actually did. So we got stuck with a lot of inventory, which we had to move ourselves."

Another experiment by the Bay was with Forsyth in 1979 buying for fall 1980. GMO felt that Pierre Cardin shirts, in category 332, were a "trending commodity," which they were having trouble keeping in stock. A line budgeting system was established whereby the Bay made a seasonal commitment but held only opening inventory orders. Rates of sale parameters were set for each item for repeat purchases guidelines. This programme, somewhat similar in concept to bin stock, was arrived at largely by GMO and Forsyth on a national basis. According to Mr. Whitehead, Forsyth was an easier company than Arrow with which to establish this kind of buying arrangement, but harder than Arrow to maintain it once underway. "Forsyth's performance on our VAA was hit and miss at the time, but they've been improving their regional representation." This programme was judged by Mr. Whitehead to be a success. "We've only had some experience last spring and this fall, but it looks like sales will be up by a third. I think we'll talk to other resources about this kind of arrangement," he said, "but each deal will be different because the suppliers are different."

"The Bay's proposal is somewhat unique for us," said Mr. Griffith. "We have several issues to consider, such as timing, and order quantities. If we do this again, we need more than the usual lead time and full details on all their plans. I see some advantages for production in larger cuts and more certainty in scheduling. We would probably aim to stay one month ahead of their sales, gearing our buying and production to initial order plus a system of fill-ins adjusted as we go by rate of sale information. We haven't talked any numbers yet, so it's premature to get out my calculator. We haven't talked number of items, types (basic or more fashion-oriented), prices, advertising and promotional programmes, or, very importantly, about who bears the inventory risk."

The inventory issue was yet to be resolved. If the quantity ordered was insufficient, then several options were possible. For example, the Bay might agree to accept a substitute, or if plans and materials were in place, some of next season's numbers might be moved ahead to fill the quantity shortfall. A more difficult question was a surplus. Each party wanted the onus on the other for a surplus. "Somebody would have to carry it over to the next season or liquidate it through markdowns," stated Mr. Griffith, "and this must be worked out. Our carrying costs are no longer 11 percent, like they used to be."

"This whole idea bears careful consideration, first in concept, then we can get into the numbers," concluded Mr. Whitehead, "but the whole thing depends on the evolving relationships we have with Arrow and our other resources."

31 Bombay Canada

"The idea has tremendous possibilities but there are a lot of difficult issues to be decided in the course of putting together a viable business in Canada. Look, the concept of selling low-priced, high-quality reproductions of antique furniture based on the glory and mystique of the British Empire is not everybody's cup of tea, but I know it will work. I'm ready to put all I've got on the line, but one of the big questions is how much will it take. I know I'll have to go to the bank for a lot of money, but I don't know yet how much. However much it is, I've got to show that this is a business proposition that's worth backing."

With a good measure of entrepreneurial optimism, Mr. Robert E.M. Nourse was describing in February 1980 a new venture to which he was just about ready to give his full commitment. A letter of agreement with American principals was ready for signature, and Mr. Nourse was trying to pull together all the tenuous threads of the new business before taking the final steps.

The proposed Bombay Company of Canada would market Bombay furniture and gift products in Canada following, to the extent it was appropriate, the business practices that had been undertaken by the Bombay Co., Inc. of New Orleans, U.S.A.

The Bombay Co. Inc.

The Bombay Co. Inc. was formed in 1976 by a New Orleans businessman. Its business consisted of importing from Central America and the Far East mahogany and rosewood reproductions of fine English antique furniture. These items, all small in size, were initially marketed through advertising in prestigious magazines for mail-order delivery.

When the company was formed, it was believed that there was a growing demand for antique furniture, particularly among middle and upper middle income households. Limited availability of such items, however, had caused prices to escalate enormously. The reproduction of such antiques required a high labour content and, in developed countries, was therefore costly. The hardwood-producing nations of the world were also, coincidentally, countries with low-cost labour markets. Products imported from these countries, if shipped in a compact disassembled form, could be retailed at prices as much as 60 percent below comparable reproductions manufactured domestically.

Whether consumers would associate the low prices with inferior quality was one of the uncertainties of the market. It was concluded, however, that high quality of design and effective presentation of the product in advertising could overcome any tendency in this direction. In any event, the company achieved initial mail order success and in 1977 began wholesaling a limited number of products to selected better retailers in several major U.S. centres. In January 1979, a company-owned retail outlet was opened in New Orleans. In December 1979, the company opened a second retail outlet in New Orleans, and a third was planned for opening in Houston in early 1980.

Mail-order sales in the 1979 calendar year were $4.4 million, an increase from $2.2 million in 1978.[1] Gross margin on mail-order sales, after shipping costs, was approximately 52 percent. Advertising, at just over 18 percent of mail-order sales, was placed in approximately two dozen magazines, including *The New Yorker*, *Bon Appetit*, *Gourmet*, *Better Homes & Gardens*, *House Beautiful*, and *National Geographic*. The company also sold a four-colour catalogue displaying the full mail-order line. Approximately 60,000 copies of this catalogue were sold in 1979 at $2.00 each, roughly the cost of printing and mailing. Orders were processed by Bombay's internal computer facility.

Bombay's wholesale sales were approximately $800,000 in 1979 with a gross margin of about 26.5 percent. One indication of the success of the line was the experience of Bloomingdale's in New York City; the gift department had sales of Bombay productions in December at a level higher than total sales in the department in any previous month in history.

Retail sales in the first store, located in a suburban New Orleans shopping centre, were $640,000 in an eleven-month period, giving a very high yield for a store of 859 square feet. The second store, in the central French

---

1. All figures relating to actual sales and gross margins in this case are disguised, but essential relationships are maintained for purposes of case analysis and class discussion.

quarter of New Orleans, sold over $30,000 in its first two weeks of operation in the pre-Christmas period of December 1979.

Bombay Products

Bombay furniture products were sourced from factories in twelve countries, principally Taiwan, Malaysia, Pakistan, Singapore, Korea, Hong Kong, Honduras, and Brazil. All items were produced to designs created by Bombay. The company had a full-time purchasing representative in the Far East and was able to reduce product costs by placing orders that often represented a high proportion of the output of some of the factories. Products were shipped to New Orleans, where a new 25,000-square-foot warehouse was opened during 1979. All products were individually packed at the factories in disassembled form, thus providing compact storage and subsequent ease of handling and mailing.

The Bombay products were patterned after the many small pieces that provided finishing touches in rooms of eighteenth and nineteenth century English country houses. Bearing such names as the English Butler's Buffet, the Regency Coffee Table, and the English Officer's Field Bar, the furniture was promoted in its advertising, the catalogue, and the stores to convey a sense of remembered glory and tradition of the British Empire, or, in the words of one observer, "of Ronald Coleman sipping an afternoon sherry."

Original Georgian antique furniture was very costly in comparison to the Bombay reproductions. A George II mahogany tea table had recently sold at auction for $850. The Bombay version sold in the catalogue for $28. An employee of a well-known New York antique dealer claimed, however, that there was a definite distinction between the original and the copies. "Those tables are much lighter than ours," she said. "Old mahogany is very dense, very heavy, and that wood isn't. And there is no real workmanship involved. Ours have already survived 200 years. Let's just say those tables are certainly not put together as well as eighteenth century ones." But a Bombay manager countered, "No matter how wealthy they are, people are always looking for a bargain."

There was relatively little direct comparable competition for the Bombay line, although other small firms offered similar products. It was not entirely clear what future competition there might be. Some examples of the Bombay product line are shown in exhibit 1. In all, there were some 55 items available, mostly in mahogany and rosewood, that could be sold in Canada at prices from about $29 to $275. Because of duty, taxes, and exchange, Canadian retail prices would have to be about 50 percent higher

Exhibit 1   Examples of the Bombay Product Line

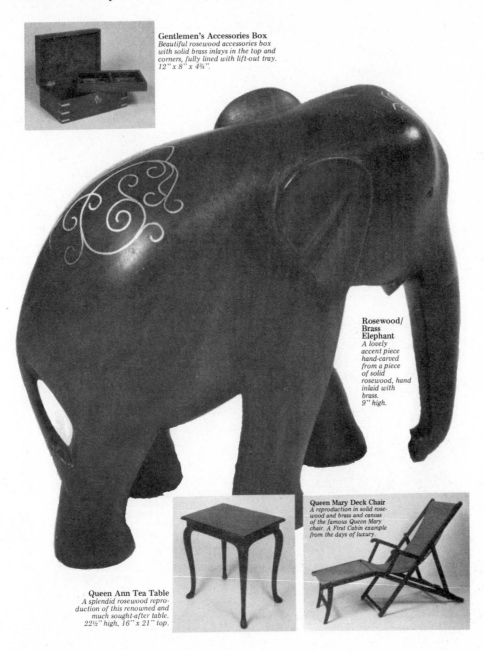

Gentlemen's Accessories Box
Beautiful rosewood accessories box with solid brass inlays in the top and corners, fully lined with lift-out tray. 12" x 8" x 4¾".

Rosewood/ Brass Elephant
A lovely accent piece hand-carved from a piece of solid rosewood, hand inlaid with brass. 9" high.

Queen Mary Deck Chair
A reproduction in solid rosewood and brass and canvas of the famous Queen Mary chair. A First Cabin example from the days of luxury.

Queen Ann Tea Table
A splendid rosewood reproduction of this renowned and much sought-after table. 22½" high, 16" x 21" top.

Exhibit 1 (continued)

Gifts for Gracious Entertaining

$49

$39

$269

English Plant Stand $49
No better way to grace a home than with plants or flower arrangements displayed on a slender stand. This reproduction of an old English plant stand makes a well-appreciated Christmas gift. 35¼" high, 11" diameter top.

Our Family Recipes $39
A true heirloom from one generation to the next. Bonded leather cover, golden parchment like paper and a small brass plaque for your family name. Space for 332 recipes and 102 menus. 10" x 12¼".

The Silver Chest $269
Handsome cabinet with top compartment and set of four drawers. Fully lined with new tarnish resistant cloth. This chest can be used for silver flatware or as an elegant collector's chest or bijoux box. 32" high, 15" x 13".

Wine Rack $25
This beautiful wine rack holds six bottles in exactly the right position to wet the cork. Brass plate for engraving can honour the owner or the wine. 15" high, 12½" x 9¾".

The English Wine Table $29
Authentic reproduction of an 18th century antique. A classic gift from The Bombay Company for any occasion, especially at Christmas. 20½" high, 13¼" diameter top.

Raffles Serving Trays $59
set of three

Set of 3 serving trays. Ideal for Christmas entertaining. Small Tray: 16½" x 10½". Medium Tray: 17¾" x 11¾". Large Tray: 19¼" x 13¼".

$25

$29

$59
set of three

Page 4

The
Bombay
Company

Exhibit 1 (continued)

Christmas Gifts with Élan

"Tole" Lamp $79

Three-candle lamp holds three 25 watt chandelier bulbs (included). The heavy base and shade are of brushed brass. A stylish and sturdy lamp that matches all small antique furniture. 13" high, 6½" wide.

Wine Table $39
(with Serpentine Marble Top)

Green serpentine marble top on detailed mahogany base. The marble is impervious to alcohol or water and requires no special care. 20" high, 12" diameter top.

The Sheraton Hall Table $219

Half round table, a masterpiece in style and finish. Elegant bombé front and fluted Sheraton legs. 30" high, 31½" x 16½" top.

Sheraton Mirror $169

The size matches the Sheraton Hall table. This bevelled glass mirror will blend with any traditional decor. Mahogany-finished hard wood frame with gold-stamped detail. 35" high, 29" wide.

Bachelor Chest $195

This reproduction of an 18th century set of drawers has a bracket foot, Sheraton drawer pulls and a nicely crossbanded top. The size: 22" high, 17" x 13" top, allows this chest to be used as a hall table, end table or even as a night table. The four-drawer facade hides two shallow upper drawers and one deep bottom drawer.

Faux Bamboo Etagère $69

Delicately turned spindles, three shelves and brass trimmed feet. Lovely stand for plants or collectables. 40½" high, 8½" square top.

$69

$169

$79

$39

$219

$109

$195

Curio Table $109

Lovely side table to display small valuables or breakable porcelain. Glass door opens at the top. The bottom of the display case is covered with pearl grey tarnish resistant cloth. 20¾" high, 18½" x 13½".

than in the United States in order for cost of goods to average a comparable 46 percent of retail.

Exclusive Rights in Canada

Mr. Nourse had been offered the exclusive rights to sell all Bombay products in Canada, including through retail, wholesale, and mail-order outlets, and to use the Bombay name, trademarks, and designs. The American company would also provide at direct out-of-pocket cost such services as computer facilities, advertising and promotional materials, and the inclusion of a Canadian name and address in all media advertising and promotional materials of the American firm.

Mr. Nourse would have the right to purchase either from the New Orleans warehouse of the American company or direct from suppliers, at the same factory prices being paid for products shipped to the United States, without an intermediary markup. In return for all rights and services, the U.S. company would hold a minority share of the Canadian company.

Supply Alternatives

Hardwood furniture products entered the United States duty-free, but for importing to Canada, the following duty rates applied:

From Most Favoured Nation countries (Taiwan, U.S.A.)	19.4%
From General Preference countries (developing countries such as Malaysia, Singapore, Pakistan, and all other countries from which Bombay imported.)	12.5%

Under the recent GATT terms, duty rates were to decline gradually by 1987 to 15.0 percent and 11.0 percent for the two categories of countries. Federal sales tax of 9 percent had to be added to the duty-paid value.

When purchasing direct from countries of origin, full-container quantities had to be ordered. Because of the compact, disassembled packaging, the minimum quantities from any one supplier were high. For example, a container could hold 1200 Butler's Tables of 3500 Tea Tables or 8000 Wine Tables. Generally, a supplier would ship a container full of one item, although there was probably an opportunity to mix items from different suppliers in one country.

Time from order placement to delivery from countries of origin would be about fourteen to eighteen weeks. International letters of credit[2] had to be provided on all purchases at time of order placement, and each factory had to be instructed in the specific documentation required by Canadian customs. Suppliers invoiced on date of shipment and presented the letter of credit for payment about 100 days later. Bank charges for providing letters of credit were small—1/4 percent to 5/8 percent of invoice—but letters of credit were considered by banks as a use of debt capacity.

If products were sourced through New Orleans, payment terms were 30 days E.O.M. Duty would apply at the level of their U.S. fair market value—in general, at the U.S. wholesale selling price. Truck freight from New Orleans would be an added cost. Mr. Nourse estimated that the savings of direct purchases over purchases through the New Orleans warehouse would be about as follows:

| From General Preference countries of origin | 16.7% reduction in landed cost of goods |
| From Most Favoured Nation countries of origin | 11.3% reduction in landed cost of goods |

Business Options

Mr. Nourse did not know to what extent he could expect the same kind of market response in Canada as Bombay had developed in its U.S. operations. He expected, first, that generally lower Canadian incomes coupled with higher product prices would combine to suppress demand somewhat. In addition, he did not think Canadians would accept a mail-order approach as readily as Americans had, since the mail-order business in Canada was generally not as well developed as in the United States, and of course Canada's 23 million people were just over 10 percent of the U.S. population.

As far as wholesaling was concerned, Canada's retail department store business was in the hands of a relatively few large chains, and there were also some dominating specialty store chains. Wholesaling to chains, if successful, offered the chance to build quick and widespread distribution and a substantial volume. It was an attractive entry route, but such a plan

2. An international letter of credit was considered by the issuing bank to be an even more serious commitment than a loan, since a loan could subsequently be called, whereas a letter of credit once issued was irrevocable. Although issuance of a letter of credit was a use of a firm's line of credit at the bank, it did not affect the firm's cash flow until date of payment.

might interfere with the development of a series of company-owned or franchised retail stores across Canada that could be visualized for the future. Wholesaling also involved financing high levels of receivables.

Mail Order

Mail-order operations were fairly straightforward, although the sales rate was very hard to forecast. Warehouse space could be rented at about $4.00 per square foot per year, and perhaps up to 2000 square feet would be needed for a full-scale successful operation. A smaller area of public warehousing could be rented at startup. A small warehouse area was needed in any event if the company used a retail store entry. An independent telephone answering service could be used to accept telephone orders at an expected cost of $1.25 per order. One person, paid about $13,000 per year, or $5.00 per hour if a part-time employee was appropriate, could probably handle a reasonable volume of mail-order business. Fringe benefits would be 10–15 percent.

The selection of magazines to reach upper middle and upper income households was less extensive than in the United States. Few national media with the required demographic profile were available, so Mr. Nourse examined statistics on a number of regional magazines, as listed in exhibit 2. The Canadian company would also benefit (at no cost) from the almost $800,000 spent annually by the New Orleans company in U.S. media. Exhibit 3 shows the Canadian circulation of a number of the U.S. magazines that were used as well as their advertising rates.

Retail Stores

If one or more retail stores were opened, a key question would be the location. About 1200–1500 square feet would be needed for selling space, and another 500–800 square feet would be needed for storage. Mr. Nourse had determined that an exclusive location such as Hazelton Lanes in central Toronto, a low-traffic but very high demographic profile shopping development, would cost about $28 per square foot plus common area charges of $11 per square foot for a total of $39. A suburban shopping centre with a wide range of stores would cost about $20 per square foot plus $7–8 for common costs.

The Toronto Eaton Centre, a large climate-controlled three-level downtown shopping development with two major department stores and about 300 other stores, was recognized as the most successful shopping complex in North America. Rental on the third level among better quality stores would be $28 per square foot plus common costs of $18 per square foot. A one-time initial allowance of $5 per square foot would be given to a new tenant toward costs of developing and building the store interior. Mr. Nourse estimated that a store would cost about $85,000, including designer fees.

Mr. Nourse decided to look very carefully at the Eaton Centre location option, since the traffic as well as the costs were extraordinarily high. He developed a comparison with the first New Orleans store in order to try to judge the sales possibilities of an available store site in the Eaton Centre. The comparison is shown in exhibit 4.

If he decided to proceed with a retailing option, then Mr. Nourse would have to develop estimates of store-operating costs in some detail. As

Exhibit 2 Circulation and Advertising Costs for Selected Canadian Magazines

Magazine	Paid Circulation	Cost of 1/3-Page Black & White or Nearest Equivalent[a]
Toronto Life	70,548	$1060
Western Living	158,669	1225
Atlantic Advocate	25,932	215
Vancouver Calendar	101,751	940
Montreal Calendar	83,362	760
Toronto Calendar	201,404	1815
City Woman	200,406	2500
Saturday Night	108,437	490
Time (Canadian)	315,000	1210
Decormag (English edition)	50,000	855
1001 Decorating Ideas	79,335	825
Canadian Home Decor	N/A	836
En Route (Air Canada)	108,750	1990
Skyward	65,000	848
The City (retail only)	310,356	960

a. One-time rate. Frequency discounts of 5–10 percent applied on multiple placements.

a rough guide, he summarized some of the main probable operating costs as follows:

Rent	Variable with site
Store manager	$25,000
Asst. mgr. and staff	$45,000 (partly variable with site and traffic level)
Supplies, insurance, telephone, etc.	$10,000
Credit card charges	4% of credit card sales
Advertising	To be decided
Delivery costs	To be contracted; parcel delivery, etc.
Miscellaneous	Probably a lot, especially at startup

Financial Requirements

If the profit potential looked good, Mr. Nourse was ready to take the plunge with the Bombay Company in Canada. Each approach that he might use to

Exhibit 3 Canadian Circulation and U.S. National Advertising Rates in Which Bombay (New Orleans) Frequently Advertised

Magazine	Total Circulation	Canadian Circulation	Percent of Total Circulation	Cost of 1/3-Page Black & White[a]
The New Yorker	504,402	15,582	3.1	$2,970
New York Magazine	407,532	2,541	0.6	2,630
Horizon	76,663	5,202	6.8	735
Bon Appetit	1,141,063	29,137	2.6	3,960
Gourmet	672,661	55,098	8.2	2,800
Better Homes & Gardens	672,661	55,098	8.2	17,610
House Beautiful	973,634	18,401	1.9	3,530
Travel and Leisure	986,689	56,546	5.8	4,990
Glamour	1,927,236	89,904	4.7	3,100
Seventeen	1,423,397	73,500	5.2	3,600
The Atlantic	347,722	22,338	6.4	1,800
National Geographic	10,244,161	842,456	8.2	32,500 (1/2 page)

a. Most U.S. magazines offered a special rate that was 20–50 percent less than figures shown for high-frequency mail-order advertisers. (There was no corresponding discount offered by Canadian magazines.)

Exhibit 4 Comparison of Draw Factors for
New Orleans Uptown Square and Toronto Eaton Centre Site

	New Orleans Uptown Square	*Toronto Eaton Centre*
Area Factors		
Metro area population	1.4 million	2.8 million
Area retail sales (annual)	N/A	$7.4 billion (1976)
Annual tourists	High	20 million
Shopping Centre Factors		
Mall type	Outdoor	Indoor
Location	Suburban	Downtown
Estimated weekly shoppers	50–75,000	750,000
Weekly shopping hours	48	63 1/2
Number of stores	80	300
Shopper profile	Upper middle	Upper middle (3rd level of Centre)
Accessibility for tourists	Poor–fair	Good
Site factors		
Visibility	Good	Good
Retail selling space	700 sq. ft.	1500 sq. ft.
Storage space	150 sq. ft.	720 sq. ft.
Sales experience		
First year sales (11 months)	$640,000	

enter the market—retail, wholesale, or mail order—had different cost and
revenue structures, different risks, and different financial requirements. In
estimating the requirements for each approach and various combinations, he
was mindful that there was likely to be some seasonality in sales. On the
basis of U.S. experience, he estimated that sales might occur as follows:

Percentage of annual sales		*Percentage of annual sales*	
January	5%	July	6%
February	5	August	7
March	8	September	9
April	6	October	11
May	7	November	14
June	7	December	15

It was apparent that all financial projections he might make would be
dependent on the strategy he developed.

CHAPTER VIII
SALES FORCE DECISIONS

For many companies, personal selling is the most important element in the marketing communications mix. Many people are directly involved in selling and in the management and support of the company's sales force and sales programmes, and these activities often require a significant expenditure. This is particularly true in industrial marketing, where personal selling tends to be the key form of marketing communication. It is not uncommon for an industrial company to spend 15 percent or more of its revenue on the sales organization. Clearly, in many situations, sales force decisions can have an important impact on the overall success and profitability of a company.

While the obvious place to begin making sales force decisions is with the company's marketing strategy, it usually pays to analyze internal and external factors first. This is important for two main reasons. After a thorough analysis, we can judge whether the role assigned to the sales force in the marketing strategy is in fact appropriate. Second, we obtain a clear picture of the buyers, their needs, and the competitive environment in which the firm must compete for sales. We should come away from this review of the firm's marketing strategy with a clear idea of the *desired selling job*. Chart 1 shows the main factors bearing on the desired selling job.

It cannot be stressed too strongly that we should know exactly what the sales force must do to be successful. Exhibit 1 gives a partial listing of the tasks a salesperson might be expected to perform. We should be able to answer the following types of questions:

1. Who are the buyers and where are they located?

2. Who in the buyer's organization will the salesperson need to deal with? How knowledgeable and sophisticated are these people?

3. What skills will the salesperson need to be effective with the buyer

Chart 1 Main Factors Bearing on the Desired Selling Job for a Manufacturer's Sales Force

and more successful than the competitor's salespeople? Will the salesperson have to supply technical assistance, service the product, and negotiate with the buyer about price or terms?

4. Is it more important for the salesperson to understand the product itself or how to apply it in a particular type of business?

5. What proportion of the salesperson's time will be spent on developing new accounts versus maintaining and improving relationships with established buyers?

6. How frequently will the salesperson need to call on the different types of accounts? How long will the calls typically last?

7. What nonselling responsibilities must the salesperson carry out? Will he or she have to service the product, make sales forecasts, provide other types of market information?

By thinking carefully about each of these questions, we will be able to develop a good understanding of the desired selling job and a very clear image of the salesperson who will be effective in it. It is then usually the role of the top sales executive in the company and the executive's staff to develop an organization and a set of policies and procedures that will result in a sales force capable of doing the desired selling job. Chart 2 provides a conceptual framework for making sales force decisions. Let us look briefly at each of the major areas in which the sales executive needs to make decisions.

Specification for Salesperson

We can determine the required tasks and desired selling job from answering the above questions. The next step is to specify the skills, qualifications, and characteristics of the ideal person to do that desired selling job. For selling expensive technical equipment, the specifications might call for the salesperson to hold a science or engineering degree and to have strong social skills in order to persuade an organizational buying committee to buy the equipment.

Organization

In most sales forces, a number of organizational issues need to be resolved. The most obvious is whether the sales force should be organized on a

Exhibit 1   Tasks That May Be Included in the Desired Selling Job

Pitch new products
Provide continual product information
Identify product applications
Explain special offers
Set up displays
Administer co-op advertising programmes
Train clerks
Take inventory
Represent company at trade shows
Negotiate sales, including pricing
Check pricing, invoicing
Monitor competitors
Relay customer suggestions to superiors
Handle defects, complaints, application problems
Get new accounts
Obtain orders
Check credit on new accounts
Collect from accounts
Monitor sales by account
Be available to accounts
Build rapport with customers
Be visible in the community

**Chart 2   A Conceptual Framework to Aid
in Sales Force Decision Making**

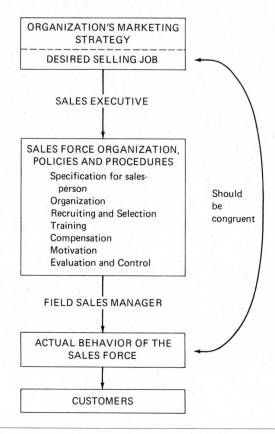

geographical, product, or market basis. Here the main question is whether
or not a salesperson can effectively handle all the company's products in a
given geographic area. If so, then an organization based on geographic territories may be satisfactory. If not, a product-based or market-based
organization may be necessary, the choice being determined largely on
whether product knowledge or market knowledge is the most critical
determinant of success. Very large sales forces often use some combination
of geographic, product, and market organization, using a product-based or
market-based organization in major, heavily competitive markets like
Toronto and a geographic organization for less concentrated market areas.
Some companies find it effective to deal with major accounts or national
accounts with a special sales force or selected salespersons. Other

organizational decisions include the number of levels of sales management, the number of people who will report to each type of manager, whether or not staff specialists (such as sales trainers) are needed, and where they should be located.

Recruiting and Selection

Once we have developed a clear picture of the desired selling job and the type of person who can fill the role, we usually have a pretty good idea where such salespersons can be found and what criteria should be used in selecting them. The resources and size of the sales force often determine whether we should try to find people who can fit almost immediately into the sales job or whether it would be better to choose the right "raw material" and train them. Large companies are more likely than small companies to choose the latter route.

Training

Almost all companies must do some training. Even companies that only hire salespeople with a good knowledge of the company's products and customers must usually train the new salespeople on the distinguishing features of their product or service, company policies, and procedures. In addition, many companies provide training covering selling skills, a thorough coverage of the buyers and their needs, and extensive product knowledge training. There is also a trend for more companies to train their experienced salespeople in order to improve their performance or to prepare them for new or more responsible positions within the sales organization. A major issue in sales training is who should do it. There are two basic approaches: doing all the training in the field or using a combination of field training and centralized training in a regional or head office. The choice should be made on the basis of the skills and knowledge to be taught in the programme, the most appropriate training methods, the resources available within the company, and the economics of the particular situation.

Compensation

The compensation system is one of the key motivational tools available to the sales executive. In developing the compensation system, it is critical to keep constantly in mind the types of behaviour and performance we are trying to encourage. The relative emphasis on salary, commissions, and bonuses can significantly affect the behaviour and performance of the salespeople; a heavy emphasis on commissions often focuses the salespeople on the short term, sometimes causing them to neglect long-term account relationships. A heavy emphasis on commissions also reduces the control the field sales manager has over his or her sales force, since this necessarily reduces the role of salary and bonuses. Yet it is these forms of financial incentive that often allow the manager to direct the salesperson's efforts in directions important to the company. Finding the right combination of salary, commissions, and bonuses and finding the right basis for computing commissions and bonuses are difficult but extremely important functions.

Motivation

Motivation is obviously a critical factor in the management of a sales force. Yet motivation is made relatively easy if the other policies and procedures and the organization are appropriate: if the right people have been selected; if they have been appropriately trained and are confident of their capabilities; if the organization of the sales force makes sense; and if the compensation system has been carefully designed. Serious deficiencies in these areas cannot be overcome by inspirational sales meetings, nonfinancial incentives, recognition programmes, and other types of motivational programmes. That is not to say that a sound motivation programme is unimportant; it can contribute positively to the success of a sales force, but it is no cure-all.

Evaluation and Control

The evaluation and control procedures in a sales force allow the sales executives to monitor the performance of the individual salespeople and other basic units in the sales force against certain standards. This information can then be fed back to the involved parties so that necessary corrective action can be taken. The standards can take a variety of forms: sales quotas, number of sales calls to be made, number of new accounts opened, salesperson knowledge, and salesperson work habits. Performance against some of these standards can be measured quite objectively, while performance against others must often rely on the subjective judgment of the field sales manager. Clearly, a good evaluation and control system can be an important motivational tool, providing the manager and the subordinate with an opportunity to identify areas of strength and weakness and to develop programmes to correct any deficiencies that are identified.

Summary

In summary, it is important to note that for the sales force to be truly effective, the organization and all the policies and procedures should be designed to encourage the salespeople to do the desired selling job. A strong programme in one area will seldom suffice, although occasionally companies seem to place excessive reliance on one area—often compensation—to achieve their objectives.

Obviously, the field sales manager plays a crucial role in most sales forces. This person is the implementer of the policies and procedures developed by the sales executive. The field sales manager often makes the final selection of salespersons, is the key person in most training programmes, sets salaries and bonuses, sets quotas, designs territories, and evaluates and motivates the salesperson. No matter how fine the policies and the procedures, if the implementer is incompetent, the organization is unlikely to attain its objectives. Thus, a great deal of attention should be paid to selecting effective field sales managers because they can spell the difference between the success and failure of most sales forces.

If the organization and the set of policies and procedures developed by the sales executive do complement each other and jointly encourage the desired behaviour and performance in the sales force, and if the field sales managers are competent, then—and only then—will the desired and the actual behaviour of the sales force be identical.

32 Super Salesman

A Role Play Exercise[1]

A great deal of what passes for sales training is product knowledge and company policy in a standard package that has been developed and taught by someone inside the company. Seldom is there sufficient emphasis on the development of basic selling skills. This case describes a selling method that can be very effective if you take time to develop and practice the skills. The method helps a salesperson to identify customer needs, to control the interview more effectively, to reduce the tension of a sales call, and to become better at gaining a commitment from prospects.

There are only four responses a customer can make to any piece of communication. He or she can express indifference, agreement, doubt, or objection. In addition to coping with each of these four customer responses, the salesperson must be able to open and close the sales call. Thus, the salesperson must develop six basic skills along with the knowledge of when to apply each skill. The flowchart in figure 1 names each basic skill and the logical order of progression. Study the flowchart and see if you understand it.

The simplest explanation of figure 1 is that for every customer reaction, the salesperson has a specific type of response to make. A salesperson who hears doubt, offers a statement of evidence and then listens to the customer's reaction. If the customer fails to indicate interest, the salesperson begins to probe concerning possible dissatisfactions with the current product. These general responses can be repeated several times until the salesperson opens up information that can be used or until it is clear

---

1.   The model for this role play was adapted, with the permission of Xerox Learning Systems, from their program ''Professional Selling Skills'' © 1976, Xerox Corporation.

that there is no possible chance for a sale. Each of the basic skills has several important parts.

Opening Statement

A good opening statement begins with a statement of general benefits associated with the type of product and concludes with a specific reference to a benefit offered by the product. For example, after the initial pleasantries, the salesperson might open with: "If you are looking for

Figure 1   Flowchart of How to Apply Basic Selling Skills

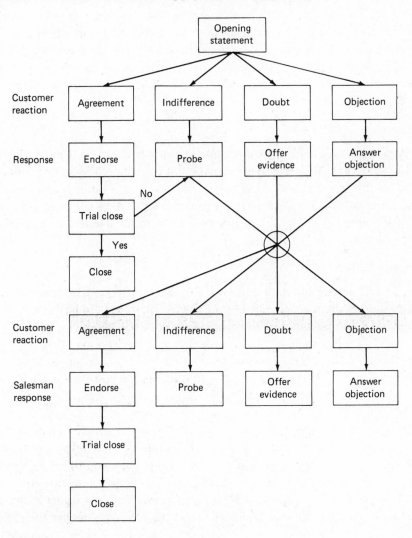

more efficient operations, the new diesel engines are much cheaper to run than the older ones. Our Workhorse D engine gives a five percent fuel saving over existing competitive makes." The salesperson tries to choose a particular benefit that will be most important to the particular customer.

Probing

Very often, it is necessary to probe (or ask questions) to determine a customer's needs or attitudes. In addition, probes can be used in such a way that they direct the discussion to areas the salesperson feels are worthwhile. A *nondirective probe* such as "Yes, can you tell me more?" is used for gathering information. A directive probe such as "Is your present machine fairly noisy?" can be used both for gathering information and directing the conversation. The main difference is the degree of specificity of the expected response. If nondirective probes are unsuccessful in prying loose needed information, the salesperson should begin to probe more directly.

Endorsing

Whenever the customer says something favourable about your product, you should agree with the customer's remark and then state how your product provides this benefit. Endorsing makes the customer's point seem important to the customer and allows you to control the discussion. For example, you might say, "Right! Our machine *is* more reliable and this avoids costly downtime."

Offering Evidence

When a customer exhibits doubt, you should restate the benefit about which the customer has doubt in your own words. This indicates that you recognize the importance of the customer's concern. Then cite the evidence source(s) such as "A recent article in *Construction Weekly*. . ." and, finally, make the conclusion about the benefit. For example, "This greater reliability means greater sales and profits for you, Ms. Smith."

Answering Objections

Objections can be categorized as simple or serious. A simple objection results from a misunderstanding about the product. Your response should be to provide the correct information. A serious objection refers to a genuine shortcoming of the product. A good way to help you decide the seriousness of the customer's objection is to restate the customer's idea in your own words. "Are you saying that this tractor has a smaller fuel tank?'' If the tractor *does* have a smaller fuel tank, you should stress other relevant product benefits. For example, ''But the more efficient operation allows this tractor to run the same hours as others—and at lower cost, which means more profit for you.''

Closing

When the salesperson feels that there is a reasonable chance for a sale, he or she should attempt to close. First the salesperson should assume that a consensus has been reached. Thus, all statement wordings are completely positive, and the customer is not given an easy opportunity to say ''no.'' At the beginning of the close, the salesperson should summarize the benefits that *were relevant to the customer. Never introduce benefits* not discussed or benefits that the customer implied were unimportant. Such statements open up new possibilities for objection rather than enhancing the product. Finally, the salesperson should ask for a commitment in a positive manner. For example, ''I can have a tractor here by the end of the week.''

The description of the skills and when to use them is necessarily rather brief. Structured role plays are a useful way to practice the skills. A simple recording-scoring system has been developed.

Draw a zigzag line down the page (figure 2). As soon as the salesperson makes the opening statement, write ''OS'' or some other shorthand to signify that he or she made an opening statement. On the customer side, categorize the customer response, such as D standing for doubt, and then write Evidence (or E) when the salesperson begins the statement of evidence. Continue scoring the customer and salesperson for the entire role play. At the end of the role play, you can review the entire selling interview in order to identify the places where the salesperson could have improved the response. However, your first task is to develop your own example of each of the skills described above. You will need them as you practice selling the Workhorse D crawler tractor. Familiarize yourself with the selling situation before you begin your role plays. Your instructor has specific role play guides for the customer.

Role Play

Product Description: The Workhorse D

The Workhorse D is a new crawler tractor, or bulldozer, made by Davis Machine in Montreal. The Workhorse D develops 200 brake horsepower and can move between 75 and 100 cubic metres of earth depending on

Figure 2   Scoring System for Role Plays

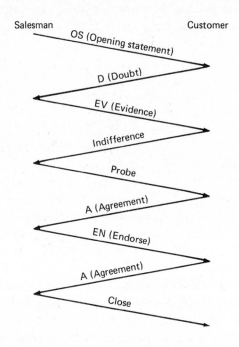

conditions. *Heavy Equipment News,* the industry trade magazine, rates the Workhorse D as "the most reliable and efficient in fuel consumption of all crawler tractors in the 180–220 horsepower range."

In tests conducted by Independent Laboratories Limited, the Workhorse D was found to have 15 percent fewer breakdowns that required stoppage of more than one hour and 10 percent fewer breakdowns requiring off-field repair, all compared to the next best competitors, Earth Mover and Attachi of Japan. The fuel consumption was "5 percent less than Earth Mover and 10 percent less than Attachi under identical operating conditions."

The relative prices for the Workhorse D and competitive models in Canada are:

Workhorse D	200 hp.	$32,000
Earth Mover D	200 hp.	$30,000
Attachi D	210 hp.	$29,500

The Davis Machine company has researched the opinions of tractor operators/owners and obtained these quotations:

"I have driven ten different models of 200 horsepower tractors and the Workhorse D is far more comfortable than the best-known make." Mr. Henri M. Lariviere, Hull, Quebec.

"Sixteen hours of continuous work and I was not tired on the Workhorse D!" Mr. Herman A. Berg, Rosetown, Saskatchewan.

"I figure my expenses in repairs and fuel alone are 5–10 percent less on the Workhorse D compared to all other equivalent size machines." Mr. James O'Drennan, Kamloops, B.C.

Product attributes	Customer benefits
Uses 5 percent less fuel than competitors under conditions of heavy, steady work	5 percent savings on operating costs
Fewer breakdowns than competitors	Less downtime, hence greater profits
Hydraulic seat (not on competitive models)	More comfort for operator, hence able to work longer, stay healthier, and feel better
High seat mount (adopted by competitors)	Extra visibility for operator, fewer mistakes
Repair and service network in Canada	Mechanics can be on site in 24 hours, which is 24 hours faster than competitors. Save downtime costs
Moves 75–100 cubic metres per hour (standard for tractors of this size)	Competitive
Lease arrangements on weekly basis	Competitors are by the month and therefore offer less financial flexibility

Customer Description

You are Mr. John White, President and major owner of White Excavating Limited in Calgary, Alberta. Your company has forty employees and annual sales of $10 million. Your company does excavation contracting for large buildings for educational institutions, the military, government, and business in Alberta.

White Excavating Limited owns ten crawler tractors, five in the 200-horsepower range, all of which are the Earth Mover brand. The firm needs two more crawler tractors in the 200-horsepower size, but you are short of cash. Hence, you must either borrow the money for the outright purchase *or* lease the equipment.

You are about thirty-five years old, hard-working, and your business is growing. You are pleasant to sales representatives as a matter of habit. The Davis Machine sales representative has made an appointment with you on the basis of a conversation at a party one week earlier.

Sales Interviewer Description

You are yourself, a sales representative for Davis Machine of Montreal, approaching Mr. John White, President of White Excavating Limited, a company that does excavation contracting in Alberta. Their customers are general contractors who in turn work for the government, the military, educational institutions, and industry. Although the company is privately owned, you estimate their annual sales at $10 million, and you know that they have about forty employees.

Until last year, there was no representation for Davis Machine in Alberta. Your objective is to have Mr. White buy or lease at least one of your crawler tractors. Mr. White met you at a party a week ago and told you that he needed two more 200-horsepower crawler tractors. You have made this appointment with Mr. White, and you are on time. This is your first meeting in his office.

While Davis Machine makes a complete line of crawler tractors, you will focus on the Workhorse D model. You have a repair and spare parts network throughout Canada. The Workhorse D is a new model with competitive advantages in fuel consumption, reliability, and worker comfort.

33 Computing Systems (Canada) Ltd.

"Bob doesn't appear to be too happy. He isn't making money, because he isn't selling. His own self-image is—well, he likes to spend money. He likes nice clothes, a nice car, and a nice house, that kind of thing, but he can't afford to live that way." These thoughts passed through Mike Hagen's mind in February 1980 as he reviewed once again the possible courses of action he might take in dealing with one of his salesmen, Bob Nichols. Mike Hagen was the District Manager in Winnipeg, Manitoba, for Computing Systems (Canada) Limited, a major full-line computer manufacturer. Mike had become increasingly concerned about Bob's performance in the last year. While the other salesmen in the district were having a very successful year, it had become quite clear to Mike that Bob was not even going to achieve his quota. Bob was thus hindering the district in its drive to meet its goals.

The Company

Computing Systems (Canada) Ltd. was the Canadian subsidiary of Computing Systems Inc., a major multinational manufacturer of a wide range of computers and peripheral equipment. The Computing Systems (Canada) Ltd. product lines were in direct competition with some of the computer lines of most other major computer manufacturers.

The head office of Computing Systems (Canada) Ltd. was located in Toronto. The Vice-President of Marketing, who was located in the Toronto head office, oversaw all the firm's marketing activities. Reporting to him were the various marketing staff groups and three regional marketing managers who coordinated the marketing activities in the western, central, and eastern regions. The Winnipeg office was located in the western region, and Mike Hagen reported to the Western Region Marketing Manager in Calgary. A partial organization chart of the Computing Systems (Canada) marketing organization is shown in exhibit 1.

The Winnipeg District

Mike Hagen had two groups of people reporting to him in the Winnipeg district. Three sales representatives reported directly to him. There were also ten programmer analysts who reported to him through the District Systems Manager. A partial organization chart of the Winnipeg branch is shown in exhibit 2.

The programmer analysts in each district were responsible for providing systems support to the firm's customers. Many of the programmer analysts worked exclusively with one customer, while the others acted essentially as systems consultants for several of the firm's smaller customers. The programmer analysts were often involved in the presales evaluation of a customer's systems requirements. In this capacity, one or more systems analysts formed a team with one of the district's sales representatives, and together they evaluated the customer's needs and developed a proposed system that they felt would satisfy these needs. Programmer analysts were compensated on a salary basis, raises being dependent on job performance.

Exhibit 1 Partial Organization Chart of Computing Systems (Canada) Limited's Marketing Department

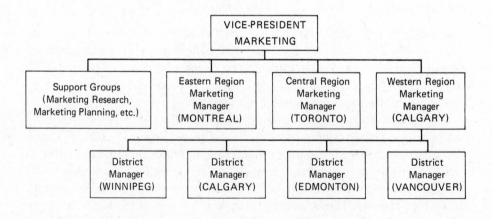

Exhibit 2   Computing Systems (Canada) Limited
Organization of the Winnipeg District

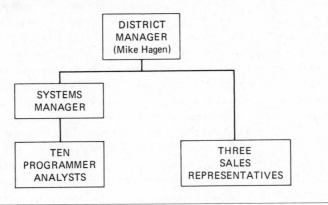

Sales Activities

When asked to describe and comment on the sales job in the computer business, Mike Hagen said:

> The sales job is broken down into prospecting, qualifying prospects, planning the sales campaign, and all those activities related to closing. Now prospecting, generally speaking, is taken rather lightly by the sales reps, and I think that is a big mistake. It's a very, very difficult activity, and it is closely related to qualifying—they dovetail very closely together. We're in the stage of the computer business where there is enough activity out there that you don't have to create demand. We qualify a prospect by saying, "Is he going to make a computer buying decision within the next six to twelve months," and if he isn't, we just keep in touch. We don't really have time to say to a prospect, "Well why don't you think of making this new application or why don't you think of buying that new equipment?" We may go in and try to develop a need if we see an area where a company could computerize, and then make a proposition and try to get their interest. But if they are not immediately interested, we forget it, because we really don't have the time or the resources to do it. So the key thing in any salesman's success is to have a very big prospect list, because you don't get 'em all. And the key thing with the prospect list is how well they are qualified. Will the guy buy from us? Are we talking to the right guy? Are they going to make the decision in the time frame they say? Timing is particularly important—if you peak out in your sales campaign to a prospect too early,

you know your competitor is going to pick up the dice. It is very competitive. So the qualifying aspect is whether you are talking to the right person, will he make the decision and does he have the guts to be the internal salesman—the person to carry the ball for you in getting others in the company, his boss and so on, to agree to the purchase. All those questions in any sales campaign are very key because the next steps cost a lot of money in terms of time and resources. So once you get the customer to the point where you can say he is a qualified prospect, you can assume he will make a decision within a reasonable period of time. We have to restrict our dealings to qualified prospects because a guy has got to make quota in the twelve-month period. That's because, unfortunately, we work on a twelve-month planning horizon.

Planning is probably one of the things that most sales-oriented people do worst—they respond to immediate conversations, interactions and stimuli. The difficult thing is to say, "Well, when are you going to do this? What are you going to do if? What are your contingency plans?" And so on. It's an easy thing really for a manager to get a salesman to put together a plan in terms of putting it down on paper and saying this is what I am going to do. The hard part is for him to do it, and discipline himself to do it when he says he is going to do it. And then to constantly ask the customer for the order, to go through trial closes to get objections. You see, in a sense, the qualifying process in our business never really ends, you never get to that point unless you have the order. So you are constantly asking questions and directing your campaign to further substantiate your qualifications. One key order we got here in Winnipeg, for example, is one where we didn't qualify until a week before we got the order. We didn't consider them really as a prospect until we got very close to the order because we hadn't been able to get to the top people.

In terms of what resources you use in this whole process (and it is not a very different process from many other sales jobs), you have got to find prospects, you have got to qualify them, you have got to plan a campaign, and you have got to hold to it. But we use a lot of different resources. My definition of the computer salesman is a coordinator of experts. We are so complex, our products have so many different uses, and we have so many different products that I can't even configure one of my own computers any more. I've only been out of it a year, and I just can't do it. Oh, I can do it basically, but there are a lot of options, pieces of equipment that I forget because I'm not close to it. So a salesman has to know hardware, software, and systems terms in a very general sense. We have systems people who vary from a very superficial sales-oriented systems guy to the highly technical detail man. As well, we have our field engineering people who actually install and maintain the equipment. We will use any one of these people in a sales campaign, and we will bring people in from Calgary or Toronto to make the sales pitches if necessary. Depending on the level of hardware and the complexity of the system, the sales rep will do his own pitching—but the key thing is to coordinate all those activities, because you just don't know it all. And if you try to know it all, you just stretch yourself too thin, and you end up being suspect because anybody who has half a brain knows that you are stretched a little thin. Another difficult thing for the salesman is getting internal people motivated to do the selling job. Salesmen also have to sell us on whether we should invest the money in the particular activity. The days are gone in the computer industry where we used to have unlimited budgets in terms of expenses. We have to be very, very profit conscious.

The point at which the systems representative comes in depends on the level of gear. We sell computers anywhere from $1000 per month to $100,000 per month. Selling covers such a wide range of activities and such a wide range of customer prospect situations that you might sell a small computer without ever getting a systems man in. You just go in and you say, "You want to computerize your payroll? No problem, we have just the package for you. It will do a super job for you. Sign here." Generally speaking, the customer doesn't know his own needs well enough to be able to really evaluate the package. Anything that you can give him is a hell of a lot better than what he currently has. So if you know a little bit about receivables and payables, you don't need a systems man, but you might bring in one or two guys to impress the customer. When you get into, say, a large system, you need a host of technical people, not just in systems but in specialized areas of systems, such as data base management, communications, and operations management. With a large system, you may have five or six computer operations raising hell, and you've got to coordinate that as a basic management function. When you only have a little main frame, you have a much simpler problem. You have only one guy, so it's not really a coordination problem. Thus the systems support a salesman needs varies dramatically from one situation to the next.

Each salesperson in Computing Systems was assigned an annual sales quota. The company used a "top-down" approach to developing sales quotas. Each year the marketing group in Toronto analyzed the anticipated levels of activity in the Canadian economy, the previous years' sales, the trends in the computer industry, and so on, to develop a reasonable sales forecast for the following year. This forecast was then broken down into sales quotas for the individual districts, and these quotas were communicated to the district managers. It was then the responsibility of the

district managers to develop quotas for the individual salespeople. Mike
Hagen felt that this method resulted in salespeople receiving reasonable, attainable quotas. In fact, Mike said that if he asked any of his salespeople
what was a reasonable quota for the next year, they usually gave him a
figure higher than the quota he would assign them.

Salespeople were compensated largely on a commission basis, receiving a commission on each sale that was related to the profitability of the
sale to the company. Generally, a salesperson's total compensation was
highly correlated with quota achievement.

The Growth of the Winnipeg Office

Mike Hagen had joined Computing Systems after graduating with an M.B.A.
degree from an eastern university in 1976. Mike had spent his first few
months with the company in its sales training course in Toronto. On completion of the course, he had become a sales representative in Toronto.
After one year with Computing Systems, Mike had been transferred to
Winnipeg as a sales representative. Initially, he was the only sales representative in Winnipeg, and he reported to the District Manager in the Calgary
office. In September 1977, two additional experienced salesmen, Jim
Cooper and Nick Johnston, were hired from outside the computer business
and joined the Winnipeg office. In 1977, Mike met his sales quota, and in
1978 he was one of the top Computing Systems salesmen in Canada. In
June 1978, Winnipeg became a separate district, and a district manager was
appointed. The District Manager then reported directly to the Western
Region Marketing Manager in Calgary. About six months after he moved to
Winnipeg, the district manager was promoted and left Winnipeg. In
January 1979, Mike Hagen was promoted to District Manager. Mike felt the
decision to promote him to District Manager had been a difficult one for
the company, since he was relatively inexperienced, having only been
employed by Computing Systems for two and one half years. Mike thus felt
he had a lot to prove in his new job, and he was anxious to prove that he
could do a superior job as District Manager.

Shortly before Mike Hagen became District Manager, Bob Nichols was
transferred to Winnipeg from Vancouver. Bob Nichols had joined the company directly after graduating from university with a B.Sc. in 1974. Bob
became a systems representative in the Vancouver office. He progressed
well in the job, and in 1975 he received a President's Award for his
outstanding performance as a systems representative during that year. Even
though Bob had spent very little time as a systems representative, his
superiors considered him to be one of the most promising systems people

in Canada. The following year, Bob requested and was granted a move from systems into sales. Bob entered the company's basic sales training programme and received part of his training in Toronto; in fact, for a couple of months, he and Mike worked in the same office in Toronto. Bob's switch into sales was motivated largely by his desire for the higher compensation a successful sales representative could earn. A few of Bob's friends from his undergraduate days, who had been quite successful financially, were also living in Vancouver, and the group of young couples was accustomed to an active social life. Bob perceived that a salesperson's compensation would allow him to lead that type of life.

Within a few months of Bob's beginning work as a sales representative, one of his customers purchased a major system, one of the largest systems that had ever been installed by Computing Systems in Canada. The sale of this system was the culmination of a major selling job by Bob and a couple of his superiors in the Vancouver office. Largely as a result of being credited with this sale, Bob won a second President's Award in 1977 for his performance as a sales representative. Bob did not have such a successful year in 1978. In the first nine months of 1978, Bob did not meet his quota, although his performance was considered acceptable. In September 1978, Bob was transferred to Winnipeg because company management felt the change of environment might result in improved sales performance. Although Mike saw very little of Bob and his wife socially after they moved to Winnipeg, he gathered from his conversations with Bob that they were adjusting reasonably well to their new life.

Mike Hagen as District Manager

When Mike Hagen assumed the job of District Manager in January, 1979, he had four salesmen reporting to him. His first year in the new job was a reasonably successful one, with the Winnipeg office making quota at a time when several other districts did not.

The quota achievement for the four salespeople in the Winnipeg district for 1978 and 1979 are shown in exhibit 3. In late 1979, Tony Webb, whose performance had been satisfactory in 1978 but marginal in 1979, was transferred to the Vancouver office. The performance of Jim Cooper and Nick Johnston both showed a significant improvement between 1978 and 1979. In 1979, they were both among the top Computing Systems salesmen in Canada.

In his short period in Winnipeg in 1978, Bob had not met his quota, which was not surprising, given that it took a few months to develop a list of prospects. However, his performance was again marginal in 1979. As

Exhibit 3 Computing Systems (Canada) Limited Sales
Performance as a Percent of Quota—Winnipeg District

Sales Representative	Percent Achievement of Quota	
	1978	1979
Tony Webb	100	81[a]
Jim Cooper	105	195
Nick Johnston	53	205
Bob Nichols	55[a]	63

a. Quota prorated for the period in Winnipeg.

Mike Hagen reviewed Bob's performance record and prospect list in
February 1980, it appeared very likely to him that Bob would not make his
quota again in 1980. From his previous discussions with Bob about his performance, he knew that Bob realized this too, although Bob would probably not openly admit it. Bob seemed uneasy at the fact that he was the
senior salesperson in the office, in terms of selling experience and yet was
performing much worse than the other salespeople in the office.

Mike felt that he had developed a good business relationship with Bob
in their eighteen months together in the Winnipeg office. Shortly after
becoming manager, Mike had assisted Bob in landing a major order. The
order had required a lot of internal selling within Computing Systems, and
Mike had spent many hours convincing Computing Systems personnel that
the deal he and Bob had worked out with the customer was a good one
from Computing Systems' point of view. Mike felt that Bob realized that he
would not have been able to do the internal selling job himself, and thus
he felt he had gained Bob's respect for his skill and efforts.

The Situation in February 1980

As he reviewed the situation in February 1980, Mike Hagen felt that there
were four possible courses of action he could take.

The first alternative was simply to ask Bob for his resignation. Mike
was personally not very happy with this alternative, since he knew there
were several Computing Systems salesmen in other districts performing
less satisfactorily than Bob. It was just that Bob's performance was incon-
sistent with Mike's goals for the Winnipeg district. He had also broached
the subject of Bob's performance with the Western Region Marketing
Manager, and he felt that his attitude and the attitude of other senior
management was that Bob was worth saving.

The second alternative that Mike was considering was transferring Bob to another district as a sales representative. Although this was probably the easiest course of action from Mike's viewpoint, it was not very satisfactory. He viewed this alternative as being neither fair to Bob nor fair to his new district manager.

The third alternative was for Mike to spend additional time with Bob trying to improve his sales performance. Mike had spent a large amount of time in the previous year accompanying Bob and each of the other salesmen on sales calls and critiquing their selling methods. In analyzing Bob's sales performance, Mike felt that Bob did an excellent job right up to the point of actually trying to close the sale. In Mike's words, "Bob doesn't have that killer instinct—to go for the throat—the real pressure that you have to exert to get some orders—the real pushing hard, brass-knuckled approach that is sometimes absolutely necessary to get an order." Mike also felt that Bob did not handle risk well and often seemed to want to "give away" the systems when he got close to the sale. Mike also believed that Bob was not very effective in doing the internal selling that had to be done inside Computing Systems. Since the computer systems packages were often customized to an individual customer's needs, the computer salesman had to convince Computing Systems management that the deal he was proposing to the customer was also a profitable one from Computing Systems' viewpoint. Mike felt Bob had a very difficult time handling the two sets of conflicting demands on him.

Mike also knew that one of Bob's goals was eventually to move into sales management; but in Computing Systems, one of the necessary conditions for promotion into sales management was a good selling track record. For this reason, he felt he should consider making further effort to develop Bob in the sales area. He wondered, however, where he would be able to find additional time to spend with Bob without neglecting the other salesmen and, even if he did spend the time, whether he would be successful.

The final alternative was to try to change Bob's career path from sales back into systems. Mike had checked with senior management about any suitable openings for Bob in other offices in Canada in a systems capacity, but there were none. Thus, any move would have to be made within the Winnipeg office. Mike thought he might be able to persuade Bob to accept a position as a senior systems analyst, but he knew that it would be an extremely difficult switch for Bob to accept. The salary Bob could earn as a senior systems analyst would be comparable to his total compensation in 1979. However, if he had been able to make quota in 1979, his total compensation as a salesman would have been about 50 percent higher than the amount he could earn as a systems analyst. The switch also had other potential problems, since he felt his systems manager would deeply resent having to take on a "loser" from sales. The personalities of Bob and the systems manager were very different, and this was also likely to be an area of further conflict. Furthermore, Mike did not feel he could discuss this alternative with the systems manager before making the decision, since he felt the systems manager would attempt to prevent the change. Mike also felt some of the other systems staff would resent a salesperson's moving into a senior systems position in the office. If it had not been for all these potential problems, Mike felt that Bob would probably do an outstanding job as a senior systems analyst.

As he weighed the pros and cons of the different alternatives in his mind, Mike wondered if there were any other alternatives he had over-looked. He was also concerned about how he should reveal his decision to Bob and to what extent he should involve the Western Region Marketing Manager and other senior company personnel. Mike knew he had to come to a decision quickly, since he was flying to Calgary in three days to see the Western Region Marketing Manager. He wanted to be able to tell his superior what course of action he planned to follow and to get his approval.

34 Canadian Pharmaceuticals Corporation Ltd.

In January 1976, Mr. David Clark, national marketing manager of the dental products division of Canadian Pharmaceuticals Corporation Ltd. (CPCL), was reviewing sales force management policies in the division. Since November 1973, nine salespeople had been hired in order to maintain a four-person sales team, and Mr. Clark had just learned that one of the remaining four salespeople had submitted his resignation. Advertisements for an additional salesperson had been run, and Mr. Clark was attempting to decide which of the applicants to hire.

Background

CPCL, a subsidiary of a large U.S. conglomerate, operated nationally out of Vancouver, British Columbia. In 1970, a Canadian medical/dental products group had been established under the joint direction of a sales manager and a marketing coordinator. By 1973, the medical/dental products group had boasted a sales force of fourteen people. In the same year, CPCL had acquired a manufacturer of in-mouth dental products and had established a separate specialized sales group for dental products. Sales by the dental products group had grown by 38 percent in 1973 and by 71 percent in 1974, but sales for the 1975 fiscal year ending October 31, 1975, had shown only an 11 percent increase over 1974. Although CPCL still held the largest market share of those branded dental products that it marketed, the sales projections of $500,000 for fiscal 1976 were well below target with no immediate signs of improvement.

Approximately 8000 dentists throughout Canada were provided with equipment and supplies by 21 manufacturers, of which about six had sales forces comparable to CPCL's. CPCL dealt through a network of five dealers, who operated an aggregate of 52 branches and provided representation with more than 250 dealer salespeople.

Upon the inception of the medical/dental products group in 1970, Mr. David Clark had been appointed marketing manager of the dental group, in addition to his existing product management responsibilities for a group of medical products and new business ventures. As marketing manager, Mr. Clark had developed the marketing plan for dental products and had implemented it. For his group of medical products, dental products, and new business, he had "bought" sales time from the medical/dental products sales force. Mr. Clark would request the number of weeks of each salesperson's time that he needed and would be charged a standard rate for it.

A separate dental products sales group had been established in November 1973, with one salesperson covering Ontario and one covering Quebec. In January 1975, a decision had been made to expand the dental sales force to four, with one salesperson covering Vancouver to Winnipeg and an additional salesperson to take one half of Ontario. Hiring had been done exclusively by the area supervisors. Mr. Clark, however, had become increasingly concerned about the continuing high rate of turnover in the sales force, for the lack of continuity had made it difficult to achieve sales goals for the dental products line. The record of sales force turnover for the dental products group since November 1973 is shown in exhibit 1.

The Sales Force

Mr. Clark commented briefly upon each of the nine salespeople:

> The two salesmen who were fired, Doucette and Holter, were just incapable of adequately carrying out the job. Ths first two reps who signed on with the dental products group, Bradford and St. Jacques,

Exhibit 1   Dental Salesperson Turnover List as of January 1976

Region	Salesperson's Name	Order of Hiring	Tenure	Reason for Leaving
Quebec	St. Jacques	1	Nov. 1973–Jan. 1975	Transferred
	Doucette	6	Feb. 1975–Apr. 1975	Fired
	Dinel	7	May 1975–Jan. 1976	Just resigned
Ontario	Bradford	2	Nov. 1973–Nov. 1974	Resigned
	Lindstrom	4	Feb. 1975–May 1975	Resigned
	Straiton	5	Feb. 1975–Jan. 1976	—
	Boynton	8	June 1975–Jan. 1976	—
West	Holter	3	Jan. 1975–June 1975	Fired
	McPhail	9	Oct. 1975–Jan. 1976	—

both came from large corporations. Bradford stayed with us for a year and then left to work for another dental products supplier in the U.S. St. Jacques transferred to selling medical products, a move that was viewed by many as a promotion because he received a $1000 increase in salary at the time.

The second Ontario rep who resigned was a woman. Lindstrom was ambitious and had great looks, but her previous employment background was extremely checkered, and she had not lasted more than five months in any previous job. She lasted only three months in this one. The Quebec salesperson who has just resigned, Dinel, says he enjoyed the challenge of the job, but the numerous small orders just didn't make sense to him. He had previously sold high ticket items of $400 to $500 per order, so a $60 order seemed not worthwhile to him.

Of the remaining three, Straiton is a particularly strong rep, and I am very happy with his performance. Boynton is very enthusiastic and has had some previous experience in selling office equipment. Unfortunately, he doesn't appear to like dentists. McPhail just joined us in June, and it's too early to fairly gauge his performance. However, he is a self-taught salesperson and extremely confident of his own abilities.

January 1976

Mr. Clark described the hiring process:

It is my responsibility to interview prospective salespeople and to train an effective sales force, although the actual hiring decision is made by our area medical/dental products supervisor. I will work closely with and train a new representative for two to three weeks to give him a basic understanding of our dental products line; but in practice it takes two to three months in the field before a rep can really communicate effectively with the dentist and the dealers.

Ideally, we look for someone with a comparable sales background who has had experience in selling under time pressure, because often the salesperson will only have five or ten minutes to present the "sales pitch" on any new product introductions, take orders on these and existing products, and ensure that there are no problems with any of our products.

The salesperson's job is to pull the product through the dealers by creating demand among the dentists. All orders are routed through the dealers. The sales pattern is repetitive; the product that accounts for about 40 percent of our sales is very similar to, and hence competes directly with, the brands offered by several of our competitors, putting a constant pressure on the salesperson to perform. I expect a salesperson to work independently and to make at least 30 calls on dentists each week, and to be able to talk with and understand the dentist on a fairly technical level. The salesman should also write five orders per week, which are then given to the dental dealer for processing. We offer about eighteen basic types of in-mouth dental products but are constantly expanding this range and introducing new lines.

The salesperson also has a responsibility to call on all his or her dealers at least once a week, to explain new product introductions, to iron out any problems, and to ensure that our brands are being adequately serviced. On occasion, a salesperson will also team up with a dealer sales rep and make joint visits to selected dentists. We have found this team to be extremely effective with our more experienced salespeople who are well versed in the technical and performance aspects of our brands. Where there is a dental research school in a territory, I also expect the salesperson to make at least monthly visits to the school. This is an excellent means of gaining brand acceptance among dentists.

After being trained, the salespeople became responsible to their area medical/dental supervisor, who, in turn, reported to the national medical/dental sales supervisor. The basic marketing plan and sales force instructions to the dental salespeople were issued by Mr. Clark. In practice, the medical/dental supervisors had responsibilities for a wide variety of products, and dental products represented only 10 percent of the total medical/dental products group sales. A partial organization chart is shown in figure 1.

A target annual income figure for each salesperson was calculated, and 95 percent of this figure was paid as a base salary. The remaining five percent of target was tied to the national sales performance of the dental products group. In a good year the national target could be exceeded, thus providing some incentive for improved performance. Average annual earnings were $14,000 for dental salesmen and $15,500 for medical products salesmen.

New Prospects

Immediately after the resignation of Dinel, Mr. Clark had advertised for a replacement in several major Quebec dailies. A copy of the advertisement is shown in exhibit 2. Fifteen people had replied to the advertisements, but Mr. Clark had been able to quickly screen out eleven as unsuitable, leaving four candidates for the job. The original letters of these four applicants are shown in exhibits 3–6. Mr. Clark's summary notes from the personal interviews with each applicant are shown in exhibit 7.

Figure 1 CPCL Organization Chart, January 1976

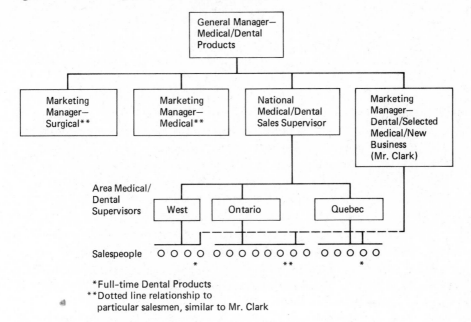

*Full-time Dental Products
**Dotted line relationship to
  particular salesmen, similar to Mr. Clark

Exhibit 2 Dental Product Sales Advertisement

Continued high sales growth has provided for a Dental Products Sales Representative to service the Quebec market.

This challenging position will appeal to a career-oriented individual who possesses an aptitude for professional sales.

Applicants should have had at least two successful years of sales experience and be fluently bilingual.

Postsecondary school education is desirable.

This position offers an attractive base salary plus an extra compensation plan, car, business expenses, comprehensive group benefits, and continuing training programme.

Please send confidential resume to:

Personnel Relations
Canadian Pharmaceuticals Corporation Limited
P.O. Box 100
Vancouver, B.C.

Exhibit 3 Application Letter from Normand Perron

Dear Sirs:

I am replying in regard to your recent advertisement concerning the position of salesman in the Quebec market. I will attempt to relate my personal background and general experience.

I am thirty years old. I have been divorced for five years and do not have any children. I am currently employed as a salesman with Lever Bros. I have worked for this company for 2 years. During this period of time, I have been responsible for selling a large variety of household consumer products.

Previous to this position, I was employed for several years by Tasti Frozen Foods. I began as a sales clerk and transferred after two years into the field as a salesman. I terminated my employment here because I was offered a job with Levers.

I have a grade 12 education with a variety of work experiences during the summer. I worked one summer as a payroll clerk for a large manufacturing firm.

The reason for my willingness to terminate my present employment is due to the fact that I am presently one of a number of salesmen and I do not see any chance for immediate advancement and increase in responsibilities. The sales manager in this area is thirty-seven, and likely to remain in this job for some time. I would prefer the possibility of future growth and development.

I have attempted to briefly outline my past history. If you would like to discuss it further, I would appreciate the opportunity to meet with you at a mutually convenient time.

Yours truly,

Normand Perron

Exhibit 4 Application Letter from Gilles Tremblay

Dear Sirs:

I am applying for the position of Sales Representative, Canadian Pharmaceuticals.

I am 22 years old, recently married and have spent two years furthering my education at the University of Montreal.

While my experience in the dental industry is limited, I have contacted several dentists in the city of Montreal recently while selling photocopiers.

Exhibit 4   (continued)

I have been employed by SCM Corporation for the last year and one month, but have just been released because of a manpower cutback.

I am living in Vancouver and I am anxious to meet with you to discuss this position further.

Sincerely,

Gilles Tremblay

Exhibit 5   Application Letter from Jean Gagnon

Dear Sirs,

I am responding to your advertisement in the January 12 edition of Le Journal. My brother sent me a copy of the newspaper.

I am 28, married with two children. For the past eight years I have worked with Simpsons-Sears in Vancouver first as a floor salesman in men's furnishings and then as a buyer. I was promoted from Vancouver to Toronto in the buying function, but we were unable to purchase a house in Toronto and my wife missed Vancouver a great deal.

After a year in Toronto, Simpsons-Sears transferred me to Vancouver and promoted me to Manager of Customer Services, where I have supervised a staff of 10 people for the past three years. Unfortunately, I do not believe that I will be able to progress to an acceptable level in the Simpsons-Sears organization. Accordingly, I am looking at other opportunities and I am willing to move wherever necessary.

I look forward to hearing from you.

Sincerely,

Jean Gagnon

Exhibit 6   Application Letter from Roger Laframboise

Dear Sirs,

I would like to meet with you concerning the job in the attached clippings from the Montreal newspapers.

I hold a B.Comm. degree, and for five years I worked as a field salesman for Campbell Soups. Six months ago, a friend and I put together a business selling scrap

Canadian Pharmaceuticals Corporation Ltd.   **547**

Exhibit 6   (continued)

steel in Montreal. Due to a variety of factors, not the least of which is the current economic climate, the business is not doing well, and I must seek alternative employment.

My ambition is to find a sales position where I can prove myself in the field over three to four years and then move up to district sales manager. If necessary, I am willing to relocate.

Yours truly,

Roger Laframboise

Exhibit 7   Mr. Clark's Additional Notes on the Applicants from Interviews

Perron:

Aggressive but not unpleasant personality, talkative, possibly fluctuating temper. Smoker. Neat appearance and enthusiastic attitude.

Expected salary around $15,000.

Quite ambitious and keen on opportunities for advancement.

Average size, 5'8", 170 lbs.

Tremblay:

Big man, 6'7", 240 lbs.

Young, confident, aggressive.

Wants $11,000.

Neat dresser.

Fair on people orientation.

Wife is working.

Frequently said, "Must talk to my wife." I interviewed wife and got her to put in writing that she is willing to relocate.

Gagnon:

Balding, 5'10", 160 lbs.

Immaculate dresser.

Strong people orientation, radiates warmth on first meeting.

Was getting $20,000, wants $22,000 to start.

Gave him a stress interview. He was comfortable.

Exhibit 7 (continued)

He and wife originally from Quebec.

I wonder about him going *out* to see people compared to them visiting him.

Held executive capacity in Vancouver United Way fund raising campaign.

Laframboise:

Mediocre appearance, 5'8", 150 lbs., 30 years old.

Good people orientation.

Seems to be a "doer."

Independent, very confident.

In middle of divorce proceedings.

Heavy smoker.

Seems very bright.

Probably very smooth salesman.

Wants $18,000.

Lady's man?

Mr. Clark was reviewing each application and wondering which of the four people to hire. He was also wondering what changes, if any, would be necessary and appropriate in the sales management of the dental products group.

35 Garrett Truck Co. Ltd.

Mr. Barton, manager of the London branch of Garrett Truck Co. Ltd., had decided to hire an extra salesperson. He believed that the three salespeople he currently employed were doing a good job but felt they were not able to give intensive enough coverage to their areas and, as a result, the potential of the district was not being fully exploited. In adding a fourth salesperson, however, Mr. Barton was faced with the decision of how to redefine sales areas and/or sales duties for the four people. (exhibit 1 shows the existing geographic divisions of the sales district.)

The Garrett Truck Co. manufactured and sold heavy-duty diesel trucks and parts as well as providing maintenance and repair service. The product line was limited to larger units (tractor only) in the price range of $27,000 to $53,000 with an average selling price of $35,000. This was somewhat higher than the industry average for comparable-sized units and, in the company's view, was maintained through the high quality of the trucks and the level of personal service and attention accorded each customer. In the year ending September 1980, the London branch sold 107 new and 64 used trucks, which, with parts and service, made up a sales total of $5,541,000 (see exhibit 2). Garrett trucks were sold throughout Canada to large and small fleet operators as well as one-unit operators; however, the London branch traditionally generated 90 percent of its sales from very small fleet operators that were located in nonurban areas and used trucks for local and long distance runs to haul a wide range of items including grain, cattle, sand and gravel, lumber, petroleum products, and freight. They tended to utilize the local servicing facilities in London provided by Garrett.

The city of London itself was not a large market for Garrett trucks, mainly because of the relatively small amount of heavy industry. In 1980, thirty-three new and twenty-one used trucks were sold to customers located within the city limits.

The London branch of Garrett Trucks had enjoyed little success selling to the major freight carriers and other major fleet operators such as oil companies, ready-mix cement firms, and large manufacturers. One reason always put forward was that many of the large operations had their headquarters in Toronto and Montreal, and truck purchase decisions were made there. Another often suggested reason was that the "Big Three" auto manufacturers, with 50 percent of their total Canadian manufacturing

Exhibit 1 Garrett Truck Co. Ltd., London Branch, Sales Territories

Exhibit 2 Garrett Truck Co. Ltd., London Branch,
Income Statement for the Years Ending September 30 (in 000's of dollars)

	1978	1979	1980
Total sales	$2865	$2988	$5541
Cost of sales	2310	2437	4700
Gross margin	$ 555	$ 551	$ 841
Expenses	505	499	676
Profit (loss) before tax	$ 50	$ 52	$ 165
Breakdown of Total Sales, $ (Units)			
New trucks	(61) $1760	(47) $1635	(107) $3689
Used trucks	(54) 390	(42) 362	(64) 555
Total trucks	(115) $2150	(89) $1997	(171) $4244
Total parts	545	731	963[a]
Total labour	170	260	334[b]
Total sales	$2865	$2988	$5541

a. Margin on parts sales about 35 percent.
b. Margin on labour about 50 percent.

capacity in Mr. Barton's sales area, had captured a large part of the major freight carrier business in the district, since deliveries of raw materials and supplies to their plants represented significant volumes for truckers.

The normal selling process was initiated by a Garrett salesperson calling on a potential customer. As most new truck buyers were fairly knowledgeable about the performance characteristics of different trucks, they generally did not need to view the truck itself but bought according to quotes given on their required specifications. In only perhaps 25 percent of sales, a customer wanted to see a truck before buying it. The salesperson's prime task then was to sell a buyer on the value of Garrett's higher-than-average quality and price. Maintenance and repair services were provided in a number of ways. The largest number of major overhauls were done at the London branch. However, two service dealers, one in Sarnia about 96 kilometres to the west, and one in Windsor about 192 kilometres to the southwest, had franchise rights to repair Garrett trucks in their area. The London branch also had a small service truck to dispatch for minor work on trucks that could not be brought to the main depot. A small number of customers had maintenance contracts with Garrett whereby for a certain fee, assessed either per hour or per kilometre, the trucks were overhauled on a set preventive maintenance schedule.

When Mr. Barton was transferred in 1977 to the London branch, which had one salesperson, he almost immediately added another. In the fall of 1979, he added a third person and simply subdivided the two existing territories to create the third territory. However, his decision to hire a fourth salesperson in the fall of 1980 involved a more complex situation, and Mr. Barton was currently considering three alternatives:

1. Divide the district into four territories as evenly as possible to give each salesperson approximately equal potential sales. The new territory would include a westerly portion of territory 1, an eastern part of territory 2, and southern part of territory 3.

2. Divide the territories, excluding the London city market, three ways, and make one salesperson the used truck manager plus giving that person sales responsibility for the city of London.

3. Leave the three territories basically unchanged geographically but assign one person the exclusive responsibility for fleet sales for the entire district.

Trade-ins were a necessary, integral part of new truck sales. Over the past three years, used trucks had accounted for just over 40 percent of all units sold by the London branch. At an average selling price of $8900, this represented over $500,000 in 1980, and yet the price barely covered the used truck department's out-of-pocket expenses (repairs, commissions) incurred plus the trade-in price. An additional factor was that used trucks were being carried in inventory for an average of one and a half months, which required a considerable amount of funds. In contrast, new truck contributions for the London branch were significant and well above the corporate average.

Mr. Barton personally had been acting as the manager for both new and used truck sales, and all the salespeople had been selling both new and used trucks. With the growth of the branch, Mr. Barton felt he needed to reduce some of his commitments and for this reason had considered establishing the position of used truck manager. In addition to relieving some of his own responsibilities and giving one of his salespeople some management experience, it would also give focus to the selling of used trucks. Under this approach, all salespeople would continue to sell used trucks at the present commission rates. However, they would need to have the deals approved by the used truck manager, who would receive an overriding commission of 1 percent on all used truck sales, plus the normal salesperson's commission on any personal sales. This manager would also be responsible for the profitability of the used truck department and thus would have authority over the price at which trade-ins would be accepted, the extent of repairs to be made, and the selling price to be charged. This meant that on any new truck sale involving a trade-in, the used truck manager would have to test and inspect the old truck and advise on an acceptable trade-in value. In addition to the foregoing, the used truck manager would be responsible for new truck sales in the city of London.

"Fleet sales" had never been high in the London branch. Mr. Barton's definition of a fleet customer was any company that operated twenty or more trucks. Although quite often these were the products of a single manufacturer, this was by no means always the case. Mr. Barton estimated that there were fifty such potential customers spread over the total district. These figures did not include those companies that bought their trucks through a Toronto- or Montreal-based head office, nor those companies that were committed to buying from one of the Big Three manufacturers. The territory estimates reflected Mr. Barton's best estimate of real market potential based on truck registration data and his knowledge of the market. The number of trucks purchased by these companies annually would amount to about 25 percent of their fleet size, some as replacements and some as additions. Of the fleet customers, six operated in the order of 150 trucks, ten operated around 50, and the remainder operated, on the average, about 25 trucks. Only 10 percent of the London branch's 1979 sales were to fleet customers, but by mid-1980 fleet sales had already exceeded that level. Mr. Barton felt that the London branch should be able to get at least 10 percent of the available fleet market. Since he felt they had 20 percent of the single-unit owner market, he was convinced that it would be difficult, but it was both possible and necessary to increase the branch's penetration of the fleet market segment. One salesperson with primary responsibility for this activity might be the answer.

One of the problems was that fleet customers not surprisingly expected larger discounts than the ordinary customer. The necessary discounts would probably exceed 27 percent. This could have considerable effect on a salesman's potential commission earnings and Mr. Barton accepted that he might have to adjust the base salary to compensate.

One of Mr. Barton's concerns was the reaction of his existing salesmen to any changes in their territories. These salesmen, with their expertise, experience and personal ties with the customers, were the backbone of the branch's operations. They earned $400/month base salary plus commissions for an average total of $35,000/year. The structure of commission payments is given in exhibit 3, and a typical month's sales by one man are shown in exhibit 4.

Exhibit 3   Garrett Truck Co. Ltd., London Branch,
Sales Commission Payments on New Trucks

Percent Discount[a]	Rate of Commission (percent)
Under 19	5
19–19.9	4.5
20–20.9	4
21–21.9	3.5
22–22.9	3
23–23.9	2.5
24–24.9	2
25–25.9	1.5
26–26.9	1
27 or higher	0.5

The average commission earned on new trucks in 1980 was 2.1 percent.
Used trucks: 2 percent on selling price.
a.   Sale price on new trucks is quoted as a percentage discount for company-estimated list price.

Exhibit 4   Garrett Truck Co. Ltd. Average Monthly Commissions
   Current average sales and commisions for one salesman in one month:

Unit sold	
New	3
Used	2
Sales dollars	
New—3 × $35,000 (avg.)	$105,000
Used—2 × $ 8,900 (avg.)	17,800
	$122,800
Commission earned	
New—105,000 × 2.1% (avg.)	$ 2,205
Used—17,800 × 2%	356
	$ 2,561
Monthly salary	400
Total monthly compensation	$ 2,961
Expenses paid to salesman	$ 270
Total selling expenses to branch	$ 3,231
Cost to sell—% of sales	2.6%

Fred, the salesperson in the southwest region (territory 2), was thirty-six years old and had sold Garrett trucks for two years. Before joining the company, he had owned his own small trucking operation. Fred was not a high-pressure salesman but sold on the basis of personal knowledge of trucks and truck driving and his understanding of the needs of small truckers. Mr. Barton characterized him as a hard-working salesman with little ambition for, or interest in, a management position.

Alan, also thirty-six, had the London city and east region (territory 1). He joined Garrett Truck in 1976 before Mr. Barton was made branch manager. Previously an insurance salesman, Al had a charming personality and a polished style but at times was considered a little "pushy" by some customers and prospects. He had no previous experience with trucks before joining Garrett, yet with what Mr. Barton considered to be at best average effort was the branch's highest paid salesperson.

Harvey, twenty-eight years old, became the third salesperson in the branch in the fall of 1979 and had the northwest region, an area not well covered previously (territory 3). He initially joined Garrett as an apprentice mechanic and, after achieving his Class A standing, rose to service foreman at the London branch before entering sales at his own request. His likeable personality and knowledge of Garrett trucks had made him a good salesperson earning a respectable commission.

Before Mr. Barton could start his search for a salesperson, he would have to receive approval from the head office. From prior conversations with his superiors, he knew that they were in favour of adding a salesperson but he still had to submit a formal proposal outlining the specific details of the job and his reasons for asking for someone to fill it.

36 General Electric Appliances

Mr. Frank Mace had recently been promoted to the position of district sales manager (B.C.) for G.E. Appliances, a division of Canadian Appliance Manufacturing Co. Ltd. (CAMCO). One of his more important duties in that position was the allocation of his district's sales quota among his five salespeople. Mr. Mace received his quota for 1978 in October 1977. His immediate task was to determine an equitable allocation of that quota. This was important because the company's incentive pay plan was based on the salespeople's attainment of quota. A portion of Mr. Mace's remuneration was also based on the degree to which his sales force met their quotas.

Mr. Mace graduated from the University of British Columbia in 1969 with the degree of Bachelor of Commerce. He was immediately hired as a product manager for a mining equipment manufacturing firm because of his summer job experience with that firm. In 1972, he joined C.G.E. in Montreal as a product manager for refrigerators. There he was responsible for creating and merchandising a product line, as well as developing product and marketing plans. In January 1975, he was transferred to Coburg, Ontario, as a sales manager for industrial plastics. In September 1975, he became administrative manager (western region), and when the position of district sales manager became available, Mr. Mace was promoted to it. There his duties included development of sales strategies, supervision of salespeople, and budgeting.

Background

Canadian Appliance Manufacturing Co. Ltd. (CAMCO) was created in 1976 under the joint ownership of Canadian General Electric Ltd. and General Steel Wares Ltd. CAMCO then purchased the production facilities of Westinghouse Canada Ltd. Under the purchase agreement, the Westinghouse brand name was transferred to White Consolidated Industries Ltd.

and became White-Westinghouse. Appliances manufactured by CAMCO in the former Westinghouse plant were branded Hotpoint.

The G.E., G.S.W., and Hotpoint major appliance plants became divisions of CAMCO. These divisions operated independently and had their own separate management staff, although they were all ultimately accountable to CAMCO management (see exhibit 1). The divisions competed for sales, although not directly, because they each produced product lines for different price segments.

Competition

Competition in the appliance industry was vigorous. CAMCO was the largest firm in the industry, with approximately 45 percent market share, split between G.E., G.S.W. (Moffatt & McClary brands), and Hotpoint. The following three firms each had 10–15 percent market share: Inglis (washers and dryers only), W.C.I. (makers of White-Westinghouse, Kelvinator, and Gibson), and Admiral. These firms also produced appliances under department store brand names such as Viking, Baycrest, and Kenmore, which accounted for an additional 15 percent of the market. The remainder of the market was divided among brands such as Maytag, Roper Dishwasher, Gurney, Tappan, and Danby.

G.E. marketed a full major appliance product line, including refrigerators, ranges, washers, dryers, dishwashers, and television sets. G.E. Appliances generally had many features and were priced at the upper end of the price range. Their major competition came from Maytag and Westinghouse.

The Budgeting Process

G.E. Appliances was one of the most advanced firms in the consumer goods industry in terms of sales budgeting. Budgeting received careful analysis at all levels of management.

The budgetary process began in June of each year. The management of G.E. Appliances division assessed the economic outlook, growth trends in the industry, competitive activity, population growth, and so forth in order to determine a reasonable sales target for the next year. The president of CAMCO received this budget, checked and revised it as necessary, and gave final approval. G.E. Appliances was considered an "invest and grow" division, which meant that it was expected to produce a healthy sales growth each year, regardless of the state of the economy. As Mr. Mace has said, "This is difficult, but meeting challenges is the job of management."

The approved budget was expressed as a desired percentage increase in sales. Once the figure had been decided, it was not subject to change. The quota was communicated back through CAMCO and G.E. Appliances, where it was available to the district sales managers in October. Each district was then required to meet an overall growth figure (quota), but each sales territory was not automatically expected to achieve that same growth. Mr. Mace was required to assess the situation in each territory, determine where growth potential was highest, and allocate his quota accordingly.

Exhibit 1 Organization Chart

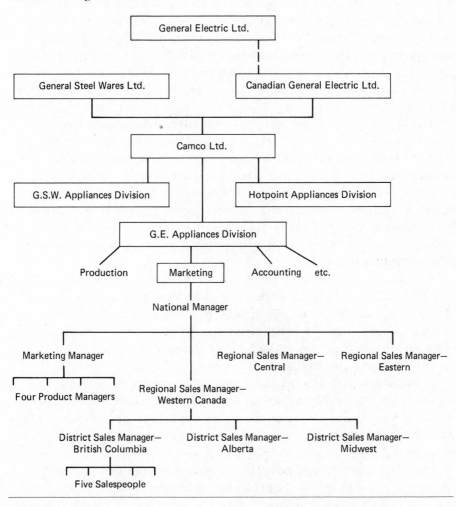

The Sales Incentive Plan

The sales incentive plan was a critical part of General Electric's sales force plan and an important consideration in the quota allocation of Mr. Mace. Each salesperson had a portion of his or her earnings dependent upon performance with respect to quota. Also, Mr. Mace was awarded a bonus based on the sales performance of his district, making it advantageous to Mr. Mace, and good for staff morale, for all his salespeople to attain their quotas.

The sales force incentive plan was relatively simple. A bonus system is fairly typical for salesmen in any field. With G.E., each salesperson agreed to a basic salary figure called "planned earnings." The planned salary varied according to experience, education, past performance, and competitive salaries. A salesperson was paid 75 percent of his or her planned earnings on a guaranteed regular basis. The remaining 25 percent of salary was at risk, dependent upon the person's sales record. There was also the possibility of earning substantially more money by selling more than quota (see table 1).

The bonus was awarded such that total salary (base plus bonus) equaled planned earnings when the quota was just met. The greatest increase in bonus came between 101 and 110 percent of quota. The bonus was paid quarterly on the cumulative total quota. A holdback system ensured that a salesperson was never required to pay back previously earned bonus by reason of a poor quarter. Because of this system, it was critical that each salesperson's quota be fair in relation to the other salespeople. Nothing was worse for morale than one person's earning large bonuses while the others struggled.

Quota attainment was not the sole basis for evaluating the salespeople. They were required to fulfill a wide range of duties including service, franchising of new dealers, maintaining good relations with dealers, and maintaining a balance of sales among the different product lines. Because the bonus system was based on sales only, Mr. Mace had to ensure that the salespeople did not neglect their other duties.

A formal salary review was held each year for each salesperson. However, Mr. Mace preferred to give his salespeople continuous feedback on their performances. Through human relations skills, he hoped to avoid problems that could lead to dismissal of a salesperson and loss of sales for the company.

Mr. Mace's incentive bonus plan was more complex than that of the salespeople. He was awarded a maximum of 75 annual bonus points

Table 1   Applicable Sales Incentive Earnings Schedule for Major Appliances and Home Entertainment Products

Sales Quota Realization (percent)	Incentive % of Base Salary (Total)	Sales Quota Realization (percent)	Incentive % of Base Salary (Total)
70	0	105	35.00
71	0.75	106	37.00
72	1.50	107	39.00
73	2.25	108	41.00
74	3.00	109	43.0
75	3.75	110	45.00
76	4.50	111	46.00
77	5.25	112	47.00
78	6.00	113	48.00
79	6.75	114	49.00
80	7.50	115	50.00
81	8.25	116	51.00
82	9.00	117	52.00
83	9.75	118	53.00
84	10.50	119	54.00
85	11.25	120	55.00
86	12.00	121	56.00
87	12.75	122	57.00
88	13.50	123	58.00
89	14.25	124	59.00
90	15.00	125	60.00
91	16.00	126	61.00
92	17.00	127	62.00
93	18.00	128	63.00
94	19.00	129	64.00
95	20.00	130	65.00
96	21.00	131	66.00
97	22.00	132	67.00
98	23.00	133	68.00
99	24.00	134	69.00
100	25.00	135	70.00
101	27.00	136	71.00
102	29.00	137	72.00
103	31.00	138	73.00
104	33.00	139	74.00
		140	75.00

broken down as follows: market share, 15; total sales performance, 30; sales representative balance, 30. Each point had a specific money value. The system ensured that Mr. Mace allocated his quota carefully. For instance, if one quota was so difficult that the salesperson sold only 80 percent of it, while the other salespeople exceeded quota, Mr. Mace's bonus would be reduced, even if the overall area sales exceeded the quota. (See Appendix A: Development of a Sales Commission Plan.)

Quota Allocation

The total 1978 sales budget for the G.E. Appliances Division was about $100 million, a 14 percent sales increase over 1977. Mr. Mace's share of the $33 million western region quota was $13.3 million, also a 14 percent increase over 1977. Mr. Mace had two weeks to allocate the quota among his five territories. He needed to consider factors such as historical allocation, economic outlook, dealer changes, personnel changes, untapped potential, new franchises or store openings, and buying group activity (volume purchases by associations of independent dealers).

Sales Force

There were five sales territories within B.C. (exhibit 2). Territories were determined on the basis of number of customers, sales volume of customers, geographic size, and experience of the salesperson. Territories were altered periodically in order to deal with changed circumstances.

One territory was comprised entirely of contract customers. Contract sales were sales in bulk lots to builders and developers who used the appliances in housing units. Because the appliances were not resold at retail, G.E. took a lower profit margin on such sales.

G.E. Appliances recruited M.B.A. graduates for their sales force. They sought bright, educated people who were willing to relocate anywhere in Canada. The company intended that these people would ultimately be promoted to managerial positions. The company also hired experienced career salespeople in order to get a blend of experience in the sales force. However, the typical salesperson was under thirty, aggressive, and upwardly mobile. G.E.'s sales training programme covered only product knowledge. It was not felt necessary to train recruits in sales techniques.

Allocation Procedure

At the time Mr. Mace assumed the job of D.S.M., he had a meeting with the former sales manager, Mr. Ken Philips. Mr. Philips described to Mr. Mace the method he had used in the past to allocate the quota. As Mr. Mace understood it, the procedure was as follows:

The quota was received in October in the form of a desired percentage sales increase. The first step was to project current sales to the end of the year. This gave a base to which the increase was added for an estimation of the next year's quota.

From this quota, the value of contract sales was allocated. Contract sales were allocated first because the market was considered the easiest to forecast. The amount of contract sales in the sales mix was constrained by the lower profit margin on such sales.

The next step was to make a preliminary allocation by simply adding the budgeted percentage increase to the year end estimates for each territory. Although this allocation seemed fair on the surface, it did not take into account the differing situations in the territories or the difficulty of attaining such an increase.

The next step was examination of the sales data compiled by G.E. Weekly sales reports from all regions were fed into a central computer, which compiled them and printed out sales totals by product line for each

Exhibit 2 G.E. Appliances Sales Territories

Territory Number	Territory Name and Salesperson	Description of Territory
9961	Greater Vancouver (Garth Rizzuto)	Hudson's Bay, Firestone, K-Mart, McDonald Supply, plus seven independent dealers
9962	Interior (Dan Seguin)	All customers from Quesnel to Nelson, including contract sales (50 customers)
9963	Coastal (Ken Block)	Eatons, Woodwards, plus Vancouver Island north of Duncan and upper Fraser Valley (east of Clearbrook) (20 customers)
9964	Independent and Northern (Fred Speck)	All independents in lower mainland and South Vancouver Island, plus northern B.C. and Yukon (30 customers)
9967	Contract (Jim Wiste)	Contract sales Vancouver, Victoria; All contract sales outside 9962 (50–60 customers)

customer, as well as other information. This information enabled the sales manager to check the reasonableness of his initial allocation through a careful analysis of the growth potential for each customer.

The analysis began with the largest accounts, such as Firestone, Hudson's Bay, and Eatons, each of which bought over one million dollars in appliances annually. Accounts that size were expected to achieve at least the budgeted growth. The main reason for this was that a shortfall of a few percentage points on such a large account would be difficult to make up elsewhere.

Next, the growth potential for medium-sized accounts was estimated. These accounts included McDonald Supply, K-Mart, Federated Co-operative, and buying groups such as Volume Independent Purchasers (V.I.P.). Management expected the majority of sales growth to come from such accounts, which had annual sales of between $150,000 and $1,000,000.

At that point, about 70 percent of the accounts had been analyzed. The small accounts were estimated last. These had generally lower growth potential but were an important part of the company's distribution system.

Once all the accounts had been analyzed, the growth estimates were summed, and the total was compared to the budget. Usually, the growth estimates were well below the budget.

The next step was to gather more information. The salespeople were usually consulted to ensure that no potential trouble areas or good opportunities had been overlooked. The manager continued to revise and adjust the figures until the total estimated matched the budget. These projections were then summed by territory and compared to the preliminary territorial allocation.

Frequently, there were substantial differences between the two allocations. Historical allocations were then examined, and the manager used his or her judgment in adjusting the figures until satisfied that the allocation was both equitable and attainable. Some factors that were considered at this stage included experience of the salespeople, competitive activities, potential store closures or openings, potential labour disputes in areas, and so forth.

The completed allocation was passed on to the regional sales manager for approval. The process had usually taken one week or longer by this stage. Once the allocations had been approved, the district sales manager then divided them into sales quotas by product line. Often, the resulting average price did not match the expected mix between higher- and lower-priced units. Therefore, some additional adjusting of figures was necessary. The house account (used for sales to employees of the company) was used as the adjustment factor.

Once this breakdown had been completed, the numbers were printed on a budget sheet and given to the regional sales manager (R.S.M.), who forwarded all the region's sheets to the central computer. The computer printed out sales numbers for each product line by salesman, by month; these figures were used as the salespeople's quotas for the next year.

Current Situation

Mr. Mace recognized that he faced a difficult task. He felt that he was too new to the job and the area to confidently undertake an account-by-account growth analysis. However, owing to his previous experience with sales budgets, he did have some sound general ideas. He also had the records of past allocation and quota attainment (exhibit 3) as well as the assistance of the R.S.M., Mr. Anthony Foyt.

Mr. Mace's first step was to project the current sales figures to end-of-year totals. This task was facilitated because the former manager, Mr. Philips, had been making successive projections monthly since June. Mr. Mace then made a preliminary quota allocation by adding the budgeted sales increase of 14 percent to each territory's total (exhibit 4).

Exhibit 3   Sales Results

Territory	Budget (× 1000)	Percent of Total Budget	Actual (× 1000)	Variance from Quota (percent)
		1975		
9967 (Contract)	2,440	26.5	2,267	(7)
9961 (Greater Vancouver)	1,790	19.4	1,824	2
9962 (Interior)	1,624	17.7	1,433	(11)
9963 (Coastal)	2,111	23	2,364	12
9965 (Ind. dealers)	1,131	12.3	1,176	4
House	84	1.1	235	
Total	9,180	100	9,299	1
		1976		
9967	2,587	26.2	2,845	10
9961	2,005	20.3	2,165	8
9962	1,465	14.8	1,450	(1)
9963	2,405	24.4	2,358	(2)
9965	1,334	13.5	1,494	12
House	52	.8	86	—
Total	9,848	100	10,398	5

Exhibit 4

Projected Sales Results 1977

Territory	Oct. 1977 Year to Date	1977 Projected Total	1977 Budget	Percent of Total Budget	Variance from Quota (projected, percent)
9967	2,447	3,002	2,859	25.0	5
9961	2,057	2,545	2,401	21.0	6
9962	1,318	1,623	1,727	15.1	(6)
9963	2,124	2,625	2,734	23.9	(4)
9965	1,394	1,720	1,578	13.8	9
House	132	162	139	1.2	—
Total	9,474	11,677	11,438	100	2

1978 budget = 1977 projection + 14% $13,312,000

Preliminary Allocation 1978

Territory	1977 Projection	1978 Budget	Percent of Total Budget
9967	3,002	3,422	25.7
9961	2,545	2,901	21.8
9962	1,623	1,854	13.9
9963	2,625	2,992	22.6
9965	1,720	1,961	14.7
House	162	185	1.3
Total	11,677	13,315	100

He then began to assess circumstances that could cause him to alter that allocation. One major problem was the resignation, effective at the end of the year, of one of the company's top salesmen, Ken Block. Mr. Block's territory had traditionally been one of the most difficult, and Mr. Mace felt that it would be unwise to replace him with a novice salesperson.

He considered shifting one of the more experienced salespeople into that area. However, that would have involved a disruption of service in an additional territory, which was undesirable because it took several months for a salesperson to build up a good rapport with customers. Mr. Mace's decision would affect his quota allocation because a salesperson new to a territory could not be expected to immediately sell as well as the incumbent, and a novice salesperson would require an even longer period of adaptation.

He was also concerned about territory 9961. The territory comprised two large national accounts and seven major independent dealers. The buying decisions for the national accounts were made at their head offices, where G.E.'s regional salespeople had no control over the decisions. Recently, Mr. Mace had heard rumours that one of the national accounts was reviewing its purchase of G.E. appliances. If they were to delist even some product lines, it would be a major blow to the salesperson, Mr. Rizzuto, whose potential sales would be greatly reduced. Mr. Mace was unsure how to deal with that situation.

Another concern for Mr. Mace was the wide variance in buying of some accounts. Woodwards, Eatons, and McDonald Supply had large fluctuations from year to year. Also, Eatons, Hudson's Bay, and Woodwards had plans to open new stores in the Vancouver area sometime during the year. The sales increase to be generated by these events was hard to estimate.

The general economic outlook was poor. The Canadian dollar had fallen to 92 cents U.S., and unemployment was at about 8 percent. The government's anti-inflation programme, which was scheduled to end in November 1978, had managed to keep inflation to the 8 percent level, but economists expected higher inflation and increased labour unrest during the postcontrol period.

The economic outlook was not the same in all areas. For instance, the Okanagan (9962) was a very depressed area. Tourism was down, and fruit farmers were doing poorly despite good weather and record prices. Vancouver Island was still recovering from a 200 percent increase in ferry fares, while the lower mainland appeared to be in a relatively better position.

In the contract segment, construction had shown an increase over 1976. However, labour unrest was common. There had been a crippling eight-week strike in 1976, and there was a strong possibility of another strike in 1978.

With all of this in mind, Mr. Mace was very concerned that he allocate the quota properly because of the bonus system implications. How should he proceed?

Appendix A: Development of a Sales Commission Plan

A series of steps are required to establish the foundation upon which a sales commission plan can be built. These steps are as follows:

A. Determine Specific Sales Objectives of Positions to be Included in Plan

For a sales commission plan to succeed, it must be designed to encourage the attainment of the business objectives of the component. Before deciding on the specific measures of performance to be used in the plan, the component should review and define its major objectives. Typical objectives might be:

Increased sales volume.

Do an effective balanced selling job in a variety of product lines.

Improve market share.

Reduce selling expense to sales ratios.

Develop new accounts or territories.

Introduce new products.

Although it is probably neither desirable nor necessary to include all such objectives as specific measures of performance in the plan, they should be kept in mind, at least to the extent that the performance measures chosen for the plan are compatible with and do not work against the overall accomplishment of the component's business objectives. Also, the *relative* current importance or ranking of these objectives will provide guidance in selecting the number and type of performance measures to be included in the plan.

B. Determine Quantitative Performance Measures to be Used

Although it may be *possible* to include a number of measures in a particular plan, there is a *drawback to using so many as to overly complicate it and fragment the impact of any one measure on the participants.* A plan that is difficult to understand will lose a great deal of its motivating force, as well as being costly to administer properly.

For components currently having a variable sales compensation plan(s) for their salespeople, a good starting point would be to consider the measures used in those plans. Although the measurements used for sales managers need not be identical, they should at least be compatible with those used to determine their salespeople's commissions.

However, keep in mind that a performance measure that may not be appropriate for individual salespeople may be a good one to apply to their manager. Measurements involving attainment of a share of a defined market, balanced selling for a variety of products, and control of district or region expenses might well fall into this category.

Listed in table A1 are a variety of measurements that might be used to emphasize specific sales objectives.

For most components, all or most of these objectives will be desirable to some extent. The point is to select those of *greatest* importance where it will be possible to establish measures of standard or normal performance for individuals, or at least small groups of individuals working as a team.

If more than one performance measurement is to be used, the relative weighting of each measurement must be determined. If a measure is to be effective, it must carry enough weight to have at least some noticeable effect on the commission earnings of an individual.

As a general guide, it would be unusual for a plan to include more than two or three quantitative measures with a *minimum* weighting of 15–20 percent of planned commissions for any one measurement.

Table A1   Tailoring Commission Plan Measurements to Fit Component Objectives

Objectives	*Possible Plan Measurements*
Increase sales/orders volume	Net sales billed or orders received against quota
Increase sales of particular lines	Sales against product line quotas with weighted sales credits on individual lines
Increase market share	Percent realization (%R) of shares
Do balanced selling job	%R of product line quotas with commissions increasing in proportion to number of lines up to quota
Increase profitability	Margin realized from sales; vary sales credits to emphasize profitable product lines; vary sales credit in relation to amount of price discount
Increase dealer sales	Pay distributor salespeople or sales manager in relation to realization of sales quotas of assigned dealers
Increase sales calls	%R of targeted calls per district or region
Introduce new product	Additional sales credits on new line for limited period
Control expense	%R of expense to sales or margin ratio; adjust sales credit in proportion to variance from expense budget
Sales teamwork	Share of incentive based upon group results

C. Establish Commission Payment Schedule
for Each Performance Measure

1. *Determine appropriate range of performance for each measurement.* The performance range for a measurement defines the percent of standard performance (R%) at which commission earnings start to the point where they reach maximum.

The minimum point of the performance range for a given measurement should be set so that a majority of the participants can earn at least some incentive pay, and the maximum should be set at a point that is possible of attainment by some participants. These points will vary with the type of measure used, and the degree of predictability of individual budgets or other forms of measurement. In a period where overall performance is close to standard, 90–95 percent of the participants should fall within the performance range.

For the commission plan to be effective, most of the participants should be operating within the performance range most of the time. If a participant is either far below the minimum of this range or has reached the maximum, further improvement will not affect his or her commission earnings, and the plan will be largely inoperative as far as that person is concerned.

Actual past experience of R%'s attained by participants is obviously the best indicator of what this range should be for each measure used. Lacking this, it is better to err on the side of having a wider range than one that proves to be too narrow. If some form of group measure is used, the variation from standard performance is likely to be less for the group in total than for individuals within it. For example, the performance range for total district performance would probably be narrower than the range established for an individual salesperson within a district.

2. *Determine appropriate reward: risk ratio for commission earnings.* This refers to the relationship of commission earned at standard performance, to maximum commission earnings available under the plan. A plan that pays 10 percent of base salary for normal or standard performance, and pays 30 percent as a maximum commission would have a 2:1 ratio. In other words, the participant can earn twice as much (20 percent) for above standard performance as he or she stands to lose for below standard performance (10 percent).

Reward under a sales commission plan should be related to the effort involved to produce a given result. To adequately encourage above-standard results, the reward:risk ratio should generally be at least 2:1. *The proper control of incentive plan payments lies in the proper setting of performance standards,* not in the setting of a low maximum payment for outstanding results that provides a minimum variation in individual earnings. Generally, a higher percentage of base salary should be paid for each 1%R above 100 percent than has been paid for each 1%R up to 100%R to reflect the relative difficulty involved in producing above-standard results.

Once the performance range and reward:risk ratio have been determined, the schedule of payments for each performance measure can then be calculated. This will show the percentage of the participant's base salary earned for various performance results (R%) from the point at which commissions start to maximum performance.

Example: For measurement paying 20% of salary for standard performance.

% base salary earned		% of sales quota
1% of base salary for each +1%R	0%	80% or below
	20%	100% (standard performance)
1.33% of base salary for each +1%R	60%	130% or above

Prepare Draft of Sales Commission Plan

After completion of the above steps, a draft of a sales commission plan should be prepared using the following outline as a guide.

Keys to Effective Commission Plans

1. *Get the understanding and acceptance of the commission plan by the managers who will be involved in carrying it out.* They must be convinced of its effectiveness in order to properly explain and "sell" the plan to the salespeople.

2. In turn, *be sure the plan is presented clearly to the salespeople* so that they have a good understanding of how the plan will work. We find that good acceptance of a sales commission plan on the part of salespeople correlates closely with how well they understood the plan and its effect on their compensation. *The salespeople must be convinced that the measurements used are factors that can be controlled by selling efforts.*

3. *Be sure the measurements used in the commission plan encourage the salespeople to achieve the marketing goals of your operation.* For example, if sales volume is the only performance measure, the salespeople will concentrate on producing as much dollar volume as possible by spending most of their time on products with high volume potential. It will be difficult to get them to spend much time on introducing new products with relatively low volume, handling customer complaints, etc. Even though a good portion of their compensation may still be in salary, you can be sure they will wind up doing the things they feel will maximize their commission earnings.

4. One good solution to maintaining good sales direction is to put at least a portion of the commission earnings in an "incentive pool" to be distributed according to the sales manager's judgment. This "pool" can vary in size according to some qualitative measure of the sales group's performance, but the manager can set individual measurements for each of the salespeople and reward each person according to how well he or she fulfills the goals.

5. If at all possible, you should test the plan for a period of time, perhaps in one or two sales areas or districts. To make it a real test, you should actually pay commission earnings to the participants, but the potential risk and rewards can be limited. No matter how well a plan has been conceived, not all the potential pitfalls will be apparent until you have actually operated the plan for a period of time. The test period is a relatively painless way to get some experience.

6. Finally, after the plan is in operation, take time to analyze the results. Is the plan accomplishing what you want it to do, both in terms of business results produced and in realistically compensating salespeople for their efforts?

37 Davgraphics Limited

"I can tell the president has been to another of those industry meetings," said Bob Piper, Sales Manager for Davgraphics. "One of the speakers talked about marketing and now he wants me to look into preparing a marketing strategy. [See exhibit 1.] Frankly, I haven't got time. Our main problem is to increase sales. What we need is to hire some proven, experienced salespeople who have accounts to bring along. We've got a good plant and good people. Marketing may be fine for toothpaste and potato chips, but we're in a different business. However, I suppose I'd better come up with a better response than that for Dave [the president]. I wonder what I should say?"

The Company

Founded in 1921 by Dave Lindsay, Sr., Davgraphics was a medium-sized family-owned full-service commercial printer located in Toronto, Ontario. Dave Lindsay, Jr. (hereafter referred to as Dave Lindsay) assumed the presidency on his father's death in 1975. Over the years, the company grew in size and gradually changed its equipment. By 1982, it offered a complete facility including artwork and design, hot and cold composition, letterpress and sheet-fed offset, and bindery services. In addition, whenever necessary, outside suppliers of graphics services were used. About 85 percent of 1981 business had been offset, using the company's one four-colour offset press, two two-colour presses, and three single-colour presses on one shift for most of the year. Davgraphics was slowly getting out of the letterpress business but had retained seven of its older presses for envelopes, numbering, and other types of jobs more suited to letterpress.

Dave Lindsay had grown up with the business. His first love was the plant, and he still liked to spend lots of time out with the presses instead

Exhibit 1   Note to Bob Piper

August 23, 1982

Bob, I attended an interesting talk last week. I wish I had notes or a tape to pass along, but neither were available. The speaker was a marketing professor. He kept saying that a firm couldn't survive without a sound marketing strategy and that marketing wasn't the same as sales. He said a company should make what it could sell, not sell what it could make.

I don't think he knew much about our business because he didn't say much about personal selling. I'll bet he doesn't even know the difference between letter-press and offset lithography. Still, he got a good reception, and my friends were saying after at lunch that we do need to do more marketing in our business.

So, Bob, would you take some time soon and let me know your thoughts about a marketing strategy for us. You might want to call Derek Lambshead at the ad agency to get his thoughts too—after all, he handles our advertising and came up with our logo.

Drop by soon.

Dave

of in his office. He had often remarked that he wanted Davgraphics to be big enough to get into web offset. To date, his plant manager, Chris Ash, had advised against this move. According to Dave Lindsay,

> We are a well-run company. I personally review internal operating and financial data every day. We've got good craftsmen and fine employees. I stress quality all the time, and that's paid off in the past. We used to be in the top 25 percent of printing firms as far as profitability is concerned, except just recently. Right now, we're in a bit of a slump. Our existing plant could handle an additional $2 million work, and we could expand even more.
>
> None of us has been to university. We're not sophisticated managers, I guess—we just follow the market and respond to it rather than trying to anticipate where the market is headed and get there first. We've changed over the years, but mostly it's been gradual. Our main problem has always been to increase sales and restore profitability.

Davgraphics served the Metropolitan Toronto area, offering all kinds of printing services. "If we specialize in anything," said Bob Piper, "it is financial printing. But that means a lot of our business is very seasonal, putting very heavy demands on all of us in March, April, May, and June. Our summers are terribly slow."

Davgraphics competed with several hundred firms in the Toronto area, although Bob Piper believed that only a handful of firms were directly competitive. "I'm also worried about the growth of in-company printing capability," he said. "It used to be that a customer company might buy a Multi, put it in the basement, and do its own small jobs. Now we're also seeing high-speed copiers and sophisticated word-processing equipment. It's a worry for all of us. And as if that wasn't enough, we've got 'instant' printers popping up all over the place."

Bob Piper commented on trends in the business:

> We used to do a lot of high-status annual reports, which gave us both profit and prestige. But the recession and the sagging stock market in the last couple of years have apparently caused many companies to cut back.
> Even more worrisome is the trend of print buyers to ask for competitive bids. In the past we did a lot of repeat business on the basis of past service or on the basis of our quality reputation. Perhaps only half of our jobs were done on a bid basis five years ago, whereas 90 percent of them are bid now. And where once we got one in three of the jobs we bid, our yield has dropped to one in five.

Davgraphics' total sales reached $4.2 million in 1981, and operating profit was $84,000. Sales in 1980 had been $4 million, and profit had been $120,000. Management had been engaged for the past several years in cost-cutting efforts. "We cut all the fat we could find," commented David Lindsay, "so I'm not sure if we can improve the bottom line any more. From now on, we'll have to concentrate on our pricing and get our volume up."

Exhibit 2 shows recent income statement ratios for Davgraphics.

Pricing

Bob Piper commented on Davgraphics pricing policies:

> Setting prices is really tough. Everything hinges on this. We don't want to give work away, and we can't have a sales force that sells on price alone. I suppose we have a reputation for being higher-priced than many of our major competitors. The salespeople have been complaining that out estimated costs have been 5–10 percent too high, which means either they give up markup and commission or lose the job.

Exhibit 2   Davgraphics Income Statement Ratios, 1977–1981
(in percent of sales except where indicated)

	1977	1978	1979	1980	1981
Sales					
$ (000)	2600	3200	3700	4000	4200
Index	100	123	142	154	162
Percent	100	100	100	100	100
Cost of goods sold					
Materials	38	38	39	39	40
Factory payroll	30	30	29	28	30
Factory expenses	8	9	9	11	10
Total	76%	77%	77%	78%	80%
Gross profit	24	23	23	22	20
Administrative expenses	10	10	9	10	11
Selling expenses[a]	6	6	7	7	7
Profit before interest and tax	8%	7%	7%	5%	2%

a.   Commission represented 4 percent of sales in 1980 and 1981.

We use a rather complicated costing system that is based on a chargeable rate for every piece of equipment and everything we do. We incorporate overheads into these rates, based on our expected chargeable time usage and capacity utilization. I don't understand it all, nor do the salespeople, but anyway we get an estimate from our fellows, then we decide on what price to charge.

I'd say our pricing was haphazard. We consider our plant capacity, what the competition is likely to do, whether we want to get started with a new customer, and very importantly, how much we think the customer is willing to pay. It's a fine line between pricing too low just to keep the presses going and pricing too high and losing the job.

We have basically three categories of work: regular, contract, and concession. Contract means repeated work like a publication such as a theatre programme. Concession means a job below our full costs. These are jobs we take primarily to keep the plant going during a slow time. All the rest are regular jobs.

We allow the salespeople to set the price in nearly all instances. We think they are in the best position to judge what price we have to meet to get the job. They have to get my approval for concessioned jobs, although I rarely say no.

Roger Moore, one of the salespeople, was not entirely happy with this system. "I feel, and so do many of the other salespeople, that our system is just too complicated. I really don't know anymore whether my jobs make money or lose money for the company. I asked John Humphrey in accounting last month about this and he said, 'Well, it depends,' and quickly lost me in his explanation. I'm not sure he really knows either."

Advertising

Davgraphics did little advertising. Infrequently, David Lindsay decided to have an ad in the *Financial Post* or in the *Globe and Mail*. These were usually relatively small, "professional card" ads suggesting that Davgraphics was a high-quality, full-service commercial printer. A two-inch, one-column ad was placed in the yellow pages, and the company delivery trucks were brightly signed. Each salesperson gave out a picture calendar with the Davgraphics name on it to customers at Christmas and any other gifts he or she felt were appropriate. While there had been some discussion of a brochure outlining Davgraphics' abilities, nothing had been done. "I don't know how you decide how much to spend or whether the money you spent was worth it," said David Lindsay, "but I keep thinking we ought to do more than just send out our salespeople."

Sales Management

Bob Piper had been promoted to Sales Manager in early 1981 when his predecessor suffered a heart attack while playing tennis. "Old J.N. was some salesman," commented Paul Gowan, one of the older salespeople.

> He could sell printing to anyone. He started in this company with Dave, Sr., and worked his way up from salesman to sales manager. He never cared about paperwork, so we didn't have to either. He used to say selling print was like selling 'faith,' which meant you had nothing tangible to sell, just press time and some services. I mean it's hard to convince a customer we're better at this than the next fellow. So, as J.N. said, selling faith requires creative salesmanship. A good print salesperson has to have all the usual qualities—good appearance, charm, and empathy with the buyer. Also, a printing salesperson has to use all the other tricks too: tickets to hockey and football games or the theatre, holiday presents, and wining and dining. When I began with Davgraphics in 1960, I didn't have any printing background, nor much knowledge of the industries I was selling to. But J.N. said that didn't matter much. He taught me to rely on my intuition and to do something extra besides all the things the competitors were doing. J.N. suggested I make sure I invited the buyer's wife and my wife to the occasion or event where he was my guest. That was a major breakthrough. I also learned that only a

Death of a Salesman

few print buyers really care about quality and service, above and beyond price and on-time delivery. These are the creative people, like those in a company's advertising department. Those people have always been my best customers.

"Paul Gowan is a typical older salesperson around here," observed Bob Piper, "and I probably couldn't change him. My predecessor wasn't a manager, he was a top salesperson. I don't like to speak poorly of him, but he didn't teach our fellows how to sell when the competition gets tough. Our oldtimers are more order-takers than salespeople. They're used to servicing the same accounts over and over. They don't like prospecting."

Bob Piper, 43, had been with Davgraphics for five years as salesperson, assistant sales manager, and then sales manager. Before joining Davgraphics, he had worked for two other printers, one in Montreal and one in Toronto. In addition to his management responsibilities for the seven salespeople, he also handled all of the "house accounts." These were previously J.N. Granger's accounts and those of his own he did not give to the other salespeople. These house accounts represented 20 percent of the company's sales in 1981. Bob Piper was paid a salary plus half the regular commission rate on the sales he handled.

"I'm still coming to grips with this job," explained Bob Piper. "For example, I've just pulled together some stats on 1981 salespeople's performance that I'm puzzling through. [See exhibit 3.] And, Dave wants me to name an assistant sales manager soon, too. He's challenged me to increase sales 15 percent in my first year, and I mean to do it."

The Sales Force

Seven salespeople constituted the sales force as of August 1982, although exhibit 3 shows eight. The eighth, Frank Howard, had been hired then fired during the last six months of 1981. "He was the stereotype of a good salesperson," explained Bob Piper, "and if he walked in here tomorrow, unknown, I'd hire him immediately. But selling print is unlike anything else and he couldn't handle it even though he'd sold office supplies very successfully previously. I don't know if he just didn't learn the business or was simply calling on the wrong customers. We really didn't try to find out. I shouldn't have hired him."

Bob Piper described his sales force as follows:

Gowan, Cassidy, and Moore have been around here a long time and were very close to J.N. They sell by being friendly, by using their personality. Oostermann is a technical man. He was one of our four customer men in the plant. Steele used to be an art director and took a degree years ago in graphic art designing. Waite used to sell for a paper company and is very creative in suggesting changes in a customer's specifications in order to get a job to fit the customer's budget.

Each of them has a favorite type of customer and is accustomed to being allowed to seek that type out. We don't organize the sales force in any way at all. It just sort of happens.

Most of the salespeople disliked prospecting. John Steele summed up the views of many of the men: "I dislike cold calls. I guess I'm lacking in self-confidence. I'm more of a service man than a stand-up salesperson. Besides, the new account bonus management has offered is a joke. It's much more important to reach quota around here."

Sales Compensation

Mark Cassidy spoke emotionally about the sales compensation programme:

We're paid a commission, with a salary plus a new account bonus and a very complicated method of payment for hours and keystrokes on concession sales. The whole thing is outlined in a 20-page document the Business Office prepared. J.N. never understood it, and if Piper does, he hasn't told us. All we know is that we get paid monthly, and it's always a surprise. I know my volume, but I'd need a C.A. to figure out my earnings. We get paid from 1 to 6.5 percent of billing price before taxes depending on the percent markup above manufacturing and sales department full costs. The higher the markup, the higher the commission rate.

Exhibit 3   Sales Force Statistics, 1980–1981

Salesperson	Age	Percent of Total Sales		Percent of Total Markup		Percent of Own Sales Concessioned	
		1980	1981	1980	1981	1980	1981
Mark Cassidy	48	7	10	11	15	27	25
Paul Gowan	56	12	14	9	11	30	33
J.N. Granger	—	20	—	5	—	50	—
Frank Howard	28	—	1	—	1	—	20
Roger Moore	52	12	15	10	10	20	22
Dan Oostermann	37	10	15	15	20	6	10
Bob Piper	43	15	20	20	10	10	40
John Steele	38	10	12	15	17	9	8
Wilf Waite	34	14	13	15	16	12	15
		100	100	100	100		

On contract sales and concession sales, we get paid a fixed amount per chargeable plant hour and another fixed amount per 15,000 key-strokes on the photocomp system. These concession rates are cut to two thirds during our four busy months, but contract rates stay the same.

We get anywhere from $25 to $250 for a new account, on top of our other compensation, depending on the size of the job. A new account is someone we haven't had for at least two years.

All our compensation is after the customer pays. I won't even get into the expense system. The company pays for authorized expenses, which means mileage and out-of-town costs mostly. It's really complicated. And, oh yes, if you miss quota three years in a row, you're fired, although that never happened with J.N.

Dan Oostermann added another concern:

In 1980, Moore and Steele sold almost the same volume, but Moore's contribution to total markup was two thirds of Steele's. That's because Moore sells lots on concession. The compensation system rewarded him within a couple of hundred dollars as much as it gave Steele and me. That's not right.

Bob Piper's Concerns

"Maybe David Lindsay is right about marketing. I'm not sure. His son, John, spent the summer here between years at university and submitted an interesting report last week." John dug through Davgraphics' dockets and other records and came up with the following data:

In 1980, 22 accounts were two thirds of our volume and in 1981, 28 accounts.

Our big accounts are declining in average size once we take out inflation over the past two years.

We only landed three accounts over $50,000 in 1980 and two last year; and 80 percent of our 1980 sales were from customers we had in 1979, and 82 percent of 1981 sales were from 1980 customers.

Our markups on financial printing are really dropping fast.

We're running less two-colour work. We're doing more four-colour and more one-colour.

It looks like our sales will be flat and our markups down for all of 1982.

"That isn't a bright picture. And the Graphic Arts Association says we'll see price increases of 6–11 percent next year but cost increases of 10–15 percent. We've just got to get volume up, but how?"

CHAPTER IX
MARKETING
COMMUNICATIONS DECISIONS

Marketing communications are the most visible and controversial activity carried on in marketing. The three main components of the marketing communications "mix" are advertising, sales promotion, and personal selling.

All of chapter 8 was devoted to personal selling and sales management because they are central components of almost any marketing strategy. However, this chapter focuses largely on advertising and sales promotion. Advertising and sales promotion can be defined as all paid, nonpersonal forms of communication that are identified with a specific sponsor. Advertising includes expenditures on radio, television, newspaper, magazines, billboards, and the yellow pages in the telephone directory. Sales promotion includes all forms of incentives such as free goods, coupons, case allowances, display allowances, sampling, demonstrations, gift items, contests, and savings stamps. Traditionally, the largest absolute dollar spenders on advertising and sales promotion tend to be big consumer products companies, such as General Foods and General Motors, followed by the federal and provincial governments. Recently, the federal government has moved to the top of the list of largest spenders. The industries that spend the highest percentage of their sales on advertising are in the drug, cosmetic, packaged food, and soap/detergent businesses.

Conceptual Framework

Each element of the marketing mix must support the product positioning. This becomes most clear whenever we attempt to communicate our products' "package of benefits" to the wholesalers, retailers, and the target segment of buyers. In chapter 4, we developed a process for positioning a product. In this chapter, we are going to elaborate on the communications aspect and add seven more steps (exhibit 1).

Exhibit 1 The Process of Marketing Communications Decisions

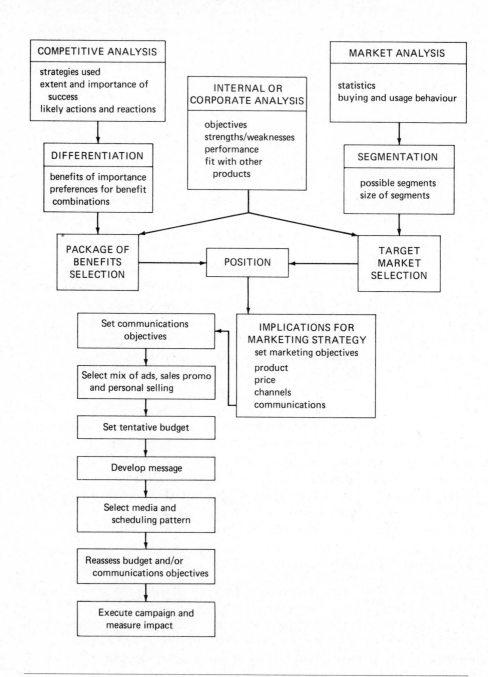

In developing a marketing communications strategy, we have to make decisions on the communication objectives; the communications "mix" of advertising, promotion and personal selling; the budget; message; media; and measurements of campaign effectiveness. As we review each decision in developing the communications programme, we can follow the seven steps listed below and make adjustments until we have all the components in harmony.

1. Set communications objectives
2. Select an appropriate mix of advertising, sales promotion, and personal selling.
3. Set tentative budget.
4. Develop message.
5. Select media vehicles and scheduling pattern.
6. Reassess budget and/or communications objectives.
7. Execute campaign and measure impact.

1. Set Communications Objectives

Communications objectives should be stated in quantifiable terms with a specific time period with reference to a specific target segment or audience. We will establish marketing objectives in terms of profits, sales, or share of market. For new products or relaunches, it is particularly useful to establish more specific communications objectives and actually to measure awareness, trial, and adoption or repeat purchase because it may provide important data for adjustments in communications or other elements of the marketing mix. For example, if awareness is low, we may have a communications problem; but if repeat purchase is low, we may have a product problem. We recognize that awareness of the product will be greater than *interest,* which will be greater than *evaluation,* which will be greater than trial or adoption. Chart 1 shows a possible set of communication response curves over time for a new product.

Communication objectives must be stated in precise, measurable terms. An objective such as "increase brand awareness" is too imprecise to be useful; an operational statement would be "achieve brand awareness and knowledge of the brand's major benefit among 85 percent of all women in the eighteen-to-forty age category within the next six months." The second statement is operational because it can be measured. In six months, a market researcher could conduct a survey to establish whether or not the objectives have been met.

Chart 1   Communication Response Curves for a New Product

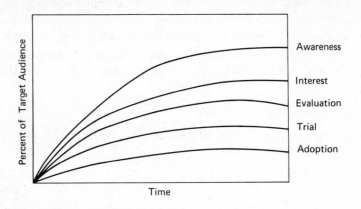

2. Select a Mix of Advertising, Sales Promotion, and Personal Selling

Some elements of the communications mix are more effective than others for particular purposes. For example, advertising is an efficient tool to create awareness of a brand and its major benefit. Sales promotion is an effective and efficient tool to obtain evaluation and trial of a product. Personal selling is *effective* in all phases of the communications hierarchy because it is human and one of the few forms of two-way communications; but because of its relatively high cost "per message delivered," marketers of consumer goods use personal selling primarily to secure the acceptance of channel members. However, in industrial marketing, personal selling plays the major role in the communications mix because the target market is identifiable, reachable, and limited in numbers, and the product may require explanation. In service marketing, the communications effort of the salesperson is frequently difficult to separate from the actual provision of the service, as in hair salons and consulting, for example. Chart 2 attempts to match the elements of the communications mix with the objectives they fulfill most efficiently.

3. Set Tentative Budget

Communication budgets are difficult to set because we have only a general idea of what response a dollar's worth of advertising or a dollar's worth of sales promotion will buy. That is why executives have adopted rule-of-thumb methods such as (1) the "all we can afford" method, (2) the percentage of sales method, and (3) the matching competitors method. For any significant budget, we prefer a fourth approach, the task method, which is to define the communications tasks we hope to accomplish and then to calculate the required budget. We prefer the task method because the process of developing the budget has logic to it, and focusing on tasks can lead to more rigorous thought and measurements.

The "all we can afford" method is weak because we may spend far too much or not nearly enough to make any significant impact. Setting a communications budget as some percent of this year's forecast sales (or last year's sales) has the merits of (1) controlling communications expenses, (2) relating this percentage to some published industry standard, and (3) taking almost no executive time to set the budget because there is little logic for debate. The main problem with the method is that it seldom focuses on the tasks to be done, and again we could be overspending or underspending. Matching competitors' budgets assumes that our situation is identical

Chart 2   Hierarchy of Communications Objectives and Communications Mix (typical examples)

Objective	Consumer Goods	Industrial Goods	Wholesalers and Retailers
Awareness	Media advertising	Trade journal advertising Personal selling	Trade journal Personal selling
Interest	Media advertising Direct mail	Publicity Direct mail Personal selling Data sheets Token gifts	Direct mail Personal selling
Evaluation	Demonstrations Comparative advertising Package	Visit suppliers' plant Data sheets Personal selling Token gifts	Supplier completes form for new listings Personal selling Token gifts
Trial	Free sample Coupons Price-off on package Personal selling contests	Test run in buyer's plant Personal selling	Case allowances Free goods Co-op advertising Display allowances
Adoption	Reassuring media advertising Package	Publicity Personal selling	Personal selling Co-op advertising Case allowances

to theirs and that they know what they are doing. One or neither may be true.

The task method of budgeting begins with a full consideration of the product positioning and proceeds to look at what type of response we might get for varying levels of communication spending (chart 3). If we know the general shape of that response curve and the contribution per unit from the product, we can set a budget that maximizes net contribution.

Several interesting phenomena are represented in the response curve in chart 3. First, there is no sales response until we reach a minimum level of spending on communication. Second, after $800,000, further expenditures actually led to a decline in sales. Unbelievable? The Anheuser-Busch brewery in the United States found that it was overspending on advertising and that by reducing their advertising expenditures, sales actually went up! Therefore, we must try to judge what the best response range will be. This is a decision in which we can use the assistance of an experienced product manager, sales manager, or account executive in an advertising agency.

4. Develop Message

The message should communicate a package of benefits to a target audience—the positioning of the product. Message development is the most critical step in establishing a particular positioning. But the message must not only communicate a distinct package of benefits, it must capture the attention and interest of the audience, and it must *persuade* the people in the target audience. With so many competing messages, we will have to be creative to gain someone's attention. The specialists who generate messages that command attention, communicate benefits, and persuade are

Chart 3   Possible Sales Response Curve to Advertising Expenditure

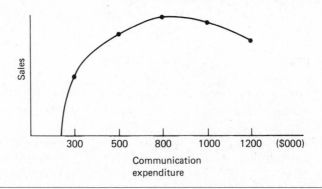

the creative people in an advertising agency. They develop their ideas inside a rigorous framework of a written positioning statement and a written copy strategy that spells out the target audience, the unique benefits of the product, the supporting evidence for the product claims, the special needs (such as colour impact or demonstration), and the desired tone, pace, and style of the communication. Even with all these guidelines, it takes great judgment to evaluate the potential effectiveness of the communication piece. Typically, two creative executions will be "on strategy," but the real difficulty is to judge their relative effectiveness. Experience may be our best friend in that kind of decision.

5. Select Media and Scheduling Pattern

We face three basic decisions: the selection of broad classes of media, the selection of specific media vehicles, and the scheduling pattern for each medium. In selecting broad classes of media, we will try to match the characteristics of the target audience with the user profiles of a variety of specific media vehicles. We can do this subject to two constraints: the creative execution and the size of the communication budget. For example, a particular theme may be better suited to print media because there is a good deal of copy and a coupon.

The second stage involves the selection of specific media vehicles, such as CFL football games or the Beachcombers. There are a number of considerations in selecting a particular vehicle, such as the match with the target audience and the efficiency of the vehicle. Specific vehicles can be compared on the basis of cost per thousand persons in the target audience who are reached. We can adjust audience size to allow for duplication between vehicles and calculate cost per thousand persons reached. We may continue this process until the budget is used up. Fortunately for us, computer algorithms have been developed to handle the many calculations made in this process.

In the third stage, we must decide the media weight and whether to (1) allocate our messages continuously throughout the period, (2) concentrate our messages in one short interval, or (3) send out bursts of messages intermittently throughout the period. Advertising executives use the concept of gross rating point (GRP) for weight and allocation decisions. A gross rating point is defined as the frequency of exposure times the percent of the target audience reached. The experts in the media department of an advertising agency may be able to apply their experience, but we might try some experiments to learn what makes the most sense for our products.

6. Reassess Budget and/or Communication Objectives

After we have allocated our budget to a schedule of specific vehicles, we should try to assess whether that schedule will meet the communications objectives we set in the first step. For example, if the objective for the target segment in the first year was 60 percent awareness, but our mix and schedule of communications appear to deliver only 40 percent awareness, we can increase our budget or lower our objectives.

7. Execute Campaign and Measure Impact

The final steps are preparation for executing the campaign and for measuring the impact. The measurement steps are the ones most frequently forgotten by managers, presumably because of the feeling that once the campaign is over, measurements cost money and there would not be much to gain but plenty to lose if the campaign was shown to have been a disaster. True, sales, share, and profit measures will be available, but it will be difficult to isolate the specific part the marketing communications contributed to meeting those objectives. Hence the need for specific *communications* objectives and measurements in order to determine how well we did so that we can do even better the next time.

Summary

In this chapter, we began with product positioning and showed how the communications strategy must support the product positioning. Then we described a sequence of seven steps we can use to develop a consistent and effective communications strategy. By harnessing our creative energies within these guidelines, we can develop effective marketing communications.

38 Kingston Transit System: "KATY's Boys. We're On Our Way"

"KATY" was the personified name of the *Kingston Transit System* (K.T.S.). "KATY'S Boys" were the drivers of the buses. "KATY'S Boys. We're on our way" was a slogan designed to spearhead an advertising campaign promoting ridership on the K.T.S.

The KATY campaign, as it was commonly called, was an extensive marketing and research programme financed by the Ontario Ministry of Transportation and Communications (M.T.C.) to measure the effectiveness and potential of using marketing principles and techniques to promote a public transit system. The KATY advertising campaign, a part of this programme, was carried out from September 1974 to May 1975.

At the conclusion of the marketing programme, there was some question among members of the Public Utilities Commission (P.U.C.), the elected officials responsible for K.T.S., as to how much the programme actually contributed to increased ridership. As a result, the P.U.C. officials decided not to contribute to the cost of continuing the programme for a further six months as desired by M.T.C. The programme was consequently terminated on June 25, 1975.

In the summer of 1977, P.U.C. officials were reviewing the results of several studies that focused on the KATY campaign in order to make a decision about whether or not to include a significant advertising component in the next K.T.S. budget.

Background on Kingston

The city of Kingston is located on the northeastern shore of Lake Ontario at the head of the St. Lawrence River. In 1974, the city had a population of 60,425 living in a largely urbanized 11-square-mile area. The city consisted of a healthy and active downtown area of commercial retail establishments. A basically radial arterial road pattern connected the downtown with several peripheral activity centres, including light industrial complexes, a community college, shopping plazas, and suburban housing communities. Kingston was also the home of a major Canadian educational institution—Queen's University. Along with several other locations, monuments, events, and activities, it recounted the traditions and historical past of Kingston as a former military stronghold and guardian of the St. Lawrence water routes.

Background and Objectives of the Kingston Transit System's Marketing Programme

Generally, most efforts to improve transit service to the community and to increase ridership were through changes to the major operating variables of the system. For example, routes, headways, and fare structures were sometimes changed; and in several cities, demand-responsive dial-a-bus systems and other special services had been introduced. These changes were all aimed at making transit more convenient to use and it was hoped that they would lead to increased ridership.

While these types of changes were undoubtedly important, there were other steps that management could take to increase ridership. Some of these steps were termed by transit management as the "marketing approach." By this, they meant an integrated effort to identify consumer needs, position products and services to meet these needs, and develop advertising and promotion programmes to communicate the products and services to the consumers. While this approach was commonly used in most consumer product and consumer service companies, its value in public transit operations was still questioned.

The M.T.C., in association with K.T.S., decided to undertake a carefully monitored demonstration project to examine the effects of a marketing programme on transit ridership. Specifically, the project was to:

1. prepare and execute a well-designed and integrated information, advertising, and promotion programme for Kingston Transit and

2. determine the effect of the marketing programme on ridership, riders' attitudes, and revenues of the system over a defined period of time.

The consulting firm of Peter Barnard Associates and the advertising agency of McKim/Benton and Bowles Ltd. were commissioned to manage this project. To achieve the objectives, a marketing programme consisting of three elements was developed. The elements were:

1. A Distinctive, Overall Advertising Approach or Theme

A vital need was to overcome the lack of public awareness of the system (almost amounting to apathy) by creating an entirely new and exciting image for K.T.S. The new image created the K.T.S. centred on the initials "KT," which, when extended to "KATY" was a personification of the transit system in the vehicle itself. The identification of the drivers as "KATY'S Boys" provided a further marketing opportunity. The accompanying slogan used with all promotional and advertising materials was "KATY'S Boys. We're on our way."

2. A New Package of Transit Service Information

This package included new "hardware" such as bus stop signs and route maps as well as information-oriented advertising. This part of the programme was aimed at communicating as clearly and precisely as possible how to get around Kingston by bus. It emphasized routes, destinations, and schedules. Each of the six fixed routes in the City of Kingston was colour-coded on the new route maps, on new bus stop signs, and on new on-bus destination signs.

New route map—The KATY guide. A new single page fold-out map was developed containing colour-coded information on all bus routes and schedules, a street index for the city, fare structures, details on the operation of the evening dial-a-bus and fixed route services and schedules, a listing of places of importance, and an explanation of the new bus stop signs and bus destination signs. The guide was distributed to all households and was available on the buses and in local retail establishments such as stores, gas stations, and banks.

KATY line. A telephone information service, separate from the general Public Utilities Commission phone number, was established to provide specific transit information to those who were uncertain about the use of the Kingston Transit System. The special phone line, 544-KATY, provided a visible and easily remembered number and was advertised as part of the overall KATY campaign theme. The person (female) who answered the phone was referred to as "KATY's Lady."

New bus stop signs. In order to help reduce passenger waiting times and thereby improve the attractiveness of Kingston Transit, a new bus stop sign was developed. Shown in exhibit 1, the bus stop sign was colour-coded by route and had on it the scheduled bus arrival time at the particular bus stop location.

Large route guide displays. A 3' × 4' full-colour copy of the KATY Guide was displayed at high activity areas in the city.

On-bus signs. A sign, colour-coded for each route, was located in the front of each bus to provide a clear description of the bus's destination.

Dial-a-bus lift line. A direct line to the evening dial-a-bus dispatcher was installed at the downtown transfer point and at one of the major shopping plazas.

3. A Campaign of Persuasion

This campaign was aimed at overcoming the negative feelings of infrequent bus users by convincing them of the benefits that Kingston Transit had to offer. It was scheduled for launching on September 15, 1974, and was divided into three components:

teaser campaign	2 weeks
launch campaign	8 weeks
sustaining campaign	28 weeks

The scheduling of the various marketing and advertising elements is shown in exhibit 2.

The teaser campaign preceded the September 15, 1974, launch date and consisted of two teaser ads. One displayed the word *KATY* without explanation and was run daily for a one-week period; the second showed the launch date *KATY, September 15* and was run daily in the second week.

On the launch date of September 15, a two-page ad appeared in the Kingston local newspaper. The ad introduced the new "KT" logo, "KATY's Boys. We're on our way." At the same time, the radio advertising campaign began with 60–second radio commercials. These ran continuously throughout the launch and sustaining campaign periods. A total of five radio commercials were developed; the scripts for one of them is shown in exhibit 3. The radio commercials were developed around the central KATY theme and incorporated a catchy jingle based upon an old vaudeville song, "K–K–K–KATY."

After the initial two-page newspaper spread, several single-page and smaller-size newspaper ads appeared. These dealt basically with the new

Exhibit 1   KATY Campaign Route Map, Bus Sign

KATY's Guide to Kingston

KINGSTON TRANSIT

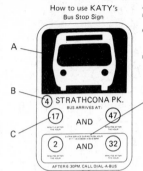

How to use KATY's
Bus Stop Sign

A ⎯⎯

B ⎯⎯

C ⎯⎯

D ⎯⎯

(4) STRATHCONA PK.
BUS ARRIVES AT:

(17)   AND   (47)

(2)   AND   (32)

AFTER 6.30PM. CALL DIAL-A-BUS

A. Bus silhouette...Colour coded for each route.

B. Number & Name...For easy identification of the route.

C. X minutes after the hour...Approximate time the bus will arrive at that stop. For example this sign states that the bus will stop there at 17 minutes and 47 minutes after each hour. (2 buses per hour.)

D. Extra Service during rush hour...Besides arriving at scheduled times (in this example, 17 minutes and 47 minutes after every hour) extra buses will be in service during posted rush-hours (in this example, 2 minutes and 32 minutes after every hour). (4 buses per hour.)

KATY's Fares

Adults . . . . 25¢ or 5 tickets for $1.00
Senior Citizens .25¢ or 20 tickets for $1.00
Students . . . . . . 15¢ or 4 tickets for 50¢
(Dial-A-Bus fare...10¢ extra)

The above fares are applicable to all of KATY's routes within Kingston.
Transfers are available on all buses for changing to intersecting routes and are subject to the conditions printed on the reverse side of each transfer.

How does "Dial-A-Bus" work?

Dial-A-Bus has been extended into new areas of the city and is now available in the whole of the city.

The city has been divided into 5 zones and buses have been allocated to each zone and will provide service every 30 minutes to any part of that zone. These 30 minute periods are known as "cycles".

All buses start from the dispatch office at the Shopping Centre or the Downtown Transfer Area at the beginning of a cycle and return there by the end of the cycle. During a cycle, each bus filter through the assigned zone, stopping at a number of addresses where pick-up has been requested. Passengers who boarded the bus earlier at the Shopping Centre or the Downtown Transfer Area at the beginning of the cycle will be dropped off at their requested destination. Once a bus has completed its run, it returns to the Shopping Centre or the Downtown Transfer Area by the shortest route ready to start out again to serve more passengers in the next cycle.

Passengers who wish to travel between two places within the same zone will not need to make a transfer but will be carried to their destination on the same bus.

Passengers who wish to travel from one zone to the other or to the "fixed routes" will transfer at the Shopping Centre or the Downtown Transfer Area to the bus operating in that zone.

Places of Importance in Kingston

	Address	Nearest Route
Municipal Buildings		
P.U.C. Offices and Service Centre	Counter St.	(2)
Kingston Memorial Centre	York	(3)
City Hall	Ontario St.	All Routes
Hospitals		
Kingston General Hospital	Stuart St.	(2)
Hotel Dieu Hospital	Sydenham St.	All Routes
St. Mary's on the lake Hospital	King St. W.	(2)
Ogwanada Hospital	Princess St.	(1) & (2)
Provincial and Federal Buildings		
Federal Gov't Bldg.	Clarence St.	All Routes
Provincial Gov't Bldg.	Princess St.	All Routes
General Post Office	Clarence St.	All Routes
Transportation		
Kingston Transit System	King St.	All Routes
Voyageur-Colonial Terminal	Division St.	(2)
Ferry-Wolfe Island	Brock St.	All Routes
Entertainment		
Hyland Cinema	Princess St.	All Routes
Odeon Cinema	Princess St.	All Routes
Capitol Cinema	Princess St.	All Routes
Grand Theatre	Princess St.	All Routes
Domino Theatre	Princess St.	All Routes
Tent Theatre(July/Aug.)	City Park	(2)
General Interest		
Pump House Steam Museum	Ontario St.	(3)
Sir J.A. MacDonald House	Centre St.	(2) & (3)
Kingston Penitentiary	King St. W.	(2)
Prison For Women	Palace Rd.	(2) & (3)
Queen's University	University Ave.	(2)
St. Lawrence College	King St. W.	(2) & (3)
Hockey Hall of Fame	York and Alfred	(3)
County of Frontenac Court House	Court St.	(2)

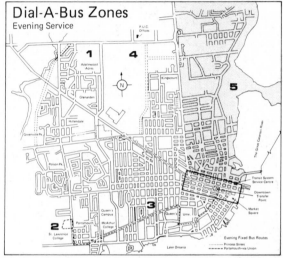

Dial-A-Bus Zones
Evening Service

Evening Fixed Bus Routes
(after 6:30 p.m.)

Route 2-Portsmouth

First bus leaves Central Business District	6:30 p.m.
Last bus leaves Central Business District	11:00 p.m.
First bus leaves St. Lawrence College	6:15 p.m.
Last bus leaves St. Lawrence College	11:15 p.m.

Route 4-Princess St.
(Downtown to Shopping Centre Only)

First bus leaves Downtown to Shopping Centre	6:30 p.m.
Last bus leaves Downtown to Shopping Centre	11:00 p.m.
First bus leaves Shopping Centre to Downtown	6:45 p.m.
Last bus leaves Shopping Centre to Downtown	11:15 p.m.

Dial-A-Bus Fares:

Appropriate Ticket plus 10¢ cash or cash fares:

Adults	35¢
Senior Citizens	35¢
Students	25¢

Call 544-4441 for Dial-A-Bus information and pick-up.

Charter Service

Kingston Transit has buses with capacities of 17 to 45 seats available for public charter. Some are equipped with public address systems. All come with KATY'S professional drivers. For more information on charter services available through KATY, call 544-KATY.

Destination Signs

Via Downtown

In the front window of each bus will be a sign indicating whether the bus is heading towards the downtown area or towards the shopping centre.

If you need help
call
544-KATY

KATY's Boys.
We're on our way.

Exhibit 2 Advertising Blocking Chart

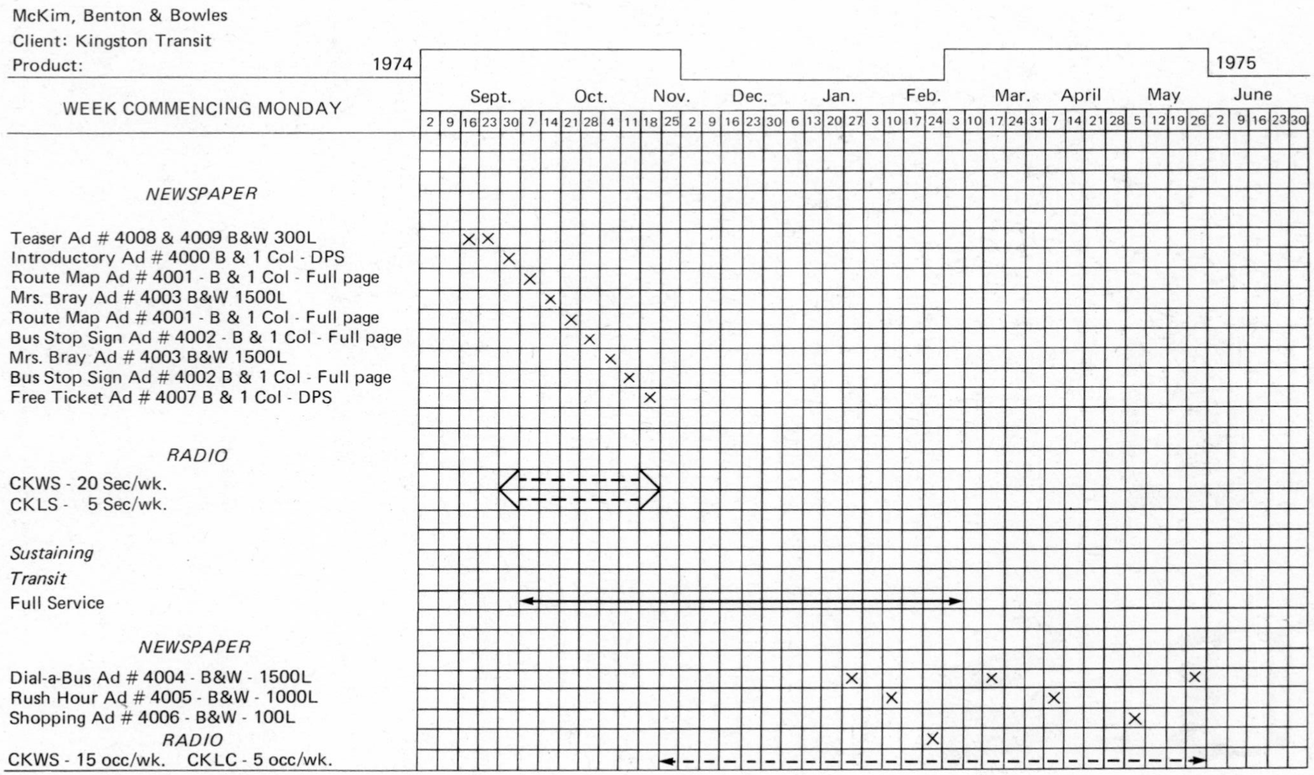
McKim, Benton & Bowles
Client: Kingston Transit
Product:
1974
1975
WEEK COMMENCING MONDAY
Sept.
Oct.
Nov.
Dec.
Jan.
Feb.
Mar.
April
May
June
2 9 16 23 30 7 14 21 28 4 11 18 25 2 9 16 23 30 6 13 20 27 3 10 17 24 3 10 17 24 31 7 14 21 28 5 12 19 26 2 9 16 23 30
NEWSPAPER
Teaser Ad # 4008 & 4009 B&W 300L
Introductory Ad # 4000 B & 1 Col - DPS
Route Map Ad # 4001 - B & 1 Col - Full page
Mrs. Bray Ad # 4003 B&W 1500L
Route Map Ad # 4001 - B & 1 Col - Full page
Bus Stop Sign Ad # 4002 - B & 1 Col - Full page
Mrs. Bray Ad # 4003 B&W 1500L
Bus Stop Sign Ad # 4002 B & 1 Col - Full page
Free Ticket Ad # 4007 B & 1 Col - DPS
RADIO
CKWS - 20 Sec/wk.
CKLS - 5 Sec/wk.
Sustaining
Transit
Full Service
NEWSPAPER
Dial-a-Bus Ad # 4004 - B&W - 1500L
Rush Hour Ad # 4005 - B&W - 1000L
Shopping Ad # 4006 - B&W - 100L
RADIO
CKWS - 15 occ/wk. CKLC - 5 occ/wk.

Exhibit 3 KATY Campaign Radio Script

Publicite McKim Advertising

client KINGSTON TRANSIT

prod./div. Introductory Commercial 2

identification Bus Stop & Route Map

docket no./dossier

length/longueur 60 Sec.

date August 22, 1974

MUSIC:	KATY's THEME
ANNCR:	KATY's new bus stop signs make missing the bus a thing of the past.
SFX:	TRAFFIC
WOMAN:	I missed a bus just yesterday. Almost ran into his rear end. Oh, excuse me.
ANNCR:	KATY's new bus stop signs tell you exactly when the next bus will arrive to make it easier than ever to catch the bus.
SFX:	WATER FRONT. WATER-LOGGED BOOTS SQUISHING TOWARD US.
H. COSELL:	. . . here comes Doug Bass, whom you may remember as the winner of last years big fish trophy award. Doug, tell us, did you catch anything today?
DOUG:	Yeah. The bus.
H. COSELL:	The bus?
DOUG:	The bus. It's the only thing worth catching today.
MUSIC:	KATY's THEME
ANNCR:	In addition to new bus stop signs, KATY's new route map will get you anywhere you want to go in Kingston.
MAN:	Cum wiz me to zee Casbah.
WOMAN:	Is that on KATY's route map?
MAN:	Zee Casbah? No.
WOMAN:	Then I'm not going.
ANNCR:	KATY's new route map gives you all the information you'd want on bus departures, transfer points, fares, and schedules. Keep yours on hand. For getting around Kingston, it's a step in the right direction.
MUSIC:	KATY's THEME
ANNCR:	KATY's BOYS. We're on our way.

information service: a route map explanatory ad and a bus stop sign explanatory ad. All graphics were designed to support the new image and the system logos and slogans. While the initial advertising was designed to help build an image, later advertising was designed merely to provide information. Two of the launch ads are shown in exhibits 4 and 5.

After the launch phase of the marketing campaign, several radio and newspaper ads were developed for, and directed toward, the infrequent rider. The purpose of this advertising was to change negative attitudes and emphasize the benefits of riding the bus. Relaxation, convenience, and adherence to schedules were featured. One of these newspaper ads is shown in exhibit 6.

The cost of the total marketing programme was $115,383. A breakdown of the costs is given in exhibit 7.

Exhibit 4   KATY Campaign Launch Ad

Meet
KATY.

Meet KATY's
boys.

Exhibit 5 KATY Campaign Launch Ad

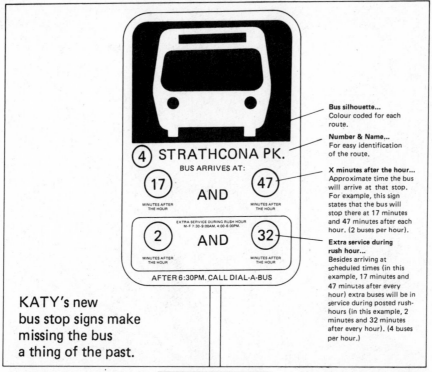

Bus silhouette...
Colour coded for each route.

Number & Name...
For easy identification of the route.

X minutes after the hour...
Approximate time the bus will arrive at that stop. For example, this sign states that the bus will stop there at 17 minutes and 47 minutes after each hour. (2 buses per hour).

Extra service during rush hour...
Besides arriving at scheduled times (in this example, 17 minutes and 47 minutes after every hour) extra buses will be in service during posted rush-hours (in this example, 2 minutes and 32 minutes after every hour). (4 buses per hour.)

KATY's new bus stop signs make missing the bus a thing of the past.

Easy. That's what we want bus riding in Kingston to be.

So we've made KATY's new bus stop signs easy to see, and easy to understand.

For starters, we colour-coded each bus route, and gave it a special name and number. And that same colour, name, and number, is what you'll find on each bus stop sign along the route. That way you know you're heading in the right direction.

But being in the right place is no good without being there at the right time. So we added times to each bus stop sign as well. In this instance, KATY will arrive every half hour

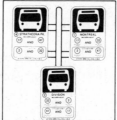

at 17 minutes and 47 minutes after the hour (give or take a couple of minutes).

Plus, during rush hours, there are buses in addition to the regular scheduled service. So we've let you know that at 2 minutes and 32 minutes after the hour KATY will be here again. That's a bus every 15 minutes or a total of four buses per hour during rush hours.

If more than one bus stops here, there'll be more than one bus stop sign.

That's easy.

Now you can always be at the right place at the right time. And still take it easy.

KATY's Boys. We're on our way.

KINGSTON TRANSIT

Exhibit 6   KATY Campaign Sustaining Ad

If you hate to take
your wife shopping,
Walter Stephens will be glad to.

But then so will Bob, Jim, Bill, in fact all of KATY's boys. Because the one thing they all have in common is they love to take ladies shopping.

And experience has taught KATY's boys that bus drivers with ladies on board need to be a little extra courteous (those big parcels sometimes need a helping hand). They need to be a little extra friendly and understanding. And as always they need to be prompt.

You've told us you really appreciate that. But then there are a few other things we're doing this year we think you'll appreciate. We've added times to our bus stop signs, so you'll know just when the bus is arriving. We've added colour codes, numbers and names to each sign so you know you're at the right stop. And we've added window signs to make it clear just where KATY's going.

After 6:30 when the regular bus routes go off, Dial-A-Bus will still take you to your door, so you won't have to call it a day shopping until 11:30 p.m.

Now what could be easier.

You'll have to admit, when it comes to shopping, KATY's boys are really easy going.

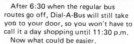

**KATY's Boys.
We're on our way.**

Kingston Transit

Exhibit 7 The Costs of the Marketing Programme

	$ Amount	Percentage
Development and management (consultants)	$ 24,917	21.6
Hardware—signs, bus logos, etc.	22,718	19.7
Community information package route guides, display maps, lift phones	21,161	18.3
Advertising and promotions (September 30/74–May 2/75)	46,587	40.4
	$115,383	100.0

Marketing Research

Some preliminary marketing research was conducted to identify the potential for transit marketing in Kingston and to prepare a proposal to be used to measure its effect.

The consultants, Peter Barnard Associates, began their work with a preliminary study of the kinds of trips people were making in Kingston, their transit usage patterns, and their attitudes toward transit. This research also determined the awareness and attitudes toward public transportation held by Kingston residents. The data for this preliminary study were gathered from a telephone survey of a random sample of Kingston households, a survey of Kingston Transit drivers, and focus group discussions held with various groups of citizens. The study was conducted in November and December 1973.

A second study conducted by the M.T.C. was designed to monitor the effects of the KATY campaign. Three cities demographically similar (see exhibit 8) to Kingston were chosen as control cities for the purposes of comparing ridership trends and public attitude toward transit. This study was conducted simultaneously in the four cities, measures being taken in December 1974 and May and June 1975.

A third study completed by a class of Queen's University Commerce undergraduate students replicated and extended much of the Barnard research. This research was compiled and completed in the fall of 1976. The longitudinal nature (exhibit 9) of the data from the three research projects provided the Public Utilities Commission officials with an opportunity to gauge the effectiveness of the KATY campaign. Exhibits 10 and 11 contain the responses of the Kingston populace at different points in time. Exhibit 12 provides data on transit usage and the degree to which riders are captive users of transit for respondents in Kingston and the control cities. Exhibit 13 contains actual ridership data for the four cities.

Exhibit 8 Basic Demographic and Transit System Characteristics
of Kingston and Three Control Cities

	Kingston	*Guelph*	*Peterborough*	*Brantford*
Population (1974)	60,482	64,100	56,923	63,035
Growth 1968–1973	5.6%	18.5%	2.9%	2.2%
Land area (sq. mi.)	10.97	26.45	20.46	17.45
Employment (1974 est)	34,407	24,704	25,665	23,669
Dwelling units (1971)	18,500	17,570	18,810	19,415
Population density (persons/sq. mi.)	5,513	2,423	2,782	3,594
Average total income per family ($) (1971)	10,379	10,677	10,637	9,515
Car ownership (1973)				
Vehicle/person	0.63	0.53	0.56	0.52
Vehicle/dwelling unit	1.88	1.70	1.65	1.67
Miles of roads (1976)	107.5	198.2	184.3	195.4
Arterial road pattern	Radial	Radial	Radial	Radial
Number of bus routes	6 + Evenings Dial-a-bus	13	10 + Trans Cab	16
Bus fleet size (1975)	39	33	32	24
Headways (min)				
Peak hours	15	30	30	30
Off-peak hours	30	30	30	30
Revenue miles (1975)	890,555	921,384	795,901	763,882
Ridership (1975)	3,611,540	4,248,417	2,273,648	2,127,306
Weekday hours of service	6:30 A.M.– 11:30 P.M.	6:15 A.M.– 11:45 P.M.	6:15 A.M.– 12:15 P.M.	6:00 A.M.– 11:30 P.M.
Adult fare (Jan. '76)				
Cash ($)	0.25	0.35	0.25	0.25
Ticket ($)	0.25	0.25	N/A	0.255
Days of service	M–F, Sat.	M–F, Sat.	M–F, Sat.	M–F, Sat.

Exhibit 9 Sequence of Events Pertinent to the KATY Campaign

Nov.–Dec. 1973	Barnard Market Research
September 1974	KATY Campaign Began
December 1974 May 1975 June 1975	M.T.C. Market Research
June 1975	KATY Campaign Discontinued
October 1976	Queen's Commerce Students Market Research

Exhibit 10 Pre-KATY Barnard (1973) and Post-KATY
Queen's (1976) Results to Similar Questions

Question: How would you say you get around Kingston most often?

Method of Transportation	Pre-KATY (1973) % of sample	Post-KATY (1976) % of sample
Bus	13.0	18.7
Car, drive myself	56.0	55.4
Car, someone else drives	12.0	8.2
Taxi	4.0	2.6
Walking	18.0	12.7
Other	1.0	2.2
	100.0	100.0
	(*n* = 200)	(*n* = 227)

$\chi^2 = 5.804$ degrees of freedom = 5

significance = 0.3257

Question: In the past three or four months, how often have you used the bus?

Frequency	Pre-KATY (1973) % of sample	Post-KATY (1976) % of sample
Not at all	56.0	48.9
Once or twice	8.0	10.1
Once a month	7.0	4.8
Twice a month	7.0	5.3
Once a week	5.0	5.3
Twice a week	5.0	5.7
Three times a week	2.0	5.7
Every working day	8.0	8.8
Every day or more	2.0	5.3
	100.0	100.0
	(*n* = 200)	(*n* = 227)

$\chi^2 = 9.890$ degrees of freedom = 8

significance = 0.2729

Exhibit 10 (continued)

Statement: I would never use the bus regularly
no matter how much they improve the service.

	Pre-KATY (1973) % of sample	Post-KATY (1976) % of sample
Really agree	16.0	19.9
Agree a bit	10.0	9.4
No particular feeling	14.0	7.8
Disagree a bit	19.0	18.4
Really disagree	41.0	44.5
	100.0	100.0
	(n = 200)	(n = 256)

$\chi^2 = 5.428$ degrees of freedom = 4

significance = 0.2461

Statement: It is easy to get around Kingston by bus.

	Pre-KATY (1973) % of sample	Post-KATY (1976) % of sample
Really agree	36.0	23.0
Agree a bit	17.0	27.3
No particular feeling	12.0	17.6
Disagree a bit	16.0	18.8
Really disagree	19.0	13.3
	100.0	100.0
	(n = 200)	(n = 256)

$\chi^2 = 16.943$ degrees of freedom = 4

significance = 0.0020

Statement: I've never really bothered to find out details about the bus service here.

	Pre-KATY (1973) % of sample	Post-KATY (1976) % of sample
Really agree	40.0	33.2
Agree a bit	13.0	19.1
No particular feeling	13.0	9.8
Disagree a bit	13.0	17.6
Really disagree	21.0	20.3
	100.0	100.0
	(n = 200)	(n = 256)

$\chi^2 = 6.595$ degrees of freedom = 4

significance = 0.1589

Exhibit 10 (continued)

Statement: In the future, people here will be more inclined to use the bus.

	Pre-KATY (1973) % of sample	Post-KATY (1976) % of sample
Really agree	60.0	20.7
Agree a bit	18.0	28.9
No particular feeling	15.0	30.1
Disagree a bit	4.0	13.7
Really disagree	3.0	6.6
	100.0	100.0
	(n = 200)	(n = 256)
	χ^2 = 76.207	degrees of freedom = 4

significance = 0.0000

Question: Thinking of the local Kingston bus system now, do you have any particular criticism to make of the system?

	Pre-KATY % of sample	Post-KATY % of sample
Yes	33	36.3
No	67	63.7
	100	100.0
	(n = 200)	(n = 267)
	χ^2 = 0.421	degrees of freedom = 1

significance = 0.5164

Statement: The bus system is confusing.

	Pre-KATY % of sample	Post-KATY % of sample
Really agree	18.0	11.7
Agree a bit	12.0	13.7
No particular feeling	24.0	24.6
Disagree a bit	18.0	21.5
Really disagree	28.0	28.5
	100.0	100.0
	(n = 200)	(n = 256)
	χ^2 = 4.014	degrees of freedom = 4

significance = 0.4041

Exhibit 11   Comparison of 1973 Barnard, 1975 M.T.C., and 1976 Queen's Responses to Similar Questions

	Pre-KATY (Barnard 1973)	KATY (M.T.C. Monitoring Report 1975)	Post-KATY (Queen's 1976)
I would never use the bus no matter how much they improve.	26%[a]	32%	29%
Might use bus if it were simpler to obtain information about schedules.	35%	13%	
Important to me that my home be close to good bus service.	67%	67%	
Think that in the future people here will be more inclined to use the bus.	78%	64%	50%
	(n = 200)	(n = 371)	(n = 256)

a.   Read: Of the total sample, 26% either said they ''Agree a bit'' or ''Really agree'' to the statement.

Exhibit 12 Comparison of Kingston Bus Ridership to That of Control Cities (M.T.C. 1974–1975)

	Ridership History of Current Transit Users							
	Kingston		Guelph		Peterborough		Brantford	
	December 1974	June 1975	December 1974	June 1975	December 1974	June 1975	December 1974	June 1975
How long have you used (name) Transit for at least one round trip a month?								
a) this is my first trip	2%	2%	1%	2%	2%	2%	1%	1%
b) I generally use the bus for less than 1 trip a month	5	6	8	8	7	8	8	12
c) less than 3 months	7	4	8	8	5	5	6	4
d) 3–6 months	15	9	8	8	8	7	8	5
e) 7–12 months	6	9	8	8	5	9	5	5
f) 1–2 years	16	15	15	15	14	14	9	13
g) more than 3 years	50	55	51	51	58	56	64	59
	100%[a]	100%	100%	100%	100%	100%	100%	100%
Would you say that you are using the (name) Bus more or less than you did this time last year?								
a) didn't use the bus last year	14%	9%	12%	12%	8%	10%	8%	6%
b) much more than last year	33	28	33	30	37	38	34	34
c) a little more	20	17	14	15	20	18	22	17
d) about the same as last year	28	32	30	34	27	28	28	35
e) a little less	3	6	6	6	5	3	5	5
f) much less than last year	1	9	4	3	3	4	3	3
	100%	100%	100%	100%	100%	100%	100%	100%
	(n = 497)	(n = 382)	(n = 663)	(n = 53)	(n = 460)	(n = 458)	(n = 435)	(n = 477)

Exhibit 12 (continued)

The Degree to Which Users Are Captive Transit Users

	Kingston		Guelph		Peterborough		Brantford	
If (name) Transit had not been available, would you have made this trip by some other means of transportation?	December 1974	June 1975	December 1974	June 1975	December 1974	June 1975	December 1974	June 1975
a) No, I would have stayed home	10%	8%	11%	8%	14%	11%	13%	12%
b) Yes, I would drive a car	13	11	13	11	16	15	12	10
c) Yes, ride as a passenger in a car	12	13	17	18	22	19	19	21
d) Yes, take a taxi	27	30	15	18	13	10	20	19
e) Yes, walk	34	29	35	35	30	38	33	34
f) Yes, other	5	9	10	10	6	7	4	5
	100%	100%	100%	100%	100%	100%	100%	100%
	(n = 520)	(n = 385)	(n = 726)	(n = 558)	(n = 488)	(n = 480)	(n = 471)	(n = 507)

608

How often have you been a *car driver* for a round trip during a recent average week?

a) I don't drive a car	73%	74%	74%	74%	66%	63%	70%	74%
b) More than 6 round trips each week	3	5	5	4	3	6	4	6
c) 4–5 round trips	4	2	3	4	7	4	4	6
d) 2–3 round trips	6	6	7	5	10	10	7	5
e) for 1 round trip	6	3	5	5	5	7	6	4
f) for less then 1 round trip each week	9	9	7	9	10	10	9	9
	100%	100%	100%	100%	100%	100%	100%	100%
	(n = 482)	(n = 378)	(n = 681)	(n = 537)	(n = 444)	(n = 447)	(n = 436)	(n = 480)

a. Percentages may not always add up to 100% owing to rounding.
Source: M.T.C. Monitoring Report.

Exhibit 13 Average Daily Ridership Trends:
Kingston, Guelph, Peterborough, Brantford

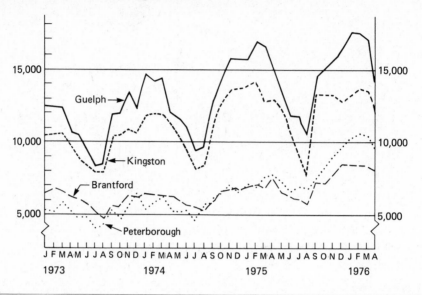

As they reviewed the results of the research studies, the management team of K.T.S. realized they had to draw some conclusions about the effectiveness of the KATY campaign and to make specific recommendations about an advertising budget for inclusion in the 1978 K.T.S. budget. Exhibit 14 contains advertising budgets for 1977 and the twelve preceding years.

Exhibit 14   Kingston Transit System Expenditures on Advertising (1965–1977)

Calendar Year	Advertising Expenditures		Advertising Expenditures as a Percent of Total Operating Costs
1965	$1809		0.31%
1966	620		0.09
1967	923		0.12
1968	735		0.09
1969	1304		0.16
1970	1557		0.17
1971	401		0.04
1972	535		0.06
1973	1239		0.12
1974	41	} excluding	0.00
1975	65	} KATY campaign	0.00
1976	123		0.01
1977	0		0

"The appropriateness of any specific rate of annual expenditure on transit marketing is not a readily definable statistic, though it would appear that some properties use roughly 1% of their operating costs as a guideline. An *ongoing* program for Kingston similar to the demonstration marketing program would be in the order of 4% of the operating costs with approximately 2.5% or roughly $30,000 going toward advertising and promotion."
Source: M.T.C. Monitoring Report.

39 Evaluating Advertisements

Advertisements are created to inform and to influence attitudes and behaviour. Because each communication situation is unique, creative pieces should be judged in terms of the objectives, strategy, and competitive environment of the particular situation rather than against other creative pieces. The following minicases give you as much information on the objectives, strategy, and competition as was available. Your task is to decide the degree to which these advertisements met the objectives and requirements of the situation.

You have a mix of advertisements by government, trade associations, and corporations with appeals involving advocacy, stimulating demand for a product category, and stimulating demand for a brand. In these campaigns, advertising would play an important role.

Print advertisements are used in three of the four minicases, not because they are simple (they are not), but merely because print is the medium of this case. Remember, too, that print takes in newspapers, magazines, transit, and billboards. For expediency, all the advertisements appear in black and white and only in the English language versions. In many cases, these advertisements were part of a larger campaign that utilized other media.

After you have noted some strengths and weaknesses of each advertisement in terms of the objectives, try to sketch out one or two advertisements you think would be better. Then you may want to go back and evaluate the entire rationale for each campaign: the objectives, strategy, and planned execution.

Boots Drugs Stores (Canada) Ltd.

Agency: MacLaren Advertising.

Boots Drug Stores (Canada) Ltd. is a chain of 160 drug stores in Ontario and the western provinces established in October 1979. In the fall of 1980,

Boots introduced their No7 Cosmetic range in Canada. The brand was imported from Boots in the United Kingdom, where it enjoyed a number two retail market position. Advertising support of No7 in the United Kingdom was aggressive, including year-round print campaigns, tactical use of television for spring/fall colour promotions, and frequent point-of-sale activity. Both Boots and No7 had top-of-mind awareness and "household word" status in the United Kingdom.

The Canadian launch of No7 was supported by nine weeks of television in Ontario and the western provinces. The 30-second spot promised a "new beautiful you" and demonstrated a range of colour cosmetics for eyes, lips, nails, and face.

In 1981, follow-up print support was planned in a major Canadian women's magazine. See the proposed advertisement for the 1981 campaign.

Marketing Objective

To increase sales of the No7 cosmetic range with Boots Drug Stores.

Advertising Objectives

1. To continue the task initiated with the fall 1980 launch, of building awareness and purchase predisposition of the total No7 line.
2. To stimulate trial and/or repeat purchase of the brand.

Selected Basic Consumer Benefit

No7 Cosmetics offer consumers a complete range of high-quality, contemporary cosmetics, which are available at a sensible price exclusively at Boots Drug Stores.

Execution

A four-colour double-page spread was judged to be the best format for the No7 announcement in order to break through the proliferation of cosmetic advertising in women's magazines. The advertisement features a "beauty shot" of a woman holding an ostrich egg (symbol of birth, newness). A prominent product shot clearly details the No7 range. The No7 image is conveyed as being stylish but timeless—sophisticated and romantic at the same time. Finally, the creative work emphasized the fact that No7 is created "for the face you choose to show."

CREATED FOR THE FACE   YOU CHOOSE TO SHOW

N°7 COSMETICS.
A TOTALLY NEW WAY TO REVEAL
YOUR EYES, YOUR LIPS, YOUR NAILS.
NO 7 COSMETICS.
FOR THE FACE YOU CHOOSE
TO SHOW.

AVAILABLE EXCLUSIVELY AT Boots DRUG STORES.

Petroleum Resources Communication Foundation (PRCF)

Agency: F.H. Hayhurst.

The Petroleum Resources Communication Foundation (PRCF) was
established in 1975 as a "vehicle through which Canada's petroleum
industry and the public can communicate on topics of mutual concern."
Its mandate has been fulfilled through a variety of mechanisms, including a
Speaker's Bureau, publications, film distribution, and paid media
advertising.

In 1981, PRCF identified its membership's key concern as increasing
government intervention in the oil and gas sector. The year began with implementation of the federal government's National Energy Program and its
takeover of several multinational companies. In September, Ottawa and
Alberta concluded an agreement that saw the two governments as the main
beneficiaries of rapidly escalating energy prices. By year end, Ontario had
joined in the nationalization game, and government policies had created
severe cash flow problems for many in the industry.

It was within this climate that PRCF commissioned the Longwoods
Research Group to carry out a program of research to develop a communications programme for the Foundation. It was recognized that in the
arena of public opinion, the federal government's actions against the
industry had a fair measure of support.

Thus the purpose of the research was twofold:

1. to find communications messages that could marshall public opinion
   on the side of the industry and away from government, and

2. to define the target group(s) for these messages, as an aid to media
   placement.

This case presents key findings from a major quantitative study fielded
in the summer of 1981. The detailed results are presented in a separate
volume, which is available from PRCF.

Ten focus group discussions were conducted among the general public
in Toronto, Montreal, and Quebec City. This was followed by a large-scale
quantitative survey, involving in-home interviews of 1486 adults across
Canada.

Issues

Canadians' concerns about the oil and gas situation were simple: they
cared about how much it cost. Two thirds of the sample mentioned price
spontaneously; and among government supporters, price was even more of

a concern. Supply was a secondary concern, with 22 percent of the sample mentioning shortages. All other concerns such as the role of government and Canadian ownership were raised by a relatively small number of individuals.

Images of Government and Private Industry

People were asked, "Who would do the better job—the federal government or private industry?" in a number of areas involving oil and gas. The federal government was the winner on ten dimensions versus three for private industry. Moreover, the federal government was ahead on the one key issue—price. Private industry won in three areas—competition, efficiency, and management—each of which ought to mean a lower price to the consumer.

If private industry had the "reasons why" for price, then why did the federal government win on the price issue? The Longwoods researchers suggested that the petroleum industry has been historically on the wrong side of the price issue; it had argued for world prices even when profits were at record levels. The Liberals made cheap oil a key promise during the 1980 election; they told the public what it wanted to hear. The petroleum industry's concern for more revenue was in direct conflict with the public's priority concern—low prices. Therefore, the petroleum industry must refocus its communications to address the public's strong emotional desire for low prices; failure to do so will lead to a perpetuation of the industry's severe image problems.

Strategy

The public simplified the complexities of the oil and gas situation down to one key question—how much does it cost? Thus, they supported import subsidies because they keep the price down. When the true cost was made visible as a tax at the pump, support disappeared. Thus, they supported some measure of government ownership until a price tag was placed upon takeovers.

> The time is now right for the industry to make its case to the Canadian public. The public is intensely dissatisfied with the federal government's management of the economy. With the recent pricing agreement, the government broke its election promise of cheap gasoline.
>
> The September 1981 agreement between Ottawa and Alberta will bring rapidly escalating oil prices for the next five years, but the terms of this agreement are unacceptable to the majority of Canadians; fewer than one in four supported the government allowing gasoline prices to reach 75 percent of world levels.

When you spend $15.00 at the gas pump, you pay $5.00 for gasoline. And $10.00 in taxes.

Of every dollar you spend for gasoline in Ontario, the petroleum industry receives 33¢. The remainder, 67¢ out of every dollar, goes to governments in the form of taxes and royalty payments.

Just thought you'd like to know.

If you'd like to know more about what the industry does with its share, write the P.R.C.F. If you'd like to know more about the sixty-seven cents, contact your M.P. or M.P.P.

A message from the 115 members of the Petroleum Resources Communication Foundation.   105,309-2nd Avenue, S.W. Calgary, Alberta T2P 0C5.

The public understands that the federal government is responsible for setting prices. Thus, we predict a backlash against the federal government, particularly in Ontario, which was counting on cheap energy to help its sagging economy. In order to rally public support on its side, the industry must deal with the public's emotional desire for low prices. It is therefore essential that the industry not voice its own concerns for more revenue in public; this message is totally unacceptable, given the current climate of public opinion. Rather, the industry must capitalize on its image strengths—ensuring competition, efficiency, and management—into a consumer benefit: lower prices for oil and gas.

The public must come to understand that rapidly escalating prices are the result of greedy taxation policies of governments, not the result of a greedy petroleum industry that wants even higher prices when profits are already seen as exorbitant. The petroleum industry is in large measure the tax collector for governments; it must be seen as such, or the industry will take the blame for the massive price increases scheduled over the next five years.

Dofasco

Agency: R.T. Kelley Inc., Hamilton.

Dofasco is Canada's second largest steelmaker. As a major corporation, Dofasco seeks to foster positive attitudes among its target audiences, who are employees, shareholders, customers, government, the business and financial community, communities in which Dofasco has operating facilities, and that broad group of people categorized as "aware Canadians."

Communications Objectives

Support and enhance perceptions of Dofasco as a people-oriented corporation, sensitive and responsive to contemporary concerns.

Strategy

Dofasco's ongoing radio campaign reaches Dofasco's target audiences with commercials based on the theme "Our product is steel. Our strength is people." The commercials present unscripted comments of employees talking about their jobs and their attitudes.

The radio campaign is supplemented by several print advertising programmes directed at various audiences.

For the "aware Canadian" group, *Macleans* was selected as the appropriate medium to "flesh out" selected radio topics.

"WE'RE PRODUCING MORE STEEL, BUT POLLUTING LESS."

—Murray Greenfield, Director, Environmental Control, Dofasco.

Since the late 1960's our steel production at Dofasco has soared. Yet, perhaps surprisingly, we have cut our net water and air pollution by more than 70%.

Here's how we did it.

Cleaning the air

Since 1970, we've invested over $60,000,000 in new air-cleaning equipment. For example, we've installed giant filters and hoods on coke ovens and on iron and steelmaking furnaces.

On our newest oxygen steel making plant, air pollution control systems capture 99% of particulate emissions.

Another achievement: 99% of the sulphur gas given off during coke production is captured and converted to sulphur.

Even simple programs like cleaning the roads get careful attention at Dofasco. Our three sweeper machines are on the job daily.

Cleaning the water

We've invested over $40,000,000 since 1970 in new and improved water treatment facilities. We'll spend another $46,000,000 by 1984.

A long-term commitment

Over the past ten years, we spent $110,000,000 on pollution control equipment—about 17% of our total net income. Over the next three years, we expect to spend another $60,000,000.

Our commitment to improving environmental control is strong. And long-term.

We don't have all the answers to pollution, but real progress has been made. We expect good results in the future, too.

Dofasco Inc.,
P.O. Box 460, Hamilton, Ontario, L8N 3J5.

Dofasco is a 96% Canadian-owned steel company employing over 11,500 Canadian men and women. Most of the steel they make is sold to Canadian manufacturers who in turn build products sold in Canada and around the world.

DOFASCO

Our product is steel. Our strength is people.

Print Execution

An editorial-style format evocative of the *Macleans'* format presents individual Dofasco employees. Headline quotes focus on Dofasco's success with regard to a contemporary issue (e.g., pollution control). Copy includes enough detail to substantiate the success claim.

Alcohol Moderation–Ontario Ministry of Health

Agency: R.T. Kelly, Inc.

In the development of the Alcohol Moderation advertising, a number of long-term health considerations were taken into account. Most salient among these were the following:

a) Despite people's tendency to overindulge, few of our audience would disagree with the wisdom of moderation. That is to say, the benefits to overall health and well-being are widely recognized— philosophically at least, if not in practice. The tone of our communication must reinforce this positive mind-set while involving moderate practices in alcohol-consuming situations.

b) There is a growing tendency toward moderation in many areas as people become increasingly aware of more positive health habits. Data suggest that the trend is away from martini lunches in favour of alcohol-free or low-alcohol beverages. Wine sales are increasing at a greater rate than liquor, and many wines on the market have less than the traditional 12 or 14 percent alcohol content. Brewers at the same time have only begun to tap the light beer market. All these factors reflect a moderation trend in favour of health. We would be wise to reinforce this trend wherever possible in our communications.

c) Peer group pressure can play a major part in helping reinforce the acceptability of moderation. Wherever possible, we should capitalize on the opportunity to invoke the influence of social acceptability, by providing role examples to which our audience can relate and/or situations with which they are familiar.

At the moment, peer group pressure is a particularly important element with the young, who tend to operate in the direction of experimentation and excessive drinking. Much of the "life style" advertising of alcoholic beverages implies to youth that drinking plays an important part in their becoming socially acceptable. Such advertising helps develop a constant source of recruits to the alcoholic beverage market.

d) Consumers who drink excessively have been conditioned to associate alcohol consumption with "good times" and sociability. As a result, anyone who drinks very little, or not at all, is somewhat suspect and may be perceived as less socially acceptable. We can turn the tables not only by invoking the principle of peer group pressure, but also by stressing the fact that many of the "good times" situations are more the by-product of moderation than overindulgence.

e) One is much more likely to accept suggestion from a friendly, supportive source than from one that is "holier than thou" in its espousal of abstinence. Every opportunity must be taken to reinforce the benefits of being oneself in a social context by verbally and visually supporting the fact that by overindulging, you are detracting from your social acceptability rather than enhancing it; reducing, not increasing your level of enjoyment. This thought we believe to be prime in establishing one's moderation patterns. The problem of moderation itself is highly personal. So must the solution be, for in the final analysis it is individual discretion and good judgment that put the philosophy of moderation into practice.

Creative Objectives

a) To make adults who consume alcohol aware that when they drink, they should do so moderately. (Problem drinkers and abstainers are not part of our target group.)

b) To provide reinforcement for the idea that it is acceptable to resist the many social pressures to drink and that it does not result in alienation from one's friends.

Creative Strategy

a) To encourage adults to practice moderation while drinking.

b) To deflate the myth that excessive drinking is an essential element in having a good time or gaining social acceptability.

c) To show moderation as an accepted way to enjoy oneself, with emphasis on personal accountability.

Media Objectives

A. Target Group
    All adults 18 + in Ontario

B. Timing
    Alcohol Moderation will be scheduled for seven weeks beginning in mid-November and will run through the Christmas/New Year's season,

Alcohol Moderation "Holiday" Television. 30-second commercial. December 2–31, 1979 (125 GRP's).

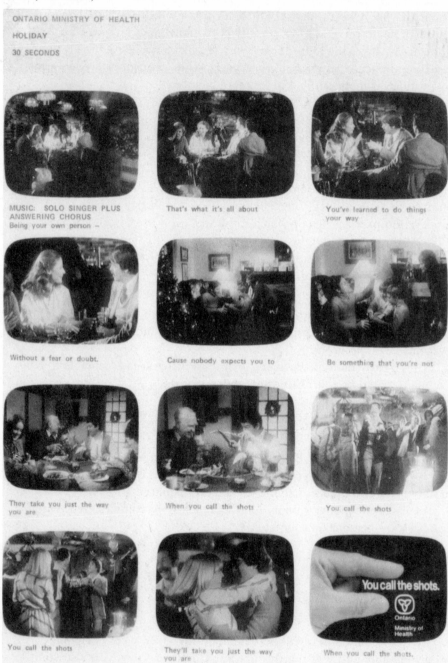

ONTARIO MINISTRY OF HEALTH

HOLIDAY

30 SECONDS

MUSIC: SOLO SINGER PLUS ANSWERING CHORUS
Being your own person –

That's what it's all about

You've learned to do things your way

Without a fear or doubt.

Cause nobody expects you to

Be something that you're not

They take you just the way you are

When you call the shots

You call the shots

You call the shots

They'll take you just the way you are

You call the shots.

When you call the shots.

Ontario Ministry of Health

Alcohol Moderation Television. 30-second commercial. October 22–December 1, 1979 (125 GRP's). January 1–19, (125 GRP's).

Alcohol Moderation (Revised). September 8, 1980–January 1981 (Sporting events). November 17, 1980–January 4, 1981 (100–150 GRP's).

Banquet scene was eliminated, and voice-over was added. Also, logo was strengthened.

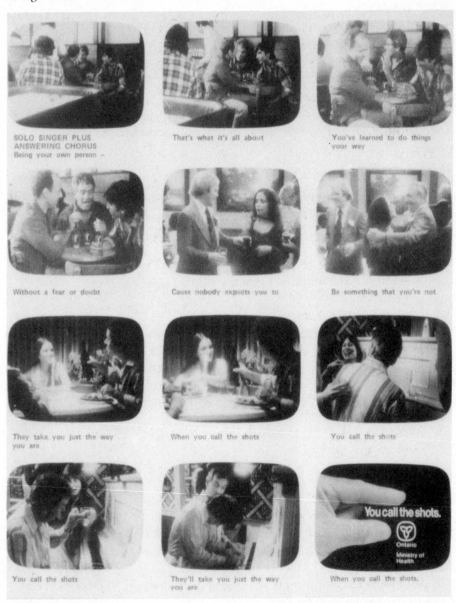

when alcohol beverage advertising is at its peak. (An estimate based on Elliot Research National Advertising Expenditures shows that beer, wine, and liquor industries spent approximately $29 million in Ontario in 1979, in measured media only. A substantial proportion of this money was expended during the last three months of the year.)

Media Strategy

Because of budget restrictions, television will be the only medium utilized for the Alcohol Moderation campaign.

Television combines sight, sound, and motion, thus providing the greatest impact of any mass medium available. Television provides excellent reach of our target group (18 +).

Commercials will also be scheduled during major sporting events to directly offset brewery advertising traditionally scheduled in these properties.

Media Recommendations

Television: Thirty-second commercials will be scheduled commencing November 17, 1980, for a seven-week period.

November 17, 1980–January 4, 1981 (7 233ks)

MARKET & G.R.P. LEVELS ARE AS FOLLOWS:

Toronto/Hamilton/St. Catharines	150
Kitchener	125
London/Wingham	125
Sudbury/Timmins/N.B.	100
Ottawa-English	125
-French	25
Kingston	100
Peterborough	100
Barrie	100
Thunder Bay	100
Sault Ste. Marie	100
Windsor	125

Level of G.R.P based on Health Skills Phase II buy. Toronto has been revised on the basis of research results, which indicated that awareness levels dropped when G.R.P. level was reduced from 170 to 115. Toronto will now be purchased at 150 G.R.P. level. (Global to be purchased as the base buy.)

Additional television spots have been purchased on NFL Football on both CITY–TV and CFTO–TV.

40 "Pick A Winner"

Consumer Sales Promotions

Consumer sales promotions are conducted by manufacturers to acquaint new users with their brand, to load existing users, and to maintain interest in the brand on the part of the sales force, the retailers, and consumers. Most consumer promotions are accompanied by a trade promotion to encourage retail display, cooperative advertising, price featuring, or any combination of these activities.

Consumer sales promotions generally are conceived by product managers and executed by a company sales force or broker. The basic concept of the sales promotion will be important in securing sales force support, retailer support, and ultimately sales. But it is not always easy to identify a winning promotion before it is conducted. Let's see how clever you are in spotting the winners. The following four cases are proposals for sales promotions. Considering the characteristics of each promotion and the surrounding circumstances, which promotions, if any, would be successful? Why? What can you generalize about the factors which are important for successful promotions?

HairCreme

The end of spring was approaching, and Ms. Catherine MacIntyre, product manager, was preparing to launch a HairCreme consumer promotion. Hair-Creme was a well known oil-based hair preparation used by men to groom their hair. MacIntyre had decided to run a national eight week in-pack bonus. The consumer would receive a free plastic comb in every package of HairCreme. The comb was valued at $0.49 retail, but each comb cost MacIntyre only $0.06. A three-ounce tube of HairCreme could be bought for $2.00, regular price, and a 4.5-ounce tube for $2.85. Although sales for all men's hairdressing products were slightly depressed at that time, a similar bonus promotion had been run on HairCreme for more than ten years. MacIntyre believed that consumers expected a promotion this year and that response again would be good.

In addition to maintaining the HairCreme existing franchise, MacIntyre had other objectives for this promotion. These were "(1) to build trade inventories, (2) to increase short term volume sold, and (3) to load the consumer." To aid the consumer promotion in achieving these objectives, MacIntyre planned to give the retailers a descriptive flyer about the promotion. Also, she would offer the retailers 5 percent off the regular case price in hopes of reducing the price at store level, and an additional 5 percent would be offered in an effort to obtain display activity or cooperative advertising. MacIntyre knew that the usual offer to the trade was between 15 and 20 percent, but she believed that HairCreme's strong brand image enabled her to offer less. In total, the promotion was likely to cost $27,000.

The three-ounce tube was packed 20 to a case, and the 4.5-ounce tube was packed 12 to the case. MacIntyre forecast that sales for the promotional period would be 15,000 cases, split evenly between the two sizes. Without the promotion, she judged that HairCreme sales would likely be 10,900 cases. In calculating this, MacIntyre considered that there were not likely to be any competitive promotions. The contribution rate for products of this type was about 45 percent, and retail margins were about 35 percent. No pretesting had been done for this promotion, other than a successful history of promotions on this brand.

Richmond Peanut Butter

As product manager for Richmond Peanut Butter, Todd Thomson had developed an "instant win" sales promotion accompanied by a $0.17 coupon, which could be redeemed on Rowntree's chocolate bars. The instant win certificate for Parker toys and games and the coupon were placed between the lid and the cardboard insert on the one-pound, two-pound, and three-pound sizes of Richmond Peanut Butter. Any certificate showing three identical animal figures entitled the bearer to $12.00 worth of Parker games. After producing the jars for the promotion with new packaging and the instant win certificates, Thomson discovered that it was somewhat difficult to pry off the cardboard facing and retrieve the certificate. However, he found that a sharp table knife would work quite well, and he did not want to delay the promotion by reordering the lids.

Thomson had several reasons for running this particular promotion. He thought it would "increase short-term volume, build trade inventories, increase the interest of the sales force, and get display activity." December was usually a low-volume period with unpromoted sales estimated at 700,000 pounds. Thomson thought he could offset the seasonal downturn by instituting a sales promotion. It would be a national promotion, run for twelve weeks, and "instant win" campaigns were becoming the most favoured type of promotion among many product managers. Because this type of promotion had been successful several times in the past, Todd decided that it was not necessary to supplement it with any point of purchase material. No major competitive activity was expected during this period.

The peanut butter market in Canada was dominated by Kraft, which held 39 percent of the market. There was a very strong brand loyalty among Kraft consumers, but multiple brand switching was usual among consumers of lesser brands. As the third major producer in terms of sales, Richmond Peanut Butter held a 10 percent market share. The average price paid to the manufacturer for Richmond Peanut Butter was $0.88 per pound, and the contribution margin was $0.16 per pound. Generally, the composition of sales was as follows:

Package size	Percent of sales	Packages per case
9 oz. (new)	4	24
1 lb.	40	12
2 lb.	40	12
3 lb.	15	6
4.5 lb.	1	6

To supplement the consumer promotion, Thomson was offering the retailers case allowances on two of the promoted sizes. The trade could get $0.75 off per case of the one-pound jar of peanut butter, $1.00 off per case of the three-pound size, and $0.80 off per case of the new nine-ounce jar. Over and above these allowances, another $5000 would go to the trade as incentive for their support of this promotion. The total cost of this promotion was expected to be $45,000, and sales on the promotion were forecast at 1,000,000 pounds. There had been no pretesting on this promotion.

Close Shaves Disposable Razors

The 1982 marketing plan called for a consumer promotion to be run on Close Shaves disposable razors in the spring. The product manager responsible for disposable razors, Fred Manno, had considered several promotions and had decided upon a bonus pack. He would offer five razors for $0.79, which was the regular price for four Close Shaves disposable razors. This bonus package would be sold nationally for twelve weeks. Manno had chosen this promotion over other promotions in order "to increase consumer trial, preempt the competition, defend against competitive sales promotions, and increase short-term volume." Manno expected that the added value of the promotional package would be the main reason for extra sales.

The disposable razor market was very competitive, and consumers were believed to be price sensitive. Manno's company had put Close Shaves on the market five years earlier, just a few years after Bic's initial introduction of disposable razors. In five years, Manno's company had managed gradually to increase their share of the disposable razor market to more than 25 percent.

In this type of market, Manno always was concerned about competitive activity. He strove at least to maintain existing market position. The competitive promotion that particularly concerned Manno was an economy-size package of twelve disposable razors for only $1.49 that a major competitor was expected to introduce. The same competitor usually offered a five-pack for $0.99. Consequently, Manno intended to enhance the Close Shave bonus pack with special artwork and packaging. He was not planning to offer the retailers any additional incentive, other than the regular promotional allowance of $2.00 per case. There would be 20 packages in a case. He had budgeted the total cost of the promotion at $45,000, including the case allowance but not counting any loss from the reduced price. On a regular nonpromoted pack, this product had a contribution rate of about 35 percent and a retail margin of 35 percent.

A special flag on the package read: "Buy 4, Get 1 Free!" Manno expected that both the sales force and the retailers would be enthusiastic about the promotion because of the consumer value of the bonus. As a result, he anticipated sales of the promotional package to be 22,500 cases plus 10,000 cases of the regular pack, as compared to 24,000 cases that he would sell without the promotion.

Tingle Oral Antiseptic

Mary Smith, product manager responsible for Tingle oral antiseptic, had just completed the plans for an eight-week national consumer promotion to be run in the early spring of 1981. The target for the promotion was existing users of Tingle mouthwash. The promotion consisted of an on-pack $1.00 coupon offer. To receive the $1.00 coupon, the consumer would have to buy a one-litre bottle of Tingle at $2.79, cut the offer off the package, put a 15-cent stamp on the envelope, and mail it to Personal Products, Inc. Personal Products would then mail a coupon worth $1.00 to the consumer, who could redeem it on the next purchase of any size of Tingle.

Tingle shared the majority of the market with Procter & Gamble's Scope. Although Tingle enjoyed strong consumer loyalty, its share of the market had been slowly eroded by Scope and some lesser brands. In addition, Personal Products had launched Tinglemint, a new mint-flavoured version of Tingle, which grew rapidly to equal Tingle's market share. Consequently, the primary objective of this promotion was "to defend against the competition." Mary also aimed to load the consumer, thereby maintaining current Tingle users and building trade inventories.

Mary expected that the promotion's sales would reach 27,000 cases, each case containing a dozen one-litre bottles. The one-litre bottle was sold only during promotions. Regular sizes were 750 ml., 500 ml., 250 ml., and 150 ml. The 500-ml. size accounted for almost half of the regular Tingle volume.

On the one-litre size, Mary was offering to the retailers case allowances of $2.50 per case plue $1.30 per case on orders exceeding 300 cases. Mary had budgeted a maximum of $80,000 to cover coupon redemptions. This cost included the retailer's handling charge of $0.07 for every coupon redeemed.

Other than Scope's promotional activity and the regular trade deals, Mary expected that there woud be very few competitive promotions. She expected to receive the maximum amount of support for this type of promotion from both the Personal Products sales force and the food and drug retailers. In the absence of any sales promotion, Mary believed that she might expect to sell about 160,000 litres at an average retail price of $3.12 per litre. At this pricing, the contribution rate was about 30 percent after average retail margins of 35 percent.

This specific promotion had not been pretested, but many coupon promotions had been run on Tingle. Mary had considered complementing the promotion with advertising but had decided that the budget was not sufficient to cover an extra $20,000 in special media.

41 Nabob Foods Ltd.

"We are going into an Ontario test market program in early July," said Mr. John Bell, Vice-President of Marketing of Nabob Foods Ltd. in May of 1979. "If we are to be successful, we must do an effective job in communicating our product benefits to ground coffee consumers. Currently, we have two new TV commercials being tested by both Clucas and Adcom. I expect to receive the test reports shortly. Once we have those results, we can make the final decision as to which commercial we will use in the test market."

The Company

Nabob Foods Ltd. was an 85-year-old company based in Burnaby, British Columbia. For many years, the firm was part of the Kelly, Douglas and Co. food products organization. Following the purchase of Kelly, Douglas by the George Weston Ltd. group in the 1970's, Nabob was sold in 1976 to Jacobs AG, a Zurich-based Swiss company and one of Europe's largest coffee manufacturers.

The Ground Coffee Market

The large majority of Nabob's business was in coffee; for many years, it had been a leading supplier in the ground coffee market in western Canada. However, this market represented only 47 percent of the total Canadian ground coffee market. In the east, Ontario represented 35 percent of total Canadian sales and $100 million in retail sales. Nabob had not been effective in penetrating this market and in 1979 had only a 3 percent market share. The market leader in ground coffee in Ontario was General Foods' Maxwell House brand, with about a 25 percent share. General Foods had been able to maintain their position in recent years with vir-

630

tually no direct advertising for the product, relying instead on the ruboff from the substantial advertising support given to Maxwell House instant coffee.

Approximately 80 percent of the Ontario ground coffee market was sold in paper bags. Vacuum tins, which represented about 20 percent of the market, provided the customer with a fresher product, but at a premium price of 20–25 percent.

Nabob's New Strategy for Ontario

In late 1978 and early 1979, John Bell and his team began work on putting together a new strategy for penetrating the Ontario market. Marketing research provided them with the information that the Nabob ground coffee products were perceived by ground coffee users as better in taste than the leading competitive coffees.

A new packaging technique had become available to Nabob that would enable the firm to provide the freshness benefits of vacuum-packed coffee without the high premium selling price. The new packaging was vacuum-sealed foil, which resulted in a stone-hard "brick" package until the vacuum seal was broken. The cost of this new packaging was higher than that of paper bags, but substantially below that of metal tins. John Bell had decided to have Nabob absorb the additional packaging cost so that the product would have the same retail price as Maxwell House.

John Bell and his team had concluded that it was important that adult women, who were the target audience for ground coffee, understand the new packaging concept in order for them to perceive the benefits of fresher and better-tasting coffee. The group had concluded further that television would be most effective in demonstrating the packaging concept.

Nabob's advertising agency, Scali, McCabe, Sloves (Canada) Ltd., developed two commercials. The scripts for these two commercials appear as exhibits 1 and 2. The creative approach for each commercial was different, as were the lengths. The reason for the difference in length was that the agency believed that the creative approach planned for the "Microphone" commercial would require 60 seconds to do an effective job of meeting the communication objectives agreed upon with Nabob.

After the two commercials were produced, each was sent out for testing by two commercial testing organizations. Adcom Research Ltd. was to do a Day-After-Recall Test (DAR). A brief description of the methodology used by Adcom is given in exhibit 3. Each test cost approximately $3000. J.E. Clucas and Associates was the second test organization,

Exhibit 1 Script for "Store" 0:30 English Commercial

Video	Audio
1. Woman walking down aisle in supermarket. She is in the coffee section. Bags. She is picking up bags and sniffing them.	
2. She picks up bag. Sniffs. Gives a nod of recognition as she can smell coffee. Puts bag down.	
3. She continues with another bag.	
4. She arrives at a section containing Nabob Sig Tradition. She sniffs. Sniffs again. Does a double take.	
5. She turns. Store manager is walking by. She holds up pack.	5. *Woman:* "I can't smell the coffee inside this Nabob pack . . .
6. She knocks her knuckles on the side of the pack several times.	. . . and (knock, knock) . . . it's as hard as a rock."
7. Store manager to the rescue. He takes pack from her.	7. *Store Manager:* "That's Nabob's new vacuum pack. Stale air can't get in, Nabob's great flavour and aroma can't get out."
8. He pulls out a pair of scissors. Snips pack.	8. *Store Manager:* "But watch this . . ." (SFX-snip. Whoosh)
9. He holds pack near her nose.	9. *Store Manager:* "Now smell . . ."
10. CU. as woman holds pack to her nose. She's entranced by the aroma.	10. *Woman:* "Mmm . . . that aroma ..."
11. Store manager and woman. Two of them sitting down drinking.	
	12. *Man:* "Well? . . ."
	13. *Woman:* "That's Nabob all right . . . but even fresher."
14. Other two women knocking Sig-Vac packs (SFX). He gets up to go to them.	
	15. *Man:* (Nods approval) "Excuse me, someone's knocking."
16. *Super:* It's hard. To be fresh.	

Exhibit 2 Script for "Microphone" 0:60 English Commercial

Video	*Audio*
	1. *Man:* "Inside these ordinary, soft paper bags . . .
	. . . is ground coffee. You can actually smell the coffee inside, on the outside."
2. Squeezes paper bag. It breaks. (SFX)	
	3. "Stale air keeps getting in, flavour and aroma keep getting out. Not good."
	4. "Inside this *extra ordinary* . . .
	5. . . . hard (knock, knock) foil vacuum pack is a truly superior blend of ground coffee . . . Nabob. Western Canada's leading fresh ground coffee."
	6. "You can't smell a thing. Stale air can't get in, so Nabob's famous flavour and aroma *can't* get out."
	7. "Listen . . ."
8. Tears paper bag in front of mike. No sound.	
9. Snips Sig-Vac. Whoosh of vacuum opening. Pack softens.	
10. He sniffs. Savours aroma. Holds pack toward screen.	10. (sniffs) "Mmm. Smell that . . . *that's* fresh aroma . . ."
	11. "Now I ask you, which one do you think makes a better, fresher cup of coffee?"
12. Move to ADC machine, Nabob pack. He savours and sips. He smiles knowingly.	12. "You're absolutely right."
13. Move in to pack and cup.	
14. Further move into same.	
15. Move to Sig ending.	

Nabob Foods Ltd. **633**

Exhibit 3 Information on the Day-After-Recall Technique

The day-after-recall technique, as applied to broadcast media, is an approach used to assess the on-air performance of commercials. Telephone interviews are held the day after the commercial is aired. The purpose of the interview is first to determine if the respondent was viewing the appropriate programming the previous evening and, for those people who qualify as viewers, to obtain recall information of various types.

The tests for the two Nabob commercials were carried out as follows:

1. The "Store" commercial was run in prime time on the same evening in seven cities: Calgary, Edmonton, Regina, Saskatoon, Winnipeg, North Bay, and Sudbury. It appeared as the first commercial in a two-minute commercial break. The "Microphone" commercial was run in prime time on another day. It was aired on the same evening in eight cities: Calgary, Regina, Saskatoon, Winnipeg, North Bay, Sudbury, Ottawa, and Kingston. It, too, appeared as the first commercial in a two-minute commercial break. Adcom monitoring of the test channel in each city for an hour before and an hour after each test commercial was aired revealed that no competitive commercials were run in these times.

2. The day/evening following airing, interviewing was carried out from centralized supervised locations in each city. The sample used in each city was generated from the current telephone directory for that city. Columns were randomly selected and start points assigned. From the start point, successive numbers were called until one interview was completed. Then another random column and start point were used.

Approximately half of the interviewing was done after 5:00 P.M. to ensure that working people were represented in the sample. Respondents, of course, were unaware before the fact that they would be called.

3. Adcom's goal was to generate a sample of 150 qualified viewers or, in Adcom's terminology, 150 members of the commercial audience. However, the amount of time required to generate this size of sample was dependent on a number of factors, a key one being the size of the viewing audience of the test show. In effect, Nabob purchased an amount of field work time. This generated a sample size of 126 for the "Store" commercial and 145 for the "Microphone" commercial.

4. The definitions used by Adcom in reporting results were as follows:

Commercial audience. Respondents in front of the television set at the time the test commercial was aired. This covers approximately four minutes.

Specific recall. Recall that can only have come from the test commercial by reason of mention by the respondent of messages or situations unique to the test commercial.

Nonspecific recall. Recall that probably comes from the test commercial and definitely does not contain recall specific to any other commercial.

Related recall. Consists of specific plus nonspecific recall as defined above.

Exhibit 3   (continued)

Unaided recall. Related recall given by the respondent after mention of the product category only.

Aided recall. Related recall given by the respondent after mention of the brand name.

Brand name only. Those who gave the brand name before the interviewer mentioned it but could recall nothing further.

Unrelated recall. Recall that definitely came from another commercial and contains nothing specific to the test commercial.

No recall. Respondents in the commercial audience who were unable to give any related recall.

Sales message recall. Recall that provides at least a minimal sales message, whether this came from audio or video. This is mainly audio in nature.

Situation recall. Recall pertaining only to the circumstances or action of the commercial. This is mainly video in nature.

and Clucas was to test the two commercials using the Clucas Diagnostic Advertising Research Technique. A brief description of the methodology used in this technique is given in exhibit 4. Each test cost approximately $5300.

Further, the "Store" commercial was run in one Western market immediately after production. By the end of May, it had been judged as successful in lifting Nabob's sales, even though share figures were not yet available. The city in which the "Store" commercial was run was not one of the test cities used by either Adcom or Clucas.

Early in June, John Bell received copies of the four research reports, which would provide him with key information on which to base his decision as to whether the Ontario test would be one commercial in one city or two test markets with one of the commercials used in each. Each of the Adcom reports was about 35 pages in length, including appendices. A selective summary of these two reports appears as exhibit 5. Each of the Clucas reports was about 65 pages long. A selective summary of these two reports appears as exhibit 6.

Exhibit 4 Information on the Clucas Diagnostic Advertising Research Technique

The Clucas Diagnostic Advertising Research Technique is used by the J.E. Clucas and Associates organization to assess the communication strengths and weaknesses of commercials in detail on a number of dimensions, as well as the overall functioning of the commercial. The test is conducted in a hotel or other kind of auditorium. The audience is those people who have responded to an invitation sent to a sample drawn in a random manner from a larger listing of the relevant target audience (e.g., electoral lists for a geographic area). The recommended minimum sample size is 100, and up to 3000 invitations may have to be sent out to yield a respondent sample of this size.

The test commercials are exposed to the audience at the end of a program of films, the audience having being told they will see "some films—very much the kind of films that you are likely to see at home on your television screen." The films are shown on a number of television sets with each member of the audience sitting with a small group of people. Lights are held at room level.

After exposure to the films, each member of the audience fills in a self-completed questionnaire. Some of the questions are preceded by the showing of individual scenes of the commercial, and the associated questions are concerned with obtaining respondent attention to and reaction towards the specific scene.

The tests for the two Nabob commercials were carried out as follows:

1. Both commercials were tested in Vancouver.

2. Nabob had a far greater market presence in Vancouver than it did in the proposed Ontario test market. Therefore, the respondents were categorized into two groups: those that stated that they had ever bought Nabob (N) and those that stated that they had never bought Nabob (R). Data analysis was done using these categories, together with the total sample, for most questions.

It was known from previous testing that the Vancouver samples responded very much more negatively to attitude questions relative to the norms, which were based primarily on respondents from Ontario, where the vast majority of Clucas testing was done. Therefore, the overall evaluative ratings were reworked so as "to represent what these scores would have been had attitudes displayed by the Vancouver sample been closer to those expressed by samples from which norm data is derived."

3. There was a sample size of 100 generated for the "Store" commercial, and a sample of 97 for the "Microphone" commercial.

4. The definitions used by Clucas in reporting results were as follows:

A. Diagnostic Data

Oral communications. The percentage of the audience that reported hearing each word in the script, word by word throughout the script.

Visual communication. The percentage of the audience that reported seeing, shot by shot, the different parts of the commercial.

Exhibit 4 (continued)

Communication objectives. (a) The percentage of the audience that reported that the commercial had succeeded in conveying the objectives of each scene. (b) Verbatims to a "Why" question asked of those who indicated that the commercial had failed in communicating a specific objective.

Audience response. (a) The proportion of the audience that reported "anything passing through your mind" the *first* time they saw each scene. (b) Verbatims of these responses grouped by subject matter.

B. Global Data About Overall Effectiveness

Product rating. Two questions, each intended to measure how the product is perceived through the "vehicle" of the commercial—in the eyes of the audience. One is an open-ended question, the second a scaled question ranging from "excellent" to "poor."

Advertiser rating. A measure that collects data on the respondent's impression of the advertiser, collected on a six-point scale.

Fatigue/wearout rating. A measure of how successfully the commercial will resist fatigue/wearout, collected on a six-point scale.

Package recognition. The proportion of the respondents who stated that they would recognize the product package if they saw it again.

Overall communication. The measure of how successful the commercial was in accomplishing its overall communications objectives—as defined by the client.

Audience sales rating. A measure that asks the respondents what they think happened to product sales in a part of Canada where the commercial was shown on T.V., with data collected on a six-point scale.

Exhibit 5 A Selective Summary of the Two Adcom Reports

A. Recall Summary

	Store	Microphone
Commercial audience		
Number	126	145
Percent	100	100
Specific unaided	9	7
Specific aided	24	5
Nonspecific unaided	1	3
Nonspecific aided	1	7
Total related recall	34	21
Brand name only (BNO)		1
Unrelated	1	8
No recall	65	70
Total BNO/unrelated/no recall	66	79
	100	100

Exhibit 5 (continued)

Related Recall Norms (12 mos. to March 31, 1979)

	Percent	*Percent Range (High-Low)*
All commercials	22	(53–5)
All English commercials	21	(48–6)
All 0:60 English commercials	*	*
All 0:30 English commercials	21	(48–6)
All English commercials for prepared and semiprepared foods/snacks/ingredients (includes coffee)	21	(47–8)

*B. Sales Message and Situation Recall***

	Store	Microphone
Commercial audience		
Number	126	145
Percent	100	100
Unduplicated total giving		
Message recall	33	21
No message recall	1	—
Total related message recall	34	21
Unduplicated total giving		
Situation recall	33	17
No situation recall	1	4
Total related recall	34	21

C. Communication Objectives Recall

	Store	Microphone
Commercial audience		
Number	126	145
Percent	100	100
Nabob Coffee comes in a new vacuum pack	21	
Nabob Coffee is fresher tasting than before	23	

*Insufficient data

**The original report provided detailed diagnostic data on unduplicated responses by dimensions of sales message/situation.

Exhibit 5 (continued)

	Store	Microphone
Nabob Coffee comes in a hard vacuum pack		3
Nabob Coffee is fresher		13
Nabob Coffee tastes better		5
Unduplicated total recalling any communication objective	30	17
Related recall not on communication objective	4	4
BNO/unrelated/no recall	66	79
Total	100	100

Related Communication Norms (12 mos. to March 31, 1979)

	Percent	Percent Range
All commercials	16	(44–3)
All English commercials	16	(44–3)
All 0:60 English commercials	*	*
All 0:30 English commercials	16	(44–3)
All English commercials for prepared and semiprepared foods/snacks/ingredients (includes coffee)	16	(44–3)

D. Total Remembering Commercial

	Store	Microphone
Commercial audience		
Number	126	145
Percent	100	100
Total related recall	34	21
Respondents remembered the commercial only when prompt was read to them	34	46
Total respondents remembering the commercial	68	68

Total Remembering Respondents Norm (12 mos. to March 31, 1979)

	Percent	Percent Range
All English commercials	62	(85–35)

*Insufficient data

Exhibit 5 (continued)

E. Attitudes Toward the Commercial

	Provided Related Recall		Remembered Only When Commercial Prompt Read		Total	
	Store	Micro-phone	Store	Micro-phone	Store	Micro-phone
Total remembering commercial						
Number	43	31	43	67	86	98
Percent	100	100	100	100	100	100
Liked it very much	28	35	16	24	22	28
Liked it a little	53	62	63	42	58	48
Did not like it very much	9	3	5	9	7	7
Did not like it at all	5	—	5	6	5	4
Not sure/refused	5	—	12	19	8	13
	100	100	100	100	100	100
Index*	48	65	46	43	47	51
Unduplicated mentions of something disliked/hard to believe/confusing	40	19	35	15	37	16
Something disliked	16	13	23	4	20	7
Something hard to believe	33	3	26	15	29	11
Something found confusing	2	6	—	—	1	2
Nothing disliked/hard to believe/confusing	60	81	65	85	63	84
	100	100	100	100	100	100

Attitudes Norms (12 mos. to March 31, 1979)

	Percent	Percent Range
All English unduplicated		
Disliked/hard to believe/confusing	20	(51–2)
Disliked	10	(43–1)
Hard to believe	12	(37–0)
Confusing	2	(11–0)

*The index is free to vary from − 100 to + 100. The following weights have been assigned:

Liked it very much	+ 2	Did not like it very much	− 1
Liked it a little	+ 1	Did not like it at all	− 2

Exhibit 5 (continued)

	Index Number	Index Range
All English index of liking/disliking	50	$(80-(-18))$

F. Sample Information

	Store	Microphone
Commercial audience		
Number	126	145
Percent	100	100
Respondents female	100	100
Age distribution		
12 and under		
13–19	5	1
20–24	25	13
25–29	26	10
30–34	16	16
35–39	6	10
40–44	6	6
45–49	8	8
50–54	5	11
55–59	2	13
60 and over	—	12
No answer/refused	2	1
	101[a]	101[a]
Marital status		
Single	15	12
Married	79	70
Widowed	1	13
Divorced/separated	3	5
No answer/refused	2	—
	100	100

a. Total greater than 100 owing to rounding.

Exhibit 6 A Selective Summary of the Two Clucas Reports

A. Overall Communication Summary

	Store			Microphone		
	Nabob (N)	Rest (R)	Total	Nabob (N)	Rest (R)	Total
Base						
Number	52	48	100	47	50	97
Percent	100	100	100	100	100	100
Average over commercial	70	67	69	68	69	69

Percent Reporting Hearing Each Word in Script, Word-by-Word Throughout the Script

Norm: 51

B. Visual Communication and Audience Response Summaries

	Duration (secs.)	Visual Communication (%)	Audience Response (%)
(i) Store			
Scene I			
Woman	5	100	80
Pack	2	84	80
Scene II			
Man/woman	6	99	
Pack	2	91	63
Man-woman	4	89	
Scene III			
Man/woman	8	97	71
Pack	3	83	
	30		
Average:		92	71
Norm:		84	58
(ii) Microphone			
Scene I			
Man/pack	16	96	77
Scene II			
Man	4	97	
Pack	5	96	73
Man	12	88	

Exhibit 6 (continued)

	Duration (secs.)	Visual Communication (%)	Audience Response (%)
Scene III			
1st package	3	78	
2nd package	4	93	73
Man	3	93	
Scene IV			
Man	9	95	63
Pack	4	87	
	60		
Average:		91	72
Norm:		84	58

C. Communication Objectives for a Selected Scene and Over All Scenes

(i) Store

"The *first* time you saw it, did this scene succeed in conveying to you that . . ."

Scene III	%N	%R	%T
The coffee really tastes fresh	88	77	83
More than one customer was discovering that Nabob pack is hard	83	88	85
In the last shot a Nabob pack was shown	75	69	72
Average over *three* scenes:	79		
Norm:	71		

(ii) Microphone

"The *first* time you saw it, did this scene succeed in conveying to you that . . ."

Scene I	%N	%R	%T
The commercial was about ground coffee	85	82	84
A pile of ground coffee packages was shown	83	84	84
In the pile there were several different brands	60	60	60
The coffee was packaged in soft paper bags	79	82	82
With this sort of package you can smell the coffee; it lets out flavour/aroma	87	74	80
Average over *four* scenes:	77		
Norm:	71		

Exhibit 6 (continued)

D. Overall Communication Objectives

"The *first* time you saw it, did the commercial *as a whole* succeed in conveying to you that . . ."

	Store			Microphone		
	%N	%R	%T	%N	%R	%T
The commercial was advertising Nabob coffee	100	92	96	94	84	89
It was ground coffee	71	63	67	94	92	93
It has really good flavour	83	77	80	79	66	72
It has really good aroma	90	85	88	89	80	85
It is packed in foil	81	75	78	85	86	86
It is vacuum packed	92	90	91	96	88	92
This seals in the flavour and aroma	88	94	91	89	84	87
It preserves freshness the regular type of paper package cannot match	77	69	73	91	84	88
It makes a better, fresher cup of coffee	87	71	79	77	68	72

E. Package Recognition

	Store			Microphone		
	%N	%R	%T	%N	%R	%T
Recognized pack	67	48	58	89	66	77

Norm: 68

F. Unadjusted Overall Indicators

Sales Rating

"This commercial has been shown in one T.V. area of Canada. Which of the following things do you think actually happened to sales of Nabob coffee as a result of showing the commercial?"

	Store			Microphone		
	%N	%R	%T	%N	%R	%T
Sales increased considerably	18	4	11	15	12	13
Sales increased quite a bit	22	23	22	36	32	34
Sales increased slightly	27	29	28	26	40	33
Sales did not change	33	38	35	21	16	19
Sales decreased slightly	0	6	3	2	0	1
Sales decreased considerably	0	0	0	0	0	0
Weighted ratings sales	31	12	21	39	41	40
Product weighted rating	62	28	46	68	57	63
Advertising weighted rating	4	−19	− 8	11	1	9
Fatigue/wearout weighted rating	−8	−33	−20	−1	−11	−7

Exhibit 6 (continued)

G. Adjusted Overall Indicators

Rating	Store	Microphone	Norm
Sales	27	47	40
Product	49	66	61
Advertiser	0	12	32
Fatigue/wearout	– 16	0	22

H. Sample Information

	Store	Microphone
All respondents		
Number	100	97
Percent	100	100
Sex		
Male	0	2
Female	100	98
Age		
16–24	21	22
25–34	35	37
35–44	17	17
45–54	15	19
55 and over	12	5
	100	100
Annual Household Income		
Less than $7,500	10	13
$7,500–$9,999	8	10
$10,000–$14,999	38	20
$15,000–$19,999	13	18
$20,000–$24,999	10	21
$25,000 or more	20	19
No answer/refused	1	1

42 Nestlé and the Infant Food Controversy

In October 1978, Dr. Fürer, Managing Director of Nestlé S.A., head-quartered in Vevey, Switzerland, was pondering the continuing problems his company faced. Public interest groups, media, health organizations, and other groups had been pressuring Nestlé to change its marketing practices for infant formula products, particularly in developing countries. Those groups had used a variety of pressure tactics, including a consumer boycott in the United States over the past eight years. Critics of Nestlé charged that the company's promotional practices were not only abusive but also harmful, resulting in malnutrition and death in some circumstances. They demanded that Nestlé put a stop to all promotion of its infant formula products to both consumers and health personnel.

Nestlé management had always prided itself on its high quality standards, its efforts to serve the best interests of Nestlé customers, and its contribution to the health and prosperity of people in developing countries. Nestlé management was convinced their infant formula products were useful and wanted; they had not taken the first signs of adverse publicity in the early 1970's very seriously. By 1978, massive adverse publicity appeared to be endangering the reputation of the company, particularly in Europe and North America. Despite support from some health officials and organizations throughout the world, Nestlé Management in Vevey and White Plains, New York (U.S.A. headquarters) were seriously concerned. Dr. Fürer had been consulting with Mr. Guerrant, President of Nestlé U.S.A., in an effort to formulate a strategy. Of immediate concern to Nestlé management was the scheduled meeting of the National Council of Churches (U.S.A.) in November 1978. On the agenda was a resolution to support the critics of Nestlé who were leading the consumer boycott against Nestlé products in the United States. The National Council of Churches was an important, prestigious organization, a fact that caused

* Courtesy IMEDE Management Development Institute, Lausanne, Switzerland.

Nestlé management to fear that NCC support of the boycott might further endanger Nestlé.

Also of concern was the meeting of the World Health Organization (WHO) scheduled in fall 1979 to bring together the infant food manufacturers, public interest groups, and the world health community in an attempt to formulate a code of marketing conduct for the industry. Nestlé management, instrumental in establishing this conference, hoped that a clear set of standards would emerge, thus moderating or eliminating the attacks of the public pressure groups.

Dr. Fürer was anxious to clear up what he thought were misunderstandings about the industry. As he reviewed the history of the formula problem, he wondered in general what a company could do when subjected to pressure tactics by activist groups and in particular what Nestlé management should do next.

Nestlé Alimentana S.A.

The Swiss-based Nestlé Alimentana S.A. was one of the largest food products companies in the world. Nestlé had 80,000 shareholders in Switzerland. Nestlé's importance to Switzerland was comparable to the combined importance of General Motors and Exxon to the United States. In 1977, Nestlé's worldwide sales approximated 20 billion Swiss francs. Of this total, 7.3 percent were infant and dietetic products; more specifically, 2.5 percent of sales were accounted for by infant formula sales in developing countries.

Traditionally a transnational seller of food products, Nestlé's basic goal had always been to be a fully integrated processor in every country in which it operated. It aimed at maintaining an important market presence in almost every nation of the world. In each country, Nestlé typically established local plants, supported private farms and dairy herds, and sold a wide range of products to cover all age groups. By the end of 1977, Nestlé had 87 factories in the developing countries and provided 35,610 direct jobs. Nestlé management were proud of this business approach and published a 228-page book in 1975 entitled *Nestlé in Developing Countries*. The cover of this book carried the following statement:

> While Nestlé is not a philanthropic society, facts and figures clearly prove that the nature of its activities in developing countries is self-evident as a factor that contributes to economic development. The company's constant need for local raw materials, processing and staff, and

the particular contribution it brings to local industry, support the fact that Nestlé's presence in the Third World is based on common interests in which the progress of one is always to the benefit of the other.

Although it neither produced nor marketed infant formula in the United States, the Nestlé Company Inc. (White Plains) sold a variety of products such as Nescafe, Nestea, Crunch, Quik, Taster's Choice, and Libby, McNeil & Libby products throughout the United States.

With over 95 percent of Nestlé's sales outside of Switzerland, the company had developed an operating policy characterized by strong central financial control along with substantial freedom in marketing strategy by local managers. Each country manager was held responsible for profitability. Through periodic planning meetings, Nestlé management in Vevey ("the Centre") reviewed the broad strategy proposals of local companies. One area of responsibility clearly reserved to Vevey was the maintenance of the overall company image, although no formal public relations department existed. Marketing plans were reviewed in part by Vevey to see if they preserved the company's reputation for quality and service throughout the world.

Nestlé and the Infant Formula Industry

The international infant formula industry was composed of two types of firms, pharmaceutically oriented ones and food processing ones. The major companies competing in the developing countries were as follows:

	Company	*Brands*
(a) Pharmaceutical		
(U.S.)	Wyeth Lab (American Home Products)	SMA, S26, Nursoy
(U.S.)	Ross Lab (Abbott Laboratories)	Similac, Isomil
(U.S.)	Mead Johnson (Bristol-Myers)	Enfamil, Olac, Prosobee
(b) Food processing		
(U.S.)	Borden	New Biolac
(Swit.)	Nestlé	Nestogen, Eledon, Pelargon
(U.K.)	Unigate	Nan, Lactogen

In addition to these six firms, there were about another dozen formula producers chartered in 1978 throughout the world.

The basic distinction between pharmaceutically oriented formula producers and food processing oriented producers lay in their entry point into the formula business. In the early 1900's, medical research laboratories of major pharmaceutical firms developed "humanized formulas," leading their parent companies into marketing such products. Essentially, a humanized formula was a modification of normal cow's milk to approximate more closely human milk. Generally speaking, the food processing companies had begun offering infant food as an extension of their full milk powdered products and canned milk.

As early as the 1800's, Nestlé had been engaged in research in the field of child nutrition. In 1867, Henry Nestlé, the founder of the company and the great-grandfather of infant formula, introduced the first specifically designed, commercially marketed infant-weaning formula. An infant-weaning formula is basically a cereal and milk mixture designed to introduce solids to a child of 5–6 months of age.

As of the 1860's, both Nestlé and Borden had been producing sweetened and evaporated milk. Nestlé very quickly recognized the need for better artificial infant food and steadily developed a full line of formula products in the early 1900's (for example, Lactogen in 1921, Eledon in 1927, Nestogen in 1930). Although it was a food processing company, Nestlé's product development and marketing were supervised by physicians.

In the United States during the early 1900's, the infant formula products developed by the medical laboratories were being used primarily in hospitals. Over time, the industry developed the distinction of formula products for "well babies" versus those for "sick babies." In the latter category would be included special nutritional and dietary problems, such as allergies to milk requiring babies to have totally artificial formulas made from soybeans. Approximately 2 percent of industry volume was formula designed for "sick babies."

In the late nineteenth century and the early twentieth century, Nestlé developed a commanding position in the sweetened and evaporated milk market in the developing countries (also referred to as "the Third World"). Demand for these products was initially established among European colonials and gradually spread throughout the world and into the rising middle classes in many nations. Nestlé's early marketing efforts focused on switching infant feeding from the previously common use of sweetened and condensed milk to a more appropriate product, humanized infant formula.

By promoting through doctors (medical detailing) a full product line, Nestlé achieved an overwhelmingly dominant market position in the European colonies, countries that later became independent "Third World" countries. Meanwhile, most of the competition developed quickly in the industrialized countries, so much so that Nestlé stayed out of the U.S. formula market entirely. Not until late in the 1950's did significant intense competition, mainly from American multinationals, develop in Nestlé's markets in developing countries. These markets, with their high birth rates and rising affluence, became increasingly attractive to all formula producers. After the entry of American competitors, Nestlé's share of markets began to erode.

As of 1978, Nestlé accounted for about one third to one half of infant formula sales in the developing countries while American companies held about one fifth. The size of the total world market for infant formula was not exactly known because data on shipments of infant formula were not separated from other milk products, especially powders. Some sources "guesstimated" world sales to be close to $1.5 billion (U.S.), half of that to developing countries.

Traditional Methods of Promotion

Several methods had been used over the years to promote infant products in developing countries. Five major methods predominated:

1. *Media advertising.* All media types were employed, including posters in clinics and hospitals, outdoor billboards, newspapers, magazines, radio, television, and loudspeakers on vans. Native languages and English were used.

2. *Samples.* Free sample distribution, either direct to new mothers or via doctors, was relatively limited until competition increased in the 1960's. Mothers were given either formula or feeding bottles or both, often in a "new mother's kit." Doctors in clinics and hospitals received large packages of product for use while mother and baby were present. The formula producers believed that this practice helped educate new mothers on the use of formula products, and hopefully, initiated brand preference. In some instances, doctors actually resold samples to provide an extra source of income for themselves or their institutions.

3. *Booklets.* Most formula marketers provided new mothers with booklets on baby care, which were given free to them when they left the hospitals and clinics with their newborn infants. These booklets, such as Nestlé's *A Life Begins,* offered a variety of advice and advertised the formula products and other infant foods, both Nestlé and home-made.

4. *Milk nurses.* Milk nurses (also known as "mothercraft nurses") were formula producer employees who talked with new mothers in the hospitals and clinics or at home. Originally, they were all fully trained

nurses instructed in product knowledge and then sent out to educate new mothers on the correct use of the new formula products. This instruction included the importance of proper personal hygiene, boiling the water, and mixing formula and water in correct quantities. These became a major part of many firms' efforts; for example, at one time, Nestlé had about 200 mothercraft employees worldwide. The majority of milk nurses were paid a straight salary plus a travel allowance; but over time, some were hired on a sales-related bonus basis. Some companies, other than Nestlé, began to relax standards in the 1960's and hired nonnursing personnel who dressed in nurses' uniforms and acted more in a selling capacity and less in an educational capacity.

5. *Milk banks*. Milk bank was the term used to describe special distribution outlets affiliated with and administered by those hospitals and clinics that served very low income people. Formula products were provided to low income families at much reduced prices for mothers who could not afford the commercial product. The producers sold products to those outlets at lower prices to enable this service to occur.

PAG 23

Nestlé management believed the controversy surrounding the sale of infant formula in developing countries began in the early 1970's. Many international organizations were concerned about the problem of malnourishment of infants in the developing countries of South Asia, Africa, and Latin America. In Bogota (1970) and Paris (1972), representatives of the Food and Agricultural Organization (FAO), the World Health Organization (WHO), UNICEF, the International Pediatric Association, and the infant formula industry, including Nestlé, all met to discuss nutrition problems and guidelines. The result was a request that the United Nations Protein-Calorie Advisory Group (PAG), an organization formed in 1955, set guidelines for nutrition for infants. On July 18, 1972, the PAG issued Statement 23 on the "Promotion of Special Foods for Vulnerable Groups." This statement emphasized the importance of breast-feeding, the danger of overpromotion, the need to take local conditions into account, the problem of misuse of formula products, and the desirability of reducing promotion but increasing education.

Statement 23 included the following statements:

Breast milk is an optimal food for infants and, if available in sufficient quantities, it is adequate as the sole source of food during the first four to six months of age.

Poor health and adverse social circumstances may decrease the output of milk by the mother . . . in such circumstances supplementation of breast milk with nutritionally adequate foods must start earlier than four to six months if growth failure is to be avoided.

It is clearly important to avoid any action which would accelerate the trend away from breast-feeding.

It is essential to make available to the mother the foods, formulas, and instructions which will meet the need for good nutrition of those infants who are breast-fed.

Nestlé management regarded PAG 23 as an "advisory statement," so management's stance was to see what happened. None of the developing countries took any action on the statement. Nestlé officials consulted with ministers of health in many developing countries to ask what role their governments wished Nestlé to play in bringing nutrition education to local mothers. No major changes were requested.

At the same time, Nestlé Vevey ordered an audit of marketing practices employed by its companies in the developing nations. On the basis of reports from the field, Nestlé Management in Vevey concluded that only a few changes in marketing were required, which they ordered be done. In Nigeria, the Nigerian Society of Health and Nutrition asked Nestlé to change its ads for formula to stress breast-feeding. Nestlé complied with this request, and its ads in all developing countries prominently carried the phrase "When breast milk fails, use . . ."

The British Contribution

In its August 1973 issue, the *New Internationalist,* an English journal devoted to problems in developing countries, published an article entitled "The Baby Food Tragedy." This was an interview with two doctors: Dr. R.G. Hendrikse, Director of the Tropical Child Health Course, Liverpool University, and medical researcher in Rhodesia, Nigeria, and South Africa and Dr. David Morley, Reader in Tropical Child Health, University of London. Both doctors expressed concern about the widespread use of formula among impoverished, less literate families. They claimed that in such cases, low family incomes prevented mothers from buying the necessary amount of formula for their children. Instead, they used smaller quantities of formula powder, diluting it with more water than recommended. Further, the water used was frequently contaminated. The infant thus received less than adequate nutrition, indeed was often exposed to contaminated formula. The malnourished child became increasingly susceptible to infections, leading to diarrheal diseases. Diarrhea meant that the child could assimilate even less of the nutrients because neither the child's stomach nor intestines were working properly. This vicious cycle could lead to death. The two doctors believed that local conditions made the use of commercial infant formula not only unnecessary, but likely difficult and dangerous. Breast-feeding was safer, healthier, and certainly less expensive.

The article, in the opinion of many, was relatively restrained and balanced. However, it was accompanied by dramatic photographs of malnourished black babies and of a baby's grave with a tin of milk powder placed on it. The article had a strong emotional impact on readers and reached many people who were not regular readers of the journal. It was widely reprinted and quoted by other groups. The journal sent copies of the article to more than 3000 hospitals in the developing nations.

The two doctors interviewed for the article had mentioned Nestlé and its promotional practices. Accordingly, the editors of the *New Internationalist* contacted Nestlé S.A. for its position. The company response was published in the October issue of the *New Internationalist* along with an editorial entitled "Milk and Murder."

Nestlé S.A. responded in part as follows:

> We have carefully studied both the editorial and the interviews with Dr. Hendrickse and Dr. Morley published in the August edition of the *New Internationalist*. Although fleeting references are made to factors other than manufacturers' activities which are said to be responsible for the misuse of infant foods in developing countries, their readers would certainly not be in a position to judge from the report the immense socio-economic complexities of the situation. . . .
>
> It would be impossible to demonstrate in the space of a letter the enormous efforts made by the Nestlé organization to ensure the correct usage of their infant food products, and the way in which the PAG guidelines have been applied by the Nestlé subsidiaries. However, if the Editor of the *New Internationalist* (or the author of the article in question) wishes to establish the complete facts as far as we are concerned, then we should be happy to receive him in Vevey on a mutually agreeable date in the near future. We should certainly welcome the opportunity to reply to some of the sweeping allegations made against Nestlé either by implication or by specific references.

The editors of the *New Internationalist* refused the invitation to visit Nestlé's Vevey headquarters. Further, they maintained that PAG 23 guidelines were not being observed and did not have any provisions for enforcement.

In March 1974, War on Want published a pamphlet entitled *The Baby Killer*. War on Want was a private British group established to give aid to Third World nations. In particular, they were devoted "to make world poverty an urgent social and political issue." War on Want issued a set of recommendations to industry, governments, the medical profession, and others to deal with the baby formula problem as they saw it (see exhibit 1).

The Baby Killer was written by Mike Muller as an attempt to publicize the infant formula issue. Mr. Muller expanded on the *New Internationalist* articles and, in the view of many observers, gave reasonable treatment to the complexity of the circumstances surrounding the use of formula products in the developing countries. On the whole, it was an attack against bottle-feeding rather than an attack against any particular company.

Part of *The Baby Killer* was based on interviews the author had with three Nestlé employees: Dr. H.R. Müller, G.A. Fookes, and J. Momoud, all of Nestlé S.A. Infant and Dietetics Division. These Nestlé officials argued that Nestlé was acting as responsibly as it could. Further, they said, that abuses if they existed could not be controlled by single companies. Only a drastic change in the competitive system could check abuses effectively.

Exhibit 1 War on Want's Recommendations

Industry

1. The serious problems caused by early weaning onto breast milk substitutes demands a serious response. Companies should follow the Swedish example and refrain from all consumer promotion of breast milk substitutes in high risk communities.
2. The companies should cooperate constructively with the international organisations working on the problems of infant and child nutrition in the developing countries.
3. Companies should abandon promotions to the medical profession which may perform the miseducational function of suggesting that particular brands of milk can overcome the problems of misuse.

Governments of developing countries

1. Governments should take note of the recommendations of the Protein Advisory Group for national nutrition strategies.
2. Where social and economic conditions are such that proprietary infant foods can make little useful contribution, serious consideration should be given to the curtailment of their importation, distribution, and/or promotion.
3. Governments should ensure that supplies are made available first to those in need—babies whose mothers cannot breast-feed, twins, orphans, etc.—rather than to an economic elite, a danger noted by the PAG.

Exhibit 1 (continued)

British Government

1. The British Government should exercise a constructive influence in the current debate.
2. The Government should insist that British companies such as Unigate and Glaxo set a high standard of behaviour and it should be prepared to enforce a similar standard on multi-nationals like Wyeth who export to developing country markets from Britain.
3. The British representative on the Codex Alimentarius Commission should urge the Commission to consider all aspects of the promotion of infant foods. If necessary, structural alterations should be proposed to set up a subcommittee to consider broader aspects of promotion to enable the Commission to fulfill its stated aims of protecting the consumer interests.

Medical profession

There is a need in the medical profession for a greater awareness of the problems caused by artificial feeding of infants and of the role of the medical profession in encouraging the trend away from breast feeding.

Other channels

Practicing health workers in the Third World have achieved startling, if limited, response by writing to local medical journals and the press about any promotional malpractices they see and sending copies of their complaints to the companies involved. This could be done by volunteers and others not in the medical profession but in contact with the problem in the field.

In Britain, student unions at a number of universities and polytechnics decided to ban the use of all Nestlé's products where they had control of catering following the initial exposé by the *New Internationalist* magazine. Without any clear objective, or coordination, this kind of action is unlikely to have much effect.

However, if the companies involved continue to be intransigent in the face of the dangerous situation developing in the Third World, a more broadly based campaign involving many national organisations may be the result. At the very least, trade unions, women's organisations, consumer groups, and other interested parties need to be made aware of the present dangers.

There is also a clear need to examine on a community scale, how infant feeding practices are determined in Britain today. There is a long history of commercial persuasion, and artificial feeding is now well entrenched.

As has been shown, there are still risks inherent in bottle feeding even in Britain. The available evidence suggests that both mother and child may do better physically and emotionally by breast feeding. An examination of our own irrational social practices can help the Third World to throw a light on theirs.

Mr. Muller apparently was not impressed by this argument, nor did he mention Nestlé management's stated willingness to establish enforceable international guidelines for marketing conduct. In *The Baby Killer,* Mr. Muller revealed that he was convinced that Nestlé was exploiting the high birth rates in developing countries by encouraging mothers to replace, not supplement, breast-feeding by formula products. Mr. Muller offered as support for his stance a quotation from Nestlé's 1973 Annual Report:

> . . . the continual decline in birth rates, particularly in countries with a high standard of living, retarded growth of the market. . . . In the developing countries our own products continue to sell well thanks to the growth of population and improved living standards.

Dr. Fürer's reaction to *The Baby Killer* was that Mr. Muller had given too much weight to the negative aspects of the situation. Mr. Muller failed to mention, for example, that infant mortality rates had shown very dramatic declines in the developing countries. Some part of these declines were the result of improved nutrition, Dr. Fürer believed, and improved nutrition was partly the result of the use of formula products. Despite his strong belief that Nestlé's product was highly beneficial rather than harmful, Dr. Fürer ordered a second audit of Nestlé's advertising and promotional methods in developing countries. Again changes were made. These changes included revision of advertising copy to emphasize further the superiority of breast-feeding, elimination of radio advertising in the developing world, and cessation of the use of white uniforms on the mothercraft nurses.

At the same time, on May 23, 1974, WHO adopted a resolution that misleading promotion had contributed to the decline in breast-feeding in the developing countries and urged individual countries to take legal action to curb such abuses.

The Third World Action Group

In June 1974, the infant formula issue moved into Switzerland. A small, poorly financed group called the Third World Action Group, located in Bern, the capital of Switzerland, published in German a booklet entitled *Nestlé Kills Babies (Nestlé Totet Kinder).* This was a partial translation of the War on Want publication *The Baby Killer.* Some of the qualifying facts found in Mr. Muller's booklet were omitted in *Nestlé Kills Babies,* while the focus was changed from a general attack on bottle-feeding to a direct attack on Nestlé and its promotional practices.

Nestlé's top management was extremely upset by this publication. Dr. Fürer immediately ordered a follow-up audit of Nestlé's marketing practices to ensure that stated corporate ethical standards were being observed. Nestlé management also believed that the infant formula issue was being used as a vehicle by leftist, Marxist groups intent on attacking the free market system, multinational companies in general, and Nestlé in particular. Internal Nestlé memoranda of the time reveal the material available to management that supported their belief that the issue went beyond infant formula promotion. For example:

> Having a closer look at the allies of the AG3W [Third World Action Group] in their actions, we realized that they happen to have the same aim. There are common actions with the leninist progressive organizations (POCH), who are also considered to be pro-Soviet, with the Swiss communist party (PdA) and the communist youth organization (KJV), as well as with the revolutionary marxist alliance (RML). Since the AG3W has tried to coordinate the support of (only pro-communist) liberation movements with representatives of the communist block, it is not surprising that they also participate at the youth festival in Eastern Berlin.

> Third World Action Group (AG3W), *Der Zurichbieter,* August 15, 1973.

Believing the issue to be clearly legal, Nestlé management brought suit in July 1974 against thirteen members of the Third World Action Group and against two newspapers who carried articles about *Nestlé Kills Babies.* Nestlé charged criminal libel, claiming that the company had been defamed because "the whole report charges Nestlé S.A. with using incorrect sales promotion in the third world and with pulling mothers away from breast-feeding their babies and turning them to its products." More specifically, Nestlé management claimed the following were defamatory:

The title "Nestlé Kills Babies."

The charge that the practices of Nestlé and other companies are unethical and immoral (written in the introduction and in the report itself).

The accusation of responsibility for the death or permanent physical and mental damage of babies by its sales promotion policy (in introduction).

The accusation that in LDC's, the sales representatives for baby foods are dressed like nurses to give the sales promotion a scientific appearance.

The trial in Bern provided the Third World Action Group with a great deal of publicity, giving it a forum to present its views. Swiss television in particular devoted much time to coverage of the trial and the issues involved. The trial ended in the fall of 1976. Nestlé management won a judgment on the first of the libel charges (because of lack of specific evidence for the Third World Action Group), and the activists were fined 300 Swiss Francs each. Nestlé management dropped the remaining charges. In his judgment, the presiding judge added an opinion that became well-publicized:

> . . . the need ensues for the Nestlé company to fundamentally rethink its advertising practices in developing countries as concerns bottle feeding, for its advertising practice up to now can transform a life-saving product into one that is dangerous and life-destroying. If Nestlé S.A. in the future wants to be spared the accusations of immoral and unethical conduct, it will have to change its advertising practices. . . .

The Controversy Spreads

While the trial was in process, various interest groups from all over the world became interested and involved in the infant formula controversy. In London, England, Mr. Mike Muller founded the Baby Foods Action Group. Late in 1974, the World Food Conference adopted a resolution recommending that developing nation governments actively support breast-feeding. The PAG had been organizing a number of international regional seminars to discuss all aspects of the controversy. For example, in November 1974, during the PAG regional seminar in Singapore, the PAG recommended that the infant formula industry increase its efforts to implement Statement 23 and cooperate to regulate their promotion and advertising practices through a code of ethics.

The world health organizations kept up the pressure. In March 1975, the PAG again met:

> . . . to discuss together the problem of deteriorating infant feeding practices in developing countries and to make recommendations for remedying the situation. The early discontinuance of breast-feeding by mothers in low-income groups in urban areas, leading to malnutrition, illness and death among infants has been a serious concern to all.

In May 1975, WHO at its fourteenth plenary meeting again called for a critical review of promotion of infant formula products.

In response, representatives of the major formula producers met in Zürich, Switzerland, in May 1975 to discuss the possibility and desirability of establishing an international code of ethics for the industry. Nine of the manufacturers, with the notable exceptions of Borden, Bristol-Myers, and Abbott, created an organization called the International Council of Infant Food Industries (ICIFI) and a code of marketing conduct. This code went into effect November 1, 1975. Some firms also adopted individual codes, including Nestlé, with standards higher than the ICIFI code.

The ICIFI code required that ICIFI members assume responsibility to encourage breast-feeding, that milk nurses be paid on a strict salary basis and wear company uniforms, and that product labels indicate breast milk as the best infant food. At this time, Nestlé began to phase out use of mass media for infant formula in developing countries but continued to distribute educational materials and product information in the hospitals and clinics. Nestlé management believed that such advertising and promotion was of educational value—to ensure proper use of formula and to decrease usage of sweetened and condensed milk for infant feeding.

ICIFI submitted its code of ethics to the PAG, which submitted it to a number of third parties. On the basis of their opinions, the PAG refused to endorse the code, saying that it did not go far enough, that substantial amendments were required. ICIFI rejected these suggestions because of difficult antitrust considerations, so the PAG withheld its approval of the code.

An important exception to ICIFI membership was Abbott Laboratories. While Abbott representatives had attended the meeting that led to the establishment of ICIFI, they decided not to join. Abbott, having recently had difficulties with the U.S. Food and Drug Administration regarding the marketing of cyclomates and artificial sweeteners, felt that ICIFI was not an adequate response to the public pressure:

> . . . the most important area is to reduce the impact of advertising on the low-income, poorly educated populations where the risk is the greatest. The ICIFI code does not address this very important issue.
>
> Our company decided not to join ICIFI because the organization is not prepared to go far enough in answering this legitimate criticism of our industry. We feel that for Abbott/Ross to identify with this organization and its code would limit our ability to speak on the important issues.

Abbott acted largely independently of the other producers. Later, in 1977, Abbott management announced its intention to commit about $100,000 to a breast-feeding campaign in developing nations and about $175,000 to a task force on breast-feeding, infant formula, and Third World countries.

Developments in the United States

Although Nestlé U.S. neither manufactured nor marketed formula, management found itself increasingly embroiled in the controversy during the mid-1970's. The first major group to bring this matter to the public was the Interfaith Center on Corporate Responsibility (ICCR). The ICCR, a union of fourteen Protestant denominations and approximately 150

Catholic orders and dioceses, was a group concerned about the social responsibility behaviour of corporations. The ICCR advised its members on this topic to guide decisions for the members' combined investment portfolio of several billion dollars. Formerly known as the Center of Corporate Responsibility, the ICCR was established under the tax-exempt umbrella of the American National Council of Churches when the U.S. Internal Revenue Service revoked the CRR tax exemption.

The ICCR urged its members to investigate the marketing practice of the leading American formula producers, American Home Products, Abbott Laboratories, and Bristol-Myers. Stockholder groups demanded from these companies, as they were entitled to do by American law, detailed information regarding market shares, promotion and advertising practices, and general company policies concerning the infant formula business.

Nestlé management believed that the ICCR was interested in ideology more than in baby formula. As support, they pointed to a statement made in a January edition of ICCR's *The Corporate Examiner:*

> . . . the motivations, ethos, and operations of transnational corporations
> are inimical to the establishment of a new economic order. Both justice
> and stability are undermined in the fulfillment of their global vision.

Perhaps the major vehicle used by ICCR to get attention was a half-hour film entitled *Bottle Babies.* Well-known German filmmaker Peter Krieg began this film shortly after the Bern trial began. Nestlé Vevey management believed that the film was partially sponsored by the World Council of Churches to provide a public defence for the Third World Action Group position. Most of the filming was done in Kenya, Africa in 1975 in a "documentary" style, although Nestlé management pointed out that the film was scripted and, in their opinion, highly emotional and misleading. A letter (exhibit 2) that Nestlé management later received written by Professor Bwibo of the University of Nairobi supported management's views about the *Bottle Babies* film.

ICCR distributed copies of the *Bottle Babies* film to church groups throughout the United States. Typically, the film was shown to a gathering of church members followed by an impassioned plea to write letters of protest and a request for funds to further the campaign. Since the film singled out Nestlé for attack in its last ten minutes, Nestlé became symbolic of all that was wrong in the infant formula controversy in the minds of these religious groups. Nestlé management, however, were seldom asked for nor given an opportunity to present their position on the issues.

While Nestlé felt the growing pressure of *Bottle Babies,* the major American formula producers faced a variety of ICCR-shareholder in-

Exhibit 2

14th April, 1978

Miss June Noranka
644 Summit Avenue
St. Paul
Minnesota 55105

Dear Miss Noranka:

Following your visit to Kenya and my office I write to inform you, your group, your colleagues and any other person interested that the film Peter Krieg filmed in this department and the associated teaching areas, did not represent the right aspects of what we participated in during the filming.

The film which was intended to be a scientific and educational film turned out to be an emotional, biased and exaggerated film—and failed to be a teaching film. It arouses emotions in people who have little chance to check these facts. No wonder it has heated the emotions of the Activists groups in America and I understand now spreading to Europe. I wish I was in an opportunity to be with your groups and we view the film together and I comment.

As a pediatrician, I would like to put on record that I have not seen the Commercial baby food companies pressurise anybody to use their brands of milk. As for Nestlé, we have discussed with their Managing Directors, starting much earlier than the time of the film in 1971, as to the best way of approaching baby feeding and discussed extensively advertisement especially the material to be included. The directors have followed our advice and we are happy with their working conditions.

We are interested in the well being of our children and we are Medical Scientists. So anything of scientific value we will promote but we will avoid imagined exaggerated and distorted views.

I am taking the liberty to copy this letter to Mr. Jones, Managing Director of Food Specialty in Nairobi, who produce and makes Nestlé's products here for his information.

Yours sincerely,

Nimrod O. Bwibo
Professor & Chairman

---

itiatives. ICCR requested detailed information from American Home Products, Abbott Laboratories, and Bristol-Myers. Each company responded differently.

American Home Products. After refusing to release all the information ICCR requested, American Home Products (AHP) faced a resolution to be included in its proxy statement. ICCR dropped the resolution the day before printing, when AHP management agreed:

to provide the requested information;

to send a report to its shareholders saying that many authorities believe that misuse of infant formula in developing countries could be dangerous, that the company promotes breast-feeding while making available formula for mothers who cannot or do not choose to breast-feed, that the company would promote to medical professionals only, and that AHP was a member of ICIFI, which was developing a voluntary code of promotional practices.

Abbott Laboratories. After a year and a half of meetings with ICCR, Abbott released most of the information ICCR wanted. Still, to obtain the rest of the data, ICCR shareholders filed a shareholder resolution. This proposal received less than the 3 percent of the vote required by the Securities and Exchange Commission (SEC) in order to resubmit the proposal at a later time. Thus, it was not resubmitted.

Bristol-Myers. Bristol-Myers would not cooperate with ICCR, so one church shareholder with 500 shares, Sisters of the Precious Blood, filed a shareholder resolution in 1975 asking that the information be released. After receiving 5.4 percent of the vote and having aroused the concern of the Ford Foundation and the Rockefeller Foundation, it appeared the resolution would be launched again the next year. In August 1975, Bristol-Myers management published a report "The Infant Formula Marketing Practices of Bristol-Myers Co. in Countries outside the United States." The 1976 proxy included the Sisters' resolution and a statement entitled "Management's Position." The Sisters maintained that the statement was false and misleading and filed suit against management; statements appearing in a proxy statement are required by law to be accurate.

In May 1977, a U.S. district court judge dismissed the case, saying the Sisters had failed to show irreparable harm to themselves as the law requires. The judge would not comment on the accuracy of the company's proxy report. The nuns appealed with the support of the SEC. In early 1978, the management of Bristol-Myers agreed to send a report outlining the dispute to all shareholders and agreed to restrictions on company marketing practices, including a ban on all consumer-directed promotion in clinics, hospitals, and other public places and a stop to using milk nurses in Jamaica.

In 1977, Abbott management agreed to revise their code of marketing conduct and to eliminate the use of nurses' uniforms by company sales people despite the fact some were registered nurses.

ICCR and its supporters also persuaded Representative Michael Harrington, Democrat from Massachusetts, to cosponsor a federal resolution requiring an investigation of U.S. infant formula producers.

The campaign against the formula producers took on a new dimension in mid-1977. A group at the University of Minnesota called the Third World Institute, led by Doug Johnson, formed the Infant Formula Action Coalition (INFACT) in June 1977. INFACT members were encouraged by ICCR and the Sisters of the Precious Blood but felt that significant progress would not be made until Nestlé was pressured to change. INFACT realized that legal and shareholder action against a foreign-based company would be futile, so on July 4, 1977, INFACT announced a consumer boycott against those infant formula companies whose marketing practices INFACT found abusive. Despite the boycott's original target of several companies, Nestlé was the main focal point, especially after the other major companies made concessions to ICCR. INFACT began the boycott in front of Nestlé's Minneapolis offices with a demonstration of about 100 people. INFACT urged consumers to boycott over forty Nestlé products.

Nestlé management in White Plains was not sure what response to take. Nestlé U.S. was not at all involved with infant formula but was genuinely concerned about the publicity INFACT was getting. Nestlé S.A. management, on the other hand, originally did not think the boycott campaign would amount to anything, believing that it was a project of some college kids in the United States based on misinformation about events in other parts of the world.

In September and October 1977, Nestlé senior managers from Vevey and White Plains met with members of INFACT, ICCR, the Ford Foundation, and other interested groups. Nestlé management had hoped to resolve what they thought was a problem of poor communication by explaining the facts. Nestlé management argued that the company could not meet competition if it stopped all promotion, which would mean less sales and less jobs in the developing nations. Further, management claimed, "We have an instructional and educational responsibility as marketers of these products and, if we failed in that responsibility, we could be justly criticized." INFACT members stated they found the talks useful in clarifying positions but concluded Nestlé was unwilling to abandon all promotion of its formula products.

In November 1977, INFACT decided not only to continue the boycott, but also to increase it to a national scale. INFACT held a conference in Minneapolis on November 2–4, for more than 45 organizers from 24 cities. These organizers represented women's groups, college hunger-action coalitions, health professionals, church agencies, and social justice groups. A clearinghouse was established to coordinate boycott efforts and information collection. The group also agreed to assist ICCR in its shareholder pressure campaign and to press for congressional action. Later, INFACT petitioned all U.S. government officials, state and federal, for support of the boycott. On November 21, the Interfaiths Hunger Coalition, a group affiliated with INFACT, demonstrated in front of Nestlé's Los Angeles sales office with about 150 people chanting "Nestlé kills babies." This demonstration received prominent media coverage, as did other boycott activities. The combination of INFACT's boycott, ICCR's shareholder efforts, the exhibition of *Bottle Babies,* and the strong support of other U.S. activists (including Ralph Nader, Cesar Chavez, Gloria Steinem, and Dr. Benjamin Spock), resulted in an increasingly high profile for the infant formula controversy, even though Nestlé management believed there had been as yet no adverse effect on sales.

In early 1978, an unofficial WHO working group published the following statement:

> The advertising of food for nursing infants or older babies and young children is of particular importance and should be prohibited on radio and television. Advertising for mother's milk substitutes should never be aimed directly at the public or families, and advertising for ready-made infant food preparations should show clearly that they are not meant for less than three-month old infants. Publicity for public consumption, which should in any case never be distributed without previous recommendation by the competent medical authority, should indicate that breast milk should always constitute the sole or chief constituent of food for those under three months. Finally, the distribution of free samples and other sales promotion practices for baby foods should be generally prohibited.

Nestlé management met again with INFACT representatives in February 1978. No progress was made in reconciling the two sides. Nestlé management could not accept statements from INFACT such as:

> The corporations provide the product and motivate the people to buy it, and set into motion a process that may cause the death of the baby. The corporations are responsible for that death. When the outcome is death, the charge against the corporation is murder.

Nonetheless, management learned what INFACT wanted:

Stop all direct consumer promotion and publicity for infant formula.

Stop employing "milk nurses" as sales staff.

Stop distributing free samples to clinics, hospitals, and maternity hospitals.

Stop promoting infant formula among the medical profession and public health profession.

To further publicize their campaign, INFACT representatives and their allies persuaded Senator Edward Kennedy, Democrat from Massachusetts, to hold Senate hearings on the infant formula issue in May 1978. CBS decided to make a TV report of the entire affair. To prepare for the hearings, INFACT organized a number of demonstrations across the United States. At one meeting on April 15, 1978, Doug Johnson said:

> The goal of the Nestlé's Boycott Campaign and of the entire infant formula coalition is to get the multinationals to stop promotion of infant formula. We're not asking them to stop marketing; we're not asking them to pull out of—out of the countries; we're simply asking them to stop the promotion, and in that I think we're—we're in agreement with a number of prestigious organizations. The World Health Organization recently asked the corporations to stop consumer advertising and to stop the use of free samples, and the International Pediatric Association did that several years ago. So, I think we're asking a very reasonable thing: to stop promoting something which is inappropriate and dangerous.

CBS filmed these demonstrations but did not air them until after the Kennedy hearings.

The Kennedy Hearings and CBS Report

Senator Kennedy was chairman of the Subcommittee on Health and Scientific Research on Infant Nutrition. Both critics and members of the infant formula industry appeared before the Kennedy Committee in May 1978. Nestlé S.A. management decided not to send headquarters management or management from Nestlé U.S. Instead, they asked R. Oswaldo Ballarin, President and Chairman of Nestlé, Brazil to represent Nestlé at the hearings. Dr. Ballarin, a highly regarded technical expert on nutrition, began with a statement prepared by Nestle U.S., but Senator Kennedy soon interrupted him as the following excerpt from the testimony indicates:

DR. BALLARIN: United States Nestlé's Company has advised me that their research indicates this is actually an indirect attack on the free world's economic system: a worldwide church organization with its stated purpose of undermining the free enterprise system is at the forefront of this activity.

SENATOR KENNEDY: Now you can't seriously expect . . . (Noise in background: gavel banging.) We'll be in order . . . we'll be in order now please. We'll be in order. Uh, you don't seriously expect us to accept that on face value, after we've heard as . . . as you must've, Doctor . . . if I could just finish my question . . . the . . . the testimony of probably 9 different witnesses. It seemed to me that they were expressing a very deep compassion and concern about the well-being of infants, the most vulnerable in this . . . face of the world. Would you agree with me that your product should not be used where there is impure water? Yes or no?

DR. BALLARIN: Uh, we give all the instructions . . .

SENATOR KENNEDY: Just . . . just answers. What would you . . . what is your position?

DR. BALLARIN: Of course not. But we cannot cope with that.

SENATOR KENNEDY: Well, as I understand what you say, is where there's impure water, it should not be used.

DR. BALLARIN: Yes.

SENATOR KENNEDY: Where the people are so poor that they're not gonna realistically be able to continue to purchase it, and which is gonna . . . that they're going to dilute it to a point, which is going to endanger the health, that it should not be used.

DR. BALLARIN: Yes, I believe . . .

SENATOR KENNEDY: Alright, now . . . then my final question is . . . is what do you . . . or what do you feel is your corporate responsibility to find out the extent of the use of your product in those circumstances in the developing part of the world? Do you feel that you have any responsibility?

DR. BALLARIN: We can't have that responsibility, sir. May I make a reference to . . .

SENATOR KENNEDY: You can't have that responsibility?

DR. BALLARIN: No.

Dr. Ballarin's testimony continued (for example of excerpts, see exhibit 3), but Nestlé management believed that little attention was paid to it. Mr. Guerrant, President of Nestlé U.S., was very angry and wrote a letter to Senator Kennedy on May 26, 1978, protesting against the way he had treated Dr. Ballarin (exhibit 4).

CBS aired its program on July 5, 1978. Again Nestlé management was upset. In their view, CBS had selected portions of the testimonies to make Nestlé management look inept and confused. Mr. Guerrant wrote a letter of protest to CBS president Richard Salant (exhibit 5).

Exhibit 3   Further Excerpts from Dr. Ballarin's Testimony

Nestlé recognized that even the best products will not give the desired results if used incorrectly. We, therefore, placed great weight on educational efforts aimed at explaining the correct use of our product. Our work in this field has received the public recognition and approval of the official Pediatric Associations in many countries. Such educational efforts never attempt to infer that our product is superior to breast milk. Indeed, we have devoted much attention to the promotion of breast-feeding, and educational material has always insisted that breast-feeding is best for the baby.

Nevertheless, many factors militate against exclusive breast-feeding in the rapidly growing cities of Brazil as well as other developing countries, and our products are seen today as filling a valid need, just as they did when they were first introduced over 50 years ago. In recognition of this, all such products are subject to strict price control, while in many countries which do not have a local dairy industry, they are classified as essential goods and imported free of duty. In many cases, official agencies establish what they consider to be a fair margin for the manufacturers.

It must be stressed that many problems remain to be solved. Our production is far from reaching the total needs of the population. Hence, many mothers in the poorer population groups continue to supplement breast-feeding with foods of doubtful quality. Owing to the lack of adequate medical services, especially in the rural areas, misuse of any supplement can occur and we are very conscious of the need to improve our efforts. These efforts depend on continued cooperation between the infant food industry and health professionals. We have to be more and more conscious of our responsibility to encourage breast-feeding while researching new foods and safer methods for feeding babies who cannot be exclusively breast-fed. The dilemma facing industry and the health service alike, is how to teach these methods without discouraging breast-feeding.

Exhibit 4   Excerpts from Mr. Guerrant's Letter to Senator Kennedy

I am angry but more important deeply concerned about the example of our governmental processes exhibited this week by the Human Resources Subcommittee on Health and Scientific Research.

It was the general consensus of several people in the audience that your position toward the manufacturers was "you are guilty until you prove your innocence." Objectivity would have been more becoming, Senator.

Secondly, it seemed equally probable that prior to the hearing the prepared statements were reviewed and you were quite prepared to rebuff Dr. Ballarin on his statement "undermining the free enterprise system." Unaccustomed to television

Exhibit 4 (continued)

and this type of inquisition, Dr. Ballarin, who appeared voluntarily, was flustered and embarrassed.

Probably, for this gathering, the statement was too strong (though nothing to compare with their theme "Nestlé kills babies") and should have been more subtle. But the point is well made, and your apparent denial of this possibility concerns me.

As you may know, this whole issue gained its greatest momentum a few years ago in Europe fostered by clearly identified radical leftist groups. Their stated purpose is opposition to capitalism and the free enterprise system. I submit that they are not really concerned with infants in the third world but are intelligent enough to know that babies, especially sick and dying, create maximum emotional response. Further, they are clever enough to know that the people most easy to "use" for their campaign, to front for them, are in churches and universities. These are good people, ready to rise against oppression and wrong-doing without, regrettably, truthful facts for objective research. I know, as my father is a retired Presbyterian minister, and I have a very warm feeling toward members of the church, Protestant and Catholic.

People with far left philosophies are not confined to Europe and are certainly represented in many accepted organizations here and abroad. (Please take the time to read the enclosed report of the 1977 Geneva Consultation of the World Council of Churches.) Associated with the World Council is the National Council of Churches, and one of their units is the Interfaith Centre for Corporate Responsibility. One of their major spokespersons appears to be Leah Margulies, who was present in your hearing.

Now, just briefly to the very complex infant food issue. As the U.S. Nestlé Company does not manufacture or sell any infant food products, we are unhappy with the attempted boycott of our products—at least 95% of these manufactured in the U.S. The jobs and security of about 12,000 good U.S. employees are being threatened.

From our associates in Switzerland, and Nestlé companies in the third world, we have gathered hundreds of factual documents. Neither Nestlé nor the U.S. companies in this business claim perfection. Companies are comprised of human beings. However, virtually every charge against Nestlé has proved to be erroneous. Distorted "facts" and just pure propaganda have been answered by people with undeniable integrity and technical credentials. Quite some time ago, because of the accusations, Nestlé world headquarters in Switzerland studied every facet of their total infant food business, made immediate changes where warranted and established new and very clear policies and procedures regarding the conduct of this business.

I might add that Nestlé infant foods have undoubtedly saved hundreds of thousands of lives. There is not even one instance where proof exists that Nestlé infant food was responsible for a single death. The products are as essential in the third world as in the industrialized world. Though the accusers use some statements

Exhibit 4 (continued)

by apparently qualified people, there is an overwhelming amount of data and number of statements from qualified medical, technical and government representatives in the third world confirming Nestlé's position.

At your hearing this week were the same identical charges made against Nestlé and the others years ago. These people will not recognize the changes made in marketing practices nor the irrefutable facts of the real infant health problems in the third world. They continue to push the U.S. Nestlé boycott and continue to distribute the fraudulent film "Bottle Babies." (Please read Dr. Bwibo's letter enclosed.) Sincere, well-meaning church people continue to be used, as they have not had all the real facts available for analysis.

The above situation made me believe that the organizers must have some motivation for this campaign other than what appears on the surface. If it could possibly be what I think, then our representatives in government should proceed with caution, thorough study and great objectivity, as your ultimate position can be of critical consequence. I am not a crusader, but I do feel the free enterprise system is best.

Exhibit 5   Excerpts from Mr. Guerrant's Letter to CBS President Salant

In the first minute of the program the infant formula industry has been tried and convicted of causing infant malnutrition. The remainder of the program is devoted to reinforcing Mr. Myer's conclusion. Tools of persuasion include the emotionality of a needle sticking in a child's head and the uneasy answers of cross-examined industry witnesses who are asked not for the facts but to admit and aplogize for their "guilt."

But CBS Reports chose to concentrate on the "rhetoric of concern" and the claims which permeate the rhetoric. Industry's response to the rhetoric is not glamorous but hits into the root causes of infant malnutrition—the poverty, disease and ignorance existing in the areas of developing and developed countries. Those conditions are not easy for anthropologists, economists, scientists or medical people to trace or explain. And certainly the reasons for them are not as identifiable as a major corporation. But in thirty minutes Mr. Myers and Ms. Roche identified four companies as a major reason for infant malnutrition.

One way Nestlé has attempted to meet the responsibility is by making capital investments in and transferring technology to the developing countries. Nestlé began this effort in 1921 in Brazil and now has almost 40,000 local employees working in 81 manufacturing facilities in 25 developing countries. Not only does Nestlé have a beneficial impact on those directly employed, the company also encourages and assists the development of other local supporting industries, such as the dairy industry and packaging plants.

Exhibit 5 (continued)

Another way Nestlé meets its responsibility is to work with local governments and health authorities in educating consumers. Clinics, pamphlets, posters, books and product labels emphasize the superiority of breast feeding, demonstrate proper sanitation and diet for breast feeding, and show in words and pictures how to correctly use formula products.

Neither of these positive approaches was covered in CBS Reports nor was there mention of the fact that infant mortality has declined worldwide over the past thirty years, nor that lack of sufficient breast milk is a major cause of infant malnutrition, nor that tropical diseases cause millions of deaths per year in developing countries. Any one of these facts would have provided some balance to the Myers-Roche report.

Following the Kennedy hearings, representatives of Nestlé S.A., Abbott, Bristol-Myers, and American Home Products met privately with Senator Kennedy to explore a suggestion for a further hearing. Meanwhile, the President of ICIFI wrote Kennedy, pointing out that this was an international and not a U.S. domestic issue—and should therefore be discussed at a forum sponsored by WHO. Kennedy accepted ICIFI's suggestion and requested the Director General of WHO to sponsor a conference at which the question of an international code could be discussed.

A consensus emerged that a uniform code for the industry was required and that Kennedy and ICIFI would suggest that WHO sponsor a conference with that aim in mind. The conference would be comprised of WHO officials, ICIFI members and other companies, health and government officials from the developing countries, and all appropriate concerned public groups. WHO accepted the idea and announced the conference date in the fall of 1979. Shortly after Nestlé management met with Kennedy, the National Council of Churches, comprised of about thirty major religious groups in the United States, announced that the question of supporting INFACT and ICCR would be discussed and decided at the NCC national conference in November 1978.

The Situation in October 1978

Dr. Fürer knew that all senior Nestlé management felt personally attacked by critics of the industry. Not only was this the first major public pressure campaign ever encountered by Nestlé, but also Nestlé management felt its critics were using unfair tactics. For example, again and again they saw in boycott letters and articles a grotesque picture of a wizened child with a formula bottle nearby. Eventually, this picture was traced to Dr. Derrick Jeliffe, an outspoken critic of the industry. He admitted to *Newsweek* that he had taken the picture in a Caribbean hospital in 1964. Even though it seemed that the media and many respected companies were against Nestlé, Dr. Fürer stated publicly:

> No one has the right to accuse us of killing babies. No one has the right to assert that we are guilty of pursuing unethical or immoral sales practices.

Nonetheless, under U.S. law, a company is regarded as a public person, which meant that the First Amendment applied; that is, Nestlé could not get legal relief against charges made by the critics unless the company could prove that those charges were both wrong and malicious.

Further, Dr. Fürer was struck by the fact that all the demands for change were coming from developed countries. In fact, Nestlé had received many letters of support from people in the developing countries (exhibit 6). Mr. Ernest Saunders, Nestlé Vice-President for infant nutrition products, summarized his view as follows:

> Government and medical personnel tell us that if we stopped selling infant foods we would be killing a lot of babies.

Exhibit 6 Examples of Support for Nestlé

1. I have been associated with the medical representatives of Nestlé in Kenya for the last five years. We have discussed on various occasions the problems of artificial feeding, in particular the use of proprietary milk preparations. We have all been agreed that breast feeding should always come first. As far as I am aware, your representatives have not used any unethical methods when promoting Nestlé products in this country.

> M.L. Oduori, Senior Consultant
> Pediatrician
> Ministry of Health
> Kenyatta National Hospital, Nairobi
> Kenya, Dec. 23, 1974

2. You are not "killing babies," on the contrary your efforts joined with ours contribute to the improvement of the Health Status of our infant population.
   We consider your marketing policies as ethical and as not being opposite to our recommendations. We note with pleasure that you employ a fully

Exhibit 6 (continued)

qualified nurse and that during discussions with mothers she always encourages breastfeeding, recommending your products when only natural feeding is insufficient or fails.

> Dr. Jerry Lukowski
> Chief Gynecologist, Menelik Hospital
> Ethiopia, Dec. 3, 1974

3. Over several decades I have had direct and indirect dealings with your organisation in South Africa in relation to many aspects of nutrition among the non-white population who fall under our care, as well as the supply of nutriments to the hospital and peripheral clinics.

    I am fairly well aware of the extent of your Company's contributions to medical science and research and that this generosity goes hand in hand with the highest ethical standards of advertising, distribution of products and the nutrition educational services which you provide.

    At no time in the past have my colleagues or I entertained any idea or suspicion that Nestlé have behaved in any way that could be regarded as unethical in their promotions, their products or their educational programmes. On all occasions when discussion of problems or amendments to arrangements have been asked for, full cooperation has been given to this department.

    Your field workers have given and are giving correct priorities in regard to breast feeding, and, where necessary, the bottle feeding of infants.

    The staff employed to do this work have shown a strong sense of responsibility and duty towards the public whom they serve, no doubt due to the educational instruction they have themselves received in order to fit them for their work.

> S. Wayburne, Chief Pediatrician
> Baragwanath Hospital
> Associate Professor of Pediatrics,
> Acting Head of Department of Pediatrics,
> University of Witwatersrand/South Africa
> Dec. 18, 1974

4. I have read about the accusation that "Nestlé Kills Babies" and I strongly refute it, I think it is quite unjustifiable.

    In my experience I have never seen any mother being advised to use artificial milk when it was not necessary. Every mother is advised to give breast foods to her baby. It is only when there is failure of this, then artificial foods are advised.

    I being a working mother, I have brought up my five children on Nestlé Products and I do not see anything wrong with them. I knew I would have

Exhibit 6   (continued)

found it difficult to carry on with my profession if I had nothing to rely on like your products.

Your marketing policies are quite in order as I knew them and they are quite ethical. As they stress on breast milk foods first and if this is unobtainable then one can use Nestlé's Products.

> Mrs. M. Lema, Nursing Officer
> Ocean Hospital
> Dar-es-Salaam/TANZANIA
> Dec. 16, 1974

5. On behalf of the Sisters of Nazareth Hospital, I thank you heartily for your generous contribution in giving us the Nestlé products in a way that we can assist and feed many undernourished children freely cured and treated in our hospital.

Trusting in your continuous assistance allow me to express again my sincerest thanks, and may God bless you.

> Nazareth Hospital
> Nairobi, Kenya
> September 9, 1978

6. I am very grateful for this help for our babies in need in the maternity ward.

Another mission has asked me about this milk gift parcels, if there would be any chance for them. It is Butula Mission and they have a health centre with beds and maternity and maternal child health clinics. There is a lot of malnutrition also in that area, so that mothers often do not produce enough milk for their babies. It would be wonderful if you could help them also.

> Nangina Hospital
> Medical Mission Sisters
> Funyula, Kenya
> June 15, 1976

7. As a doctor who has practiced for eighteen years in a developing country, I was angered by the collection of half-truths, judiciously mixed with falsehoods put out by the Infant Formula Action Coalition as reported in the *Newsweek* article on breast-feeding. Whether we like it or not, many mothers cannot or will not resort to breast-feeding. I do not believe that advertising has played any significant part in their decision. It is an inescapable necessity that specific, nutritionally balanced formulas are available. Otherwise, we would witness wholesale feeding with products that are unsuitable.

Exhibit 6 (continued)

I carry no brief for companies like Nestlé, but have always found it to be a company with the highest regard to ethical standards. Infant formulas have saved many thousands of lives. What alternative are their critics proposing?

D.C. Williams, M.D.
Kuala Lumpur
Malaysia

8. Surely, Nestlé is not to blame. There have been similar problems here but through the efforts of the Save the Children Fund and government assistance, feeding bottles can only be purchased through chemists or hospitals by prescription. In this way, the decision of whether to breast-feed or not is decided by qualified personnel.

I would think that Americans would have better things to do than walk around disrupting commerce with placards.

Gail L. Hubbard
Goroka, Papua New Guinea

Dr. Fürer also believed that the scientific facts underlying the breast versus bottle controversy were not being given adequate attention (for example, see exhibit 7), nor were the changes Nestlé and the other companies had made. Nestlé's policies regarding infant formula products were apparently not well known. Exhibit 8 includes excerpts from the latest edition, dated September 1, 1977.

Exhibit 7 Examples of Supplementary Information on Breast-Feeding Versus Bottle-Feeding*

1. Findings of the Human Lactation Center (HLC)

The HLC is a scientific research institute, a nonprofit organization dedicated to worldwide education and research on lactation. The HLC entered the breast/bottle controversy between the infant formula industry and the anti-multinational groups in an attempt to clarify certain issues. Eleven anthropologists, all women, studied infant feeding practices in eleven different cultures, ranging from a relatively urbanized Sardinian village to a very impoverished Egyptian agricultural village. Their findings:

Poverty is correlated with infant morbidity (disease). Child health is associated with affluence.

*Source: Nestlé memoranda.

Exhibit 7 (continued)

Infant mortality had decreased in the three decades prior to 1973 when food prices began to escalate.

Breast milk is the best infant food but breast-feeding exclusively for most *under-nourished* women in the less developed countries is inadequate beyond the baby's third month. Lack of sufficient food after this time is a major cause of morbidity and mortality whether or not the infant is breast-fed.

Mixed feeding is an almost universal pattern in traditional cultures; that is, breast-feeding and supplementary feeding from early on and often into the second year.

The preferred additional food for the very young child is milk. Most milk is fresh milk, unprocessed.

Most women still breast-feed, though many do not. The popular assumption that breast-feeding is being reduced has not been verified.

Third World women with the least amount of resources, time or access to health care and weaning foods, have no choice but to breast-feed.

More than half the infants they bear do not survive due to lack of food for themselves and their children.

Women who are separated from close kin, especially the urban poor, lack mothering from a supportive figure. They find themselves unable to lactate adequately or lose their milk entirely. Without suitable substitutes, their infants die.

Middle class women in the less-developed countries, market women, the elite and professional women are moving towards bottle feeding with infant formula in much the same way women turned from breast- to bottle-feeding in the western countries.

The current literature on breast-feeding in the developing countries is meager. Information on mortality, the incidence of breast-feeding, the content of infant food, and the amount of breast milk, tend to be impressionistic reports by well-meaning western or western trained persons often unaware of the complexities of feeding practices and insensitive to the real-life situation of the mothers. Judgments for action based on these inconclusive data could be dangerous.

Mothers have a sensitive and remarkable grasp of how best to keep their infants alive. Neither literacy nor what has been called "ignorance" determine which infants live and which die except as they are related directly to social class.

In seeking solutions to the problems of infant well-being in the developing world, we must listen to the mothers and involve them in the decisions which will affect their lives.

2. *The Feeding of the Very Young: An Approach to Determination of Policies,* report of the International Advisory Group on Infant and Child Feeding to the

Exhibit 7 (continued)

Nutrition Foundation, October 1978:

"Two basic requirements of successful feeding are: (1) adequate milk during the first four to six months of life, and (2) adequate complementary foods during the transition to adult diets. It is imperative that all societies recognize these requirements as a major component of nutrition policy. The extent to which mothers are able to meet both of these requirements will vary under different cultural and sociological circumstances. In all societies there will be some proportion of mothers who will not be able to meet them without assistance, and policy must be developed to protect those children who are at risk of malnutrition resulting from inadequacy in either one or both of these basic requirements."

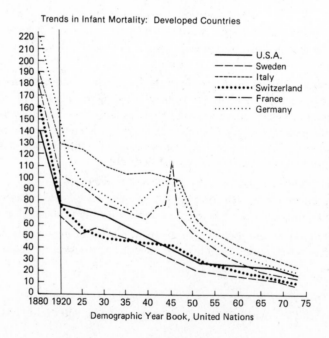

Trends in Infant Mortality: Developed Countries

Demographic Year Book, United Nations

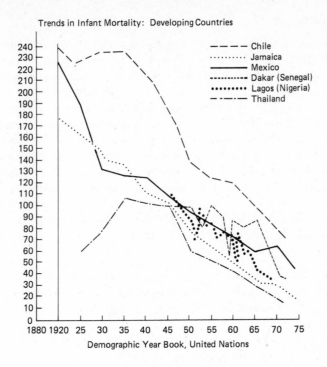

Trends in Infant Mortality: Developing Countries

Demographic Year Book, United Nations

Exhibit 8   Excerpts from Nestlé Directives on Infant and Dietetic Products Policy

Infant Milks

It is recognized that breast milk is the best food for a baby. Our baby milks are therefore not intended to compete with breast milk, but to supplement breast feeding when the mother's own milk can no longer cover the baby's needs or to replace it when mothers cannot, or elect not to, breast-feed.

Three to four months after birth, the quantities of breast milk produced by the average mother become insufficient to satisfy the growing needs of the baby. The baby needs a supplement of water and food. From this moment on, in the poor communities of developing countries this baby is in danger because water is sometimes polluted and local foods, like plantain or manioc, are nutritionally inadequate, they are starchy foods with little food value and a young baby cannot digest them. Thus the highest infant mortality occurs precisely in areas where babies receive only mother's milk plus a supplement of unboiled local water and/or starchy decoctions.

This is not a Nestlé theory. This is a fact known by every Third World doctor and recently scientifically demonstrated by British researchers working in Africa.

Exhibit 8 (continued)

The alternative to traditional local supplement is a properly formulated breast milk substitute, preferably a humanized formula. It is true that there is a risk of misuse, but these risks exist with a local supplement too, although the baby has a better chance of survival when the starting point is of high quality.

It is precisely to reduce the risks of misuse and thereby increase the chances of survival that we had developed over the years a comprehensive programme of information and education: contact with doctors, educative advertising, booklets, nurses; all this had the purpose of making the alternative to local supplements known and ensuring a proper and safe use of our products when needed. Nestlé policies are designed to avoid the unnecessary replacement of breast milk.

The real issue is not: Breast milk versus formula, as so often pictured, but: Breast milk + formula + education versus traditional foods like manioc.

Products must be in line with internationally recognized nutritional criteria and offer definite consumer benefits.

Distribution Policy

It is a rule that PID products are never sold to mothers directly by us; distribution aims at making products available to prescribers and users under optimum safety and price conditions.

Within the limits set by the law and by the distribution structure, we practice mixed distribution (pharmacies and general food stores) and use the normal market channels. On the other hand, dietetic specialties and products designed for delicate or sick babies, which are basically sold on medical prescription, are sold only through pharmacies, unless special local conditions warrant mixed distribution.

Communication Policy—Direct Contacts with Mothers

Medical representatives must not enter into direct contact with mothers, unless they are authorized to do so in writing by a medical or health authority and provided that they are properly qualified. Films may be shown with the agreement of the medical or public health authorities concerned.

Visits to mothers in their homes are not allowed unless the responsible medical authority has made a written request for a visit to take place.

Personnel Policy

The main task of the medical promotion personnel consists in contacting the medical and paramedical professions and hospitals. They are not concerned with direct sales to mothers and cannot sell dietetic products other than, exceptionally and exclusively, to the trade or institutions.

Specialized training must be given to such staff, to enable them to render a genuine service to the medical and paramedical professions and give them scientific and unbiased information on product characteristics and utilization.

No sales-related bonus will be paid to any staff engaged in medical promotion or having direct contact with mothers. If a bonus is to be paid, it must depend on elements other than sales, such as, for example, personal qualities, qualifications, etc.

Many members of management believed the attack against Nestlé was ideologically based. They gathered information about and quotations from many of the activist groups to support their position (for example, see exhibit 9). Whatever their foundation, the critics seemed to Dr. Fürer to be

Exhibit 9 Examples of Comments Concerning the Ideology of the Activist Groups*

Sue Tafler and Betsy Walker, "Why Boycott Nestle?" in *Science for the People* January/February 1978:

> Unfortunately, the power in many developing countries is not held by the people themselves, and local ruling elites often want to encourage corporate investment. . . . What the boycott will not do is overthrow capitalism. . . . The boycott can unite well-meaning groups that see themselves as apolitical with more openly political groups. . . . We can have the effect of politicizing others working in the coalition. If Nestlé does make some concessions to the demand of the boycott, the sense of victory can give encouragement to the organizers of the boycott to continue on to larger struggles.

T. Balasusiya, Centre for Society and Religion, Colombo, Sri Lanka, participant at the World Council of Churches meeting, January 1977:

> The capitalist system is the main cause of the increasing gap and within that system multinationals are a main form. Ideology of wealth is the practical religion of capitalist society. Churches are legitimizers of the system, so their first job is self-purification. There can be no neutrality between money and God.
>   Our function is not to judge persons, but we have to judge systems. . . . What alternative solutions do countries propose that have rejected the capitalist system, e.g., U.S.S.R., China, Cuba, Tanzania? Capitalism is inherently contradicatory to the Gospel.

M. Ritchie, at a conference "Clergy and Laity Concerned," August 1978:

> It's not just on babies, it's not just multinational corporations, it's class conflict and class struggle. Broadening the constituency both of people interested in the infant formula issue but also how the infant formula campaign and the people there link up completely in terms of support and action with other types of campaigns . . . .
>   I think ultimately what we're trying to do is take an issue-specific focus campaign and move it in conjunction with other issue-specific campaigns into a larger very class wide very class-conscious campaign and reasserting our power in this country, our power in this world.

Douglas Johnson of INFACT, at an address in Washington, September 1978:

> Our hope is that we can use this [boycott] campaign as the forerunner of legislation for control of multinational corporations.

Source: Nestlé internal memoranda.

gaining publicity and momentum. INFACT claimed at least 500 separate action committees in the United States and support in about 75 communities in Canada, as well as support in about 10 other countries. "The movement is snowballing," reported Gwen Willens of INFACT. "We're getting over 300 letters of support every day."

As Dr. Fürer consulted with senior management in Nestlé, he wondered what further steps Nestlé might take to deal with the controversy surrounding the marketing of infant formula products in the developing countries.

CHAPTER X

MARKETING STRATEGY FORMULATION: REVIEW AND PREVIEW

A major purpose of this book has been to assist you in the formulation of marketing strategy. We have approached this objective by giving you an overview of marketing decision making and then immersing you in the details of analysis and decision for various components of the marketing programme. This chapter tries to integrate all the preceding chapters by discussing marketing strategy in terms of programmes and plans and the process of developing marketing plans. At the outset, these words deserve some clarification.

A *marketing strategy* refers to the formulation of objectives and a marketing programme (an integrated set of marketing activities designed to achieve these specified objectives).

A *marketing plan* refers to a written document detailing a marketing programme, its rationale, its implementation, and provisions for review of its performance.

Marketing planning refers to the process whereby programmes and plans are formulated, assessed, revised, and communicated.

A marketing strategy is imbedded in a marketing plan; therefore, we will confine our attention in this discussion to marketing plans and marketing planning.

The Marketing Plan

Marketing plans may be prepared for brands, product lines, or even entire companies. Such plans may refer to a variety of time periods and range in size from a couple of pages to volumes. In each instance, however, a plan is designed to provide:

1. a set of marketing and financial objectives for the next time period;

2. the reasons why these objectives can and should be met, given the marketing environment of the firm;
3. the marketing activities (programme) necessary to meet these objectives;
4. a detailed plan of action (implementation plan) to put the programme into effect;
5. contingency plans in the event that the marketing environment or the firm's resources change during the implementation period; and
6. provisions for evaluation of the programme's performance both during and by the end of the period involved.

Exhibit 1 contains a suggested format for a marketing plan. This is only a suggestion, as the format for a particular plan should be tailored to the specific needs of the users.

Exhibit 1   A Suggested Format for a Marketing Plan

  I. "Management summary": of the major dimensions of the marketing programme suggested and the implications for the firm's financial resources and performance.
 II. A review of the market situation
    A. Buyer
       1. level of primary demand; trends, determinants
       2. nature of selective demand; sensitivity to various marketing approaches.
    B. Competition
       1. identification, by type, of relevant competitors; trends
       2. share of market and other competitive performance measures
       3. competitive programmes and anticipated changes in programmes
    C. Channels
       1. identification, by type, of channels that are important; trends
       2. nature of channel behaviour; sensitivity to various marketing approaches
    D. Technology
       1. Changes affecting people, institutions, products, communication, etc.
    E. Government and the public interest
       1. laws: trends, enforcement patterns
       2. expectations; responsibilities; bargaining arena
III. A review of the firm/product/brand situation
    A. Performance
       1. past goals; results to date on dimensions such as market share, awareness, trial, repeat purchase rates, and contribution

Exhibit 1 (continued)

    B. Resources audit
       1. financial strengths and weaknesses
       2. skills: marketing, people, production, and R & D
    C. Organization
       1. nature of organization and implications for incentives, authority,
          responsibility, and accountability for decisions and changes in decisions
    D. Existing programme
       1. product, price, channels, and communications strategies summarized
          for the past and current periods
    E. Critique of performance
       1. firm/product/brand performance (versus past objectives) explained in
          terms of events and activities that affected it

  IV. A review of problems and opportunities for the future
    A. Opportunities
       1. factors that will enable the firm to realize equal or improved marketing
          performance during the next period
    B. Problems
       1. factors that may jeopardize future improvements in marketing
          performance
    C. Objectives
       1. what specific goals for the next period (in particular) and future
          periods (in general)
       2. priorities if goals contradictory (e.g. profit margin versus market share;
          penetration of existing markets versus market development effort)

   V. Programme formulation
    A. Overview
       1. outline of the basic strategy, stripped to its essentials in terms of posi-
          tioning selection and critical activities to achieve marketing success;
          this is sometimes referred to as the "core strategy"
    B. Product strategy
       1. branding, features, etc.
    C. Pricing strategy
       1. to channels, to buyers, margins, etc.
    D. Channels strategy
       1. retailers/wholesalers to use, incentives and controls, etc.
    E. Communications strategy
       1. mix of methods, messages, media, timing, and measurement
    F. Research strategy
       1. information needs to improve decisions
       2. cost versus value of such information
       3. plans and procedures to gather information to improve marketing pro-
          gramme decisions

Exhibit 1   (continued)

VI. Financial implications of the programme
   A. Revenues
      1. amount and timing
   B. Expenses
      1. variable, fixed, discretionary distinctions
      2. may include: cost of goods, media and production, sampling, promotion, trade allowances, market research, sales force, physical distribution, and administration
   C. Investments
      1. inventory, receivables, advertising, and sales training
   D. Statements
      1. income (profit and loss) for past and future
      2. budget (and/or cash flow statement)
      3. balance sheet (sometimes not included)

VII. Programme implementation
   A. Determination of what will be done, by whom, when, where
   B. Manpower recruiting, training, controlling, directing and compensating
   C. Coordination with other areas/departments of the company

VIII. Programme performance
   A. Information system
      1. who gets what information, for what purpose, when, about the performance of all or part of the programme
   B. Additional research
      1. tests, studies, etc. proposed to add to information usually gathered about programme performance and reasons for that performance

IX. Contingency plans
   A. Situation changes
      1. probable versus possible development in market situation (e.g. change by competition) and in company situation (e.g. change in financial support); indicators to give earliest possible warning of these changes
   B. Importance of changes
      1. what changes mean for programme performance either in total or in part
   C. Alternate plans
      1. what to do if the changes occur to maintain or improve marketing performance

X. Appendices
   A. Financial exhibits
   B. Research exhibits
   C. Sales call plans, media schedules, promotion cycles and sales promotion schedules.

There are several very important points to remember about a marketing plan:

1. It is a working document, prepared with the expectation that it will be changed as circumstances warrant. It is not intended to be bound in leather, embossed, put on a shelf, and ignored. Accordingly, the plan should be prepared with flexibility and change in mind.

2. There is a marked difference between conciseness and brevity. A marketing plan should be concise (to the point), but it may or may not be brief (short). The level of detail appropriate is governed by simple rules: as specific and operational as possible, and as understandable as possible.

3. A marketing plan is both a marketing and a financial document. A critical part of the plan is a review and preview of marketing revenues and costs in the form of financial statements. A marketing plan should always contain an income statement for past performance (except for new product introductions) and a projected income statement for anticipated future performance. Further, a budget should be provided, showing both expenses expected and investment required.

4. A marketing plan is a communication device and should be both written and discussed thoroughly. Quite simply, it outlines "what to do, why, how, and what if." Mr. Murray Cayley, a senior manager at Petrocanada, prepared the following diagram to demonstrate the ways in which a plan is a communication device (chart 1).

Chart 1   A Plan as a Communication Device

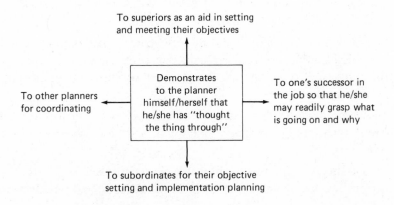

To superiors as an aid in setting and meeting their objectives

To other planners for coordinating

Demonstrates to the planner himself/herself that he/she has "thought the thing through"

To one's successor in the job so that he/she may readily grasp what is going on and why

To subordinates for their objective setting and implementation planning

5. Marketing plans vary immensely according to the complexity of the market and of the company. Plans also vary significantly for a continuing product versus a new product. A new product plan includes four distinct components:

> justification for engaging in the new business (i.e., "go" versus "no go");
>
> an introductory strategy (i.e., what to do first and why);
>
> an expansion strategy (e.g. a regional roll-out strategy); and
>
> a continuing strategy (similar to the "existing" product plan).

Marketing Planning

Part of the benefits of marketing planning is the disciplined thinking and interactive discussions required to develop a plan. Marketing planning should be a continuous process of assessing the situation in terms of problems and opportunities, and improving one's marketing programme in light of this situation analysis.

Marketing planning is a vital part of corporate planning, which also includes financial planning, production planning, etc. While we have tried to outline in simple terms how to prepare a marketing plan, you must recognize that planning is not an easy process; planning efforts frequently fail. Here are some common pitfalls that account for marketing planning failures:

1. Marketing planning not integrated with corporate planning. (It must be.)
2. Marketing planning regarded as a staff, rather than a line management activity. (Both should be involved.)
3. Management expects too much the first time they try planning. (It takes several attempts before planning works well, so start with modest expectations and build the system up gradually.)
4. Management expects the plans to come true, rather than treating them as guidelines that need to be changed as time passes. (Too often, one finds lots of effort preparing the plan and too little effort keeping the plan up to date.)
5. Marketing planning done infrequently, haphazardly or too hurriedly. (Good plans are not prepared overnight or on a crash basis once every five years.)
6. "Hope sheets" (guesses, wishful thinking) confused with careful forecasting and financial projections. (Be realistic and practical.)

Summary

In short, the quality of a marketing plan (and the process by which it is prepared) depends on the weakest aspect of it. Astute managers periodically review not only their marketing plans, but also their planning processes. Improved planning leads to improved marketing programmes, which lead to improved implementation of marketing programmes, which leads to improved marketing performance. The purpose of this book is to improve marketing performance in Canada. We are confident that the skills that you learned from the textual chapters and have practiced with the cases will enable you to meet and triumph over the challenges involved in marketing decision making in Canada and in other parts of the world.

43 Canadair Challenger Jet

Mr. James Taylor and Mr. Harry Halton were taking a last minute look at the marketing strategy developed for Canadair's new Challenger business jet. Mr. Taylor was head of Canadair Inc., the Challenger's marketing arm, located in Westport, Connecticut. Mr. Halton, the Executive Vice-President, was the Chief Engineer, responsible for the design and production of the Challenger at Canadair's Montreal plant. The Challenger was being touted as the world's most advanced business aircraft, incorporating the latest technologies to achieve high speed, longest range, greatest fuel economy, and greatest seating space and comfort. It was early July 1976, and the President of Canadair, Mr. Fred Kearns, wanted senior management's consensus on product design, pricing, advertising, and approach to selling.

The preliminary design of the Challenger was generally complete, but Mr. Halton continued to receive suggestions for additional features from Mr. Taylor and his marketing group, from prospective customers, and from project engineers. Rather than build prototype models by hand, Mr. Halton had decided to begin setting up a full-scale production line. Eventually, three preproduction models of the Challenger would be constructed for testing and demonstration.

Canadian management was considering a number of pricing options. Some executives advocated a very competitive initial price to hasten customer orders, with subsequent price increases. Another group of top executives believed that the Challenger should bear a premium price to reflect its superiority and to recover $140 million in development costs. The advertising agency's proposed copy for the Challenger's print advertisements was feared to be too controversial, and the marketing group wondered whether some "softening" of the copy might be advisable. Selling direct to customers, selling direct to customers with a supplementary dealer network, or selling entirely through a dealer network were three possible approaches to sales. Finally, executives recognized that plans for service facilities required to maintain the Challenger "in the field," which could mean anywhere in the world, were very sketchy.

Canadair executives wanted 50 orders by September 30, 1976, before committing fully to the Challenger programme. However, the major marketing decisions had to be finalized before the sales blitz could begin. If sales by September 30 fell in the range of 30–40 units, management might grant an extension on the deadline. However, sales of fewer than 30 units would probably result in scrapping the Challenger programme.

General Background

Canadair's objective was to sell 410 units, or 40 percent of the market for large business jets over the period 1978–1988. Business jets were changing the way companies conducted business, as executives learned the competitive advantages that a corporate aircraft could provide. What critics had once scorned as a "toy of executive privilege" was increasingly seen as a desirable and advantageous management tool. "Probably more than ever, most businessmen agree with Arco's vice-chairman Louis F. Davis, that 'there's nothing like face-to-face communications to keep a business running.'"[1] One observer commented:

> As big as corporate flying has become in recent years, there are strong signs that its role will continue to expand rapidly in years to come. Of the largest 1000 U.S. companies, only 502 operate their own airplanes, versus 416 five years ago. That leaves a sizable virgin market, which sales people from a dozen U.S. and foreign aircraft builders are tripping over each other to develop.[2]

Competitors were skeptical that the Challenger could meet its promised specifications. The unloaded Challenger would weigh only 17,100 pounds compared to 30,719 for the Grumman Gulfstream II (GII), a head-on competitor that was the biggest corporate jet flying, yet still provide a wider cabin. The Challenger would be propelled by less powerful engines than the GII, yet theoretically would fly faster and consume only 50 percent as much fuel. "The Canadians seem to know something the rest of the industry doesn't," commented Ivan E. Speer, Group Vice-President of

1. "Corporate Flying: Changing The Way Companies Do Business," *Business Week*, February 6, 1978, p. 64.
2. *Ibid.*, p. 62.

Aerospace at Garret Corp., the major builder of corporate jet engines.[3] The Challenger was to be powered by Avco-Lycoming engines, a competitor to the Garret Corp.

More simply, it was not known how well the Challenger would fly. Although Canadair had made jets for the military, the company had never built a business jet. Beyond these concerns, production problems could arise with a project of this nature and magnitude, but little could be done to anticipate how and when these problems would occur.

Company Background

Originating as the aircraft division of Canadian Vickers Ltd. in the 1920's, Canadair assumed its own identity in 1944 following a reorganization brought about by the Canadian government. In 1947, Canadair was acquired by Electric Boat Company of Groton, Connecticut, forming the basis for an organization that became General Dynamics Corp. in 1952. Canadair reverted to Canadian government ownership in January 1976 under a government plan for restructuring the Canadian aerospace industry. In 1975, *Interavia* magazine described Canadair as follows:

> Once a flourishing company, Canadair is the "sick man" of the national aerospace industry; employment has steadily dropped since 1970, when 8,400 were on the books, and could fall below 1,000 sometime this year unless new work is found rapidly.[4]

However, uneven employment was characteristic of the entire aircraft industry. In terms of deliveries, quality, innovation, and steady profits, Canadair had an enviable record. Located at Cartierville Airport in St. Laurent, Quebec, approximately ten miles from the centre of Montreal, the plant was one of the largest and most versatile aerospace-manufacturing facilities in Canada. Canadair's activities included the design and development of new aircraft and contracting for major modifications to existing types of aircraft. Subcontracts for the manufactured component parts and subassemblies for military and commercial aircraft in production such as the Boeing 747 accounted for a substantial volume of the company's business (table 1).

Exhibit 1 supplies data on earnings for Canadair from 1973 to 1976. Canadair's President reflected on the activities of the company:

> We at Canadair are not really known as a major influence in the international aerospace industry. For various reasons, we have been a major

3. *Ibid.*, p. 64.
4. *Interavia*, February 1975, p. 150.

Table 1   Canadair's Sales from 1973 Through 1976 by Class of Business

	1976 est.		1975		1974		1973	
	$000	%	$000	%	$000	%	$000	%
Aircraft	20,410	46	15,520	42	38,808	68	22,006	63
Component subcontracts	7,783	17	6,716	18	2,945	5	2,967	9
Surveillance systems	9,367	21	6,958	19	9,620	17	8,542	25
Other	7,034	16	7,938	21	5,744	10	1,113	3
Total	44,954	100	37,132	100	57,117	100	34,628	100

subcontractor or producer of other people's aircraft over a large span of our existence, and our native designs have not been more than a small portion of our overall effort. You may imagine that the elder statesmen of the aerospace industry smiled indulgently when they heard about this radical new aircraft that Canadair was developing.

The Canadian Aerospace Industry[5]

The Canadian aerospace-manufacturing industry had specialized capabilities for the design, research and development, production, marketing, and in-plant repair and overhaul of aircraft, aero-engines, aircraft and engine subsystems and components, space-related equipment, and air and ground-based avionic systems and components.

Approximately 100 companies were engaged in significant manufacturing work, but 40 companies accounted for 90 percent of the industry's sales in 1975. Three companies, including Canadair, were fully integrated, having the capability to design, develop, manufacture, and market complete aircraft or aero-engines. With aggregate sales of $785,000,000 in 1976, the Canadian aerospace industry shared fifth place in western world sales with Japan, after the United States, France, the United Kingdom, and the Federal Republic of Germany.

It was economically impractical for Canadian industry to manufacture all the diverse aerospace products demanded on the Canadian market. Through selective specialization, the Canadian industry had developed product lines in areas related to Canadian capabilities and export market

5. *Sources: A Report By The Sector Task Force On The Canadian Aerospace Industry*, June 30, 1978, Chairman D.C. Lowe.

Exhibit 1 Canadair Limited and Subsidiaries

	Year Ended December 31			
	1976[a]	*1975*	*1974*	*1973*

CONSOLIDATED STATEMENT OF INCOME
(thousands of dollars)

	1976[a]	1975	1974	1973
Sales	$44,594	$37,132	$57,117	$34,628
Cost of Sales	41,325	42,421	53,264	31,702
Income (loss) from operations	$ 3,269	$ (5,289)	$ 3,853	$ 2,926
Other Income (Expense):				
Interest income	$ 240	$ 260	$ 248	$ 356
Miscellaneous income	9	30	61	71
Interest expense	(2,056)	(3,203)	(1,755)	(1,001)
	$ (1,807)	$ (2,913)	$ (1,446)	$ (574)
Income (loss) from operations before provision for income taxes, loss on discontinued operations of a subsidiary, extraordinary items, and share of earnings of Asbestos Corporation Limited	$ 1,462	$ (8,202)	$ 2,407	$ 2,352
Provision for Federal and Provincial Income Taxes	642	6	1,122	1,056
Income (loss) before loss on discontinued operations of a subsidiary, extraordinary items, and share of earnings of Asbestos Corporation Limited	$ 820	$ (8,208)	$ 1,285	$ 1,296
Loss on Discontinued Operations of a Subsidiary	(385)	(165)	(260)	(280)
Income (loss) before extraordinary items and share of earnings of Asbestos Corporation Limited	$ 435	$ (8,373)	$ 1,025	$ 1,016
Extraordinary Items:				
Income tax reduction	$ 638	$ —	$ 1,100	$ 1,041
Gain on exchange	—	1,957	—	—
Provision for disposal of a subsidiary company's assets	(988)	—	—	—
Total extraordinary items	$ (350)	$ 1,957	$ 1,100	$ 1,041

a. Estimated results for 1976.

Exhibit 1 (continued)

	Year Ended December 31			
	1976^a	1975	1974	1973
Income (loss) before share of earnings of Asbestos Corporation Limited	$ 85	$ (6,416)	$ 2,125	$ 2,057
Share of Earnings of Asbestos Corporation Limited	—	7,368	6,063	520
Net Income	$ 85	$ 952	$ 8,188	$ 2,577

CONSOLIDATED STATEMENT OF EARNED SURPLUS (DEFICIT)
(thousands of dollars)

Balance at Beginning of Year	$(14,059)	$ 49,683	$41,495	$38,918
Net income	85	952	8,188	2,577
	$(13,974)	$ 50,635	$49,683	$41,495
Dividend paid	$ —	$ 25,000	$ —	$ —
Unrecovered portion of investment in Asbestos Corporation Limited, representing the excess of carrying value over the amount paid by General Dynamics Corporation	—	39,694	—	—
	$ —	$ 64,694	—	—
Balance at End of Year	$(13,974)	$(14,059)	$49,683	$41,495

a. Estimated results for 1976.

penetration. In 1975, 80 percent of the industry's sales were in export markets, an achievement attained under strong competitive conditions.

The Canadian industry was fully exposed to the competitive forces of the international aerospace market. Its hourly labour rates were in some cases higher than those in the United States. The industry's export market penetration was vulnerable to the economic forces associated with competitors' industrial productivity improvements. The industry, like most world aerospace industries, was manufacturing high-cost and high-risk products. There were many hazards: a relatively long-term payback cycle, sporadic government purchasing decisions, tariff and nontariff barriers, monetary inflation, and rapid technological obsolescence.

Aerospace industries throughout the world generally received government support, particularly in the areas of research, development, and equipment modernization. For example, the U.S. aircraft industry benefited from the annual $10 billion Department of Defence budget and the annual $6 billion NASA budget. By contrast, during the nine years ended March 31, 1976, the Government of Canada had provided $349 million to the Canadian aerospace industry through several programmes. In short, the Canadian aircraft industry was not subsidized.

There were indications in 1976 that the Canadian aerospace industry was entering a growth cycle. The trend lines of Canadian sales and exports encouraged an optimistic outlook.

The Business Jet Industry

Continued expansion of business aircraft activities was expected to continue into the 1980's in what business aviation officials described as the "best growth climate in years."[6] Booming sales of business aircraft in Europe, the Middle East, and Africa were giving rise to a belief that the business aircraft was becoming a true business tool in these regions, much as it had in the United States about a decade earlier.

All forecasts pointed to an enormous upsurge in the sale of business jet aircraft. Exhibit 2 graphs the trends in the U.S. business jet industry from 1956 to an estimate of 1976 and beyond. Exhibit 3 illustrates the trends in world deliveries of all corporate aircraft from 1965 to 1975, with delivery estimates through 1981. Many factors were contributing to increase the desire for private business aircraft:

Commercial airlines were reducing service drastically as they added the "jumbo" jets. In six years, the number of U.S. cities served by commercial airlines dropped from 525 to 395.

97 percent of all scheduled air carrier passengers in the U.S. flew out of only 150 airports.

Flights were packed with tourists and other occasional travelers. This made it difficult to obtain reservations and impossible to work en route. The amount of executive time spent traveling was increasing, and most of this travel time was being wasted.

Corporate planes provided the management of many companies with new flexibility and shortened reaction time in special situations.

6. *Aviation Week and Space Technology*, September 11, 1978, pp. 46–56.

Exhibit 2 Growth Trends in U.S. Business Flying

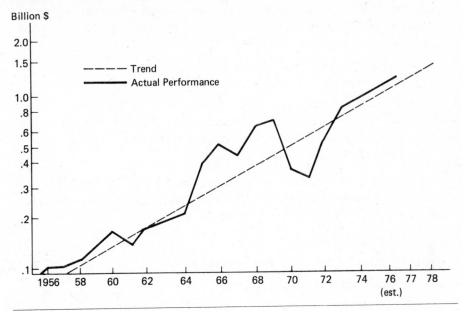

Source: Aviation Week and Space Technology.

Exhibit 3 Unit Worldwide Corporate Jet Deliveries (All Models)

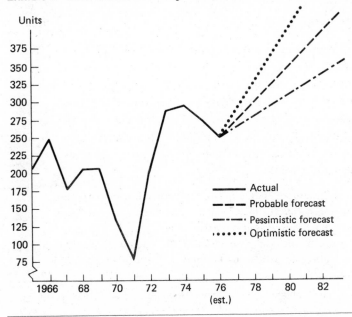

Cost savings could be achieved; for example, Xerox flew 15,000 employees per year on a company-owned shuttle plane between its Stamford headquarters and its Rochester (N.Y.) plant, saving $410,000 annually over commercial air fares.

There was growing concern for the security and protection of top executives from the growing incidence of airplane hijackings.

Finally many organizations were trading up to newer or larger aircraft to replace outdated, older equipment. Essentially, technology permitted such improvements over the aircraft of ten years earlier (for example in fuel economy) that the buyers could easily justify the update.

To cash in on the business jet bonanza, several manufacturers were planning to introduce new models. The following business jets would be on the market in some fashion by 1979:

Canadair's Challenger (large category)

Dassault-Breguet Falcon 50 (large category)

Grumman Gulfstream III (large category)

Rockwell's Sabreliner 80A (medium category)

Cessna's Citation III (medium category)

Gates Learjet's 54/55/56 series (medium category)

Corporate Aircraft Categories

More than 100 different aircraft models were offered to the business flyer.[7] Hence, the selection of the right aircraft for an individual company was a complex task. John Pope, Secretary of the National Business Aircraft Association, emphasized this advice: "Any aircraft selected involves a compromise, because the worst error you can make is buying more aircraft than you need and underutilizing it."[8] The general categories in order of performance and price were: single-engine piston, multiengine piston, turboprop, turbojet, and turbofan.

> Single-engine piston aircraft, while not usually considered "corporate," did provide starting points for many smaller companies, as well as individuals who combined business and pleasure flying. . . . Multiengine piston aircraft were the next step up, offering the additional security and performance afforded by a second engine. . . . Piston-engine twins

7. "Corporate Aviation: The Competitive Edge," *Dunn's Review*, January, 1979, p. 89.
8. *Ibid.*

were considered excellent entry-level aircraft for smaller corporations, with a relatively high percentage owner-flown. . . . Turboprop aircraft were referred to by some as "turbojets with propellers attached." . . . Turboprops used significantly less fuel than pure jets but could easily cost more than $1 million.[9]

Turbojet and turbofan aircraft flew faster and, for the most part, farther than the other aircraft. A turbojet was not usually a first-time purchase for a smaller company. Prices in this category ranged from $1 million to $7.5 million. The turbofans offered greater low-altitude efficiency than the turbojets. The Challenger, JetStar II, Falcon 50, and Gulfstream II and III were turbofans.

The following rules of thumb were often used to determine the suitability of different planes for different flying needs:

Average distance per flight (miles)	Appropriate type of aircraft for this distance
150–200	single-engine piston
200–500	multiengine piston and smaller turboprop
500–750	turboprops and small turbojets
750–1000	small turbojets
1000–2000	medium-size turbojets
2000–4000	large turbofans and large turbojets

Corporate Jet Competition

The Falcon 50, Gulfstream II and III, and JetStar II seemed to compete directly against the Challenger. Exhibit 4 summarizes sales by segment and model from 1965 to 1975. A schematic layout of each competitive plane is shown in exhibits 5 and 6. Exhibit 7 compares the salient product differences for the Challenger and its competitors.

Falcon 50

The new Dassault-Breguet Falcon 50, with its flight testing scheduled for completion by October 1978 and certification expected in December 1978, was slightly ahead of the Challenger programme. The Challenger would probably not be certified until August 1979. Flight tests of the Falcon 50 had shown that its performance figures were better than expected in terms of landing strip required and rate of climb. The Falcon 50 was essentially a modification of the medium-sized Falcon 20, which had been introduced fourteen years earlier.

9. *Ibid.*

Exhibit 4 Worldwide Corporate Jet Deliveries (units)

Model	1965	1966	1967	1968	1969	1970	1971	1972	1973	1974	1975	1976 Prices (000's)
Small Jet Market												
Citation I								52	81	85	69	$ 918
Falcon									1	21	26	$1905
Lear 23	80	18	1									—
Lear 24		24	26	28	33	20	10	16	21	22	18	—
Lear 25				18	25	18	14	23	45	40	14	$1315
Lear 35/36										4	47	$1679
Hansa			3	6	14	4	1	1	5			—
Sabre 40	26	31	5	5	1	6						—
Corvette										6	5	—
Westwind #1151/52/54	30	50	25	10	12	5	4	11	12	12	4	—
Total Small Jets	136	123	60	67	85	53	29	103	165	190	183	
Medium Jet Market												
Hawker Siddely 125	43	58	20	32	39	32	18	24	24	25	13	$2075
Sabre 60			11	20	14	6	9	4	4	20	9	$2200
Sabre 75								6	1	10	19	$2406
Falcon 20	14	43	63	38	25	18	7	24	46	17	29	$3005
Total Medium Jets	57	101	94	90	78	56	34	60	75	72	70	
Large Jet Market												
JetStar	18	22	18	18	11	2	4	10	6	1	0	$5035
Gulfstream			2	35	36	17	14	14	17	18	20	$5500
Total Large Jets	18	22	20	53	47	19	18	24	23	19	20	
Grand Total	211	246	174	210	210	128	77	194	284	290	273	

Exhibit 5 Cabin Floor Outline

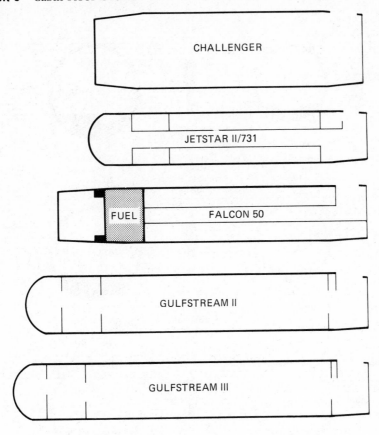

CHALLENGER

JETSTAR II/731

FUEL   FALCON 50

GULFSTREAM II

GULFSTREAM III

Challenger data based on engineering statistical analysis.

Exhibit 6

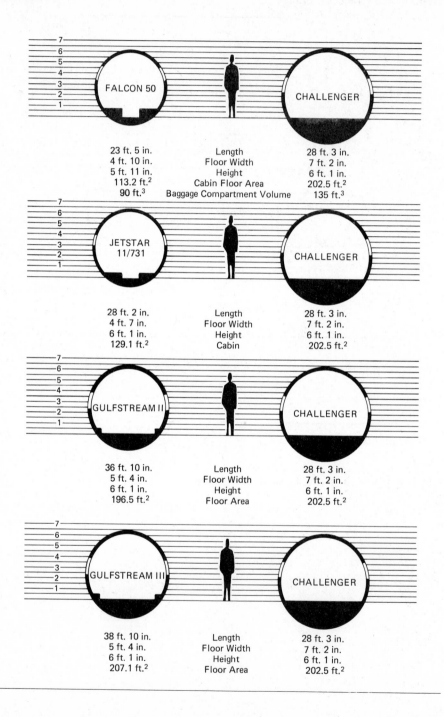

23 ft. 5 in.	Length	28 ft. 3 in.
4 ft. 10 in.	Floor Width	7 ft. 2 in.
5 ft. 11 in.	Height	6 ft. 1 in.
113.2 ft.^{2}	Cabin Floor Area	202.5 ft.^{2}
90 ft.^{3}	Baggage Compartment Volume	135 ft.^{3}

28 ft. 2 in.	Length	28 ft. 3 in.
4 ft. 7 in.	Floor Width	7 ft. 2 in.
6 ft. 1 in.	Height	6 ft. 1 in.
129.1 ft.^{2}	Cabin	202.5 ft.^{2}

36 ft. 10 in.	Length	28 ft. 3 in.
5 ft. 4 in.	Floor Width	7 ft. 2 in.
6 ft. 1 in.	Height	6 ft. 1 in.
196.5 ft.^{2}	Floor Area	202.5 ft.^{2}

38 ft. 10 in.	Length	28 ft. 3 in.
5 ft. 4 in.	Floor Width	7 ft. 2 in.
6 ft. 1 in.	Height	6 ft. 1 in.
207.1 ft.^{2}	Floor Area	202.5 ft.^{2}

Exhibit 7 Comparative Specifications

	Operating Cost Per Nautical Mile	Maximum Range	Cruising Speed	Fuel Consumption 100 nm at Cruise Speed	Noise Decibels[1] Take-off	Sideline	Approach	Current 1976 Price U.S. (000)	Passenger Capacity	Date of Entry on the Market	Production Rate/Mth
Challenger	$ .93	3900 nm	547 mph	4160 lb	78	87	90	$4100[2]	15	late 1979	8
JetStar II	$1.25	2800 nm	538 mph	7250 lb	N/A	N/A	N/A	$5345	10	1961 (updated)	1
Gulfstream III	$1.16	3600 nm	534 mph	6410 lb	90	102	98	$6200	12	August 1979	2
Gulfstream II	$1.26	3187 nm	541 mph	7723 lb	90	102	98	$5500	10	1969	2
Falcon 50	$1.06	3550 nm	528 mph	6200 lb	87	94	97	$5750	10–12	early 1979	2

1. 1979 FAA 36 Regulation: Take-off, 89; Sideline, 94; Approach, 98.

2. Initial proposal for first 50 units.

Source: Canadair comparative advertising material (based on statistical analysis) and company records.

The new Falcon 50 would be available for delivery by March 1979, and its performance in terms of projected operating cost per mile and range was second only to the Challenger. The print advertisement (exhibit 8) for the Falcon 50 claimed that it would be the fastest business jet in the world, although this statement was disputed by the calculations made by Canadair engineers. Mr. Halton and Mr. Taylor believed that the Falcon 50 would be around for some time, although its fuel consumption would be a major competitive disadvantage.

Gulfstream II and III

The Gulfstream II first flew in October 1966 and represented the latest technology at the time of its certification. Its turbojet engines were powerful but consumed considerably more fuel than used in the more recent high-bypass turbofans used by the Challenger. In addition, engine noise was high both inside and outside the cabin. Since 1966, 173 Gulfstream II's had been sold around the world.

Grumman had accelerated developmental work on a new Gulfstream III to replace the Gulfstream II in response to new demands on the market and the news of the Challenger. The Gulfstream III would be an aerodynamically modified version of the Gulfstream II, but it would use the same engines. The first prototype of the Gulfstream III was scheduled for completion in August 1979, and the first production unit was scheduled for delivery in March 1980. A print advertisement showing the Gulfstream II is shown in exhibit 9.

JetStar II

The JetStar II, available since January 1976, was a reengineered version of the original JetStar, which had been certificated in 1961. Although the new engines of the JetStar were turbofans, they were medium-bypass fans and not as efficient as high-bypass fans in minimizing fuel consumption. More than 112 JetStars had been sold since 1961.

According to a company spokesman, Lockheed-Georgia anticipated no new changes to its JetStar II in order to meet forthcoming competition from the Challenger, Falcon 50, and Gulfstream III. Lockheed was still attempting to determine its market share in the larger-cabin business fleet, with the performance and acceptance of the three new aircraft still unknown. JetStar II's were being built at the rate of one per month and the earliest promised delivery date was June 1978.[10] The JetStar II print advertisement was aimed directly at the Challenger.

10. *Aviation Week and Space Technology, op. cit.*

Exhibit 8

THE NEW FALCON 50

LONG FLIGHTS. SHORT FIELDS.
VERY VERSATILE.

Long-range jets are big. And because they *are* big, they must use big landing fields. They must take big strides. Use big amounts of fuel.

But all this has changed. And the new Falcon 50 has changed it.

For here is the *longest* long-range jet. It can take one giant step of more than 3,500 miles. Los Angeles to Hawaii? Of course. And longer flights. Much longer.

Yet it also handles extremely short fields. And it takes short hops as easily as it takes those giant steps.

In a word, it's *versatile*. The most versatile jet in the sky.

Short field. Long field. Short flight. Long flight. Name it. The remarkable new Falcon 50 lets *you* decide.

And this Falcon offers other formidable features. Features that will change the way management travels—all over the world.

Here's the first three-engine business jet. Advantage? Three engines are *very* reassuring. Especially over jungles and oceans.

The Falcon 50 boasts a new silhouette. Not big. But intelligently sized. With conservation in mind. In tune with the times. Seats 10-12. How often do you fly more?

It's the fastest long-range business jet.

The strongest—with the widest margins of reliability built right in.

The newest. Yet solidly based on the famous Falcon family. An *evolutionary* plane. Yet every feature's tried and true.

Perhaps now is the time to look into the newest development in executive travel: The long-range, three engine Falcon 50.

The complete story is yours for the asking. Just request it on your letterhead. Write Field Aviation Company, Ltd., Toronto International Airport, P.O. Box 6023, Toronto, A.M.F., Ontario L1P 1B9 Canada.

The Falcon 50:
Brand New. Tried and True.

Exhibit 9

The Challenger Programme

Early in 1976, much of Canadair's subcontract work was nearing completion, and Canadair was not selling enough of its own CL-215 water bombers to fill the gap. Canadair executives needed an ambitious project if they were to meet government demands for eventual self-sufficiency. Mr. Halton commented:

> We knew that we needed to do something in the general-aviation business and a market-research study indicated that business aviation would be a growth market. In November 1975, Fred Kearns talked with Bill Lear about his concept of an advanced business aircraft based on two known pieces of technology, the supercritical wing used on military aircraft and the high-bypass fanjet engine. In January 1976, I met with Bill Lear, and by March 1976 we were negotiating options on the Lear design. Jim Taylor was hired in April 1976 to head up the marketing for the new aircraft and by May he had arranged a selling seminar to which he invited 200 chief pilots and senior corporate officers to Canadair's plant to unveil the Challenger concept.

Bill Lear, who built the first business jet in 1961, had developed the original concept of the Challenger around an 88-inch-diameter fuselage. Representatives of the business market for the jet responded to the design encouragingly. However, Canadair decided to change the Lear design drastically for a number of reasons, one of them a fuel tankage problem. Also, at the original meeting with 200 chief pilots and executive officers, potential customers expressed demands for roominess. Consequently, Canadair engineers redesigned the jet with a 106-inch fuselage. As it happened, the extra width made the plane capable of seating four abreast. Lear disassociated himself from the Challenger program in response to this change and dubbed the Canadair design "Fat Albert." Canadair executives recognized the possibility of creating a "stretch" version of the Challenger that perhaps could carry up to 50 passengers.

It was clear at the beginning of 1976 that in order to finance the project, at least $70 million would have to be raised in addition to the company's own $70 million. Projects with this degree of leverage were not uncommon in the aerospace industry, and the Canadian government agreed to *guarantee* a $70-million Eurobond for Canadair.

The Challenger's most salient product benefits as conceived by Canadair's marketing and engineering staff were:

Large wide-body cabin: excellent size for executive, air taxi, third-level carriers, and cargo.

Fuel economy: lowest operating cost per nautical mile compared with direct competition.

Long range: long single-stage flight or numerous short-stage flights without refueling.

Competitive speeds: very competitive, high cruise speed in long-range configuration.

Low noise levels: most closely meets FAA standards for 1979.

Market Forecast

Canadair was already building a test model for fatigue tests, a test model for static tests, and three preproduction models for the eventual production plan, which would be as follows:

1979	6 units
1980	50 units
1981	80 units

The first test unit was expected to fly by April 1978, and the preproduction models were to be available for delivery by the end of 1979. This production plan was adopted in response to an analysis of the market trends for this category. Table 2 traces the market history of jet sales in the medium and large categories.

The United States was the major market for corporate aircraft. Table 3 summarizes the geographic distribution of corporate aircraft sales during 1966–1975.

On the basis of this history, Canadair's marketing staff first calculated pessimistic, probable, and optimistic worldwide sales forecasts for the medium and large jet category from 1978 to 1988, judged to be the Challenger's sales life (table 4).

Table 2   Market History (units):
Sales of Medium- and Large-Size Jets
(Gulfstream II, JetStar, Falcon 20, HS 125)

1966:	123	1971:	43
1967:	103	1972:	72
1968:	123	1973:	93
1969:	111	1974:	62
1970:	69	1975:	51

Ten-year total: 850 units

Canadair executives then narrowed this down to a forecast for Challenger sales only (table 5).

The most probable sales estimate for this period represented a 40 percent share of the probable world market during 1978–1988. In the

Table 3   Distribution of Sales, 1966–1975 (All Corporate Planes)

	Units	Percent
North America	565	66.5
Europe	189	22.2
Central and South America	25	2.9
Asia	24	2.8
Africa	37	4.4
Oceania	10	1.2
	850	100

Table 4   Worldwide Business Jet Sales Forecast, 1978–1988 (Challenger Category, Executive Configuration Only)

	Pessimistic	Probable	Optimistic
North America	600	625	675
Europe	200	225	275
Central and South America	25	40	65
Asia	25	40	65
Africa	50	75	95
Oceania	10	15	20
	910	1020	1195

Table 5   Challenger Sales Forecast, 1978–1988 (Executive Configuration Only)

	Pessimistic	Probable	Optimistic
North America	150	250	300
Europe	55	80	105
Central and South America	15	20	25
Asia	15	25	35
Africa	20	30	50
Oceania	5	5	10
	260	410	525

midterm, Canadair executives could consider a stretched version of the Challenger for the commuter and freight market. Adding this version would raise the probable forecast to 560 units, the pessimistic to 333, and optimistic to 750 units. The average variable cost per unit for the first 200 units was projected to be $4.1 million per jet, but variable costs per unit were expected to show some improvement because of the experience curve effect after the first 200 jets. Exhibit 10 shows a pro forma cash flow for the first 250 Challengers that might be produced. No cost or investment data had been generated on the stretched Challenger model.

Pricing

The marketing staff had prepared several pricing options for the Challenger. It was necessary to finalize pricing for the first 50 orders and work out a *general* pricing plan for the rest of the projected sales. Exhibit 11 contains data on the existing competitive prices and the marketing staff's best estimate of future pricing moves by the competition.

One pricing option for the first fifty orders was to undercut the competition by $1.2 million, setting the price at $4.1 million per Challenger. To some executives, a $1.2 million discount seemed large for such a superior product, even though the Challenger had flown only "on paper." They pointed out that all new aircraft faced this issue of confidence and that most buyers understood the process of designing an all-new aircraft and the process of gearing up a volume production system. Because the break-even volume under the low-price option was larger than the probable sales forecast, the price was expected to rise after the first fifty orders.

Alternatively, the Challenger could be priced at parity with the competition. In this case, the price would probably increase in step with inflation and the pricing of competitive products.

Some executives suggested that the Challenger's superior product characteristics required a premium price even in the short run. They believed that the Challenger could maintain a premium over competitive prices in the long run.

The purchase price for each Challenger would include training for captains, maintenance training for mechanics, programmed maintenance assistance from Montreal, and service and support from any of the three planned service facilities. Bill Lear, who had done the initial Challenger design, would receive 5 percent of the *sale* price of the first fifty units sold, 4 percent on the second fifty, and 3 percent on all orders beyond the first hundred.

Exhibit 10   CL 600 Challenger Pro Forma[a] Cash Flow Profile as of June 1976 ($000)

Activity Time Span	Sept. 76–Dec. 79 not assignable	Dec. 77–Oct. 80 Lot #1 Aircraft 1–50	Apr. 79–Aug. 81 Lot #2 Aircraft 51–100	Feb. 80–Apr. 82 Lot #3 Aircraft 101–150	Oct. 80–Jan. 83 Lot #4 Aircraft 151–200	Jul. 81–Dec. 83 Lot #5 Aircraft 201–250	Total
Labour, overhead cost	$ 86,400	$ 72,460	$ 29,350	$ 26,350	$ 24,980	$ 25,315	$ 264,855
Material, equipment cost	20,925	81,148	94,970	107,450	113,045	126,100	543,638
Other costs (rentals, service)	21,600	17,550	925	713	760	750	42,298
Programme support cost	6,075	18,936	10,440	11,100	12,784	14,475	73,810
Marketing		5,030	2,744	2,938	3,390	3,836	17,938
Finance		31,326	10,700				42,026
Total cost	135,000	226,450	149,129	148,551	154,959	170,476	984,565
Revenue		205,000	225,500	238,500	253,000	268,000	1,190,000
Cumulative	(135,000)	(156,450)	(80,079)	9,870	107,911	205,435	205,435
Date #1 aircraft ordered		Jul. 76					
Anticipated date last aircraft ordered		Nov. 76	Apr. 78	Oct. 79	Apr. 81	Oct. 82	
Delivery date #1 aircraft		Nov. 79					
Anticipated date last aircraft delivered		Sept. 80	Aug. 81	June 82	May 83	Apr. 84	
Assumed average price per aircraft		4,100	4,510	4,770	5,060	5,360	4,750

a. These data are presented for case study purposes only and do not purport to represent actual estimating data.

Exhibit 11   Expected Pricing Movement in the Large Jet Market ($000's)

	1976 Current Price[a]	Expected BCA Price[b]							
		1977	1978	1979	1980	1981	1982	1983	1984
Challenger[c]	$4100	$	$	$	$	$	$	$	$
JetStar II	5345	5195	5611	6057	6544	7068	7633	8244	8900
Gulfstream III	6200	?	—	—	—	—	—	—	—
Gulfstream II	5500	5900	6354	6844	7371	7938	8549	9208	9910
Falcon 50	5750	5750	5750	5750	6153	6583	7044	7537	8060

Source: Company records.
a. Average BCA equipped prices.
b. Smith and Taylor were less certain of pricing activity after 1980.
c. Initial proposal for first 50 units.

The following terms of purchase were proposed:

1. Each customer would be required to make a 5 percent deposit for each plane ordered. All deposits would be placed in escrow with accrued interest at the Canadian prime rate (10 percent in 1976).
2. One year before delivery, the customer would pay 30 percent of the purchase price.
3. Six months before delivery, the customer would pay 30 percent again.
4. The customer would pay the final 35 percent of the purchase price upon delivery.

Service

After-sale service was an important purchase criterion for the customer. Canadair executives tentatively had decided to build three factory-owned service centres, which would service only Challengers. Their cost, $4.5 million each, was included in the planned $140-million investment. One centre would be located in Hartford, Connecticut, where Canadair's U.S. sales office was located, one in the southwestern United States, and one in Europe. The selection of these locations was based on the projection that these areas would provide the majority of Challenger sales. Only technical personnel would operate from these facilities.

The service facilities would have to be completed in time to service the first jets as they were sold at the end of 1979. Canadair would have to service early Challenger buyers very well to enhance its credibility and improve sales prospects. There was some concern at Canadair about whether factory-owned centres were the best way to provide service. Some corporate jet manufacturers such as Gulfstream and Hawker-Siddely utilized service distributors. Hence, the 200 Hawker-Siddely 125's in the United States were serviced by a distributor network of fourteen outlets. This method of servicing, if chosen by Canadair, would eliminate the $4.5 million investment in each service facility; but because the Challenger was technically more advanced than its competition, special in-house expertise might offer certain advantages and would not require handing over technical information to distributors who serviced competitive aircraft.

Advertising and Promotion

The advertising and promotion budget for the Challenger programme in 1976 was set at about $2.5 million. Because the Challenger was a new and unproven airplane, the marketing staff and its advertising agency had decided to mount a print advertising campaign in the leading technical and business magazines to support the sales force's personal selling activities. Domestic and international advertising campaigns were planned for journals such as *Professional Pilot*, *Business Week*, *Business and Commercial Aviation*, *Interavia*, and the *Wall Street Journal*. All of the Challenger's competitors advertised in these journals, trying to reach the executive in charge of purchasing a business jet and the pilot who would be flying the jet.

To achieve high readability scores for their advertising, Canadair executives were prepared to use a bold, confident and "challenging" theme. Examples of the proposed advertisements are shown as exhibits 12 and 13. This copy differed markedly from what the competition typically employed. Of the total advertising and promotion budget, $625,000 was to be allocated to print advertising.

Studying the competition's advertising copy, Mr. Taylor sensed that the competition had already begun to react to the Challenger programme. This was particularly evident in the Gulfstream II and JetStar II advertisements. Still, the Canadair marketing group was worried that its own bold campaign could backfire and damage the credibility of the Challenger by taking pot shots at the competition, especially when the Challenger had no flight tests to back it up. If their theme proved inappropriate, they could quickly develop other themes and advertisements. In any case, the advertising agency would be paid 10 percent of the expenditures for media space.

To reinforce the print advertising campaign, brochures and other sales literature were printed. An active direct mailing programme could be used to solicit inquiries from potential prospects. The Challenger would also be promoted through press releases and press conferences, pilot seminars,

Exhibit 12

This business jet design is so advanced, it's making the competition airsick.

Enter the Canadair Challenger. Not just another business jet, but the first new concept in business jets in about 20 years.

And we're not just saying that with empty words.

We're sending forth this solid challenge:

We challenge any business jet to fly as fast.

We challenge any business jet to offer as much range.

We challenge any business jet to fly as efficiently.

We challenge any business jet to match our wide-body comfort.

And now, we'd like to plunge into some specifics, demonstrating why our competition is feeling a bit queasy at the moment.

The Challenger challenges the JetStar II.

The Challenger is really much more of a star than the JetStar II. It will carry 17% less fuel, yet travel 1,400 statute miles further.

The Challenger will be faster, quieter, 40% less expensive to operate. As well as a sprawling 25 inches wider.

The Challenger challenges the Falcon 50.

Compared to the Challenger, the Falcon 50 is a bird of a different feather. The Challenger will fly up to 35 mph faster (N. Y. to L. A. in 5 hours and 11 minutes).

The Challenger will also fly 1,000 miles further, be quieter, and burn 20% less fuel while doing so.

As for the inside story, the Challenger will have 42% more cabin volume than the Falcon 50, and 76% more baggage space.

The Challenger challenges the Gulfstream II.

The Challenger will carry 40% less fuel, yet travel 900 miles further.

The Challenger will be about ⅓ less expensive to operate.

And the Challenger will be easy to take in still another way. Noise. We'll be significantly quieter than the Gulfstream II. And because we'll be 10 inches wider, we'll even challenge their cabin for passenger comfort and room.

How we're meeting the challenge.

We're meeting the challenge of the Challenger by discarding the hand-me-down technology that the competition uses.

Our business jet will incorporate the most sophisticated and proven technology currently available.

That includes the Lycoming ALF-502 turbofan with a 5 to 1 high bypass ratio. Its power will provide us with the best thrust-to-weight relationship of any commercially obtainable plane.

We also bring you a new wing. An advanced, yet proven, airfoil concept that will delay the formation of shock waves.

So prepare yourself for this shock: we'll not be just faster than any business jet, we'll be faster than a DC-10.

The company that's behind all this is Canadair, makers of over 3,800 aircraft, 580 supersonic.

For more information on the Challenger, formerly known by the drawing board name LearStar, write to Jim Taylor at Canadair Inc., Dept. A, 274 Riverside Avenue, Westport, Conn. 06880. Or call him at (203) 226-1581.

You'll become convinced that the Challenger, the business jet that's making the competition airsick, can be a very healthy investment for your company.

CABIN		GULFSTREAM II	JETSTAR II/731	FALCON 50
LENGTH	28.25 ft.	36.8 ft.	28.2 ft.	23.2 ft.
WIDTH	8.16 ft.	7.3 ft.	6.5 ft.	6.2 ft.
HEIGHT	6.1 ft.	6.1 ft.	6.1 ft.	5.8 ft.
VOLUME	1150 ft.³	1460 ft.³	850 ft.³	700 ft.³

Challenger is head and shoulders above the rest.

canadair challenger

We challenge any business jet to match it.

All performance figures in this advertisement for CHALLENGER are based upon wind tunnel tests and engineering statistical analysis with flight testing to begin in early 1978.

Exhibit 13

Our competition wastes a lot of energy.

And they'll be wasting a lot more when they try to explain these figures.

On a 1,000 nautical mile trip, the *challenger* will burn:

- **36% less fuel than a JetStar II.**
- **45% less fuel than a Gulfstream II.**
- **20% less fuel than a Falcon 50.**
- **11% less fuel than a Falcon 20F.**

These are the numbers that add up to trouble for the competition.

The numbers that prove the Challenger will be the business jet that not only outperforms all the rest, but outconserves all the rest of the full-cabin business jets.

The environment will save. You will save. And with fuel costs taking off even faster than a Challenger, we don't have to tell you what the savings will be.

Our economy isn't a con.

The same engine that will let us go so fast (N.Y. to L.A. in 5 hours, 11 minutes) is also what will use up our fuel so slowly.

It's the Lycoming ALF-502 turbofan with a 5 to 1 high bypass ratio. This design means exceptional fuel efficiency.

So does our new wing. An advanced configuration that will delay the formation of shock waves. So drag, which is such a drag, won't drag as much. And lift will be lifted. So the Challenger will fly faster, further, and more economically than any other business jet.*

Our economy will also apply to maintenance. The Challenger's engine is fully modular for on-airframe servicing. Meaning our engine is a snap to fix. You won't be paying $1,000 for labor to replace a $50 part.

Tomorrow's plane without yesterday's technology.

Scratch the twenty-year-old technology the competition embraces. The Challenger is being built from scratch. Incorporating all the latest proven aspects of both design and technology.

Even our cabin is a big idea. The Challenger will be the first wide-body business jet. Almost a full foot wider than any other, and two spacious feet wider than most.

Now who's behind all this, you ask? Canadair. Canadair has built over 3,800 aircraft, 580 supersonic.

There's much more detailed information on the Challenger, formerly known by the drawing board name LearStar, and Jim Taylor has it. Write to him at Canadair, Dept. A, P.O. Box 6087, Montreal, Canada H3C3G9. Or call him at (514) 744-1511.

He'll spend all the time you need talking about the plane that will expend so little energy.

canadair challenger

We challenge any business jet to match it.

*All performance figures in this advertisement for CHALLENGER are based upon wind tunnel tests and engineering statistical analysis with flight testing to begin in early 1978.
© CANADAIR 1977

photography, and newsletters, so that magazine articles would chronicle the progress of the Challenger engineering and marketing activities.

All competitors generally used this kind of promotion, but with varying degrees of intensity and success. The Falcon 50 marketers had used comparative advertising but had made no mention of the Challenger in their advertising. Canadair executives believed that this obvious exclusion was an attempt by the Falcon 50 people to present the Challenger as unworthy of consideration. The JetStar II and Gulfstream II advertising did not use comparative approaches.

Exhibit 14 contains rate and reach data for full-page advertisements (the typical size in the large-jet business) in publications typically used by corporate airplane advertisers. Media space could be purchased as early as the third week in July.

The Selling Task

President Kearns described the selling process this way:

> Each sale *is* different. It isn't like going to the military with a proposal and finding that you have just won a competition and the armed forces are going to buy 225 of your airplanes in the very first contract. It isn't like going to the airlines and selling batches of ten or a dozen transports at once, all to the same specifications, with the same number of seats and the same colours inside and on the tail! It is, in fact, a matter of doing a complete presentation and proposal for every single prospect you approach. We start out with a prospect list made up of present business aircraft operators plus other major corporations throughout the world who do not yet operate any aircraft. These organizations often have the need but we in the industry have yet to prove it to them. We gather data on the companies. We get an idea of their current needs by talking to their pilots, or we make some estimates if they have never operated an aircraft.
>
> We study the trips their people make, the points they routinely travel between, the longest and shortest flights, how many go on each trip, etc. Gradually a picture emerges to show us each prospect's specific requirement. And armed with that study, we approach the prospects with our sales proposals.

The first pitch was usually made to a firm's pilot. Pilots generally had only veto power and not purchase power, but their acceptance was crucial. The salesperson had to determine how much he or she would be able to use the pilot to make the sale. Mr. Taylor described three possibilities:

1. The pilot is strongly in your favour. He would act like an in-house salesman for you.

2. The pilot is unsure. The first task is to move him to neutral and then improve his and management's attitudes.

3. The pilot is against the product right off, clearly the least-preferred situation. The first task here is to cool him off and try to get to the chief executive officer and sell him first.

The salesperson had to be very perceptive in assessing to what degree the influencers on the selling decision would be involved and finding out who exactly would make the final decision.

Prospects were identified with the assistance of a *Business and Commercial Aviation*[11] study that measured the impact of company aircraft in the top 1000 U.S. industrials as compiled by *Fortune* magazine.

This summary of the business performance of the Fortune 1000 industrials showed that the aircraft operators, for whatever reason, were more efficient. The 514 aircraft-operating companies controlled 1778 aircraft in 1975, an increase of 125 over 1974. This study concluded that

> nearly one-half of the nation's biggest corporations are not operators
> even though their dollar volume of business indicates a cash flow that
> would support capital equipment such as an aircraft. In some cases, the
> nature of a firm's activities precludes the need for travel to locations
> not well served by public transportation; for others, the scheduling flex-
> ibility and effective utilization of personnel afforded by business avia-
> tion is not a strong incentive in the firm's type of business endeavors.
> But there are many corporations, we suspect, where the concept of
> business aircraft still is not appreciated or fully understood, and it is in
> this area that a greater knowledge of corporate aviation is needed.[12]

Hence, part of the selling task involved giving a potential customer an education in the advantages of corporate-owned aircraft in general before making a pitch for a particular model.

Another study identified companies owning the most expensive and largest fleets in the United States (table 6).

The Men Behind The Selling Task

Mr. James Taylor, 55, had been hired by Canadair in April 1976 to market the Challenger concept to the corporate market. Mr. Taylor's fascination

11. Arnold Lewis, "Business Aviation and the Fortune 1000," *Business and Commercial Aviation*, December 1978, pp. 1–4.
12. *Ibid.*

Exhibit 14 Print Advertising Rate Data[a]

Publication	Edition	Circulation (000's)	Distribution	Full Page (1 time)	Half Page	Frequency Discount 7 times	13 times
Wall Street Journal	Eastern	606	Daily	$14,101	$ 7,050		
	Midwest	458		11,366	5,683		
	West	289		7,958	3,534		
	Southwest	168		4,049	2,024		
	North America	1500		36,265	18,132		
Business Week	International	59	Weekly	$ 2,450			
	European	31		1,710			
	Northeast	218		6,180			
	Midwest	182		5,120			
	Pacific Coast	131		3,640			
	Southwest	51		1,480			
	Southeast	66		1,900			
	North America	738		9,000		10%	5%
Fortune	North America	600	Bi-Weekly	$13,710			
	Eastern	201		7,000			
	Midwestern	159		5,130			
	Southeastern	60		2,610			
	Southwestern	48		2,210			
	Western	115		3,820			
	International	70		4,020			
	European	46		3,070		8%	4%
Forbes	North America	665	Monthly	$10,990		7%	4%

						Frequency Discount		
					3 times	5 times	7 times	13 times
Dunn's Review	Eastern	Monthly	90	$ 3,405				
	Central		86	2,665	7%	6%		
	Southern		32	1,515			5%	
	Western		40	1,160				
	All		248	5,405				
Aviation Week and Space Technology	All North America	Weekly	97	$ 4,343	2.5%	1.8%		4%
Business and Commercial Aviation	All North America	Monthly	50	$ 2,850		11%		6%
Flight International[b]	All	Weekly	47	$ 1,670		6%		6%
Interavia[b]	All	Monthly	3	$ 390	14%	22%		

a. All rates are noncontract rates; all rates are black and white ads.

b. International circulation.

Source: Standard Rate and Data Service.

Table 6 The Most Expensive Corporate Fleets

Company	Number of Airplanes	Fleet Value (millions of dollars)
Coca-Cola	5	17.2
3M Co.	7	16.2
Rockwell International	21	15.6
Mobil	28	14.4
IBM	9	13.2
Atlantic Richfield	20	13.0
General Motors	14	12.8
United Technologies	14	12.3
Exxon	16	11.3
Tenneco	26	11.1
ITT	13	10.9
Shell	24	9.7
Diamond Shamrock	3	9.0
Gannett	4	8.9
General Dynamics	5	8.8
U.S. Steel	4	8.8
Conoco	19	8.7
Texaco	8	8.3
Time	9	8.2
Johnson & Johnson	7	8.1
Marathon Oil	14	8.0

Data: Aviation Data Service Inc.

with aircraft went back many years. His father had been a test pilot in World War I and II. James Taylor had scored successes for the Cessna Aircraft Corp. and the French-based Dassault-Breguet Aircraft Corp. When Mr. Taylor joined Dassault in 1966, the "Fan Jet Falcon 20" soon became the industry sales leader in terms of both units and dollars. In 1966, Lear had sold 33 jets worldwide through 200 dealers, but in 1967, Mr. Taylor and his four salesmen sold 45 Falcon 20's in North America without the assistance of any dealers. Mr. Taylor believed in direct sales rather than a dealer network because, as he put it,

> It is a narrowly defined market. When I sell direct, I have better control over hiring, training, the territory, and the price. I like to bring prospects in for seminars, take a mock-up to key cities, and make extensive use of direct mail.

Joining Cessna in March 1969, he became the architect behind the highly successful "Citation" marketing and product support programmes, which transformed the aircraft into the world's most successful business jet in its initial four years of production.

Mr. Taylor brought three key people with him to Canadair. Mr. Bill Juvonen had been with Mr. Taylor on three previous marketing programmes including the Falcon 20 and the Citation. He became the Vice-President of Sales responsible for Canada and the United States west of the Mississippi. Mr. Dave Hurley had spent five years with Cessna and had worked with Mr. Taylor on two programmes. He became the Vice-President of Sales responsible for the eastern half of the United States. Barry Smith had been the Director of Corporate Marketing Services for Atlantic Aviation, a company that serviced and distributed such corporate jets as the Gulfstream II, the Hawker-Siddely 125, and the Westwind. He had later worked for James Taylor in the same capacity on the successful Cessna Citation programme. Mr. Taylor immediately hired him as Vice-President, Marketing Services. Mr. Smith would be responsible for advertising, direct mail, and all the "inside" marketing services. These four men made up the marketing team that would have to sell 50 Challengers before September 30, 1976.

Final Questions

The Challenger's design was undergoing constant modification. Mr. Taylor described the Chief Engineer, Mr. Halton, as

> the most open-minded engineer I've ever met. For example, one of our
> customers suggested an APU (auxiliary power unit) system to assure
> power to the cabin electricals in flight. Harry designed in the APU
> system. Similarly, traditional aircraft use DC electricals, but there are
> customer advantages in using AC. Harry put in AC. When Harry cannot
> accommodate one of our design suggestions, he always has good
> reasons and he takes the time to tell us. Normally, a chief pilot would
> not want you talking to his boss, but with the Challenger, some pilots
> not only are talking to their bosses, they are relaying information to us
> and to them.

However, it was time to finalize the design and move ahead on a production system that would produce 80 aircraft per year.

Although Mr. Taylor had been very successful using a direct sales approach, other companies made extensive use of dealer networks, particularly in foreign countries. The "five percenters" (agents) in foreign countries also raised the issue of controlling their selling practices, especially in countries where bribery was almost a standard practice.

The pricing strategy and promotion strategy would have to provide fairly rapid market penetration. Advertising and service expenditures already comprised $16 million of the investment budget; changes in these expenditures would have to promise compensating paybacks. There had to be a high probability that the proposed marketing plan would deliver the sales forecast for the Challenger. Mr. Taylor smiled and commented wryly to his aides, "This is going to have to be the biggest selling job in history. I think we can count on working six days a week, fourteen hours a day from now until September 30th."

Two manufacturers were rumoured to be looking at the Challenger statistics to see how best to compete with this wide-body turbofan. Messrs. Taylor, Halton, and Kearns sat down on the morning of July 4, 1976, to review the Challenger strategy for the next three months and the longer term.

44 S.C. Johnson—The Agree Line

As Mel Liston reviewed the latest material received from the firm's advertising agency, he felt very pleased that his recommendations on product positioning had been approved by senior management. These recommendations centered around a new targeting strategy for Agree Shampoo and Agree Creme Rinse and Conditioner that would shift marketing effort away from the "all women, aged 18 to 45" segment toward the "teenage female" segment of the market. As Product Manager of the Agree line at S.C. Johnson & Son, Ltd., in Brantford, Ontario, his current task was to develop a comprehensive marketing communications programme aimed at the new target audience for the fiscal year (FY) 1980–1981. It was May 1980, and he would have to make strategic decisions on advertising, consumer sales promotion, and trade promotion within the next few weeks in order to finalize a plan that could be implemented by July 1, the start of the new fiscal year.

Company Background

S.C. Johnson & Son, Ltd., better known as Johnson Wax, was founded in 1886 in Racine, Wisconsin, as a manufacturer of parquet flooring. When customers became concerned with the care and protection of their flooring, Johnson began making and selling a prepared paste wax. The popularity of parquet flooring began to fade, and by 1917 the company was concentrating solely on floor wax and other wood finishing products. The Canadian operation was created in 1920, by which time there were also plants in England and Australia.

By 1980, the company had grown into a two billion dollar corporation with operations in 41 countries and 110 distribution centres around the world. At that time, 78 percent of the company's sales were derived from the Consumer Products Group which was comprised of the U.S. Division and the International Division. The Canadian company was part of the latter group, although it had a separate management structure and research facilities. This arrangement ensured a high degree of autonomy in decisions related to marketing, finance, and research and development. Some products were developed in Canada—for example, Glade Flo-Thru Air Freshener and Super Soap—and these were frequently adopted by other subsidiaries. Other products were developed abroad and were later marketed in Canada.

Until the late 1970's, Johnson's primary emphasis was on floor and furniture care products. These were relatively mature markets that, in recent years, had suffered a slow but steady decline. Two reasons accounted for this slowdown: no-wax floors were becoming increasingly popular, and consumers' attitudes toward floor and furniture care were softening with the growth of low-maintenance chrome, glass, and wood veneer products. At this time, Johnson controlled over two thirds of the shrinking floor market. The company responded to these trends by improving and repositioning existing products as well as by adding new products to the line. Although the company believed that these tactics helped it to maintain a market leadership position, management recognized that it would have to look farther afield in order to sustain existing sales and profitability.

New Market Opportunity

Personal care products were designated by Johnson as a key growth area at this time, and the firm began to explore the possibility of entering these markets. Market research indicated that after-shampoo products had grown recently by more than 20 percent per year despite the fact that users were apparently dissatisfied with the feel of their hair after using these oily conditioning products. Research findings suggested that consumers wanted control and softness in hair that both looked and felt clean. Owing to its wide-ranging R&D program, Johnson had developed the technology to formulate a unique creme rinse product that was 99 percent oil free[1] but still conditioned hair. The company had recently hired personnel who were experienced in the production and marketing of hair care products.

Agree Creme Rinse and Conditioner (CRC), was first launched in the United States in 1976. During the fall of that year, marketing research was

---

1. The 1 percent oil component was included to provide a fragrance base. At that time, a major competing brand, Tame, contained approximately 40 percent oil.

undertaken in Canada to develop profiles of typical shampoo and/or CRC consumers. Findings from the "Usage and Attitude Study" indicated that 95 percent of all Canadians used a shampoo product, with women accounting for the heaviest usage. The rate of usage varied, however, from once a day to once a week or less. In addition, the study found that 40 percent of all women used CRCs "some of the time."

Agree CRC was then introduced in Canada in June 1977 and became the Canadian CRC market leader by 1979 (see exhibit 1). Some of its success was due to Johnson's Canadian advertising budget, set at $700,000[2] in the launch year compared to $868,000 for all other firms in the CRC industry, including $200,000 spent by Gillette on its CRC product, Tame, the market leader prior to Agree's introduction. The Johnson product was also successful because of its superior formulation, which was emphasized in its advertising (see exhibit 2). Finally, a large-scale sampling promotion[3] contributed to the early success of Agree CRC.

The extraordinary success of Agree CRC prompted Johnson to introduce a second Agree product. Johnson entered the large, highly competitive and fragmented shampoo market early in 1978, almost a year after its Agree CRC introduction (see exhibit 3). Agree shampoo was formulated to clean hair more thoroughly than most of the shampoos then on the

Exhibit 1   S.C. Johnson—Agree, Creme Rinse and Conditioner Market Shares 12 Months Ending Sept./Oct. 1975–1979 (percent)

Brand	1975	1976	1977	1978	1979
Tame	23.3	23.5	18.1	13.7	11.2
Clairol (total)[a]	18.3	16.2	13.2	9.1	10.8
Alberto Culver	9.4	8.0	—	—	—
Breck Clean Rinse	4.0	3.9	—	—	—
Revlon Flex	—	5.2	11.7	11.4	13.3
Wella Balsam	—	—	5.2	6.0	7.8
Agree	—	—	—	13.5	13.8
All others	45.0	41.6	47.0	41.0	40.0

a. Includes: Herbal Essence, Balsam, and Clairol Conditioner.

Source: Company records.

2. Many of Johnson's figures have been disguised, but basic relationships have not been altered significantly.

3. During the sampling campaign, 3/4-ounce sachets were distributed in a full national mailing to approximately 3.2 million Canadian households.

Exhibit 2 S.C. Johnson—Agree, 1977 Advertisement
for Agree Creme Rinse and Conditioner

Exhibit 3 S.C. Johnson—Agree,
Market Shares of Shampoos, Early 1978

Leading Brands	Share
Head & Shoulders	16
Johnson & Johnson Baby Shampoo	12
Clairol Herbal Essence	5
Breck Golden	6
Revlon Flex	4
Short & Sassy	3
Earth Born	3

Sales by Formula Type	
Dandruff medicated segment	20%
Cosmetic segment	
(including baby shampoos)	80%

Note: The total shampoo category consisted of
over 150 brands and more than 700 sizes and
types.
Source: Company records.

market. The slogan, "Helps stop the greasies between shampoos" combined with the Agree name helped to make the new shampoo number three in the market within six months, close behind Head & Shoulders and Johnson & Johnson (J & J) Baby Shampoo.

By 1979, most other CRC's on the market were reformulated to be oil-free, thus converting Agree's main benefit into a generic one. Management recognized the potential threat posed by this move and began to consider alternative steps that could be taken to prevent any erosion of Agree's market share.

Product Management

S.C. Johnson employed a product management system to guide the strategic plans and activities of the firm's marketing department. Under this system, the director of marketing delegated responsibility for specific groups of products to group product managers (e.g., personal care products, furniture and floor care, etc.), who, in turn, reassigned responsibility for one or more brands within the group to product managers and assistant product managers.

Product managers at Johnson adhered to a well-defined policy governing new product development. Under this policy, a new product was permitted to lose money during its introductory year(s) but was expected to achieve annual corporate profitability goals thereafter. Because the CRC and the shampoo had been introduced at different times, the goal for the full Agree line had been set at 11 percent in FY 1979–1980. A target of 12.5 percent had been set for FY 1980–1981.

From the inception of Agree shampoo in 1978 to late 1979, Agree CRC and shampoo were handled by two separate product managers within Johnson. The rationale for this division of responsibility reflected management's belief that the competitive environments for CRC's and shampoos were quite distinct during that period. This policy resulted in the development of separate advertising and pricing strategies for Agree CRC and shampoo.

During the latter part of 1979, market analysis was undertaken by S.C. Johnson to identify and describe Agree CRC and shampoo users (see exhibit 4). Management was quite surprised to discover that the user base for Agree was not women aged 18–45, but primarily girls in the 12–24 age group. This study also showed that there was as high as 65 percent cross-usage between the Agree CRC and shampoo brands, one of the highest nationally, although they were not advertised as being essential to one another. Interestingly, earlier advertising tracking studies had indicated that approximately 24 percent of viewers of any Agree shampoo commercial recalled it as one for Agree CRC and vice-versa.

In view of these research results, the product management group for Agree became increasingly convinced that consumers seemed to think about Agree products as a unit. As a result, the separate product manager positions for Agree CRC and shampoo were combined in order to achieve economies of scale and to foster better communications. As part of this integration, management decided that Agree products eventually would share a common pricing strategy together with joint trade and consumer promotions. Since Agree products would now be viewed as a family, advertising would be scheduled to alternate between shampoo and CRC. The combined FY 1979–1980 sales for these products were estimated to total $12 million at retail.

Mel Liston had recently been appointed product manager for both Agree CRC and shampoo products. As a result of the 1979 market research study, he believed that repositioning Agree would strengthen its chances for continued success. In particular, the information pertaining to the current user base for Agree products led Mel Liston to define the primary target market as girls in the 12–18 age bracket and the secondary target market as women aged 19–24. New advertising copy and media schedules

Exhibit 4 S.C. Johnson—Agree, Shampoo/CRC Markets, Importance by Sex and Age Group

Group	Population (millions)	Percent Who Use	Frequency of Use Per Year	Number of Uses (millions)	Adjusting Factors	Equivalent Volume Used	Percent of Volume Represented	Percent of Volume of Agree Used
A. Hair Conditioner Market: Importance by Sex and Age Group								
Females								
12–18	1.35	80	200	216	1.25	270	23	32
19–24	1.37	93	157	200	1.1	220	19	10
25–34	1.96	84	134	220	1.0	220	19	13
35–54	2.60	87	98	221	0.75	166	15	15
55+	2.33	85	70	138	0.60	83	7	4
Males								
13–34	5.2	57	53	157	1.0	157	14	24
35+	4.8	42	11	22	0.8	18	3	2
B. Shampoo Market: Importance by Sex and Age Group								
Females								
12–18	1.35	100	260	351	1.25	439	15	23
19–24	1.37	100	239	327	1.1	360	12	8
25–34	1.96	100	208	407	1.0	407	14	11
35–54	2.60	100	175	455	0.75	341	11	12
55+	2.33	100	95	221	0.6	132	4	3
Males								
13–34	5.2	99	175	900	1.0	900	30	37
35+	4.8	97	102	474	0.8	380	14	6

Source: Company records.

aimed at implementing the revised strategy for Agree were requested from Johnson's advertising agency.

Mel Liston said, "If we're going to be the 'bubble gum' shampoo, we have to gear most of our plans to this new market. We must change our thinking in order to fully exploit our knowledge of the consumer base for Agree."

The Agree Market

By May 1980, both Agree CRC and Agree shampoo were being offered on a continuous basis in three regular sizes and three formulas (see exhibit 5). A fourth size, 50 ml, was offered each year, although mainly as a back-to-school trial size. This trial size was typically offered in promotional packages containing other personal care products sold by a variety of companies.

At that time, there were at least 150 kinds of shampoos and 80 CRC's on the market. Less than half of them were branded, and of these, only

Exhibit 5 S.C. Johnson—Agree, Types, Sizes, and Colours of Agree Products, 1980

CRC's

Formula Name	Bottle Colour	Sales Volume (percent)
Extra Body with Balsam	Orange	27
Regular Formula	Green	41
For Extra Oily Hair	Yellow	32

Shampoos

Formula Name	Shampoo Colour (bottle is clear plastic)	Sales Volume (percent)
Extra Gentle	Orange	29
Regular	Green	40
Oily Hair	Yellow	31

Size	Type
50 ml	trial (promotional only)
225 ml	regular
350 ml	family
450 ml	economy (introduced in Feb. 1980)

Source: Company records.

about ten were supported by any advertising or consumer promotion. The rest were "price brands," reasonably priced, acceptable products that were low priced to consumers and were promoted heavily to the trade. Two of the more familiar of the price brands were Unicare and Suave.

Market share estimates for the different shampoo and CRC sizes are summarized in exhibit 6. By May 1980, the total CRC market in Canada had reached almost $37.5 million and was growing at an annual rate of approximately 20 percent. At that time, Agree CRC was the leading brand in the category, with sales of $5.2 million at retail representing almost 13.8 percent of the total CRC market in dollar terms. The total shampoo market had risen to almost $108 million with a growth rate of about 12 percent per year. Agree was second in terms of market share with sales amounting to $6.8 million or close to 6.3 percent of the total shampoo market. The 350-ml size bottle accounted for the bulk of total Agree sales, both in the CRC and shampoo categories (see exhibit 6).

The Consumer

Company sales records indicated that by May 1980, consumers purchased 75 percent as much Agree CRC as shampoo. Buying habits for these two items were quite different from those associated with Johnson's other products. For example, a 1979 market research study indicated that purchase frequency was relatively high—every few weeks as opposed to every few months. If the product that the consumer wanted was not on the shelf, she would rarely postpone her purchase until the following week. Instead, she normally would switch to another brand.

According to the 1979 study, the consumer typically owned about three brands at a time. Many of the purchasers, principally women, apparently believed that they became sensitized[4] to one particular brand after a while. Consequently, they would try another brand in their "evoked brand set," those four or five brands which they were prepared to buy at any one time. Since people tended to rotate between brands within their own set, a key objective of management was to encourage users to come back to Agree more often, thereby ensuring its position as the brand with the highest frequency of use in the category. Purchases tended to be made largely on impulse, particularly for conditioners, which generally were considered to be less essential in the household than shampoos.

4. As a rule, people consider their hair care requirements to be highly unique. After repeated uses of any single brand, many people gradually become concerned that the brand no longer works as effectively as it once did. It is this concern that prompts brand-switching behaviour.

Exhibit 6 S.C. Johnson—Agree, Market Shares for Agree Shampoo/CRC

	Share of $ Sales		Share of Volume Sales	
	1979–1980 to Date[a]	*Percent Change from 1978–1979*	*1979–1980 to Date*	*Percent Change from 1978–1979*
A. *Shampoo*				
Total market volume	107,742,000	11	6,725[b]	1
Total Agree	6.3	32	5.5	37
50 ml	0.1		0.1	
225 ml	1.5		1.1	
350 ml	4.1		3.7	
450 ml	0.7		0.6	
Head & Shoulders	16.5	22	10.8	16
J & J	7.6	2	7.9	(7)
Body on Tap	3.5	66	3.6	64
Revlon Flex	5.8	22	5.6	15
All others	60.3	6	67.4	(5)
B. *CRC*				
Total market volume	37,455,600	21	2,034.4	12
Total Agree	13.8	19	14.5	15
50 ml	0.3		0.5	
225 ml	2.8		2.4	
350 ml	6.1		6.5	
450 ml	4.6		5.2	
Tame	8.0	(2)	10.9	(11)
Silkience	2.9	N[c]	1.2	N[c]
Revlon Flex	10.5	43	12.0	29
Condition II	4.0	N	6.1	N
All others	60.8	10	55.3	1

a. Based on approximately ten months of sales. FY 1979–1980 ends on June 30.
b. Represents the liquid measure of millions of cases of twelve 350-ml bottles.
c. New; no data for year ago.
Source: Company records.

Sales and Distribution

When Agree CRC was first introduced in 1977, Johnson's distribution system was oriented primarily toward the food trade. However, the launch of Agree, a personal care item, underscored the need for greater dependency on the drug trade in order to obtain widespread distribution for this type of product. Management decided to partially realign its field sales effort in order to place increased emphasis on the drug trade. By 1980, more than 97 percent of the drug stores in Canada were included as part of the Johnson distribution system. Food stores constituted the primary outlets for Agree products, followed by drug and mass merchandising outlets, such as Woolco, K-Mart, and Zellers (see exhibit 7).

Johnson had clear objectives for shelf management. In particular, it sought to have the eighteen different bottles arranged at the retail outlet in a "billboard" or "ribbon effect" for maximum eye-catching appeal. Inserts and shelf talkers[5] were frequently included to increase the likelihood of eye contact (see exhibit 8). Most retail outlets did not, in fact, carry every size and formula of the Agree line, despite aggressive sales force efforts to achieve this stocking pattern.

Johnson maintained its own sales force of approximately 80 people, who were required to sell all of its products, including Agree. By May 1980, additional penetration of distribution channels was no longer a primary objective. However, it was recognized that continued trade support would depend, in part, upon the frequency and quality of both consumer and trade promotions. Sales representatives were well trained and

Exhibit 7   S.C. Johnson—Agree, Sales Percentages by Outlet Type

	Food	Drug	Mass Merchandise
Industry shampoo sales, 1978	43[a]	42	15
Industry CRC sales, 1978	36	42	22
Agree shampoo sales, 1979–1980	47.4	35.5	17.0
Agree CRC sales, 1979–1980	35	46.3	18.5

a. To be read: "43% of all units sold were purchased in food stores."
Source: Company records.

5. Case inserts are written instructions indicating where to stock the brand on the shelf. Shelf talkers are small signs attached to the front of a shelf on which the product is stocked.

Exhibit 8 S.C. Johnson—Agree, Case Insert (Top) and Shelf Talker (Bottom)

Stock Agree next to Tame as shown
for maximum shelf movement

Yellow Bottle
for Extra Oily Hair

Green Bottle
Regular Formula

Orange Bottle
Extra Body with Balsam

"I used
to get
the
greasies."

"With
Agree
I can
forget
the
greasies."

New **Agree** TM.
Creme Rinse & Conditioner
helps stop the greasies

were compensated by a salary plus incentives scheme, where the incentives included things like free trips and prizes. Management attempted to provide strong support for the sales force through regular meetings and discussions and by furnishing selling aids. Some of the Johnson products which the sales group sold, for example, "Raid" and "Off," were seasonal. In the case of Agree, however, the variation per season was slight, averaging 3 or 4 percent higher in midsummer and 1 or 2 percent lower in winter.

Pricing

When Agree CRC was first introduced, the retail price was pegged to that of the leading brand, Tame. The regular cost to the retailer initially was $12.86 per case for one dozen 225-ml bottles and $16.94 per case for 350-ml size bottles. At that time, retail selling prices ranged from $1.39 to $1.79 for the 225-ml size and from $1.79 to $2.39 for the 350-ml size. By

May 1980, trade costs and suggested retail selling prices for Agree CRC were as follows:

Bottle size	Trade cost (per case)	Suggested retail selling prices
225 ml	$14.65	$1.59–$1.79
350 ml	$19.20	$2.09–$2.29
450 ml	$23.50	$2.59–$2.79

The suggested retail selling prices for Agree CRC provided trade margins in the 23–31 percent range.

By May 1980, trade costs and suggested retail selling prices for Agree shampoo were as follows:

Bottle size	Trade cost (per case)	Suggested retail selling prices
225 ml	$16.55	$1.79–$1.99
350 ml	$24.25	$2.59–$2.79
450 ml	$28.00	$2.99–$3.19

Suggested retail selling prices for Agree shampoo typically provided trade margins in the 23–27 percent range.

The initial pricing strategy for Agree CRC was to introduce the product at a consumer price equal to that of Tame, or to Gillette Earth Born if Tame was not stocked in a particular outlet. A similar pricing strategy was pursued for Agree shampoo in that the pricing objective was parity with Johnson & Johnson Baby Shampoo, or with Clairol Herbal Essence if the former was not available. Over the next few years, Agree CRC and shampoo moved to a slight premium price relative to the top selling brands.

Advertising

Mel Liston was about to set a marketing communications budget that would include expenditures for advertising, consumer promotion, and trade promotion. As a starting point, he examined the budgets for the fiscal years 1978–1979 and 1979–1980 (see exhibit 9). In doing so, however, he recognized that some important factors had changed in the interim. For example, deal and promotional costs had been higher in FY 1978–1979 than in the following year because of the introductory expenses incurred for the launch of Agree shampoo. Although the current year was estimated to be slightly below target, his projected budget for FY 1980–1981 would still have to provide for a pretax profit level of at least 12.5 percent.

Exhibit 9 S.C. Johnson—Agree, Mel Liston's P&L Worksheet
for His 1980–1981 Budget (CRC and Shampoo Combined)

	1978–1979 $000	Percent of NS	1979–1980[a] $000	Percent of NS	1980–1981 $000	Percent of NS
Net sales	8158	100	9300	100		100
Cost of goods sold[b]	2941	36	3160	34		33
Gross profit	5217	64	6140	66		
Advertising	1875	23	1578	17		
Consumer promotion	816	10	553	6		
Deals	1225	15	1197	13		
Other[c]	890	11	920	10		
Total promotion	4806	59	4248	46		
Functional expenses[d]	900	11	927	10		
Operating profit	489	(6)	965	10		≥ 12.5

a. Projected from mid-May to June 30 year end.
b. Includes labour, materials, standard overhead.
c. Includes external marketing services, sales meetings, agency fees.
d. Overhead allocations and fixed costs.
Source: Company records.

Foote, Cone & Belding, Johnson's advertising agency was requested to prepare scripts that would direct advertising toward the new target audience. The agency created material that it felt would be effective and then made suggestions about how to use the advertising package, for example, the level of frequency required to achieve maximum impact with a particular audience. The agency commission would be included in Mr. Liston's budget as a fixed percent of his expected net revenue (see exhibit 9).

The primary marketing objective was to maintain or increase current sales levels for Agree. To meet this goal, Mel Liston believed that it would be necessary to achieve a 90 percent awareness level for Agree within the new primary target audience of women aged 12–18. A secondary target audience was defined as women aged 19–24, and he hoped to achieve at least a 60 percent awareness level for this group.

Research undertaken by the advertising agency on Canadian teens' and young women's television viewing habits indicated a national weekly reach of 99 percent for the 12–18 age bracket and 98 percent for the 19–24-year-old group, with average weekly viewing times of 21.3 and 21.5 hours, respectively. One of the tasks facing Mel Liston was to select specific programmes and parts of the day, e.g., 4:00–9:00 P.M., that achieved optimal viewing levels within the budget that he set. He felt that consumer magazine advertising was important as a support vehicle to television, since magazines provided increased reach against the light television viewer (see exhibit 10).

The agency proposed a television commercial for each Agree product, scripts for radio advertising, and layouts for print media. Total media costs to run the television commercials on a complete network daily basis were estimated at $1.05 million for 52 weeks if late afternoon time slots were scheduled versus $1.6 million for a prime time insertion schedule. These figures incorporated a discount, which could range from 10 to 15 percent

Exhibit 10   S.C. Johnson—Agree, Media Plan Excerpts

A. *Quintile Analysis*

The quintiles of the 1980–1981 media plan were compared with the quintiles of a television-only campaign, which would run for 52 weeks with a 45 percent weekly reach. The target group was women aged 12–18.

TV Watcher Quintile	TV Only % Total Impressions	Index	TV/Consumer Magazines % Total Impressions	Index
1 + 2 (light)	15.9	100	25.9	163
3 (medium)	21.5	100	33.6	156
4 + 5 (heavy)	62.6	100	40.6	70

B. *Publication Costs* (for full-page ads)

Publication	Cost/Insertion (s)	Total Readers Women 12–18 (000)	CPM[a] ($)
Chatelaine (E)	15,078.15	350	43.08
Flare	5,174.80	224	23.10
Homemaker's	14,614.00	176	83.03
Chatelaine (F)	4,996.85	42	118.97
Madame au Foyer	4,199.13	27	155.52
Clin d'Oeil	1,921.50	60	32.01

The above analysis reflects the fact that the inclusion of consumer magazines provides increased reach against the light TV viewer. In addition, the multimedia schedule provides a more even distribution of impressions against the light, medium, and heavy quintiles.

a. Cost per thousand impressions.
Source: Foote, Cone and Belding.

on a full 52-week purchase. In keeping with Agree's younger image, the agency recommended a fast-paced, exciting commercial featuring a strong musical beat, which appeared to be favoured by teens.

The product management group also considered radio advertising, which had been directed mainly at the "teen" segment of the Agree market during the previous two years. In FY 1979–1980, Johnson ran a seven-week radio campaign (see exhibit 11). For FY 1980–1981, it was estimated by the agency that the media cost for 27-station national radio would amount to approximately $35,000 per week.

Exhibit 11   S.C. Johnson—Agree, Agree Radio Plan

Target Group: Primary   teens   12–18
Target Group: Secondary   women   19–24

Reach Objective: 55% weekly
Announcements: 30 seconds
Duration: 7 weeks

Market	No. of Stations	No. of Weekly Announcements for Each Product
Vancouver	2 CKLG/CFUN	40
Victoria	1 CKDA	20
Calgary	1 CKXL	25
Edmonton	1 CHED	25
Regina	1 CJME	25
Saskatoon	1 CKOM	25
Winnipeg	2 CKRC/CFRW	35
Toronto	3 CHUM-FM/CFTR/CHUM	50
Hamilton	1 CKOC	25
Ottawa	2 CFRA/CFGO	45
Kitchener	1 CHYM-AM	30
London	1 CJBK	25
Montreal		
English	2 CKGM/CHOM-FM	40
French	2 CKLM/CKAC	30
Quebec City	2 CHOI-FM/CFLS	50
Halifax	1 CJCH	20
St. John/Moncton	2 CFBC/CKCW	20
St. John's	1 VOCM	20

Source: Company records.

Since its introduction, Agree had been promoted regularly in magazines, and newspapers. During the launch periods, seven American and three Canadian magazines had carried full-page colour advertisements for Agree. In Canada, Johnson had paid for the Canadian material and had received the American magazine spillover, estimated at approximately $200,000 per year, at no cost, although it was recognized that U.S. advertising would still be directed at the historical U.S. target audience, women aged 18–45.

As Mel Liston began to work on developing a marketing communications programme for FY 1980–1981, he tried to imagine a profile of a typical teen girl and the type of advertising she would be most likely to notice. Studies on women 18 years old and over had shown that heavy users of hair products were not necessarily heavy watchers of television. However, he wondered how applicable this result was, given the age disparity with the Agree primary target group. There was even less statistical information on magazine readership in the target age group. Thus, Mel Liston wondered whether or not the reading habits of the typical girl consumer would justify spending a significant part of his budget on print advertising, in either magazines or newspapers. If a decision was reached to run a print campaign, he believed that any print advertising that did appear would have to be young and vibrant like the ads that the agency was proposing for the coming year (see exhibit 12).

Consumer Promotion

Johnson had introduced its Agree products with heavy consumer promotion. The CRC was introduced with a six-month sampling campaign, which consisted of a direct mailing to approximately three million potential users of a 3/4-ounce plastic sachet good for about two uses. This was followed by a second six-month campaign which included 400,000 3/4-ounce plastic sachets and 15-cent coupons using a cross-promotion[6] with Close-Up toothpaste. Agree shampoo was introduced by using similar sachets to 3.2 million homes, and this campaign included a fact book and another 15-cent coupon. The net effective coverage of these promotional events was approximately 50 percent of Canadian homes.

Another launch promotion for Agree consisted of 3/4-ounce pouches of free shampoo, which were attached to CRC bottles. One million of these pouches were distributed free to stores, in addition to 1.5 million

---

6. Cross-promotions are samples, coupons, etc., placed on or inside the package of a non-competing product usually sharing the same market as the promoted brand.

Exhibit 12   S.C. Johnson—Agree, 1980–1981 Proposed Print Ad

50-ml samples, which were prepriced at 39 cents each. The unit cost to Johnson was 5 cents per sachet of CRC and 7 cents per sachet of shampoo. Bulk distribution costs were estimated at $30 per thousand. Although sales for each product increased significantly during the trial period, the cost to Johnson of distributing such high quantities of free or virtually free merchandise was very high.

After Agree CRC and shampoo had been launched, other consumer promotion opportunities were considered. Refund campaigns were run twice during FY 1979–1980. Coupons that offered 50 cents off the next purchase were distributed in bulk mailings and in magazines directed toward homemakers. Cash refunds of one dollar were later offered in exchange for two Agree labels. The redemption rates were 3 percent and 2 percent, respectively. This coupon programme proved rather disappointing, since there was little, if any, change in sales volume during the promotion period.

In 1979, Agree in the United States had been packaged with a free Warner-Lambert razor, normally sold at $3.69. Although the perceived value of this "gift" was high, the impact on sales during the promotion period was disappointing. After calculating the total cost of the distributed premiums, this campaign was responsible for a substantial loss incurred by American Agree. A similar promotion was tried in the United States six months later. Free pantyhose were attached to Agree products. During the promotion period, sales remained relatively stable. However, the result of this promotion was less damaging to profits than the free razor campaign, since the cost to Johnson was only 40 cents per pair of pantyhose. Despite these results, Mel Liston was unwilling to describe either of the premium campaigns as a failure, since other longer-term objectives such as increases in usage frequency and brand loyalty appeared to have been met. Furthermore, in judging any sales promotion campaign, he realized, as a general rule, that most promotion events did lose money during the deal period.

One promotion being considered by Mel Liston was an "instant win" tag, whereby the purchaser would be notified if she had won a free pair of Jordache jeans. Jordache would be asked to supply the jeans free in exchange for being featured in advertising and in-store promotion. Other costs for this contest would include plastic prize tickets, special labels, backer cards, and labour. Some of these expenses would overlap into the trade promotion category. Total promotional costs for the Jordache Sweepstakes were estimated at $120,000, at least $20,000 of which would include store items such as end aisle displays.

Mel Liston believed that consumer promotions were important merchandising devices, since all consumers who learned about such offers could take advantage of them. In contrast, trade promotions, particularly off-invoice allowances, were important to retailers, but the benefits from these deals were not necessarily passed along to consumers in the form of lower prices. The primary objective of a consumer promotion was to induce the consumer to buy Agree more often, perhaps every other time, rather than every fourth or fifth time.

Since the product was in the non-price-sensitive 50 percent of the market where consumers tended to buy on impulse, Mel Liston felt that non-price promotions might be very effective. Deals such as bonus packs were nondiscretionary in that anyone who bought the product received the bonus. However, Mr. Liston wondered whether bonuses were merely a way to subsidize or reward the already loyal purchaser. In his mind, it was unclear whether or not larger amounts of an untried product would, in fact, induce trial.

As Mel Liston began to think about consumer promotion plans for the coming year, he recognized the importance of establishing a clearly defined personality for Agree CRC and shampoo. One possible promotion event consisted of a contest that would offer as the grand prize a rock group concert at the winner's school or community center. Although somewhat unusual, this type of promotion might reinforce the image he was trying to project for Agree. He said, "We want a commercial image with an underlying message which tells the kids that the music and the special Agree products are mainly for them; they're not something meant to appeal to the whole family." Other consumer promotion possibilities included couponing and redemption ideas. For example, one opportunity under consideration was cross-ruff couponing, perhaps on Pledge or Flo-Thru Air Freshener or one of the company's other home care products.

Trade Promotion

Trade spending was something that companies such as Johnson felt they *had* to do; it was not truly discretionary. As part of each year's budget, a percent of sales dollars was set aside in order to meet shelf space objectives. The FY 1979–1980 discretionary pool of funds was set at 7.9 percent of projected sales. Without special deals, there might be insufficient reason for stores to try to sell Agree instead of competing brands.

Johnson allocated funds to trade promotion for two main reasons. First, trade deals were viewed as essential simply to get and keep products listed. A variety of trade deals were possible such as off-invoice allowances (e.g., $1.20 off each case ordered during the deal period). During FY 1979–1980, trade spending varied widely both in the CRC and shampoo markets (see exhibit 13).

The other reason for trade spending was related to cooperative advertising. Contributions to these programmes normally were calculated according to a formula that included some percent of a retailer's previous sales, typically around 2 percent. Advertising "slicks"[7] (see exhibit 14) were provided to retailers to encourage their active participation in co-op advertising campaigns.

To encourage retailers to sell stock at "feature prices" from time to time, S.C. Johnson provided off-invoice allowances (also called deal money) to the trade. Deal money was occasionally passed on to consumers as reduced prices but frequently was viewed by the retailer as a means to increase the trade margin. For example, Mel Liston estimated that only 40–50 percent of all stock sold on deal to the trade was actually retailed at the "feature price." The balance was sold at the regular price, thereby increasing the retailer's trade margin. It seemed to Mel Liston that a large number of retailers were more concerned about obtaining deal money than about an extensive advertising campaign that the manufacturer might undertake to build a longer-term brand franchise.

Although advertising was sometimes cut if fourth-quarter sales were disappointing, trade deals hardly ever were cut. The risk of suffering a loss in shelf positioning was considered too great to justify a reduction in trade promotion activity. Retailers typically tried to buy and stock up at the end of a deal period to keep annual inventory costs down as much as possible. Retailer expectations regarding trade deals were not expected to change in FY 1980–1981.

The Task

As Mel Liston began to think about developing a comprehensive marketing communications program for the Agree line in FY 1980–1981, he remembered that the first step in the process was to establish a set of clear and specific objectives against which campaign results could be measured. In addition, he understood that decisions about advertising, consumer promotions, and trade deals were highly interrelated. Thus, overall success in implementing the revised positioning strategy for Agree CRC and shampoo

7. Advertising "slicks" are reproducible copy and pictures supplied by manufacturers to participating retailers during a cooperative advertising campaign.

Exhibit 13 S.C. Johnson—Agree, Selected Promotional Influences
for Major Brands, July/August 1979 to March/April 1980 (3 Periods)

A. *Shampoo*

	Agree			Head & Shoulders			Johnson & Johnson			Body on Tap			All Others		
	1979 July Aug.	1979 Nov. Dec.	1980 Mar. Apr.	1979 July Aug.	1979 Nov. Dec.	1980 Mar. Apr.	1979 July Aug.	1979 Nov. Dec.	1980 Mar. Apr.	1979 July Aug.	1979 Nov. Dec.	1980 Mar. Apr.	1979 July Aug.	1979 Nov. Dec.	1980 Mar. Apr.
Sales share	6.4	5.4	5.7	9.5	10.8	10.1	7.3	7.3	8.6	4.0	3.3	3.9	72.7	73.1	71.7
Deal % of market[a]	2.8	1.2	0.4	0.1	0	0	0.5	0.8	0.4	1.5	0.5	1.0	7.5	7.0	6.4
	(43.8)	(22.2)	(7.0)	(1.0)	(0.0)	(0.0)	(6.8)	(10.9)	(4.7)	(37.5)	(15.2)	(25.6)	(10.3)	(9.6)	(8.9)
TV advertising ($000)	12.9	40.8	181.2	157.5	152.8	151.1	186.2	2	169.8	24.6	28.3	115.3	456	283	856
Radio advertising ($000)	139	3.7	0	31.3	7.0	36.2	0	0	10.9	0	0	0	5	2	15
Press advertising ($000)	0	0	17.2	13.7	16.2	7.4	0	0	0	7.1	0	11.0	105	46	220
Total advertising volume ($000)	152	45	198	203	176	195	186	2	181	31.8	28.3	126.3	566	331	1091
Advertising share[b]	13.4	4.6	11.1	17.8	31.3	10.9	16.4	0.2	10.1	2.8	5.0	7.1	49.7	58.8	60.9
Co-op share:[c]															
Food	32	20	31	35	30	34	53	61	59	29	1	10			
Drug	48	44	72	64	64	86	56	57	76	41	20	31			
Mass merchandiser	83	10	59	113	46	95	64	87	102	64	29	55			
Displays share:[d]															
Food	9	6	8	16	7	8	6	14	13	3	2	4			
Drug	13	16	21	21	20	19	19	17	19	7	7	15			
Mass merchandiser	34	3	50	25	22	28	28	45	50	9	10	43			

744

B. CRC

	Agree			Revlon Flex			Silkience			Tame			Condition II			All Others		
	1979 July/Aug.	Nov./Dec.	1980 Mar./Apr.	1979 July/Aug.	Nov./Dec.	1980 Mar./Apr.	1979 July/Aug.	Nov./Dec.	1980 Mar./Apr.	1979 July/Aug.	Nov./Dec.	1980 Mar./Apr.	1979 July/Aug.	Nov./Dec.	1980 Mar./Apr.	1979 July/Aug.	Nov./Dec.	1980 Mar./Apr.
Sales share	15.6	15.1	13.7	14.5	11.1	12.8	2.7	4.5	6.1	9.2	10.3	9.2	7.1	8.1	6.2	50.9	51.8	51.2
Deal % of market[a]	4.6	5.3	2.1	6.0	2.1	1.4	0	0	0	1.3	2.5	1.1	1.5	2.6	0.9	10.5	11.2	9.9
	(29.5)	(35.1)	(15.3)	(41.4)	(18.9)	(10.9)	(0.0)	(0.0)	(0.0)	(14.1)	(24.3)	(11.9)	(21.1)	(32.1)	(14.5)	(20.6)	(21.6)	(19.3)
TV advertising ($000)	33.7	243.8	0	58.9	7.3	0	133.0	100.8	75.7	0	0	85.1	11.8	5.8	8.9	124.6	81.5	41.3
Radio advertising ($000)	47.5	0	0	0	0	0	0	0	0	0	0	0	0	0	0	1.8	0	0
Press advertising ($000)	0	0	0	0	0	0	0	19.0	30.4	0	35.1	5.2	0	10.4	28.0	71.8	7.6	99.8
Total advertising volume ($000)	81.1	243.8	0	58.9	7.3	0	133.0	119.8	106.1	0	35.1	90.3	11.8	16.2	37	198.2	89.1	141.1
Advertising share[b]	16.8	47.7	0	12.2	1.4	0	27.5	23.4	25.6	0	6.9	21.8	2.4	3.2	8.9	41.0	17.4	43.7
Co-op share:[c]																		
Food	19	9	15	19	5	14	7	14	15	13	17	17	1	7	6			
Drug	36	31	43	15	21	29	45	40	46	29	28	26	27	42	32			
Mass merchandiser	53	16	32	40	10	33	29	26	29	44	26	50	31	45	36			
Displays share:[d]																		
Food	9	4	2	5	5	7	3	8	8	13	7	6	1	4	1			
Drug	20	15	18	17	12	19	13	24	12	22	23	5	10	14	8			
Mass merchandiser	37	22	50	40	16	21	19	13	7	34	6	18	15	35	21			

a. The Neilsen Market Survey defines a deal as any package/price configuration that is different from the company's regular market configuration. The figures in the row are the proportion of brand sales that were sold on deal. For example, during July/August 1979 in the shampoo market, approximately 43.8% (6.4 ÷ 2.8) of Agree shampoo sales were "on deal," compared to 22.2% (5.4 ÷ 1.2) of sales for Agree during November/December 1979.

b. Advertising share denotes Agree share of total advertising expenditures on the product category during each period. For example, the calculation for July/August 1979:

$$12.9 + 139.0$$

$$\overline{(12.9 + 139.0) + (157.5 + 31.3 + 13.7) \ldots + (456.0 + 5.0 + 105.0)} = 13.4\% \text{ (rounded)}$$

c. Co-op share is supplied by A.C. Neilsen. It is a period result defined as the number of stores which did co-op advertising (i.e., newspapers, flyers) weighted by their sales importance to the shampoo category. For example, in July/August 1979, food stores doing 32% of shampoo sales in the food trade had co-op advertising on Agree.

d. Display share is the unweighted percent of stores that had display activity when the store was audited by A.C. Neilsen at the end of the bimonthly period. For example, at the end of August 1979, 9% of food stores had Agree on display. Display is defined by Neilsen as the product being somewhere in the store other than its normal shelf position.

745

Exhibit 14 S.C. Johnson—Agree, Example of an Advertising Slick